HARVARD ECONOMIC STUDIES

HARVARD UNIVERSITY PRESS

HARVARD ECONOMIC STUDIES

VOLUME LX

THE STUDIES IN THIS SERIES ARE PUBLISHED BY THE DEPARTMENT OF
ECONOMICS OF HARVARD UNIVERSITY, WHICH, HOWEVER, ASSUMES
NO RESPONSIBILITY FOR THE VIEWS EXPRESSED

LONDON : HUMPHREY MILFORD

OXFORD UNIVERSITY PRESS

THE COMMERCIAL PAPER HOUSE
IN THE UNITED STATES

BY

ALBERT O. GREEF

CAMBRIDGE
HARVARD UNIVERSITY PRESS
1938

PRINTED AT THE HARVARD UNIVERSITY PRESS

CAMBRIDGE, MASS., U.S.A.

TO

E. V. M.

PREFACE

OPEN-MARKET dealings in commercial paper have been carried on in the United States for approximately a century and a half, and dealers in promissory notes have bought and sold hundreds of millions of dollars of such obligations in the open market each year during the greater part of the period since the Civil War. But despite the fact that the business of buying and selling open-market notes is as old as commercial banking in this country, and attained a position of some importance in our financial system more than fifty years ago, there is probably no financial institution in the United States with whose operations the general public is less familiar today than with those of the modern commercial paper house. Even some commercial bankers, in fact, are unaware of the existence in this country of the system of financing which the operations of dealers in promissory notes make possible. With these circumstances in mind, and in the hope of making some contribution toward a fuller and more widespread understanding of the rôle which the commercial paper house has come to play in the functioning of our financial system, the writer undertook several years ago a more detailed and comprehensive study of the commercial paper business than any which had been made theretofore. The results of the study begun at that time are presented in this volume.

The purpose of this study is threefold: to give an account of the development of the commercial paper business in the United States from its origins in the eighteenth century down to the close of the year 1935, to describe in some detail the organization and the practical operations of the modern commercial paper house, and to indicate the economic significance of a financial institution which is found in no other country than the United States. With this purpose in view I have divided the study into three parts. In Part I some of the main developments in the commercial paper business from the closing years of the eighteenth century to the beginning of 1936 have been traced. The methods used by commercial paper dealers in carrying on their operations in open-market notes and the various forms of organization which they maintain for this purpose have been described in Part II. Such related matters as the classes of obligations bought and sold by dealers in commercial paper, the classes of concerns issuing such obligations, the buyers of open-market notes, the practices followed by banks in buying "outside" paper, and the operations of commercial paper houses other than dealing in promissory notes have also been considered in Part II. In Part III the rôle played by the commercial paper house in the functioning of the financial system has been indicated and an appraisal of the services performed by dealers in open-market obligations has been given.

A large part of the factual material included in this study was secured by means of a field investigation which was begun in the summer of 1930 and continued at irregular intervals over a period of six years. In the course of this investigation I interviewed all the dealers in commercial paper who were currently reporting their "outstandings" to the Federal Reserve Bank of New York, officers of branch offices maintained by most of the more important of these dealers, and a number of smaller dealers whose operations in open-market paper were comparatively unimportant. I also interviewed officers or other representatives of each of the Federal Reserve banks and a number of bankers in each of the Federal Reserve districts. This field investigation was supplemented by correspondence with commercial paper dealers and bankers in all sections of the country and by an examination of the voluminous literature relating to commercial paper and commercial paper houses which is available in financial and other libraries in Boston and New York. It is believed, therefore, that this study of the commercial paper house and its work is based on a thorough examination of all the most important sources of information concerning the business of buying and selling promissory notes in the open market.

I have received valuable suggestions and advice in preparing this study from Professors J. F. Ebersole, S. E. Harris, O. M. W. Sprague, and J. H. Williams of Harvard University and from

Mr. C. E. Fraser, vice president of Massachusetts Distributors, Incorporated, and Mr. E. V. McKey of Weil, McKey, Pearson and Company. I have also received helpful suggestions from Professors H. H. Burbank and A. P. Usher of Harvard University and from Mr. J. N. Thorne of Goldman, Sachs and Company. To practically all the commercial paper dealers in the country I am indebted for their patience in answering innumerable questions relating to the business of buying and selling open-market notes. Without their cordial coöperation this study could not have been completed in its present form. I wish also to acknowledge my indebtedness to various dealers in Boston and New York for permission to reproduce the note offering lists, etc., shown in Exhibits 4 and 5 and 8 to 16; to officers of the Federal Reserve banks and of leading commercial banks in each of the Federal Reserve districts for furnishing information concerning banks' practices in selecting and purchasing open-market notes and various related matters; to the Federal Reserve Bank of New York for permission to reproduce Chart I, as well as for supplying figures of commercial paper "outstandings" and other data relating to the commercial paper business; and to the National Credit Office of New York for furnishing information relating to the classes of concerns using the open market and losses on purchases of open-market paper. Charts II to IX were prepared by Mr. Richmond F. Bingham, Instructor in Business Statistics, Harvard Graduate School of Business Administration.

A. O. G.

CONTENTS

EXHIBITS

CHARTS

TABLES ACCOMPANYING TEXT

TABLES INCLUDED IN FOOTNOTES

PART I

DEVELOPMENT OF THE COMMERCIAL PAPER
BUSINESS IN THE UNITED STATES

CHAPTER I

THE NOTE BROKERAGE BUSINESS BEFORE THE CIVIL WAR

THE PURPOSE of the three chapters included in Part I is to give an account of the development of the business of dealing in open-market commercial paper in the United States from the closing years of the eighteenth century, the earliest years for which records of this business are readily available, down to the beginning of 1936. In the present chapter the development of open-market dealings in commercial paper during the period before the Civil War will be traced. Since throughout the whole of this period dealers in such paper generally acted as brokers, rather than out-right buyers and sellers of negotiable instruments, the purpose of this chapter, more specifically, is to present an account of the rise and earlier development of the note brokerage business in this country. In the following chapter the development of the commercial paper business from 1861 to 1914, the period in which operations in open-market paper became nation-wide and the evolution from the earlier note broker to the modern commercial paper house was completed, will be traced. In Chapter III some of the main developments in the commercial paper business during the brief but eventful period from 1914 to 1936 will be indicated.

1. RISE OF THE NOTE BROKERAGE BUSINESS: DEALINGS IN COMMERCIAL PAPER DURING THE EIGHTEENTH CENTURY

The modern commercial paper house, with its branch offices or elaborate correspondent system, its highly efficient credit department, its large capital, its hundreds of borrowing customers, representing trading and manufacturing enterprise in nearly every state in the Union, and its no less numerous and widely distributed clientele of "paper-buying" banks, is the product of nearly a century and a half of gradual development. Acting, as it does, as an intermediary "between the borrowing public and the less qualified capitalist" — to use Bagehot's phrase — it depends for its existence upon its ability to "find" or originate, and then to sell to banks or other buyers, a volume of carefully selected short-term commercial paper large enough to be profitable. Its main operations of buying and selling can be conducted only at a very considerable expense. Its remuneration, on the other hand, is but moderate — a gross commission amounting as a rule to no more than ¼ of 1 per cent of its sales. If its open-market operations are to be carried on at a profit, therefore, it must handle each year a volume of paper amounting to many millions of dollars. Hence not until comparatively recent years, when business concerns of many different classes and in many different localities had begun to seek relatively large amounts of short-term credit in the open market, and banks in various parts of the country had accumulated correspondingly large amounts of surplus funds which they were willing to place in "outside" loans, could any such elaborate organizations as the larger of the modern commercial paper houses have found a profitable field of operations in this country.

Dealings in negotiable credit instruments, however, were being carried on in the United States many years before the appearance of the modern commercial paper house. The exact date when such dealings began is not known, but it is certain that they began much earlier than seems generally to have been supposed. It is possible that merchants in the larger towns may occasionally have offered bills of exchange or promissory notes for sale in the market through some intermediary agent even as early as the colonial period. The use of both these types of negotiable instruments seems to have become fairly common by that time.[1] Even as early as about 1704,

---

[1] J. J. Klein, "The Development of Mercantile Instruments of Credit in the United States," *Jour. of Accountancy*, vol. XII (Oct. 1911), p. 34. An account of the origin and development of negotiable instruments of credit was not considered within the compass of the present study. This subject is discussed in a number of treatises on negotiable instruments. The following articles also may be mentioned in this connection: F. D. Chester, "On Early Moslem Promissory Notes," *Jour. Amer. Orient. Soc.*, vol. XVI (1896), pp. xliii–xlvii; C. A. Conant, "The Development of Credit," *Jour. Pol. Econ.*, March 1899, pp. 161–181; G. H. Conder, "Bills of Exchange: The Part They Have Played in English Banking, Past and Present," *Jour. Inst. of Bankers*, vol. X (Oct. 1889), pp. 405–441; W. S. Holdsworth, "The Origins and Early History of Negotiable Instruments," *Law Quar. Rev.*, vol. XXXI (Jan., April, and Oct. 1915), pp. 12–29, 173–186, 376–388, and vol. XXXII (Jan.

in fact, the larger colonial merchants were selling domestic bills of exchange to fellow merchants and others who wished to make remittances to distant towns.[2] It is probable, however, that during this period merchants as a rule dealt with one another directly in buying and selling bills of exchange, whether domestic or foreign;[3] and any sales of bills or notes in the market through intermediary dealers must have been more or less sporadic transactions and inconsiderable in volume. Neither any large supply of negotiable paper nor any considerable demand for it as an investment could have developed when industry and trade were so unimportant as they remained throughout the colonial period,[4] and commercial banks did not even exist.[5] If, as has been said, there was "no money market on this side of the Atlantic until after the Revolution,"[6] any open market for commercial paper must have been

---

1916), pp. 20–37; Edward Jenks, "On the Early History of Negotiable Instruments," *ibid.*, vol. IX (Jan. 1893), pp. 70–85; Klein, *op. cit.*, vol. XII (Sept. and Oct. 1911), pp. 321–345, 422–449; A. H. Pruessner, "The Earliest Traces of Negotiable Instruments," *Amer. Jour. Semit. Lang. and Lit.*, Jan. 1928, pp. 88–107; Frederick Read, "The Origin, Early History, and Later Development of Bills of Exchange and Certain Other Negotiable Instruments," *Can. Bar Rev.*, vol. IV (Sept. and Dec. 1926), pp. 440–459, 665–682; A. P. Usher, "The Origin of the Bill of Exchange," *Jour. Pol. Econ.*, June 1914, pp. 566–576, and "The Parisian Bill Market in the Seventeenth Century," *ibid.*, Dec. 1916, pp. 985–1002.

[2] J. T. Adams, *Provincial Society — 1690–1763*, p. 48. Adams cites the case of Benjamin Faneuil, a New York merchant, who advertised in the Boston *News-Letter* (issue of April 26–May 3, 1708) in 1708 that he could supply bills of exchange to "merchants or others" who had money in New York and wished to remit to Boston.

[3] A. H. Cole, "Evolution of the Foreign-Exchange Market of the United States," *Jour. Econ. and Bus. Hist.*, May 1929, p. 387. According to Professor Cole, no intermediary dealer was required, and even advertising bills for sale in newspapers was generally unnecessary (p. 389).

[4] During the colonial period, manufactures "were still largely in the handicraft stage, and goods were produced primarily for local and home use. Manufacturing proper, that is, the production of goods outside the home for sale in the market or for export, never developed very far."
Foreign trade "was of greater immediate importance than domestic commerce and was of greater economic significance throughout the whole of the colonial period." Most of the colonial trade "was really barter." (E. L. Bogart, *Economic History of the American People*, pp. 120–121, 142, 161.)

[5] Commercial banks were not organized in this country until after the colonial period. A colonial bank was not a bank of discount and deposit, but " 'simply a batch of paper money,' whether organized by private individuals or by public authority" (D. R. Dewey, *Financial History of the United States*, 9th ed., p. 24).

[6] M. G. Myers, *The New York Money Market*, I, 3.

narrowly limited throughout the entire colonial period.

During the remaining years of the eighteenth century dealings in negotiable paper must undoubtedly have increased to some extent, along with increasing activity in industry and trade. At any rate, during this period the first commercial banks were organized in this country and began to discount bills of exchange and promissory notes, and actual records of dealings in such paper during the decade of the 1790's are available.

The Bank of North America, the first commercial bank to be organized in the United States, was chartered by Congress in 1781 and "put in operation" by Robert Morris in Philadelphia in the same year. Besides making large advances to the government, it carried on "a considerable business in the discount of commercial paper." [7] Three years later the Bank of New York began business in New York City, without a charter. It exercised the functions of discount, issue, and deposit.[8] The Massachusetts Bank, "apparently the first commercial bank to do business in New England," was also organized in 1784. It "accepted notes for discounting twice a week" when it began business.[9] Within the next eight years eight more commercial banks, mentioned by Sumner, were organized in various parts of the country: the Bank of Maryland, chartered in 1790; the Bank of Providence, founded in 1791; and the Union Bank of Boston, the Hartford Bank, the Bank of Albany, the Bank of Richmond, the Bank of Alexandria (Virginia), and the Bank of South Carolina (unchartered), all founded in 1792.[10] The establishment of banking institutions like these in different sections of the country meant a considerably broader potential market for commercial paper; and it seems more than a coincidence that the earliest dealings in promissory notes of which any record is readily available cannot be traced back much farther than 1793, a year

[7] Horace White, *Money and Banking* (5th ed.), pp. 244–245.

[8] *Ibid.*, pp. 248–249, 252.

[9] M. H. Foulds, "The Massachusetts Bank, 1784–1865," *Jour. Ec. and Bus. Hist.*, Feb. 1930, p. 256. That commercial banking was still a pioneer business as late as 1784 seems clearly shown by the fact that both the Bank of New York and the Massachusetts Bank sent representatives to Philadelphia to "learn the system used by the bank of North America" (*ibid.*, p. 257).

[10] W. G. Sumner, *A History of Banking in the United States*, p. 20.

later than the establishment of the last of the eleven banks mentioned above.

Of these early dealings in commercial paper perhaps the best evidence is furnished by certain early law cases. A Maryland case mentions "dealers in negotiable paper" who seem to have been dealing in both bills of exchange and promissory notes in Georgetown, D. C., in 1793, and perhaps even earlier.[11] About the same time promissory notes were being bought and sold in Charleston, South Carolina, also, as two other early cases clearly indicate.[12] One of these cases makes mention both of note brokers and of their practice of "sending notes into the market for sale."[13] Even before this time there may have been dealers in negotiable paper in New York. It is said that Nathaniel Prime, supposed to have

[11] ". . . there had existed at George Town from the year 1793 . . . a practice among banking corporations, merchants, and dealers in negotiable paper, of demanding payment of unpaid notes and bills, on the fourth day after the time limited for payment . . ." (*Bank of Columbia* v. *Fitzhugh*, 1 Harris and Gill, Md., 239, 240–241).

[12] *Payne* v. *Trezevant*, 2 Bay (S. C.) 23, and *Foltz* v. *Mey*, 1 Bay (S. C.) 486.

[13] *Payne* v. *Trezevant*. It is stated in this case that a Mr. House, "a broker," in December 1794, "was applied to by the defendant to raise him 500 l. [£] on loan for four months, for the use of which he would give 80 l. [£] at the rate of four per cent. a month." House, "knowing that Mr. Moses Sarcedas was at that time in the habit of lending money, went to him, and asked him if he would advance the 500 l. [£] to the defendant, for the time and upon the terms before mentioned, to which he agreed." House then went to the defendant, got the note for £580, payable to himself, sold it to Sarcedas for £500, and turned the £500 over to the defendant.

Charles N. Simons, "a broker" called as a witness by the plaintiff, swore that "it had been a very customary thing in Charleston, ever since the establishment of the banks, to send notes into the market for sale, and that these were not considered as loans, but sales of notes" (pp. 25–27).

". . . the late practice of brokers and usurers in Charleston, since the establishment of the banks, (for it never was customary before), of sending notes into the market for sale, as it was termed, at five per cent. a month" is mentioned in this case as an indirect means of evading the act against usury (p. 29).

An actual case in which a promissory note was "negotiated" — i.e., presumably, sold — in the market in Charleston (probably in 1794 or earlier) at a discount of 5 per cent a month is given in *Foltz* v. *Mey*, 486–487.

These two cases are of interest in that they show not only that there were note brokers and at least a limited open market for commercial paper in Charleston by 1794, but also that the buyers of such paper included both banks and private capitalists, and that neither of these classes of buyers was by any means averse to exacting a high rate of return on purchased paper. As will be shown later, this practice of "shaving" notes became widespread by about 1820. It has survived in various localities in the United States down to the present time.

been "in early life a coachman to the rich William Gray, an emi-
nent merchant in Boston," began business as a broker "in a very
small way" (presumably in New York) at an early date, and that
the "ex-coachman shaved notes, and got bravely ahead." In 1796
he is said to have entered the brokerage business in New York as
"Nathaniel Prime, Stock and Commission Broker, No. 42 Wall
street [sic]." [14] Two early law cases furnish additional evidence
that there were note brokers in New York State before 1800.[15]
Still further evidence is supplied by Exhibit 1, a copy of an advertisement by G. W. Cornwell. This advertisement appeared in
the New York *Commercial Advertiser* of May 8, 1799.[16]

Thus far sufficient evidence has been presented to indicate that
dealings in negotiable paper had been begun in a few of the more
important commercial towns in the United States by about 1790,

[14] Walter Barrett, *The Old Merchants of New York City* (1st series), pp. 10–11.
Thirty years later, in 1826, the firm of Prime, Ward, and King was organized.
The members of this organization are said to have been the first "large genuine
private bankers" in New York (*ibid.*, pp. 10–11, 16).

[15] *Jones* v. *Hake*, 2 Johnson (N. Y.) 60, and *Wilkie* v. *Roosevelt*, 3 Johnson
(N. Y.) 66.
In the first of these cases it is stated that the maker of a promissory note, "in
order to raise money, sent it to one Haskin, a money broker, who had often obtained money for him before." Haskin, acting as an agent, sold the note to one
Herriman, at a discount of 2 per cent a month (*Jones* v. *Hake*, 60).
The second case states that one Goodrich (presumably before 1799) "had been
in the practice of receiving notes from Mark & Co. for the purpose of raising
money, by discounting them, in the market." Goodrich himself, however, discounted the note concerned in this case — at the rate of "about 3¼ per cent. per
month" (*Wilkie* v. *Roosevelt*, 66).
Though these cases do not state where Haskin and Goodrich carried on their
operations, it is probable that both brokers bought and sold negotiable paper in
New York City.

[16] The following advertisement also appeared in the same issue of the *Commercial
Advertiser*:

MOSES LOPEZ,
IS removed to no. 29 Ann-street, where he
continues transacting the BROKERS BUSINESS —
he returns his most sincere thanks for the encour-
agement he has met with from his friends and the
public, and craves a continuance of their favors,
assuring them he shall make it his study to discharge
the trust reposed in him with fidelity and punctuality.

While the nature of Lopez' business is not specifically stated, it is quite possible
that the operations he was carrying on were similar to those of Cornwell.

EXHIBIT 1

ADVERTISEMENT OF G. W. CORNWELL, 1799 *

G. W. CORNWELL,

Takes the liberty to offer his services in the *Money Brokerage and Negociating Business.*

HE has opened an office solely for that purpose, at no. 7 Garden-street, a few doors west of the Post-Office; where the utmost care and attention will be paid to the interests of those who may apply to him, and the strictest delicacy observed. His office will be kept open during the summer season from 9 in the morning till half past 3 in the afternoon, and such persons as wish to purchase or sell Negociable Paper, Stock, Bills of Exchange, &c. will most certainly be accommodated by applying to this office.

May 1   tf

* Published in the New York *Commercial Advertiser*, May 8, 1799, p. 3.

if not earlier.[17] A summary description of the commercial paper business during the period before 1800 may now be given. Throughout the whole of this period dealings in negotiable paper were probably confined to the more important trading and financial centers. Moreover, the volume of such paper bought and sold in the market, limited as it was by the comparatively slight development of trading and manufacturing activity, the small number of commercial banks, and probably also by serious currency evils, undoubtedly remained relatively small. As a rule, dealers in negotiable paper no doubt acted as brokers, though in some few cases they may have bought paper outright. If they acted as brokers only, they received a commission as remuneration for their services. If, on the other hand, they bought paper outright, they had the opportunity of making a further gain if they were able to sell the same paper at a rate lower than that at which they had discounted it. It is quite possible that in some cases their remuneration may have consisted entirely in such differences between buying and selling rates. Little is known concerning the classes of negotiable instruments they handled except that such paper included both promissory notes and bills of exchange, that the notes were probably as a rule indorsed, and that both bills and notes were bought and sold at rates of discount much higher than those which have prevailed in more recent years. It seems probable that they obtained their supplies of paper in the main from merchants in various lines of trade. Such merchants, it is practically certain, were by no means always the makers of notes which they offered to dealers. In a number of cases they must merely have indorsed notes which they had received in the ordinary course of trade and turned them over to note brokers for sale in the market. What-

---

[17] Both Boston and Philadelphia had become important trading and financial centers before the close of the eighteenth century. In fact, it is said that the first money market in America "developed in Philadelphia rather than in New York," and that Philadelphia remained the leading money market in the United States until about 1836, when the charter of the Second Bank of the United States expired (Myers, *op. cit.*, pp. 3, 9). It is probable, therefore, that dealings in negotiable paper began in Boston and Philadelphia about as early as in Charleston and New York, though the writer found no positive evidence of such dealings in the former two towns before 1800.

ever may have been the sources of supply of the negotiable paper they handled, dealers in such paper sold it both to the few banks which were organized before 1800 and to the comparatively few private capitalists who had surplus funds available for investment in notes or bills yielding relatively high rates of return. Finally, it should be pointed out that dealers in commercial paper during the eighteenth century did not confine their operations to the purchase and sale of such paper exclusively. Some of them dealt also in stocks, as the advertisements of Nathaniel Prime and G. W. Cornwell indicate; and indeed the range of operations of these early dealers is said to have been wide enough to include, in addition, the purchase at a heavy discount of notes issued by out-of-town banks, and even a general "negotiating" or commission business.[18]

2. GROWTH OF THE NOTE BROKERAGE BUSINESS, 1800–1861

It has been shown that dealers in several of the leading commercial centers of the United States had begun to buy and sell commercial paper in the market before the close of the eighteenth century. With the rapid development of trading and industrial activity of all kinds, the improvements in means of transportation and communication, and the increase in the number and capital of banking institutions, which took place in the period from 1800 to the outbreak of the Civil War, dealings in open-market paper gradually increased in volume and spread to other parts of the country than those already mentioned. References to such dealings accordingly become more frequent in the early years of the nineteenth century.

One of the earliest of these references is an advertisement of

---

[18] Myers, *op. cit.*, p. 56, and Klein, *op. cit.*, Nov. 1911, p. 532. It will be recalled that, in the advertisement shown in Exhibit 1, G. W. Cornwell offers his services in the "Negociating Business" and in the purchase and sale of "Negociable Paper, Stocks, Bills of Exchange, &c." (italics are the writer's) ; and that Nathaniel Prime in 1796 called himself a "Stock and Commission Broker."

According to Klein, dealers in commercial paper toward the beginning of the nineteenth century "were not brokers, but either general commission merchants, or, in some instances, probably men of means who had their own capital to invest" (*loc. cit.*). Such dealers in some instances may very well have been "general commission merchants" or "men of means who had their own capital to invest"; but Klein appears to be mistaken in maintaining that they were not brokers.

Abraham Pinto, which is said to have appeared in the New York *Commercial Advertiser* of April 15, 1801. In this advertisement Pinto states that he will buy and sell on commission " 'all kinds of United States Funded Debt, Shares in the different Banks, Insurance Shares, Bills of Exchange, Negotiable Notes, &c. Also, Merchandize in general at no. 30 Mill-street.' " [19] He is said to have been typical of a class of "stock and exchange brokers" who early in the nineteenth century were buying and selling foreign and domestic bills of exchange, selling bank notes, transferring stocks, and the like.[20] Evidently he was acting as a general commission broker, and in this capacity exercising functions of as wide a range as those advertised in the same city two years earlier by G. W. Cornwell. Operations of the same general character were being carried on at the same time by at least two other New York brokers also, E. Benjamin and P. C. Waterbury, whose advertisements appeared in the New York *Commercial Advertiser* early in 1801. Copies of such advertisements are shown in Exhibits 2 and 3, respectively. References to other early dealers in negotiable paper in New York State may be found in two cases decided in the New York Supreme Court early in the nineteenth century. The first of these cases mentions a note broker who was dealing in commercial paper at least as early as 1810;[21] the second, two bill brokers who were buying and selling such paper by 1814, and probably earlier.[22] Presumably all three dealers were carrying on their operations in New York City.

New York is not the only state in which commercial paper was being bought and sold in the market in the early years of the nineteenth century. Evidence derived mainly from early law cases indicates that dealings in negotiable instruments were also being

---

[19] Cole, *op. cit.*, p. 392. The present writer was unable to find this advertisement in the *Commercial Advertiser* of April 15, 1801. Other advertisements of Pinto, however, may be found in earlier issues of the same journal. The following appeared in the issue of January 1, 1801, p. 1:

ABRAHAM PINTO,
Stock & Money Broker.
No. 30 Mill-Street.
N.B. Goods Bought and Sold on Commission.

[20] Cole, *loc. cit.*   [21] *Woodhull* v. *Holmes,* 10 Johnson (N. Y.) 231.
[22] *Munn* v. *Commission Co.,* 15 Johnson (N. Y.) 44.

carried on shortly after 1800 in Massachusetts, Pennsylvania, and Maryland.

Two cases decided in the Massachusetts Supreme Court mention "brokers" who were buying and selling promissory notes in that state at least as early as 1807.[23] The earlier of these cases states that the maker and the payee of a promissory note, "to raise money," delivered the note "to one Bartlett a broker, to negotiate in the market," and that this note "was originally made to sell in the market." [24] Two other cases, decided somewhat later in the same court, indicate that there were note brokers and at least a limited open market for commercial paper in Boston by 1816, and bill brokers in Boston and Philadelphia by the following year.[25] The first of these two cases contains the significant statements that "one Sumner, a broker," sold a promissory note to the plaintiff at a discount of 1 per cent a month, such "being the rate at which good commercial paper was then passed on the exchange," and that many other notes "of the like description" were made by the maker of this note about the same time and "delivered to brokers to be discounted." [26]

Dealings in negotiable paper in Pennsylvania can be traced back at least as far as 1801. In Philadelphia, indeed, such operations must have been begun in the eighteenth century, since that city was for years the leading money market in the country. At any rate, an early law case supplies evidence of dealings in commercial paper, presumably in Philadelphia, at the beginning of the following century. In this case it is stated that one Ross, "a broker," sold a thirty-day promissory note to the plaintiff in 1801 "in exchange for land." [27]

In Maryland both bills of exchange and promissory notes were being bought and sold in the market about the same time. By

---

[23] *Churchill* v. *Suter*, 4 Mass. 156, and *Widgery* v. *Munroe et al.*, 6 Mass. 449.

The latter case states that "a broker" sold to the plaintiff, at a discount of 2¼ per cent a month, "an accommodation note between the maker and endorsers, to enable the maker to raise money on it as a security" (pp. 449–450).

[24] *Churchill* v. *Suter*, 156–157.

[25] *Boardman* v. *Gore et al.*, 15 Mass. 331, and *Nevins et al.* v. *De Grand*, 15 Mass. 436. [26] *Boardman* v. *Gore et al.*, 331–332.

[27] *Mussi* v. *Lorain*, 2 Browne (Penn.) 56.

EXHIBIT 2

ADVERTISEMENT OF E. BENJAMIN, 1801 *

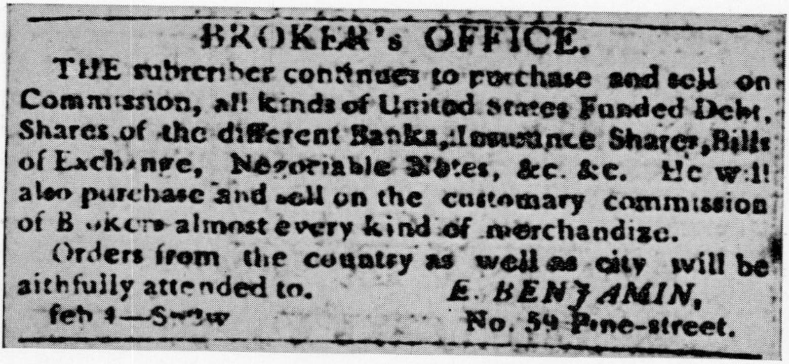

BROKER's OFFICE.

THE subscriber continues to purchase and sell on Commission, all kinds of United States Funded Debt, Shares of the different Banks, Insurance Shares, Bills of Exchange, Negotiable Notes, &c. &c. He will also purchase and sell on the customary commission of Brokers almost every kind of merchandize.

Orders from the country as well as city will be faithfully attended to.   E. BENJAMIN,

feb 4—S~3w   No. 59 Pine-street.

* Published in the New York *Commercial Advertiser*, March 14, 1801, p. 4.

EXHIBIT 3

ADVERTISEMENT OF P. C. WATERBURY, 1801 *

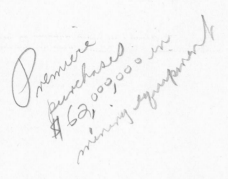

BROKER's OFFICE.

P. C. WATERBURY informs his friends and the public that he has again commenced the business of *INSURANCE BROKER*, at his office, no, 99, Water-street. From long experience and information in that line, his employers may be assured of accuracy, dispatch and punctuality. He also buys and sells on Commission, the Stock of the United States, Bank and Insurance Stock, Bills of Exchange, &c.

nov 13   tf

* Published in the New York *Commercial Advertiser*, January 1, 1801, p. 4.

1803, two years after he had begun business as a linen importer, Alexander Brown, founder of the house of Alexander Brown and Sons of Baltimore, was dealing in bills of exchange in that city.[28] References may be found also to other dealers, presumably both note and bill brokers, who were buying the paper of Baltimore merchants in the same year.[29] Two law cases decided some years later supply further evidence of open-market operations in commercial paper, including both bills and notes, in Maryland before 1820.[30]

Even as early as 1818 the practice of "shaving" notes seems to have become fairly common in various parts of the country. References to "note-shaving" and "note shavers" or "money brokers" appear rather frequently in *Niles' Weekly Register* during the years 1818 and 1819. From articles published in this periodical it may be inferred that "note shavers" were plying their trade by 1818 not only in the larger cities, but also in smaller towns, and even in the sparsely settled regions of what was then the West.[31]

[28] Cole, *op. cit.*, p. 390. The sons of Alexander Brown later established affiliated houses similar to the original Baltimore house — in Philadelphia in 1818, and in New York in 1825. In the case of all three houses, dealings begun originally in merchandise gradually declined in importance as compared with dealings in bills of exchange. By about 1830 all three houses apparently "had become specialized 'merchant-bankers'" (*ibid.*, p. 391).

[29] It is said that, because of inadequate banking facilities in their city — as evidenced by the fact that Baltimore banks early in 1804 were rejecting some $120,000 of good commercial paper every week — merchants seeking accommodation in Baltimore about 1803 "were compelled to patronize brokers who charged them excessive rates"; and that the lack of banking facilities and the consequent excessive rates accounted in large measure for a considerable decline in Baltimore's trade in 1803 (A. C. Bryan, *History of State Banking in Maryland*, p. 22; and J. W. Randall, "The Centenary of Maryland's First Banking Corporations," *Proc. Md. Bankers' Assoc.*, 1904, p. 50).

[30] *Sauerwein* v. *Brunner*, 1 Harris and Gill (Md.) 477, and *Gaither* v. *Lee*, 2 Cranch, C. C. 205. An account of the latter case is given in *Niles' Weekly Register*, vol. XVIII (July 1, 1820), p. 328.

[31] Cf. the following:

"Alas! where shall they [farmers] go to find this asylum from brokers and speculators? The borders of the Mississippi, the Missouri, Illinois, Ohio, Kentucky, and Tennessee, are infested by this pernicious *fry*" ("The Paper System — No. III," *Niles' Weekly Register*, vol. XIV, May 9, 1818, p. 183).

"*Description!* — I asked a friend who returned from ———— the other day — what was the state of business there? 'Every body is fully employed,' said he. How so? 'Every man who has 100 dollars is *shaving,* and every one that wants $100 is trying to get *shaved,* and you find a broker's office in every street. *Shavers and*

The business of these early "money brokers" or "note shavers" apparently consisted in discounting, at rates which would now seem absurdly high, notes and bills of merchants or others who could not obtain sufficient accommodation from banks, and then either selling such paper to banks or other buyers at lower rates, or if it could not be rediscounted, holding it to maturity.[32] Not only "private capitalists" but banks and bank directors themselves seem to have been busily engaged in "shaving" notes in this early period, and indeed for some years later.[33] In the earlier years of the nineteenth century banks are said often to have charged usurious rates on paper they bought through brokers, on the pre-

---

shavees are the bulk of the male population, and many females are also busy in such matters' " (*ibid.*, vol. XVII, Nov. 20, 1819, p. 185). See also vol. XIV, six other articles on "The Paper System," and "Paper System. The Farmer and the Broker" (Aug. 22, 1818), pp. 426–428; vol. XVI, "Brokers" (May 8, 1819), p. 179; and vol. XVII, "Shaving" (Oct. 9, 1819), p. 85.

[32] The nature of the business in which these early "money brokers" were engaged is indicated by the following:

"The principal business of the money broker is discounting notes — *shaving* them . . . that is . . . buying them at as great a discount as possible — no matter what the laws say on the subject. I am told that in ordinary cases where the security is good, and the paper undoubted, they don't charge more than two per cent. a month discount; but this is really a piece of moderation I think quite creditable" ("The Paper System — No. II," *Niles' Weekly Register*, vol. XIV, May 2, 1818, p. 155).

It should be remembered, of course, that the risks involved in the purchase of paper of the classes handled by these early "note shavers" probably corresponded pretty closely as a rule with the high rates at which such paper was discounted.

[33] Cf. the following:

". . . many, I will not say a majority of the bank directors, are leagued with these brokers, and employ the discounts they receive, in his very dirty shop, in shaving notes through his agency; thus escaping the odium, while they receive the gains of such vile degradation" (*ibid.*).

". . . speculators bolster up brokers, brokers are cats-paws to bank directors" ("The Paper System — No. VII," *Niles' Weekly Register*, vol. XIV, June 20, 1818, p. 285).

"Shaving Notes without any Capital. — In the . . . trial in the Supreme Court, recently, of the case of Luke Green against Peleg W. Gardiner, . . . Doyle testified that while he was cashier of the Grocers' and Producers' Bank, one of the Directors of that bank, now deceased, was in the habit [presumably about 1850 or later] of buying paper of the bill-brokers, giving therefor his check payable some days ahead, and before it came due would get the same discounted to pay his check. Sharper practice than this was never sworn to in a court of law. Men frequently transact a large business without capital; but we never before heard of a man shaving notes without money. — Providence Journal" (*Bankers' Mag.*, Jan. 1858, p. 577).

tense that they had to pay the broker a commission.[34] With or without such a pretense, their practice of charging usurious rates on paper bought in the market seems to have continued at least as late as the 1850's. In a treatise on currency and banking published in 1840 Raguet mentions "discounting notes in the market, through the instrumentality of brokers, at usurious interest, instead of discounting them at lawful interest, in the regular way," as one means which some banks were using to secure more than the legal rate of return on their loanable funds. As one example, he cites the case of a New York bank which "discounted at usurious interest out of doors, the very notes that had been offered to the bank and been rejected by the board of directors."[35] The same practice is mentioned in a treatise published in Philadelphia in 1854.[36]

During the 1820's dealings in bills of exchange and/or promissory notes attained sufficient importance to engage the attention not only of individual brokers but also of banking houses and commercial banks. By about 1823 the New York office of S. & M. Allen, a partnership established in that city in 1815, had begun to buy and sell bills of exchange and "notes of hand on all sections of

[34] Klein, *loc. cit.*

[35] Condy Raguet, *A Treatise on Currency and Banking*, p. 109.
Another means by which banks then evaded usury laws and increased their profits was to give preference in their discounting to customers who agreed to "leave in the bank, never to be drawn for, a certain proportion [sometimes as high as 20, 30, or 40 per cent] of the amount borrowed; by which virtually the bank receives interest for money or credit which it does not lend. . . . Borrowers upon such terms are seldom to be found amongst the most responsible traders, but can always be had in abundance amongst that class of needy men, who, without such a facility, would be obliged to borrow in the open market at a higher rate of interest" (*ibid.*, p. 105).
By that time, and doubtless many years before 1840, banks were deducting in advance all or part of the interest they charged on their loans (*ibid.*, pp. 85, 90, 104).
The passages in Raguet's treatise referred to above indicate that by 1840, and very probably a number of years earlier, commercial banks' practices in discounting notes and acceptances in important respects had become the same as those of the present; and that borrowing in the open market at that time generally involved higher charges than borrowing direct from banks — a circumstance which in later years was to be reversed.

[36] "Another way [by which "bank speculators" "make money"] is to refuse discounts of unexceptionable paper at their banking office at legal rates, and buy up the same paper, through brokers or agents, at two, three, and four per cent. a month" (E. T. Freedley, *A Practical Treatise on Business*, p. 177).

the country," as well as stocks and foreign bills of exchange.[37] Four years later, in 1827, the Second Bank of the United States began to buy and sell bills of exchange on a large scale, and by about 1830 "stock banks" also had begun to deal in such paper.[38]

Dealings in open-market paper during the ten years following very probably increased in volume. At any rate, there are records of such dealings within this decade not only in the states already mentioned but also in Louisiana; and toward the close of this period quotations of rates on open-market commercial paper in various cities began to appear in a leading financial periodical. Operations of note brokers in Massachusetts in 1831 and 1837 are mentioned in two cases decided in the supreme court of that state;[39] and "brokers and others taking bills and notes," in a work on negotiable instruments published in Boston in the latter year.[40] By 1834 Connecticut banks were buying notes and bills of exchange in New York and other cities. Some of this paper they purchased through other banks. Whether or not they bought either notes or acceptances through brokers also is not stated, but it is reasonable to suppose that they were using the services of such intermediary dealers at that time.[41] At all events, just three years later the Exchange Bank, a Connecticut institution, "through brokers in New York, purchased two parcels of Notes to the amount of $45,000, at a discount of 18 per cent per annum for the time they had to run, which was from 38 to 105 days." [42] Banks

---

[37] H. M. Larson, "S. & M. Allen — Lottery, Exchange, and Stock Brokerage," *Jour. Ec. and Bus. Hist.*, May 1931, p. 439. The main business of this firm before 1823 had been the selling of lottery tickets (*ibid.*, p. 424).

[38] A. H. Cole, *op. cit.*, pp. 394, 403.

An earlier writer, Professor John McVickar, seems to have been of the opinion that there was no important class of dealers in foreign exchange in the United States as late as 1829; for in a pamphlet published in that year he predicted that such "a class of bill merchants; men devoted to the business of foreign exchanges" would probably be established in this country "in the course of time" (*Considerations upon the Expediency of Abolishing Damages on Protested Bills of Exchange* — pamphlet — p. 36).

[39] *Dana* v. *Underwood*, 19 Pickering (Mass.) 99, and *Lobdell* v. *Baker*, 1 Metcalf (Mass.) 193. See also *Lobdell* v. *Baker*, 3 Metcalf 469.

[40] B. F. Foster, *A Practical Summary of the Law and Usage of Bills of Exchange and Promissory Notes*, p. 32.

[41] *Report of the Committee Appointed by the Legislature to Visit and Examine the Banks in Connecticut*, 1837, pp. 12–13.   [42] *Ibid.*

in Louisiana also were probably using the services of brokers about the same time, since a case decided in the supreme court of that state in 1840 mentions an exchange and note broker (presumably of New Orleans), and the judge who delivered the opinion of the court stated that brokers were then buying and selling "paper on their own account, and on that of others" in Louisiana.[43] Even before 1840 — as early as 1837, in fact — rates on open-market commercial paper in leading cities were being quoted in the *Financial Register of the United States*,[44] a fact which seems to indicate that by such time a fairly broad market for bills and notes had developed in each of these cities.

Up to this time the market for such paper doubtless remained primarily a local market, to be found in each of a number of the larger cities. Within the next ten years, however, as the operations of bill brokers and note brokers increased in volume and extended to communities beyond their own immediate localities, the market for commercial paper seems to have become increasingly intersectional in character. The purchase of bills and notes in New York and other cities by Connecticut banks during the 1830's has already been noted. Beginning about 1840, the bank commissioners of Connecticut, and of New Hampshire and Massachusetts as well, frequently refer to the purchase of commercial paper in New York or Boston by banks in their states.[45] They often condemn the practice of making such "foreign loans," on the ground that a bank's funds should be lent to borrowers in its own com-

---

[43] *Nott* v. *Papet*, 15 La. 306.

[44] See, for example, the issue of Oct. 25, 1837 (vol. I), p. 129.

In the period before 1861, and for some years later, the terms "business paper," "mercantile paper," and "commercial paper" were used interchangeably. Rates on such paper were often referred to as "street" rates or rates "out of doors." Borrowing "in the street" seems to have meant borrowing in the open market from any one, whether a banker, private capitalist, or any one else, willing to advance funds at relatively high rates to persons who found it impossible or inconvenient to obtain the required accommodation from banks direct. In at least some cases borrowers "in the street" no doubt negotiated directly with the ultimate lenders, instead of using the services of brokers.

With the terms "street rates" or rates "out of doors" may be compared the expression "up-the-alley rates," sometimes used in New York to indicate rates on "commercial paper" of inferior grade.

[45] H. E. Miller, *Banking Theories in the United States before 1860*, pp. 181–182, 212, and D. R. Dewey, *State Banking before the Civil War*, pp. 200–205.

munity. The view that banks should lend to local borrowers, rather than extend credit to outsiders, was commonly held in New England and various other states throughout the entire period from 1800 to 1861. A number of states during this period even passed laws restricting the amounts banks could lend to persons living in other states or prohibiting them from making any loans to such persons at all.[46] While this prejudice against "outside" loans, and the legislation to which it gave rise, probably operated to restrict to some extent the purchase of paper in the open market, banks nevertheless continued to place surplus funds in such "foreign loans." The purchase of paper in New York by "banks from out of town" is mentioned again in 1845, in an article in the *Bankers' Magazine*.[47] New York banks themselves, as well as "large monied houses in Wall street [*sic*]," seem to have been discounting, about as early as 1840, notes payable received by local wholesale dealers in payment for goods sold to retailers in "all quarters of the Union." [48] Within the next ten years, moreover, commercial paper was being sent from cities like Boston to other leading commercial centers for discount. Presumably some of this paper, as well as some of the retailers' paper just mentioned, was handled by brokers.[49]

Further evidence of the growth of the commercial paper business during the decade from 1840 to 1850 is furnished by numerous references to dealers or dealings in bills and notes in periodicals and law cases and by the increasing frequency with which quotations of commercial paper rates may be found after 1840. Bill brokers (presumably in New York in both cases) are mentioned in *Hunt's Merchants' Magazine* [50] in 1843, and in the

---

[46] Dewey, *op. cit.*, pp. 200–206; Miller, *op. cit.*, pp. 181–182, 212; and M. G. Myers, *The New York Money Market*, I, 46.

The view that it is the duty of a commercial bank to lend primarily to persons or concerns in its own community, rather than buy commercial paper in the market, is still held in various sections of the country.

[47] "Money Market. — 18th November, 1845," *Bankers' Mag.*, Nov. 18, 1845, p. 74.

[48] "Monthly Financial and Commercial Article," *U. S. Dem. Rev.*, Oct. 1842, p. 434.

[49] "Review of the Month," *Bankers' Mag.*, April 1849, p. 644, and "Notes on the Money Market," *ibid.*, May 1849, p. 708.   [50] April 1843, p. 370.

Bankers' Magazine [51] in 1845, and by 1850 dealing in commercial paper seems to have become an established business in New York. An article published in the *Journal of Commerce* in the latter year and reprinted in the *Bankers' Magazine* speaks of the "introduction of a regular system of street discounts, and the classification of business paper at regular rates, which ordinarily change only when the money market fluctuates materially." It then points out the significant change in the commercial paper business which the introduction of this "regular system" involved:

Formerly, no person went into the street for loans, except he was pressed for funds, or wished to rid himself of doubtful assets, and the notes thus offered were hawked around privately, until some capitalist was tempted to make the purchase. Now, at some of the principal brokers', every name has its price, and the holder may dispose of his bill at once, or limit it and leave it for the inspection of purchasers. [52]

Toward the close of this decade activities of "private capitalists" in the Boston market are mentioned rather frequently in the *Bankers' Magazine*. Law cases decided in the supreme courts of Maine and Louisiana about the same time indicate that commercial paper was being bought and sold in those states also during the 1840's. [53] Additional evidence of such activity in "Wall Street," "State Street," and most of the other leading financial centers, is supplied by the fact that quotations of commercial paper rates in various cities may be found more frequently in financial periodicals during this period than in the decade preceding. Even the modern expression, "prime paper," was being used in connection with such quotations as early as 1846. [54]

During the remaining ten odd years of the period considered in this chapter, the main developments in the note brokerage business seem to have been similar to those already noted. The number of

---

[51] Nov. 11, 1845, p. 58.

[52] "Out-Door Capital," *Bankers' Mag.*, Dec. 1850, p. 505.

[53] *Baxter* v. *Duren*, 29 Maine 434, and *Conrey* v. *Hoover*, 10 La. Ann. 437. In the first of these cases one Wood testified "that he had been a broker in Portland for a number of years past" (i.e., before 1849). In the second case two dealers testified that they had been brokers (presumably in New Orleans) since about 1843.

[54] "The street rates for prime paper [in New York] may be quoted at 10 @ 12 per cent" ("The Money Market," *Bankers' Mag.*, April 14, 1846, p. 415).

dealers, whether individual brokers or banking houses, increased; dealings in bills and notes were extended to cities as far west as St. Louis; the market for commercial paper broadened, and the volume of paper bought and sold undoubtedly increased;[55] and by 1861 the purchase and sale of bills and notes had become an established business in a number of cities besides New York.

As was indicated above, the latter city had become the leading money market in the United States by about 1836, and by 1850 "a regular system of street discounts" had been introduced in Wall Street. From this time on, New York seems to have retained the primacy it had won in earlier years not only as a money market in general but also as a market for commercial paper.[56]

---

[55] Unfortunately even estimates of the total volume of commercial paper sold in the United States each year do not become available until some time after the Civil War. The nearest approximation the writer could find to such an estimate for any year during the period before 1861 was the statement (in the article on "The Wall Street Note Brokers," quoted on p. 21) that in 1851 there were "many *millions* under the control of these brokers." In the earlier years of the nineteenth century the total volume of paper sold must indeed have been small, as seems to be indicated both by the small number of commercial banks then existent and by the small amount of their capital. In 1806 Blodget published in his *Economica* a list of all the banks concerning which he was able to collect information. This list, which he admitted was incomplete, included only forty-seven banks. In a supplementary list he included twenty-one additional banks. The total capital of these institutions he estimated at $45,000,000 (Samuel Blodget, *Economica: A Statistical Manual for the United States of America*, pp. 158–160). Obviously, sixty-eight banks with such a total capital could furnish but a comparatively small demand for open-market paper. It is true that the number of state banks increased rapidly between 1811 and 1816 and in later years, and it is said that banks were actively discounting both bills and notes by about 1820; yet in 1818, when the Suffolk Bank was chartered, there were only seven banks in Boston (Dewey, *Financial History of the United States*, 9th ed., p. 144; *Fleckner* v. *The Bank of the United States*, 8 Wheaton 338, 341, 349; Horace White, *Money and Banking*, 5th ed., p. 294). Even as late as 1851 the total loans of New York City banks were estimated at only $65,000,000, and those of Boston banks at only $35,000,000 (*Bankers' Mag.*, Feb. 1851, p. 694). Hence the annual volume of commercial paper bought and sold in the market in the decade preceding the Civil War, while much greater than the aggregate amount handled in any year during the eighteenth century, was doubtless considerably smaller than the corresponding figure for almost any year since 1900.

[56] The importance of New York as a money market in the early 1850's is indicated by the following excerpts from articles in a leading financial journal:

"The concentration of capital at New York, from all quarters of the Union, as well as from New England, enables that great city to give *a tone* to the money circle of other cities" ("Notes on the Money Market," *Bankers' Mag.*, Feb. 1851, p. 694).

"It is fully conceded that New York is now the grand centre of commercial and

Perhaps the best evidence of the importance of Wall Street as a center of dealings in open-market paper during the decade before the Civil War is afforded by the numerous references to dealers or dealings in such paper in various periodicals. One of the most interesting of these references is the following brief article on "The Wall Street Note Brokers," which appeared in the *Wall Street Journal* in 1851:

This class of our citizens have assumed an importance in our community, that deserves more than a passing notice. They are fast taking the place of the banks, for whom many of them act as agents. Formerly they were known by the name of *shavers*, and were looked upon as almost out of the pale of *commercial* respectability. A change has come over the spirit of the feeling, and they are now looked upon in the same light as they are in Europe — as parties holding a position second only to the banks themselves; and persons now find it quite as easy to drop into the office of a respectable bill broker, and obtain the facilities he [*sic*] has been accustomed to ask hat in hand from a bank, without going through the degrading means they insist on. There are many *millions* under the control of these brokers, and as a body they are worthy of all trust. Some, though, cannot forget the *old leaven,* particularly found in the region of Jone's Court, who still merit the old-fashioned name of shavers from 3 to 10 per cent a month — men bringing the name of a broker into disrepute, which though they acquired wealth by the misery and ruin of their customers, still reek on, and cannot forget their origin. These *gentlemen* prove but an exception to the general *modern* high character which the bill brokers hold.[57]

Other references to dealers or dealings in commercial paper in New York during this decade appear so frequently that they must be summarized briefly. In 1851 large amounts of "business paper" are said to have been "daily discounted in New York for Boston account, with much advantage to the sellers," because of more favorable rates in the former city.[58] At least some part of this

monetary movements in this country; and it is there that both borrowers and lenders congregate for the heavy operations of the day. Both Boston and Philadelphia assume the condition of the New York market as a criterion for themselves, and as the rates rise or fall in Wall Street, so they rise or fall in the other cities" ("Notes on the Money Market," *ibid.*, April 1852, p. 839).

[57] Reprinted in *Hunt's Merch. Mag.*, Nov. 1851, p. 622.

[58] "Notes on the Money Market" (Dec. 26, 1851), *Bankers' Mag.*, Jan. 1852, p. 587.

paper must have been sold through brokers. Two years later mention is made of the purchase by "private capitalists" of "a large amount" of commercial paper which New York banks had rejected because a new state law, "requiring the publication of weekly returns from our city banks," had "induced them generally to curtail their discount line." [59] Similar purchases are mentioned again in 1856.[60] In 1853 a "loan broker" [61] and bill brokers [62] are mentioned. In 1855 the purchase of "prime paper from the brokers" by New York banks was noted.[63] The purchase of paper by brokers themselves in the years 1854–1856, and again in 1858 and 1859, is noted in various issues of the *Bankers' Magazine* for these years. In 1858 mention is made of the investment of $20,000 in "'good endorsed business paper'" in New York by a "'capitalist in the country.'" [64] In the same year Henry Clews, one of the best-known dealers in commercial paper during the Civil War period and later, began business in Wall Street.[65] Numerous quotations of commercial paper rates become available during this decade. In connection with such quotations, the modern expression, "prime commercial paper," was used as early as 1852;[66] and by 1859 a rather detailed classification of short-term money rates had appeared in a leading commercial and financial periodical.[67] In the same year a Philadelphia banking house, in a letter to the editor of the *Bankers' Magazine*, stated that since "the *panic* [of

[59] "Notes on the Money Market," *Bankers' Mag.*, Sept. 1853, p. 274.
[60] "Notes on the Money Market," *ibid.*, Nov. 1856, p. 414.
[61] *Hunt's Merch. Mag.*, Oct. 1853, p. 455.
[62] "Notes on the Money Market," *Bankers' Mag.*, Nov. 1853, p. 442.
[63] "Notes on the Money Market," *ibid.*, March 1855, p. 742.
[64] "Permanent Investment," *ibid.*, Jan. 1858, p. 577.
[65] Henry Clews, *Twenty-eight Years in Wall Street*, p. 5.
[66] "Notes on the Money Market," *Bankers' Mag.*, Dec. 1852, p. 494.
[67] "The rate of money . . . may be quoted as follows: —

	Oct. 25th	Nov. 24th	Dec. 6th	Dec. 14th
Loans on call, stock securities	3 a 3½	3⅛ a 4	3½ a 4½	3½ a 4½
Loans on call, other securities	3½ a 4½	4 a 5	5 a 6	4 a 5
Prime indorsed bills, 60 days	4½ a 5	4¾ a 5	4½ a 5½	4 a 5
Prime indorsed bills, 4 to 6 mos.	5 a 6	5½ a 6	5 a 6	5 a 6
First-class single signatures	5 a 7	5½ a 7	5 a 6	6 a 7
Other good commercial paper	7 a 8	7 a 8	7 a 8	7 a 8
Names not well known	8 a 10	8 a 10	8 a 10	8 a 10"

("Commercial Chronicle and Review," *Hunt's Merch. Mag.*, Jan. 1859, p. 76.)

1857] (so called) the note brokers have become very necessary to banks and bankers," and suggested that a list of all the note brokers "generally deemed reliable" in New York would be valuable to insert in the next issue of the *Bankers' Register*.[68]

After New York, Boston was perhaps the next most important market for commercial paper in the decade before the Civil War. As early in this period as September 1850 the firm of Gilmore, Blake, and Ward was formed in the latter city "to carry on a banking and foreign exchange business." Within the next few years this firm was succeeded by several others, the last of which, organized in April 1858, took the name of Blake Brothers and Company.[69] Under this name the firm became one of the leading dealers in commercial paper; and for many years, until it gave up operations in such paper in 1930, it had the distinction of being the oldest commercial paper house in the country. An advertisement of a predecessor firm is shown in Exhibit 4, and the announcement of the formation of the later firm in Exhibit 5. These exhibits indicate the variety of operations in which this firm and its predecessors were engaged. Besides Blake Brothers and Company, numerous other dealers were carrying on similar operations in State Street during this same period. A Boston almanac lists four note brokers in its "Boston Business Directory" as of November 1856.[70] The *Boston Directory for the Year 1857* lists nine "note brokers," [71] and the *Directory* for 1860, twenty-eight such dealers.[72] The range of operations of these brokers in some cases

[68] The editor announced in reply: "The information desired, although merely local and not appreciated by persons at a distance, will be added to our *Bankers' Register* for the coming year; also a list of note brokers in Philadelphia and Boston" ("Correspondence of the Bankers' Magazine. I. List of Note Brokers," *Bankers' Mag.*, July 1859, p. 58). Such lists of note brokers, however, were evidently not published in the *Bankers' Register* for 1860.

Other references to brokers or their dealings in commercial paper, too numerous to mention, may be found in various issues of the *Bankers' Magazine* for 1859 and later years.

[69] Blake Brothers and Company, "A Word about Blake Brothers & Co." (typewritten paper), p. 1.

[70] *The Boston Almanac for the Year 1857*, p. 92. This list was undoubtedly incomplete.

[71] Page 389.

[72] Page 471.

was about as wide as that of Blake Brothers and Company, as is indicated by the two advertisements included in Exhibit 6.[73] At least some of these dealers seem to have carried on a rather active business, for their operations attracted the attention of the press, of the Boston Board of Trade, and of the Massachusetts state bank commissioners. An article in the Boston *Herald*, reprinted in *Hunt's Merchants' Magazine* in 1857, spoke with disapproval of excessive borrowing at high rates in the open market by "the young trader." [74] In a memorial to the Massachusetts House of Representatives in the same year, the Boston Board of Trade contrasted borrowing by local merchants and manufacturers "in the *legitimate* way," from banks, with borrowing "in the illegitimate way," through brokers.[75] More or less similar views were expressed by the Massachusetts bank commissioners in their annual reports of 1859 and 1860.[76]

[73] These advertisements appeared in the *Massachusetts Register for the Year 1859*. It will be noted that, though both dealers were carrying on exactly the same kinds of operations, Perkins described himself as a stock and *note* broker, while the firm of Dupee, Beck, & Sayles preferred the term *bill* broker. Throughout the period before the Civil War, and for many years later, the two terms were used synonymously, as were "bill brokerage" and "note brokerage." The terms "bills" and "notes" also have often been used interchangeably in this country, however inaccurate such use may be.

[74] "Of Paying Extra Interest for Money," *Hunt's Merch. Mag.*, Aug. 1857, p. 262. Reliable quotations of rates on prime commercial paper, comparable to the rates quoted in more recent years, are probably not available for any year of the period considered in this chapter. There can be little question, however, that rates on promissory notes sold in the market were generally higher in the years before the Civil War than such rates have been during most of the years since 1860. This conclusion is supported by Chart 1.

[75] "Increase of Banking Capital," *Bankers' Mag.*, May 1857, p. 902.

[76] Dewey, *State Banking before the Civil War*, p. 202.

In their report for 1860 these commissioners stated that banks often discount paper for brokers "in the regular way, and at legal rates; but not infrequently, we are led to believe, the managers [of a bank] go with its money into the street, and buy notes, as any private citizen would do, at rates of discount much beyond the legal rates" (*Annual Report of the Bank Commissioners of Massachusetts*, 1860, p. 138).

The commissioners had "not a word to utter against that most respectable and useful class of business men" (note brokers), but conceived "their legitimate business to be auxiliary to that of the banks, in drawing capital from private sources, and supplying it to the demands of trade." If these brokers drew "their principal capital" not from "private sources," but from the banks, in the opinion of the commissioners they became an "unnecessary class of middle-men" (*ibid.*, pp. 137–138).

EXHIBIT 4

ADVERTISEMENT OF BLAKE, HOWE & CO., 1856

BLAKE, HOWE & CO.,

GEO. BATY BLAKE, JOHN RICE BLAKE, JAS. MURRAY HOWE.

Bankers & Dealers in Exchange,

Brokers and Negotiators of Stocks,

NO. 4, CORNER OF STATE STREET, BOSTON.

B., H. & CO. draw Bills upon Messrs. GEORGE PEABODY & CO., LONDON, for any amount from £1 upwards, and payable at from one to sixty days' sight, at the lowest market rates. They also buy Bills of Exchange, or sell them for their owners on commission. Circular Letters of Credit on Messrs. Geo. Peabody & Co. will be furnished to travellers in Europe or along the Mediterranean Sea. For freight or other moneys deposited with their correspondents in England —on terms which will be explained at their office,—an equivalent will be paid in Boston at the current rate of Exchange, less a charge of one-half of one per cent., being half the usual banker's commission.

B., H. & CO. give their attention, also, to the purchase and sale of Stocks, at the Brokers' Board and elsewhere, both in Boston and, by their agents, in New York and the Southern cities. As they confine themselves to a *strictly* commission business in this department, investors and others may be sure of an impartial and undivided attention to their interests.

Good Commercial Paper is also bought and sold at the most favorable rates. Capitalists preferring this kind of investment will find a most undoubted security with a remunerating rate of interest; while banks and other moneyed institutions can employ their funds both safely and profitably, with a confidence of receiving them again in money at short intervals.

EXHIBIT 5

ANNOUNCEMENT OF BLAKE BROTHERS & COMPANY, 1858

Blake Brothers & Company

The undersigned have associated themselves under the firm of _Blake Brothers & Company_, and will continue the Banking Business at No _28 State Street_ Merchants Bank Building. They offer their services for the purchase and sale of securities and in particular for the negotiation of _Commercial Paper_ & _Sterling Exchange_

Boston April 1, 1858

Geo. E. Baty E. Blake

John K. Blake

Saml Bradford

inside one week

EXHIBIT 6

ADVERTISEMENTS OF BOSTON BROKERS, 1859 *

DUPEE, BECK, & SAYLES,

STOCK & BILL BROKERS,

41 State Street, Boston,

Buy and sell on Commission, State, City, and Town Securities, Railroad and other Bonds, Manufacturing, Bank, and Railroad Shares; negotiate business paper and loans on Stock collaterals.

D., B., & S. give particular attention to the Mines of Lake Superior, and are prepared to furnish reliable information respecting them. A monthly review of the Stock and Money Market, with quotations of all the current securities, will be sent to any address desired.

JAMES A. DUPEE.   **JAMES BECK.**   **HENRY SAYLES.**

T. HENRY PERKINS,

STOCK AND NOTE BROKER,

NO. 19 STATE STREET,

BOSTON,

Buys and sells on Commission, State, City, and Town Securities, Railroad and other Bonds, Manufacturing, Bank, and Railroad Shares; negotiates business paper and loans on Stock collaterals.

The latest information respecting the Mines at Lake Superior will be furnished on application, and orders for purchase or sale of Shares in Mining Companies promptly attended to.

* Published in the *Massachusetts Register for the Year 1859*, pp. 6 and 7 of the "advertising department."

During this same period operations in negotiable paper were being carried on more or less actively in other leading financial centers also, and in some of the smaller cities as well. As early as 1855 a banking house in Hartford, Connecticut, was advertising its services in negotiating commercial paper.[77] By the following year there was at least one "bill broker," and there were also dealers engaged in "buying and selling negotiable paper and dealing in uncurrent money," in Buffalo.[78] Even earlier in this period banking houses in Philadelphia were advertising their buying of "business paper," [79] and it will be recalled that a Philadelphia banking house stated in 1859 that, since the panic of 1857, note brokers had become "very necessary to banks and bankers." Dealings in bills and notes no doubt continued active in Baltimore, as well as Philadelphia, during this decade. Advertisements of a number of dealers in the former city may be found in various periodicals in the few years preceding the Civil War. One such advertisement is shown in Exhibit 7.[80] Toward the close of this period a case involving the liability of "a public bill and note broker" of Baltimore in the negotiation of a forged note attracted considerable attention.[81] By 1854 a banking house in Washington, D. C., was advertising its services in the negotiation of "first-class business paper of the District." [82] As early as the first year of the same decade a number of brokers seem to have been actively engaged in Cincinnati " 'in shaving notes or getting them shaved' ";[83] and three years later quotations of commercial paper rates "in the

---

[77] *The Merchant's and Banker's Almanac for 1855.*

[78] *Brown* v. *Montgomery*, 20 N. Y. 287–288.

[79] *The Merchant's and Banker's Almanac for 1854*, p. v of "Bankers' Magazine Advertising Sheet."

[80] An advertisement of another Baltimore dealer, Johnston Brothers and Company, may be found in the *Bankers' Mag.*, vol. VI, n.s., 1856–57 (page number not given).

[81] *Fisher* v. *Rieman et al.*, 12 Md. 497. See also "Legal Miscellany. I. Liabilities of Note Brokers — Forgeries," *Bankers' Mag.*, Dec. 1856, pp. 459–462; "Liabilities of Brokers in the Negotiation of Forged Mercantile Paper," *ibid.*, pp. 488–489; and "Liabilities of Brokers in the Negotiation of Forged Notes," *Hunt's Merch. Mag.*, Dec. 1856, pp. 737–738.

[82] *The Merchant's and Banker's Almanac for 1854*, p. xiii of "Bankers' Magazine Advertising Sheet."

[83] "Banking in Cincinnati," *Bankers' Mag.*, May 1851, p. 882.

money market" of that city appeared in a leading commercial and financial journal.[84] Operations in bills and notes were being carried on by a number of brokers in New Orleans also during this period, as is indicated by five cases decided in the Louisiana Supreme Court.[85] A statement made in one of these cases seems to indicate that New Orleans had attained a position of some importance as a "bill market" by 1852.[86] By 1860 the sale of "good Southern bills" — called also "pets of brokers" — in Louisville is said to have become "one of the regular features of the city's trade."[87] By this time also there were note brokers and bill brokers in St. Louis,[88] and "banking houses" which handled insurance as well were advertising their dealings in "business paper" both in St. Louis and in Quincy, Illinois.[89] Hence dealing in commercial paper had become an established business not only in the East, but also in some of the more important cities in the South and the Middle West, before the outbreak of the Civil War.

3. OPERATIONS OF DEALERS IN COMMERCIAL PAPER, 1800–1861

In the preceding section some of the main developments in the note brokerage business in the period from 1800 to 1861 were indicated. It was pointed out there that during this period the market for commercial paper broadened considerably, the volume of such paper bought and sold undoubtedly increased, and dealing in bills and notes became an established business in states as far west as Illinois and Missouri. We may now consider some more

[84] "Cincinnati Money and Exchange Market in 1853–4," *Hunt's Merch. Mag.*, Nov. 1854, p. 615.

[85] *Conrey* v. *Hoover*, 10 La. Ann. 437; *Fonda* v. *Garland*, 7 La. Ann. 201; *Greenwood* v. *Lowe*, 7 La. Ann. 197; *Séré* v. *Faurès*, 15 La. Ann. 189; and *Winston* v. *Tufts*, 10 La. Ann. 23.

[86] "Acceptances [bills drawn by planters on New Orleans factors and accepted by the latter] to the amount of many hundreds of thousands of dollars, are thus . . . no doubt, thrown into the New Orleans bill market annually" (*Greenwood* v. *Lowe*, 198).

[87] "Long Credits," *Hunt's Merch. Mag.*, June 1860, p. 768.

[88] *Thompson* v. *McCullough*, 31 Mo. 224.

[89] See the advertisement of the National Insurance Company of St. Louis in *The Merchants' and Bankers' Almanac for 1861*; and that of the Quincy Savings and Insurance Company in *The Merchant's and Banker's Register for 1860* (page numbers not given).

EXHIBIT 7

ADVERTISEMENT OF JOSIAH LEE & CO., 1854 *

JOSIAH LEE & CO., BANKERS,

AND DEALERS IN

FOREIGN AND DOMESTIC EXCHANGE,
BALTIMORE, MD.

———◆———

They will make collections on every part of the United States, at the lowest rates; negotiate Loans; buy and sell Stocks and Commercial Paper; and transact any business relating
to general Banking.

THE FIRM CONSISTS OF

WM. F. DALRYMPLE,
J. H. CARTER, late Cashier, }
GERARD GOVER.

* Published in *The Merchant's and Banker's Almanac for 1854*, p. vii of
advertisements.

technical matters relating to operations of dealers in negotiable paper in this same period, such as classes of paper handled, methods of buying and selling, buyers of open-market paper, the compensation received for their services by those who handled such paper, and other operations of dealers than the purchase and sale of bills and notes.

One of the main problems, as well as one of the most important functions, of the dealer in negotiable paper has always been that of originating or "finding" a supply of credit instruments both adequate in quantity and satisfactory in quality. This problem of selecting desirable paper in some respects undoubtedly became more complicated after 1800, as the market for such instruments broadened and dealers sought their stock in trade from sources more and more remote from their own local communities. In form, however, this stock in trade, from whatever sources obtained, remained the same during this period as it had been in the eighteenth century; that is, it comprised both bills of exchange and promissory notes. Of these two classes of paper, whether discounted by banks for their own customers directly or purchased through brokers, notes seem to have been more important than bills of exchange both in the earlier and in the later part of this period. During the first quarter of the nineteenth century the promissory note, secured as a rule either by one or two indorsements or by such collateral as real estate, stocks, or bonds, is said to have been the "usual form" of business paper discounted by banks directly.[90] The trade acceptance seems not to have been used much in this country until after 1816, when the Second Bank of the United States was organized. The Second Bank purchased large amounts of acceptances for its own account, encouraged other banks to buy them by maintaining a market for such trade bills, and through its branch offices furnished a convenient means of collecting acceptances at maturity. By 1846 trade bills are said to have become very popular in the New York market for commercial paper.[91] After 1836, however, when the Second Bank was closed, there was no bank or group of banks in the United States

[90] M. G. Myers, *The New York Money Market*, I, 46, 48.
[91] *Ibid.*, p. 203.

which had any strong interest in encouraging the use of acceptances. Promissory notes, on the other hand, were widely used in
domestic trade, and continued to be much more important than
bills of exchange for this purpose throughout the period before the
Civil War.[92]

Whatever the form of the instruments they bought and sold,
dealers probably secured the greater part of the negotiable paper
they handled during this period, as well as in the years before
1800, from merchants in the larger cities. Dry-goods jobbers and
wholesale dealers in hardware in New York and Boston, for instance, seem to have been among the largest borrowers in the open
market. Wholesale grocers also probably used the open market
to some extent.[93] In many cases these jobbing merchants and
others in various lines of trade, instead of issuing their own notes,
merely indorsed notes receivable which they had taken in payment
for goods sold and turned these notes over to brokers for sale in
the market.[94] Paper drawn by manufacturers in Massachusetts,

[92] Myers, *The New York Money Market*, I, 49–51. Cf. the following:
"Commerce, in its broadest sense, is carried on by promissory notes. The multiplication of this form of credit is beyond all control. It loads every department
of trade, from pins and needles up to cargoes of grain and cotton. It represents ships,
railroads, manufactories, public and private contracts" (J. S. Gibbons, *The Banks
of New York*, New York, 1858, p. 214).

"In the United States the promissory note has become the favorite sort of
negotiable paper, and in transactions for the purchase and sale of merchandise these
instruments are the common and usual forms of settlement of accounts" ("Banking
in the United States. II. Of Bills of Exchange and Promissory Notes," *Bankers'
Mag.*, Sept. 1860, p. 170).

[93] One of the best-known dealers in commercial paper in New York during this
earlier period referred to the paper he was buying in the years immediately preceding
the Civil War as "merchants' acceptances and receivables" (Henry Clews, *Twenty-
eight Years in Wall Street*, p. 78).

In a case argued in the Massachusetts Supreme Court in 1840, mention is made
of three promissory notes which were sold by a broker in the market. All three
notes were described as "New York business paper" (*Lobdell* v. *Baker*, 1 Metcalf,
193–194). References to the "business paper" of New York and Boston wholesale
dealers in dry goods, hardware, and groceries may be found in various issues of the
Bankers' Magazine in the decade before the Civil War.

[94] "The merchants at that time [1857] would go to these discount firms [two
other New York dealers in commercial paper who were rivals of Henry Clews] and
leave their receivables, bearing their endorsements, on sale there" (Clews, *op. cit.*,
p. 78).

In this earlier period wholesale dealers in New York and other large cities customarily sold large amounts of goods, on credit terms varying from four to twelve

Rhode Island, and Connecticut on their New York agents or factors was being sold in the New York market by 1860.[95] The rate on "railroad paper" in Boston was quoted as early as 1850, and apparently some such paper was being sold in the open market by that time.[96] Besides these classes of paper, note brokers were also handling eight-months' "tobacco notes," [97] bills drawn by Southern planters on their New Orleans factors and accepted by the latter,[98] and "Cuban acceptances" — drafts drawn (presumably) by Cuban exporters on American merchants who bought sugar and tobacco from them.[99]

---

months, to retailers in various parts of the country, and accepted the latters' notes of hand in payment. As a result of this practice, these wholesale dealers often had fairly large amounts of "receivables" among their current assets, and the sale of these notes to banks direct, or indirectly through brokers, afforded a convenient means of financing these credit transactions (Francis Burritt, 'Banking on Short Dated Paper," *Bankers' Mag.*, Jan. 1859, 532–533; "Monthly Financial and Commercial Article," *U. S. Dem. Rev.*, Oct. 1842, p. 434; "Notes on the Money Market," *Bankers' Mag.*, March 1855, p. 743, and Dec. 1857, p. 510).

The following excerpt from an address of a former Comptroller of the Currency before the Illinois Bankers' Association in [presumably] 1892 indicates the extent to which long-term commercial credits were used in the period before the Civil War:

"Three decades ago [about 1860] the sale of commodities by the manufacturer to the wholesale dealer was upon long time, the wholesale dealer giving long credit to the retailer, and the latter to the consumer, and in nearly every case a note of hand closed each transaction. . . . Weeks were consumed in the transportation of these supplies, months were employed in selling them at a large profit on credit to the consumer, and time seemed to be merging into eternity before the cash was actually paid over by the consumer, and, passing through various transmutations, finally reached the hands of the distant manufacturer.

"All along this devious, obscure, and almost interminable line of credits, the promissory note or bill of exchange constituted the convenient and unfailing medium for settlement. The bills thus brought into existence furnished the larger part of the commercial and business paper, which filled to repletion the note cases of the banking houses, whose aid was necessarily invoked" ("Banks and Commercial Paper," *Bradstreet's*, vol. XX, Dec. 31, 1892, p. 838).

[95] "Notes on the Money Market," *Bankers' Mag.*, June 1860, p. 972, and Aug. 1860, p. 165.

From this method of financing may have developed later the New England textile mills' practice of selling their promissory notes, with a commission house's or selling agent's indorsement, in the open market.

[96] "Notes on the Money Market," *Bankers' Mag.*, Sept. 1850, p. 262.

[97] H. C. Cabell, "Banking at the South, with Reference to New York City," *Hunt's Merch. Mag.*, March 1860, p. 318.

[98] *Greenwood* v. *Lowe*, 7 La. Ann. 197–198.

[99] J. J. Klein, "The Development of Mercantile Instruments of Credit in the United States," *Jour. of Accountancy*, vol. XII (Nov. 1911), pp. 535–536.

According to Klein, various dealers by about 1850 had begun to specialize in the classes of commercial paper they handled (*ibid.*, p. 535).

Just what proportion of these various classes of paper was single-name, and what bore one or more indorsements, is not known, but the greater part of the promissory notes sold in the market during this period was no doubt indorsed paper. As early as about 1857, however, the modern practice of making notes payable to the order of the promisor, and thus negotiable without indorsement by the holder, was noted in one or two of the larger cities.[100]

Modern practice was also being followed in this earlier period with respect to the maturities of these several classes of instruments: then as well as now, paper was being issued with maturities ranging from sixty days to six months or more.

It was pointed out above that the broadening of the area throughout which dealers sought their supplies of negotiable instruments made the problem of selecting desirable paper somewhat more complicated in this period than it had been in the years before 1800. The increasing variety in the classes of open-market paper which has just been indicated no doubt produced a similar effect. Both the methods of selecting bills and notes, however, and other operating methods of dealers in such instruments remained essentially about the same in the later as in the earlier of these two periods. Since they still continued to procure the larger part of their stock in trade in their own localities, these dealers could acquire a more or less close personal familiarity with the affairs of many of their borrowing customers. They of course made no such elaborate credit investigations, however, as those on which

---

[100] According to Gibbons, this practice "originated with the commission merchants" (presumably in New York). Gibbons condemns this practice on the ground that it enabled various merchants to sell "in 'the street,'" without any responsibility therefor, excessive amounts of "receivables" given them by customers to whom they had sold excessive amounts of goods (Gibbons, *op. cit.*, p. 375).

Klein states that after the crisis of 1857 a number of business men in one city (presumably Baltimore), not wanting to assume the contingent liability involved in discounting ordinary promissory notes or acceptances, refused to take such paper but agreed to receive, instead, notes made payable to the order of their debtors and indorsed by these debtors themselves. At least some of this paper was then sold in the market in the city concerned. (Klein, *op. cit.*, Nov. 1911, p. 528.)

It may be noted that in such cases indorsement in blank was a symptom of a more or less doubtful credit position of the maker, whereas in modern times the ability of a concern to sell its paper in the open market with only a blank indorsement is generally a reliable indication of a strong financial position and a high credit rating.

the modern commercial paper house bases the selection of the obligations it handles. Even unaudited financial and operating statements were then practically unknown, and in selecting the paper they handled dealers perforce continued to rely mainly on their judgment of the character and ability of their borrowing customers. Their other main operations, the actual buying and selling of the bills and notes they selected, also remained essentially unchanged. As was stated earlier in this chapter, dealers in negotiable paper generally acted as brokers, rather than as outright buyers and sellers of bills and notes, throughout the whole of the period before the Civil War. It was for this reason that they were called "note brokers" or "bill brokers." In their capacity as brokers they of course made no commitment to purchase themselves the paper they accepted for sale, as the modern commercial paper house does; instead, they would agree to try to find a buyer for such paper and to put their borrowing customer in funds only after they had sold his bills or notes and received payment therefor.

This practice of buying and selling bills and notes on a brokerage basis obviously involved less responsibility than the modern commercial paper house's practice of buying outright practically all the paper it handles. Probably the most significant difference between the earlier note broker and the commercial paper house of the present time, indeed, lies in the fact that the former did not, whereas the latter does, assume the responsibility of buying and paying for commercial paper before selling it. It is of some importance, therefore, to note that in at least some cases dealers had begun to buy bills and notes outright even before 1860. In fact, "brokers" in Louisiana (presumably in New Orleans) are said to have been buying and selling "paper on their own account, and on that of others" as early as 1840.[101] It is probable that dealers in other parts of the country also were occasionally buying bills or notes outright about the same time. Some years later, in 1857, Henry Clews is said to have introduced the practice of buying paper "out and out" in New York City. The method of purchas-

---

[101] *Nott* v. *Papet*, 15 La. 306, 309–310.

ing notes and acceptances which he "inaugurated" may best be described in his own words:

At the time I visited Washington [early in 1861] my firm was more largely engaged in dealing in mercantile paper than any other branch of Wall Street business.

I had inaugurated the system at the time [1857] of my advent to the "Street" of buying merchants' acceptances and receivables out and out, the rate being governed by the prevailing ruling rate for money, with the usual commission added.

It was by this method that my firm soon became the largest dealers in mercantile paper, which business had formerly been controlled by two other firms for at least a quarter of a century, and whose old fogy methods were by my innovations easily eclipsed.

The merchants at that time would go to these discount firms and leave their receivables, bearing their indorsements, on sale there, and only when sold by piece-meal could they obtain the avails thereof.

The more expeditious plan that I adopted, which was to give these negotiators a check at sight, seemed generally to merit their approbation, and enabled me to command the situation in that line of business, very much to the chagrin of my competitors.[102]

Once he had procured a supply of paper from his borrowing customers, whether by outright purchase or through the much more common consignment arrangement, the dealer in this earlier period as a rule then called on his prospective buying customers in person and offered them the actual bills or notes he had for sale.[103]

These customers in the main were probably banks, though merchants in New York and "private capitalists" in New York, Boston, and other cities evidently bought fairly large amounts of paper also.[104] Both incorporated banks and private bankers are

[102] Clews, op. cit., p. 78.

[103] Klein, op. cit., Nov. 1911, p. 534, and Myers, op. cit., p. 56.

According to Miss Myers, banks took the initiative in buying commercial paper only in exceptional cases, as in May 1850, when a number of New York banks, to keep their funds employed, were forced to buy paper "in the street."

In the case of Henry Rieman and Sons v. William Fisher, decided in the Superior Court of Baltimore in 1856, it was stated that the defendant, "a public bill and note broker" of Baltimore, "was in the habit of bringing to the counting-room of the plaintiffs a large number of notes at a time, for the purpose of selling them to the plaintiffs" (Bankers' Mag., Dec. 1856, p. 459). This statement succinctly describes the practice of the typical dealer in bills and notes in this earlier period.

[104] Banks, "other moneyed institutions," and capitalists are mentioned as buyers of commercial paper in the advertisement of Blake, Howe & Co. shown in Exhibit 4.

said to have been actively discounting bills and notes, at least some of which were undoubtedly purchased in the market, as early as about 1820.[105] Some years later, according to Klein, merchants (presumably in New York City in the main) who had surplus capital at certain seasons began to buy large amounts of commercial paper maturing at times when they would need such capital in their own business again. A number of these traders are said to have continued to invest surplus funds in open-market paper after their retirement from active business; and some few of these retired merchants, having found time "hanging too heavily on their hands," even to have begun to collect the business paper of their friends and offer it for discount to bank officials whom they knew.[106] The activities of other "private capitalists" are mentioned rather frequently in the *Bankers' Magazine* and other periodicals during this period. Apparently they often bought, at rates of discount correspondingly high, bills or notes which had been rejected by commercial banks as undesirable.[107] In a number of cases they

[105] In the case of *Fleckner* v. *The Bank of the United States* (8 Wheaton 338), decided in the United States Supreme Court in 1823, it was stated that "the great object of the trade of banking, as it is carried on by the private bankers and incorporated companies, is to discount bills and notes" (341). In his opinion in this case, Associate Justice Story said: "It is notorious that banking operations are always carried on in our country discounting notes [*sic*]. The late [First] Bank of the United States conducted, and all the state banks now conduct, their business in this way" (349).

[106] Klein, *op. cit.*, Nov. 1911, p. 535.

Mr. Elkan Naumburg, who was then a dry-goods merchant in Baltimore, bought paper in the market during the panic of 1857. Nearly forty years later, in 1894, he and several associates founded in New York the house which later took the name of E. Naumburg and Company. (See Exhibit 8.) This organization was for years one of the leading dealers in commercial paper.

[107] This is indicated by the following excerpts from articles in the *Bankers' Magazine*:

"A few thousand dollars more are wanted to make some persons easy. Their business is too extended, and they grasp at too much. They complain of the banks for not granting all that is asked, when we all know that the latter are bound by self-interest to do all that prudence permits. It is only in self-defence when a bank turns down the offerings for discount, and thus throws its customers upon private capitalists" ("Notes on the Money Market," *Bankers' Mag.*, Jan. 1850, p. 579).

"The [Boston] banks are not able to do [i.e., discount] one half the paper that offers — consequently large amounts are thrown into the hands of private capitalists" (*ibid.*, April 1850, p. 866).

"The [New York] banks are enabled to discount nearly all the acceptable paper that offers, so that . . . very little paper of a good stamp finds its way to the brokers" (*ibid.*, Oct. 1858, p. 318).

seem to have acted as "note shavers," or dealers in such paper, buying it at high rates and then either selling it at a profit or, if necessary, holding it to maturity.

As compensation for their services in finding these various classes of buyers for the paper they handled, dealers as a rule charged their borrowing customers a commission. When they purchased bills and notes outright they had the opportunity of making an additional gain if able to sell such paper at a rate lower than that at which they had bought it. It is possible that they may at times have purchased paper at a flat rate, without commission, and therefore have depended for their remuneration entirely on differences between their buying and their selling rates. Among so-called "private capitalists" and "note shavers," as distinguished from banking houses and other large dealers, this practice was probably by no means uncommon in a period when "spreads" between buying and selling rates were much wider than at present. In some cases note brokers are said to have charged their borrowing customers directly both a commission and a "shave." [108] Just what rate or rates of commission were most commonly charged is not certain, but it is safe to say that rates were less uniform, showed a wider range, and were as a rule higher in this earlier period than at present. Mention is made of commissions of ¼ and ½ of 1 per cent in the *Bankers' Magazine* in 1845, but it is not clear that these were commissions being charged by dealers in open-market paper.[109] Bill brokers (presumably in New York) are said to have been charging commissions of ⅛ to ¼ of 1 per cent in 1844.[110] It is possible that these rates, which happen to be also the rates most commonly charged by commercial paper houses in more recent years, were influenced by the rate charged for selling stock on the New York Stock Exchange.[111] In New Orleans, bill brokers

---

[108] Cabell, *op. cit.*, p. 318.

[109] "Money Market," *Bankers' Mag.*, Dec. 1845, p. 162.

[110] "The individual brokers, standing between the sellers and buyers of the bills, transact the business for the difference of ⅛ @ ¼ per cent, and the utmost uniformity must be preserved" ("Monthly Commercial Chronicle," *Hunt's Merch. Mag.*, June 1844, p. 560). The uniformity mentioned above seems not to have characterized rates of commission charged by other dealers than those referred to in this quotation.

[111] The brokers who "drew up the first informal agreement for a Stock Exchange"

during the decade before the Civil War were charging a maximum commission of 1 per cent of the face of the bills they sold, as is stated in two cases decided in the Louisiana Supreme Court in 1855.[112] While most of the rates mentioned above were those charged by "bill brokers," generally no distinction was made between bill brokers and note brokers in this earlier period, and it is reasonable to suppose that dealers charged commissions ranging approximately from $\frac{1}{4}$ of 1 per cent to 1 per cent for handling notes as well as bills during the period before the Civil War.

The financing of the operations by which these commissions were earned constituted no serious problem during this period. Since the typical dealer acted as a broker, and consequently paid for his customers' paper only after he had sold it, he required no capital for purchasing or carrying his stock in trade. Even a dealer who bought bills or notes outright needed no considerable capital for this purpose unless he purchased large amounts of paper at a time or was unable to dispose of his stock in trade as promptly as he had expected. In some cases, however, brokers apparently resorted to banks to secure a part of the funds they required to carry on their operations, and pledged as security for their loans the paper they were handling, just as the modern commercial paper house does. Mention is made of such borrowing in the *Bankers' Magazine* in 1859,[113] and, about the same time, of call loans secured by "strictly prime paper" or "negotiable paper" as collateral.[114] While the purposes of such loans are not definitely stated, it seems probable that the borrowed funds were used in the first case to finance dealings in bills and notes, and that the proceeds of the call loans were used to finance other operations, par-

---

in New York (about 1792) agreed to charge a commission of not less than $\frac{1}{4}$ of 1 per cent. This commission was based on the selling value of stock until Nov. 7, 1840, when it was changed to $\frac{1}{4}$ of 1 per cent of the par value (Myers, *op. cit.*, p. 16).

The same rate of commission — "$\frac{1}{4}$ per cent. on what is usually considered the par value" — was being charged by members of the Boston Stock Exchange some years later ("Brokers' Board," *Bankers' Mag.*, March 1856, p. 695).

[112] *Conrey* v. *Hoover*, 10 La. Ann. 437, and *Roubieu* v. *Palmer*, 10 La. Ann. 320.

[113] "The bill brokers are borrowers [presumably from New York banks] to some extent on pledge of their receivables at from 6 to 7 per cent" ("Notes on the Money Market," *Bankers' Mag.*, Dec. 1859, p. 495).

[114] *Ibid.*, Feb. 1859, p. 669, and March 1860, p. 749.

ticularly the purchase of securities, in which a number of dealers also engaged during this period.

In concluding this account of the operations of bill and note brokers in the period from 1800 to 1861, it should be pointed out that the "other operations" of various dealers remained as wide in range as those of some of the brokers of the eighteenth century. Some of the smaller dealers, or "note shavers," probably combined the "shaving" of bank notes with the purchase of commercial bills and notes at a heavy discount, particularly in the earlier decades of the nineteenth century.[115] As late as 1849 a broker in New York is said to have been acting as a "general commission broker" — soliciting orders for the purchase and sale of stocks and real estate, as well as "exchange and business paper." [116] Dealing in such "business paper" was often only one part of a general banking business, including also dealing in domestic and foreign exchange, the purchase and sale of securities, and in some cases even the handling of insurance, which various private banking houses were organized to carry on during this period.[117]

It might therefore be supposed that, so far as the development of a class of dealers specializing in handling short-term negotiable paper is concerned, there were no events worth recording in the period before the Civil War. It will be recalled, however, that the firm of Henry Clews, a leading New York dealer, not only had begun to buy bills and notes outright as early as 1857 but also by 1860 had become "more largely engaged in dealing in mercantile paper than any other branch of Wall Street business." Dealing in open-market paper also became an important part of the business of a number of other private banking houses which were organized in various cities some years before 1860. Such banking houses, in fact, were the largest dealers in bills and notes in this earlier

---

[115] Bryan refers to Maryland bank note brokers of 1818, 1841, and 1858 as "bill brokers," "note brokers," and "note shavers" (A. C. Bryan, *History of State Banking in Maryland*, pp. 68, 108, 121).

[116] Klein, *loc. cit.*

[117] See Exhibits 4–7; and advertisements of the Quincy Savings and Insurance Company and the National Insurance Company, which may be found, respectively, in *The Merchant's and Banker's Register for 1860* and *The Merchants' and Bankers' Almanac for 1861* (page number not given in either case).

period; and, if they also carried on important operations in stocks and bonds, they did not in this respect differ materially from some of the leading commercial paper houses of the present, which "specialize" in handling not only short-term credit instruments but long-term securities as well.

CHAPTER II

THE COMMERCIAL PAPER BUSINESS FROM 1861 TO 1914

IN THE preceding chapter it was shown that by 1860 dealing in open-market paper had become an established business in states as far west as Illinois and Missouri. During the period from the following year to that in which the Federal Reserve banking system was established, the business of buying and selling promissory notes in the open market, under such favorable conditions as those resulting from a great expansion in industry and trade, rapid improvements in means of transportation and communication, and a great increase both in national wealth and in the number and capital of independent unit banks, developed at a more rapid rate than in the period which has just been considered. The purpose of the present chapter is to give an account of some of the main developments connected with this business from 1861 to 1914.

1. TERRITORIAL EXPANSION OF DEALINGS IN OPEN-MARKET PAPER

One of these main developments was the rapid expansion of dealers' operations to the newer and more remote sections of the country, which was greatly facilitated by important improvements in means of communication. During the eighteen years from the outbreak of hostilities between the North and the South to the resumption of specie payments in 1879 the operations of all dealers, it is true, were perforce curtailed to some extent. Even during this period of inconvertible paper currency, however, the purchase and sale of bills and notes was carried on actively in Boston, New York, and other leading financial centers, as is indicated by the fact that twenty-four Boston "note brokers" are listed in *The Massachusetts Register and Directory* for 1867,[1] and about forty New York "note and bill brokers" in *The Bankers'*

[1] Page 403.

Directory of the United States and Canada for 1876–77.[2] Within about a generation after the Civil War dealers were also carrying on their operations in a number of cities much farther west. They were combining dealings in commercial paper with security brokerage and other operations in Indianapolis by 1871 and in Louisville by 1875.[3] Private banking houses were dealing in commercial paper in Chicago by about 1880.[4] Some twenty years later, in 1902, it is estimated that there were ten commercial paper houses in the same city.[5] As early as 1887 it was said that there were "dealers long established in the business" in Milwaukee, and that this business was "no longer an experiment in the West."[6] In Minnesota (presumably in Minneapolis or St. Paul) at least one "note-broker" was plying his trade as early as 1875.[7] Twenty years later there were some nine or ten such brokers in Minneapolis. By 1881 "bankers and brokers" were buying and selling notes and stocks and bonds in Kansas City.[8] About thirty years later a dealer began business in Wichita, Kansas. Bankers in Dallas, Texas, reported in 1930 that dealings in open-market paper were probably begun there before 1910. By about the same time dealers finally completed their progress across the continent and began operations in financial centers on the Pacific Coast. Dealers and bankers in San Francisco, Los Angeles, and Seattle gave 1900 as the approximate date of the earliest operations in open-market paper in those cities. One of the larger commercial

[2] Pages 149–159.

[3] See the advertisement of Snyder and Moore in *The Merchants' and Bankers' Almanac* for 1871, p. xxxv of advertisements; and that of Galt and Shotwell in *The Banker's Almanac and Register for 1875*, p. 37 of advertisements.

[4] This information was furnished by two Chicago dealers in 1930.

Unless the contrary is indicated by specific references to printed material, statements of fact made by the writer in this and the following chapters are based on information obtained by personal interviews or correspondence with dealers and bankers in all sections of the country.

[5] *Investment Banking in Chicago*, Bulletin No. 39, Bureau of Business Research, University of Illinois, p. 8.

[6] W. H. Baker, "Commercial Paper," *Proc. Amer. Bankers' Assoc.*, 1887, p. 47.

[7] *Farmers' and Mechanics' Bank* v. *Baldwin*, 23 Minn. 198–200.

[8] See the advertisement of Whipple, Cowherd, and Company in *The Banker's Almanac and Register for 1881*, p. 20 of advertisements; also *Hamlin* v. *Abell*, 120 Mo. 188, 196, and "The Liability of Investment Brokers in the Sale of Commercial Paper," *Banking Law Jour.*, May 1894, p. 388.

paper houses opened an office in San Francisco in 1907 or 1908,[9] and by about 1910 this same concern and one other house had opened offices in Seattle. Dealings in Portland seem to have been begun somewhat later than in the former two cities. By 1913, the close of the period considered in this chapter, it could be said that the larger commercial paper houses had branches or representatives "in all large cities" in the United States.[10]

In this rather rapid extension of operations to the more remote sections of the country, most of the twenty-five houses which presumably were the largest dealers in commercial paper in 1931, or earlier dealers to whom they were successors, took a more or less active part. All but two of these houses (or predecessor dealers), in fact, were established before the end of this period.[11] Some of

[9] One officer of this organization gave 1907 as the year in which this office was opened; other officers gave 1908 as the date. According to R. A. Foulke, a branch office was opened in San Francisco in 1906, and this was the "first representation" on the Pacific Coast (*The Commercial Paper Market*, p. 102).

[10] J. A. Broderick, "Registration of Commercial Paper," *Bankers' Home Mag.*, Nov. 1913, p. 43.

[11] An announcement of the establishment of a firm whose successor became one of the largest commercial paper houses in the country is shown in Exhibit 8.

The distribution of the twenty-five houses by cities and the years in which they were established are shown in the following enumeration:

1. Boston: Four houses.
   One established in 1879.
   One about 1899, as the successor of a stock brokerage house which was organized about 1885 and began to deal in commercial paper some five years later.
   Two in 1921. Of these two, one was the successor of two earlier concerns established in 1894 and 1906, respectively.
2. Hartford: One house, established some time after 1888 as the successor of an earlier concern which began business in that year.
3. New York: Eight houses.
   One established in 1885. This firm, from the time of its establishment to May, 1931, when it was dissolved, acted as a broker only; i.e., it never bought paper outright.
   One some time after 1885, as the successor of a firm founded in 1869.
   One some time after 1894, as the successor of a firm organized in that year. (See Exhibit 8.)
   One some time after 1897, as the successor of a partnership established in Boston about that time. This house established semi-independent branches in Boston and Chicago, and became closely affiliated through capital ownership with a house in St. Louis and the San Francisco house mentioned below. For the purposes of this study the New York house, together with all its branches and the St. Louis house, have been treated as a single organization. The San Francisco house has also been regarded as a single

EXHIBIT 8

ANNOUNCEMENT OF NAUMBURG, LAUER & CO., 1894

NAUMBURG, LAUER & CO.

BANKERS & BROKERS

6 WALL STREET.

ELKAN NAUMBURG.   WALTER W NAUMBURG.
EMANUEL LAUER.   WILLIAM E. LAUER

Dictated.

Commercial Paper a Specialty

New York,   January 1st, *18*7 4

Dear Sir :

In enclosing our card we wish to inform you particularly that our specialty will be the MERCANTILE NOTE BUSINESS.

This branch of finance is not a new field for us. During our long mercantile career we have bought for our firm and for various institutions, large amounts of paper, and have found the percentage of loss to be insignificant.

Supported by this experience, and by what we have learned from other extensive purchasers, we feel justified in saying that no investment has shown itself to be safer than judiciously selected mercantile paper.

Our senior partners have been identified for a long term of years with the mercantile community on the one hand, and with banks and bankers on the other. Therefore we believe ourselves warranted in assuming that our firm has exceptional facilities for conducting this business successfully.

Submitting the above for your consideration, we remain,

Yours truly,

Naumburg Lauer Co

them, to be sure, have remained down to recent years comparatively small concerns, with but one office and a more or less localized business. On the other hand, some of the larger houses have
at one time or another maintained branch offices, representatives,
or correspondent relations in all the more important financial
centers, and through similar arrangements still originate and sell
commercial paper in practically all sections of the country. The
activities of these houses were of course supplemented by those of
a number of other concerns, both large and small, which also began
business during this period but later discontinued their operations
in open-market paper.

This expansion of dealers' operations from the larger financial

---

organization, though it was probably about as closely affiliated with the
New York firm as the St. Louis house was.

One in 1916, by a dealer who had entered the commercial paper business
in 1907 but later discontinued operations on his own account.

One in 1922, as the successor of four earlier firms, the first of which was
founded about 1876.

One in 1925, as the successor of three earlier firms, the first of which was
established in 1874.

One which made New York its main office in 1928, but was established
originally in Boston in 1894.

4. Philadelphia: Two houses.
   One established some time after 1866, as the successor of a firm founded in
   that year.
   One in 1893.

5. Chicago: Four houses.
   Two established some time after 1880, as the successors of private banking
   houses organized somewhat earlier. The larger of these two dealers was
   also the immediate successor of another commercial paper house.
   One in 1893.
   One about 1930, as the successor of at least two earlier concerns, the first
   of which was established about 1905.

6. Minneapolis: One house, established about 1925, as the successor of a concern
   organized in 1895.

7. St. Louis: One house, established in 1907, as the successor of a firm founded
   in 1902.

8. New Orleans: Two "houses."
   One of these was an investment banking organization established in 1920,
   as the "security affiliate" of a commercial bank.
   The other was the "commercial paper department," organized about 1910,
   of a similar bank which was established in 1902.

9. Wichita, Kansas: One house, established about 1923, as the successor of a
   dealer who began business about 1911.

10. San Francisco: One house, established about 1922, as the successor of a New
    York house's branch office which was opened about 1907.

centers of the East to the Middle West, and thence across the continent to leading cities along the Pacific Coast, implied a corresponding growth in the practice of borrowing in the open market, as well as that of buying outside paper as a short-term investment for surplus funds of banks. Since by means of the telegraph, correspondence, and traveling representatives, dealers could establish contacts with both borrowing and buying customers in localities far removed from any of their offices, both these practices, in fact, could develop years in advance of the time when those who handled negotiable paper found the establishment of offices in such localities advisable. It is not surprising, therefore, that both practices seem to have become nation-wide some years before commercial paper houses had covered the entire country with their main or branch offices. The expansion of their operations implied, further, a corresponding growth in the volume of paper handled by dealers each year. These developments will now be considered in turn.

2. GROWTH OF OPEN-MARKET BORROWING

It is said that years ago "many merchants were timid to be known as borrowers" in the open market.[12] This attitude, however, did not deter a great number of merchants and other borrowers who could not obtain sufficient accommodation from their own local banks, or else could secure such accommodation only at rates less attractive than those offered by dealers, from seeking short-term credit in the market during the period under consideration. As early as 1873 nearly a hundred different concerns at a time, representing trading or manufacturing enterprise not only in the East, but in the South and Middle West as well, were offering their notes for sale through a Boston dealer.[13] By the following year open-market borrowing seems to have become practically nation-wide, for another Boston dealer was then offering for sale

[12] W. W. Naumburg, "Commercial Paper," *N. Y. Times*, "Annual Financial Review," Jan. 7, 1912, p. 25.

[13] See Exhibit 12. This exhibit and Exhibits 9–11 and 13–15, which are copies of some of the earliest available note offering lists issued by commercial paper dealers, have been placed at the end of this chapter.

the single-name paper of concerns from Burlington, Vermont, to Mobile, New Orleans, and Galveston, and from Boston to San Francisco.[14] Three years later the "merchants of the larger cities of the [Middle] West," including St. Paul, Minneapolis, and Omaha, are said to have been looking to the "note brokers of New York and Boston for the placing of their paper." [15] By 1884, according to a Canadian banker, even a few concerns in his country were occasionally borrowing through "brokers," though the "brokers" apparently were Canadian rather than American.[16] The same banker observed that American firms and corporations in nearly every state in the Union were then borrowing in the open market on their "one-name unsecured bills" (that is, promissory notes).[17] This phenomenon was noted also by bankers of St. Louis [18] and Philadelphia [19] in 1904 and 1905, respectively.

Other indications of the extent to which borrowers in various parts of the country were resorting to the open market toward the beginning of the present century were the increasing tendency on the part of borrowers to "divide" their accounts among several dealers, and the increasing competition between dealers and banks and among dealers themselves. As early as 1901 "not a few concerns" were using the services of "two or more brokers to sell their paper on the market." [20] In the following year some concerns were offering their notes "in half a dozen different markets by as many

[14] See Exhibit 13.

[15] J. H. Burroughs, "Investing in Commercial Paper," *Bankers' Home Mag.*, Feb. 1907, p. 38.

[16] George Hague, "One-Name Paper," *Proc. Amer. Bankers' Assoc.*, 1884, p. 67.

[17] *Ibid.*, p. 68.

[18] "As money has become plentiful in the South and West, these note brokers have extended their operations, and now, I might be safe in saying that there go out daily from St. Louis or from Chicago anywhere from one to half a dozen circular letters to banks all over the South and West, offering them paper made by Tom, Dick and Harry, issued in territory extending from Maine to California, and from Washington to Florida" (H. P. Hilliard, address — without title — before the Michigan Bankers' Association, *Proc. Mich. Bankers' Assoc.*, 1904, pp. 69–70).

[19] "In every large city there is an enormous business transacted each day in the buying and selling of notes made by individuals, firms, and corporations located in every part of the United States" (T. W. Andrew, "Banking Methods — Ancient and Modern," *Proc. S. C. Bankers' Assoc.*, 1905, pp. 72–73).

[20] S. R. Flynn, "A Twentieth Century Credit System," *Proc. Mich. Bankers' Assoc.*, 1901, p. 28.

different brokers";[21] and before the close of this period, in 1911, there are said to have been many instances of borrowers' "using one brokerage house in the South, one in the West, another in New York and another in the East." [22] The competition of "the festive note-broker" for the borrowing accounts of their customers was being keenly felt by bankers in the Middle West nearly twenty years before this time, as is indicated in an address delivered by a banker of Dubuque, Iowa, in 1892.[23] From about 1890 on to the close of this period bankers in various parts of the country not infrequently found occasion to express their disaffection toward such competition, especially during periods of low money rates, apparently overlooking the fact that the real rivalry was not between "broker" and banker, but rather between banks in one locality and all other banks willing to buy outside paper originated in that locality.[24] They found occasion also to complain against the growing competition among dealers themselves, for the struggle of the latter to secure new borrowing accounts made all the more intense their competition with bankers.[25] This rivalry among

---

[21] J. B. Forgan, "Branch Banking," an address (1902) reprinted in W. H. Hull (editor), *Practical Problems in Banking and Currency*, p. 249.

[22] J. B. Martindale, "The Business of a Commercial Bank and How to Safeguard the Investment of Its Funds," *Proc. Amer. Bankers' Assoc.*, 1911, p. 704.

[23] "Until recently, western bankers were able to maintain their loaning rates regardless of the depressions of the eastern markets, but now there has arisen an element which wages constant war on established rates. It is the festive note-broker, who, with his eastern capital, steps in to disturb the harmonious relations between banker and borrower, and just at a time when there seems to be an opportunity to dispose of idle funds at a profitable rate, the banker is confronted with the alternative of cutting his rate or seeing his loans going to outside dealers" (J. K. Deming, "Modern Methods of Soliciting Business," *Proc. Iowa Bankers' Assoc.*, 1892, p. 21).

[24] The following quotation describes the situation as it appeared to a Chicago banker in 1908:
"In the matter of loans the banks are no longer the closest competitors of one another. When money is in active demand and interest rates are high there is no occasion for close competition among banks for loans, and the note broker is all but out of an occupation; but when money is easy the broker, as a dispenser of credit, is in strenuous conflict with the banks, and he becomes an active and expensive rival" (J. T. Talbert, "Commercial Credits," *Proc. N. Y. Bankers' Assoc.*, 1908, p. 85).

[25] The effect of such competition on rates obtainable by banks on direct loans to customers was pointed out in the same address by the banker referred to in n. 24:
"The competition of brokers among themselves for the paper of good concerns constitutes to the bank a two-edged sword, for not only are interest rates depressed on brokers' paper, but the recession in rates necessarily becomes effective on the whole body of loans carried by a bank" (*ibid.*, pp. 85–86).

dealers had become very active by 1908. A committee on credit information appointed by the American Bankers' Association reported in that year that such competition was heedless and demoralizing, and extended to "splitting" commissions (that is, charging borrowing customers less than the usual commission for placing their paper with banks or other buyers) and at times even to "sacrificing them altogether" to "obtain notes of a quality useful in dressing up lists of offerings and assisting in the sale of less desirable paper." [26]

3. Growth of the Practice of Investing Banks' Funds in Open-Market Paper

In thus actively competing against one another to secure new borrowing accounts in all sections of the country, dealers themselves may be said in a sense to have created a demand for the paper they handled. As they induced more and more concerns to borrow in the open market — that is, indirectly from many banks, located in many different parts of the United States, instead of directly from only a few banks in their own immediate localities — many banks whose best customers began to seek short-term credit in the much broader open market accumulated surplus funds which they could not advantageously employ in direct advances to local borrowers. For such banks the dealer in negotiable paper could then perform a valuable service. Handling credit instruments of convenient maturities and denominations, and both safer and more liquid than the majority of their local loans, he could offer these banks a highly desirable form of investment for the funds they had formerly been advancing as direct loans to their own local customers. As Professor Phillips has said, the situation "was and remains a peculiar one and goes far to explain the rapid spread of the note brokerage system." [27] First banks in a few localities invested surplus funds in short-term paper originated in other parts of the country. This resulted in the accumulation of

[26] Report of Committee on Credit Information, *Proc. Amer. Bankers' Assoc.*, 1908, p. 198.
[27] C. A. Phillips, *Bank Credit*, p. 135.

surplus funds which banks in the latter communities could then advantageously place in outside paper issued in still other localities, as well as in those where the purchase of such paper originally began. There was thus a close interrelation between the growth of the practice of investing banks' funds in commercial paper and that of borrowing in the market: the purchase of outside paper stimulated open-market borrowing, and the latter in turn stimulated further purchases of notes issued for sale through dealers.

This interaction of forces, and consequently the growth of the whole system of open-market financing, it may be observed, were conditioned by the banking system under which they developed. If, instead of a large number of widely scattered and comparatively small local independent unit banks, a nation-wide system of branch banking had grown up in this country, even the largest borrowing concerns could have obtained in the form of direct loans from a single institution all the accommodation they required; and banks could advantageously have invested in such loans a larger proportion of their short-term loanable funds. Under such circumstances, the system of open-market financing would never have reached the position of importance it actually attained in this country some years before the close of the last century.

Since in the earlier part of this period both the activities of dealers and the greater part of the banking resources of the country were concentrated mainly in the financial centers of the East, it would be natural to expect that the demand for commercial paper as an investment for banks' funds would for some years after 1860 be furnished in the main by Eastern banking institutions. Such seems in fact to have been the case. Purchases of paper by New England banks, including country banks and savings banks, are mentioned in the *Bankers' Magazine* in 1866, 1869, 1870, and 1872;[28] and in a case decided in the Massachusetts Supreme Court in 1878, the defendants, who were commercial paper "brokers" in Boston, offered to prove that "for many years a very large portion" of the business of national banks (presum-

[28] *Bankers' Mag.*, Feb. 1866, p. 670; Dec. 1869, p. 485; Aug. 1870, p. 158; and Sept. 1872, p. 236.

ably those in the Boston district in particular) had "consisted in buying commercial paper." [29] A few years later the banks of Hartford and Providence, which had more "banking capital" than could be "profitably employed locally," were also investing "large sums through note-brokers." [30] In New York, national banks were "buying good paper in the open market at 8 @ 12 per cent." before 1867,[31] and three years later the purchase of "mercantile paper" by "country banks" and "Savings banks" in the same state is mentioned in the *Bankers' Magazine*.[32] Apparently banks in other sections of the country remained comparatively small buyers of bills and notes until about 1876. At any rate, a New York dealer in 1930 expressed the opinion that "the market" for commercial paper as late as 1876 was practically confined to banks of New England, New York State, the Atlantic Coast, and a part of Pennsylvania, and this opinion agrees rather closely with a statement made in the *Bankers' Home Magazine* in 1907.[33]

As was indicated in the preceding chapter, however, banks not only in the East but in some of the more important cities of the South and the Middle West as well had begun to buy paper in the market by 1860; and this method of investing surplus funds spread rather rapidly to the newer sections of the country some time after 1875. Probably by the latter year, and certainly by 1884, even banks in Canada were buying some paper through American or Canadian "brokers." [34] Not many years later probably at least some banks in most of the states in the Mississippi Valley were buying promissory notes in the market, though of course the practice of banks in different cities was by no means uniform in this respect. Banks in St. Louis, which in later years

---

[29] *Attleborough National Bank* v. *Rogers*, 125 Mass. 339, 342.

[30] A. S. Bolles, *Practical Banking* (1884 ed.), p. 63.

[31] "National Banks Not Authorized to Establish Branches, or to Buy Commercial Paper at More than Seven Per Cent," *Hunt's Merch. Mag.*, Feb. 1867, p. 167.

[32] *Bankers' Mag.*, Aug. 1870, p. 158.

[33] "Thirty years ago [1877] most of the banks that bought commercial paper were those, with hardly an exception, located east of the Alleghanies. . . . The banks of New England, Eastern Pennsylvania, New Jersey and New York, were the main buyers" (Burroughs, *op. cit.*, pp. 38–39).

[34] "A Discount Registry," *Bankers' Mag.*, Dec. 1875, p. 480; and Hague, *op. cit.*, p. 68.

invested large sums in open-market obligations, are said to have been opposed to the purchase of such paper until "after the financial strain in that center in 1897." [35] A New York dealer stated in 1931 that banks in Kansas City also bought but little paper until after 1897. According to a banker of Minneapolis, banks in that locality did not purchase any considerable volume of promissory notes until after the panic of 1893 and the collapse of a real estate boom which had begun in the 1880's. Some ten years later, however, banks in Minnesota towns of but moderate size were "supplementing their reserves with purchased paper of the highest grade." [36] About the same time it is said that many bankers in North Dakota "were familiar with commercial paper," and that the seasonal buying of such paper as an investment for surplus funds of banks was "in general practice throughout the Northwest." [37] Nebraska banks, including those in the interior of the state, had begun to buy short-term notes by 1900.[38] Banks in Kansas were investing surplus funds in this manner about the same time.[39] In Tennessee, and probably some other Southern states also, banks apparently bought but comparatively little paper until after 1894.[40] According to bankers of Dallas, Texas, banks in that state were buying open-market paper by about 1900; and nine years later an officer of a New York bank could say that his institution had "purchased, in one day, over one-quarter million

[35] "The Commercial Paper Business," *Fed. Res. Bull.*, Aug. 1921, p. 922.

A New York dealer who opened a branch office in St. Louis about 1902 reported that banks in that city were not buying much paper at that time and were even opposed to dealings in open-market obligations, on the ground that such operations tended to reduce rates they could charge on direct loans to customers.

[36] A. C. Anderson, address as president of Minnesota Bankers' Association, *Proc. Minn. Bankers' Assoc.*, 1904, p. 11.

[37] E. M. Stevens, "Commercial Paper," *Proc. N. D. Bankers' Assoc.*, 1903, pp. 29, 31.

[38] S. H. Burnham, address (without title) on commercial paper, *Proc. Neb. Bankers' Assoc.*, 1903, p. 188, and E. Royse, "The Critical Season in Banking in Nebraska," *ibid.*, p. 366. See also G. W. Wattles, "Quick Assets" (a discussion), *ibid.*, 1904, p. 116.

[39] G. A. Rogers, "Loaning Money," *Proc. Kan. Bankers' Assoc.*, 1905, pp. 138–139, and J. Q. Royce, "An Analysis of Banking Conditions in Kansas," *ibid.*, 1906, p. 61. See also "A Study in Bank Investments," a discussion led by C. L. Brokaw, *ibid.*, 1908, pp. 39–41.

[40] G. N. Henson, "Selection of Loans," *Bankers' Mag.*, Feb. 1894, p. 613.

[$250,000 of] commercial paper for a Texas bank." [41] About the same time it was said that the "operations of the many great houses now dealing in commercial paper" were "well known" to bankers in Arizona.[42] Even before 1909 banks in the more important cities along the Pacific Coast had begun to invest surplus funds in outside paper. A New York dealer who opened a branch office in San Francisco about 1907 stated that banks in that city were then investing some of their funds in this manner. According to a banker of Los Angeles, banks in that locality had but small amounts of surplus funds available for such investment until after 1903. Purchases of paper in the Pacific Northwest began about the same time. An officer of one of the leading banks in Portland reported that he began to buy paper for his institution about 1900. On the other hand, a Boston dealer who visited Portland and Seattle in 1907 stated that banks in those cities, with the exception of a single institution, were even at that time "loaned up" with local real estate loans and other advances to borrowers in their own immediate localities, were buying practically no outside paper, and were carrying practically no secondary reserves of any other description.[43]

This rather hasty review will perhaps suffice to indicate the rapid expansion of the market for commercial paper in the years from 1875 to 1900. Just when the practice of buying short-term notes as an investment for surplus funds of banks became nationwide would be difficult to state precisely. As early as 1887 it was said that "the buying and selling of commercial paper has become a distinct branch of the banking business, and an important auxiliary to bankers." [44] By 1901 even many "small country banks" are said to have become "heavy purchasers of market paper." [45]

[41] W. O. Jones, "The Ideal Country Banker," *Proc. N. C. Bankers' Assoc.*, 1909, p. 137.

[42] J. K. Lynch, "Modern Tendencies and Ancient Principles," *Proc. Ariz. Bankers' Assoc.*, 1909, p. 50.

[43] Cf. with the following statement in an address of a New York banker before the Oregon Bankers' Association in 1908: ". . . your particular section of our country is beginning to attract the attention of dealers in commercial paper" (Jones, "The Ideal Country Banker," *Proc. Ore. Bankers' Assoc.*, 1908, p. 66).

[44] W. H. Baker, "Commercial Paper," *Proc. Amer. Bankers' Assoc.*, 1887, p. 45.

[45] Flynn, *op. cit.*, p. 33.

Four years later, according to a well-informed bank officer of New York, bankers were buying the open-market paper "of their home merchants" at rates lower than they were willing to take on direct loans to such borrowers.[46] In 1906 a St. Louis banker who traveled rather extensively through various parts of the country reported that he "found the South, Southwest, North, Northwest and West purchasing commercial paper at from 4 to 5½ per cent," and that such cities as St. Paul, Minneapolis, Denver, Dallas, Nashville, Memphis, and Little Rock, "as well as many others that might be enumerated," had "become a field for the commercial note broker who heretofore confined himself to selling his securities practically east of the Alleghany Mountains, with the exception of Chicago and St. Louis." [47] Two years later the New York banker mentioned just above, in an able address before the Illinois Bankers' Association, affirmed that the Southern states were the only part of the country not buying open-market paper to any great extent by that time.[48] In the same year a Chicago banker stated that "the carefully selected notes of solvent merchants, manufacturers and corporations . . . are now almost universally purchased . . . by mercantile banks throughout the country," and that "the market for commercial paper under ordinary conditions is wide and nearly continuous." [49] By 1911 the Superintendent of Banks of Minnesota could say that "the market for commercial paper extends over the length and breadth of this land, excepting some portions of the southern states." [50] As a matter of fact, from the evidence which has been presented in this section it would probably be safe to conclude that the market for such paper had become very nearly nation-wide some ten years earlier than indicated in the address of this official. Certainly at

[46] J. G. Cannon, *Bank Credits. No. 2* (pamphlet containing reprint of an address before the New Jersey Bankers' Association, 1905), p. 5.

[47] F. J. Wade, "What Causes Fluctuation in Money Rates?" *Proc. N. Y. Bankers' Assoc.*, 1906, pp. 35–36.

[48] Cannon, *Buying Commercial Paper* (pamphlet containing reprint of the address referred to), pp. 5–6.

[49] J. T. Talbert, "Commercial Paper," *Proc. Minn. Bankers' Assoc.*, 1908, pp. 42, 44.

[50] K. S. Chase, "Registration of Commercial Paper," *Proc. Minn. Bankers' Assoc.*, 1911, p. 31.

least some banks in practically all the larger cities of the United States had begun to buy promissory notes through dealers by 1900; and by a year or so after the panic of 1907, when the merits of carefully selected outside paper as an investment for banks' funds were proved beyond a doubt, it is probable that the market for such paper had become virtually as wide as it has been at any subsequent time.

4. GROWTH IN THE ANNUAL VOLUME OF OPEN-MARKET PAPER HANDLED BY DEALERS

The growth of the practices of borrowing in the market and investing banks' surplus funds in outside paper, which has just been traced, implied a corresponding growth in the total volume of commercial paper bought and sold by dealers each year. While accurate figures of such total volume have never been published, and even at present are not obtainable, there can be no question that the annual volume of paper handled by dealers in this period, as compared with that purchased by banks and other buyers in the years before 1861, increased considerably.

During the earlier years of this period, however, the growth in dealers' annual turnover was interrupted by the outbreak of the Civil War and its effects on industry, trade, and finance — both public and private. Obviously the disruption of economic relations between the North and the South, and such accompanying disturbances as extraordinarily high money rates, numerous failures of trading concerns — particularly wholesale dry-goods houses, many of which had probably been borrowing in the open market to finance the sale of large amounts of goods on long credit terms to retail dealers in the South — the suspension of specie payments, and the general uncertainty overhanging and discouraging trading and manufacturing enterprise throughout the country, were circumstances by no means favorable for any expansion of operations in commercial paper.[51] Under the conditions pre-

[51] Indications of the disturbances which a prolonged and severe struggle between the Northern and the Southern states might be expected to produce in the country's leading money markets were observed in New York as early as November 1860, several months before Fort Sumter was fired on. Pressure began to be felt in the

vailing for some months before and a somewhat indefinite period
after the actual outbreak of hostilities between the North and the
South, both borrowing in the market and buying open-market
paper as an investment were hazardous undertakings, as may be
readily inferred from the account given by Henry Clews, a leading
New York dealer,[52] of the adroit — if not too scrupulous — manner in which he dealt with the contingencies confronting his business in the first few months of 1861.

Early in that year Clews went to Washington to negotiate with
Secretary Chase in regard to the purchase of an issue of government bonds. While there he got the impression that "war was inevitable," and that "the contest would be long and bloody." He
therefore sent a dispatch to his firm in New York, urging this
concern to "lose no time in selling off all the mercantile paper on
hand." He himself hastily returned to New York to dispose of
this paper: "I went vigorously to work, and succeeded in unload-
ing all but ten thousand dollars of short time notes made by Lane,
Boyce & Co., and a note of $500 of Edward Lambert & Co." Very
soon after he had accomplished what he calls "this very desirable
work of shifting my burden, and distributing it in a more equable
manner on the shoulders of others, but at higher rates than I
paid," news reached New York that Fort Sumter had been fired
on. Thereupon "the wildest scenes of excitement and consterna-
tion were witnessed in Wall Street and throughout the entire business community. . . . The two firms whose papers I was unable
to dispose of were about the first to fail, and before the maturity
of any of the balance of the paper which I had successfully negoti-

---

stock market about the beginning of November and soon spread to "the general
discount market." Private capitalists were "frightened out of the market." Holders
of bills "found it difficult to procure loans, as usual, on the security of mercantile
paper." By the thirteenth the discount market "became blocked up." Brokers
"confined their energies to attempts to sell such paper as they had on hand, while
the negotiation of any fresh notes was impossible." Money "became very scarce and
dear." Paper even of "the best houses met but a limited sale at 12 per cent., while
that of houses heretofore rated number one, was hawked around the market at 18
and even 24 per cent." By about the middle of December, "an almost complete
cessation of operations in the open discount market" was reported. ("Notes on the
Money Market," *Bankers' Mag.*, Dec. 1860, p. 499; Jan. 1861, p. 588; and Feb. 1861,
p. 669).   [52] See pp. 22, 31-32.

ated both the drawers and endorsers thereon, without a single exception, all collapsed." [53]

Under such conditions both the supply of open-market paper and the demand for it as an investment inevitably fell off to an appreciable extent, and dealers in bills and notes were forced to curtail their operations correspondingly. The business of dealers in New York began to decline as early as November 1860,[54] and remained comparatively small in volume for at least the next two years [55] and probably for some time thereafter. Just how long after 1861 operations in commercial paper remained restricted is not certain, but the war and the disturbances to which it gave rise probably continued to exert a more or less retarding influence on the growth of dealers' sales until about 1879, when specie payments were resumed.

At the beginning of the period considered in this chapter the total annual volume of short-term credit instruments handled by dealers was undoubtedly small as compared with the figures attained in later years. Early in 1862 it was estimated that the total investment of American banks in commercial paper then outstanding amounted to $700,000,000, and, on the assumption that the average maturity of the instruments concerned was three months, that these banks were then investing $2,800,000,000 a year in such paper.[56] If even as much as one-seventh of the latter figure could be taken to represent the amount of open-market paper purchased by banks and other buyers combined, the total annual volume of dealers' sales thus estimated would in 1862 have been considerably smaller than the figures reached before the close of the last century. Five years later, in 1867, a number of failures among "prominent grocers, dry goods houses, and tea dealers" occasioned

[53] Henry Clews, *Twenty-eight Years in Wall Street*, pp. 74–75, 78–79.

It will be recalled that this dealer bought paper outright. Those who acted as brokers only — that is, bought outright none of the bills or notes they handled — obviously were not confronted at that time with the risks from which Clews thought it advisable to extricate himself in the manner described.

[54] See n. 51, pp. 51–52.

[55] "Commercial Chronicle and Review," *Hunt's Merch. Mag.*, Jan. 1861, p. 78; and "Notes on the Money Market," *Bankers' Mag.*, June 1861, p. 946; Aug. 1861, p. 158; Nov. 1861, p. 398; Dec. 1861, p. 477; and March 1862, p. 751.

[56] "Notes on the Money Market," *Bankers' Mag.*, Feb. 1862, pp. 653–654.

"some loss of confidence in commercial paper," and therefore, it is probable, some reduction in dealers' sales also.[57] A decision made early in the same year by Deputy Comptroller Hulburd, to the effect that national banks are "not authorized to buy commercial paper in the open market at a rate greater than seven per cent," also probably tended to restrict such sales to some extent.[58] The crisis of 1873 followed shortly thereafter, and no doubt exerted a more powerful influence in the same direction. No considerable growth in dealers' annual volume during the years of depression which succeeded this crisis would be expected; yet it is said that "after the depression of 1873 set in, merchants and other business men began to rely more largely than before on note-brokers to raise them the funds needful to transact business," and that the commercial paper business increased "enormously" in the ten years ending about the middle of 1884.[59] Some support for this statement is furnished by the author of a well-known work on banking published in the latter year. According to this writer, the business of the "note broker" had by that time become "a very large one." The same author says that Alonzo Follett, a New York dealer who failed in 1882, had at that time nearly $10,000,000 of notes in his office, and had been selling about $100,000,000 of paper a year; and, further, that a bank president (presumably of New York) estimated at the same time that New York City banks were then buying $1,000,000 of open-market paper a day.[60] It is of course impossible to verify the accuracy of these figures, but they would seem to be rather exaggerated. At any rate, banks are said to have decreased their purchases of paper shortly thereafter, as a result of losses sustained from the failure of "several large leather concerns" in 1883 and a number of dry-goods houses in the following year.[61]

[57] *Bankers' Mag.*, July 1867, p. 79.
[58] "National Banks Not Authorized to Establish Branches," *Hunt's Merch. Mag.*, Feb. 1867, pp. 167–168.
[59] "The New York Banks and Their Customers," *Bankers' Mag.*, Aug. 1884, pp. 81–82.   [60] Bolles, *op. cit.*, pp. 64–65.
[61] "The New York Banks and Their Customers," *Bankers' Mag.*, Aug. 1884, pp. 82–83, and "Notes on the Money Market," *ibid.*, p. 157. See also Bolles, *op. cit.*, pp. 63, 66; and "Scrutiny of Commercial Paper," *Rhodes' Jour. of Banking*, Dec. 1883, p. 1048.

During the remaining years of this period, however, dealers' sales undoubtedly increased to a considerable extent. A prominent "note broker" of New York is said to have sold about $250,000,000 of commercial paper in the six years ending about November 1892, or about $42,000,000 a year;[62] and a large increase in the business of the "note broker" during the 1890's and the earlier years of the present century was noted in addresses by bankers of the Middle West in 1908 and 1912.[63]

One reason why the supply of negotiable paper increased during this time was the fact that a number of concerns in the South and the West found it advisable to take advantage of rates appreciably lower than those charged by their own local banks. Even about as late as 1900 there were wide differences in the discount rates charged by banks in different sections of the country, and concerns in the South and the West found it distinctly advantageous to supplement loans obtained direct from local banks at high rates with credit obtained indirectly from banks in the East at rates considerably lower.[64] Probably the main reason for the increase in the

[62] Cannon, *Bank Credits* (pamphlet containing reprint of an address delivered at the Drexel Institute, 1892), p. 39.

[63] Talbert, "Commercial Credits," *Proc. N. Y. Bankers' Assoc.*, 1908, p. 85; and N. E. Franklin, "Commercial Paper," *Proc. S. D. Bankers' Assoc.*, 1912, p. 127.

[64] R. M. Breckenridge, "Branch Banking and Discount Rates," *Bankers' Mag.*, Jan. 1899, p. 44, and "Discount Rates in the United States," *Pol. Sci. Quart.*, March 1898, p. 130.

The wide differences in discount rates charged by banks in different sections of the country a few years before 1900 are indicated in a table included in the first of these two articles (p. 44). This table shows average discount rates charged by banks in forty-three cities on "first-class two-name commercial paper" during the years 1893–1897. The average "lower" and "higher" rates charged in twelve of these cities were as follows:

City	Lower Rate	Higher Rate
Boston	3.83%	5.05%
New York	4.41	5.36
Philadelphia	4.64	6.01
Savannah	7.99	9.75
Atlanta	8.00	8.00
Birmingham	8.00	9.86
Houston	8.00	8.00
Salt Lake City	8.00	10.00
Portland (Oregon)	8.00	10.00
Tacoma	9.27	11.13
Seattle	9.96	11.96
Denver	10.00	11.67

demand for open-market paper was the growing realization on the part of bankers of the desirability of such paper as a short-term investment. The safety and certainty of payment of carefully selected unsecured single-name notes purchased in the market were demonstrated to the satisfaction of a number of bankers during the late 1880's, at the time of the panic of 1893, and in the years immediately following, and undoubtedly encouraged the policy of carrying commercial paper as a secondary reserve.[65]

Just how great an expansion of dealers' operations in the early years of the present century resulted from the growing popularity of commercial paper both as a means of raising short-term capital and as an investment for surplus funds of banks is not known, but the annual volume of sales by dealers no doubt attained substantial proportions by 1907. A New York banker in 1906 gave "upwards of five hundred millions of dollars" as an estimate of the volume of paper then being sold "in the course of a year by the note brokers of this city."[66] If this estimate may be taken as approximately accurate, it seems safe to conclude that the total volume of sales by all dealers in the United States had by 1907 reached a figure in excess of $1,000,000,000 a year.

However large this volume may have become by that time, sales

[65] The losses on about $250,000,000 of paper purchased by banks from a New York dealer during the years 1886 to 1892 are said to have amounted only to about $500,000 or 1/5 of 1 per cent (Cannon, *loc cit.*).

Cannon states also that a large bank in New York lost only $37,000, or about 1/20 of 1 per cent, on $71,700,000 of paper bought from about 1891 to about 1895 (*Losses from Bad Debts* — pamphlet containing reprint of an address before the New York Bankers' Association, 1895 — p. 11).

According to a Chicago dealer, the president of a bank in that city stated that his total losses on more than $50,000,000 of paper purchased during some five years ending about 1902 amounted to less than $500, or only about 1/1,000 of 1 per cent (Noble Crandall, address — without title — on commercial paper, *Proc. Neb. Bankers' Assoc.*, 1903, p. 187).

Such low ratios of losses as those just enumerated were probably exceptional, and banks which bought paper without making careful credit investigations sometimes suffered fairly heavy losses.

[66] S. S. Conover, "The Credit Man in a Bank," *Banking Law Jour.*, April 1906, p. 311.

In this same article Conover states that the "purchasing of commercial paper from brokers in the open market has come in these days to be a great business," and that the "note brokerage business in New York has . . . greatly increased within recent years" (pp. 311–312).

by dealers seem to have expanded more rapidly after 1907 than before.

Even as late as that year many bankers looked askance at commercial paper, and probably no small number of them were actually hostile to the operations of the dealer. During the last few months of 1907, however, the safety and liquidity of judiciously selected open-market paper in times of serious financial stress were brought home in a striking fashion to bankers in all sections of the country. At a time when stocks and bonds of the highest grade could be sold only at a heavy sacrifice, and call loans could not be converted into cash at all, millions of dollars of "purchased" promissory notes were paid promptly at maturity, without loss to the holders and without request for renewal. Banks which owned substantial amounts of such notes maturing from October to December were indeed in a fortunate position. It may not be true, as has been said, that "no paper buying bank failed during the panic of 1907";[67] but it is certain that the prompt payment of outside paper then held in their portfolios enabled many banks to meet pressing demands for cash and for additional loans which they would have found it impossible to satisfy had their secondary reserves consisted entirely of high-grade listed securities and call loans.

It is said also that commercial paper stood the New York Clearing House banks in good stead at this time in connection with the issue of clearing house loan certificates. Nearly 73 per cent of the collateral held against these certificates, in fact, is said to have consisted of such paper.[68]

[67] W. H. Kniffin, *Commercial Banking*, II, 691.

[68] Cannon, *Clearing House Loan Certificates and Substitutes for Money Used during the Panic of 1907* (pamphlet containing reprint of an address delivered before the Finance Forum, New York City, 1910), p. 30. Presumably the commercial paper mentioned in this address was open-market paper, though Cannon makes no specific statement to this effect.

Numerous examples of the safety and "liquidity" of such paper during the panic of 1907 might be cited. Only a few will be given here:

". . . a prominent and reliable firm of note brokers of whom I recently made inquiry, informed me that during the first twelve days of the money panic of 1907 — at its very peak — they had maturing through their office something more than ten million dollars' worth of bought paper, every single dollar of which was promptly paid without renewal" (J. H. Case, "The Desirability of Commercial Paper as a Bank Investment," *Proc. N. J. Bankers' Assoc.*, 1912, p. 32).

The record for prompt payment established under such trying circumstances by unsecured promissory notes purchased through dealers was indeed impressive, and unquestionably brought about a considerable expansion of the market for such paper during the remaining years of this period. As early as 1908 it was estimated that dealers' sales had reached the figure of $2,000,000,000 a year,[69] but such a figure seems overstated by several hundred million dollars. Much more exaggerated is an estimate, ascribed by a South Dakota banker to "statisticians," that by 1912 "over five billion dollars' worth of Commercial Paper" was "being discounted by National Banks alone, each year." [70] An estimate made in 1913, that total sales of such paper amounted in 1912 to about $1,700,000,000, representing the obligations of 2,500 to 3,000

"A member of a prominent commercial paper house in New York informed me . . . that out of between $4,000,000 and $5,000,000 of commercial paper negotiated by his house and maturing in sixty days of the panic, every dollar was met at maturity, with the exception of a short renewal upon $7,500 . . . which has since been paid.

"A partner in another commercial paper house related . . . that in one day in October last $1,560,000 of paper sold by his house matured, every dollar of which was promptly paid upon that particular date" (W. O. Jones, "The Ideal Country Banker," *Proc. Ore. Bankers' Assoc.*, 1908, pp. 65–66).

"The president of a National bank in a certain Pennsylvania city stated that during October and November (in the very heart of the panic) he had over $2,000,000 of commercial paper mature, every dollar of which was paid upon its due date, with the exception of a short extension granted upon one piece of $5,000" (*ibid.*, p. 65).

See also C. R. Burnett, "Commercial Paper" (lecture to the credit class of the Richmond Chapter, American Institute of Banking, Dec. 8, 1921); F. W. Crane, "Commercial Paper Purchased from Brokers," *Proc. Ill. Bankers' Assoc.*, 1916, p. 130; F. K. Houston, *Commercial Paper — Its Uses and Abuses* (pamphlet containing reprint of an address before the convention of Reserve City Bankers, Baltimore, 1917), p. 4; A. H. Lindsay, *Commercial Paper* (pamphlet containing reprint of an address before Group 7, Wisconsin Bankers' Association, La Crosse, Wisconsin, 1913), pp. 3–4; McCluney and Company, pamphlet (without title) containing reprint of parts of letters in which twenty-one different banks state their experiences with "purchased" paper which matured during the panic of 1907; National Credit Office, *The Story of Commercial Paper* — No. 1 (pamphlet), p. 2; E. Naumburg, *Basis of Sound Banking* (pamphlet), p. 1; O. J. Sands, *Commercial Paper as a National Asset* (pamphlet containing reprint of an address before the National Association of Credit Men, Cincinnati, 1913), p. 3; and E. H. Sensenich, "Commercial Paper as a Secondary Reserve," *Proc. Idaho Bankers' Assoc.*, 1914, p. 113, and "Convertible Assets, the Secret of the Strong Bank," *Proc. Mont. Bankers' Assoc.*, 1914, p. 30.

[69] W. A. Law, "Co-operation in Commercial Credits," *Proc. Pa. Bankers' Assoc.*, 1908, p. 43.   [70] Franklin, *op. cit.*, p. 128.

borrowing concerns, is unquestionably a closer approximation to the actual volume being handled by dealers at that time.[71] About the same time a well-known Chicago banker gave $1,500,000,000 as approximately "the greatest volume of commercial paper afloat in this country at any one time." [72] If we may assume that the average maturity of such paper was then somewhere between four months and six months, average "outstandings" of $1,500,000,000 would be equivalent to annual sales of about $3,600,000,000 — a figure which would seem to be considerably overstated. This same banker estimated, further, that the annual volume of dealers' sales probably doubled or trebled in the five-year period from 1909 to 1914.[73] Such estimates as these also seem too liberal. In the same year a banker of Milwaukee reported that as many as six houses were then each handling more than $100,000,000 of paper a year; and, from figures supplied by "two of the most important brokerage firms in this country," estimated that annual sales by all dealers had reached a figure somewhere between $1,000,000,000 and $3,000,000,000.[74] A few months later a Richmond banker gave $1,750,000,000 as an estimate of such sales.[75] In the same year, 1913, it was reported that more than two-thirds of all state banks and trust companies in New York State were buying paper in the market, and the purchase of outside paper by New York banks apparently had become of sufficient importance to justify the Banking Department of that state in undertaking to investigate the "character and financial responsibility" of the dealers through whom such banks were then investing their surplus funds.[76] Since banks in all other sections of the country also had begun to buy such paper even some years before this time, it would seem safe to

[71] J. A. Broderick, "Registration of Commercial Paper," *Bankers' Home Mag.*, Nov. 1913, p. 42. See also E. E. Agger, "The Commercial Paper Debate," *Jour. Pol. Econ.*, July 1914, p. 665, n. 1; and "For Check on Notes," *N. Y. Times*, Sept. 21, 1913, Part 7, p. 15.

[72] C. B. Hazlewood, "Commercial Paper as a Secondary Reserve for West Virginia Banks," *Proc. W. Va. Bankers' Assoc.*, 1913, p. 84.

[73] *Ibid.*, p. 91.

[74] Lindsay, *op. cit.*, p. 3.

[75] Sands, *op. cit.*, p. 5.

[76] Report of N. Y. State Superintendent of Banks, 1913, pp. 8–9. See also Broderick, *op. cit.*, p. 42.

infer that the total volume of sales by dealers had by the close of this period reached a figure of approximately $2,000,000,000 a year.

Some of the factors which operated to bring about the large increase in the annual volume of these sales were mentioned above. In addition to those already mentioned — in particular the use of the open market to take advantage of more favorable rates for short-term funds, and increased purchases of outside paper resulting from a growing recognition of its desirability as a secondary reserve for banks — various other factors also influenced the volume of business handled by dealers during this period.

At least two of these other influences seem to have operated in the same direction as the two just referred to. The first of these was the "campaign of education" conducted from 1908 to 1914 by those who were in favor of a reform of the currency and emphasized the "desirability of basing this reform upon commercial paper." This campaign is said to have "done much to make clear to the banks" the advantages of such paper as an investment.[77] The second of these influences was a "heavy" depreciation in the securities held by banks in the last few years of this period. This shrinkage in their investment portfolios, it is said, induced a number of banks gradually to withdraw from the bond market and replace their bonds in part with outside paper as a secondary reserve.[78]

Fluctuations in business activity also had their effects on the volume of paper sold in the market. Presumably this volume fluctuated more or less closely with changes in business activity in general, though data for any statistical demonstration of such a relationship are not available.

The influence of the financial crises or periods of money-market stringency which were among the more striking phenomena associated with fluctuations in such activity seems to have been somewhat mixed. During some of these periods, notably in 1893 and 1907, the larger and stronger open-market borrowers

---

[77] W. W. Naumburg, "Commercial Paper," *N. Y. Times*, "Annual Financial Review," Jan. 7, 1912, p. 25.   [78] Broderick, *op. cit.*, p. 43.

met their promissory notes promptly at maturity, and thus provided considerable amounts of funds at critical junctures for banks in practically all sections of the country. As was indicated above, the record which many concerns established under such circumstances for the prompt payment of their maturing obligations was one of the main factors which brought about the increase in dealers' sales in the years following 1893. A number of less ably managed concerns, on the other hand, found themselves unable to meet their obligations at such times, with the result that banks which had purchased their paper sometimes suffered fairly heavy losses. The unfortunate experiences of such banks of course had an effect on dealers' sales directly the opposite of that just noted. In times of serious financial strain, such as was felt in 1893, 1907, and 1913, even some of the strongest and most ably managed concerns no doubt succeeded in maintaining the "liquidity" of their open-market paper only through being able to shift their short-term borrowing, in part at least, to their own local banks or to their trade creditors. The "shiftability" of such short-term borrowing, in fact, probably accounted in no small measure for the advantages of purchased paper over call loans and long-term securities at such times, so far as "liquidity" is concerned. Whatever its comparative advantages as a secondary reserve for banks may be, the conditions prevailing during times of marked stringency in the money market have been such as to restrict the demand for such paper temporarily, and therefore the supply of short-term obligations which dealers have been willing to take from their borrowing customers. At such times banks have found it necessary to adopt a policy of caution in extending credit, and many banks have been "loaned up" already — particularly if they have been called on to help maintain the "liquidity" of open-market paper issued by their own customers — and therefore in no position to buy any considerable amounts of additional outside paper. Under such circumstances it is not surprising that dealers' operations have been curtailed considerably for the time being. Professor Sprague, in fact, estimated in 1910 that the commercial paper business has been reduced "very much more than one-half in an emergency like that of 1893 or 1907." [79] Somewhat similar effects were observed also in 1873, 1883, and 1913: in each of these years, as well as in 1893 and 1907, a number of concerns which had been borrowing in the open market found that their "note brokers" were able to serve them as "fair-weather friends" only.[80] Thus the conditions prevailing during all the major financial crises of the last fifty years of this period tended to restrict considerably, for the time being, the demand for outside paper, and therefore the supply of it offered for sale by dealers. Within a comparatively short time after 1893, 1907, and 1913, however, this tendency seems to have been more than offset by the increased demand for such paper resulting from the promptness with which in those years concerns borrowing in the open market met their maturing obligations.

Besides those already considered, three other factors operated to restrict to some extent the volume of paper sold by dealers during this period. The first of these was the view, held by at least some bankers in all parts of the country, and even more strongly by many of their borrowing customers, that the loanable funds of local banks should be used, so far as is consistent with safety and a satisfactory rate of return, to foster local enterprises. Expressions of this view, which was held rather widely during the preceding period also, may be found as late as 1889 and 1914;[81] and even at present it continues to limit to some extent the demand for out-

---

[79] O. M. W. Sprague, *History of Crises under the National Banking System*, p. 302. In an article published some five years later Professor Sprague speaks of the market for commercial paper as being "completely suspended" in the financial crises preceding that of 1914 ("The Crisis of 1914 in the United States," *Amer. Ec. Rev.*, Sept. 1915, p. 520). With this may be compared the following statement, relating to the year 1893: "Scarcely anything is done in commercial paper, and the few transactions made are at such rates as can be agreed upon" ("The Financial Situation," *C. and F. Chron.*, July 29, 1893, p. 162).

[80] J. K. Lynch, "Seven Years' Financial Schooling," *Proc. Ariz. Bankers' Assoc.*, 1914, p. 33; Sprague, "The Crisis of 1914 in the United States," *Amer. Ec. Rev.*, Sept. 1915, p. 520, and *History of Crises under the National Banking System*, p. 84; Ralph Van Vechten, address as president of Clearing House Section, American Bankers' Association, *Proc. Amer. Bankers' Assoc.*, 1913, p. 518; article on discounting paper at banks, *Rhodes' Jour. of Banking*, April 1883, p. 292; and "The New York Banks and Their Customers," *Bankers' Mag.*, Aug. 1884, p. 83.

[81] "Out-of-Town Paper," *Rhodes' Jour. of Banking*, June 1889, p. 521, and Sensenich, "Commercial Paper as a Secondary Reserve," *Proc. Idaho Bankers' Assoc.*, 1914, p. 117.

side paper by banks in all sections of the country. The second of these factors was the competition of various commercial banks with regular dealers in the origination and sale of commercial paper. Throughout practically the whole of this period banks in various sections of the United States at least occasionally sold unsecured promissory notes of their own customers to correspondent or other banks, and purchases of such notes reduced *pro tanto* the amounts of paper which the latter banks were able to buy through regular dealers. During the latter years of this period, indeed, some few banks even acted as regular dealers in commercial paper. The operations of such banks obviously had an effect on total sales by dealers directly the reverse of that just noted. The third factor was the development of certain abuses in the commercial paper business, particularly such practices as taking promissory notes for sale without any careful preliminary credit investigation, inducing comparatively small concerns, whose credit accommodation should have been confined to loans from their own local banks, to borrow in the open market as well, and encouraging larger concerns to seek excessive amounts of short-term credit in the market. As a result of such practices, which were confined in the main to irresponsible note brokers or small dealers, as distinguished from commercial paper houses, a number of banks occasionally suffered fairly heavy losses. Such losses, moreover, were incurred even in periods when business conditions in general were favorable; and, though they resulted in many cases from carelessness on the part of the buying banks themselves, they unquestionably led to some reduction in purchases of outside paper by these and other banks. They led also to widespread criticism of abuses connected with the commercial paper business, and finally, as one of a number of remedies proposed for such abuses, to a movement for the registration of all promissory notes sold in the open market.[82]

The growth of the commercial paper business — as indicated by the rapid expansion of dealers' operations, the growth of the practices of borrowing in the open market and investing surplus funds of banks in outside paper, and the increase in the annual volume

[82] See pp. 396–397.

of dealers' sales — was one of the main developments of this period. Significant developments took place also with respect to the organization maintained by the dealer for carrying on his business, the classes of credit instruments he handled, the classes of borrowers from whom he procured and investors to whom he sold these obligations, his methods of conducting his operations in commercial paper, the practices in buying and methods of credit investigation followed by the banks to which he sold the greater part of this paper, and the other operations in which he engaged. These developments will be considered in the remaining pages of this chapter.

5. DEVELOPMENT OF MORE ELABORATE ORGANIZATIONS BY DEALERS

At the beginning of this period, and indeed for some years later, many dealers in negotiable paper carried on their operations with only the simplest form of organization. Most dealers were then brokers who confined their activities in the main to their own immediate localities. Such credit investigations as they made were very simple, as also were their methods of buying and selling the paper they handled; and for the successful conduct of their affairs they required no more than a single office and perhaps the assistance of a clerk or two. Besides a comparatively large number of these smaller note brokers, a smaller number of private banking houses were also buying and selling bills and notes at that time. These banking houses operated on a larger scale and in a wider territory than the smaller brokers, and for this reason required a correspondingly more elaborate organization. As they extended their operations to more and more remote localities, and began to handle an increasing volume of business, these and other large dealers found it advisable to adopt newer and more effective methods of making credit investigations and buying and selling paper. In order to accomplish these purposes, and to carry on more effectively their operations other than dealing in short-term negotiable instruments, the larger houses began to maintain more and more elaborately organized main offices and to establish, in addition, branch offices, correspondent relations, or other arrangements for representation, in other parts of the country. It is true that a fairly large number of small dealers were still buying and selling open-market paper as late as 1913, and that some of these smaller dealers were carrying on their business with but a single office and one or two assistants. These dealers, however, confined their operations largely to their own localities, and handled but a small proportion of the total volume of paper then being sold each year. The bulk of the commercial paper business, even at that time, was being handled by a comparatively small number of the larger houses. For some years before 1913, in fact, various forces had been operating to bring about a concentration of this business in the hands of the larger dealers; and, in order to handle effectively an increasing proportion of the total volume of paper bought and sold each year, these larger dealers found it necessary before the close of this period to build up organizations scarcely less elaborate than those maintained by the largest commercial paper houses in more recent years.[83]

6. Changes Relating to Classes of Paper Handled by Dealers

During this same period important developments took place with respect also to classes of negotiable instruments handled by dealers. It was stated in the preceding chapter that throughout the period before the Civil War the promissory note remained a much more important credit instrument in domestic trade than the trade bill, and that the greater part of the promissory notes sold in the market were indorsed or double-name paper. For a number of years after 1861 dealers continued to buy and sell both domestic bills of exchange and double-name promissory notes, but the proportions of both these classes of paper sold in the market began to decline shortly after the outbreak of the Civil War. The decline which began at that time, moreover, continued more or less

---

[83] The organization of the modern commercial paper house is described in Chap. IV. Because of the similarity of structure between the larger houses of the present and those of the preceding thirty years, no detailed description of the organization maintained by the larger dealers was considered necessary in this or the succeeding chapter.

steadily throughout the remaining years of the last century; and by 1900 these two classes of paper had been largely replaced by promissory notes bearing the name of the maker only.

The volume of trade bills handled by dealers seems not only to have been smaller than that of double-name promissory notes at the beginning of the period considered in this chapter, but also to have declined more rapidly than the latter in succeeding years. Exhibits 9 and 10 indicate that a leading Boston dealer was offering acceptances for sale in 1867 and 1869.[84] "Note brokers" in New York and Boston were selling trade bills in 1878,[85] and no doubt in later years also, and a "broker in commercial paper" was dealing in both notes and acceptances in New Jersey (presumably) about as late as 1890.[86] About ten years later, however, the trade bill is said to have "fallen so law" that it was being used as a means of forcing the collection of slow and doubtful accounts,[87] and early in 1914 it was estimated that domestic acceptances were then being used in less than 3 per cent of the credit transactions in the United States.[88] Since only a comparatively small volume of such instruments was being drawn after about 1890, and most concerns able to borrow in the open market would not have needed to resort to the use of trade bills, it seems reasonable to conclude that the volume of acceptances handled by the larger dealers in open-market paper had dwindled to insignificant proportions a number of years before the close of this period.[89]

The other form of negotiable instrument handled by dealers during this period, the promissory note, included the two well-known classes of single-name and double-name, or indorsed paper. Of these two classes, the latter was undoubtedly more common at

[84] Exhibit 11 may indicate that a leading New York dealer was offering bills as well as notes for sale in 1872, though the term "drawer" may be used in this offering list as synonymous with "indorser."

[85] "Inquiries of Correspondents. III. The Purchase of Notes by National Banks," *Bankers' Mag.*, June 1878, p. 984.

[86] *Danforth et al.* v. *National State Bank of Elizabeth*, 48 Fed. 271.

[87] M. G. Myers, *The New York Money Market*, I, 316.

[88] "Commercial Paper," *Annalist*, Mar. 9, 1914, p. 293.

[89] In this connection it may be pointed out that the paper advertised for sale in the offering lists shown in Exhibits 12–15 apparently consists altogether of promissory notes.

the beginning of this period, though some single-name notes were sold in the market before 1860.[90] According to Klein, single-name and indorsed open-market paper were "about evenly divided" toward the close of the Civil War,[91] but this view seems to exaggerate the importance of unindorsed paper at that time. As Exhibit 12 indicates, many of the promissory notes offered for sale in the market were still being indorsed as late as 1873. According to dealers in New York and Boston, moreover, the open-market paper bought and sold in those cities was preponderantly double-name paper until about 1885.[92] It should be noted also that the Boston dealers whose offering list is shown in Exhibit 14 were advertising "full lines of Endorsed Paper for sale" as late as 1886; and that about one-half of the notes listed in Exhibit 15, an offering sheet issued by a leading firm of New York dealers in 1893, were indorsed obligations. During and after the Civil War period, however, the practice of selling single-name paper in the market gradually became more common.[93] The growth of the custom of issuing unindorsed notes is said to have been particularly rapid in the decade from 1882 to 1892.[94] In the latter year a well-informed New York banker estimated that two-thirds of all the paper then being purchased by banks in his city was single-name paper. This same banker stated also that about the only trades in which transactions were still being settled by promissory notes at that time were the jewelry, tobacco, and rubber trades, and a few others in which staple products were handled.[95] A dealer who began business in Chicago in the following year reported that the first paper he handled consisted of notes receivable which local manufacturers and jobbers and other merchants had taken in payment for goods

[90] See p. 30.

[91] J. J. Klein, "The Development of Mercantile Instruments of Credit in the United States," *Jour. of Accountancy*, Jan. 1912, p. 46.

[92] In an article published in a New York newspaper in 1914, it is stated that the use of two-name paper was "practically abandoned" in the New York market by 1884 ("Double-Name Paper," *N. Y. Evening Post*, Mar. 14, 1914, p. 3). This statement without question underestimates the importance of double-name paper at that time.

[93] It is said that when single-name open-market paper was "first [?] introduced, soon after the Civil War period," it was criticized as a " 'kiting operation' " (*ibid.*).

[94] J. G. Cannon, *Bank Credits* (pamphlet), pp. 36–37.   [95] *Ibid.*, pp. 37–38.

sold, but that these local business men began to offer their own single-name paper for sale in the market some time after 1893.[96] A New York dealer estimated in 1930 that about 75 per cent of the paper being sold in the market in 1894 was single-name, and that the remaining 25 per cent consisted mainly of notes receivable which jobbers in the hardware, grocery, dry-goods, tobacco, and leather trades had taken in payment for goods sold to retail dealers. During the remaining years of this period dealers continued to handle some double-name paper, but, as compared with single-name notes, indorsed obligations seem to have declined in importance more or less steadily after 1894. A Nebraska banker noted in 1903 that dealers' offering lists included but very little "trade paper," or indorsed notes receivable.[97] The heavy preponderance of single-name open-market paper was noted also a few years later by a number of writers, one of whom, a Chicago banker, pointed out that the activities of dealers by 1908 had "all but done away with the necessity which existed in former times to issue trade paper." [98] By about that time, and certainly by the close of this period, single-name promissory notes had to a very large extent displaced indorsed obligations as a means of raising short-term capital, whether in the open market or through direct loans from banks.[99]

[96] A. G. Becker, *Commercial Paper* (pamphlet containing reprint of a paper read before the Chicago and Cook County Bankers' Association, 1923), pp. 3, 5–6.

[97] C. F. Bentley, "Commercial Paper as an Investment for Country Bankers," *Proc. Neb. Bankers' Assoc.*, 1903, p. 180.

[98] J. T. Talbert, "The New Currency Law," *Proc. Ohio Bankers' Assoc.*, 1908, p. 79. See also two other addresses by Talbert: "Commercial Credits," *Proc. N. Y. Bankers' Assoc.*, 1908, pp. 84–85, and "Commercial Paper," *Proc. Minn. Bankers' Assoc.*, 1908, p. 44; and Cannon, *Buying Commercial Paper* (pamphlet), p. 4; K. S. Chase, "Registration of Commercial Paper," *Proc. Minn. Bankers' Assoc.*, 1911, p. 31; and J. L. Laughlin, "The Aldrich-Vreeland Act," *Jour. Pol. Econ.*, Oct. 1908, p. 511.

[99] Klein estimated that the proportion of double-name time paper to the total loans and discounts of national banks declined from about 56 per cent in 1889 to about 33 per cent in 1913, whereas the proportion of single-name time paper increased from about 5 per cent in 1879 to about 20 per cent in 1913 ("Commercial Importance of Single Name Paper," *Annalist*, Mar. 23, 1914, p. 361). He does not explain in this article why the total of both single-name and double-name time paper should constitute such a small proportion of the loans and discounts of these banks.

In an article published about the same time it was stated that the H. B. Claflin Company was about the only prominent New York firm still borrowing on double-

Some of the more important forces which brought about the gradual decline in the use of trade bills and double-name promissory notes, and the displacement of both these classes of credit instruments by notes bearing the name of the maker only, may now be considered.

These forces may be traced back to the Civil War period or the years immediately following. For a number of years before the war retail dealers in many parts of the country had been in the habit of visiting once or twice a year some large trading center, such as New York or Boston, to select stocks of merchandise sufficient to satisfy their customers' requirements over periods varying from a few months to a year. Since the turnover of their goods was slow, and they could not conveniently make cash payments

name paper ("Double-Name Paper," *N. Y. Evening Post*, Mar. 14, 1914, p. 3).

About a month earlier a leading dealer (presumably of New York) is said to have calculated that, of $30,000,000 of paper which was actually sold in the market, only $300,000, or 1 per cent, was double-name ("99 Per Cent. One-Name Paper," *N. Y. Times*, Feb. 11, 1914, p. 13).

In a brief prepared (presumably) in the same year, the Merchants' Association of New York stated that the bill of exchange "in nearly all branches of trade in manufactured goods," and the promissory note "in settlement of trading accounts receivable," both became obsolete "many years ago." The only exceptions noted were cases of "forced trade sales at auction," in which notes or bills were "given in payment mostly by second and third rate debtors, all other preferring, in ordinary times, to settle on short time." The Association stated, further, that such promissory notes as were then (about 1914) being given for merchandise accounts were "quite well understood to represent settlements of overdue accounts receivable, or extensions granted to weak debtors"; that strong houses hesitated to indorse and sell these notes, knowing that they were "the least liquid of all their receivables" and that "a transaction of this kind, disclosed," would "besmirch their own credit"; and that on the average from one-fourth to one-third of such notes went to protest and were paid by the indorser ("Brief of the Merchants' Association of New York on Commercial Paper for Discount by the Federal Reserve Banks" — typewritten paper issued about 1914 — pp. 9–10). If the total amount of such "trade paper" being issued at the close of this period was small, the proportion of it which represented indorsed or double-name obligations was undoubtedly a negligible quantity. Obviously the sale of such low-grade paper in the open market would have been difficult.

According to Professor Laughlin, the practice of taking promissory notes in payment for goods sold, and then indorsing these notes and discounting them at banks, had practically disappeared by 1914 ("The Banking and Currency Act of 1913. II," *Jour. Pol. Econ.*, May 1914, p. 425).

In an article in the same issue of this journal, Professor Sprague pointed out that by 1914 single-name paper and bank acceptances had to a large extent "taken the place of double-name mercantile paper all over the world, except in France" ("Commercial Paper and the Federal Reserve Banks," p. 438).

for large orders at time of purchase, they customarily offered in payment for their purchases their own promissory notes with maturities ranging from about four months to a year, or accepted bills drawn on them by the sellers. The latter, in turn, commonly indorsed these notes or bills and discounted them at their own local banks or sold them to note brokers.[100] The outbreak of hostilities between the North and the South early in 1861, and the financial and other disturbances to which the war gave rise, for the time being practically put an end to this system of conducting trade based on long credit terms. In a period when the value of the depreciated and inconvertible greenbacks was fluctuating widely, it was obviously hazardous to contract to pay or to receive fixed sums of money at any very distant date in the future. Under such circumstances, business men found it advantageous to reduce the length of credit terms to periods of thirty to sixty days, to buy and sell for cash so far as possible, and to encourage prompt payments of accounts through the offer of substantial discounts for cash.[101] The rates of discount offered were in many cases appreciably higher (figured on an annual basis) than the rates at which merchants could borrow from their banks. Hence it was clearly to the advantage of these dealers, if their own resources were insufficient to allow them to pay cash for goods purchased, to obtain from their local banks the accommodation required for this purpose. Not long after the close of the Civil War some of the larger merchants apparently began to seek credit for the same purpose in the open market also. It is said that, in order to take

[100] See pp. 28–29.

[101] According to Klein, most transactions during the Civil War period were either cash transactions or those involving terms of thirty days ("The Development of Mercantile Instruments of Credit in the United States," *Jour. of Accountancy*, Jan. 1912, p. 45). Cf. the following statement from the annual report of the Secretary of the Treasury for 1865: ". . . trade is carried on much more largely for cash than was ever the case previous to 1861" (p. 11).

It is said that the great bulk of sales by jobbers to Western and Southern buyers were being made in 1865 "on short time, say from sixty days to four months," and that buyers in most cases were anticipating payment, to take advantage of liberal cash discounts offered ("The Present State of Trade and Credit," *C. and F. Chron.*, Sept. 9, 1865, p. 325).

For a discussion of credit operations during the Civil War period, see W. C. Mitchell, *A History of the Greenbacks*, pp. 374–376.

advantage of cash discounts ranging from 13 per cent to 18 per cent a year, merchants in the jobbing lines, particularly in the "larger Western centres," began to borrow in the market about as early as 1870; and that this method of financing was facilitated by "the excellent system of credit reporting" which had developed by that time.[102] Whatever the source of the funds borrowed to take advantage of cash discounts, it is obvious that in no cases where buyers paid cash at time of purchase, or shortly thereafter, would there be any occasion for the drawing of trade bills or the issuance of promissory notes which sellers, if they wished to discount such obligations, would generally have to convert into double-name paper by indorsement. The drawing of trade bills, in fact, was clearly impracticable in cases where sellers offered their customers the option of taking cash discounts or paying in effect appreciably higher prices at some later time; for in such cases they could not readily ascertain in advance what methed of payment their customers would elect.

It is clear also that the practice of selling goods on open account, and encouraging prompt payment through the offer of cash discounts appreciably greater than the cost at which buyers could obtain short-term advances on their single-name promissory notes from banks, had advantages that enabled it to survive the disturbed conditions under which it developed.[103] This distinctively American practice, in fact, became even more widespread after 1878 than it had been during the period of inconvertible greenback currency; and, as it became more and more general, exercised an increasingly important influence in restricting the use of trade bills and double-name promissory notes.[104] This influence re-

---

[102] E. D. Page, "The Proposal to Dehumanize Trade," *Annalist*, Mar. 16, 1914, p. 324.

[103] A good brief discussion of the advantages of the "cash discount — open account — single-name paper" system, as contrasted with the trade acceptance method of financing, may be found in *Trade Acceptances — Supporting and Opposing Arguments* (pamphlet issued in 1918 by the Chamber of Commerce of the United States), pp. 14–24.

[104] The extent to which the practice of taking advantage of cash discounts offered was being followed in this country by 1908, and its influence in restricting the supply of trade acceptances and "trade paper" (or notes receivable), are indicated in the following:

mained active throughout the closing years of the period considered in this chapter.

Two other factors which accounted for the decline in the use of trade bills were closely connected. The first of these was a change in the methods of distribution which took place some time after the close of the Civil War. As improvements in means of communication and transportation were developed, and as competition in various trades and industries became more active, many concerns, instead of waiting for buyers to come to them, began to send traveling salesmen out to call on prospective customers. Buyers thereafter no longer found it necessary to visit the larger trading centers once or twice a year, as they had done before the Civil War, and order stocks of goods large enough to last for many months. Instead, with the aid of the salesmen who began to call on them more or less regularly, they could make comparatively small purchases at short intervals.[105] For the settlement of the smaller accounts which resulted from the placing of smaller orders, bills of exchange were hardly practicable. Probably many buyers also found issuing a large number of promissory notes for comparatively small sums less convenient than borrowing round amounts from banks and making settlement more promptly by means of checks. The second factor referred to above was the substitution of the doctrine of implied warranties, as a principle governing the sale of goods, for the rule of *caveat emptor* — a change which accompanied the change in methods of distribution just mentioned. So long as merchants visited the larger trading centers and personally selected the goods they bought from jobbers

---

"So universal is this practice [of taking cash discounts offered — with the aid of short-term advances from banks, if necessary] that no concern wishing to enjoy the highest standing and credit can afford, where discounts are allowed, to permit trade bills [i.e., statements of amounts due for goods purchased] habitually to run to maturity. Still less can any good concern afford to seek further time by settling such bills at maturity with notes or acceptances. . . . Thus . . . scarcely any trade paper is offered to banks for discount" (Talbert, "The New Currency Law," *Proc. Ohio Bankers' Assoc.*, 1908, p. 78).

[105] The "average size of the bills in the sales of large wholesale houses" is said to have decreased from a figure in excess of $1,000 in the 1870's to an amount less than $100 in (presumably) 1914 ("Brief of the Merchants' Association of New York on Commercial Paper for Discount by the Federal Reserve Banks," p. 9).

or wholesalers, they could hardly object to the rule that the risks involved in buying fall upon the buyer himself. When they began to order goods from samples displayed by traveling salesmen, however, it became necessary to substitute for this rule the doctrine of implied warranties, in accordance with which the seller assumes responsibility for delivering to the buyer goods conforming to the standard of the sample from which they were ordered. Where contracts of sale are governed by the latter rule, the buyer naturally hesitates to pay for goods ordered until he has had an opportunity to inspect them and ascertain whether he is entitled to any deductions on account of shortages or inferior quality of any of the merchandise received. Under such circumstances the seller cannot determine in advance the amount he can properly expect the buyer to pay for any particular shipment of goods. Hence the substitution of the doctrine of implied warranties for the older rule of *caveat emptor* made it impracticable for the seller to draw trade bills on the buyer.

The gradual displacement of trade acceptances and double-name promissory notes by single-name obligations, which has just been described, was the most important change with respect to classes of negotiable instruments handled by dealers in this period. Various other changes affecting such paper also took place during this period, such as those relating to practices in indorsing notes and to denominations, maturities, and rates. Though they were only of minor importance, these changes will now be indicated.

Practices in indorsing open-market paper from the beginning of this period until about 1900 varied considerably. In some cases dealers themselves indorsed the paper they sold.[106] In other cases borrowers whose credit standing was not of the highest secured

---

[106] A Philadelphia dealer stated in 1930 that an earlier dealer of the same city customarily indorsed the double-name "trade paper" which he began to sell after the Civil War.

Alonzo Follett, a New York note broker who failed a few years before 1884, is said to have guaranteed all the paper he sold (A. S. Bolles, *Practical Banking*, 1884 ed., p. 64).

According to a Pennsylvania banker, some dealers as late as 1897 were offering to indorse the paper they had for sale (W. H. Peck, *The Value of Commercial Paper as Quick Assets* — pamphlet containing reprint of an address before Group 3, Pennsylvania Bankers' Association, Wilkes-Barre, Penn., 1897 — p. 8).

accommodation indorsements for the notes they issued.[107] A third practice, which seems to have been rather common in Boston and New York as late as 1886, resulted from the fact that the charters of trust companies and savings banks in some states at that time required that all paper discounted by such institutions should bear at least three names. In order to comply with the provisions prescribed in these charters, dealers during the eighties often instructed minor employees — office boys, very "young men in counting-rooms, junior clerks and the men who 'take down the shutters' " —to indorse notes which were to be sold to trust companies or savings banks in such states.[108] Another practice, rather commonly followed for some thirty-five years or more after the Civil War, was that of indorsing notes receivable without recourse before selling them in the market.[109] Somewhat similar to this was the practice of indorsing notes receivable in the regular way but then securing a "release from indorsement" from the dealer who bought the paper or the customer to whom he sold it.[110] All these

---

[107] Years ago — presumably during the 1870's and 1880's — notes which were of little value of themselves but were indorsed "with gilt edge names," and thus made salable in the open market, were called "kangaroo notes." They were so called "because the strength of the notes was in the hind legs" (A. P. Brown, "Commercial Paper" — typewritten paper containing reprint of an address at the Harvard Graduate School of Business Administration, about 1922 — p. 26).

[108] C. B. Patten, *The Methods and Machinery of Practical Banking*, p. 142. See also "Practical Banking" (Part XVIII), *Rhodes' Jour. of Banking*, Jan. 1886, p. 14.

[109] Klein (*op. cit.*, pp. 46–47) states that this practice was common about as early as 1865, as well as in later years.

A Chicago dealer reports that when he began business in 1893 the local concerns whose "receivables" he bought sold such paper to him without recourse if they could (Becker, *op. cit.*, p. 5).

A Boston dealer stated in 1931 that a number of large concerns during the nineties sold their notes receivable, particularly "iron paper" and "railroad paper," to dealers without recourse.

[110] This practice is said to have been followed by coffee merchants — presumably in New York some time after the Civil War (Klein, *loc. cit.*).

According to a Boston dealer, concerns which followed this practice during the eighties and nineties sometimes secured releases from indorsement, ostensibly for "one dollar and other valuable considerations" but actually for no money payment at all, from banks which purchased their "receivables" in the market. On notes so purchased — provided indorsement by the seller would really have added value to the paper concerned — the buying bank obtained correspondingly higher rates. Bank directors, however, apparently disapproved of the practice of allowing such releases from indorsement.

various methods of indorsement were of course used in connection with double-name paper, and accordingly became less common as such paper declined in importance and single-name obligations became relatively more and more important. In connection with the latter class of paper the practice of indorsement in blank developed at an early date — some years before the Civil War, in fact.[111] Because it has the advantage of making readily negotiable a promissory note made to the order of the promisor and indorsed by him alone, this method of indorsement became more and more common during the years following the war, as the volume of single-name obligations increased and the "open account — cash discount — single-name paper" system became more and more widespread.[112] It is probably safe to say that by about 1900 most of the single-name obligations handled by dealers, and therefore a large proportion of the promissory notes sold in the open market, were being indorsed in blank.

The denominations in which commercial paper was issued during this period also underwent a change. For more than a generation after the close of the Civil War the promissory notes on which borrowing concerns raised short-term capital in the open market were issued in odd denominations, as well as for even hundreds or thousands of dollars. Both single-name and double-name notes, moreover, were issued in a great variety of different denominations, whether for odd amounts or for even hundreds of dollars, and generally the sums which borrowers agreed to repay were smaller than the amounts in which commercial paper is customarily issued at present.[113] The reason for this great variety of comparatively small denominations was that buyers often made their promissory notes out for the exact amounts of individual purchases of goods,

[111] See p. 30.

[112] According to Page, merchants began to make promissory notes payable to their own order and to indorse these notes in blank in the late seventies, as the time for resumption of specie payments drew near ("Commercial Paper as an Investment," *Bankers' Mag.*, Aug. 1911, pp. 163–169).

A few years later merchants are said to have been discounting such notes both directly at their own banks and in the market ("Credit Associations," *Rhodes' Jour. of Banking*, Jan. 1887, pp. 79–80).

[113] Some indication of the wide variety of denominations in which open-market paper was issued in the years from 1867 to 1893 is furnished by Exhibits 9–15.

and then either sold these notes to dealers or gave them to trade creditors who in turn offered them for sale in the market.[114] Banks buying commercial paper found it inconvenient, however, to record large numbers of such notes. At the same time, concerns requiring short-term advances from banks found that it was much more convenient to borrow less often but in larger round amounts. For these reasons, the practice of issuing notes for such round amounts became more and more common after about 1890, and some years before the close of this period $2,500, $5,000, and $10,000 — the amounts for which commercial paper has commonly been issued in more recent years — had probably become the most common denominations of notes offered for sale in the market.

With respect to the maturities borne by open-market paper, the changes which occurred during this period were less important. Borrowing concerns or individuals continued to issue notes with maturities ranging from about sixty days to six months or more. During the years from 1861 to 1865 and even later it was found advisable to shorten the periods for which promissory notes were issued and trade bills were drawn. Longer maturities, however, became common again some years after the Civil War. In some exceptional cases paper was made payable as late as a year from the date of issue, or even later. In other cases, also exceptional, notes were offered for sale with maturities of fewer than sixty days. The bulk of the paper handled by dealers during this period, however, undoubtedly was issued for periods falling between these two extremes.[115] Probably by about 1900, or shortly thereafter, most

[114] A former dealer of Chicago states that manufacturers and merchants who had formerly sold their notes receivable to him began some time later (after 1893) to issue their own single-name notes for sale in the market. To give them the appearance of discounted notes receivable, they issued these obligations for odd amounts. The makers of such notes "might sell me $50,000 at a time, but the denominations would be $158.60 and $485.39, and $962.73, and $1654.50 and so on." These odd denominations in some cases "had a real significance; they were the amounts of the accounts payable of my clients who would make separate notes for the precise amounts necessary to pay each individual account payable" (Becker, *op. cit.*, p. 6).

[115] A Philadelphia dealer reported in 1930 that indorsed notes receivable sold in that city some years after the Civil War sometimes ran for an entire year before maturity. Boston dealers gave the following as maturities for various classes of paper sold during the eighties and/or the nineties of the last century: Notes (pre-

paper sold in the market was being offered with maturities of from four to six months, those with which open-market notes have been most commonly issued in recent years.[116] On the whole, such maturities seem best adapted to the requirements both of borrowing concerns for short-term seasonal advances and of buying banks for a safe and liquid investment for surplus loanable funds.

The last of the minor changes mentioned above was that relating to the rates at which paper was offered for sale in the market. During the first half of this period, and particularly in years of financial strain, such rates were often much higher than any which have prevailed in recent years. An examination of Exhibits 9–15, which show note offerings listed for sale by dealers in various years from 1867 to 1893, reveals that none of these notes, with the exception of about two-thirds of those listed in Exhibit 14, were offered at less than 6 per cent, which at present would be considered a high rate. Some few even of the obligations listed in Exhibit 14 were offered at from 8 to 12 per cent, and, if an average were taken of all the rates specified in all these exhibits, it would undoubtedly be appreciably higher than the highest rate at which prime paper has sold for any length of time in any year since the close of the last century.[117] The comparatively high rates found in these exhibits resulted in part from the greater risk involved in buying

---

sumably notes receivable) of locomotive manufacturers, one year, two years, and three years; three-name notes issued by individuals for carrying securities and secured by acceptable stocks as collateral, one year; notes of cotton manufacturers and wool dealers and "shoe paper" (notes given by jobbers to shoe manufacturers and indorsed by the latter), six months; "Claflin paper" (notes receivable indorsed by the H. B. Claflin Company), two months to six months. The wide variety of shorter maturities borne by paper offered for sale in the market during the earlier years of this period is indicated by Exhibits 9–15.

[116] In 1908 a well-informed Chicago banker stated that the notes then being sold in the market were generally single-name unsecured obligations with maturities of from four to six months (Talbert, "Commercial Paper," *Proc. Minn. Bankers' Assoc.*, 1908, p. 44).

[117] In years of financial strain, open-market paper was not infrequently sold at rates which at present would be regarded as fantastically high. In November, 1873, for example, notes were offered for sale at rates as high as 18 and 24 per cent. (See Exhibit 12.) A month later dealers were buying "prime business paper" at discount rates of 10 to 15 per cent, and paper of a lower grade was being sold to yield 36 per cent (*Bankers' Mag.*, Dec. 1873, p. 500). In November of the following year notes were offered for sale at rates as high as 18, 24, and 36 per cent, though

open-market paper in the earlier years of this period. After about 1896, when not only the uncertainty caused by a depreciated paper currency but also that arising from the free-silver agitation had been brought to an end, and when both banks and dealers, with the help of more efficient credit departments, began to select commercial paper more carefully, the risks assumed by the purchaser of such paper decreased considerably. For this and various other reasons, the demand for open-market notes began to increase and the rates at which dealers were able to sell their offerings declined. During the last seventeen years of this period the monthly average of the weekly high and low rates on prime commercial paper in New York generally fluctuated around a level no higher than about 4½ per cent, which even as late as 1930 would not have been considered a high rate.[118]

7. INCREASE IN THE VARIETY OF CONCERNS USING THE OPEN MARKET

In the preceding chapter it was pointed out that merchants in the larger cities, dry-goods jobbers, wholesale dealers in hardware, wholesale grocers, and New England manufacturers were probably among the largest borrowers in the open market in the years before the Civil War. During the period from 1861 to 1914, as the practice of borrowing through dealers in negotiable paper became more common and more widespread, both the number and the variety of concerns raising short-term capital in the open market increased considerably. Merchants of the classes just mentioned

---

the obligations concerned were not prime paper. (See Exhibit 13.) In 1893 a dealer in Minneapolis bought paper at a discount rate of 17 per cent, and high-grade open-market obligations, according to a Boston dealer, were sold to yield rates even as high as 18 per cent. The latter dealer stated also that in August 1897 most paper could not be sold at any price. Even as late as 1907, according to a New York dealer, open-market paper was sold to yield 12 per cent.

[118] Yearly average rates on "prime two-name 60 to 90-day commercial paper," 1831–1920, are shown on Chart I. Monthly averages of the weekly high and low rates on prime commercial paper in New York, 1866–1935, are given in Table 1 and plotted on Chart II. Both charts indicate that rates on open-market paper after 1896 fluctuated around lower levels than those prevailing during the earlier years of the period considered in this chapter. It should be noted, however, that in the case of neither chart are the rates plotted for the earlier years strictly comparable with those plotted for later years.

apparently remained among the most important of these borrowers in the decade of the sixties. They continued, moreover, to raise relatively large amounts of short-term funds in the market throughout the remaining years of this period.[119] Other classes of bor-

CHART I *

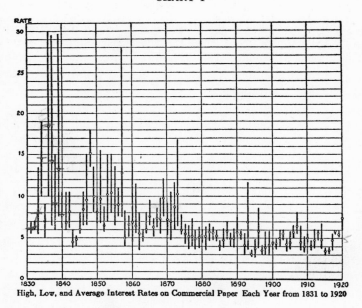

High, Low, and Average Interest Rates on Commercial Paper Each Year from 1831 to 1920

* Reproduced, with permission, from the *Monthly Review* of the Federal Reserve Bank of New York, Mar. 1, 1921, p. 3. The rates shown on the chart are "rates on prime two-name 60 to 90-day commercial paper." The vertical line plotted for each year "indicates the range between the rates prevalent in the highest month of the year and those prevalent in the lowest month." Annual average rates are indicated by the circles.

---

[119] Perhaps the best-known open-market "name" during this period was that of H. B. Claflin and Company (later called the H. B. Claflin Company), a large wholesale dry-goods house of New York. This concern sold merchandise to retail stores all over the country, accepted their promissory notes in payment, and then indorsed these notes and sold them in the market. The paper of this company, until a few days before its unexpected failure in 1914, was generally considered to be of as high a grade as any obligations offered for sale in the market. According to a Boston dealer, the rate on "Claflin paper" at one time "pretty nearly 'made' the rate on prime paper in Eastern territory." Paper indorsed by Claflin and Company is listed in Exhibits 9 and 10.

The importance of "dry-goods paper" during this period is indicated by the fact

TABLE 1

Rates on Prime Commercial Paper in New York, 1866–1935 *

(Per Cent)

Year	Jan.	Feb.	Mar.	Apr.	May	June	July	Aug.	Sept.	Oct.	Nov.	Dec.	Avg.
1866	7.95	7.75	7.70	7.40	6.55	6.20	6.40	6.10	5.45	5.70	6.85	7.00	6.75
1867	7.50	7.40	7.50	7.75	7.00	8.30	7.50	7.30	8.15	10.00	10.10	10.00	8.21
1868	7.20	7.00	7.90	8.10	7.20	6.40	7.90	6.70	6.95	7.80	10.15	9.00	7.69
1869	8.35	7.80	9.50	10.05	7.60	9.60	10.00	9.65	10.50	10.35	11.70	10.10	9.60
1870	8.95	7.50	7.50	7.15	6.05	5.10	6.25	6.95	7.00	7.05	7.15	7.35	7.00
1871	8.00	6.45	6.20	6.70	5.40	4.85	4.70	5.20	6.35	9.40	9.00	9.80	6.84
1872	9.30	8.20	8.65	8.50	7.25	6.00	6.40	7.55	10.00	11.10	12.35	10.90	8.85
1873	9.40	9.15	10.10	10.75	8.20	6.80	6.50	7.20	12.50	17.00	13.85	10.15	10.13
1874	7.40	6.00	6.15	6.30	5.60	5.65	5.90	5.45	6.25	5.80	5.60	6.00	6.01
1875	5.75	5.20	5.90	5.45	4.55	4.55	4.30	5.00	5.95	6.35	6.45	6.65	5.51
1876	6.45	5.85	5.40	5.50	5.10	4.75	3.80	3.60	4.75	5.65	5.50	5.85	5.10
1877	5.55	4.50	4.45	4.45	4.00	4.05	4.25	5.70	6.40	7.25	6.30	5.60	5.21
1878	5.85	5.35	5.15	5.35	4.45	3.80	3.60	3.80	4.60	5.45	5.15	5.05	4.80
1879	4.30	3.80	5.05	5.45	4.45	4.25	3.90	5.55	5.80	5.90	6.25	5.95	5.05
1880	5.40	5.25	5.50	5.50	5.20	4.55	4.45	5.05	5.25	5.10	5.50	6.00	5.23
1881	5.25	5.38	5.55	5.19	4.00	3.50	4.00	4.95	5.69	6.25	6.25	6.25	5.19
1882	5.60	5.62	5.62	5.06	4.85	5.19	4.62	5.65	6.75	6.65	6.50	5.88	5.67
1883	5.50	5.38	6.38	5.81	5.35	4.75	4.80	5.69	6.00	6.00	5.69	5.50	5.57
1884	4.95	4.75	4.62	4.72	5.06	5.75	5.95	5.50	5.50	5.50	5.19	5.00	5.21
1885	4.69	4.50	4.45	3.94	3.69	3.55	3.50	3.69	3.75	4.00	4.44	4.50	4.06
1886	4.31	3.91	3.88	4.25	4.06	3.85	3.94	5.25	5.81	6.06	5.90	6.00	4.77
1887	5.50	4.81	5.35	5.38	5.20	5.12	6.19	6.35	6.94	6.38	5.80	6.00	5.75
1888	5.55	4.81	5.22	5.41	4.82	4.25	4.10	4.38	5.28	5.08	4.75	4.97	4.88
1889	4.65	4.25	4.50	4.25	3.84	3.88	4.40	5.16	5.28	6.00	6.00	6.09	4.86
1890	5.39	5.04	5.50	5.14	5.06	5.00	5.08	5.61	5.71	5.89	8.20	7.38	5.75

TABLE I (*Continued*)

Year	Jan.	Feb.	Mar.	Apr.	May	June	July	Aug.	Sept.	Oct.	Nov.	Dec.	Avg.
1891	5.83	5.00	5.25	5.09	5.33	5.50	5.63	5.75	5.79	5.60	5.10	4.85	5.39
1892	4.17	3.69	3.96	3.45	3.18	2.94	3.43	4.00	4.75	5.11	5.11	5.50	4.11
1893	5.18	4.85	6.80	5.75	6.65	8.75	9.75	9.70	8.32	5.96	4.47	3.67	6.66
1894	3.50	3.25	3.00	3.15	2.91	2.89	3.00	3.09	3.28	2.72	2.81	2.88	3.04
1895	3.00	3.65	3.90	3.96	2.75	2.63	2.95	3.53	4.04	4.81	4.07	4.58	3.66
1896	6.00	5.70	5.18	5.31	4.53	4.25	5.13	7.75	8.44	8.56	5.25	3.75	5.82
1897	3.36	3.00	3.33	3.55	3.54	3.16	3.43	3.75	4.11	4.19	3.45	3.47	3.53
1898	3.35	3.13	4.69	5.75	4.63	3.22	3.63	3.64	4.14	3.39	3.31	3.05	3.83
1899	2.88	2.95	3.79	3.71	3.59	3.31	3.66	4.35	4.83	5.10	5.36	5.88	4.12
1900	4.81	4.43	4.86	4.30	3.69	3.69	4.00	4.22	4.45	5.06	4.39	4.75	4.39
1901	4.08	3.70	3.75	3.97	3.95	3.94	4.25	4.50	4.94	4.64	4.72	4.90	4.28
1902	4.56	4.00	4.37	4.53	4.54	4.42	4.64	4.82	5.58	5.90	5.71	6.00	4.92
1903	5.22	4.90	5.54	5.19	4.75	5.16	5.43	5.94	6.00	5.79	5.95	5.79	5.47
1904	4.89	4.79	4.68	4.13	3.93	3.60	3.55	3.84	4.29	4.41	4.14	4.28	4.21
1905	4.00	3.81	3.93	4.00	3.98	3.75	4.13	4.19	4.72	4.92	5.53	5.79	4.40
1906	5.06	5.04	5.28	5.44	5.33	5.25	5.48	6.00	6.56	6.30	6.25	6.25	5.68
1907	6.15	5.94	6.19	5.92	5.40	5.50	5.75	6.25	6.79	7.10	7.40	8.00	6.36
1908	6.59	5.06	5.63	4.38	3.94	3.69	3.75	3.61	3.89	4.10	4.04	3.85	4.38
1909	3.68	3.54	3.50	3.50	3.44	3.25	3.38	4.04	4.25	5.03	5.09	5.09	3.98
1910	4.75	4.44	4.50	4.75	4.75	4.81	5.38	5.43	5.53	5.56	5.50	4.66	5.00
1911	3.98	4.09	3.88	3.66	3.63	3.69	3.78	4.19	4.54	4.35	3.91	4.63	4.03
1912	3.90	3.75	4.19	4.15	4.19	4.00	4.53	5.00	5.56	5.93	5.72	6.00	4.74
1913	4.93	4.91	5.75	5.53	5.36	5.88	6.06	6.00	5.78	5.69	5.56	5.68	5.60
1914	4.53	3.84	3.88	3.73	3.88	3.84	4.40	6.34	6.70	6.44	5.50	4.35	4.78
1915	3.84	3.75	3.38	3.66	3.72	3.65	3.25	3.53	3.25	3.22	2.98	3.13	3.45

TABLE I (Continued)

Year	Jan.	Feb.	Mar.	Apr.	May	June	July	Aug.	Sept.	Oct.	Nov.	Dec.	Avg.
1916	3.13	3.13	3.13	3.13	3.13	3.63	3.97	3.73	3.38	3.38	3.50	3.91	3.43
1917	3.55	4.09	4.13	4.28	4.83	5.00	4.68	4.81	5.19	5.38	5.47	5.50	4.74
1918	5.58	5.69	5.88	5.90	5.88	5.88	5.88	5.94	6.00	6.00	5.97	5.86	5.87
1919	5.19	5.19	5.38	5.38	5.38	5.53	5.42	5.38	5.38	5.38	5.50	5.88	5.42
1920	6.00	6.41	6.68	6.81	7.16	7.72	7.84	8.00	8.00	8.00	7.94	7.88	7.37
1921	7.83	7.75	7.63	7.55	6.88	6.63	6.28	6.00	5.90	5.65	5.13	5.13	6.53
1922	4.88	4.88	4.78	4.60	4.25	4.05	3.94	3.91	4.25	4.38	4.63	4.63	4.43
1923	4.63	4.69	5.00	5.13	5.13	4.88	4.94	5.03	5.16	5.13	5.09	4.98	4.98
1924	4.88	4.78	4.59	4.63	4.23	3.91	3.53	3.23	3.13	3.13	3.28	3.56	3.91
1925	3.63	3.65	3.94	3.95	3.88	3.88	3.93	4.00	4.25	4.44	4.38	4.38	4.03
1926	4.31	4.19	4.28	4.19	4.00	3.88	3.97	4.25	4.43	4.50	4.44	4.38	4.24
1927	4.13	3.88	4.00	4.09	4.13	4.13	4.06	3.90	3.91	4.00	3.94	3.95	4.01
1928	3.88	4.00	4.15	4.40	4.55	4.70	5.13	5.39	5.59	5.50	5.38	5.43	4.84
1929	5.50	5.56	5.69	5.90	6.00	6.00	6.00	6.09	6.13	6.13	5.41	5.00	5.78
1930	4.85	4.63	4.19	3.88	3.72	3.50	3.13	3.00	3.00	3.00	2.97	2.88	3.56
1931	2.81	2.50	2.53	2.40	2.16	2.13	1.95	1.88	1.88	3.38	4.00	4.00	2.64
1932	4.00	3.83	3.53	3.38	3.00	2.78	2.56	2.38	2.13	1.98	1.63	1.63	2.74
1933	1.38	1.38	3.03	2.66	2.10	1.94	1.75	1.75	1.53	1.50	1.50	1.50	1.84
1934	1.50	1.50	1.26	1.25	1.19	1.00	1.00	1.00	1.00	1.00	1.00	1.00	1.14
1935	1.00	1.00	1.00	1.00	1.00	1.00	1.00	0.86	0.75	0.75	0.75	0.75	0.91

* Figures included in this table are averages of the weekly high and low rates in each month. For the period 1866–1889 the rates quoted are those on "prime paper," "which classification appears to include all prime short-term notes, regardless of specific maturity and number of names." For the period 1890 to March 1924 quotations are for choice double-name 60- to 90-day commercial paper. Later quotations are for 4- to 6-months' paper — presumably choice double-name until July 1930 and choice single-name thereafter. Data for the years 1866–1889 were taken from *Rev. Ec. Stat.*, Jan. 1923, p. 28; for the years 1890–1935, from Standard Statistics Company, *Base Book*, *Stand. Stat. Bull.*, Jan. 1932, p. 43, *Stat. Bull.*, April 1934, p. 6, and *Statistics*, Jan. 1936, p. 8.

rowers during the sixties included tea dealers,[120] New York coffee jobbers,[121] lumber concerns,[122] and railroads.[123] Among the more important borrowers during the next twenty years or so were "banking houses";[124] brewers;[125] dealers in leather, tobacco, silks, and diamonds;[126] railroads and concerns producing or dealing in paper, lumber, coal, iron, other metals, and rubber, or their products;[127] and, particularly in New England, boot and shoe jobbers and manufacturers,[128] cotton textile mills whose notes were commonly indorsed by the commission houses which acted as their selling agents,[129] wool dealers, manufacturers of woolen textiles, and individuals who borrowed in the market funds which they used for carrying securities.[130] During the 1890's most of these classes of

---

that a New York dealer at least as late as 1888 was advertising such paper as "a specialty" (*Banker's Almanac and Register*, 1888, p. 13 of advertisements).

[120] *Bankers' Mag.*, July 1867, p. 79.

[121] These jobbers were referred to as "Front Street names" (J. J. Klein, "The Development of Mercantile Instruments of Credit in the United States," *Jour. of Accountancy*, Jan. 1912, p. 47).

[122] A Philadelphia dealer stated in 1930 that a predecessor firm established in 1866 used to handle the double-name paper of lumber concerns.

[123] Paper of the Chicago and Great Eastern Railroad is listed in Exhibit 9.

[124] According to a former dealer of New York, Matthew Morgan's Sons and Morton Bliss and Company — the first two "names" listed in Exhibit 11 — were "banking houses" which made advances on cotton, sugar, and the like.

[125] Another New York dealer stated that "brewery paper" years ago was regarded as prime paper, and sold readily among banks — "with no financial statements and with few questions asked."

[126] C. V. Childs, *Commercial Paper and the Broker's Function* (pamphlet containing reprint of an address before the Reserve City Bankers' Association, Atlanta, 1926), p. 2.

[127] A New York "banker and note broker" was advertising in 1873 as follows: "Hardware, Metal, Iron, Rubber, Shoe, Paper and Paper-Hangings, Lumber, Coal, and Railroad Paper wanted" (*The Banker's Almanac for 1873*, p. vii of advertisements).

[128] In this earlier period Boston was one of the principal markets for "shoe paper," the greater part of which, according to dealers of that city, consisted of notes given by jobbers in various parts of the country to New England shoe manufacturers and indorsed by the latter. These obligations were regarded as prime paper. Their importance is indicated by the fact that a few dealers are said to have handled "shoe paper" only.

[129] Like "shoe paper," "mill paper" indorsed by a strong commission house was for years regarded as one of the highest grades of paper handled by dealers, and found a ready market among New England banks. Because of its prime character, it is said at one time to have been quoted separately.

[130] A Boston dealer introduced the three-name notes of such individuals, with

borrowers continued to raise short-term capital [131] through dealers, and various other classes of concerns also found it advantageous to offer their paper in the market. To mention only a few of the latter, a ferry company, a building and improvement company, a packing company, a cordage company, a type founders' company, a tanning company, a milling company, two grain elevator companies,[132] a brewing company, a girder rail company, and a fertilizer company were offering their notes for sale through New York dealers in 1893.[133] During the remaining years of the period considered in this chapter numerous other concerns, representing many different lines of trading and manufacturing enterprise,[134]

---

acceptable securities as collateral, into the open market early in the 1880's. Massachusetts savings banks, to which they offered the advantages of being a legal investment and having an entire year to run to maturity, bought large amounts of these notes. Like the collateral loan paper handled by a number of dealers at present, such obligations, strictly speaking, should not be classed as "commercial" paper.

[131] Funds raised in the open market were not always used for working capital purposes and were not always borrowed for short periods. According to a Boston dealer, "iron paper" and "railroad paper" were used during the nineties to finance the purchase and sale of cars, rails, supplies, and the like, and locomotive manufacturers sold notes with maturities ranging from one year to three years.

[132] "Grain paper" from the Northwest, according to a New York dealer, was introduced into that city early in the nineties. It is said that the dealer who introduced it "shocked the honorable banking brethren of New York City when he first went up into the great Northwest and brought back grain and flour paper to offer them" (Childs, *op. cit.*, p. 2).

By 1907 or earlier a special class of "grain paper," known as "terminal notes," was being sold in the Minneapolis district. These notes were issued presumably by grain-milling concerns or grain elevators and were secured by terminal warehouse receipts for grain. Because of their strong security, they generally sold for rates appreciably lower than those on unsecured prime paper of other classes (Northwestern National Bank of Minneapolis, *Northwestern National Bank Review*, Mar. 1917, pp. 3-4).

A New York dealer who began business in Boston in 1897 at first dealt in another class of "commodity paper," known as "cattle paper." Presumably this was issued by stock growers of the Middle West and secured by chattel mortgages on "feeder" cattle.

[133] See Exhibit 15. Shortly after 1893 a Chicago dealer was handling a comparatively large volume of single-name paper issued by concerns dealing in such staple commodities as hides, sugar, whisky, tobacco, and the like (A. G. Becker, *Commercial Paper* — pamphlet — p. 7).

[134] That trading and manufacturing concerns were two of the main classes of borrowers in the open market about 1905 is indicated by the following percentage distribution of 186 different direct bank loans "aggregating upwards of" $13,000,000,

also took advantage of the opportunity of selling their paper in the market. In 1913 it was estimated that as many as 2,500 to 3,000 concerns offered their short-term obligations for sale through "reputable brokers" in the preceding year;[135] and by the close of this period both the number and the variety of concerns borrowing in the open market had doubtless become about as large as they have been in any subsequent year.

The increase which has just been noted in the number and variety of such concerns may be regarded as one more measure of the growth of the commercial paper business discussed earlier in the present chapter. Closely connected with this growth, and with the change in the dealer's organization which was also indicated above, were certain developments relating to the actual buying and selling of commercial paper and to other operations of the dealer. An account of these developments will now be given.

8. Changes in Dealers' Methods of Buying and Credit Investigation

For a number of years after the Civil War the methods used by dealers in buying and selling open-market paper remained essentially the same as they had been in the decade preceding 1861. As compared with those employed by modern commercial paper houses, these earlier methods seem simple indeed. Before the close

---

and of some $60,000,000 of "loans placed through brokers in New York":

Class of Loan	Direct Bank Loans	Loans through Dealers
Commercial loans to manufacturers	50%	45%
" " " commission men	15	15
" " " jobbers	30	30
" " " retailers	5	10
	100%	100%

(J. G. Cannon, *Bank Credits. No. 2*, pamphlet, p. 14.)

The percentage figures given above were for 1905 or earlier. The close similarity between the two distributions will be noted: in each case about half the total funds lent were advanced to manufacturers and the other half to trading concerns. The number of loans included in the total figures, however, may not have been sufficient in either case to constitute a representative sample.

[135] "For Check on Notes," *N. Y. Times*, Sept. 21, 1913, Part 7, p. 15.

of this period, however, in order to handle more efficiently an increasing volume of business, dealers found it necessary not only to develop more elaborate organizations but also to adopt new and improved methods of carrying on their main operations.

Of the changes in their operating methods which dealers found advisable some years after the close of the Civil War, the most important were those relating to buying and credit investigation. It will be recalled that during the period before 1861 the typical dealer, instead of buying bills or notes outright, acted as a broker only; and that he was compelled to base his judgment of the quality of the paper he handled largely on his personal knowledge of the character and ability of his borrowing customers, without the aid of any such modern devices as financial and operating statements. According to traditions which have been preserved among some of the older dealers in Boston, New York, and other cities, the comparatively simple methods of operation used by brokers in this earlier period remained practically unchanged for a decade or so after the close of the war between the states. Until about 1875 dealers in New York continued to secure their stock in trade largely from local merchants with whom they were acquainted more or less closely. The "receivables" or other paper they obtained on consignment from these merchants they sold mainly to local bankers with whom they were also personally acquainted. They generally collected payment from their buying customers on delivery of the bills or notes sold. Not until they had received payment did they turn over to their borrowing customers the net proceeds realized from the sale of these obligations. Neither in buying nor in selling paper did they make use of financial statements, and such credit investigations as they made were comparatively simple.[136] Even some twenty years later a Chicago dealer who began business in 1893 was following methods of operation

---

[136] A New York dealer has given the following description of a typical small broker of New York and his operations in the early seventies:

"Dressed in the very tall silk hat and frock coat of the period, he would each business morning stop in to see some merchant friend. The call usually ended in the consignment for sale of a small batch of bills receivable. The broker put the

closely similar, except in one important respect, to those just described.[137] Not long after the resumption of specie payments in 1879, however, dealers began to adopt new methods of performing two of their main functions, buying paper and investigating the

original paper inside the hat band of his 'topper.' Then he proceeded to the Chemical, the Importers, or one of the other few big New York banks, doffed his hat with great ceremony, took out of that inner hat band the paper, and bargained at some length with the venerable banker (for bankers were all venerable in those days) as to whether the rate should be 10 or 12 per cent. No balance sheets, no credit department — merchants' paper was judged according to the maker's character and standing in the business community" (W. E. Sachs, *Commercial Paper and Its Place in Our Banking System* — pamphlet containing reprint of an address before the Kentucky Bankers' Association, Louisville, 1921 — pp. 1–2). See also Childs, *op. cit.*, p. 1; and "Commercial Paper," *A. B. A. Jour.*, Feb. 1927, p. 558.

Because they often carried around with them, in the inner bands of their tall silk hats, the bills and notes they had for sale, dealers of this earlier period have sometimes been called "hat-band brokers." A picture of one of these brokers may be found on the cover of the issue of the *American Bankers' Association Journal* referred to just above.

[137] This dealer has given an interesting account of the methods he used in dealing in commercial paper in the early nineties. Some excerpts from this account follow:

". . . the paper that I bought then — and sold without salesmen — was largely bills receivable, the notes our merchants and manufacturers took from their customers and which they sold to me without recourse, if they could, endorsed if they couldn't. I used to walk up and down Lake street [*sic*], then one of the principal business streets, and purchase the receivables of the lumber companies who had their offices there; then with these notes and others in my pocketbook, I went around selling them from bank to bank.

"Generally the entire stock of paper was in my pocketbook and if the office sold a note, a boy had to run out and find me so that the note would not be sold over again. We prided ourselves on the fact that if we took an order, delivery would be certain and prompt. . . . I will illustrate . . .: I walked in one day on Mr. D. R. Forgan — after a critical examination and discussion of the stock in trade in my portfolio he selected several notes and then asked me when he might expect delivery. I picked up a scrap of paper lying on his desk, figured the discount and said: 'Give me your check — the delivery is made.' . . .

"Some thirty years ago [about 1893], Mr. John [James?] G. Cannon of the Fourth National Bank of New York, inaugurated the practice of requiring statements from borrowers and making credit investigations. At that time and for some time after that, we bought our paper, and sold it too, on a basis of the general reputation of the borrower and our personal acquaintance with and confidence in him, or in other words, we did our business on the basis of judgment of character. On the whole, we did very well. The losses on commercial paper were really negligible and in fact it was for a time, a matter of jest among bankers that Mr. Cannon's statistical inquiries led him for a while into larger losses than any incurred by his less progressive associates.

"Many of the early statements would strike you as exceedingly funny. They were often very brief and simple. I can recall statements written in pen and ink on a

credit standing of concerns whose obligations they handled. The changes which they then began to adopt in their methods of fulfilling these two functions were two of the most important developments in the commercial paper business since the Civil War.

The first of these developments was the substitution of outright purchase for the earlier practice of buying bills and notes on a consignment or brokerage basis. This seems to have been a gradual process. As was shown in the preceding chapter, Henry Clews and a few other dealers had begun to buy paper outright even before 1860. No large proportion of the total volume of open-market obligations issued each year, however, seems to have been bought in this manner until about 1890. Even during the closing years of this period some few smaller dealers continued to act as brokers only; and indeed the practice of buying commercial paper on a brokerage basis has not yet been discontinued entirely.[138] It is probable that some dealers, before they began to buy their stock in trade in the "out and out" manner used by Henry Clews, adopted the intermediate policy of making advances on bills or notes taken on consignment, selling these obligations, and then turning over to their borrowing customers the net amounts still due them. At any rate, a number of dealers were making such

---

half sheet of note paper, reading something like this: 'I certify that my net worth is $20,000 — Signed.' Nevertheless, when we finally began to get statements, there were not lacking cases in which the first statement that came to our hands for some name that supposedly had been gilt-edged and eagerly bought for years, surprised us to the point of tears. Some very fat reputations exhibited some very sorry skeletons in those first statements. Some of them concealed skeletons" (Becker, *op. cit.*, pp. 5–6, 8–9).

This Chicago dealer began to buy paper outright from the start (*ibid.*, pp. 3–4). This was the important respect, mentioned in the text above, in which his methods of operation differed from those of the typical small broker of New York referred to in the preceding footnote.

[138] A New York dealer reported that brokerage operations in open-market paper were common in that city as late as 1890. A Chicago dealer stated in 1923 that such paper was generally handled on a brokerage basis for many years after 1893 (Becker, *op. cit.*, p. 4). The members of a Boston firm which began business about 1885 and continued operations in commercial paper until 1928 acted as brokers exclusively during this entire period of nearly forty-five years. A New York firm organized in 1885 handled open-market notes on a brokerage basis exclusively until 1931, when it retired from business.

See also pp. 283, 288–290.

advances during the 1870's and 1880's.[139] From the borrower's point of view, this method of buying paper was in some respects clearly more satisfactory than the older practice of taking his obligations for sale purely on a brokerage basis. At the same time, it was less advantageous than the practice of buying his bills or notes outright. Moreover, the business of dealing in commercial paper gradually became more competitive during the decades following the close of the Civil War. Probably for these two reasons in the main, a number of dealers began to buy paper outright not long after the resumption of specie payments in 1879. The practice seems to have become fairly common during the eighties, and was adopted by more and more dealers in the decade following. By about 1900, or shortly thereafter, it is probable that all the larger dealers were buying "out and out" a substantial proportion of their stock in trade, though many of them continued also under certain conditions to make advances against obligations taken on consignment.[140] Thus the transition from the small note broker,

[139] Advertisements of dealers who made such advances may be found in *The Merchants' and Bankers' Almanac* for 1870, p. xx of advertisements, and *The Banker's Almanac for 1873*, p. vii of advertisements.

It is said that the borrowing customers of Alonzo Follett, a New York dealer who failed in 1882, before his failure "had been in the habit of leaving their paper with him to sell, and drawing against it at convenience" ("Heavy Failure of a Note Broker," *Rhodes' Jour. of Banking*, Oct. 1882, p. 741). It is possible that some of these concerns drew against such paper in advance of its sale.

In 1884, and again in 1887, dealers are said to have been making advances on paper and also buying it outright. (A. S. Bolles, *Practical Banking*, 1884 ed., p. 64, and W. H. Baker, "Commercial Paper," *Proc. Amer. Bankers' Assoc.*, 1887, p. 46.)

As is pointed out in Chap. VII, a number of commercial paper houses of the present under certain conditions still make advances against their customers' obligations.

[140] Bolles states that "note brokers" were buying paper outright at a flat rate by 1884 (*loc. cit.*). By 1886, according to a Boston banker, the larger dealers in the larger cities were buying outright "a large proportion" of the open-market obligations they handled (C. B. Patten, *The Methods and Machinery of Practical Banking*, p. 136). In 1887 it was stated that "a responsible dealer or 'banker' (i.e., 'one who discounts notes') buys his customers' paper, and thereby becomes the owner" (Baker, *loc. cit.*). As was stated above, a Chicago dealer who entered the commercial paper business in 1893 began to buy paper outright from the start.

Of twenty-three houses which were among the largest dealers in commercial paper in 1931, fourteen were established before 1913, the close of the period considered in this chapter. Of these fourteen houses, about four began to buy paper outright during the 1880's, about seven during the 1890's, one in 1907, and one about 1910. The remaining firm in this group, from its organization in 1885 until it retired from

who acted merely as an agent, to the modern commercial paper house, which assumes the responsibility of investing its own funds in the negotiable instruments it offers for sale, and thereby performs what may truly be called a banking function, was completed some years before the close of the period considered in this chapter.

The second of the two important developments mentioned above was the adoption by dealers of improved methods of credit investigation. This development seems to have been more or less closely connected with the growth of the practice of outright buying. While it is clearly to the advantage of a dealer who expects to remain in business for any length of time, even though he act exclusively as a broker, to select most carefully the paper he offers for sale in the market, it is nevertheless reasonable to suppose that he will exercise greater care in selecting an inventory in which he invests his own funds than in assuming the lesser responsibilities involved in handling paper as a broker only.[141] At any rate, if he buys outright he will have additional incentives to investigate as carefully as possible the credit standing of all concerns whose obligations he handles.[142] Hence it seems reasonable to believe that, when they began to buy paper outright, dealers also began to

---

business in 1931, acted as a broker only. Of the nine houses which were organized after 1913, one began to buy outright about 1916 and the remaining eight during the decade ending with 1930. Four of these nine houses were successors to earlier firms, all of which had begun to buy outright by about 1900, or shortly thereafter. It is significant that twenty-two of the twenty-three houses were buying outright in 1931; and that, of these twenty-two dealers, sixteen began to buy outright from the start, five others probably did likewise, and the remaining firm within about a year after its establishment in 1879.

[141] The writer was informed in 1930, however, that a New York house which acted as a broker only would buy back from the holders any of its borrowing customers' notes not paid by the makers thereof, and that during the forty-five years it had been in business up to that time it had actually bought back about $25,000 of such paper. Of this repurchased paper, about $15,000 was eventually paid by the issuers.

[142] Unless he selects his stock in trade very carefully, the dealer who buys "out and out" may find it necessary to carry paper of a lower grade to maturity, which is not profitable, or to sell it at a loss. If such paper should not be paid at maturity, he would of course have to stand the loss on any unpaid notes in his possession at the time. Moreover, if he uses as a selling argument the fact that he considers the notes he offers for sale of such high grade that he is willing to invest his own funds in them, he would seem to have a greater moral responsibility to his buying customers in case any such paper should go to default.

pay greater attention to their methods of selecting their stock in trade. Evidence in support of this view is furnished by the fact that significant improvements relating to such methods began to be adopted during the decade of the nineties,[143] at a time when the practice of buying outright was becoming more and more common. These improvements, in turn, no doubt encouraged and stimulated a more general adoption of the latter practice.

Probably the most important development relating to credit investigation was the organization of credit departments. These were the outgrowth of credit files which at least a few dealers began to build up during the 1890's. However inadequate such files might seem today as a basis for judging the credit standing of a concern applying for short-term funds in the open market, they represented a substantial improvement over the dealer's earlier practice of carrying all his credit information in his head.[144] As the number of "names" handled by dealers grew larger, and information relating to each "name" began to accumulate in their credit files, the work of credit investigation in time became suf-

[143] "During the period of low interest rates of '94, '95, and '96, credit methods developed rapidly. At first statements came into vogue, and later, earning figures" (H. C. Smith, *Development of the Commercial Paper Broker and His Place in Banking* — pamphlet containing reprint of an address before the American Institute of Banking Credits Conference, Baltimore, 1924 — p. 4).

[144] A New York dealer gives the following account of the beginning of "a small credit information bureau" which later developed into the credit department of his firm:

"I began my business career January 1, 1894 . . . at that time the whole credit file of the firm was contained in a few manila envelopes that would not half fill a small-sized desk drawer, and which contained principally a few Agency reports. The most of the credit information then available was carried in the heads of the firm. . . .

"Absolute necessity to secure some facts and get them written down, drove me to beg the firm to allow me to start a small credit information bureau, and, under the advice of Mr. James G. Cannon, then Vice-President of the Fourth National Bank of New York, and at that time considered the leader in the development of Commercial Credits, I believe I started the first credit file in any broker's office" (*ibid.*, pp. 3–4).

Some twenty years earlier a leading firm of Boston dealers customarily recorded credit information relating to its borrowing customers in small bound books equipped with clasps and locks. When not being used, these books were kept locked. This practice reminds one of a rule of the Hartford Bank, founded at a time (1792) when every bank, as Sumner says, "was a secret society": " 'What passes in the bank not to be spoke on at any other place' " (W. G. Sumner, *A History of Banking in the United States*, p. 20).

ficiently important to justify the organization of special credit departments. Just when the first of these departments was organized is not certain, but it was probably some time before 1900; for in 1908 a well-informed New York banker stated that every "good broker" then had "a modern, up-to-date credit department," which was following methods of investigation similar to those used by commercial banks.[145] By the close of this period it is probable not only that all the larger dealers had established such departments but also that they were performing the important function of credit investigation fully as efficiently as the leading banks themselves.[146]

The organization of credit departments greatly facilitated the adoption of improved methods of credit investigation which may be traced back to the time when dealers began to buy their stock in trade outright. Even before the establishment of such departments an important beginning in the work of collecting, recording, classifying, and filing information relating to their borrowing customers had been made by those dealers who began to build up credit files during the 1890's. This work could of course be carried further by specialized departments organized expressly for the purpose. Such departments were in a position to make effective use

---

[145] Cannon, *Buying Commercial Paper* (pamphlet), p. 10.

Nine years earlier, in 1899, it was stated that even the largest commercial paper houses did not "think it important to keep well informed" with regard to the condition of concerns whose obligations they sold, and did not keep complete and up-to-date credit files. The first part of this statement appears to be mistaken; and, if dealers at that time did not maintain complete and up-to-date credit files, the carelessness of buying banks was largely responsible for this situation. The author of the statement admits this: ". . . the public [i.e., banks buying open-market paper] has not insisted on accurate information, and hence they ["note brokers"] have not taken the pains to obtain it" (Robert McCurdy, "Committee on Credits," *Proc. Amer. Bankers' Assoc.*, 1899, pp. 96–97).

The view expressed above, that the first part of McCurdy's statement appears to be mistaken, is supported by the statements of another banker some two years later: ". . . we can always find in his [the dealer's] files expert examinations of the institutions or the company whose paper he is offering, which are made at least once a year" (S. R. Flynn, "A Twentieth Century Credit System," *Proc. Mich. Bankers' Assoc.*, 1901, p. 42. The quotation is from the discussion following Flynn's address).

[146] It was stated in 1911 that the most efficient credit departments in the country were those maintained by dealers in commercial paper (E. D. Howard and J. F. Johnson, *Money and Banking*, pp. 344–345).

of the most approved methods of investigation employed by banks, including the study of reports prepared by credit agencies and information secured from trade creditors and from banks located in the borrower's community. More important than the use of such data in many cases were their own independent investigations, as a result of which they often secured closer and more detailed information concerning borrowing customers than the latter were willing to furnish their own depositary banks.[147]

In connection with such investigations they could make effective use also of another method employed by banks — securing and subjecting to detailed and careful analysis financial statements issued by their customers. Dealers in commercial paper, in fact, seem to have adopted more rapidly than most banks the practice of requiring such statements from their customers. This practice, nevertheless, like that of buying outright, developed but gradually. A New York banker who was an active leader in promoting the adoption of better methods of credit investigation among banks noted in 1891 that a large number of borrowers, including both the customers of dealers and those who sought direct advances from their own banks, appeared to be unwilling to "give the banks a full statement of their condition." [148] During the years immediately following — a period when, as a Chicago dealer remarked, "we could know all our people so well and so closely that we could guess pretty well without figures just what they were good for" [149] — there seems to have been but little change in this situation. In 1893 but few concerns, it is said, were presenting financial statements either to "note brokers" or to banks.[150] A New York dealer

[147] The close relationships which had been established by the larger dealers with their borrowing customers by 1908, and had become the basis of the important work of credit investigation, were noted as follows in an address delivered in that year: ". . . the notebroker selling the paper of a large mercantile house occupies a closer and more confidential relationship than the officers of its banks. He possesses thoroughly his client's confidence, and the heart of the house is laid bare before him to a greater degree than to the officers of its banks" (W. A. Law, "Co-operation in Commercial Credits," *Proc. Penn. Bankers' Assoc.*, 1908, p. 43).

[148] Cannon, *An Ideal Bank* (pamphlet containing reprint of an addresss before the Institute of Accounts, New York, 1891), p. 7.

[149] Becker, *op. cit.*, p. 10.

[150] William Post, "The Loan and Credit Department. I," *Bull. Amer. Inst. of Bank Clerks*, July 15, 1903, p. 102.

reported in 1930 that many borrowers as late as 1894 felt that giving such statements was "beneath their dignity" and regarded even a request for a statement as a reflection on their credit standing. The practice of offering financial figures to banks or dealers was evidently no less uncommon in the Chicago district at that time.[151] Within the next decade, however, a number of concerns began to furnish such information both to dealers and to banks from which they obtained loans direct. By 1901, if not earlier, dealers had begun to supply their buying customers with financial statements as well as other pertinent credit information.[152] Two years later it was reported that furnishing such statements had become a common practice, and that dealers of Boston, New York, and Chicago were then offering very few "names" concerning which detailed figures could not be had for the asking.[153] During the next ten years the practice of offering detailed financial information became more and more common,[154] a number of concerns

---

[151] See n. 137, p. 87.

[152] Flynn, *op. cit.*, p. 32.

[153] Post, *loc. cit.* According to Post, the practice of furnishing financial statements developed more slowly in Philadelphia than in Boston, New York, and Chicago (*loc. cit.*). This may have resulted from the fact that the commercial paper houses which established their main offices in Philadelphia were comparatively small organizations whose business was more or less localized. Such houses, whether in buying or in selling paper, would have less need for detailed financial information concerning their borrowing customers than dealers who carried on their operations on a more extensive scale.

[154] In 1908 it was stated that "the ultimate buyers [of open-market paper] rely almost invariably upon the statement of the borrower" (Law, *loc. cit.*). Two years later a St. Louis banker observed that "statements are presented with every note" offered for sale by dealers; another writer, that borrowers who would not submit financial statements had by that time been practically forced out of the market, and that "brokers now seldom have the temerity to offer paper without a statement and the other recognized references" (W. H. Lee, "Clearing House Bank Examinations," *Proc. Mo. Bankers' Assoc.*, 1910, p. 104; J. H. Puelicher, "Bank Reserves," *Proc. Wis. Bankers' Assoc.*, 1910, p. 118). In 1913 a Milwaukee banker reported that dealers were expected to furnish up-to-date statements of their borrowing customers, and usually did so (A. H. Lindsay, *Commercial Paper* — pamphlet — p. 6).

It should not be supposed, however, that all concerns borrowing in the open market in the closing years of this period were supplying purchasers of their notes with financial statements, or that the credit information offered buyers of such paper could always be relied on implicitly. A committee of the American Bankers' Association reported in 1908 that dealers had granted credits loosely upon "unverified and often unsigned statements of borrowers, supported if at all only by superficial

began to issue audited statements,[155] and coöperation between dealers and bankers in the exchange of credit data became closer.[156] The issuance of audited statements and operating figures apparently did not become common until after 1913. Before the close of this period, nevertheless, both dealers and bankers had unquestionably made important progress in securing statements of financial condition from their borrowing customers and in using such statements as an improved method of credit investigation.

9. DEVELOPMENTS RELATING TO CLASSES OF BUYING CUSTOMERS OF DEALERS

In the preceding chapter it was indicated that the buying customers of dealers in the period before 1861 included two main classes — merchants and other "private capitalists," who presumably bought a comparatively small proportion of the total volume of paper sold in the market, and private bankers and incorporated banks, which purchased the bulk of the bills and notes offered for sale by dealers. Investors of the first class continued to place surplus funds in open-market paper in the period

---

inquiries at interested banks," and that financial statements offered by dealers as a rule were "made at a date most opportune for the borrower, and not infrequently after a good deal of dressing up for the occasion" (Report of Committee on Credit Information, *Proc. Amer. Bankers' Assoc.*, 1908, pp. 197, 203). At the same time, this committee intimated that bankers themselves, because of lack of coöperation, were probably "equally responsible with brokers and borrowers for all unsound and improper practices" then connected with open-market financing (*ibid.*, p. 199). Three years later a New York banker stated that "some of the very best concerns of this country have never made, and will never make, detailed statements of their affairs." He had in mind, he explained, "a number of the choicest names appearing in the New York market, whose paper we would not hesitate to purchase in round amounts" (J. B. Martindale, "The Business of a Commercial Bank and How to Safeguard the Investment of its Funds," *Proc. Amer. Bankers' Assoc.*, 1911, p. 702). In 1913, the last year of this period, it was stated that twenty-one "leading houses" whose paper had been "floated over a wide territory" failed during the year ended September 1913, and that, of these twenty-one concerns, only one had been issuing audited financial statements (Ralph Van Vechten, address as president of Clearing House Section, American Bankers' Association, *Proc. Amer. Bankers' Assoc.*, 1913, p. 518).

[155] Puelicher, *op. cit.*, pp. 118–119.

[156] By 1911, according to a New York banker, many dealers had shown a desire to coöperate with banks and to furnish freely such information as they required, and relations between dealers and bankers were steadily becoming closer (Martindale, *op. cit.*, pp. 703–704).

after the Civil War also. Retired merchants were probably calling at note brokers' offices to buy paper as late as 1884,[157] and other "private capitalists" continued to purchase bills or notes through dealers for many years later. Even during the closing years of the period considered in this chapter, in fact, individual investors were buying at least a small volume of open-market obligations.[158] Commercial paper, however, because it is issued for comparatively short periods, and generally without security, by concerns whose center of operations may be a thousand miles or more distant from the locality of the investor, is obviously better adapted to the requirements of banks than to those of individual investors. As was to have been expected, therefore, purchases of open-market paper by banks steadily increased in importance during this period as compared with purchases by "private capitalists" or other individual buyers. This increase in the relative importance of banks as investors in such paper was the main development relating to classes of buying customers of dealers during this period. It probably began during the Civil War period, or shortly thereafter, and apparently proceeded at a rapid rate during the last quarter of the last century, as the practice of investing banks' surplus funds in outside paper spread from the East to the newer sections of the country and the annual volume of such paper sold by dealers increased. While individual investors, and probably also a certain number of trustees and business corporations, were placing surplus funds in open-market obligations as late as 1913, it is doubtless safe to say that savings banks organized under state laws which authorized the purchase of short-term notes by such institutions, and commercial banks, large and small, located in all sections of the country, by 1900 were purchasing 95 per cent or more of the total volume of paper sold by dealers each year.

---

[157] Bolles, *loc. cit.*

[158] Sales of open-market paper to "private capitalists" were mentioned by a Boston banker in a work published in 1896 but written some ten years earlier (Patten, *op. cit.*, p. 136). In 1930 a leading New York dealer reported that his organization was selling a considerable amount of commercial paper to private investors and to a dry-goods commission house in Boston after 1900; a former dealer of Philadelphia, that a considerable volume of such paper was sold to individuals in that locality in comparatively recent years.

10. Changes in Dealers' Selling Methods

As was indicated earlier in this chapter, the methods used by dealers in placing open-market paper with banks and other buying customers in the decade preceding 1861 remained practically unchanged during the years immediately following the Civil War. As late as the decade of the seventies, and probably for some years later, "hat-band brokers" [159] in New York and other cities continued to call on their customers in person and offer a varied assortment of short-term notes for sale.[160] Other dealers during this same period preferred to display their bills and notes on tables in their own offices,[161] and to let their buying customers, including both local bankers and those from out of town, take the initiative in selecting the paper they wished to purchase. Even as late as the 1890's, in fact, a number of commercial paper houses continued to sell a large part of the open-market obligations they handled to bankers who called at their offices to examine their stock in trade.[162] During the closing years of the last century, however,

[159] See n. 136, p. 87.

[160] The firm of Platt and Woodward, which began business in New York in 1874, is said to have changed the dealer's customary practice of offering actual promissory notes for sale to prospective customers "by keeping the endorsed bills receivable in their safe and letting their patrons buy from long lists of names" ("Double-Name Paper," *N. Y. Evening Post*, Mar. 14, 1914, p. 3). Presumably the "lists of names" referred to were "inventory slips" (i. e., slips of paper showing the amount, maturity, and name of the maker of each note), rather than dealers' note offering lists; for dealers in New York and Boston had begun to issue note offering lists before 1874. (See Exhibits 9–12.) At least twenty years later, however, one of the leading dealers of Chicago was still selling, and delivering at the time of sale, the actual promissory notes making up his stock in trade (see n. 137, p. 87).

[161] O. M. Bogart, a prominent New York note broker of the Civil War period, is said to have displayed his paper in much the same way as that used by modern department stores in displaying their merchandise. He had banks send representatives to his office every day to look over the notes which had come in on the day preceding. These representatives would examine at leisure the paper offered for sale and select any which they wished to buy for their banks ("Double-Name Paper," *N. Y. Evening Post*, Mar. 14, 1914, p. 3).

According to New York dealers, Bogart handled relatively large amounts of dry-goods paper and prime brewery paper. Some of the "names" he was offering for sale in the early 1870's are listed in Exhibit 11. His firm is said to have failed in 1884. Its failure, however, was connected with its dealings in securities, rather than its operations in commercial paper.

[162] During the nineties, according to a New York dealer, "country bank officers, very largely, came to the brokers' offices to buy their paper" (Smith, *op. cit.*, p. 5).

perhaps because competition in their business was growing keener, dealers who formerly had sold such obligations almost entirely "over the counter" began to send traveling salesmen out to call on prospective buying customers.[163] From then on to the close of the period considered in this chapter sales through such representatives steadily increased in relative importance; and though dealers continued even after 1913 to sell a certain amount of paper "over the counter," [164] by the close of this period they had come to rely in the main, as modern commercial paper houses do, on more aggressive methods of selling. Most of the methods now employed by dealers, in fact, were adopted some years before 1913. Note offering lists, specifying the makers and indorsers of notes and the drawers and acceptors of bills offered for sale in the market, together with the rates, denominations, and maturities borne by such paper, were issued as early as 1867.[165] Two years later dealers were making use of the telegraph in connection with the distribution of their offerings.[166] By about 1893 some of them had established correspondent relations similar to those maintained by a number of the leading commercial paper houses at present.[167] Dealers also began to make use of written correspondence and the telephone at an early date. Thus by about 1900 they were using practically all the methods of distribution employed by the larger dealers in more recent years.

[163] A New York dealer reported in 1930 that the firm which was the predecessor of his organization sent out its first salesmen in 1892, and that other dealers who had previously been selling "over the counter" also began to send out salesmen to call on prospective buyers about the same time. By 1908 a "number of wealthy and able firms" are said to have been distributing commercial paper "throughout the country . . . oftentimes through . . . several score of salesmen" (Law, *op. cit.*, p. 42). It may be doubted, however, that many dealers were employing so large a number of salesmen at that time.

[164] Dealers in New York and Boston stated in 1930 that bankers used to call at their offices to select open-market paper as late as 1925. A Philadelphia dealer reported in the same year that his organization, which succeeded a firm established in 1866, had never employed salesmen to call on prospective buyers.

[165] See Exhibit 9.

[166] It may be noted that the house which issued the offering list shown in Exhibit 10 invited prospective buyers to "telegraph by numbers" for any of the listed notes or bills they wished to purchase. See also Exhibits 12–15.

[167] A Chicago dealer stated that his organization had "broker correspondents" in New York and Boston at an early date — presumably about as early as 1893, the year in which he entered the commercial paper business (Becker, *op. cit.*, p. 4).

In addition to the changes in selling methods which have just been mentioned, commercial paper houses also adopted during this period the practice of selling notes "on option." In accordance with this practice, a dealer allows a banker who has purchased open-market paper from him a period varying from about one week to about seventeen days in which to investigate the credit standing of the maker of the notes. If the results of the investigation prove to be satisfactory, it is understood that the banker will keep the paper; if, on the contrary, he should not be satisfied with the results of his inquiries, he is allowed the option of returning the notes to the dealer within the period agreed upon and receiving from the latter a check for the face amount less the discount to maturity. This practice was devised as a convenient means of enabling bankers first to secure outside paper in which they were interested, and then to decide later on, after they had had time to examine more carefully its desirability as an investment, whether they wished to keep it. Without some such arrangement as this, they might have wasted an undue amount of time in investigating notes which in the meanwhile, before they could complete their investigations, would have been sold to banks or other buyers in other localities. Just when dealers first introduced the practice of allowing their customers to purchase paper on option is not certain, but Boston "brokers" seem to have been granting options, occasionally at least, during the 1870's, and more commonly during the decade following.[168] Within the next twenty years the practice

---

[168] From the facts stated in *Attleborough National Bank* v. *Rogers*, 125 Mass. 339–341 (decided in the Massachusetts Supreme Court in 1878), it may be inferred that H. A. Rogers and others, "brokers" in Boston, were in the habit of allowing banks which purchased open-market obligations from them the option of either keeping or returning such paper after their boards of directors had met to determine its desirability as an investment. At any rate, this firm of dealers allowed the bank involved in this case an option of this kind.

A dealer who began business in Boston about 1885 stated that banks at that time were commonly taking advantage of the option privilege, even in buying paper of concerns with respect to whose credit standing they were already well informed. According to this dealer, abuse of the option privilege by banks was then by no means uncommon, especially in periods of rising money rates. In such periods, banks which had bought paper at lower rates would return it to dealers and buy other notes, or some other investment, which would yield them a higher return. Even in recent years some banks have abused the option privilege.

292101

ther parts of the country, and by 1910 it is probable
larger dealers were extending the option privilege to
customers.[169]

11. CHANGES IN BANKS' METHODS OF BUYING AND CREDIT INVESTIGATION

No less important than the changes just described in dealers'
methods of buying and selling open-market obligations were certain changes adopted by banks during this same period in their
methods of selecting such paper as an investment for their surplus
funds. The changes which banks found it advisable to introduce
in their methods of selecting outside paper, indeed, were in some
respects closely similar to those adopted by dealers themselves.
Like those adopted by dealers, moreover, they were introduced at
a comparatively late date and were the outgrowth of much simpler
practices which had been followed for a number of years.

The significance of these changes may be more readily appreciated if a brief account is first given of the practices followed by
banks in buying paper for a generation or so after the close of the
Civil War. During that period most banks can hardly be said to
have followed any methodical procedure at all in selecting short-
term notes or bills offered for sale in the market. According to
New York dealers, in fact, some bankers, presumably as late as
the 1880's, are said to have bought such obligations "by the
inch," [170] without attempting to investigate their desirability as an

[169] In 1901 it was stated that banks in the larger money centers were generally
buying paper with the option privilege (Flynn, *op. cit.*, pp. 32–33). Five years later
it was reported that banks in New York and elsewhere were buying open-market
obligations on options of a week or ten days (S. S. Conover, "The Credit Man in a
Bank," *Banking Law Jour.*, April 1906, p. 312). By 1914, according to an Oregon
banker, the customary option periods allowed by dealers had come to be seven to
ten days in the case of banks located in the East, and twenty days in the case of
institutions in the Far West, which required more time for completing credit investigations (E. H. Sensenich, "Commercial Paper as a Secondary Reserve," *Proc. Idaho
Bankers' Assoc.*, 1914, p. 115). (See also H. P. Hilliard, address — without title —
before the Michigan Bankers' Association, *Proc. Mich. Bankers' Assoc.*, 1904, p. 71;
and "Double-Name Paper," *N. Y. Evening Post*, Mar. 14, 1914, p. 3.) These option
periods are about the same as those granted by dealers in more recent years.

[170] It is said that these bankers would indicate a distance of half an inch or so
along the tip of a pencil and say to the dealer whose offerings they were buying,
"I'll take that much paper," meaning enough notes to make a pile about half an
inch high. This practice was known as buying paper "by the inch."

investment; and one banker is said to have selected the notes he purchased according to their color and appearance. In judging the desirability of obligations issued or indorsed and sold in the market by local borrowers, bank officers were compelled to rely largely on their personal knowledge of the character and ability of the maker or indorser. In buying outside paper issued or indorsed by concerns with whose affairs they were not familiar, they could make some use of the services of mercantile credit agencies, but even after the close of the last century continued to depend to a large extent upon the recommendations of dealers and correspondent banks.[171] They made but little use of financial state-

---

[171] In 1892 it was estimated that "fully seven-eighths of the paper sold in New York" was "purchased upon the simple recommendation of the note broker" (Cannon, *Bank Credits* — pamphlet — p. 37).

That bankers in Boston, occasionally at least, were buying paper in the same manner two years later is indicated by the following excerpt from an address by a New York dealer:

". . . it was no simple task for a young salesman, just starting in business [early in 1894], to know much about what he was selling. I remember going to Boston to sell some paper, before I had been at work four weeks, and I had a few offerings of double named paper. The bank president — a genial, kindly old fellow — asked me about my names and picked out one of the double named notes to inquire as to the facts. My memory as to this particular name was a blank. I was wholly stumped, and told him truthfully that I knew nothing about the name, but that I was sure, if it was offered by my firm, it was good. He laughed, bought the paper, and I am glad to tell you that it was paid at maturity" (Smith, *op. cit.*, p. 4).

The dependence of small banks, in purchasing open-market paper, on information furnished by larger banks, was noted in 1901 (Flynn, *op. cit.*, p. 44). Ten years later they were still using very simple methods in selecting such paper, as the following quotation indicates:

"The banker who manages the small bank . . . makes little effort, as a rule, to decide for himself the worth of any paper offered him. He usually asks the opinion of the note broker as to which are the best names and checks this up with the information received from his correspondent banker" (K. S. Chase, "Registration of Commercial Paper," *Proc. Minn. Bankers' Assoc.*, 1911, p. 32).

Even in recent years, as a matter of fact, many country banks have either used equally simple methods of selecting outside paper or followed the still simpler practice of arranging with their city correspondent banks to purchase such paper for them. The latter practice seems to have become rather common by about 1900. In 1907 it was stated that a single Chicago bank was buying about $125,000,000 of commercial paper for its country correspondent banks every year (W. G. Schroeder, address — without title — *Proc. Okla.-Ind. Ter. Bankers' Assoc.*, 1907, p. 64). The figure given, however, would seem to be rather exaggerated. Some city banks about that time may have been making a charge for buying paper for their country correspondent banks, though in recent years it has not been customary to make any such charge (C. L. Brokaw, "A Study in Bank Investments," *Proc. Kan. Bankers' Assoc.*, 1908, p. 39).

During the years following 1900, and probably for some years before the close

ments before 1890,[172] and very few even of the larger city banks had organized efficient credit departments before 1900.[173] As a former dealer of Chicago has pointed out, the function of the modern bank credit department in selecting open-market paper was performed as late as the 1890's by bank directorates representing a rather wide range of business interests. Each director was supposed to be particularly well informed with respect to conditions in his line of business, as well as the credit standing of concerns engaged in the same trade or industry, and therefore qualified to pass judgment on the desirability of short-term notes which such concerns offered for sale in the market.[174] In a number of cases, in fact, individual directors assumed the responsibility of purchasing outside paper for their banks,[175] though purchase of such paper by boards of directors as a whole [176] or by individual bank offi-

---

of the last century also, many small country banks expected their city correspondents not only to purchase outside paper for them but also to maintain its "convertibility" thereafter; i.e., to repurchase it from them on demand (E. M. Stevens, "Commercial Paper," *Proc. N. D. Bankers' Assoc.*, 1903, p. 31; Brokaw, *op. cit.*, p. 40; and C. B. Hazlewood, "Commercial Paper as a Secondary Reserve for West Virginia Banks," *Proc. W. Va. Bankers' Assoc.*, 1913, p. 86). In some cases they evidently expected the dealers through whom they had purchased such paper to maintain its "convertibility" for them by enabling them to resell it to some other buyer (G. A. Rogers, "Loaning Money," *Proc. Kan. Bankers' Assoc.*, 1905, p. 138).

[172] According to Moulton, financial statements were probably "first used in procuring loans" in the late seventies, and were not commonly used even by the larger banks (presumably in connection either with making advances to customers direct or with buying paper in the market) until the nineties (H. G. Moulton, "Commercial Banking and Capital Formation," *Jour. Pol. Econ.*, June 1918, p. 646).

[173] Cannon, "Uniform Statement Blanks and Credit Department Methods," *Proc. Amer. Bankers' Assoc.*, 1899, p. 174.

[174] Becker, *op. cit.*, pp. 4–5.
It is said that banks buying open-market paper in this earlier period were constantly seeking for their directorates men who had a "large acquaintance" in many lines of business and were therefore in a position to recommend desirable outside paper for purchase (Cannon, *Buying Commercial Paper* — pamphlet — p. 9).

[175] Becker, *loc. cit.*

[176] During the period from about 1870 to about 1890, according to Boston dealers, commercial paper salesmen were in the habit of submitting lists of note offerings to New England banks on days when their boards of directors met. These directors, most of whom were business men, would meet early in the morning on "discount days" of their banks, and would themselves select from these lists any outside paper in which surplus funds of their institutions were to be invested. As a rule, they would not purchase any notes which any one of their number considered undesirable.
In this earlier period New England banks rarely bought open-market paper on any other days than those known as "discount days." Banks in Boston and other

cers [177] was probably more common, particularly in the case of smaller banks.

This brief description will suffice to indicate that banks in this earlier period customarily bought open-market paper without any careful preliminary investigation. During the decade of the nineties, however, some at least of the larger banks began to adopt more careful methods of investigating the credit standing not only

---

cities generally designated two days a week as "discount days"; country banks and those in the smaller towns and cities, one day a week only. About the beginning of the period considered in this chapter, even banks in New York generally set aside only two days a week for discounting commercial paper, whether offered directly by their own customers or indirectly through dealers. Gibbons stated in 1858 that the "general practice of Bank Board Directors in New York" was to meet on two stated days of the week, called *Discount Days*," to "act on the notes offered for discount" on the days immediately preceding, which were known as "*Offering Days*" (J. S. Gibbons, *The Banks of New York*, p. 200). In the following year, of a total of fifty-four New York banks only two were discounting paper daily. The remaining fifty-two each had two "discount days" a week ("Banks of the City of New York," *Bankers' Mag.*, Jan. 1860, pp. 556–557).

The practice of setting aside one or two days a week as regular "discount days" originated toward the close of the eighteenth century, when the earliest commercial banks in the United States were being established. The Massachusetts Bank, which received its charter from the Massachusetts Legislature early in 1784, "accepted notes for discounting twice a week" when it began business (M. H. Foulds, "The Massachusetts Bank, 1784–1865," *Jour. of Ec. and Bus. Hist.*, Feb. 1930, pp. 256, 259). The Bank of New York, which began business in 1784, was "making discounts" on two days a week in 1786 (Horace White, *Money and Banking*, 5th ed., pp. 248–249). The Bank of Hartford, organized in 1792, apparently had but one "discount day" a week in that year (P. H. Woodward, *One Hundred Years of the Hartford Bank*, p. 21). By 1816 banks in Boston generally had two regular "discount days" a week (*Boston Directory* for 1816, pp. 240–242).

[177] During the decades of the seventies and eighties, when dealers themselves often called on their buying customers in person, there was more bargaining between dealers and individual bank officers in the purchase and sale of commercial paper than was common after the market for such paper became nation-wide, commercial paper rates became more nearly uniform throughout the country, and relations between dealers and bankers became more impersonal. As an example of the kind of negotiation in which dealers and bankers in the Boston district are said to have engaged during this earlier period may be mentioned the practice known as buying and selling paper at an average rate. A banker wishing to invest surplus funds in outside paper would examine a dealer's offerings, pick out the notes in which he was interested, and ask the dealer at what rate he would sell the whole batch of selected notes. He would not take time to look at the rate on each individual note, nor would he allow the dealer time to examine each note before specifying a selling rate for the entire lot. The dealer would therefore have to make the best guess he could as to what he would consider a satisfactory rate. The banker might accept the rate offered by the dealer or bargain for a somewhat higher rate. Sometimes he would agree to accept the offered rate if the dealer would "sweeten" the collection of notes

of concerns whose obligations they purchased in the market but also of those to which they granted direct advances. One reason for their adoption of improved methods of selecting outside paper at this time was the fact that in earlier years they had occasionally suffered appreciable losses on such paper. Probably another reason was that a number of them began to increase their purchases of open-market obligations after 1890, and consequently found it worth while to give more time and attention to the selection of notes whose prompt payment at maturity could reasonably be expected. It will be recalled, moreover, that dealers themselves began to adopt improved methods of credit investigation about the same time; and their success in eliminating undesirable credit risks no doubt to some extent encouraged bankers to endeavor to adopt more effective methods of selecting outside paper. In fact, the improved methods which bankers found it advisable to employ were closely similar to those which dealers themselves were using. It is true that many banks, particularly the smaller country institutions, continued even after 1913 to rely mainly on the recommendations of correspondent banks and dealers. City banks, however, began to make more and more effective use of reports of credit agencies and of bank and trade "checkings." About the same time, the larger of these banks began also to organize credit departments and to secure whenever possible, and subject to careful analysis, financial statements issued by concerns whose paper they bought in the market.

The latter two developments, which made possible the substitution of accurate and detailed information for what previously had often been little better than conjecture or opinion, were no less important than similar changes which dealers had also begun to

---

by adding to it some very high-grade low-rate paper. In practically all cases of buying paper at an average rate the banker would of course pay the dealer either somewhat more or somewhat less for the batch of notes than he would have paid had he bought each note separately in the usual manner.

In some cases, according to Boston dealers, banks preferred to buy paper at an average rate of not less than, say 4 per cent, rather than some notes at lower and some at higher rates. They could then tell their regular customers that they made no loans at rates lower than 4 per cent, and could use this fact as an argument for keeping rates charged these customers up to such a figure as a minimum.

adopt. Such changes in credit practice, however, seem to have developed but gradually among even the larger city banks. Up until about 1890, according to a well-informed banker of New York, only one or two banks in that city had credit departments, and the work of these departments "consisted principally in noting up what certain directors had to say about the notes purchased." [178] In 1892, after a careful investigation, this same banker found that there were not more than half a dozen banks in the United States with credit departments; [179] and even as late as 1899 he could state that, though all mercantile houses of any consequence in this country had "thoroughly equipped" credit departments "in charge of a competent man," the number of bank credit departments could be "counted almost upon the fingers of your two hands." [180] In no small measure because of his own activity in the promotion of better credit methods, [181] however, more and more bankers in various sections of the country during the next ten years or so began to

[178] Cannon, *Buying Commercial Paper* (pamphlet), pp. 6–7.

Probably one of the first bank credit departments established in this country was that organized by Mr. Buell, president of the Importers' and Traders' National Bank of New York, about 1883. Easy conditions prevailing in the money market at that time are said to have induced a number of merchants to borrow rather heavily through dealers and to use the funds so obtained in ventures which "too often proved disastrous." As a result, banks which had purchased the paper of such borrowers suffered losses. To protect itself against losses of this kind, the Importers' and Traders' National Bank began to investigate more carefully the credit standing of concerns whose open-market obligations it was considering for purchase. In particular, it began to ask for information concerning the amounts of their bills and accounts payable, mortgages on real estate, other liabilities, cash on hand, good bills and accounts receivable, merchandise, and real estate and other assets, as well as for other similar information ("Scrutiny of Commercial Paper," *Rhodes' Jour. of Banking*, Dec. 1883, p. 1048). (See also M. G. Myers, *The New York Money Market*, I, 325, and E. Naumburg, "A Danger in Two-Name Paper," *Annalist*, Mar. 23, 1914, p. 361.)

[179] Cannon, *op. cit.*, p. 7.

[180] Cannon, "Uniform Statement Blanks and Credit Department Methods," *Proc. Amer. Bankers' Assoc.*, 1899, p. 174.

[181] In the address referred to in the preceding footnote, Cannon proposed resolutions that the American Bankers' Association should approve the system of credit departments for banks and that its secretary should prepare and set up in his office a model credit department and furnish information relating to its operation to members of the Association. These resolutions were unanimously adopted (*ibid.*, pp. 176–177). Cannon was for many years vice-president of the Fourth National Bank of New York. He organized in this institution, presumably some years before 1899, one of the earliest bank credit departments established in this country (C. A. Phillips, *Bank Credit*, p. 145).

realize the advantages to be gained from establishing special departments for making credit investigations; and by 1911 it was stated that "almost every bank of size and prominence" was "equipped with a complete credit department." [182] The investigations of such departments were facilitated by the growth of the practice of buying and selling open-market paper on option, briefly described in the preceding section, and by the development of closer coöperation between dealers and bankers in the exchange of credit information. Like those organized about the same time by dealers, moreover, these credit departments were able to make effective use of financial statements in the selection of commercial paper. As was stated above, in buying outside paper banks made but little use of such statements before 1890. Up until that time, indeed, dealers themselves did not as a rule secure any detailed financial information from their borrowing customers and, even if they had been called on to do so, could seldom have furnished their buying customers with financial statements. During the decade of the nineties, however, both dealers and bankers made important progress in securing more accurate and detailed credit information;[183] and by about 1900, or shortly thereafter, banks which requested them were able to secure from leading dealers financial statements of most of the concerns whose paper they handled.[184] Thus some years before the close of the period considered in this chapter the larger banks, as well as the leading dealers, had developed and were making more or less effective use

---

[182] Chase, *op. cit.*, p. 35.

A fuller discussion of the development of bank credit departments in the United States may be found in Phillips, *op. cit.*, pp. 142–152.

[183] Early in 1895 the New York State Bankers' Association recommended that its members request their borrowing customers to furnish written and signed financial statements on uniform statement blanks. Nearly all groups of this association adopted such statement blanks. Similar blanks were adopted by bankers' associations of other states not long afterward, and by the National Association of Credit Men in 1898. In 1899 James G. Cannon proposed a resolution that the American Bankers' Association prepare a uniform statement blank which could be used by all its members. This resolution was unanimously adopted; and in the same year the association also adopted a uniform statement blank (Cannon, *Buying Commercial Paper* — pamphlet — pp. 7–8, and "Uniform Statement Blanks and Credit Department Methods," *Proc. Amer. Bankers' Assoc.*, 1899, pp. 176–177).

[184] Flynn, *op. cit.*, p. 32, and William Post, "The Loan and Credit Department. I," *Bull. Amer. Inst. of Bank Clerks*, July 15, 1903, p. 102.

of practically all the facilities and methods of credit investigation which have been employed in the selection of open-market paper in recent years.

12. COMPENSATION RECEIVED BY DEALERS

The development of more elaborate organizations and the adoption of the practice of outright buying and of more careful methods of credit investigation, which have been described in earlier sections of this chapter, involved an appreciable increase in dealers' costs of operation, particularly in the later years of the period from 1861 to 1914. Partly as a result of increasing competition among themselves, however, and partly also, perhaps, because of the force of custom, dealers endeavored to meet these rising costs through increasing the volume of their operations and the turnover of their capital, rather than through changing the form or increasing the amount of the compensation charged for their services.

They continued as a rule to receive their compensation in the form of a commission paid by their borrowing customers. The rates of commission they charged during the earlier years of this period probably ranged from about ¼ to ½ of 1 per cent, though in some cases rates as high as 1 per cent of the face amount of the notes handled may have been charged.[185] Later on, as competition among dealers grew keener, rates tended to fall somewhat and to

[185] In the case of *Farmers' and Mechanics' Bank* v. *Baldwin*, 23 Minn. 198–200, it is stated that the rate of commission received by one Patterson, "a note-broker" (presumably of St. Paul or Minneapolis), for selling certain notes in 1875 was ½ of 1 per cent. This rate, however, evidently was higher than those commonly received by dealers in the larger cities in the early eighties. By 1884, if not a number of years earlier, ¼ of 1 per cent had probably become the rate most commonly charged by the larger dealers (A. S. Bolles, *Practical Banking*, 1884 ed., p. 64). None of a large number of dealers interviewed by the writer in 1930 and 1931 could state precisely when or why this particular rate was established. As was pointed out in the preceding chapter, rates charged by dealers in negotiable paper before the Civil War may have been influenced by the rate, ¼ of 1 per cent, charged for selling stock on the Stock Exchanges of New York and Boston. During the period from about 1865 to about 1874 it is said that many city (national) banks which were unwilling to send national bank notes back to their correspondents for redemption sold these notes to brokers at a discount of 1/10 to ¼ of 1 per cent (Myers, *op. cit.*, p. 404). The rates of discount charged by these brokers may have had some influence on the commission rates charged by dealers in open-market paper in the years following the close of the Civil War.

show a narrower range of variation. As early as 1884 dealers in the larger cities were accepting rates as low as ⅛ of 1 per cent for handling some classes of paper.[186] Within the next twenty years or so competition had become so active that they were willing occasionally to sell some high-grade notes at no charge to the maker whatsoever, in order to secure choice "accounts" or to retain such accounts previously secured.[187] In such cases they bought paper at a flat or net discount rate of, say 3 per cent, and took a chance on being able to sell it at a rate sufficiently lower to be profitable. According to a Philadelphia dealer, this practice of buying at a net rate, without commission, developed in the earlier years of this period, at a time when those who bought and sold paper in the market could make substantial gains from the "spread" between their buying and selling rates alone.[188] It is probable, however, that the larger dealers more commonly combined the practice of

[186] According to Bolles, the commission of "note brokers" in large cities in 1884 was generally ⅛ of 1 per cent, but was ¼ of 1 per cent for "negotiating" leather paper, dry-goods paper, and tea paper (Bolles, *loc. cit.*). It may be doubted, however, that dealers during the 1880's as a rule received a commission no higher than ⅛ of 1 per cent.

[187] The Committee on Credit Information of the American Bankers' Association reported in 1908 that, in order to secure high-grade paper, dealers were "splitting" commissions (i.e., charging borrowing customers less than the regular rates for selling their notes in the market) and "sometimes sacrificing them altogether" (Report of Committee on Credit Information, *Proc. Amer. Bankers' Assoc.*, 1908, p. 198). (See also J. T. Talbert, "Commercial Paper," *Proc. Minn. Bankers' Assoc.*, 1908, pp. 46–47.) A Boston dealer reported in 1931 that after about 1905 the rate of commission for selling high-grade paper in the Boston and New York districts fell below ¼ of 1 per cent, and that the average commission received by his organization in subsequent years did not exceed 1/7 of 1 per cent of its sales of such paper.

[188] According to a dealer of Minneapolis, it was possible as late as about 1893 to buy paper in that district at a flat rate of 8 per cent and sell it at 4½ per cent. It may be noted that a "spread" of 3½ points on six-months' paper would yield the dealer a gross profit seven times as great as the commission of ¼ of 1 per cent which commercial paper houses commonly charge for their services at present. (The "spread" just mentioned would be at the rate of 3½ per cent a year; a commission of ¼ of 1 per cent on six-months' paper amounts to ½ of 1 per cent a year.)

As was indicated in the preceding chapter, the practice of buying paper at a flat rate, without commission, probably developed in the period before the Civil War, particularly among "private capitalists" and "note shavers." It was noted by Bolles as early as 1884, and by Conover some twenty years later, in 1906 (Bolles, *loc. cit.*; Conover, *op. cit.*, p. 311). By the latter year, even in periods of falling money rates, dealers as a rule could hardly expect to make from selling notes bought at a net rate any speculative profit much in excess of a commission of ¼ of 1 per cent.

charging a commission with that of making whatever additional gain was possible from selling paper at rates lower than those at which they had purchased it.[189] In any case, after about 1896, when commercial paper rates began to fall below the levels which had prevailed in the earlier years of this period, the spread between dealers' buying and selling rates, and therefore the gains which could be realized from differences between these rates, declined also.

Thus during the later years of this period the compensation received by dealers — whether in the form of a straight commission, a speculative profit arising from differences between buying and selling rates, or a combination of both these sources of income — declined both in amount and in range of variation. By 1913, if not some years earlier, it is probable that this remuneration had become about as nearly uniform, and did not as a rule exceed, that which commercial paper houses receive for their services at present.

13. Methods Used by Dealers in Financing Operations in Open-Market Paper

For some years after the close of the Civil War the financing of the operations from which dealers derived the several forms of income just described remained a relatively simple problem. So long as they conducted their operations on a comparatively small scale, required no elaborate organizations for selecting or selling their stock in trade, and in buying and selling bills and notes acted

[189] One of the partners of a commercial paper house of Boston stated in 1931 that years ago — presumably from about 1875 to about 1895 — dealers in that district could buy paper at 6 per cent, plus a commission of ¼ of 1 per cent, and sell it at 5 per cent. In such cases they could therefore make, on six-months' paper, a gross profit of ¾ of 1 per cent of their sales, or a gain three times as great as the rate of commission commonly received by modern commercial paper houses.

Despite the comparatively high rates of gross profit which could be made on sales of open-market paper as late as the 1890's, the earnings of dealers in this earlier period were sometimes by no means excessive in amount. A Boston dealer who began business in 1879, and for a year or so acted as a broker only, is said to have made less than $600 in commissions during his first year of operations (A. P. Brown, "Commercial Paper" — typewritten paper — p. 7). According to an officer of a New York commercial paper house, a dealer who could make net profits of as much as $1,000 to $1,500 a year in the period after the panic of 1893 was fortunate.

as brokers only, dealers needed practically no capital other than the nominal amount which sufficed to meet their current operating expenses.

With the expansion of their operations and the adoption of the practice of outright buying, which began after about 1880, this situation began to change. The selection of an increasing volume of open-market obligations by more careful and detailed methods of credit investigation and the sale of this paper over a constantly widening market area could be effected only by the development of larger and more elaborate organizations, and involved no inconsiderable increase in dealers' distribution costs and administrative and other overhead expenses. To meet these increased expenses more capital was required. The adoption of the practice of buying paper outright, instead of on a brokerage basis, increased still further the amount of capital dealers needed to carry on their operations.[190]

To obtain this additional capital, however, they were not compelled to resort to any new methods of financing; instead, they found it possible to continue to employ the simple methods which they had used in the period before 1861 and have likewise found satisfactory in the period since 1913. More specifically, they continued to draw on their own private resources, to reinvest in their business part of their earnings from operations, and to obtain from commercial banks short-term advances secured by open-market paper. The extent to which individual dealers relied on each of these sources of capital of course varied considerably, since it depended on the amount of their own personal resources, the financial results of their operations, their policies with respect to the dis-

[190] At the same time it may be observed that the developments just mentioned produced other effects which operated to limit the amount of additional capital required by dealers. The adoption of the practice of outright buying doubtless stimulated to some extent (and was in turn no doubt to some extent promoted by) the development of the more effective methods of selecting and selling open-market paper which were made possible by the development of larger and more elaborate organizations. The adoption of these improved methods enabled dealers to offer their buying customers paper of a higher grade, and to dispose of their stock in trade more readily; and therefore to maintain a high rate of turnover of their capital, or, in other words, to reduce to a relatively small figure the amount of capital required for transacting a given volume of business each year.

position of net earnings, the volume of their business, and the like. It would accordingly be impossible to state which method of financing was being used most extensively at any particular time. It may be said, however, that dealers as a rule no doubt preferred to supply their own capital so far as possible, rather than resort to the use of borrowed funds, and that the practice of borrowing from banks to finance their operations in open-market paper became more common in the later than it was in the earlier years of this period. As early as 1882 one of the leading dealers in New York, it is true, is said to have borrowed from a bank in that city, "against good commercial paper collateral," as much as $100,000 at one time;[191] but dealers undoubtedly made more extensive use of bank loans after about 1890, when the volume of their business began to increase and they began to buy outright an increasing proportion of the paper they handled, and when banks became more familiar with the open-market system of financing and presumably more willing, as a consequence, to make short-term advances against open-market paper as collateral. While no figures of the total amounts of such advances made in any one year are available, it is probable that the practice of borrowing substantial sums from commercial banks, particularly in periods of greatest activity in the commercial paper business, had become common among the larger dealers some years before 1913, the close of the period considered in this chapter.

14. "OTHER OPERATIONS" OF DEALERS

In the preceding sections of this chapter it has been shown that the organizations maintained by dealers, as well as their methods of selecting, buying, and selling their stock in trade, though they remained practically unchanged for some years after the close of the Civil War, nevertheless underwent significant changes in later

---

[191] The dealer was Alonzo Follett, "a heavy note broker of Wall Street," who is said to have borrowed the amount mentioned from the Manhattan Company Bank shortly before his failure in 1882. Though he was unable to take up the loan when called upon, the bank was secured by the commercial paper which he had offered as collateral ("Heavy Failure of a Note Broker," *Rhodes' Jour. of Banking*, Oct. 1882, p. 741).

years, and by 1913 had become closely similar to those which
modern commercial paper houses have found most effective. A
somewhat similar development took place with respect also to the
"other operations" — that is, operations other than the purchase
and sale of open-market paper — in which many dealers engaged
during this period.

As was indicated in the preceding chapter, dealing in short-term
negotiable instruments in the years immediately preceding the outbreak of the Civil War was often only one part of a general banking business carried on by private banking houses whose range of
operations was sufficiently wide to include, in addition, dealing in
domestic and foreign exchange, the purchase and sale of stocks
and bonds, and even the handling of insurance. For some fifteen
years or more after the close of the war between the states a number of dealers continued to follow this policy of combining operations in open-market paper with other dealings more or less diverse
in character. In 1868, for instance, a Boston note broker was acting
also as the selling agent of a manufacturing company;[192] and in
the decades of the seventies and eighties dealers in other cities were
combining the purchase and sale of commercial paper with one or
more classes of such other operations as a general banking business
or dealings in securities, real estate and mortgage paper, or real
estate itself.[193] Not long after 1879, moreover, a Boston dealer

---

[192] See the advertisement of Watson Gore, Jr., in the *Boston Directory* for 1868,
p. 926.

[193] In 1873 a New York dealer was also carrying on a general banking business
and dealings in securities. (See advertisement of Edward Haight and Company,
Bankers' Mag., June 1873, p. 9 of advertisements.) Dealers in Indianapolis about
the same time were combining operations in open-market paper with handling real
estate mortgage investments on commission or with security brokerage and dealings
in real estate. (See advertisements of Snyder and Moore, *The Merchants' and
Bankers' Almanac* for 1871, p. xxxv of advertisements, and J. A. Moore and Brother
and D. E. Snyder and Company, *Bankers' Mag.*, June 1873, p. 22 of advertisements.)
In 1875 dealers in Louisville were also acting as bond and stock brokers and dealing
in mortgage and real estate paper. (See advertisement of Galt and Shotwell, *The
Banker's Almanac and Register for 1875*, p. 37 of advertisements.) In St. Louis
during the 1870's and in Kansas City during the early 1880's there were "bankers
and brokers" who were buying and selling "notes" and stocks and bonds. In addition, these St. Louis dealers were buying gold and "effecting" loans "with Undoubted
Real Estate Security," and those of Kansas City were conducting a general banking
business, buying and selling real estate on commission, and lending money on real

who entered business in that year began also to handle collateral loans, which differed from ordinary open-market loans in that they were used by individuals for carrying securities, rather than for commercial or industrial purposes.

After about 1880, however, a trend toward greater specialization of function on the part of dealers became apparent. As the total annual volume of paper sold in the market began to increase, a number of new houses were organized for the express purpose of dealing in open-market obligations, and houses which formerly had carried on a wider range of operations began to confine their activities more and more to dealing in promissory notes, or in such obligations and securities issued for longer terms. It is significant that, of the twenty-five houses which were the largest dealers in 1931, twenty-three began to deal in open-market paper from the beginning, one within a year after it was established, and the remaining concern within eight years after its organization.[194] Of all these houses, moreover, only the latter was carrying on a general banking business, and this concern's dealings in open-market paper never became an important part of its operations. It is true that a number of houses established originally for the express purpose of dealing in open-market paper later on assumed other functions

---

estate for non-residents. (See advertisements of Matthews and Whitaker, *The Banker's Almanac and Register for 1878*, p. 27 of advertisements, and Whipple, Cowherd and Company, *The Banker's Almanac and Register for 1881*, p. 20 of advertisements. See also *Hamlin* v. *Abell*, 120 Mo. 188, 196, and "The Liability of Investment Brokers in the Sale of Commercial Paper," *Banking Law Jour.*, May 1894, p. 388.) During the early 1880's two private banking houses in Chicago were dealing in commercial paper and real estate mortgages. Both these concerns later on gave up their banking business and their dealings in mortgages and became leading dealers in open-market paper in the Chicago district. In 1883 a St. Louis concern established in 1871 was buying and selling securities and "Real Estate and first-class Commercial Paper." (See advertisement of P. F. Keleher and Company, *The Banker's Almanac and Register for 1883*, p. 22 of advertisements.)

[194] Of these twenty-five houses, nine began business after 1913, but six of these nine succeeded earlier concerns established before the close of the period considered in this chapter. Apparently only two of the twenty-five houses were not organized originally for the express purpose of dealing in open-market paper, though two others succeeded private banking houses established in Chicago early in the 1880's. Of the former two houses, one was organized in 1920 as the "security affiliate" of a commercial bank in one of the larger cities of the South. The other was organized about 1910 as the "commercial paper department" of a similar institution established in the same city in 1902.

also. During the later years of this period, however, an increasing proportion of the business of buying and selling promissory notes in the market came under the control of two classes of houses which specialized in a limited number of operations. Dealers of the first class confined their activities mainly to buying and selling commercial paper. Those of the second class carried on in addition one or more classes of other operations, the most important of which were security brokerage and the origination and distribution of long-term securities. Thus the "other operations" which leading dealers were carrying on during the closing years of this period differed in one respect from those of the earlier private banking houses, but in other respects resembled those both of these earlier dealers and of commercial paper houses of the present. In being comparatively restricted in range, they differed from those of a number of earlier dealers. At the same time, in being in some cases relatively unimportant but in others the most important part of the business of those who bought and sold short-term paper in the market, they resembled both those of earlier dealers and those of modern commercial paper houses as well. Finally, both in their range and in their character they were closely similar to those of the houses which at present handle the bulk of the open-market obligations sold in the United States each year.

EXHIBIT 9

Note Offering List of Blake Bro's. & Co., 1867

LIST OF PAPER PROPOSED FOR DISCOUNT

Blake Bro's & Co., Bankers,

No. 28 STATE STREET, BOSTON, MASS.,

AND

No. 17 WALL STREET, NEW YORK.

Subject to Chance of Previous Sale.

BOSTON, JUNE 24 1867

NO.	RATE	PROMISER OR ACCEPTOR	DRAWER OR ENDORSER	DUE	AMOUNT
1	6¼	Hest Tillinghast & Co	A Lippmans	Nov.9	6000
2					9000
3		H J Gardner & Co	Newark Woolen Mills	Dec.9	4500
4			Bellville Printing Co	Oct. 1	7500 5000
6					10000
7		Bowers Beeckman & Co	James B Hall	Nov.14	5000
8					10000
9		Sutton Smith & Co	H H Stevens	,, 13	5000
10					10000
11		,,	Hall & Vezin	Oct.15	5000
12					5000
13		Thomas Howe	John B Turner	Oct.21	4000
14					5000
15		Fabbri & Chauncey	John Collins	Dec.18	5000
16					5000
17		Gardner Bacon & Co	A Sessums & Co	Aug. 7	15000
18		Nathan Matthews	Thomas Upham	Oct.17	5000
19					11000
20	7	Sprague Colburn & Co	E & R E Spalding	Dec.6	5000
21					10000
22		Jordan Marsh & Co	Adriatic Mills	Oct.17	5000
23					10000
24		Stanfield Wentworth & Co	G Reynolds Agent	Dec.10	3000
25	7¼	Business Paper Endorsed	H B Claflin & Co	Sept.	50000
26		Turnbull Slade & Co	R R Andrews	Nov.16	5000
27					5000
28		,,	Reynolds & Bartlett	Oct.20	5000
29					6000
30		Glidden & Williams	Meader & Swain	,, 26	5000
31					10000
32		Oliver Ames & Sons	,,	Aug.16	5000
33					10000
34		Chicago & Gt Eastern R.R.	Hinkley & Williams Works	Oct.25	5039

EXHIBIT 10

Note Offering List of Blake Bro's. & Co., 1869

LIST OF PAPER PROPOSED FOR DISCOUNT BY

Blake Bro's & Co., Bankers,

No. 28 STATE ST., BOSTON, MASS.,

— AND —

NO. 52 WALL STREET, NEW YORK.

Subject to Chance of Previous Sale.

BOSTON, October 8, 1869.

No.	RATE.	PROMISOR OR ACCEPTOR.		DRAWER OR ENDORSER.	DUE.		AMOUNT.
1	9	Almy & Co.	Acc.	Slade Woolen Co.	Feb.	2	10,000
2	9½	John A. Griswold & Co.	End.	John A. Griswold & Erastus Corning of Albany, N. Y.	"	21	5,000
3		" " "		" "	"	21	10,000
4	10½	William Dwight.		Ind. Cinn. & Lafayette R. R. Co. & H. C. Lord	Dec.	1	10,000
5		" "		" "	"	31	5,000
6	10½	F. Skinner & Co.		John S. Barry & Co.	Dec.	4	10,000
7		" " "		" " "	"	11	10,000
8	10½	Ames Plow Co.	Acc End.	Oliver Ames & Sons, Oakes Ames,	Feb.	8	10,000
9		" "		" "	"	"	5,000
10		" "		" "	"	"	3,000
11		" "		" "	"	"	10,000
12	10½	Hoyt, Spragues & Co.		Atlantic DeLaine Co.	"	4	5,000
13		" "		" " "	"	"	10,000
14	10½	Leland, Allen & Bates,		Methuen Woolen Mills.	"	"	6,000
15		" " "		" "	"	11	4,000
16		" " "		Hyde Park Woolen Co.	"	11	4,000
17		" " "		" " "	"	15	6,000
18	12	Business Notes,	Endorsed.	H. B Claflin & Co. Nov., Dec. &	Jan.		50,000
19	10	N. C. Munson.		Nathan Matthews & Thomas Upham.	Feb.	8	15,000
20		" "		" "	"	8	3,000
21	10	A. G. Farwell & Co.		N. C. Munson.	Dec.	8	15,000
22		" " "		" "	"	23	16,886
23	10½	Samuel G. Reed,		Charles H. Tyler,	Nov.	18	5,100
24	11	Richards & Co.		Charles A. White,	Nov.	20	5,000
25		" "		" "	Dec.	7	5,000
26		" "		" "	"	16	5,000
27	12	Sprague, Colburn & Co.		J Stevens & Co.	Dec.	4	4,000
28		" "		Ontario Mills,	"	2	5,000
29	12	Jenkins, Vaill & Peabody,		James H. Prentice,	Nov.	4	5,000
		PLEASE TELEGRAPH BY		NUMBERS IF WANTED.			

EXHIBIT 11

NOTE OFFERING LIST OF O. M. BOGART & CO., 1872

Geo. M. Bogart & Co.
3 Nassau Street
New York

We offer for discount   March 16 '872

Maker	Drawer	Date	Amount	Rate
1 Mathew Morgan's Sons	Single	May 6	10000	Each 7
2 Morton Bliss & Co	C B Barclay Pt	Aug 28	1018 2	7
3 Spaulding Hunt & Co	C W Searing N Y	July 5	5000	7½
4 Harding Colby & Co	Phoenix Woolen Co	" 5	5000	7½
5 Thomas & Co	Weguman & Co	" 9	4000	7½
6 E L Holbrook & Co	Grafton Mills	" 17	5000	8
7 Spaulding Hunt & Co	Auburn Woolen Co	Aug 12	5000	8
8 Hoyt Splague & Co	City Mill & Co	July 12	5000	8½
9 Amidown Lane & Co	J Stearns	" 18	5000	8½
10 Isaiah McCoy's Sons	Single	" 13	5000	8½
11 Wm Fishing & Co	" July 8 5000	" 8	5000	8½
12 Bliss & Allen	Merllico Co	" 15	2000	8½
13 Pomeroy & Skinner	N Adams Mfg Co	" 23	5200	8½
14 do	M Blackington & Co	June 29	5000	8½
15 William Turnbull & Co	C S Kittredge	July 10	5000	Each 8½
16 W M Huntington & Co	Mill Brook Co	June 27	5000	8½
17 Seth B Hunt & Co	Schaghticoke Co	July 25	5000	8½
18 Woodward Baldwin & Co	Lagato Factory	June 24	5000	8½
19 C H & F D Blake	A H Turner	July 4	5000	8½
20 Clifford Devoe & Co	J McMahon & Co	May 22	10000	8½
21 Chace Sherwell & Co	C Holt & Rice	June 28	5000	8½
22 Geo O Lyle & Co	N Y O Midland R R	" 15	5000	Each 8½
23 Tillinghast Wright & Co	Bogue & Wager	July 10	3300	8½
24 Hoyt Splague & Co	Atlantic Delaine Co	June 17	5000	8½
25 Lindsley & Rees & Co	Single	July 14	5713	9
26 Haight Halsey & Co	"	Aug 12	2640	
27 Gregory & Co I City	End to Dudley & Gregory	July 18	4694	
28 Kingsbury Abbott & Co	Single	June 7	1973	
29 Anneborn & Co	" July 13 — 4950	July 11	4885	
30 Browning King & Co	" Aug 19 — 3684	Aug 18	1919	
31 W C Browning & Co	" 19 — 2409	" 18	3008	
32 Hehle & Heerlein	"	May 16	6320	
33 Peet Sale & Dowling	"	June 28	2792	
34 Eastman Beylon & Brigton	June 17 — 3833	" 24	3209	
35 Mer Britton White Sale Co	End F N Norell	July 10	5000	10
36 J L Spellman & Bro	Ingls May 23 — 1800	May 31	1800	
37 Shortridge & Co	Aug 19 — 1229	Aug 8	1276	
38 David Valentine & Co	" 12	2072	
39 John Mott & Co	June 17 — 2417	" 26	1737	
40 Greene Guerin & Davey	" 12 — 2134	June 6	3216	
41 Carhart Whitford & Co	"	July 18	2060	
42 Chic Goodwin Miller & Co	Aug 18 — 1477	Aug 27	3408	
43 Guttwaite Lewis Miller	"	July 11	1700	
44 Beale Splague & Co	June 17 — 2819	July 21	2164	12
45 Cochran McLean & Co	" 14 — 1591	" 9	1591	
46 Geo W Beale & Co	" 14 — 2730	June 5	2730	
47 Buchholter & Keeler	" 14 — 2034	" 16	1087	
48 Richard Patrick & Co	May 18 — 3377	May 12	2100	
49 United States Match Co	End Giles Wales & Co	Sep 13	2971	Each

EXHIBIT 12

NOTE OFFERING LIST OF W. F. LAWRENCE, 1873

NOTES OFFERED FOR SALE
BY
W. F. LAWRENCE,
BANKER AND NOTE BROKER,

85 (former No., 41) DEVONSHIRE STREET,   BOSTON.

Subject to chance of previous sale. Telegraph numbers wanted.

P. O. Box, 2554.   Nov. 17, 1873

No.	Rate.	PROMISOR.	ENDORSER.	When Due.	Am't.
1	12	F. Shaw & Bro. ....(Boston)	Endorsed	May 8	7900
2	12	Davis Bros. & Co. ....do.	do.	April 22	1727
3	12	James Skinner & Co. ....do.	do.	Mar 4	1937
4	12	Z. Einstein Bros. & Co.....(Boston)	do.	Feb 24	4704
5	12	C. C. Houghton & Co. ...(Worcester)	do.	Mar 24	1962
6	12	Converse & Stanwood......(Boston)	do.	Jan 7	2020
7	12	A. Houghton & Co. ......(Worcester)	do.	Mar 11	2701
8	15	Jenkins, Lane & Sons......(Boston)	do.	Feb 27	7905
9	15	Bay State Shoe & Leather Co. (N. Y.)	do.	Mch 12	2162
10	12	L. Pullam ....(N. Brookfield)	do.	Feb 26	900
11	12	W. E. Schmertz & Co. ...(Pittsburg)	do.	Jan 4	5675
12	12	do. ....do.	do.	Feb 15	5871
13	12	D. Lytle & Co. ....(Cincinnati)	do.	18	2500
14	12	do. ....do.	do.	Jan 24	2500
15	12	do. ....do.	do.	15	2500
16	12	Niles T. Stickney & Co. ....(Oshkosh)	do.	Feb 19	895
17	12	O. A. Childs & Co. ....(Cleveland)	do.	Jan 20	2697
18	12	R. & J. Cummings & Co. ...(Toledo)	do.	7	1590
19	12	Fogg, Houghton & Coolidge..(Boston)	do.	Feb 27	1308
20	15	D. A. Drury & Co. ....(Spencer)	do.	Mar 11	2415
21	12	H. Childs & Co. ....(Pittsburg)	do.	Feb 18	1969
22	12	Pancoast, Sage & Morse...(Rochester)	do.	Dec 30	1186
23	12	Hill, Terry & Mitchell....(Memphis)	do.	Feb 4	3441
24	12	R. E. Bigelow & Co. ....(Paxton)	do.	Mar 13	1267
25	12	E. Jones & Co. ....(Spencer)	do.	Feb 11	2504
26	12	Newell Bros. ....(New York)	do.	Mar 9	2107
27	15	Appleton, Noyes & Co. ...(St. Louis)	do.	May 15	2729
28	15	R. L. White & Co. ....(Louisville)	do.	April 16	1104
29	15	Vinnedge, Jones & Co. ...(Indianap's)	do.	Feb 27	1660
30	15	Currier, Sherwood & Co. ..(New York)	do.	Jan 8	1500
31	13½	Hill & Rowe..............(Boston)	do.	18	1392
32	12	Powers, Gaston & Co. ....(New York)	do.	April 19	919
33	13½	Cook, Nettle & Co. ......(Nashville)	do.	Feb 19	969
34	15	Harvey & Keith. ....(Louisville)	do.	23	1500
35	13½	Bixco & Birnie. ....(Springfield)	do.	April 15	900
36	12	W. H. & S. L. Emery......(Boston)	do.	Jan 27	1753
37	12	Rice, Kendall & Co. ....(Boston)	Wm. Russell & Son	Jan 20	5000
38	15	do.	do.		5000
39	16¼	Webster Woolen Mills. ....(Webster)	Leland, Allen & Bates.	8	4401
40	13½	W. E. Schmertz & Co. ...(Pittsburg)	Bales & Halcom.	April 13	1600
41	18	Wm. C. Berry, Jr. ....(Boston)	T. Emerson Sons.	Mar 10	350
42	18	Shaw, Wheelock & Co. (Auburn, Me.)	Adams, Lowe & Newton.	Feb 19	926
43	18	S. W. & E. Nash. ....(Weymouth)	do.	Mar 20	1650
44	24	M. Harris & Bro. ....(Richmond)	Pulsifer, Rook & Co.	22	800
45	15	Shriver, Rook & Co. .....(Baltimore)	do.	April 22	1729
46	15	A. W. Clapp & Co. ....(Boston)	Endorsed.	7	800
47	15	C. J. Bishop & Co. ....(Boston)	E. G. Gove & Son.	Feb 10	1500
48	15	W. R. Ramsdell. ....(Boston)	E. G. Cook.		1500
49	12	Thomas E. Proctor. ....(Boston)		April 23	2874
50	12	Converse & Stanwood. ......(Boston)		Feb 9	2458
51	12	do. ....do.		16	2458
52	15	Joseph Davis & Co. ....(Lynn)		20	765
53	15	Wood, Prentice & Co. ....(Troy)		21	1066
54	12	Henry Poor & Son. ....(Boston)		Mar 27	2672
55	12	do.		8	2500
56	18	Reed & Clossen. ....(Boston)		31	1001
57	15	C. C. Houghton & Co. ...(Worcester)		Dec 18	2800
58	15	do. ....do.		Dec 18	2800
59	18	Currier, Sherwood & Co. ..(New York)		Jan 5	2200
60	15	Appleton, Noyes & Co. ...(St. Louis)		9	1522
61	18	Vinnedge, Jones & Co. (Indianapolis)		Feb 8	1189
62	18	Brown & Brother ....(Lynn)		April 18	452
63	18	B. E. Paxon & Co. ....(Boston)		Dec 19	892
64	18	C. J. Bishop & Co. ....(Boston)		Feb 4	1820
65	18	do. ....do.		18	1820
66	24	Studwell Bros ....(New York)		Mar 7	475
67	18	Murray, Meade & Co. ....(New York)		Feb 26	868
68	24	Melius, Trask & Ripley...(New York)		Dec 18	1737
69	24	D. Schafer & Co. ....(New York)		29	482
70	24	Walker, Short & Co. ....(Boston)		22	871
71	18	Canedy & Titus ....(N. Adams)		Feb 12	1118
72	18	A. M. Smith & Co. ....(Turner)		Jan 18	460
73	24	Goodwin, Davis & Co. ...(Rochester)		Mar 30	995
74	15	Geo. L. Thayer & Co. ......(Boston)		Mar 13	5098
75	18	Lamereux, Dreas & Co. ..(St. Louis)		April 1	2000
76	24	John A. Smith & Co. ......(Turner)		Dec 23	507
77	24	do. ....do.		Jan 18	502
78	24	Pulsifer, Rook & Co. ......(Auburn)		Dec 26	981
79	24	Henry Damon ....(Boston)		Feb 25	411
80	18	E. & A. H. Batcheller & Co. ..(Boston)		Feb 24	5558
81	18	do. ....do.		Mar 14	4654
82	15	Gates & Kendall ....(Boston)	Endorsed.	Jan 13	1118
83	18	Canedy & Titus ....(N. Adams)		Feb 8	925
84	15	Benedict, Hall & Co. ....(New York)		Feb 19	3871
85	15	Everett, Lane & Co. ......(Boston)	Jenkins, Lane & Son.	Mar 10	1560
86	18	Hathaway Soule ....(New Bedford)		18	500
87	18	J. W. Belcher. ....(Randolph)		Feb 11	820
88	18	E. G. W. Cartwright ....(Haverhill)		Dec 5	574
89	15	Tenney & Co. ....(Methuen)	Bryant & King.	Feb 19	1060
90	21	D. A. Drury & Co. ....(Spencer)		Mar 11	2445
91	18	Adams, Lowe & Newton....(Boston)		April 19	454
92	18	Sudebaher & Hyman....(New York)		Feb 4	1470
93	24	Calvin Rew & Co. ......(Haverhill)		Mar 14	1050
94	18	A. N. Saunders. ....(Boston)		Feb 10	525
95	18	Aaron Claflin & Co. ....(New York)	Claflin & Thayer	Feb 28	5000
96	24	J. H. Alden. ....(Boston)		Mar 4	1593
97	24	J. F. Comstock & Co. ...(St. Louis)		Feb 4	3550
98	15	Gideon Burton & Co.		Mar 11	2167
99	18	C. J. Bishop & Co. ....(Boston)		14	1160
100	15	Franklin Upton & Co........do.		Feb	800

CHAPTER III

THE COMMERCIAL PAPER BUSINESS FROM 1914 TO 1936

IN CHAPTER II an account was given of some of the main developments in the commercial paper business from 1861 to 1914. It was shown that the operations of dealers and the practices of borrowing in the open market and investing surplus funds of banks in outside paper became nation-wide some years before 1913, and it was estimated that by 1914 the volume of paper sold in the market had probably increased to about $2,000,000,000 a year. It was pointed out also that by about 1900 probably all the larger dealers were buying outright a substantial proportion of the open-market obligations they handled, and that the widespread adoption of the practice of outright buying marked the completion of the transition from the early note broker to the commercial paper house of modern times.

During the twenty-two years following the passage of the Federal Reserve Act the commercial paper business continued to follow some of the main trends of development described in Chapter II. Dealers continued to improve their methods of investigating the credit standing of their borrowing customers, and improvements in their methods of selecting the short-term obligations they offered for sale to banks and other buying customers stimulated further growth of the practice of outright buying. For some years after 1913, moreover, the annual volume of paper bought and sold in the market seems to have increased, though probably at no very rapid rate. In 1920, however, the total volume of business handled by dealers began to decline. The decline at first was gradual, and in fact was interrupted temporarily by moderate increases in several of the following years; but within the brief period from 1920 to 1934 total sales by dealers shrank from nearly $2,700,000,000 a year to a figure probably not much in excess of $225,000,000. This unprecedented decline, following a long period of gradual growth in the annual volume of dealers' sales, may be regarded as the most important development in the commercial paper business during the years from 1914 to 1936. Accordingly changes in the total annual volume of sales by dealers, together with the forces which operated to bring these changes about, will be discussed at some length in the present chapter. Certain general effects of these changes on the commercial paper business will be considered next, and then the more important changes in the organizations and methods of operation used by dealers will be indicated. In the remaining pages of this chapter an account will be given of the activities of a committee of the Investment Bankers' Association of America, known as the Commercial Credits Committee, which was organized in 1924 for the purpose of bringing about an improvement in conditions in the commercial paper business.

1. Changes in the Total Volume of Open-Market Paper Handled by Dealers Each Year

By the close of the period considered in the preceding chapter total sales of commercial paper in the open market had probably reached a figure of about $2,000,000,000 a year.[1] During the crisis which followed the outbreak of the World War in 1914 purchases of open-market paper no doubt fell off to a considerable extent. According to such estimates as are available, however, sales by dealers increased again in the years immediately following 1914. Early in 1915 a New York dealer stated that the amount of open-market obligations outstanding "runs somewhere between $800,-000,000 and $1,200,000,000, the higher figure being more likely

---

[1] The president of the National Association of Credit Men stated in 1914 that he had received $750,000,000 as an estimate of the amount of commercial paper "in the market at any one time," and approximately "two and one-half times that amount," or about $1,875,000,000, as an estimate of the total annual sales of such paper (C. E. Meek, address on credit, *Proc. Ky. Bankers' Assoc.*, 1914, p. 53). In 1931 a Boston banker who formerly had been connected with a leading commercial paper house gave about $700,000,000 as an estimate of the average amount of open-market obligations outstanding in 1914. If it is assumed that the average maturity of such obligations was five months, this figure would be equivalent to annual sales of nearly $1,700,000,000.

to be correct." [2] If the average of these two figures may be accepted as approximately accurate, and if the maturity of such paper averaged about five months, total sales by dealers at that time amounted to about $2,400,000,000 a year. During the following year, according to an estimate given by a St. Louis banker, approximately 2,500 borrowing concerns sold a total of $3,000,000,000 of commercial paper in the open market.[3] In 1918 it was estimated that the purchased paper "annually held by the commercial banks of the United States" amounted to more than $4,000,000,000.[4] Both the latter two estimates, however, seem excessive.

For the period from July 1918 to date, figures of the amount of commercial paper outstanding at the end of each month, as reported by leading dealers to the Federal Reserve Bank of New York, are available. Though not complete, they include all but a small part of the total amount of open-market paper outstanding [5] and may be used to arrive at more accurate estimates of total sales by dealers each year than those given above. The figures reported to the Federal Reserve Bank of New York for the seventeen and one-half years ending with December 1935 are given in Table 2 and plotted on Chart III. Estimates of annual sales by dealers during the same period, based on the assumption that the average matu-

[2] H. C. Smith, *The Federal Reserve Regulations as to Commercial Paper and their Application to Existing Methods of Credit* (pamphlet), p. 18.

[3] F. K. Houston, *Commercial Paper — Its Uses and Abuses* (pamphlet), p. 2. In the same year a Chicago banker stated that "the National Banks alone discount nearly 7 billions" of open-market paper "every year" (J. M. Hurst, "Interest on Balances and its Regulation by Open Market Rates," *Proc. Idaho Bankers' Assoc.*, 1916, p. 64). This figure, however, is without doubt considerably exaggerated.

[4] H. G. Moulton, "Commercial Banking and Capital Formation," *Jour. Pol. Econ.*, July 1918, p. 710.

[5] According to dealers in New York and in Boston, the amount of "commercial paper outstanding" reported by commercial paper houses to the Federal Reserve Bank of New York includes (1) all notes which such houses have bought outright and (2) in case they have merely made advances against purchased paper, instead of paying for it in full at time of purchase, such a proportion of this paper as they have already paid for by means of these advances.

In recent years practically all dealers of any importance have reported their "outstandings" to the Bank. About the only dealers who have not been reporting are those whose operations have been confined in the main to their own immediate localities.

TABLE 2

COMMERCIAL PAPER OUTSTANDING, 1918–1935 *

(Millions of Dollars)

	1918	1919	1920	1921	1922	1923	1924	1925	1926	1927	1928	1929	1930	1931	1932	1933	1934	1935
Jan.		934	1,296	909	704 b	807	818	820	654	551	576 c	407	404 g	327	109 k	85	108	171
Feb.		944	1,264	870	718	838	867	820	655	577	567	411	457	315	104 l	84	117	177
Mar.		1,028	1,207	831	760	864	889	813	668	606	570	387	529	311	107 m	72 p	133	182
Apr.		1,049	1,212	796	792	867	871	801	663	599	571	351	553	307	110 n	64	139	173
May		1,056	1,136	779	791	888	852	776	668	582	541 d	304	541	312 i	111	60	142 r	173
June		1,046	1,063	736	795	885	864	759	652	579	503	274	527	298	103 o	73 q	151	159
July	874	1,062	1,032	695	805	854	879	727	655	569	483	266	528	295	100	97	168	164
Aug.	871	1,127	1,038	681	807	830	911	722	638	591	458	267	526	275	108	107	188	177
Sept.	863	1,186	1,064	677	805	803	915	708	612	600	430	265	513	251	110	123	192 s	183
Oct.	838	1,200	1,055 a	667	775	815	925	684	593	611	427	285	485	213 j	113	130	188	180
Nov.	871	1,193	1,038	685	748	799	888	666	566	603	421	315 f	448 h	176	109	133	178	178
Dec.	881	1,186	948	663	722	763	798	621	526	555	383 e	334	357	120	81	109	166	171

a Previous to October 1920 the monthly totals for 30 firms are based on per cent change in totals of 11 known firms.

b 26 firms.	f 22 firms.	j 20 firms.	n 16 firms.	r 12 firms.
c 25 firms.	g 21 firms.	k 19 firms.	o 15 firms.	s 13 firms.
d 24 firms.	h 20 firms.	l 18 firms.	p 14 firms.	
e 23 firms.	i 21 firms.	m 17 firms.	q 13 firms.	

* As at close of business, last day of each month. Figures given are those for paper maturing within seven months, reported as outstanding by leading dealers to the Federal Reserve Bank of New York. Such figures include practically all the open-market commercial paper outstanding. They are published currently in the *Monthly Review* of the Federal Reserve Bank of New York and in the *Federal Reserve Bulletin*.

CHART III *

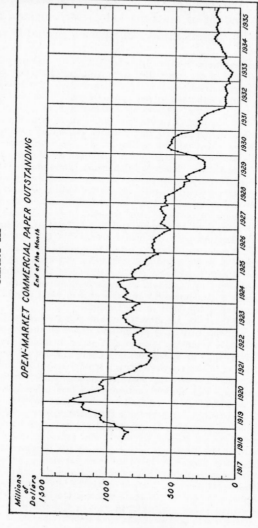

OPEN-MARKET COMMERCIAL PAPER OUTSTANDING

End of the Month

* Based on figures in Table 2.

rity of the paper they handled was five months,[6] are given in Table 3.[7]

As is indicated by these two tables and the accompanying chart, the average amount of open-market paper outstanding and total annual sales by dealers during this period probably reached their

---

[6] Leading dealers interviewed in 1930 and later years gave about five months as the average maturity of the paper they were handling. If it may be assumed that the bulk of the open-market paper sold each year runs for five months, total annual sales by dealers can be estimated by multiplying average "outstandings" for the year in question by 12/5, or 2.4. Figures so obtained can at best be no more than approximate. They are subject to the error involved in assuming that the bulk of the paper handled by dealers has the maturity mentioned and that the average amount of such paper outstanding during any year can be accurately ascertained by averaging the amounts of "outstandings" reported by dealers at the end of each month. Actually, maturities change with changing conditions in the money market and in business in general, and for periods of some length may commonly be either six months or longer or four months or shorter. Moreover, an estimate of the average amount of commercial paper outstanding during any year obtained by averaging the amounts of "outstandings" reported by leading dealers at the end of each month is less than the true figure, because (1) some of the smaller dealers do not report to the Federal Reserve Bank of New York, (2) figures reported to the Bank are those for notes maturing within seven months only, and (3) such figures are simply those of obligations which happen to be outstanding on twelve particular dates — the end of each month — and it is well known that concerns borrowing in the open market ordinarily endeavor to improve the appearance of their balance sheets by reducing to a minimum the amounts of their notes payable outstanding on statement dates, particularly June 30 and December 31.

[7] The figures in this table are lower than some other estimates that are available for certain years of this period. A publication issued by the American Acceptance Council states that the volume of open-market paper outstanding in the years before 1920 "was often as high as $1,800,000,000" (American Acceptance Council, *Facts and Figures Relating to the American Money Market*, p. 29). If the *average* amount of paper outstanding in those years had been as high as $1,800,000,000, total sales by dealers would have been about $4,000,000,000 a year, a figure which seems rather high. In 1922 a Chicago dealer estimated that average "outstandings" of leading dealers for the years 1919–1921 were more than $900,000,000 — which would be the equivalent of sales of more than $2,000,000,000 a year — and that the total volume of paper handled by all houses in 1920 "was probably about $3,000,000,000" (Walter McAvoy, "The Economic Importance of the Commercial Paper House," *Jour. Pol. Econ.*, Feb. 1922, p. 78). About the same time a Boston dealer secured from "six different note brokerage houses" estimates of the annual volume of paper sold by "legitimate brokers who are not afraid to buy the notes they sell." The average was between $2,000,000,000 and $3,000,000,000 (A. P. Brown, "Commercial Paper" — typewritten paper — p. 27). In 1925 a Chicago dealer stated that the total volume of paper sold each year was more than $2,000,000,000 (H. W. Murray, "What Is Commercial Paper?" *Mid-Continent Banker*, Aug. 1925, p. 23). Two years later the house with which this dealer was connected gave about the same figure as an estimate of the amount of open-market paper which banks were buying each year (A. G. Becker and Company, *Commercial Paper* — advertising pamphlet

TABLE 3
ESTIMATES OF AVERAGE AMOUNTS OF COMMERCIAL PAPER OUTSTANDING
AND OF ANNUAL SALES BY DEALERS, 1918–1935
(*Millions of Dollars*)

Year	Estimated Average Amounts of Paper Outstanding *	Estimated Annual Sales by Dealers †
1918 ‡	866	2,078
1919	1,084	2,602
1920	1,113	2,671
1921	749	1,798
1922	768	1,843
1923	834	2,002
1924	873	2,095
1925	743	1,783
1926	629	1,510
1927	585	1,404
1928	494	1,186
1929	322	773
1930	489	1,174
1931	267	641
1932	105	252
1933	95	228
1934	156	374
1935	174	418

* Figures in this column are yearly averages of the "outstandings" reported by leading dealers to the Federal Reserve Bank of New York at the end of each month.

† Figures in this column were obtained by multiplying those in the preceding column by 12/5, or 2.4, on the assumption that the average maturity of promissory notes sold in the open market is about five months.

‡ Estimates for 1918 are based on "outstandings" reported for the last six months of that year.

— p. 6). Foulke has given the following figures as annual sales by dealers during the years 1919–1929:

Year	Annual Sales of Commercial Paper
1919	$3,180,000,000
1920	3,263,000,000
1921	2,196,000,000
1922	2,254,000,000
1923	2,557,000,000
1924	2,683,000,000
1925	2,277,000,000
1926	2,016,000,000
1927	1,873,000,000
1928	1,581,000,000
1929	1,029,000,000

(R. A. Foulke, *The Commercial Paper Market*, p. 19.)

peaks in 1919 and 1920. In the latter year one of the largest houses in the Middle West sold about $500,000,000 of promissory notes for its borrowing customers,[8] and one of the leading dealers in the East probably handled a volume of business equally large. Average "outstandings" and total sales of most other dealers also were probably higher in 1920 than in any other year of this period.[9] Total "outstandings" of leading dealers at the end of January 1920 reached a figure of $1,296,000,000, the highest figure which has been recorded since the Federal Reserve Bank of New York began to collect such data.[10]

In the following month, however — some nine months before direct loans of banks to customers began to show any substantial reduction [11] — the amount of paper outstanding began to decline. The decline continued almost without interruption until January 1922, when a seasonal increase over the figure for the end of the year was again recorded. Total sales by dealers also declined to a considerable extent within this two-year period. During the next three years "outstandings" and total sales increased to some extent. At the end of October 1924 the amount of paper outstanding reached a total of $925,000,000, the highest figure which has been reported since December 1920. In 1925 "outstandings" and esti-

[8] On single days in 1920 this house occasionally sold as many as 200 to 300 different notes, ranging in denomination from $2,500 to $500,000, and sometimes bought and sold as much as $3,000,000 of the paper of a large mail order house — whose account, moreover, was a "split" or "divided" account (i.e., was at the same time being handled also by another dealer, who sold the notes of the concern in question in a different section of the country). The maximum amount of commercial paper issued by any one borrowing customer of this Middle Western dealer, and outstanding on any one date — about $26,000,000 — was presumably reached in the same year.

[9] One house in the Middle West reported that it has sometimes sold as much as $600,000 of open-market paper a day for several consecutive days; another, that it has occasionally sold as much as $1,000,000 of paper on a single day. Presumably the business of both these dealers was most active in 1920. At any rate, sales by the former dealer reached a total of $72,000,000 in 1920, but declined to $57,000,000 in 1925 and still further in later years.

[10] Total "outstandings" at the end of January 1920 would no doubt have been higher had not certain dealers during that month discouraged their customers from borrowing in the open market extensively (Federal Reserve Bank of New York, *Report on Business Conditions*, Jan. 20, 1920, p. 3).

[11] Federal Reserve Bank of New York, *Mo. Rev.*, Jan. 1922, p. 4. In August, September, and October 1921, as well as in April 1922, funds borrowed in the open market were used to a considerable extent to reduce direct loans from banks (*ibid.*, Sept. 1921, p. 2, Nov. 1921, p. 2, and June 1922, p. 3).

mated total sales by dealers began to decline again.[12] The decline continued, with only temporary interruptions of a seasonal character, for approximately five years. By the end of June 1927 the estimated amount of open-market paper outstanding, which five years earlier had been 2 per cent of the total loans and investments of all banks in the United States, fell to 1 per cent of such earning assets.[13] At the end of September 1929 leading dealers reported

[12] Snyder estimated that sixty- to ninety-day open-market commercial paper in 1925 probably constituted "scarcely 1 per cent of the total amount of money loaned in one form or another in the United States," and that loans on open-market paper amounted to "considerably less than 10 per cent of the total of commercial loans" (Carl Snyder, "The Influence of the Interest Rate on the Business Cycle," *Amer. Econ. Rev.*, Dec. 1925, pp. 684, 689). As a matter of fact, only a relatively small proportion of the total amount of paper sold by dealers each year is ordinarily issued with maturities as short as sixty to ninety days; and even if the total amount of open-market paper outstanding be considered, instead of that with maturities of sixty to ninety days only, open-market loans seem to have been relatively even less important in 1925 than Snyder's estimates would indicate. On June 30, 1925, the loans and discounts (including rediscounts), overdrafts, and investments of 28,841 banks (commercial banks, savings banks, loan and trust companies, and private banks) alone amounted to $49,334,105,000 (*Annual Report of the Comptroller of the Currency*, 1926, p. 102). The estimated amount of open-market commercial paper outstanding on the same date — $759,000,000 — was only about 1.5 per cent of the former figure. While figures of "the total of commercial loans" are not available, the loans and discounts (including rediscounts), other than loans secured by real estate, of these same banks amounted at the end of June, 1925, to $31,836,-398,000 (*ibid.*, 1925, p. 104). This total probably included at least $16,000,000,000 of "commercial loans." The $759,000,000 of open-market paper outstanding on the same date was therefore presumably less than 5 per cent of such advances by these banks alone.

[13] This is indicated by the following table:

APPROXIMATE DISTRIBUTION OF LOANS AND INVESTMENTS OF ALL BANKS
IN THE UNITED STATES ON JUNE 30, 1922, AND JUNE 30, 1927
(*Amounts in Millions of Dollars*)

	1922	1927	Increase or Decrease (−)	Percentage Distribution of Total 1922	1927
Total loans and investments ...	40,105	54,372	14,242	100	100
Loans to customers	25,228	33,912	8,659	63	62
Open-market portfolio, total ..	14,877	20,460	5,583	37	38
Investments	12,525	17,217	4,692	31	32
Loans to brokers in New York City	1,328 *	2,275	947	3	4
Acceptances purchased *	229	389	160	1	1
Commercial paper purchased *	795	579	−216	2	1

* Estimated
Source: *Fed. Res. Bull.*, March 1928, p. 169.

"outstandings" of only $265,000,000, the lowest figure recorded up to that time. During the next seven months the figures reported by dealers increased rapidly. The increase, however, proved to be but temporary, and was followed by an equally rapid decline which continued for nearly two years. Both in 1931 and in 1932, for the first two times since 1921, the figures reported by leading dealers at the end of January failed to show an increase from the seasonal low point generally reached at the close of the year. During 1932 "outstandings" fluctuated around a level slightly above $100,-000,000 until December. At the end of that month they fell to $81,000,000, or nearly 20 per cent below the lowest figure previously recorded. The total reported amount of purchased paper held by all Federal Reserve member banks also fell to a new low point on the same date. As recently as September 24, 1930, these banks had held as much as $523,000,000, or 2.1 per cent of their total loans, in the form of promissory notes purchased through dealers; but at the end of 1932 their total holdings of such outside paper amounted only to $93,000,000, or no more than 0.6 per cent of their total loans.[14] Reported "outstandings" declined still further

[14] See Tables 16 and 17.

It may be noted that the amounts of outside paper held by these banks on various call dates in recent years have exceeded the figures of "outstandings" reported to the Federal Reserve Bank of New York for the same dates by leading dealers. This is shown by the following table:

PURCHASED PAPER HELD BY ALL FEDERAL RESERVE MEMBER BANKS ON SELECTED CALL DATES COMPARED WITH "OUTSTANDINGS" REPORTED BY LEADING DEALERS
(Millions of Dollars)

Call Date	Purchased Paper Held by All Federal Reserve Member Banks	"Outstandings" Reported by Leading Dealers
Dec. 31, 1928	390	383
Dec. 31, 1930	366	357
June 30, 1931	384	298
Dec. 31, 1931	140	120
June 30, 1932	122	103
Sept. 30, 1932	115	110
Dec. 31, 1932	93	81
June 30, 1933	87	73
June 30, 1934	200	151
Dec. 31, 1934	232	166
Dec. 31, 1935	272	171

(Figures in this table were taken from Tables 2 and 16.)

As Professor Beckhart has indicated, one reason for discrepancies of the kind

during the spring of 1933. By the end of May they had fallen to $60,000,000, the lowest figure which has been recorded to date, and by the end of June Federal Reserve member banks' holdings of purchased paper had also fallen to the lowest total which has yet been reported, or $87,000,000. In the latter month, however, the downward trend in "outstandings" was interrupted, and figures reported by dealers increased rather steadily thereafter until they reached a total of $192,000,000 at the end of September 1934. During the remaining fifteen months of the period under consideration "outstandings" fluctuated around a level of about $175,-000,000. Estimated annual sales by dealers from 1925 to 1936 followed the same general trend as "outstandings." They declined rather steadily until the latter part of 1929, increased substantially in 1930,[15] declined at a rapid rate in the following two years, fell in 1933 to about $225,000,000 — a volume probably lower than total sales for any year since the Civil War period — increased rapidly in 1934, and in the following year reached a total of about $420,000,000.

---

shown in this table is that banks buy some outside paper from dealers other than those who report their "outstandings" to the Federal Reserve Bank of New York (B. H. Beckhart, *The New York Money Market*, III, 236). Some banks in recent years have bought promissory notes from the smaller, non-reporting dealers, from other banks, or even from the issuing concerns direct, as well as from the larger reporting dealers. Two other reasons for such discrepancies are that only paper maturing within seven months is included in the reported figures and that a number of banks class as purchased commercial paper notes which they buy direct from two or three large finance companies.

[15] The business of at least two of the larger houses, which no doubt benefited to some extent from the fact that by 1930 a number of other houses had discontinued operations in commercial paper, was very active for the first eight months of that year. Toward the close of July 1930 one of these houses sold $3,500,000 of commercial paper on a single day. Total sales of the other house are said to have been about as large for the first eight months of that year as for any corresponding period since its organization. On the other hand, sales of various other dealers were much smaller even in 1930 than in 1925 or any year of the decade preceding. A Boston dealer estimated that the "commercial paper" business of his company for the first six months of 1930 amounted to less than its "collateral loan" business. Another dealer of the same city stated that, whereas in the late 1880's a commercial paper house would have four or five salesmen who spent all their time calling on the fifty-two banks which were then to be found in Boston, as well as other salesmen who called only on country banks in the surrounding territory, in 1930 one salesman alone could in a single day submit to all the banks in Boston all the "names" currently being offered for sale by his company. Another illustration of the decline

2. Reasons for Changes in the Annual Volume of Paper Handled by Dealers

The forces which brought about the changes that have just been indicated in the volume of open-market financing from 1914 to 1936 may now be considered.

It will be recalled that estimated annual sales by dealers reached a figure of approximately $2,000,000,000 a year by the close of the preceding period, declined in 1914, and then increased in the years immediately following until they attained a peak of nearly $2,700,000,000 in 1920.

The decline in the first year of the period considered in this chapter may be accounted for in the main by the recession in business activity which occurred in 1914 and the financial crisis which followed the outbreak of the World War in the same year.[16]

---

in the commercial paper business after 1925 was given by a New York dealer, who stated that, whereas a decade or so earlier he alone had sold $15,000,000 of paper in a single year, in 1930 the entire volume of sales his company was handling was only about half that amount.

Two houses furnished figures of their total sales for some of the years after 1924. Sales of one of these houses were as follows:

Year	Total Sales
1925	$57,000,000
1926	39,000,000
1927	43,000,000
1928	39,000,000
1929	45,000,000
1930	45,000,000 *

(* Estimated about the middle of August on the basis of sales up to that time.)

Sales of the other house are given in the following table:

Year	Sales through Own Offices	Sales through Correspondents	Total Sales
1926	$37,883,600	$6,802,500	$44,686,100
1927	35,743,400	4,775,000	40,518,400
1928	18,747,400	4,382,500	23,129,900
1929	6,557,500	57,500	6,615,000
1930	599,000 *	—	599,000

(* Sales through one of company's offices up to September 1.)

In 1928 this house discontinued the policy of competing actively against other houses for new business, and toward the close of that year it decided to discontinue operations in open-market paper as soon thereafter as it conveniently could. These facts in the main account for the rapid decline in its sales after 1927.

[16] According to Professor Sprague, purchases of commercial paper were reduced considerably during this crisis, "but the market was never completely suspended as

The increase in dealers' sales from 1915 to 1921 resulted largely from the same conditions as those which promoted the growth of open-market financing in earlier years. Business activity was sustained at comparatively high levels, and wholesale commodity prices rose rapidly, during most of this six-year period. Conditions such as these were clearly favorable for an increase in the supply of open-market paper. Borrowing in the market was encouraged also by the comparatively low rates prevailing on commercial paper from 1915 to about the middle of 1917.[17] Even as late as 1919 commercial paper rates were lower than rates charged customers by banks in selected cities, as is shown by a comparison of Tables 1 and 4 and by Chart IV; and the cost of financing through dealers probably did not discourage open-market borrowing to any considerable extent until after the middle of 1920, when the rate on prime paper rose to 8 per cent, or 1 per cent higher than the rate charged customers by banks in selected Northern and Eastern cities.[18] Conditions were also favorable for an increase in the demand for open-market paper during the six years from 1915 to 1921. The safety and liquidity of unsecured promissory notes purchased through dealers were again demonstrated during the financial crisis of 1914,[19] yields on such obligations, as is indicated by an examination of Tables 1 and 5 to 9 and Charts V and VI, compared favorably with those obtainable on bankers' bills,

---

in former crises." Many concerns which customarily borrowed in the open market are said to have resorted to their own banks for loans at that time, partly from necessity, but often because prevailing commercial paper rates were so high that it was advisable to borrow for shorter periods than were customary in the case of open-market loans (O. M. W. Sprague, "The Crisis of 1914 in the United States," *Amer. Ec. Rev.*, Sept. 1915, p. 520).

[17] See Table 1 and Chart II.

[18] See Chart IV.

[19] The cashier of one of the larger New York City banks stated that after July 1, 1914, "when the [New York] stock exchange closed, resulting in call loans as well as collateral time loans being converted into almost fixed investments, our commercial paper proved the most liquid assets we had" (F. K. Houston, *Commercial Paper — Its Uses and Abuses* — pamphlet — p. 4). Cf. the following: "After the closing of the stock exchange, commercial paper purchased from note brokers became the only class of loans which could be reduced [by banks] without bringing pressure to bear upon regular customers. . . . Commercial paper was obviously more liquid than other loans" (Sprague, "The Crisis of 1914 in the United States," *Amer. Ec. Rev.*, Sept. 1915, pp. 514, 520).

TABLE 4

RATES CHARGED CUSTOMERS BY BANKS IN PRINCIPAL CITIES, 1919–1935 *

(*Per Cent*)

	1919	1920	1921	1922	1923	1924	1925	1926	1927	1928	1929	1930	1931	1932	1933	1934	1935
New York City																	
Jan.	5.54	5.93	6.71	5.50	4.82	5.21	4.16	4.64	4.66	4.56	5.74	5.64	4.24	4.71	4.12	3.58	2.83
Feb.	5.36	6.00	6.78	5.48	4.91	5.07	4.43	4.68	4.56	4.44	5.73	5.35	4.31	4.71	4.11	3.43	2.90
Mar.	5.46	6.00	6.70	5.43	4.98	5.06	4.53	4.62	4.56	4.59	5.81	5.22	4.20	4.72	4.88	3.31	2.64
Apr.	5.56	6.09	6.64	5.46	5.32	4.98	4.48	4.62	4.63	4.72	5.85	4.91	4.17	4.69	4.33	3.39	2.61
May	5.43	6.00	6.68	5.06	5.27	4.89	4.38	4.66	4.63	4.97	5.88	4.74	4.11	4.55	4.24	3.42	2.69
June	5.45	6.00	6.43	4.93	5.21	4.64	4.36	4.58	4.60	5.09	5.93	4.59	4.13	4.61	4.10	3.30	2.66
July	5.49	6.43	6.21	5.16	5.29	4.21	4.46	4.38	4.56	5.38	5.88	4.48	4.05	4.42	3.93	3.30	2.61
Aug.	5.49	6.36	6.25	4.66	5.18	4.09	4.36	4.62	4.41	5.56	6.05	4.41	3.97	4.45	3.97	3.33	2.67
Sept.	5.49	6.57	6.11	4.70	5.33	4.20	4.57	4.81	4.44	5.63	6.06	4.29	3.93	4.30	3.79	3.26	2.72
Oct.	5.63	6.57	5.93	4.74	5.37	4.41	4.62	4.85	4.49	5.63	6.08	4.26	4.27	4.35	3.76	3.28	2.72
Nov.	5.56	6.71	5.96	4.82	5.39	4.13	4.61	4.79	4.35	5.56	5.86	4.17	4.67	4.12	3.52	3.22	2.77
Dec.	5.61	6.36	5.68	4.86	5.21	4.29	4.70	4.79	4.50	5.63	5.74	4.16	4.64	4.22	3.48	3.18	2.61
Eight other Northern and Eastern cities																	
Jan.	5.79	5.99	6.99	6.08	5.34	5.53	4.80	5.14	4.99	4.73	5.87	5.88	4.61	5.07	4.89	4.65	4.08
Feb.	5.67	6.15	6.95	5.89	5.38	5.38	4.79	5.11	4.98	4.76	5.86	5.66	4.63	5.13	4.84	4.49	4.02
Mar.	5.66	6.32	6.94	5.77	5.52	5.37	4.89	5.15	4.88	4.81	5.91	5.47	4.62	5.14	5.39	4.52	4.05
Apr.	5.72	6.68	6.99	5.46	5.49	5.31	4.92	5.17	4.90	4.91	6.00	5.22	4.57	5.10	5.09	4.52	3.99
May	5.59	6.79	6.94	5.43	5.54	5.26	4.95	5.07	4.95	5.04	6.09	5.13	4.55	5.14	4.99	4.39	3.88
June	5.70	6.98	6.97	5.43	5.45	5.12	4.95	4.87	4.93	5.36	6.02	5.06	4.49	5.13	4.97	4.30	3.78
July	5.75	7.01	6.93	5.31	5.47	5.09	4.90	4.92	4.90	5.57	6.08	4.81	4.48	5.05	4.82	4.15	3.87
Aug.	5.75	7.01	6.59	5.27	5.64	4.80	4.98	4.91	4.87	5.59	6.11	4.79	4.47	5.12	4.68	4.12	3.79

TABLE 4 (Continued)

	1919	1920	1921	1922	1923	1924	1925	1926	1927	1928	1929	1930	1931	1932	1933	1934	1935
Sept.	5.76	6.98	6.62	5.12	5.59	4.87	5.04	5.08	4.77	5.80	6.24	4.74	4.48	5.03	4.65	4.11	3.75
Oct.	5.76	7.00	6.65	5.20	5.57	4.87	5.16	5.15	4.79	5.80	6.25	4.75	4.62	4.96	4.51	4.13	3.75
Nov.	5.77	7.00	6.32	5.38	5.51	4.80	5.20	5.07	4.82	5.82	6.12	4.66	4.87	4.88	4.54	4.08	3.63
Dec.	5.86	6.97	6.19	5.44	5.48	4.87	5.17	5.09	4.76	5.91	5.94	4.68	4.91	4.88	4.59	3.98	3.67
Twenty-seven Southern and Western cities																	
Jan.	6.11	6.16	7.10	6.56	5.90	6.02	5.57	5.56	5.72	5.53	5.94	6.12	5.50	5.61	5.60	5.40	4.95
Feb.	6.03	6.26	7.11	6.46	5.91	5.91	5.55	5.65	5.71	5.53	5.96	6.04	5.43	5.61	5.56	5.39	4.84
Mar.	6.02	6.43	7.13	6.35	5.83	5.89	5.61	5.62	5.65	5.54	6.04	5.98	5.40	5.64	5.66	5.40	4.85
Apr.	6.01	6.47	7.09	6.22	5.94	5.89	5.61	5.65	5.57	5.54	6.07	5.86	5.36	5.63	5.68	5.34	4.80
May	6.00	6.56	7.06	6.23	5.92	5.79	5.58	5.61	5.59	5.56	6.10	5.75	5.26	5.64	5.66	5.28	4.79
June	5.91	6.88	7.05	6.13	5.91	5.69	5.59	5.54	5.54	5.67	6.16	5.69	5.34	5.62	5.62	5.19	4.76
July	5.98	7.00	7.04	6.04	5.96	5.63	5.59	5.54	5.52	5.77	6.17	5.62	5.30	5.63	5.54	5.07	4.58
Aug.	5.94	6.99	7.03	6.02	5.98	5.57	5.60	5.56	5.53	5.80	6.22	5.57	5.28	5.68	5.53	5.05	4.63
Sept.	5.93	7.07	6.96	5.94	5.94	5.55	5.55	5.60	5.61	5.82	6.27	5.54	5.32	5.63	5.55	5.04	4.51
Oct.	5.96	7.04	6.85	5.89	5.95	5.47	5.53	5.66	5.56	5.87	6.29	5.53	5.38	5.56	5.50	5.05	4.55
Nov.	5.95	7.08	6.74	5.94	5.99	5.53	5.55	5.67	5.56	5.90	6.29	5.49	5.53	5.55	5.42	4.93	4.51
Dec.	6.10	7.07	6.67	5.90	5.99	5.53	5.61	5.68	5.60	5.91	6.20	5.42	5.56	5.60	5.43	4.92	4.55

* Figures given in this table are weighted averages of prevailing rates charged by reporting Federal Reserve member banks to their own customers. All averages are computed from rates reported for 3 types of customers' loans — commercial loans and demand and time loans on securities. "The method of computing the averages takes into account (a) the relative importance of each of these 3 types of loans and (b) the relative importance of each reporting bank, as measured by total loans. In the 2 group averages the average rate for each city included is weighted according to the importance of that city in the group, as measured by the loans of all banks in the city." Figures included in this table were taken from *Annual Report of the Federal Reserve Board*, 1931, p. 82, and 1934, p. 137; and *Fed. Res. Bull.*, Feb. 1936, p. 98.

CHART IV *

RATES ON PRIME COMMERCIAL PAPER IN NEW YORK
COMPARED WITH
RATES CHARGED CUSTOMERS BY BANKS IN PRINCIPAL CITIES

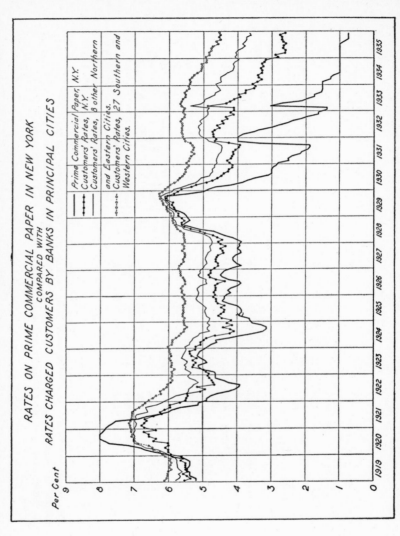

* Based on figures in Tables 1 and 4.

TABLE 5
Rates on Prime Ninety-day Bankers' Acceptances, 1919–1935 *
(Per Cent)

Year	Jan.	Feb.	Mar.	Apr.	May	June	July	Aug.	Sept.	Oct.	Nov.	Dec.	Avg.
1919	4.25	4.25	4.25	4.25	4.25	4.25	4.26	4.28	4.25	4.25	4.52	4.95	4.33
1920	5.37	5.50	6.00	6.00	6.13	6.25	6.25	6.25	6.25	6.25	6.23	6.25	6.06
1921	5.94	5.97	5.98	5.67	5.69	5.59	5.25	5.00	4.94	4.49	4.27	4.16	5.25
1922	3.95	4.00	3.73	3.32	3.18	3.07	3.00	3.00	3.12	3.72	4.00	4.00	3.51
1923	3.98	3.99	4.00	4.14	4.13	4.13	4.13	4.13	4.13	4.13	4.13	4.13	4.10
1924	4.09	4.07	4.04	3.95	3.29	2.45	2.01	2.10	2.33	2.21	2.37	2.89	2.98
1925	3.00	3.08	3.25	3.14	3.17	3.25	3.25	3.27	3.50	3.50	3.50	3.50	3.28
1926	3.67	3.63	3.63	3.42	3.20	3.32	3.38	3.57	3.88	3.88	3.79	3.83	3.60
1927	3.69	3.69	3.63	3.63	3.63	3.63	3.50	3.13	3.13	3.25	3.25	3.25	3.45
1928	3.36	3.51	3.52	3.81	3.94	4.05	4.32	4.62	4.50	4.50	4.50	4.50	4.09
1929	4.84	5.15	5.34	5.46	5.48	5.49	5.16	5.13	5.13	5.01	4.23	3.90	5.03
1930	3.96	3.77	3.07	2.91	2.48	2.09	1.88	1.88	1.88	1.88	1.88	1.88	2.46
1931	1.58	1.39	1.50	1.43	1.01	0.88	0.88	0.88	0.98	2.47	2.99	3.00	1.58
1932	2.85	2.78	2.51	1.39	0.92	0.86	0.75	0.75	0.75	0.59	0.50	0.39	1.25
1933	0.33	0.47	2.49	0.81	0.50	0.38	0.48	0.45	0.25	0.25	0.39	0.62	0.62
1934	0.50	0.50	0.31	0.20	0.19	0.19	0.19	0.19	0.19	0.17	0.13	0.13	0.24
1935	0.13	0.13	0.13	0.13	0.13	0.13	0.13	0.13	0.13	0.13	0.13	0.13	0.13

* For the period 1919–1934, figures included in this table are monthly averages of daily quotations in New York; for 1935, prevailing rates. Quotations for the period 1919–1934 were taken from *Annual Report of the Federal Reserve Board, 1927*, pp. 95–96, 1931, p. 79, and 1934, p. 134; for 1935, from *Fed. Res. Bull.*, Feb. 1936, p. 98.

TABLE 6

RATES ON CALL LOANS, NEW YORK STOCK EXCHANGE, 1866–1935 *

(Per Cent)

Year	Jan.	Feb.	Mar.	Apr.	May	June	July	Aug.	Sept.	Oct.	Nov.	Dec.	Avg.
1866	5.50	6.25	5.60	5.50	5.20	5.00	4.80	3.70	4.25	4.40	6.00	6.50	5.22
1867	7.00	5.85	6.00	5.90	4.50	6.15	4.50	4.25	5.60	11.45	6.50	9.00	6.39
1868	5.50	4.70	16.70	17.40	5.70	3.80	4.00	3.70	4.60	7.35	35.00	20.55	10.75
1869	18.40	6.60	7.00	6.75	6.75	30.10	6.90	6.40	7.00	5.65	6.30	9.60	9.79
1870	6.15	5.50	5.40	5.50	4.70	4.40	5.00	5.20	5.50	5.10	5.40	8.40	6.35
1871	15.40	4.50	4.50	5.70	4.10	3.00	3.00	2.55	4.85	7.05	6.60	8.15	6.62
1872	14.10	14.90	16.40	36.25	7.35	4.50	3.60	4.15	35.20	9.30	12.30	58.65	18.06
1873	10.55	18.00	21.35	87.50	6.10	4.70	3.70	4.60	72.05	31.20	13.50	10.75	23.67
1874	5.50	4.10	4.00	4.20	3.15	2.75	2.65	2.50	2.70	2.95	3.00	3.80	3.44
1875	2.75	2.50	3.95	3.55	2.75	2.35	2.65	2.05	2.45	3.30	4.20	5.10	3.13
1876	5.25	3.60	3.85	3.70	3.20	2.60	2.05	1.85	1.95	3.10	3.95	5.05	3.35
1877	6.45	3.30	2.95	3.70	2.45	1.75	2.20	3.25	4.35	7.15	5.40	8.65	4.30
1878	7.05	4.75	4.90	6.45	3.40	2.60	1.75	1.80	2.30	5.05	3.80	4.50	4.03
1879	2.60	3.05	5.95	4.40	3.80	3.30	2.95	9.20	12.55	40.10	45.80	10.30	12.00
1880	6.20	4.65	15.25	16.15	4.05	3.00	2.50	2.65	2.50	2.85	22.00	11.10	7.74
1881	4.81	50.12	17.15	4.44	3.30	3.19	3.44	15.60	7.97	13.55	8.12	18.28	12.50
1882	8.56	9.47	4.51	5.39	3.00	3.56	3.00	3.95	7.87	6.80	10.75	4.62	5.96
1883	4.50	4.12	10.87	6.68	3.55	2.00	2.10	2.62	2.44	2.70	2.00	2.25	3.82
1884	1.90	1.87	1.75	2.10	163.4	4.00	1.90	1.75	1.80	1.94	1.44	2.25	15.51
1885	1.18	1.44	1.30	1.37	1.44	1.25	1.31	1.50	1.55	2.12	3.44	2.75	1.72
1886	2.12	2.06	2.65	2.37	2.87	3.35	2.25	6.05	6.37	5.06	5.90	28.69	5.81
1887	4.18	3.55	5.05	6.12	5.20	33.26	1.75	5.15	5.12	4.19	4.60	5.00	7.18
1888	3.50	2.69	2.75	2.62	1.80	1.50	1.40	1.62	2.81	2.60	2.56	4.12	2.50
1889	3.30	2.31	3.06	3.70	2.44	3.00	3.55	3.87	4.81	9.60	7.25	9.87	4.73

TABLE 6 (*Continued*)

Year	Jan.	Feb.	Mar.	Apr.	May	June	July	Aug.	Sept.	Oct.	Nov.	Dec.	Avg.
1890	8.75	3.87	4.50	4.25	4.80	4.75	4.75	10.10	6.75	4.75	6.80	5.00	5.75
1891	3.90	2.88	2.87	3.25	4.20	3.25	2.37	2.00	4.13	4.60	4.37	2.94	3.39
1892	2.40	2.00	2.00	2.00	1.50	1.31	1.85	1.69	3.88	5.40	5.31	6.95	3.02
1893	4.00	3.00	8.50	5.30	3.88	5.75	9.20	5.75	4.87	2.37	1.75	1.23	4.63
1894	1.03	1.00	1.07	1.13	1.09	1.02	1.00	1.00	1.00	1.00	1.00	1.37	1.06
1895	1.19	1.62	2.10	2.19	1.34	1.17	1.47	1.05	1.56	3.65	2.02	4.56	1.99
1896	5.12	3.95	3.50	3.13	2.55	1.94	2.22	4.10	5.69	9.80	6.25	1.95	4.18
1897	1.78	1.62	1.63	1.56	1.40	1.19	1.20	1.25	1.62	2.60	1.81	2.92	1.73
1898	2.50	1.78	1.62	2.85	2.09	1.25	1.25	1.56	3.47	2.25	2.06	2.38	2.09
1899	2.72	2.47	4.10	5.12	3.75	2.62	4.47	3.31	5.72	7.55	8.00	10.10	4.99
1900	4.50	2.37	3.60	3.06	2.03	1.73	1.52	1.32	1.61	3.34	4.95	5.06	2.93
1901	3.37	1.97	2.27	4.13	6.50	4.31	4.75	2.45	4.34	3.38	4.10	6.25	3.99
1902	4.47	2.37	3.94	4.63	5.85	2.84	3.69	3.60	10.00	8.90	4.87	6.81	5.16
1903	5.75	2.87	5.50	5.55	2.45	2.55	3.20	2.03	2.22	2.70	5.19	5.50	3.79
1904	2.34	1.81	1.78	1.42	1.63	1.15	1.05	0.89	1.41	2.03	2.63	3.20	1.78
1905	2.22	2.25	1.20	3.25	2.47	2.45	2.28	2.00	3.32	4.63	8.37	14.20	4.05
1906	9.87	4.31	4.90	9.50	4.19	3.40	3.16	4.00	9.37	4.81	7.30	9.50	6.19
1907	6.94	3.88	6.10	2.37	2.36	3.12	4.94	3.05	4.00	9.25	19.80	14.60	6.70
1908	4.75	1.81	1.91	1.66	1.70	1.53	1.28	1.06	1.31	1.45	1.75	2.90	1.93
1909	1.81	2.25	1.84	1.92	1.84	1.88	1.82	2.12	2.52	4.05	4.59	5.00	2.64
1910	4.69	2.77	2.82	3.54	3.63	2.78	2.60	1.53	1.84	2.93	3.50	3.28	2.99
1911	3.44	2.34	2.34	2.33	2.28	2.38	2.38	2.34	2.30	2.28	2.50	4.05	2.58
1912	2.50	2.22	2.43	3.16	2.75	2.75	2.91	2.88	4.59	5.22	6.43	6.25	3.67
1913	3.53	3.31	4.07	3.56	2.77	2.37	2.18	2.32	2.90	3.31	4.25	4.50	3.26
1914	3.18	1.88	1.91	1.84	1.83	1.84	2.41	6.50	7.00	6.80	5.81	3.60	3.72

TABLE 6 (*Continued*)

Year	Jan.	Feb.	Mar.	Apr.	May	June	July	Aug.	Sept.	Oct.	Nov.	Dec.	Avg.
1915	2.35	1.97	1.97	2.13	2.00	1.84	1.83	1.88	1.91	1.95	1.97	1.98	1.98
1916	1.90	1.88	2.03	2.08	2.19	2.88	3.10	2.25	2.75	2.63	2.69	4.48	2.57
1917	2.03	2.31	2.25	2.41	2.84	4.50	3.50	2.88	4.48	3.66	3.88	5.20	3.33
1918	4.44	4.94	5.15	3.81	4.69	5.02	5.75	5.80	6.00	6.00	5.78	5.45	5.24
1919	4.87	5.02	5.05	5.36	5.34	6.30	6.45	5.30	5.62	7.45	10.43	8.06	6.27
1920	8.61	9.38	8.13	7.43	7.10	7.47	8.39	7.26	7.07	7.79	7.78	7.00	7.78
1921	6.72	7.27	6.83	6.54	6.78	5.98	5.58	5.56	5.12	5.23	4.97	5.14	5.98
1922	4.52	4.90	4.22	3.97	3.90	3.72	3.86	3.75	4.34	4.73	4.89	4.65	4.29
1923	4.32	4.82	5.14	4.87	4.70	5.00	5.06	4.97	4.93	4.75	4.80	4.86	4.85
1924	4.39	4.33	4.04	4.21	3.38	2.25	2.10	2.00	2.07	2.32	2.42	3.49	3.08
1925	3.32	3.60	3.97	3.86	3.82	3.97	4.09	4.19	4.62	4.87	4.75	5.32	4.20
1926	4.33	4.85	4.55	4.06	3.81	4.15	4.27	4.52	5.02	4.75	4.56	5.16	4.50
1927	4.32	4.03	4.13	4.18	4.26	4.33	4.05	3.68	3.83	3.90	3.60	4.38	4.06
1928	4.24	4.38	4.47	5.08	5.70	6.21	6.05	6.87	7.26	6.98	6.67	8.60	6.05
1929	7.05	7.06	9.10	8.89	8.91	7.70	9.23	8.23	8.50	6.43	5.44	4.83	7.61
1930	4.64	4.32	3.69	4.00	3.12	2.62	2.20	2.21	2.19	2.00	2.00	2.23	2.94
1931	1.57	1.50	1.55	1.52	1.45	1.50	1.50	1.50	1.50	2.10	2.50	2.70	1.74
1932	2.65	2.50	2.50	2.50	2.50	2.50	2.08	2.00	2.00	1.35	1.00	1.00	2.05
1933	1.00	1.00	3.32	1.37	1.00	1.00	1.00	0.98	0.75	0.75	0.75	0.94	1.15
1934	1.00	1.00	1.00	1.00	1.00	1.00	1.00	1.00	1.00	1.00	1.00	1.00	1.00
1935	1.00	1.00	1.00	0.64	0.25	0.25	0.25	0.25	0.25	0.29	0.75	0.75	0.56

* Figures for the period 1866–1889 are averages of the high and low rates for each week; those for later years, averages of daily renewal rates. Data included in this table were taken from Standard Statistics Company, *Base Book, Stand. Stat. Bull.*, Jan. 1932, p. 42, and *Stat. Bull.*, April 1933, p. 9; *Annual Report of the Federal Reserve Board*, 1927, pp. 95–96, 1931, p. 79, and 1934, p. 134; and *Fed. Res. Bull.*, Feb. 1936, p. 98.

TABLE 7

Rates on Sixty- to Ninety-Day Time Loans, New York Stock Exchange, 1890-1935 *

(Per Cent)

Year	Jan.	Feb.	Mar.	Apr.	May	June	July	Aug.	Sept.	Oct.	Nov.	Dec.	Avg
1890	4.69	4.63	5.05	4.88	5.40	4.56	4.75	5.60	6.00	6.00	6.00	6.00	5.30
1891	5.16	4.38	4.63	4.25	5.35	4.38	4.22	5.25	5.47	5.18	4.69	4.32	4.77
1892	3.38	2.91	3.44	2.85	2.32	2.44	2.80	2.75	4.38	5.20	5.31	5.33	3.76
1893	4.81	4.00	6.00	5.80	5.81	5.38	6.60	6.60	5.90	4.81	3.47	2.40	5.13
1894	2.35	2.47	2.25	2.31	1.81	1.75	1.75	2.13	2.20	1.94	2.25	2.38	2.13
1895	2.25	3.13	3.35	3.42	2.38	1.88	2.16	2.81	2.63	2.93	2.50	4.13	2.80
1896	6.00	5.30	3.75	3.88	3.00	2.94	3.44	5.80	6.00	7.10	4.53	2.95	4.56
1897	2.44	2.31	2.66	2.50	2.25	2.13	1.95	2.47	2.94	3.15	2.75	3.30	2.57
1898	2.81	2.69	4.47	5.40	3.63	2.63	2.50	2.69	3.63	2.63	2.75	2.98	3.23
1899	2.75	2.88	3.95	3.81	3.17	3.00	3.60	4.22	5.15	5.17	5.75	6.00	4.12
1900	5.00	4.06	4.55	3.50	3.00	3.05	3.06	3.35	3.69	4.97	4.44	4.78	3.95
1901	3.91	3.38	3.15	4.00	4.45	3.56	4.31	4.24	5.06	4.69	4.65	5.28	4.22
1902	4.58	4.00	4.00	4.21	5.08	4.29	4.53	4.65	5.94	6.00	5.97	6.00	4.94
1903	4.94	4.54	5.63	5.21	3.95	4.19	4.45	4.91	4.94	5.02	5.81	5.59	4.93
1904	4.00	3.58	3.08	2.60	2.63	2.19	2.21	2.16	2.93	3.32	3.69	3.68	3.01
1905	2.88	3.00	3.22	3.40	3.16	2.99	2.99	3.05	4.05	4.74	5.83	6.18	3.42
1906	5.32	4.93	5.32	5.74	4.90	4.37	4.30	5.18	7.16	5.97	7.23	8.22	5.72
1907	5.82	5.23	6.16	4.30	3.83	4.21	4.80	5.99	5.57	6.39	13.60	10.55	6.37
1908	5.83	4.21	3.49	2.79	2.69	2.21	2.13	2.30	2.41	2.84	3.21	3.16	3.11
1909	2.57	2.66	2.55	2.42	2.48	2.46	2.23	3.02	3.49	4.53	4.91	4.68	3.17
1910	4.30	3.60	3.80	3.99	3.93	3.33	3.62	3.37	4.21	4.59	4.76	3.91	3.95
1911	3.36	3.06	2.76	2.67	2.68	2.73	2.77	3.04	3.30	3.31	3.52	4.10	3.11
1912	2.88	2.70	3.25	3.49	3.13	3.12	3.40	3.84	5.44	5.65	5.94	5.95	4.07
1913	4.09	4.50	5.41	4.30	3.86	4.04	4.34	4.14	4.45	4.83	4.94	5.09	4.50

TABLE 7 (*Continued*)

Year	Jan.	Feb.	Mar.	Apr.	May	June	July	Aug.	Sept.	Oct.	Nov.	Dec.	Avg.
1914	3.65	2.88	2.93	2.72	2.52	2.38	2.79	7.63	7.00	6.50	5.20	3.88	4.17
1915	3.12	2.76	2.73	2.77	2.77	2.81	2.59	2.68	2.62	2.59	2.60	2.46	2.71
1916	2.69	2.69	2.76	2.82	2.81	3.32	3.88	3.07	3.16	3.24	3.12	4.24	3.15
1917	3.15	3.71	4.21	3.82	4.45	4.74	4.30	4.39	5.47	5.54	5.39	5.51	4.57
1918	5.61	5.72	6.00	6.00	6.00	5.78	5.69	5.90	6.00	6.00	6.00	5.72	5.87
1919	5.18	5.32	5.50	5.79	5.58	5.79	6.00	5.95	5.88	6.15	6.50	6.60	5.85
1920	7.25	8.13	8.19	8.10	8.25	8.06	8.28	8.72	8.41	7.89	7.85	7.30	8.04
1921	6.60	6.81	6.75	6.68	6.60	6.75	6.20	6.00	5.65	5.38	5.19	5.13	6.14
1922	4.75	4.85	4.74	4.41	4.19	4.13	4.30	4.22	4.44	4.71	4.96	4.93	4.55
1923	4.66	4.85	5.23	5.31	5.11	4.88	5.13	5.25	5.44	5.31	4.99	4.94	5.09
1924	4.75	4.72	4.67	4.31	3.94	3.26	2.75	2.52	2.81	2.68	3.21	3.34	3.58
1925	3.64	3.66	4.05	3.85	3.63	3.80	3.94	4.38	4.45	4.78	4.93	4.99	4.18
1926	4.77	4.63	4.70	4.19	4.03	4.13	4.38	4.67	4.93	4.95	4.64	4.69	4.56
1927	4.47	4.38	4.40	4.36	4.31	4.44	4.34	3.98	4.11	4.25	4.05	4.15	4.27
1928	4.34	4.51	4.61	4.93	5.19	5.73	5.94	6.30	6.97	7.09	6.88	7.63	5.84
1929	7.65	7.69	8.00	8.60	8.70	8.16	7.90	8.88	8.94	7.88	5.44	4.83	7.72
1930	4.70	4.66	4.16	4.05	3.41	2.88	2.68	2.50	2.44	2.38	2.16	2.28	3.19
1931	1.91	1.69	1.88	1.88	1.56	1.38	1.40	1.44	1.65	1.03	3.44	3.40	2.07
1932	3.56	3.63	3.18	2.44	1.59	1.50	1.44	1.38	1.28	1.03	0.53	0.50	1.84
1933	0.50	0.66	2.80	1.19	0.88	0.88	1.11	1.05	0.62	0.63	0.77	1.01	1.01
1934	1.00	0.88	0.88	0.88	0.88	0.88	0.88	0.88	0.88	0.88	0.88	0.88	0.89
1935	0.88	0.88	0.88	0.61	0.27	0.25	0.25	0.25	0.25	0.31	1.00	1.00	0.57

* Figures given are averages of the weekly range of rates on loans secured by mixed collateral. Quotations included in this table were taken from Standard Statistics Company, *Base Book*, *Stand. Stat. Bull.*, Jan. 1932, p. 43, *Stat. Bull.*, April 1934, p. 6, and *Statistics*, Jan. 1936, p. 8.

TABLE 8

YIELDS ON LIBERTY AND TREASURY BONDS, 1919–1935 *

(Per Cent)

Year	Jan.	Feb.	Mar.	Apr.	May	June	July	Aug.	Sept.	Oct.	Nov.	Dec.	Avg.
1919	4.67	4.75	4.77	4.78	4.72	4.74	4.78	4.83	4.78	4.77	4.88	4.96	4.79
1920	4.98	5.09	5.14	5.35	5.65	5.59	5.63	5.73	5.63	5.36	5.54	5.76	5.45
1921	5.48	5.55	5.52	5.48	5.49	5.49	5.47	5.40	5.28	4.98	4.73	4.54	5.37
1922	4.54	4.58	4.44	4.30	4.27	4.25	4.18	4.18	4.22	4.33	4.43	4.42	4.35
1923	4.41	4.41	4.49	4.51	4.48	4.44	4.43	4.43	4.45	4.50	4.44	4.41	4.45
1924	4.32	4.29	4.29	4.24	4.15	4.01	3.94	3.92	3.95	3.93	3.98	4.05	4.09
1925	4.04	4.02	4.02	3.96	3.93	3.90	3.95	3.98	3.98	4.02	4.04	4.04	3.99
1926	4.04	4.01	3.98	3.94	3.93	3.90	3.93	3.95	3.96	3.95	3.91	3.84	3.95
1927	3.60	3.58	3.48	3.47	3.44	3.47	3.48	3.45	3.44	3.43	3.39	3.34	3.46
1928	3.35	3.36	3.30	3.32	3.35	3.40	3.50	3.56	3.54	3.55	3.48	3.53	3.44
1929	3.59	3.66	3.76	3.67	3.67	3.71	3.68	3.72	3.70	3.67	3.45	3.46	3.65
1930	3.51	3.50	3.40	3.46	3.41	3.37	3.37	3.38	3.37	3.34	3.32	3.34	3.40
1931	3.33	3.40	3.39	3.38	3.31	3.30	3.32	3.34	3.42	3.71	3.69	3.92	3.46
1932	4.27	4.11	3.92	3.74	3.77	3.78	3.65	3.57	3.54	3.54	3.55	3.48	3.74
1933	3.19	3.29	3.44	3.43	3.31	3.22	3.20	3.21	3.20	3.22	3.46	3.53	3.31
1934	3.50	3.32	3.21	3.12	3.01	2.94	2.85	2.99	3.20	3.08	3.05	2.97	3.10
1935	2.83	2.73	2.69	2.64	2.61	2.61	2.59	2.66	2.78	2.77	2.73	2.70	2.70

* Figures given are averages of daily rates. For the period 1919–1926 the yield is calculated on Liberty bonds (3 issues — 2d, 3d, and 4th 4¼%) only. Beginning with 1927, Liberty bonds are excluded, and for the 6 years ending with 1932 the average yield is calculated on 3 issues of Treasury bonds to their last redemption dates. The Treasury bond issues used were the 3¾%, 4%, and 4¼%, maturing in 1956, 1954, and 1952, for the period January 1927–March 1928; and for the period April 1928–December 1932, the 3⅜%, 3¾%, and 4%, the last redemption dates of which are 1947, 1956, and 1954. Figures for the years 1933–1935 are averages, computed by the Treasury Department, of yields of all outstanding Treasury bonds except those due or callable within 8 years. In computing the latter averages "the yield used at each date for each bond callable before maturity is the lower of two computed yield figures, the one based upon redemption at the earliest call date and the other based upon redemption at maturity." For bonds selling above par and callable at par before maturity, "yields computed on the basis of redemption at the first call date are the ones that are used, while for bonds selling below par yields to maturity are used."

Data included in this table were taken from Standard Statistics Company, *Base Book, Stand. Stat. Bull.*, Jan. 1932, p. 45, and *Stat. Bull.*, April 1933, p. 9; *Annual Report of the Federal Reserve Board*, 1927, pp. 95–96, 1931, p. 79, and 1934, p. 185; and *Fed. Res. Bull.*, June 1934, p. 322, and Feb. 1936, p. 99.

TABLE 9

STANDARD STATISTICS COMPANY'S INDEX OF HIGH-GRADE BOND YIELDS, 1900–1935 *

(Per Cent)

Year	Jan.	Feb.	Mar.	Apr.	May	June	July	Aug.	Sept.	Oct.	Nov.	Dec.	Avg.
1900	4.16	4.15	4.13	4.12	4.14	4.15	4.16	4.16	4.17	4.17	4.14	4.10	4.15
1901	4.10	4.09	4.06	4.05	4.06	4.04	4.06	4.08	4.07	4.08	4.07	4.08	4.07
1902	4.05	4.05	4.05	4.01	4.02	4.03	4.04	4.06	4.07	4.09	4.11	4.11	4.06
1903	4.12	4.11	4.14	4.17	4.17	4.21	4.26	4.32	4.33	4.32	4.35	4.33	4.24
1904	4.32	4.31	4.33	4.28	4.28	4.25	4.22	4.20	4.19	4.15	4.16	4.12	4.23
1905	4.08	4.06	4.06	4.07	4.07	4.07	4.06	4.06	4.05	4.06	4.07	4.06	4.06
1906	4.07	4.08	4.11	4.12	4.15	4.16	4.19	4.23	4.25	4.24	4.24	4.26	4.18
1907	4.26	4.30	4.34	4.36	4.38	4.45	4.47	4.55	4.59	4.68	4.87	4.83	4.51
1908	4.75	4.69	4.70	4.65	4.59	4.56	4.55	4.50	4.47	4.45	4.40	4.34	4.55
1909	4.34	4.32	4.34	4.32	4.32	4.32	4.32	4.32	4.33	4.34	4.35	4.36	4.33
1910	4.35	4.37	4.38	4.42	4.44	4.47	4.49	4.50	4.48	4.46	4.46	4.45	4.44
1911	4.43	4.43	4.43	4.43	4.40	4.41	4.41	4.43	4.45	4.45	4.45	4.44	4.43
1912	4.44	4.42	4.43	4.45	4.44	4.44	4.44	4.45	4.46	4.48	4.51	4.51	4.46
1913	4.51	4.52	4.55	4.60	4.64	4.69	4.72	4.70	4.68	4.69	4.70	4.72	4.64
1914	4.64	4.58	4.56	4.57	4.57	4.54	4.58	....	Exchange		Closed	....	4.58
1915	4.68	4.67	4.68	4.65	4.67	4.70	4.71	4.71	4.71	4.66	4.57	4.55	4.66
1916	4.53	4.52	4.53	4.54	4.55	4.55	4.56	4.56	4.54	4.50	4.48	4.49	4.53
1917	4.45	4.51	4.54	4.63	4.72	4.77	4.81	4.85	4.96	5.01	5.10	5.19	4.80
1918	5.19	5.16	5.20	5.28	5.25	5.27	5.28	5.31	5.35	5.30	5.08	5.08	5.23
1919	5.14	5.14	5.18	5.20	5.17	5.17	5.20	5.30	5.32	5.28	5.39	5.48	5.25
1920	5.50	5.64	5.65	5.81	6.00	6.10	6.11	6.06	5.95	5.81	5.86	6.03	5.88
1921	5.80	5.88	5.91	5.90	5.91	6.00	5.97	5.85	5.76	5.69	5.50	5.29	5.79
1922	5.17	5.13	5.07	4.97	4.94	4.93	4.87	4.81	4.77	4.82	4.90	4.87	4.94
1923	4.86	4.89	4.97	5.00	4.98	4.98	5.01	4.99	5.02	5.02	5.01	5.01	4.98
1924	4.95	4.95	4.96	4.95	4.90	4.84	4.80	4.80	4.78	4.77	4.76	4.78	4.85

TABLE 9 (*Continued*)

Year	Jan.	Feb.	Mar.	Apr.	May	June	July	Aug.	Sept.	Oct.	Nov.	Dec.	Avg.
1925	4.78	4.76	4.76	4.72	4.67	4.66	4.69	4.72	4.72	4.73	4.74	4.70	4.72
1926	4.66	4.63	4.63	4.61	4.58	4.58	4.60	4.59	4.60	4.60	4.56	4.55	4.60
1927	4.54	4.53	4.51	4.47	4.46	4.51	4.51	4.48	4.45	4.43	4.42	4.40	4.47
1928	4.38	4.38	4.37	4.38	4.42	4.50	4.54	4.59	4.57	4.57	4.55	4.59	4.49
1929	4.60	4.65	4.69	4.69	4.69	4.73	4.73	4.74	4.76	4.73	4.70	4.63	4.69
1930	4.64	4.65	4.56	4.55	4.54	4.52	4.49	4.43	4.41	4.41	4.46	4.55	4.52
1931	4.43	4.44	4.41	4.43	4.43	4.45	4.44	4.50	4.70	5.12	5.14	5.76	4.69
1932	5.77	5.82	5.62	5.93	6.34	6.64	6.42	5.57	5.35	5.50	5.68	5.75	5.87
1933	5.59	5.73	6.25	6.38	5.78	5.37	5.15	5.12	5.28	5.39	5.72	5.63	5.62
1934	5.25	4.90	4.74	4.61	4.56	4.47	4.45	4.55	4.63	4.51	4.48	4.40	4.63
1935	4.32	4.32	4.41	4.34	4.32	4.26	4.13	4.13	4.20	4.28	4.18	4.11	4.25

* Figures given are arithmetic averages, based on the means of monthly high and low prices, of the yields to maturity of 60 high-grade bonds — 15 industrial, 15 railroad, 15 public utility, and 15 municipal. "Beginning April 30, 1930, the average yield is computed from Wednesday's closing prices, the monthly index consisting of an average of the four or five weekly indexes for the month." Data included in this table were taken from Standard Statistics Company, *Base Book*, *Stand. Stat. Bull.*, Jan. 1932, p. 125, *Stat. Bull.*, April 1934, pp. 27–29, and *Statistics*, Jan. 1936, pp. 29–30.

New York Stock Exchange call and time loans, and United States government and other high-grade bonds,[20] and more and more bankers became familiar with these advantages of outside paper as an investment for their secondary reserves.

After 1913 both the supply of open-market paper and the demand therefor were affected by a new factor — the operations of the Federal Reserve banking system. It is of course impossible to isolate the effects of this new factor, but in the writer's opinion the operations of the Reserve system also promoted, at least indirectly, the growth of open-market financing from 1915 to about 1921.

The direct effects of the new banking system on the supply of commercial paper seem to be more difficult to determine than its influence on the demand for notes handled by dealers. Presumably it affected the supply of open-market obligations in the main through its influence in the development of an acceptance market in the United States and its effects on short-term money rates other than rates on acceptances.

Section 13 of the Federal Reserve Act authorized member banks to accept bills of exchange, and the Federal Reserve system has from the beginning fostered the growth of an acceptance market in this country. This policy has probably resulted in some substitution of acceptance financing for borrowing through commercial paper houses, and therefore in some reduction in the supply of notes which dealers would otherwise have offered for sale.[21] In

[20] Commercial paper is purchased on a discount basis, and the price paid for it is a net price, without any deductions for brokers' commissions or other charges. Consequently the yields on such paper, as compared with those on all the alternative investments for banks' funds mentioned in the text, except bankers' bills (and any time loans on which interest was deducted in advance), were really more favorable than Charts V and VI would indicate.

According to a St. Louis dealer, "a large host of country banks learned to buy" commercial paper "in the years 1918, 1919, and 1920, when rates were 7% and 8%" (James McCluney, "Distribution of Commercial Paper" — typewritten paper — p. 2). Rates on *prime* paper, however, did not reach 7 and 8 per cent until 1920.

[21] In this connection see statement (b) of the Federal Reserve Bank of Dallas in *Operation of the National and Federal Reserve Banking Systems* (Hearings before a Subcommittee of the Committee on Banking and Currency, U. S. Senate, 71st Congress, 3d Session, pursuant to Sen. Res. 71), Part 6, p. 861; and L. E. Clark, *Central Banking under the Federal Reserve System*, p. 378.

PRIME BANKERS' ACCEPTANCES AND CALL AND TIME LOANS

K

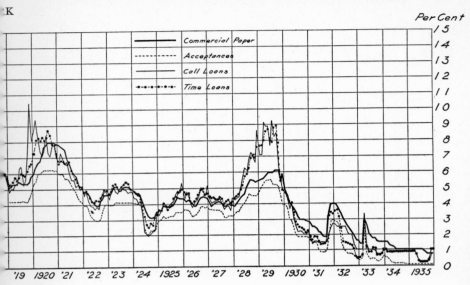

*

DE CORPORATION AND MUNICIPAL BOND YIELDS AND YIELDS
ASURY BONDS

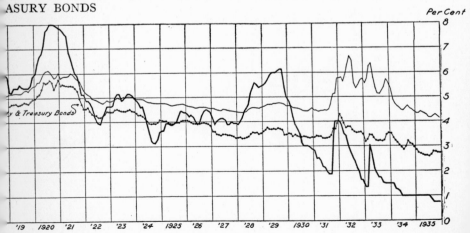

RATES ON PRIME COMMERCIAL PAPER COMPARED WITH RATES O[

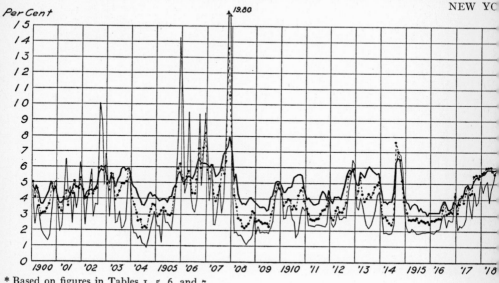

Per Cent

* Based on figures in Tables 1, 5, 6, and 7.

CHART V

RATES ON PRIME COMMERCIAL PAPER COMPARED WITH HIGH–GRA

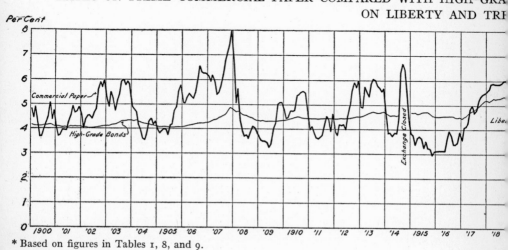

Per Cent

* Based on figures in Tables 1, 8, and 9.

the main, however, acceptances are used for financing transactions of a different character from those commonly financed through promissory notes. Hence the Reserve system's policy of promoting the development of the American acceptance market has probably had no important direct effect in restricting the supply of commercial paper.[22]

It is probable also that the new banking system has had no very important influence on the supply of such paper through its effects on short-term money rates other than those on acceptances. Four such effects attributed to the Reserve system are that it has operated to diminish the spread between rates on sixty- to ninety-day and those on four- to six-months' commercial paper;[23] to reduce seasonal fluctuations in commercial paper rates;[24] to bring about a decline in rates on such paper relative to other open-market rates;[25] and to reduce the spread between rates charged by banks in different sections of the country on direct loans to customers.[26] Of these four effects, the first two probably have had but little influence on the total annual volume of dealers' sales. The diminution in the spread between rates on sixty- to ninety-day notes and those on instruments with maturities of four to six months would lower the relative cost of borrowing for longer periods, and the reduction in seasonal fluctuations in commercial

[22] This matter is discussed further on pp. 154, 157, 164.

As late as 1921 a number of houses dealing in commercial paper were dealing in acceptances also ("Dealing in Acceptances," *Fed. Res. Bull.*, Oct. 1921, p. 1169). Hence any decline in their commercial paper business which may have resulted from the growth of acceptance financing was probably offset to some extent by an increase in the volume of acceptances they handled.

[23] W. R. Burgess, *The Reserve Banks and the Money Market*, 1st ed., pp. 281–285.

[24] B. H. Beckhart, *The New York Money Market*, III, 248; B. H. Beckhart, J. G. Smith, and W. A. Brown, *The New York Money Market*, IV, 517–518. See also the charts, *ibid.*, pp. 512, 524, and 528.

[25] Burgess, *op. cit.*, p. 281, and "Steadier Interest Rates under the Federal Reserve System," *A.B.A. Jour.*, July 1925, p. 13; W. W. Riefler, *Money Rates and Money Markets in the United States*, p. 48.

[26] Burgess, *The Reserve Banks and the Money Market*, 1st ed., pp. 287–288. For a somewhat different conclusion, so far as the period 1919–1930 is concerned, see C. O. Hardy, *Credit Policies of the Federal Reserve System*, pp. 301–303.

Professor Beckhart has pointed out that the spread between the rates in question had begun to grow narrower even before the establishment of the Reserve system (Beckhart, *op. cit.*, p. 247).

paper rates would tend to make the cost of borrowing in the open market more nearly uniform throughout the year; but probably neither of these two effects would of itself lead to any considerable increase in the annual volume of open-market financing.[27] The third effect would tend to encourage borrowing through commercial paper houses, as opposed to any competitive methods of financing subject to the influence in question,[28] and so to increase the supply of dealers' offerings, but the decline in commercial paper rates would at the same time make such offerings less attractive to banks and therefore tend to reduce the demand for open-market paper. The last of the four effects mentioned above has probably had some influence in reducing the supply of open-market paper, since it has tended to reduce the cost of borrowing direct from banks in certain localities as compared with that of obtaining funds indirectly through dealers. This influence would counteract that of a decline in commercial paper rates relative to other open-market rates. Hence it seems safe to conclude that the establishment of the new banking system had no important influence, through any direct effects it may have had on the supply of commercial paper, in bringing about the growth in the annual volume of dealers' sales from 1915 to 1921. Any important effect it may have had in increasing the supply of notes offered for sale by dealers seems

[27] The reduction in seasonal fluctuations in commercial paper rates, however, did have an effect on dealers' profits. According to dealers in New York and Chicago, commercial paper houses used to make a speculative profit from buying their customers' notes late in the fall, after rates had risen, and selling them in January, after rates had fallen. After 1914, as seasonal fluctuations in rates declined, opportunities for making such speculative gains became less common.

[28] The "other open-market rates" in which Burgess holds that the Federal Reserve system has brought about a decline, relative to rates on open-market commercial paper, are rates on New York Stock Exchange call and sixty- to ninety-day time loans. Probably Riefler also meant rates on stock exchange call and time loans by "other open-market rates," though he does not specify what he would include under the latter term. With the exception of acceptance financing, issuing notes direct to the purchasers thereof, and selling secured notes through dealers who specialize in handling collateral loans, raising capital for purchasing or carrying securities through stock exchange call or time loans is about the only method of short-term open-market financing which competes directly with borrowing through commercial paper houses; and it competes with the latter method of financing only to the extent that commercial paper houses handle the "collateral loan" paper mentioned below in Chap. V, § 2.

rather to have been the indirect result of its influence in increasing the demand for outside paper by banks.

That the new banking system did bring about such an increase in demand, and thereby promote the growth of open-market financing during the years immediately following 1914, there can be little question. In making commercial paper with a maturity of not more than ninety days eligible for rediscount by the Federal Reserve banks for their member banks, Section 13 of the Federal Reserve Act in effect created a broader and more continuous market for notes handled by dealers and thus gave them a greater degree of liquidity than they had possessed at any previous time.[29] The Federal Reserve Board and the Reserve banks, moreover, have promoted a more widespread use of financial statements [30] and the development of more careful methods of credit investigation both by banks and by dealers, and this policy has resulted in an improvement in the quality of paper offered for sale by dealers. Finally, the reduction of the legal reserve requirements provided for under Section 19 of the Federal Reserve Act released for investment funds which a large number of banks, particularly country banks, had previously held idle as reserves or kept as balances

[29] In making commercial paper, but not loans secured by stocks and bonds, eligible for rediscount, the Federal Reserve Act gave the former an advantage over collateral loans (other than call loans) as an investment for banks' funds. At the same time, however, in authorizing member banks to accept bills of exchange the Act made available for banks a form of investment even safer and more liquid than promissory notes handled by dealers. Comparative risks and yields considered, prime bankers' bills are in my opinion a less advantageous form of investment for banks' funds than prime commercial paper. Nevertheless the availability of the former has to some extent restricted the demand for promissory notes offered for sale by dealers since 1914.

It may be noted that the market for commercial paper would have been made even broader had the Federal Reserve banks been authorized not only to rediscount such paper for their member banks but also to purchase promissory notes in the open market. Since they were not authorized to buy such obligations in the market, and neither dealers nor banking institutions customarily repurchase any considerable amount of promissory notes which banks or other buyers have obtained through dealers, the market for commercial paper has remained essentially a "one-way" market.

[30] The policy of the Federal Reserve Board and the Federal Reserve banks with respect to the requirement of financial statements is summarized in S. E. Harris, *Twenty Years of Federal Reserve Policy*, I, 273–274. See also Hardy, *op. cit.*, pp. 266–269.

with larger correspondent institutions. Thus the Reserve banking system has operated to increase the demand for open-market promissory notes, both by enhancing the attractiveness of such obligations as an investment for banks' funds and by increasing the supply of funds available for investment in outside paper; and the increase in demand resulting from the new banking system was undoubtedly a factor of some importance in bringing about the increase in open-market financing from 1915 to about 1921.[31]

Before the close of 1920 the trend which the annual volume of such financing had been following for some six years was rather sharply reversed. After reaching a peak in January 1920, commercial paper "outstandings" began to decline during the following month, and within two years shrank nearly 50 per cent. Sales by dealers probably began to decline a few months after "outstandings," though estimated total sales — largely, no doubt, as

---

[31] The probable effects of the establishment of the Federal Reserve banking system on the commercial paper business were discussed in three articles published early in 1914. Professor Sprague expressed the opinion that in the future a solvent borrower would feel more certain that his paper could always be marketed by his "note broker," and that banks would purchase a greater amount of open-market obligations than in the past, since they would prefer to use purchased paper for rediscounting purposes rather than the obligations of their own customers (O. M. W. Sprague, "The Federal Reserve Act of 1913," *Quar. Jour. Econ.*, Feb. 1914, pp. 245, 248, and "Commercial Paper and the Federal Reserve Banks," *Jour. Pol. Econ.*, May 1914, p. 443). A Chicago dealer predicted that city banks which previously had bought large amounts of promissory notes through dealers would in the future have "little or no surplus funds" to invest in such obligations, but that the decreased demand of these banks would be more than offset by increased purchases of commercial paper by country banks (R. C. Schaffner, "The Relation of the New Currency Act to the Work of Commercial Paper Houses," *Jour. Pol. Econ.*, April 1914, pp. 359–364). The expectation that country banks would increase their purchases of outside paper after 1913 was confirmed by the experience of a dealer in St. Louis (James McCluney, "Distribution of Commercial Paper" — typewritten paper — p. 2). It is doubtful, however, that annual purchases of such paper by city banks declined to any great extent between 1914 and 1921. The Chicago dealer mentioned just above predicted also that the Federal Reserve Act would probably "open a new field for the commercial paper house — namely, that of dealing in bank rediscounts" (Schaffner, *op. cit.*, p. 364). While it is true, as Schaffner says, that dealing in notes previously discounted by banks for their own customers would merely offer "another opportunity for the broker to exercise his function of acting as a medium between borrower and lender," probably none of the larger commercial paper houses have engaged in operations of this character. About as late as 1925, however, a few small dealers in the South were buying customers' notes from local banks and selling these obligations to other banks in the South or in other sections of the country.

a result of unusual activity in the commercial paper market during the earlier months of the year — actually increased about $70,-000,000 in 1920. In the following year estimated total sales decreased nearly 33 per cent. Both "outstandings" and annual sales increased to some extent from 1922 to 1925, but declined more or less steadily from 1925 to the latter part of 1929. "Outstandings" increased rapidly thereafter until May 1930 and then declined with about equal rapidity to the beginning of 1932. They continued to decline, though more slowly, from January 1932 to the end of May 1933, when they fell to $60,000,000, the lowest figure which has yet been reported. After May 1933 they increased rather steadily until, at the end of September of the following year, they reached a total of $192,000,000. During the remainder of 1934 and throughout 1935 they fluctuated within the rather narrow range of $159,000,000 and $188,000,000. Estimated annual sales by dealers increased substantially in 1930, declined rapidly in the next two years, fell in 1933 to about $225,000,000 — a volume probably smaller than the corresponding figure for any year since 1865 — increased at a rapid rate in 1934, and rose in the following year to a total of about $420,000,000. Thus within the short space of fourteen years the annual volume of open-market financing reached its peak, reversed its upward trend, and then declined to a figure probably lower than that for any year since the Civil War period.

This unprecedented decline in the volume of open-market financing resulted mainly from forces which operated to restrict the supply of commercial paper, and only to a lesser extent from those which tended to limit the demand for such paper as an investment. The influence of some of these forces will be considered next, and then some of the factors which accounted for such increases in dealers' sales and "outstandings" as occurred from 1922 to 1925 and in later years of the period considered in this chapter will be indicated.

The supply of commercial paper declined more or less steadily from about the middle of 1920 to about June 1933, and remained comparatively small thereafter to the close of 1935, largely because many concerns which had a credit standing strong enough to permit their borrowing in the open market required decreasing amounts of short-term accommodation during this period; and because, in order to obtain substantial proportions of such accommodation as they required, such concerns resorted to other methods of financing than borrowing through dealers.

For the decline in the amounts of short-term credit which these concerns required during this period, a number of reasons may be given.

In the first place, business activity was at a low level during the depression of the early 1920's, the recessions in 1924 and the latter part of 1927, and the depression which began in the latter part of 1929. Trading and manufacturing concerns obviously need less working capital in periods such as these, and accordingly reduce their short-term borrowings. Declining business activity was undoubtedly an important factor in bringing about the rapid decline in the figures reported by dealers in 1920 and 1921, and again in 1930 and 1931, as well as the still further reduction in "outstandings" from January 1932 to June 1933.

Secondly, reduced business activity during the years mentioned just above was accompanied by falling prices. From June 1920 to the end of 1921 the Bureau of Labor Statistics' index number of wholesale commodity prices fell from 167 to 93. During the next eight years it never rose above 105, and from the beginning of 1930 to March 1933 it dropped from 93 to 60, a figure 64 per cent below that for June 1920. Under such conditions, concerns borrowing in the open market clearly required reduced amounts of working capital, including that obtained through dealers, to handle a given physical volume of business.

In the third place, during the years following 1920 the practice of hand-to-mouth buying became more common — a development which was aided by improvements in railroad transportation services. As a result of the precipitous decline in prices which began about the middle of 1920, many manufacturing and mercantile concerns suffered heavy inventory losses; and, in order to minimize the risks of such losses in the future, as well as losses from style changes, these and other concerns endeavored thereafter to reduce the size of their inventories. The adoption of this policy of hand-to-mouth buying increased the marketing and handling expenses of many companies, but it undoubtedly enabled a number of concerns to reduce the amounts of their open-market borrowing for the purpose of financing their current operations.[32]

A final reason why many concerns of the size and standing required for borrowing in the open market needed decreasing amounts of short-term credit during this period is that they strengthened their current position to an unusual extent in the years following 1921.[33] Many corporations followed dividend policies which enabled them to reinvest in their own undertakings substantial proportions of their large net earnings during this period. Others took advantage of unusually favorable conditions

[32] For a discussion of hand-to-mouth buying, see L. S. Lyon, *Hand-to-Mouth Buying; Recent Economic Changes in the United States*, I, 343–361; and H. R. Tosdal, "Hand-to-Mouth Buying," *Harv. Bus. Rev.*, April 1933, pp. 299–306.

[33] The following figures, taken from a "composite balance sheet" of 433 leading American industrial corporations, indicate the strong current position of a large group of industrial concerns as of the close of each year from 1927 to 1933:

($000,000's omitted)

	1927	1928	1929	1930	1931	1932
Cash and equivalent	3,135	3,799	3,658	3,645	3,578	3,361
Total current assets	10,803	11,924	12,659	11,733	10,250	8,946
Total current liabilities	2,168	2,450	2,685	2,108	1,587	1,378
Net working capital	8,635	9,474	9,974	9,625	8,663	7,568

(Figures taken from Standard Statistics Company, *Standard Earnings Bull.*, July 19, 1933, p. 3. See also Beckhart, *op. cit.*, p. 169; F. A. Bradford, "Cash Burdened Corporations," *A.B.A. Jour.*, Jan. 1932, pp. 465–466; Lauchlin Currie, "The Decline of the Commercial Loan," *Quar. Jour. Econ.*, Aug. 1931, pp. 699–706; Hardy, *op. cit.*, pp. 269–271; "Corporation Balance Sheets, End of 1928, Show Improvement," *C. and F. Chron.*, June 1, 1929, p. 3591; and *Recent Economic Changes in the United States*, II, 681–683.)

Boston dealers gave the writer the following two examples of the strong current position in recent years of corporations which formerly borrowed large amounts of funds in the open market: A cordage company, which during the World War period used to have as much as $13,000,000 of commercial paper outstanding at a time, stopped borrowing in the market by about the end of 1928, began to place loans in the call money market about the same time, and toward the close of 1930 had $2,000,000 in cash. A tobacco company, which during the years 1918–1921 occasionally had as much as $20,000,000 of open-market paper outstanding at one time, had more than that amount in cash and government bonds about the beginning of 1931.

in the security markets and issued large amounts of long-term securities — in some cases with the assistance of houses through which they had previously been issuing promissory notes for sale in the open market. As is indicated by Table 10, which gives figures of new capital flotations of selected groups of enterprises for the fifteen years ending with 1935, the volume of such new financing was particularly heavy during the years immediately preceding 1930. In 1929 these concerns issued new stock alone in an amount almost equal to the exceptionally large volume of their total security issues for the preceding year. By following such financial policies as these, a number of companies were able to liquidate their short-term notes payable entirely or to fund them into obligations with longer maturities.[34] Some concerns even became embarrassed with surplus liquid resources, and found it expedient in 1928 and 1929 to lend in the security markets at high rates on call funds which they had but a short time before obtained on unusually favorable terms in these very markets. Brokers' loans made by reporting Federal Reserve member banks in New York City "for account of others" increased to a very considerable extent

[34] The increase in the volume of long-term financing during the years preceding 1930 was promoted not only by favorable conditions in the security markets but also by such developments as the following: improvements in methods of production involving the use of increasing amounts of fixed capital; the spread of large-scale enterprise in the fields of production and merchandising; and reduction by a number of concerns of seasonal peaks in their operations (*Recent Economic Changes in the United States*, II, 683). Still another factor was responsible for at least some part of the increase in the volume of such financing from 1922 to about 1930. This was the policy, followed by a number of business concerns, of replacing short-term advances from banks with long-term securities, in order to avoid embarrassment of the kind experienced in 1920 and 1921 as a result of inability to meet maturing bank loans (Hardy, *op. cit.*, p. 270). (See also Currie, *op. cit.*, pp. 703–707.)

Long-term financing is mentioned as one of the factors bringing about the decline in the volume of open-market borrowing in 1927 and the years immediately preceding in the *Monthly Review* of the New York Federal Reserve Bank (Aug. 1926, pp. 3–4; Sept. 1927, p. 67). See also G. G. Munn, "New Problems of Investing Bank Funds," *Bankers' Mag.*, Jan. 1929, pp. 16–17, and "The Trend toward Long Term Investments," *ibid.*, Feb. 1929, pp. 182–183.

As an instance of the replacement of open-market borrowing by longer-term financing, a Boston dealer reported that a company manufacturing cotton and woolen textiles, which some years ago used to have as much as $19,000,000 of its commercial paper outstanding at one time, retired all its open-market obligations about the middle of 1926 with the proceeds of an issue of five-year notes.

TABLE 10

New Capital Flotations of "Other Industrial and Manufacturing" and "Miscellaneous" Enterprises in the United States, 1921-1935 *

Years Ending December 31	Long-Term Bonds and Notes	Short-Term Bonds and Notes	Stocks	Total Corporate Securities	Per Cent of Total		
					Long-Term Bonds and Notes	Short-Term Bonds and Notes	Stocks
1921	$ 393,146,700	$ 21,592,166	$ 48,574,500	$ 463,313,366	85	5	10
1922	498,687,200	6,600,000	136,232,102	641,519,302	78	1	21
1923	347,523,500	12,685,500	287,569,580	647,778,580	54	2	44
1924	288,153,900	53,141,800	183,654,223	524,949,923	55	10	35
1925	482,985,000	56,808,750	465,649,593	1,005,443,343	48	6	46
1926	663,283,000	91,457,195	399,439,923	1,154,180,118	58	7	35
1927	1,075,451,200	83,697,000	538,084,096	1,697,232,296	64	4	32
1928	842,661,000	44,217,000	1,284,885,464	2,171,763,464	39	2	59
1929	560,761,339	60,820,000	2,167,059,782	2,788,641,121	20	2	78
1930	336,436,910	115,475,000	359,386,217	811,298,127	42	14	44
1931	119,392,000	80,433,000	46,819,262	246,644,262	48	33	19
1932	2,525,000	12,710,500	11,861,200	27,096,700	9	47	44
1933	1,725,000	5,175,000	136,494,072	143,394,072	1	4	95
1934	2,908,000	7,008,000	33,177,399	43,093,399	7	16	77
1935	247,103,250	10,730,000	88,427,798	346,261,048	71	3	26

* Figures of new corporate issues given in this table include comparatively small amounts of Canadian and/or foreign securities for all years except 1932 and 1935. They were taken from the *Commercial and Financial Chronicle*, Jan. 19, 1929, pp. 316-317, Jan. 18, 1930, p. 366, Jan. 14, 1933, p. 229, and Jan. 11, 1936, p. 193. The table includes figures for two classes of concerns only — "other industrial and manufacturing" and "miscellaneous" enterprises — since presumably such concerns are more likely to borrow in the open market than most enterprises included in the other ten classifications used by the *Chronicle*.

during these two years, as is shown by Table 11;[35] and at least some part of the rapidly rising total of such loans represented investments of corporations which, far from requiring short-term credit accommodation to finance their own operations, became lenders in the short-term money market themselves.[36]

The factors just considered brought about a reduction in the supply of commercial paper through limiting the demand for short-term credit in general. The supply of such paper was further restricted through the competition of alternative methods of financing with borrowing through dealers. These alternative methods of financing included direct borrowing from banks, acceptance financing, and financing through discount or finance companies.

Of these other methods of financing, direct borrowing from commercial banks was the most important. Numerous consolidations of smaller banks into larger organizations took place during the years following 1920, and branch and group banking systems were organized or expanded in various sections of the country. These larger organizations, with increased resources, were able in many cases to furnish all the credit accommodation which their customers required. After 1920, however, many borrowing concerns required decreasing amounts of short-term credit; and consequently banks throughout the country began to compete more actively with dealers, as well as with one another, in supplying the reduced accommodation required by such concerns. The competition of banks with dealers was perhaps most effective in such

---

[35] Brokers' loans "for account of others" are discussed in Beckhart, *op. cit.*, Chap. VI, and L. H. Haney, L. S. Logan, and H. S. Gavens, *Brokers' Loans*, Chap. VIII.

The decline in this class of loans after October 1931 resulted mainly from an amendment to the constitution of the New York Clearing House Association. This amendment, which became effective on Nov. 16, 1931, provided that no member of the Association (and no non-member clearing through a member) should make or attend to the service of any loan secured by stocks, bonds, and/or acceptances for the account of any lender other than a bank, banker, or trust company (*Fed. Res. Bull.*, Dec. 1931, p. 657). About a year and a half later Federal Reserve member banks were prohibited by Section 11 of the Banking Act of 1933 from acting as agents in making brokers' loans for non-banking organizations.

[36] In this connection see *C. and F. Chron.*, Mar. 10, 1934, pp. 1659–1660.

TABLE 11

BROKERS' LOANS MADE BY REPORTING FEDERAL RESERVE MEMBER BANKS
IN NEW YORK CITY, 1926–1935 *

(Millions of Dollars)

Date	Total	For Own Account	For Account of Out-of-Town Banks †	For Account of Others
1926 — January	3,126	1,259	1,281	585
February	3,119	1,182	1,329	608
March	2,800	1,051	1,173	576
April	2,467	905	1,035	528
May	2,452	913	998	541
June	2,517	973	944	600
July	2,607	960	1,000	646
August	2,720	948	1,073	699
September	2,783	974	1,128	682
October	2,698	866	1,106	726
November	2,615	819	1,048	748
December	2,698	887	1,045	766
1927 — January	2,778	933	1,104	741
February	2,733	841	1,127	765
March	2,816	901	1,091	824
April	2,866	929	1,131	806
May	2,933	936	1,191	805
June	3,115	1,077	1,180	858
July	3,096	1,032	1,188	877
August	3,181	1,048	1,225	908
September	3,261	1,061	1,285	916
October	3,392	1,103	1,326	962
November	3,441	1,175	1,276	990
December	3,621	1,282	1,354	985
1928 — January	3,802	1,342	1,470	990
February	3,784	1,167	1,500	1,117
March	3,761	1,064	1,450	1,247
April	4,062	1,193	1,616	1,252
May	4,414	1,272	1,628	1,514
June	4,360	1,048	1,568	1,744
July	4,232	929	1,543	1,760
August	4,239	835	1,522	1,881
September	4,417	887	1,607	1,924
October	4,701	933	1,720	2,048
November	5,102	1,105	1,749	2,248
December	5,193	1,114	1,760	2,319
1929 — January	5,408	1,173	1,801	2,434
February	5,555	1,082	1,817	2,656
March	5,679	1,071	1,729	2,879
April	5,477	934	1,649	2,893
May	5,491	861	1,665	2,965
June	5,383	895	1,548	2,940

TABLE 11 (*Continued*)

Date	Total	For Own Account	For Account of Out-of-Town Banks †	For Account of Others
July	5,841	1,198	1,651	2,992
August	6,069	993	1,786	3,290
September	6,540	1,048	1,850	3,642
October	6,498	1,257	1,639	3,602
November	4,023	1,090	779	2,154
December	3,391	888	713	1,790
1930 — January	3,351	844	862	1,644
February	3,459	942	971	1,546
March	3,741	1,210	1,100	1,430
April	4,115	1,557	1,183	1,376
May	4,030	1,665	1,062	1,302
June	3,825	1,831	917	1,078
July	3,224	1,631	747	846
August	3,150	1,659	692	798
September	3,174	1,676	750	748
October	2,769	1,675	537	557
November	2,249	1,357	435	458
December	2,013	1,266	339	407
1931 — January	1,798	1,132	329	337
February	1,759	1,186	290	283
March	1,858	1,335	264	259
April	1,824	1,322	271	231
May	1,644	1,279	191	174
June	1,464	1,110	181	173
July	1,434	1,062	204	168
August	1,342	951	226	165
September	1,268	943	174	151
October	921	674	90	157
November	802	588	124	90
December	655	554	88	13
1932 — January	544	473	65	6
February	495	417	72	6
March	531	432	94	5
April	500	423	70	7
May	436	385	44	7
June	377	342	29	6
July	335	309	18	8
August	344	319	17	8
September	409	385	19	5
October	411	389	16	6
November	354	336	12	6
December	393	377	12	4

TABLE 11 (*Continued*)

Date	Total	For Own Account	For Account of Out-of-Town Banks †	For Account of Others
1933 — January	380	365	11	4
February	433	416	10	7
March	398	373	18	7
April	399	374	21	4
May	578	555	17	6
June	755	712	36	7
July	919	806	105	8
August	877	747	122	8
September	847	741	98	8
October	779	663	111	5
November	722	610	106	6
December	759	632	121	6
1934 — January	802	657	137	8
February	889	731	149	9
March	886	736	148	2
April	975	813	156	6
May	936	765	163	8
June	1,016	845	165	6
July	1,042	871	168	3
August	827	670	156	1
September	776	633	142	1
October	746	612	133	1
November	713	573	139	1
December	784	639	144	1
1935 — January	777	635	140	2
February	756	614	140	2
March	839	696	141	2
April	803	714	86	3
May	878	858	19	1
June	883	865	18	–
July	908	893	15	–
August	868	853	15	–
September	886	871	15	–
October	848	836	12	–
November	870	859	11	–
December	970	956	14	–

* Loans (secured by stocks and bonds) made to brokers and dealers in securities. Figures given in this table are monthly averages of figures reported each week. Figures for 1926–1934 were taken from *Annual Report of the Federal Reserve Board*, 1927–1934; those for January–October 1935, from *Fed. Res. Bull.*, Nov. 1935, p. 748; those for November and December 1935 were supplied by the Division of Research and Statistics of the Board of Governors of the Federal Reserve System.

† Member and non-member banks outside New York City (domestic banks only).

periods as the early part of 1921, when rates on commercial paper were appreciably higher than rates charged customers by banks in principal cities, and from July 1928 to December 1929, when commercial paper rates were nearly as high as the latter rates.[37] It also operated to reduce the volume of open-market financing, however, in periods when rates on commercial paper were comparatively low, as in 1925[38] and the earlier part of 1927[39] and throughout the greater part of the period 1930–1935. In the latter period, when the demand for commercial loans by their own customers declined to a very considerable extent, some of the larger city banks offered certain of the best-known open-market "names" rates on direct loans no less attractive than those at which such concerns could borrow through dealers.[40]

The total volume of financing through the remaining two methods mentioned above increased to a considerable extent during the years following 1920, but probably neither acceptance financing nor financing through discount or finance companies had more than a limited influence in restricting the supply of commercial paper.

Such figures of total bankers' acceptances outstanding as are available for the period from 1917 to 1936 are given in Table 12 and plotted on Chart VII. As this table and the accompanying chart indicate, the total amount of acceptances outstanding increased

[37] See Chart IV.

According to a Boston dealer, a number of concerns which encountered difficulty in obtaining sufficient short-term credit in the open market in 1920 increased their lines of credit with commercial banks thereafter.

[38] H. C. Burke, Jr., "Credit Risk in Commercial Paper," *Texas Bankers' Record*, June 1926, p. 64.

[39] Federal Reserve Bank of New York, *Mo. Rev.*, Mar. 1927, p. 19.

[40] Even as early as 1926 and the years immediately preceding, banks in the larger cities are said to have offered extremely large "lines of discount" to their regular customers at rates lower than those at which the same concerns could borrow in the market ("Report of Commercial Credits Committee," *Proc. Inv. Bankers' Assoc. Amer.*, 1926, pp. 109–110). As a matter of fact, the business of commercial paper houses is likely to be affected more adversely by the competition of banks in periods of very low money rates than in periods when commercial paper rates are relatively high. At any rate, competition of banks with dealers was probably more active from about the middle of 1930 to the close of 1935 — a period in which rates on short-term loans, particularly in the open market, were unusually low — than during any preceding period of the same length.

TABLE 12

BANKERS' ACCEPTANCES OUTSTANDING, 1917–1935 *

(*Millions of Dollars, at End of Each Month*)

Year	Jan.	Feb.	Mar.	Apr.	May	June	July	Aug.	Sept.	Oct.	Nov.	Dec.
1917	...	...	...	...	...	...	...	...	...	...	...	450
1918	...	...	...	...	...	...	...	...	...	...	...	750
1919	...	...	...	...	...	...	...	...	...	...	...	1,000
1920	...	...	...	799	...	...	...	...	...	...	...	1,000
1921	...	...	...	664	...	...	...	...	...	...	...	600
1922	...	...	...	416	...	...	...	...	...	...	...	600
1923	...	...	...	524	...	...	...	...	...	...	...	650
1924	...	...	...	618	...	...	...	...	...	...	...	821
1925	835	808	800	757	680	608	569	555	607	674	690	774
1926	788	767	746	721	685	622	600	583	614	682	726	755
1927	774	785	809	811	775	751	741	782	864	975	1,029	1,081
1928	1,058	1,056	1,085	1,071	1,041	1,026	978	952	1,004	1,123	1,200	1,284
1929	1,279	1,228	1,205	1,111	1,107	1,113	1,127	1,201	1,272	1,541	1,658	1,732
1930	1,693	1,624	1,539	1,414	1,382	1,305	1,350	1,339	1,367	1,508	1,571	1,556
1931	1,520	1,520	1,467	1,422	1,413	1,368	1,228	1,090	996	1,040	1,002	974
1932	961	919	911	879	787	747	705	681	683	699	720	710
1933	707	704	671	697	669	687	738	694	715	737	758	764
1934	771	750	685	613	569	534	516	520	539	562	561	543
1935	516	493	466	413	375	343	321	322	328	363	387	397

* Totals for 1917 to 1920 are estimated; those for later years are based on surveys of the American Acceptance Council. Figures included in this table were taken from the American Acceptance Council, *Facts and Figures Relating to the American Money Market* (1931), p. 39; and *Accept. Bull.*, Jan. 1932, p. 34, Feb. 1933, p. 17, Feb. 1934, p. 19, Mar. 1935, p. 14, and Feb. 1936, pp. 14–15.

CHART VII *

COMMERCIAL PAPER AND BANKERS' ACCEPTANCES OUTSTANDING

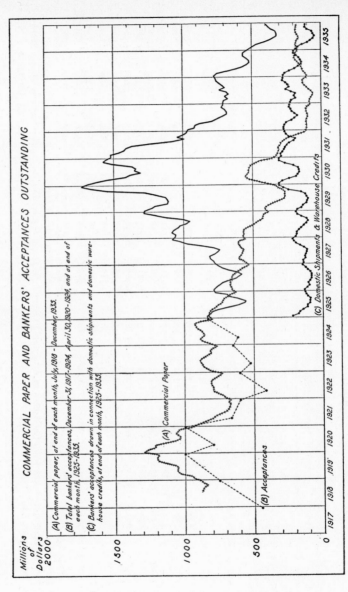

(A) Commercial paper, at end of each month, July, 1918 - December, 1935.
(B) Total bankers' acceptances, December 31, 1917 - 1924, April 30, 1920 - 1924, and at end of each month, 1925 - 1935.
(C) Bankers' acceptances drawn in connection with domestic shipments and domestic warehouse credits, at end of each month, 1925 - 1935.

(A) Commercial Paper

(B) Acceptances

(C) Domestic Shipments & Warehouse Credits

Millions of Dollars
2000
1500
1000
500
0

1917 1918 1919 1920 1921 1922 1923 1924 1925 1926 1927 1928 1929 1930 1931 1932 1933 1934 1935

* Based on figures in Tables 2, 12, and 13.

at a rapid rate from September 1926 to 1930, when commercial paper "outstandings" were more or less steadily declining; and, though it fell off at a rapid rate during most of the period from 1930 to 1936, nevertheless remained appreciably above the comparable figure for commercial paper throughout this six-year period. Rates on prime bankers' bills, moreover, were lower by ½ of 1 per cent or more than rates on prime commercial paper during practically the entire period from 1921 to 1936.[41] It might be supposed, therefore, that a substantial proportion of the increase in the amount of bankers' bills outstanding after 1926 represented a shifting from borrowing through commercial paper houses to acceptance financing. For the most part, however, bankers' acceptances are used in financing foreign-trade, rather than domestic, transactions; whereas commercial paper is used mainly in financing the manufacture and distribution of goods within the United States.[42] Table 13 shows the amount of bankers' bills outstanding, classified according to the purposes for which they were drawn, from 1925 to 1936. Of the six classes of acceptances shown in this table, only two — bills used for financing domestic shipments and those drawn in connection with domestic warehouse credits — were used for financing transactions within the United States; and, as both Table 13 and Chart VII indicate, these two classes of bills together constituted only a small proportion of the total amount of acceptances outstanding during this period.

Figures of the total amount of financing through trade acceptances in recent years are not available. So far, however, the use of such acceptances in this country has been confined largely to concerns whose credit standing has not been of the highest. Such concerns are not in a position to sell their promissory notes in the

---

[41] See Chart V.

[42] See R. H. Bean, "Acceptance Market Facts," *Accept. Bull.*, Jan. 31, 1929, pp. 3–4; B. H. Beckhart and J. G. Smith, *The New York Money Market*, II, 190–191; *Facts and Figures Relating to the American Money Market* (published by the American Acceptance Council), p. 29; *Operation of the National and Federal Reserve Banking Systems* (Hearings before a Subcommittee of the Committee on Banking and Currency, U. S. Senate, 71st Congress, 3d Session, pursuant to Sen. Res. 71), Part 6, p. 845; and statement of the Federal Reserve Bank of Boston, *ibid.*, p. 861.

TABLE 13

CLASSIFICATION OF BANKERS' ACCEPTANCES OUTSTANDING, 1925–1935 *

(Millions of Dollars, at End of Each Month)

	Imports	Exports	Dollar Exchange	Based on Goods Stored in or Shipped between Foreign Countries	Domestic Shipments	Domestic Warehouse Credits	Total Domestic Shipments and Warehouse Credits	Total
1925								
Jan.	$273	$317	$ 27	$ ...	$ 42	$176	$218	$835
Feb.	297	308	15	13	28	147	175	808
Mar.	297	302	19	14	26	143	168	800
Apr.	296	288	18	8	30	117	147	757
May	275	261	17	13	23	92	114	680
June	253	222	14	8	25	87	112	608
July	254	191	13	13	19	79	98	569
Aug.	254	182	13	12	19	75	94	555
Sept.	283	205	16	14	15	74	90	607
Oct.	290	246	15	13	23	87	110	674
Nov.	285	256	16	14	24	95	119	690
Dec.	311	297	19	17	26	103	129	774
1926								
Jan.	324	283	20	30	28	103	131	788
Feb.	326	280	19	32	21	90	111	767
Mar.	334	257	17	38	19	80	100	746
Apr.	330	235	18	35	19	84	103	721
May	316	224	16	35	16	77	94	685
June	282	209	15	33	15	69	84	622
July	273	196	16	31	17	68	85	600
Aug.	262	186	15	33	17	69	86	583

TABLE 13 (*Continued*)

	Imports	Exports	Dollar Exchange	Based on Goods Stored in or Shipped between Foreign Countries	Domestic Shipments	Domestic Warehouse Credits	Total Domestic Shipments and Warehouse Credits	Total
Sept.	272	195	18	36	14	79	93	614
Oct.	277	235	21	38	20	90	110	682
Nov.	281	260	21	40	20	105	125	726
Dec.	284	261	26	40	29	116	145	755
1927								
Jan.	293	272	24	43	33	108	141	774
Feb.	302	275	23	44	25	116	141	785
Mar.	320	285	22	55	18	109	127	809
Apr.	309	285	24	64	21	108	129	811
May	299	271	20	61	16	108	125	775
June	294	261	19	58	19	100	119	751
July	293	250	23	59	17	100	116	741
Aug.	286	261	27	72	16	119	136	782
Sept.	290	297	31	79	21	147	167	864
Oct.	309	343	31	98	22	172	194	975
Nov.	304	376	31	111	22	186	208	1,029
Dec.	313	391	28	131	21	197	218	1,081
1928								
Jan.	318	386	30	130	21	173	194	1,058
Feb.	320	383	29	138	19	168	187	1,056
Mar.	328	389	29	152	21	166	187	1,085
Apr.	333	379	25	161	19	153	172	1,071
May	318	383	25	162	19	133	152	1,041
June	329	361	25	174	20	117	137	1,026

TABLE 13 (*Continued*)

	Imports	Exports	Dollar Exchange	Based on Goods Stored in or Shipped between Foreign Countries	Domestic Shipments	Domestic Warehouse Credits	Total Domestic Shipments and Warehouse Credits	Total
July	319	352	25	164	18	100	118	978
Aug.	316	353	24	152	15	92	108	952
Sept.	321	370	28	171	15	99	115	1,004
Oct.	314	416	32	207	15	138	154	1,123
Nov.	317	449	32	221	18	163	181	1,200
Dec.	316	497	39	243	16	174	190	1,284
1929								
Jan.	319	467	46	267	18	162	180	1,279
Feb.	341	422	47	264	18	137	154	1,228
Mar.	360	387	50	267	17	124	141	1,205
Apr.	324	377	45	249	16	99	116	1,111
May	326	381	47	243	15	95	110	1,107
June	323	368	56	264	14	88	102	1,113
July	316	368	49	280	15	99	114	1,127
Aug.	330	370	52	325	16	107	123	1,201
Sept.	328	397	46	347	17	137	155	1,272
Oct.	351	480	72	395	23	220	243	1,541
Nov.	363	523	76	417	20	260	280	1,658
Dec.	383	524	76	441	23	285	308	1,732
1930								
Jan.	336	510	67	471	20	289	309	1,693
Feb.	335	475	63	470	26	256	282	1,624
Mar.	314	466	58	467	15	219	235	1,539
Apr.	296	429	57	443	18	171	189	1,414

TABLE 13 (*Continued*)

	Imports	Exports	Dollar Exchange	Based on Goods Stored in or Shipped between Foreign Countries	Domestic Shipments	Domestic Warehouse Credits	Total Domestic Shipments and Warehouse Credits	Total
May	295	406	61	442	21	158	179	1,382
June	276	373	50	442	19	145	164	1,305
July	260	380	48	495	29	137	167	1,350
Aug.	255	357	54	502	26	145	172	1,339
Sept.	241	364	63	499	27	174	201	1,367
Oct.	244	407	58	533	31	235	266	1,508
Nov.	243	422	56	544	34	274	307	1,571
Dec.	221	415	52	561	35	271	306	1,556
1931								
Jan.	214	400	65	549	35	257	292	1,520
Feb.	212	398	71	544	34	261	295	1,520
Mar.	212	390	62	520	37	246	282	1,467
Apr.	211	360	73	507	33	238	271	1,422
May	207	361	75	505	28	236	264	1,413
June	202	349	69	494	29	225	254	1,368
July	186	330	52	423	35	202	237	1,228
Aug.	178	276	43	391	28	175	202	1,090
Sept.	174	257	37	338	28	162	190	996
Oct.	173	261	38	330	24	214	238	1,040
Nov.	158	254	34	298	18	239	258	1,002
Dec.	158	222	31	296	16	251	267	974
1932								
Jan.	150	207	34	298	17	254	272	961
Feb.	142	195	26	284	17	254	271	919

TABLE 13 (*Continued*)

	Imports	Exports	Dollar Exchange	Based on Goods Stored in or Shipped between Foreign Countries	Domestic Shipments	Domestic Warehouse Credits	Total Domestic Shipments and Warehouse Credits	Total
Mar.	129	205	23	287	20	248	267	911
Apr.	118	199	17	294	20	231	251	879
May	103	184	15	269	18	199	217	787
June	97	173	13	271	14	179	193	747
July	85	162	15	265	14	163	178	705
Aug.	76	152	11	250	17	175	192	681
Sept.	73	156	8	234	14	198	212	683
Oct.	81	157	6	231	16	206	222	699
Nov.	81	161	9	232	16	221	237	720
Dec.	79	164	10	228	14	215	230	710
1933								
Jan.	71	166	11	237	13	209	222	707
Feb.	71	174	9	231	13	206	219	704
Mar.	73	175	8	230	10	174	184	671
Apr.	77	176	10	234	10	189	199	697
May	77	174	9	225	11	173	184	669
June	80	168	9	213	14	203	217	687
July	86	168	10	219	16	240	256	738
Aug.	95	160	4	206	14	215	229	694
Sept.	103	171	4	199	15	223	238	715
Oct.	99	185	5	195	14	238	252	737
Nov.	98	200	4	180	14	264	278	758
Dec.	94	207	4	182	14	263	277	764
1934								
Jan.	89	225	5	175	13	263	276	771
Feb.	98	203	4	184	13	248	261	750

TABLE 13 (*Continued*)

	Imports	Exports	Dollar Exchange	Based on Goods Stored in or Shipped between Foreign Countries	Domestic Shipments	Domestic Warehouse Credits	Total Domestic Shipments and Warehouse Credits	Total
Mar.	103	186	3	168	11	215	226	685
Apr.	103	164	3	158	11	175	186	613
May	100	150	3	152	10	153	163	569
June	97	145	4	148	9	132	141	534
July	94	135	4	144	8	130	138	516
Aug.	89	140	4	141	9	138	147	520
Sept.	94	138	4	137	9	158	157	539
Oct.	93	147	4	133	8	177	185	562
Nov.	89	148	2	127	7	187	194	561
Dec.	89	140	2	119	8	186	194	543
1935								
Jan.	86	133	3	114	8	171	179	516
Feb.	92	123	3	109	9	157	166	493
Mar.	101	122	2	106	8	126	134	466
Apr.	103	114	2	99	8	88	96	413
May	107	100	2	91	8	68	76	375
June	102	94	2	89	9	48	57	343
July	99	86	3	86	9	37	46	321
Aug.	102	81	4	83	9	43	52	322
Sept.	102	77	4	79	8	58	66	328
Oct.	106	75	4	82	10	88	98	363
Nov.	105	84	3	84	11	101	112	387
Dec.	107	94	2	84	11	99	110	397

* Figures included in this table were taken from the American Acceptance Council, *Facts and Figures Relating to the American Money Market* (1931), pp. 42–43; and *Accept. Bull.*, Jan. 1932, p. 34, Feb. 1933, p. 17, Feb. 1934, p. 19, Mar. 1935, p. 14, and Feb. 1936, pp. 14–15.

market. On the other hand, concerns which are able to borrow in the market prefer to obtain in this manner or through direct borrowing from banks such amounts of short-term credit as they require, rather than through accepting trade bills drawn on them.[43]

Hence it may be concluded that, despite the efforts of the Federal Reserve system to promote the growth of acceptance financing in the United States, such financing had no very important effect in reducing the supply of commercial paper during the period from 1921 to 1936.

The effect of the third method of financing mentioned above, like that of acceptance financing, can only be estimated. There are reasons for believing, however, that the increase in financing through discount or finance companies was also a factor of but minor importance in restricting the supply of commercial paper during this period. A large part of the loans of finance companies are extended direct to consumers. In making such loans, these companies obviously do not compete against commercial paper houses directly, though in some cases they have probably taken over financing services which manufacturing and trading concerns formerly offered their own customers with the aid of working

---

[43] Cf. the following: ". . . a great many business men in good credit standing refuse or object to placing their names as acceptors or to pledging acceptances which they have received to their banks when borrowing. They are proud of their ability to obtain clean credit and are very anxious to maintain the standing of their good names. . . . Probably the great majority of concerns have been able to get credit if merited on a straight note basis" (W. L. Gray, "For Wider Use of Trade Acceptances," *Barron's*, Mar. 13, 1933, p. 16).

Since 1914 strenuous attempts have been made from time to time to stimulate the use of trade acceptances in the United States, but so far such attempts have met with no great success. (In this connection see the statements of Messrs. R. H. Bean and R. M. Coon in *Operation of the National and Federal Reserve Banking Systems*, Part 3, pp. 456, 474–475, 477–478; and C. O. Hardy, *Credit Policies of the Federal Reserve System*, pp. 247–248.) As late as the spring of 1932 a campaign to promote the use of trade acceptances was undertaken by various interested organizations, bankers, and other business men. Some increase in the volume of acceptance financing undoubtedly resulted from this attempt to galvanize the domestic bill of exchange into an unaccustomed activity. Probably only a small part, if any, of this increase, however, represented a shifting to this method of financing from that of financing through commercial paper dealers. (For an account of some of the developments connected with this recent attempt to stimulate the practice of financing through trade acceptances, see the issues of the *Acceptance Bulletin* from May to August 1932, inclusive.)

capital obtained from open-market loans and direct loans from banks. The only direct way in which finance companies compete against commercial paper houses in supplying short-term credit is through discounting "receivables." Some concerns of the kind able to borrow in the open market have no doubt occasionally raised certain amounts of cash through discounting some of their "slow" accounts receivable with finance companies. Except in periods of unusually high money rates, however, the cost of this method of borrowing is likely to be appreciably higher than that of borrowing in the market or from banks direct. Furthermore, a concern which discounts its "receivables" is in effect pledging specific assets which, if good, are likely to be among the most current it has and, if of doubtful collectibility, involve a contingent liability so much the heavier; and therefore cannot at the same time readily borrow in the open market. For these reasons the practice of discounting "receivables" is as a rule confined largely to concerns which are not in a position to borrow through commercial paper houses. About the only other way in which finance companies compete against such houses affects the supply of commercial paper less directly than the discounting of "receivables" does. Some of the larger companies issue and sell to banks and other investors their collateral trust notes or their unsecured promissory notes with shorter maturities. The availability of such alternative investments at attractive rates has at times undoubtedly restricted the demand for open-market commercial paper, and has therefore tended indirectly to reduce the volume of open-market borrowing to some extent. On the other hand, a number of finance companies have in recent years marketed their unsecured notes through commercial paper houses and thereby added to the supply of open-market paper. It seems safe to conclude, therefore, that neither the direct nor the indirect competition of finance companies with dealers in promissory notes had any important influence in restricting the supply of commercial paper during the period under consideration.

A final reason for the reduction in the supply of such paper during the years following 1920 is that a number of concerns which formerly borrowed comparatively large amounts of working capital through dealers found it necessary after about 1924 either to reduce their open-market borrowing to a considerable extent or to discontinue it entirely. Probably the most important classes of such concerns were those in the textile and leather industries and wholesale grocers and other middlemen. Some years ago concerns of the first two classes were among the largest borrowers in the market, and their paper was regarded as a choice short-term investment, particularly by banks in New England. Because of depressed conditions in the textile and leather industries after about 1924, however, a number of concerns of both these classes found it necessary to resort to other methods of obtaining such working capital as they required.[44] Wholesale grocers and other middlemen encountered similar conditions during this period. As a result of the growth of chain stores and the development of other direct merchandising methods, many such dealers are said to have been driven out of business.[45] Others were more successful in withstanding the competition of the more direct methods of merchandising, but were not in a position to borrow in the open market so heavily as they had done in earlier years.[46]

The various forces which operated to reduce the supply of commercial paper were more important in bringing about the decline in open-market financing from about the middle of 1920 to about

[44] B. F. Martin, "Recent Movements in the Commercial-paper Market," *Harv. Bus. Rev.*, April 1931, p. 366. See also Lauchlin Currie, "The Decline of the Commercial Loan," *Quar. Jour. Econ.*, Aug. 1931, p. 706; and Federal Reserve Bank of New York, *Mo. Rev.*, Aug. 1926, pp. 3–4, Mar. 1927, p. 19, and Sept. 1927, p. 67.

[45] B. H. Beckhart, *The New York Money Market*, III, 245; Report of Economic Policy Commission, American Bankers' Association, 1930, p. 15; and Prentice Welsh, "Commercial Paper from the Borrower's Standpoint," *Bankers' Mag.*, July 1930, pp. 33, 35.

[46] The coöperation of the Federal Reserve system with the Treasury's program of keeping afloat a large volume of Treasury certificates may also have reduced the supply of open-market commercial paper to some extent after about 1920. Hardy maintains that the joint policy of the Treasury and the Reserve banks with regard to short-term government securities "has been a powerful factor undermining the commercial paper market and obstructing the growth of the bill market," but it is not clear whether or not he would include open-market notes in "commercial paper" in this connection (Hardy, *op. cit.*, p. 291). In the opinion of the present writer the policy in question has had no great influence either in restricting the supply of open-market notes or in limiting the demand for such obligations as an investment for banks' funds.

June 1933, as well as in restricting the volume of such financing thereafter to the close of 1935, than those which tended to limit the demand for open-market obligations as an investment. Many banks, to be sure, bought little or no outside paper during this entire period, preferring to invest their loanable funds in unsecured direct advances to their own customers, local loans secured by real estate or listed stocks and bonds, stock exchange call and time loans, acceptances, finance company paper, short-term government securities, or various classes of long-term securities. In a number of cases where smaller banks were consolidated to form larger institutions, or were brought under the control of branch, chain, or group banking systems, the resulting larger organizations, partly because they could secure a greater diversification in loans to local borrowers, found it expedient to purchase smaller total amounts of paper through dealers than these smaller banks had been buying in earlier years. Other banks which purchased substantial amounts of open-market obligations during this period nevertheless placed increasing proportions of their resources in some of the alternative investments mentioned above. During the years immediately preceding 1930 banks which had bond departments or subsidiary investment companies also found profitable employment for increasing amounts of funds in security dealings. Except in periods when demands by banks' own customers for direct loans were unusually heavy, however, as in parts of 1920, 1928, and 1929, and when rates on New York Stock Exchange call and time loans were appreciably higher than rates on prime commercial paper, as during the greater part of both the latter two years, dealers encountered but little difficulty in finding a market for all such paper they could obtain. Even in 1928 and 1929, and also in years when rates on prime paper fell to figures so low as to be unattractive to many country banks, as in 1924 and each of the six years ending with 1935,[47] the main problem of dealers was that

[47] About the middle of November 1932 some high-grade four- to six-months' paper was sold at 1¼ per cent, and some choice paper with a maturity shorter than ninety days at 1 per cent (Federal Reserve Bank of New York, *Mo. Rev.*, Dec. 1932, p. 90). At that time the latter rate was probably the lowest at which commercial paper had ever been sold in the United States. In May and September 1935 dealers sold some prime paper maturing in not more than four months at ½ of 1 per cent (*ibid.*, June 1935, p. 43, and Oct. 1935, p. 75).

of securing an adequate supply of high-grade notes, rather than finding a market for such obligations among banks.

As a matter of fact, had dealers been able to secure larger port-folios of high-grade notes during the years from 1921 to 1936, commercial banks would undoubtedly have been willing to pur-chase considerably larger amounts of outside paper during this period. For reasons closely similar to those which accounted for the decline in open-market borrowing, many banks during the years following 1920 encountered increasing difficulty in finding employ-ment for their loanable funds in short-term self-liquidating ad-vances to their own customers,[48] and consequently were confronted with the problem of finding alternative investments for their sur-plus funds. Since indirect advances through dealers correspond most closely to direct advances by banks to their own customers, and are also safer and more liquid than the latter class of loans, there can be little question that many banks would have placed larger amounts of their surplus funds in open-market obligations if a larger supply of prime paper had been available during this period.

As may be inferred from an examination of the tables and charts shown on the following pages, however, large numbers of banks were unable during the later years of this period to find employ-ment either in advances through dealers or in other forms of short-term self-liquidating loans for as large a proportion of their earning assets as they had invested in such loans in earlier years. Table 14 shows that the proportion of total loans of all reporting Federal Reserve member banks to their total loans and investments de-clined from about 79 per cent in 1920 to about 60 per cent in 1932, and in 1935 fell to about 40 per cent; and that the proportion of their "all other loans" — which in this case include direct loans for industrial and commercial purposes to their own customers, open-market loans, and loans on real estate — to their total loans declined from 68 per cent in 1920 to less than 52 per cent in 1930, and increased only to about 61 per cent during the next five years. The changes in the amounts of their earning assets shown in this table are plotted on the accompanying Chart VIII. Table 15 shows

[48] For a discussion of the decline in banks' commercial loans during the years following 1920, see Currie, *op. cit.*, pp. 699–709.

TABLE 14

LOANS AND INVESTMENTS OF ALL REPORTING FEDERAL RESERVE MEMBER BANKS, 1920-1935 *

(Amounts in Billions of Dollars)

YEAR	TOTAL LOANS AND INVESTMENTS	TOTAL LOANS Amount	TOTAL LOANS Per Cent of Total Loans and Investments	LOANS ON SECURITIES Amount	LOANS ON SECURITIES Per Cent of Total Loans	ALL OTHER LOANS Amount	ALL OTHER LOANS Per Cent of Total Loans	TOTAL INVESTMENTS Amount	TOTAL INVESTMENTS Per Cent of Total Loans and Investments
1920	16.90	13.38	79.2	4.28	32.0	9.11	68.0	3.52	20.8
1921	15.40	12.12	78.7	3.81	31.4	8.32	68.6	3.28	21.3
1922	15.21	11.12	73.1	3.86	34.7	7.26	65.3	4.09	26.9
1923	16.34	11.87	72.6	4.12	34.7	7.75	65.3	4.47	27.4
1924	17.20	12.46	72.4	4.46	35.8	8.00	64.2	4.75	27.6
1925	18.80	13.58	72.2	5.34	39.3	8.25	60.7	5.22	27.8
1926	19.56	14.31	73.2	5.72	40.0	8.59	60.0	5.25	26.8
1927	20.40	14.84	72.8	6.17	41.5	8.68	58.5	5.56	27.2
1928	21.86	15.80	72.3	6.89	43.6	8.91	56.4	6.05	27.7
1929	22.60	16.88	74.7	7.65	45.3	9.23	54.7	5.72	25.3
1930	22.88	16.78	73.3	8.13	48.5	8.64	51.5	6.10	26.7
1931	22.17	14.60	65.9	6.68	45.8	7.92	54.2	7.57	34.1
1932	19.09	11.35	59.9	4.77	42.0	6.58	58.0	7.65	40.1
1933	16.48	8.51	51.6	3.69	43.4	4.82	56.6	7.97	48.4
1934	17.56	8.00	45.6	3.37	42.1	4.63	57.9	9.56	54.4
1935	19.98	8.02	40.1	3.12	38.9	4.90	61.1	11.96	59.9

* The absolute figures given in this table are averages of monthly averages of the figures reported by Federal Reserve member banks each week. The original monthly averages may be found in *Annual Report of the Federal Reserve Board*, 1931, p. 110, 1932, p. 136, 1933, p. 190, and 1934, pp. 158-159; and *Fed. Res. Bull.*, Dec. 1935, p. 806, and Jan. 1936, p. 24.

CHART VIII *

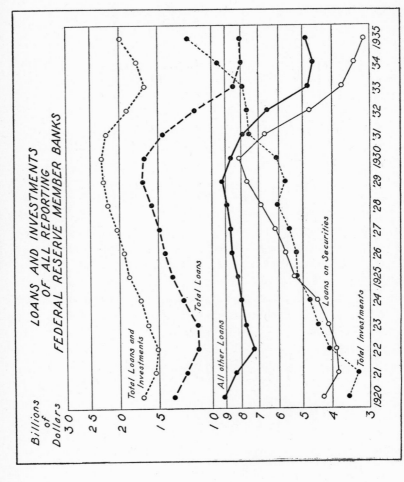

LOANS AND INVESTMENTS
of ALL REPORTING
FEDERAL RESERVE MEMBER BANKS

* Based on figures in Table 14. Logarithmic scale.

that from June 30, 1925, to June 30, 1928, the loans on securities of all Federal Reserve member banks and their loans secured by real estate increased, respectively, from 33 per cent to 37 per cent and from 11 per cent to 13 per cent of their total loans, while their loans "otherwise secured and unsecured" decreased from 56 per cent to 50 per cent of the total figures. Tables 16 and 17 give for all dates for which they are available in the years preceding 1936 figures showing a more detailed classification of loans and investments of all Federal Reserve member banks. Table 17 shows that from October 3, 1928, to the end of 1935 the total loans of all Federal Reserve member banks decreased from 69.6 per cent to 40.6 per cent of their total loans and investments. The following changes in the proportions of various earning assets of these banks to their total loans during this period are also worth noting: the increase in loans secured by stocks and bonds in 1929 and the following two years; the increase in loans secured by real estate; the decline in loans "otherwise secured and unsecured," or direct advances for commercial and industrial purposes to these banks' own customers; the increase in acceptances in 1931, 1932, and 1934; and the decline in open-market commercial paper and brokers' loans in 1932. The changes in the amounts of these six classes of their earning assets given in Table 16 are shown graphically on Chart IX. It may be noted also that the proportion of United States government securities to total investments increased substantially during this period.[49]

[49] Tables 16 and 17 show that Federal Reserve member banks' holdings of United States government securities increased from $4,386,000,000 to $6,540,000,000, or approximately 50 per cent, from Oct. 3, 1928, to Dec. 31, 1932, and at the latter date constituted more than 53 per cent of their total investments. The unusually large proportion of their earning assets invested in such securities as of the end of 1932 reflected not only the difficulty of finding suitable employment for their loanable funds in short-term commercial and industrial loans but also their desire to maintain a large proportion of their resources in a highly liquid form. Had the proportions of their "collateral loans," loans secured by real estate, and unsecured commercial and industrial loans which were then in a "frozen" state been smaller, they would doubtless have been carrying smaller amounts of government securities. By the close of 1935 their holdings of such securities had increased to $12,269,000,000, or to nearly three times the corresponding figure for October 3, 1928, and constituted almost 70 per cent of their total investments. The substantial increase in the proportion of their holdings of government securities to their total earning assets since 1933 has resulted primarily from their inability to find more attractive alternative outlets for abnormally large amounts of surplus loanable funds.

TABLE 15

CLASSIFICATION OF LOANS OF ALL FEDERAL RESERVE MEMBER BANKS ON JUNE 30, 1925–1928 *

(Amounts in Millions of Dollars)

YEAR	TOTAL LOANS	LOANS ON SECURITIES		ALL OTHER LOANS				
		Total	Per Cent of Total Loans	Total	Secured by Real Estate		Otherwise Secured and Unsecured †	
					Amount	Per Cent of Total Loans	Amount	Per Cent of Total Loans
1925	20,655	6,718	33	13,937	2,338	11	11,599	56
1926	22,060	7,321	33	14,740	2,650	12	12,090	55
1927	22,938	8,156	35	14,782	2,926	13	11,856	52
1928	24,303	9,068	37	15,235	3,068	13	12,167	50

* Including loans to other banks and open-market loans (*i.e.,* "street loans," or loans to brokers and dealers in securities in New York, and commercial paper and acceptances purchased in the open market).

† Includes overdrafts; excludes acceptances of other banks and bills of exchange or drafts sold with indorsement.

Source: *Fed. Res. Bull.,* Dec. 1928, p. 882.

TABLE 16

CLASSIFICATION OF LOANS AND INVESTMENTS OF ALL FEDERAL RESERVE MEMBER BANKS ON CALL DATES, 1928-1935

(Millions of Dollars)

Call Date	Total Loans and Investments	Total Loans	Loans to Banks	Loans to Other Customers — Total	Secured by Stocks and Bonds	Secured by Real Estate	Otherwise Secured and Unsecured	Open-Market Loans — Total	Acceptances Payable in U.S.	Acceptances Payable Abroad	Commercial Paper	Loans to Brokers in N.Y.*	Investments — Total	U.S. Government Securities	Other Securities
1928 — Oct. 3	34,929	24,327	548	21,242	6,646	3,089	11,507	2,537	80	101	457	1,899	10,604	4,386	6,218
Dec. 31	35,684	25,158	538	21,462	7,348	3,123	10,991	3,158	109	103	390	2,556	10,529	4,312	6,217
1929 — Mar. 27	35,393	24,945	548	21,903	7,540	3,123	11,240	2,494	146	93	376	1,879	10,448	4,454	5,994
June 29	35,711	25,659	670	22,517	7,734	3,164	11,618	2,472	108	90	249	2,025	10,052	4,155	5,898
Oct. 4	35,914	26,150	640	23,249	8,109	3,152	11,988	2,276	93	70	228	1,885	9,749	4,022	5,727
Dec. 31	35,934	26,150	714	23,193	8,488	3,191	11,515	2,243	212	80	291	1,660	9,784	3,863	5,921
1930 — Mar. 27	35,056	25,118	527	21,494	7,730	3,170	10,595	3,097	175	79	499	2,344	9,937	4,085	5,852
June 30	35,656	25,213	535	21,565	8,061	3,155	10,349	3,113	170	71	507	2,365	10,442	4,061	6,380
Sept. 24	35,472	24,738	466	21,010	7,864	3,163	9,982	3,262	205	62	523	2,472	10,734	4,095	6,639
Dec. 31	34,860	23,871	631	21,007	7,942	3,234	9,831	2,233	315	55	366	1,498	10,989	4,125	6,864
1931 — Mar. 25	34,729	22,840	446	19,940	7,423	3,220	9,298	2,454	361	101	361	1,630	11,889	5,002	6,886
June 30	33,923	21,817	457	19,257	7,117	3,216	8,922	2,103	389	113	384	1,217	12,106	5,343	6,763
Sept. 29	33,073	20,875	599	18,713	6,842	3,149	8,722	1,563	268	70	296	928	12,199	5,564	6,635
Dec. 31	30,575	19,261	790	17,570	6,290	3,038	8,244	901	146	41	140	575	11,314	5,319	5,996
1932 — June 30	28,001	16,587	573	15,267	5,292	2,894	7,081	747	313	34	122	278	11,414	5,628	5,786
Sept. 30	28,045	15,924	457	14,497	5,086	2,885	6,527	970	407	34	115	414	12,121	6,356	5,755
Dec. 31	27,469	15,204	444	13,905	4,848	2,862	6,195	855	375	30	93	357	12,265	6,540	5,726
1933 — June 30 †	24,786	12,858	330	11,337	3,917	2,372	5,049	1,191	291	25	87	788	11,928	6,887	5,041
Oct. 25	24,953	13,059	297	11,523	3,809	2,364	5,349	1,239	303	24	164	748	11,894	6,801	5,093
Dec. 31	25,220	12,834	287	11,315	3,772	2,359	5,185	1,232	223	37	132	840	12,386	7,254	5,132
1934 — Mar. 5	26,548	12,706	225	11,093	3,644	2,382	5,067	1,388	350	26	157	855	13,842	8,848	4,995
June 30	27,175	12,523	153	10,884	3,517	2,357	4,931	1,566	264	20	200	1,082	14,652	9,413	5,239 ‡
Oct. 17	27,559	12,292	149	10,782	3,325	2,297	5,161	1,361	276	30	253	802	15,267	9,895	5,372
Dec. 31	28,150	12,028	155	10,509	3,297	2,273	4,940	1,362	256	31	232	843	16,122	10,895	5,227
1935 — Mar. 4	28,221	11,953	133	10,420	3,215	2,250	4,955	1,399	235	34	255	875	16,318	11,021	5,298
June 29	28,285	11,928	119	10,369	3,123	2,277	4,969	1,440	201	17	247	975	16,857	11,429	5,427
Nov. 1	29,301	11,841	94	10,465	3,064	2,279	5,122	1,282	154	27	260	841	17,460	11,844	5,615
Dec. 31	29,985	12,175	98	10,548	3,089	2,284	5,175	1,529	181	29	272	1,047	17,810	12,269	5,541

* Loans (secured by stocks and bonds) to brokers and dealers in securities in New York City.

† Beginning June 30, 1933, figures relate to licensed banks only.

‡ An estimated small amount of Home Owners' Loan Corporation bonds guaranteed by the United States government as to both interest and principal is included in "Other Securities."

Source: *Fed. Res. Bull.*, Nov. 1930, p. 753, Mar. 1933, p. 140, and Mar. 1936, p. 160.

TABLE 17

PERCENTAGE DISTRIBUTION OF LOANS AND INVESTMENTS OF ALL FEDERAL RESERVE MEMBER BANKS ON CALL DATES, 1928–1935 *

CALL DATE	TOTAL LOANS TO TOTAL LOANS AND INVESTMENTS	LOANS TO BANKS TO TOTAL LOANS	LOANS SECURED BY STOCKS AND BONDS TO TOTAL LOANS	LOANS SECURED BY REAL ESTATE TO TOTAL LOANS	LOANS OTHERWISE SECURED AND UNSECURED TO TOTAL LOANS	ACCEPTANCES TO TOTAL LOANS	OPEN-MARKET COMMERCIAL PAPER TO TOTAL LOANS	LOANS TO BROKERS IN NEW YORK TO TOTAL LOANS	TOTAL INVESTMENTS TO TOTAL LOANS AND INVESTMENTS	U. S. GOVERNMENT SECURITIES TO TOTAL INVESTMENTS	OTHER SECURITIES TO TOTAL INVESTMENTS
1928—											
Oct. 3	69.6%	2.3%	27.3%	12.7%	47.3%	0.7%	1.9%	7.8%	30.4%	41.4%	58.6%
Dec. 31	70.5	2.1	29.2	12.4	43.7	0.8	1.6	10.2	29.5	41.0	59.0
1929—											
Mar. 27	70.5	2.2	30.2	12.5	45.1	1.0	1.5	7.5	29.5	42.6	57.4
June 29	71.8	2.6	30.1	12.3	45.3	0.8	1.0	7.9	28.2	41.3	58.7
Oct. 4	72.8	2.4	31.0	12.1	45.8	0.6	0.9	7.2	27.2	41.3	58.7
Dec. 31	72.8	2.7	32.5	12.2	44.0	1.1	1.1	6.4	27.2	39.5	60.5
1930—											
Mar. 27	71.7	2.1	30.8	12.6	42.2	1.0	2.0	9.3	28.3	41.1	58.9
June 30	70.7	2.1	32.0	12.5	41.0	1.0	2.0	9.4	29.3	38.9	61.1
Sept. 24	69.7	1.9	31.8	12.8	40.3	1.1	2.1	10.0	30.3	38.1	61.9
Dec. 31	68.5	2.6	33.3	13.5	41.2	1.6	1.5	6.3	31.5	37.5	62.5
1931—											
Mar. 25	65.8	2.0	32.5	14.1	40.7	2.0	1.6	7.1	34.2	42.1	57.9
June 30	64.3	2.1	32.6	14.7	40.9	2.3	1.8	5.6	35.7	44.1	55.9
Sept. 29	63.1	2.9	32.8	15.1	41.8	1.6	1.4	4.4	36.9	45.6	54.4
Dec. 31	63.0	4.1	32.6	15.8	42.8	1.0	0.7	3.0	37.0	47.0	53.0

TABLE 17 (Continued)

Call Date	Total Loans to Total Loans and Investments	Loans to Banks to Total Loans	Loans Secured by Stocks and Bonds to Total Loans	Loans Secured by Real Estate to Total Loans	Loans Otherwise Secured and Unsecured to Total Loans	Acceptances to Total Loans	Open-Market Commercial Paper to Total Loans	Loans to Brokers in New York to Total Loans	Total Investments to Total Loans and Investments	U. S. Government Securities to Total Investments	Other Securities to Total Investments
1932 —											
June 30	59.2	3.5	31.9	17.4	42.7	2.1	0.7	1.7	40.8	49.3	50.7
Sept. 30	56.8	2.9	31.9	18.1	41.0	2.8	0.7	2.6	43.2	52.5	47.5
Dec. 31	55.3	2.9	31.9	18.8	40.7	2.7	0.6	2.4	44.7	53.3	46.7
1933 —											
June 30	51.9	2.6	30.4	18.5	39.3	2.4	0.7	6.1	48.1	57.7	42.3
Oct. 25	52.3	2.3	29.2	18.1	40.9	2.5	1.3	5.7	47.7	57.2	42.8
Dec. 30	50.9	2.2	29.4	18.4	40.4	2.0	1.0	6.6	49.1	58.6	41.4
1934 —											
Mar. 5	47.9	1.8	28.7	18.7	39.9	3.0	1.2	6.7	52.1	63.9	36.1
June 30	46.1	1.2	28.1	18.8	39.4	2.3	1.6	8.6	53.9	64.2	35.8
Oct. 17	44.6	1.2	27.0	18.7	42.0	2.5	2.1	6.5	55.4	64.8	35.2
Dec. 31	42.7	1.3	27.4	18.9	41.1	2.4	1.9	7.0	57.3	67.6	32.4
1935 —											
Mar. 4	42.3	1.1	26.9	18.8	41.5	2.3	2.1	7.3	57.7	67.5	32.5
June 29	41.4	1.0	26.2	19.1	41.6	1.8	2.1	8.2	58.6	67.8	32.2
Nov. 1	40.4	0.8	25.9	19.2	43.3	1.5	2.2	7.1	59.6	67.8	32.2
Dec. 31	40.6	0.8	25.4	18.8	42.5	1.7	2.2	8.6	59.4	68.9	31.1

* Figures in this table were computed from those given in Table 16.

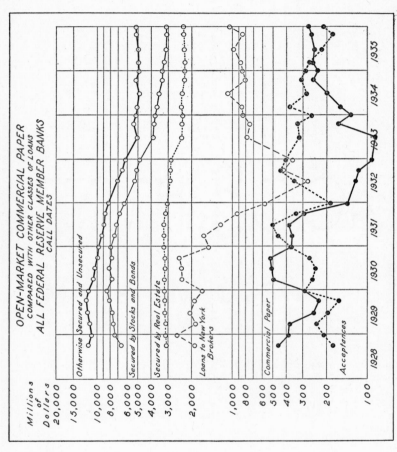

CHART IX *

OPEN-MARKET COMMERCIAL PAPER
COMPARED WITH OTHER CLASSES OF LOANS
ALL FEDERAL RESERVE MEMBER BANKS
CALL DATES

Millions
of
Dollars
20,000
15,000
10,000
8,000
6,000
5,000
4,000
3,000
2,000
1,000
800
600
500
400
300
200
100

Otherwise Secured and Unsecured
Secured by Stocks and Bonds
Secured by Real Estate
Loans to New York Brokers
Commercial Paper
Acceptances

1928   1929   1930   1931   1932   1933   1934   1935

*Based on figures in Table 16. Logarithmic scale.

Thus it is clear that distinct changes took place in the distribution of the earning assets of commercial banks throughout the country during the years following 1920. The decline in their holdings of open-market commercial paper was accompanied by a parallel decline, brought about by similar forces, in their short-term commercial and industrial loans to their own customers. As a consequence, they were forced to seek employment for increasing amounts of surplus funds in both short-term and long-term loans quite different in character from the self-liquidating advances to which, according to conservative banking traditions at any rate, the extension of credit by commercial banks should in the main be confined. Hence they invested increasing proportions of their resources in "collateral loans," in loans secured by real estate, and in government and other securities. Far from remaining commercial banks strictly so called, they became in effect investment trusts.[50]

The decline in the volume of open-market financing which has been considered at some length in the preceding pages was interrupted by increases in reported commercial paper "outstandings" and in estimated sales by dealers during the years from 1922 to 1925, and again in 1930, and both "outstandings" and dealers' sales increased to some extent from about the middle of 1933 to the end of 1935. Some of the more important reasons for the increased activity in the commercial paper market during these years will now be indicated.

Probably the main reason for the increase in the volume of open-market financing which began in 1922 was the revival of business activity following the depression of 1920 and 1921. Business recovered rather rapidly during 1922 and the first few months of 1923, and, though declining, continued fairly active throughout the remaining months of the latter year. A slight increase in

---

[50] For a discussion of changes in the earning assets of commercial banks from about 1920 to about 1930 see D. M. Dailey, "Bank Credit during the Last Decade," *Bankers' Mag.*, Oct. 1930, pp. 497–502; V. P. Lee, "Country Bank Investment Trends," *ibid.*, Feb. 1930, pp. 183–187; and G. G. Munn, "New Problems of Investing Bank Funds," *ibid.*, Jan. 1929, pp. 15–17, and "The Trend toward Long Term Investments," *ibid.*, Feb. 1929, pp. 181–185.

activity in the early part of 1924 was followed by a minor recession, but after about the middle of the year business again became more active. Wholesale commodity prices, moreover, rose steadily from January 1922 to April 1923, and from the latter month to the beginning of 1925 fluctuated within a fairly narrow range. Under these circumstances many trading and manufacturing concerns required increasing amounts of short-term credit; and, since commercial paper rates during the greater part of this period were distinctly lower than rates charged on direct loans to customers by banks in principal cities,[51] such concerns found it advantageous to obtain increasing amounts of working capital through dealers. The demand for open-market paper also became more active during this period. Banks in New York and other large cities bought relatively little outside paper during the greater part of 1920 and 1921; but toward the close of the latter year, after the demands of their customers for direct accommodation had declined, and they had reduced their own borrowings from Federal Reserve banks, they began to buy open-market paper more actively again.[52]

Both the supply of such paper and the demand for it as an investment for banks' funds increased again in 1930. Between November 1929 and about March 15, 1930, 125 additional concerns are said to have borrowed funds in the open market.[53] The open-market financing of these concerns, as well as increased financing through dealers by other concerns in 1930, is probably to be accounted for in the main by the moderate increase in business activ-

---

[51] See Chart IV. According to a New York banker, the cost of borrowing through commercial paper houses was for some time before February 1923 even less than that of acceptance financing, and a number of the largest and best-known users of bankers' acceptances consequently abandoned the use of the latter in that period and borrowed in the commercial paper market (M. H. Fry, "The Future of the Acceptance Market," *Accept. Bull.*, Feb. 1923, pp. 9–10).

[52] Federal Reserve Bank of New York, *Mo. Rev.*, Jan. 1922, p. 4.

About the middle of 1922, in order to find employment for surplus funds, New York banks are said in some instances to have found it necessary to purchase open-market notes issued by their own customers (*ibid.*, July 1922, p. 3). It is probable that at least part of these surplus funds were accumulated as the result of the repayment, with the aid of funds obtained in the open market in the fall of 1921 and the spring of 1922, of direct loans to their own customers (*ibid.*, Sept. 1921, p. 2; Nov. 1921, p. 2; and June 1922, p. 3).

[53] "More Discounting Paper," *N. Y. Times*, Mar. 16, 1930, p. 20 N.

ity during the earlier months of the year and the precipitous decline in commercial paper rates which began toward the close of 1929. The rise in business activity proved to be of but short duration, however, and its influence in bringing about an increase in the supply of open-market obligations was limited accordingly. Such influence as it had was limited further by the fact that wholesale commodity prices declined steadily throughout 1930. The effect of the decline in commercial paper rates in encouraging the issue of increased amounts of open-market obligations, on the other hand, was more lasting. Throughout the entire year such rates remained distinctly below those charged on customers' loans by banks in principal cities, even though the latter declined rapidly also.[54] After the stock-market crash late in 1929, moreover, conditions became less favorable for the issue of long-term securities, particularly common stocks. Hence a considerable part of the increase in the supply of open-market paper in 1930 presumably represented a shifting from direct bank loans and the issue of long-term securities to indirect bank loans through dealers as a means of raising working capital. For the increase in the demand for open-market paper during 1930, three reasons may be given. In the first place, a number of banks encountered increasing difficulty after 1929 in finding advantageous employment for their loanable funds in commercial and industrial loans to their own customers.[55] Secondly, a number of country banks whose loans to their customers on collateral security became after November 1929 "to an unfortunate degree 'frozen' " wished to strengthen their positions by building up secondary reserves of commercial paper.[56] Finally, rates on New York Stock Exchange call and time loans declined even more precipitously after the stock-market

---

[54] See Chart IV.

[55] Tables 16 and 17 show that the loans "otherwise secured and unsecured" of all Federal Reserve member banks — the class of loans which includes the greater part of their direct advances for commercial and industrial purposes to their own customers — were smaller on each of the four call dates in 1930, both in absolute amounts and in proportion to their total loans, than on the corresponding dates in 1929. The reverse was true of their holdings of open-market commercial paper.

[56] "Report of Commercial Credits Committee," *Proc. Inv. Bankers' Assoc. Amer.*, 1930, p. 144.

crash than rates on prime paper,[57] and a considerable number of banks in 1930 no doubt shifted some part of their resources from loans of the former two classes to promissory notes purchased through dealers.[58]

Increased business activity, rising commodity prices, and the comparatively low cost of borrowing through dealers were probably the factors which were most influential in bringing about such increases in the volume of open-market financing as occurred in the years 1933–1935. Business activity increased at an extraordinarily rapid rate from April to August 1933, and rather rapidly also from December 1933 to May 1934 and during the last five months of 1935. Commodity prices during these three years increased more or less steadily, the Bureau of Labor Statistics' index number of wholesale commodity prices rising from 61 in January 1933 to 81 in the third quarter of 1935. Under these conditions many companies required increased amounts of working capital for purchasing inventories and meeting current operating expenses; and a number of these concerns found it expedient to borrow through dealers the additional amounts of short-term funds they required, as is indicated by the facts that the number of open-market borrowers increased in 1934 and 1935 and the average amount borrowed through dealers by companies using the open market increased in each of the years 1933–1935.[59] Raising capital in this

---

[57] See Chart V.

[58] Tables 16 and 17 show that loans of Federal Reserve member banks to brokers in New York were higher, both in absolute amounts and in proportion to their total loans, on each of the first three call dates in 1930 than on the corresponding call dates in 1929, and that the figures for Dec. 31, 1930, were only slightly lower than those for the last call date in 1929. Brokers' loans of non-member banks, on the other hand, probably declined earlier and at a more rapid rate in 1930 than those of member banks. Figures to support such a conclusion are not available, but most non-member institutions are "country" banks, and it is well known that these banks as a rule endeavor to secure appreciably higher rates of return on their earning assets than were obtainable on New York Stock Exchange call and time loans during the greater part of 1930. In any case it may be noted that brokers' loans made by reporting Federal Reserve member banks in New York for account of out-of-town banks, including both member and non-member institutions, declined rapidly during the last eight months of 1930. (See Table 11.)

[59] See Table 19.

Hardy and Viner hold that the failure of bank loans to increase from the end of 1932 to about 1935 was due in large part to the fact that "many business men had

manner was stimulated to some extent by the comparatively low cost of open-market financing. Rates on prime commercial paper were on the average lower during these three years than they had been in any preceding period of the same length, and were much lower than rates charged on direct loans to customers by banks in principal cities of the United States.[60] As a matter of fact, in all cases where the commercial paper house's commission charge has been ¼ of 1 per cent or less, and the accepting bank has charged not less than the prevailing minimum commission of 1½ per cent a year for its services, the cost of borrowing through commercial paper houses on six-months' notes has during the greater part of the period since the fall of 1933 been less even than that of acceptance financing. Some part of the increase in the volume of dealers' sales from the fall of 1933 to 1936 consequently represented a shifting from acceptance financing to borrowing through commercial paper houses.[61]

Conditions with regard to the demand for open-market notes were also such as to encourage increased borrowing through dealers during the years 1933–1935. The demand for commercial paper

----

unutilized cash resources which they could draw upon to finance such expansion as has taken place" (C. O. Hardy and Jacob Viner, *Report on the Availability of Bank Credit in the Seventh Federal Reserve District*, p. v). The failure of the volume of open-market financing to increase at a more rapid rate since 1932 may likewise be regarded as due, in part at least, to the same fact.

[60] See Chart IV. The comparatively low rates prevailing on commercial paper are mentioned in the *Monthly Review* of the Federal Reserve Bank of New York (Oct. 1933, p. 74) as a factor encouraging increased borrowing in the open market in the fall of 1933. As was pointed out above, however, some of the larger city banks have in recent years offered certain open-market borrowers rates on direct loans as attractive as those at which these concerns have been able to borrow through commercial paper houses.

During the first half of 1933 the volume of open-market financing is said to have increased because of the reduction in the number of banks and in the capital resources of many banks during the preceding few years ("Commercial Paper Comes Back," *Jour. of Com.*, July 23, 1934, p. 2). There was probably little increase, if any, however, in the volume of such financing before the second quarter of 1933, and very few concerns with a credit standing high enough to enable them to borrow in the open market would have found it impossible to obtain from their own banks all the short-term credit accommodation they required.

[61] In this connection see "Acceptance Credit Costs," *Accept. Bull.*, Oct. 1933, pp. 1–2; "The Monthly Review," *ibid.*, p. 9; "Commercial Paper Comes Back," *Jour. of Com.*, July 23, 1934, p. 2; and n. 1, p. 386.

remained very active throughout this period, despite the fact that rates on prime paper were at extraordinarily low levels. A large Eastern house, in fact, placed open-market notes with a greater number of banks in 1935 than in any preceding year in its history; and, as Table 17 indicates, Federal Reserve member banks were holding larger proportions of their earning assets in the form of purchased paper on the four call dates in 1935 than on the corresponding dates in any preceding year for which their holdings of open-market notes have been reported. The sustained demand for outside paper by banks during the years 1933–1935 is to be accounted for by the same conditions which were responsible for the active demand for purchased paper in earlier years. More specifically, banks in general continued to possess large amounts of surplus funds which they could not advantageously place in direct loans to their own customers and therefore had to employ in some other manner;[62] and, of the various alternative short-term investments available for these surplus funds, open-market obligations remained one of the most attractive throughout the period under consideration. Yields on prime paper were appreciably lower than those on Liberty and Treasury bonds and high-grade corporation and municipal bonds during the years 1933–1935,[63] but were distinctly higher than those on short-term government obligations; and during most of this period they were also higher than those on such other short-term investments as prime bankers' acceptances and New York Stock Exchange call and time loans.[64] Moreover, open-market notes proved to be an exceptionally safe investment throughout the years 1933–1935. No losses at all were

[62] Such funds were increased in the case of a number of banks by Section 11 (b) of the Banking Act of 1933, which prohibited the payment by member banks of interest on demand deposits. As a consequence of this prohibition, the demand for open-market paper, both by interior banks and by other corporations, is said to have "broadened considerably" in July and August 1933 ("Commercial Paper Increase Probable," *Wall St. Jour.*, Aug. 28, 1933, p. 7). Increased purchases of open-market notes with funds formerly kept as bankers' (or other corporations') balances in the leading money markets were probably offset to some extent, however, by decreased purchases of outside paper on the part of banks from which such balances were withdrawn.

[63] See Chart VI.

[64] See Chart V.

reported on such obligations during this period, whereas even a number of bankers' acceptances were not paid at maturity in 1933, and banks incurred heavy losses both on direct loans to customers and on long-term securities in each of the three years from 1933 to 1936.[65]

3. Effects on the Commercial Paper Business of the Decline in Dealers' Sales After 1920

In Section 2 of this chapter it was estimated that annual sales of open-market paper increased gradually from about $2,000,000,000 in 1913 to nearly $2,700,000,000 in 1920, and then declined more or less steadily within the next thirteen years to about $225,000,000. This unprecedented decline in dealers' annual sales had important effects on the business of buying and selling commercial paper, some of which will be pointed out in the following pages.

The most direct of these effects was a serious reduction in dealers' profits. When it is considered that in 1920 two of the leading dealers each probably sold $500,000,000 of open-market paper, and thereby probably earned in gross commissions about $1,250,000 each, whereas the total gross commissions on the $225,000,000 of paper sold in the market in 1933 probably amounted to no more than about $560,000, it becomes apparent that the decline in dealers' annual sales involved a serious reduction in their gross earnings. Since they were unable to reduce their expenses correspondingly, it involved also a considerable reduction in their net operating income. This decline in their net earnings may be regarded as the most important effect of the decline in their annual sales volume after 1920, for most of the other effects of their decreasing sales volume which are worth noting resulted directly from the reduction in these net earnings.

Among these other effects, probably the most important which resulted directly from the reduction in dealers' profits were the discontinuance of operations in open-market paper by a number of houses, combination of the interests of some houses with those of one or more other houses, greater concentration in the commercial

[65] See Tables 28 and 29.

paper business, and certain changes in the organizations and methods of operation used by dealers.

Discontinuance of operations in commercial paper was resorted to by a number of houses as an extreme measure after other methods of dealing with the problem of declining profits had proved unsuccessful. Some concerns whose dealings had been confined almost exclusively to buying and selling open-market paper discontinued operations entirely and retired from business. Other houses gave up their dealings in commercial paper but continued various other classes of operations in which they were engaged at the time.[66] As a result of the withdrawal of houses of both these classes, the number of dealers was reduced considerably between 1921 and 1936.

A comparatively small number of houses continued their operations in commercial paper throughout the later years of this period. Some of these houses after about 1924 became more interested in other operations, including dealings in securities, which were more profitable than buying and selling commercial paper, and devoted their energies mainly to developing these more profitable branches of their business. Others took active measures both to increase their sales of open-market paper and to reduce their costs of operation.

As a means of accomplishing the latter purpose, a number of houses effected a combination of their interests with those of one or more other houses. The most common method of effecting such a combination of interests was the establishment of correspondent relations by one dealer with one or more other dealers. Through

---

[66] An account of an Eastern house which adopted this policy is given in "Hampton, McLaren, and Company," a finance case prepared by the present writer for use in the Harvard Graduate School of Business Administration.

Houses which discontinued operations in commercial paper generally turned over the accounts of their borrowing customers to some other dealer or dealers. In some cases they turned over such accounts without charge; in others, they probably charged either a lump sum for the transfer of their good will to the other dealer or dealers or a certain percentage of the commissions earned by the latter over some stated period from sales of paper issued by their new customers.

Some concerns which had formerly been borrowing in the open market discontinued the practice of raising working capital in this manner when dealers who had been handling their accounts gave up operations in commercial paper.

such an arrangement the associated dealers could offer their buying customers a wider variety of open-market "names" and reduce the number of offices required for handling a given volume of business. Another method of consolidating the interests of one house with those of another was a merger of the two houses concerned. Two New York houses, both of which were among the largest dealers in the country, effected such a merger in February 1932,[67] and about a month later two of the most active dealers in New England completed arrangements for a similar merger.

As a result of the discontinuance of operations by a fairly large number of dealers and of mergers of the kind just mentioned, the business of buying and selling promissory notes in the market during the later years of the period considered in this chapter became concentrated in the hands of a very small number of the larger houses. Even before 1913 the bulk of the commercial paper business was probably being handled by fewer than thirty dealers, but during the period from 1914 to 1936 concentration of control in this business became much closer. In 1917, according to a banker of St. Louis, there were "over sixty recognized brokers," of whom a third were "national in their scope." [68] Foulke estimated that a few years before 1927 there were only thirty-nine dealers in the country, but that twenty-seven new dealers began operations during the years from 1924 to 1928.[69] In the same study he estimated that in 1931 there were twenty-one large houses and "from nineteen to about forty-five small, local brokerage houses" which were "active intermittently from one year to another." [70] In August of the same year another writer stated that "commercial paper sales of the entire country" were "concentrated among a primary group of 17 important commercial paper brokers, and a secondary

[67] An account of this merger was given in the *New York Times* of Feb. 9, 1932, p. 37.

[68] F. K. Houston, *Commercial Paper — Its Uses and Abuses* (pamphlet), p. 2.

[69] R. A. Foulke, *The Commercial Paper Market*, p. 99. These twenty-seven new "brokers" were small dealers "engaged principally in the local distribution of the collateral trust notes of one or two important finance companies, or the open market paper of a few prominent cotton mills."

[70] *Ibid.*, p. 108. The forty-five smaller houses included five Southern banks which occasionally sold the notes of their own customers in the market and two securities companies affiliated with banks.

group of 15 small houses." [71] Through personal interviews with practically all the dealers in the country, however, the present writer found that even in the earlier part of 1931 there were only twenty-five dealers of any importance at all. At least eight of these twenty-five, moreover, were comparatively small dealers, and consequently the number of important houses in that year did not exceed seventeen at the most. Of these seventeen houses, probably fifteen were then handling 90 per cent or more of the annual volume of sales of commercial paper. During the years 1931 and 1932 a relatively large number of houses discontinued operations in such paper, and at the end of the latter year only fifteen houses were reporting their "outstandings" to the Federal Reserve Bank of New York. Of these fifteen concerns, at least five were handling practically no commercial paper at that time; and of the remaining ten houses, nine were handling the bulk of the small volume of paper then being bought and sold in the market. Three years later only thirteen dealers were reporting their "outstandings," [72] though six other non-reporting concerns, including a San Francisco corporation which acts only as a correspondent for a large New York house, were also dealing in open-market obligations at that time. Of the thirteen "reporting" dealers, one had really discontinued operations in open-market notes before the close of 1935, another is now handling little, if any, commercial paper, and two are comparatively small concerns. The six non-reporting dealers mentioned just above are also comparatively small houses. At present, therefore, there are only nine large dealers, and these leading nine houses probably handle at least 90 per cent of the total volume of notes being issued for sale in the open market. Hence, though competition in buying and selling open-market obligations has remained very active, concentration of control has in recent years become almost as close in the commercial paper business as in the business of dealing in acceptances.

[71] L. M. Read, *The Story of Commercial Paper* (pamphlet), p. 5.

[72] The decline in the number of dealers reporting to the Federal Reserve Bank of New York after 1920 is shown in Table 2. Actually, two of the thirteen houses just referred to in the text discontinued reporting their "outstandings" to the Federal Reserve Bank of New York after the close of 1933, but both these houses were carried on the list of reporting dealers until about the end of 1936.

Besides bringing about a considerable reduction in the number of houses dealing in open-market paper, and therefore the increasing concentration of control in this business which has just been noted, the decline in the annual volume of commercial paper sales after 1920 also had certain effects on the organizations and methods of operation used by dealers. These effects will be pointed out in the following section.

4. CHANGES IN THE ORGANIZATIONS AND METHODS OF OPERATION USED BY DEALERS

In the preceding chapter it was stated that by 1913 dealers had developed organizations and operating methods closely similar to those used by the larger commercial paper houses in more recent years. As this statement implies, changes in the methods of carrying on their operations used by dealers during the years from 1914 to 1936 were less important than those described in the preceding chapter. Some of the changes they found it advisable to adopt in their organizations and methods of operation during the period from 1914 to 1936 are nevertheless worth noting. These will now be briefly indicated. No attempt will be made at this point, however, to give any detailed description of either the organizations or the operating methods used by commercial paper houses in recent years, for matters such as these can be considered more conveniently in the chapters immediately following.

Such changes as took place in the organizations used by dealers from 1914 to 1936 resulted mainly from changes in the annual volume of their sales. During the earlier years of this period, when their sales were gradually increasing, a number of houses built up larger and more complex organizations than they had maintained before 1914. In some cases they increased the number of their branch offices;[73] in others, they relied more on establishing cor-

---

[73] According to a St. Louis banker, most of the large houses were maintaining branch offices in all the larger cities in the United States by 1917 (Houston, *op. cit.*, p. 9). A New York dealer stated that his house had sixteen offices at the close of the World War (H. C. Smith, "Commercial Paper Broker and His Place in Modern Banking," *Proceedings*, Departmental Conferences, American Institute of Banking, Baltimore, July 1924, p. 469). Presumably fifteen of these offices were branches of the main office in New York. This same house was one of the two New York houses whose merger in February 1932 was mentioned above.

respondent relations with other dealers,[74] or on maintaining sales representatives in various cities, in order to secure a nation-wide distribution of their borrowing customers' paper. After about 1925, however, as the volume of their sales trended steadily downward, most of the houses which remained in business found it necessary to contract the size of their organizations, and therefore to close one or more of their branch offices and to reduce their personnel. Some dealers substituted correspondent relations or the services of sales representatives for the branch offices they closed; others either discontinued one or more of their correspondent connections or dispensed with the services of sales representatives they had formerly been maintaining in one or more cities at some distance from their main offices. On the other hand, as was indicated in the preceding section, two houses early in 1932 each effected a merger of their interests with those of another house; and the resulting organization in each case was presumably somewhat larger than either of the combining houses before the merger.

Certain operating methods of dealers, as well as their "other operations," were also affected by the decline in their sales.

Their methods of selling remained practically the same throughout the period under consideration, but after 1924 most houses found it necessary to reduce their sales staffs to a considerable extent; and during the later years of this period some dealers adopted the policy of allotting open-market notes to their buying customers, that is, distributing their restricted supplies of such obligations among a large number of banks, rather than trying to sell each individual bank as much outside paper as it wishes to purchase. The methods which dealers used in financing their operations also remained practically the same during the years from

---

[74] In October 1923 six of the larger houses, the main offices of which were maintained, respectively, in Boston, New York, Chicago, Minneapolis, St. Louis, and San Francisco, established "a reciprocal correspondent agreement" ("Securities Firms to Co-operate," *N. Y. Times*, Oct. 11, 1923, p. 32). Two of the original members of this system later changed their firm names, and three others discontinued operations in commercial paper entirely. The place of the latter three dealers, however, was taken by two other houses; and, with these modifications, the original association has remained to date the most important correspondent system in the country.

1914 to 1936. During the later years of this period, however, when the demand for their limited supplies of open-market paper was so great that they could turn over their portfolios as often as every day, they required less assistance from banks than formerly in financing purchases of their stock in trade.

On the "other operations" of certain houses, the effects of the decline in their sales volume were more important. As their earnings from operations in commercial paper declined, a number of dealers became more interested in certain other classes of operations which under conditions then prevailing were more profitable. Some houses gave up dealings in open-market paper entirely, in order to devote their energies exclusively to developing these more profitable other classes of operations. Neither these houses nor those which continued to deal in commercial paper, however, added any more than a small number of new classes of operations to those in which they were already engaged. The effect of the decline in their sales of open-market paper was rather to induce them to develop more intensively a limited number of operations which various houses had been carrying on for some years, such as dealing in long-term securities and acting as brokers in the purchase and sale of stocks and bonds. It may be noted also that the greater interest which certain houses took in developing one or more classes of "other operations" was to some extent a cause, as well as an effect, of the decline in their sales of open-market paper; for in their efforts to develop more intensively these more profitable other classes of operations some houses undoubtedly neglected their commercial paper business.

Most of the changes which remain to be noted in the methods used by dealers in carrying on their operations from 1914 to 1936 might more accurately be described, not as actual changes in methods, but rather as further developments of practices which the larger houses had adopted some years before 1914.

Throughout the period considered in this chapter the larger dealers continued to handle in the main the same class of paper as that which constituted the bulk of their stock in trade during the closing years of the preceding period — namely, unsecured single-name promissory notes. Most dealers also bought and sold small amounts of double-name obligations. In addition to these two classes of notes, a number of houses handled bank acceptances and a smaller volume of trade acceptances for a few years after the passage of the Federal Reserve Act, thereby acting as discount houses as well as commercial paper houses. Both the volume of acceptance financing and the gross profits from handling acceptances were so small, however, that practically all commercial paper dealers discontinued operations in both bankers' and trade bills within a few years after the close of the World War.[75] During the later years of the period under consideration the volume of double-name notes bought and sold by dealers dwindled to insignificant proportions. Hence by about 1930 practically the only class of paper they were handling was single-name promissory notes, most of which were unsecured.[76] They continued to obtain such obliga-

[75] As late as October 1921 it was stated that most of the "regular dealers" in acceptances were also handling either commercial paper or stocks and bonds or both ("Dealing in Acceptances," *Fed. Res. Bull.*, Oct. 1921, p. 1169). The number of these so-called "regular dealers," however, seems to have been small (*ibid.*, p. 1167). Some two years later it was reported that commercial paper houses were not dealing in trade acceptances "to any extent worthy of mention" (S. P. Meech, "Recent Tendencies in Credit Relations between Commercial Paper Houses and Business Concerns," *Univ. Jour. Bus.*, Dec. 1923, p. 69). The author of a monograph on the American acceptance market published in October 1935 states that most acceptance dealers, besides dealing in bankers' bills, also buy and sell commercial paper. Similarly, the authors of a work on international money markets published earlier in the same year state that "discount houses and acceptance dealers" buy and sell commercial paper as well as acceptances. Actually, however, no acceptance dealer of any importance has handled open-market notes since about 1925.

In reply to the question of the Reserve Bank Organization Committee as to what classes of paper the Federal Reserve banks should recognize as eligible for rediscount with them, the New York Clearing House recommended early in 1914 that the Federal Reserve Board should discourage the use of merchants' single-name promissory notes "by penalizing them," and "encourage the use of European forms of commercial paper," i.e., acceptances ("Commercial Paper," *Annalist*, Mar. 9, 1914, pp. 293–294). Fortunately, however, such single-name notes were not excluded from the category of eligible paper. If they had been, dealers in commercial paper after 1914 would doubtless have handled a larger volume of bankers' and trade acceptances.

[76] In 1915 it was estimated that "fully 90%" of the commercial paper sold in the market was single-name (*Commercial Paper and Bills of Exchange of the World*, p. 13). In 1930 a number of dealers estimated that about 95 per cent of the open-market notes they were handling were single-name obligations.

tions from a wide variety of trading and manufacturing concerns in all sections of the country, though from 1926 to 1934 the number of their borrowing customers declined rather rapidly.[77] Through greater use of audited financial statements,[78] independent credit investigations of their own, and the establishment of closer contacts with their borrowing customers, they continued also to

[77] See Table 19.

[78] In 1915 an Ohio banker stated that probably more than half the concerns borrowing in the open market were giving "certified reports of condition" (L. F. Kiesewetter, "Audited Statements" — pamphlet — p. 13). Some nine years later a New York dealer reported that financial statements being issued by borrowers in the open market in almost every case bore the certificate of a certified public accountant (E. C. King, "How Banks Should Buy Commercial Paper," *Proc. N. J. Bankers' Assoc.*, 1924, p. 69). In the spring of 1936 several of the largest dealers reported that all their borrowing customers were furnishing audited financial statements every year. As the following table indicates, the proportion of open-market borrowers furnishing such statements has been steadily increasing in recent years, and since 1933 has exceeded 92 per cent.

OPEN-MARKET BORROWERS FURNISHING AUDITED FINANCIAL STATEMENTS, 1931–1935 *

YEAR	NUMBER OF CONCERNS BORROWING IN OPEN MARKET	OPEN-MARKET BORROWERS FURNISHING AUDITED FINANCIAL STATEMENTS	
		Number	*Proportion*
1931	1,239	935	75.7%
1932	651	550	84.5
1933	548	509	92.9
1934	625	585	93.6
1935	654	623	95.3

* Figures included in this table were supplied by the National Credit Office of New York. The records of the latter show that 672, or 97.1 per cent, of the 692 concerns which borrowed in the open market in 1936 were furnishing audited financial statements.

One reason why the practice of furnishing audited financial statements became more common after 1913 was that an increasing number of banks began to insist on having such statements from concerns whose open-market paper was offered for sale to them. As early as 1914 the Association of Reserve City Bankers "resolved unanimously to favor," in buying such paper, concerns which were furnishing audited statements (Kiesewetter, *op. cit.*, p. 1). The failure of the H. B. Claflin Company about the middle of the same year, at a time when some $34,000,000 of promissory notes bearing its indorsement were outstanding, no doubt induced a number of other bankers to adopt a similar policy. At any rate, some two years later an Illinois banker noted that, as a result of "steady pressure of the banks," the auditing by public accountants of statements issued by borrowers in the open market was increasing (F. W. Crane, "Commercial Paper Purchased from Brokers," *Proc. Ill. Bankers' Assoc.*, 1916, p. 134).

increase their efficiency in selecting the paper they handled. Most houses probably bought outright a somewhat greater proportion of the obligations issued by their borrowing customers, and all the larger dealers sold an increasing proportion of the notes they handled to commercial banks.

Competition between dealers and banks for the borrowing accounts of concerns with a high credit standing became very active during the closing years of this period. At the same time, however, coöperation between the larger commercial paper houses and their buying customers became closer, particularly in the exchange of credit information. Partly for this reason, banks as well as dealers became more proficient in selecting the open-market paper they purchased.

5. Activities of the Commercial Credits Committee

Competition of dealers with one another during the period from 1914 to 1936 was no less active than their competition with commercial banks. Some ten years before the close of this period, however, a committee of the Investment Bankers' Association of America, known as the Commercial Credits Committee, was organized for the purpose of bringing about some measure of coöperation among dealers and hence an improvement in conditions in the commercial paper business. An account of the activities of this committee follows.

The Commercial Credits Committee was established in 1924. According to the president of the Investment Bankers' Association of America, the purpose of the committee was to be "the consideration of the problems of those of our member houses who deal in commercial Paper and short-time credits."

The first meeting of the committee, which was attended by representatives of nine commercial paper houses, was held in the spring of 1925. This meeting "was probably the first occasion on which the leading commercial paper houses had ever met on common ground for a general discussion of their problems."

The chairman of the committee was requested to confer with the important commercial paper houses not represented at this meeting, and to ask them to be prepared to state their views on the various matters under discussion at a meeting to be held in New York thirty days later.

This second meeting, which was held on May 27, 1925, was attended by representatives of practically all the leading commercial paper houses. At this meeting it was suggested that "a permanent commercial paper group be formed, to function under the auspices of the Investment Bankers Association"; and that all commercial paper houses not already members thereof be invited to join the association, and through such membership to join in the deliberations of the commercial paper group and assist in carrying out its plans and policies. An organization committee of seven members was then appointed to carry out these suggestions.

On July 15 this committee sent to all commercial paper houses a letter "setting forth the contemplated program" and suggesting the appointment of four permanent subcommittees to consider the various problems confronting dealers in open-market paper. The favorable response with which this letter met led to the appointment by the organization committee of the four subcommittees in question. The latter were called, respectively, the Committee on Competitive Methods, the Committee on Remuneration for Services Rendered, the Committee on Relations with Banks, and the Committee on Publicity.

The names of these four subcommittees indicate in a general way four of the main problems which in the opinion of the Commercial Credits Committee required the joint consideration of the various houses dealing in commercial paper in the summer of 1925.

The most important of these problems was that connected with a certain competitive practice which, though perhaps not "unfair," had "a very unsettling effect" on the commercial paper business and was no doubt disapproved by the majority of houses. This was the practice, resorted to by some dealers, of striving to secure the accounts of other dealers "by wholesale offers of money at rates definitely below the market."

The next most important problem was that of securing an adequate gross commission. Despite the fact that the expenses of conducting their operations had risen appreciably during the years following 1914, the "recognized" commission of dealers had remained ¼ of 1 per cent. Because of competition among dealers themselves, as well as that between dealers and banks willing to lend at low rates to their own customers, the commissions actually received by dealers were often less than the "recognized" rate of compensation.[79]

The third problem, like the first two, was one of long standing. It arose in connection with the practice of allowing banks the option of returning purchased paper if, after investigation, they regard it as unsatisfactory. During the years following 1913, as well as in the preceding period, a number of banks either showed carelessness in failing to observe the terms of option agreements or deliberately abused the option privilege.

The last problem referred to above was less important. This was the problem of securing "a certain amount of publicity" for the purpose of acquainting a larger group of merchants and manufacturers with the advantages of open-market financing and a larger number of bankers with the advantages of commercial paper as a short-term investment. The Commercial Credits Committee believed that this publicity should be secured through addresses and articles by dealers, bank officers, and prominent merchants using the open-market method of financing.[80]

After the appointment of the four subcommittees mentioned above, the committee endeavored to bring about an improvement in conditions in the commercial paper business by securing the coöperation of as large a number of houses as possible in dealing with the main problems then confronting this business. While its efforts in this direction were not entirely successful, it nevertheless

---

[79] In Chap. II it was pointed out that the practice of "splitting" commissions, which has the same effect on the compensation received by dealers as buying paper at rates below those prevailing in the market, was not uncommon in the closing years of the period from 1861 to 1914. During the years immediately following 1914 both these practices seem to have been rather common, though they were doubtless condemned by most of the leading dealers (Houston, *op. cit.*, p. 15).

[80] The account of the activities of the committee which has been given up to this point is based on its first annual report, which was issued in typewritten form in December 1925.

did succeed in establishing "standards of business and rules of conduct which were of mutual benefit" to all houses belonging to the Investment Bankers' Association of America.[81]

Before the end of May 1926 it was able to report that it had already brought about an improvement in competitive conditions sufficient to justify its existence.[82] It did not succeed, however, in inducing all dealers to discontinue the practice of striving to secure competitors' accounts through offering to buy the paper of certain concerns at rates definitely lower than those prevailing in the market.[83] It recognized that excessive competition of this sort was one of the causes of the unsatisfactory situation with respect to commissions, and that such a situation could be improved only by a general agreement among dealers themselves.[84] It recognized

---

[81] "Interim Report of the Commercial Credits Committee," *I.B.A. of A. Bull.*, May 29, 1929, p. 73.

[82] "Report of Commercial Credits Committee," *ibid.*, May 29, 1926, p. 212.

[83] Offers to buy open-market paper at rates below the market have been called "baiting propositions." The practice of making such offers no doubt became less common after 1931; for in that year the large Eastern house which had been most aggressive in making "baiting" offers retired from business, and during the last few years, instead of relying to the same extent as formerly on competitive rate-underbidding as a means of securing new accounts, dealers have stressed primarily the services they are able to offer their borrowing customers (J. N. Eaton, "Rate Competition," *Mo. Bull. Robert Morris Associates*, July 1936, p. 45). It should be noted that it is sometimes difficult to state precisely what should be considered as "the market rate" for the paper of a concern wishing to borrow in the market. In such cases what may appear to be a purchase of paper at rates below the market may not have been intended as such at all by the dealer concerned.

[84] "Interim Report, Commercial Credits Committee," *I.B.A. of A. Bull.*, Mar. 31, 1925, p. 179.

If a dealer buys paper at a rate below the market and has to sell it at the market rate, he of course suffers a loss as a result of these buying and selling operations alone. Such a loss, however, may be reduced, offset, or more than offset by his commission for selling the paper concerned. The shorter the maturity of the paper, the smaller any such loss will be, provided, as is commonly the case, the dealer's commission remains the same regardless of the maturity of the paper.

A similar method of competition, which certain dealers continued to use even during the later years of the period from 1914 to 1936, consists in buying open-market paper at a net or flat discount rate, with no commission charge. If a dealer buys paper at such a rate and sells it at the same rate, he of course merely "swaps dollars": he suffers no actual loss on the transaction, but forgoes the opportunity of making his customary commission. As an example of the use of this method of competition within recent years, the following instance may be cited: About the middle of 1930, in order to secure a choice account then being handled by one of its competitors, one of the largest houses in the country is said to have bought

also that both the rates at which commercial paper houses buy
open-market notes and the commissions they can charge for handling such obligations are affected by the competition of banks
willing to make direct loans at low rates to their own customers.
Most dealers, in fact, believed that such competition "regulates as
much as any other factor the commercial-paper rate" and the commission which the commercial paper house can charge.   Hence the
committee in 1926 temporarily abandoned "any concerted effort"
to raise commissions.[85]   In dealing with the problem of options, the
committee was probably able to secure more effective coöperation
on the part of the various commercial paper houses.   It had stated
in December 1925, in its first annual report, that it regarded the
practice of granting options as "unsound in principle and unfair
in its application," but doubted the feasibility of attempting to
eliminate it completely at that time.[86]   After studying the problem
early in the following year, it apparently came to the same conclusion; for it made various recommendations and suggestions de-
signed to bring about greater uniformity of practice in the matter
of allowing options,[87] but did not recommend that the practice of

$5,000,000 of the paper of a leading flour-milling company on a net rate basis, with
no expectation of making a commission or any other immediate gain from the sale
of such paper.

[85] "Report of Commercial Credits Committee," *Proc. Inv. Bankers' Assoc. Amer.*,
1926, pp. 109–110.

[86] Page 2 of typewritten copy of this report.

[87] Such recommendations, which the committee proposed should go into effect
on Mar. 1, 1926, included the following:

1. That options should be granted for credit investigation only, and only on
special request of the purchasing bank; and that they should be a definite contract
between the commercial paper house and the bank, "covering in each case the sale
of specific notes."

2. That the following "uniform form of option" should be adopted: "The
above notes may be returned by delivery at our office during banking hours on or
before .... This option is given for credit investigation only. Please do not mark
these notes until the above option has expired."

3. That options should date from the day on which the sale of commercial paper
is confirmed to the buying bank — not from the day on which such paper is actually
delivered.

4. That options should expire within a period not exceeding ten days, except
in the twelfth Federal Reserve district, where the option period should be reduced
from twenty to seventeen days.

5. That the practice of granting extensions or renewals of options should be
discouraged as unnecessary and detrimental to the best interests of commercial

allowing banks to purchase commercial paper on option be discontinued entirely.

During the years following 1926, as a result, perhaps, of the decline in dealers' annual sales and of the failure of certain dealers to take any active interest in its work, the committee seems to have become less active. In July 1931 only about five houses were formally represented on the committee, and since 1934 it has issued no annual report on its activities. In the spring of 1936, however, though the number of commercial paper dealers was then much smaller than it was in 1931, six houses were represented on the committee; and a number of dealers not members of the Investment Bankers' Association of America have continued to send representatives to the committee's meetings and to coöperate with houses belonging to the association in the endeavor to maintain high standards of business ethics and practice in the commercial paper business.

---

paper houses; and that commercial paper houses should grant such extensions or renewals "only in the most exceptional cases."

6. That granting options subject to the receipt of new balance sheet figures should be discontinued. [Many houses had already discontinued this practice.] ("Report of Commercial Credits Committee," *I.B.A. of A. Bull.*, May 29, 1926, pp. 212–213.)

PART II
ORGANIZATION AND OPERATION OF THE COMMERCIAL PAPER HOUSE

CHAPTER IV

THE ORGANIZATION OF THE COMMERCIAL PAPER HOUSE

In Chapter II an account was given of the organizations and methods of operation used by dealers during the period from 1861 to 1914, and in the following chapter some of the more important changes in such organizations and operating methods during the period from 1914 to 1936 were indicated. No attempt was made in these chapters, however, to describe in detail either the organizations or the methods of operation used by dealers in recent years. The purpose of Part II is to furnish a more detailed description of both the organization and the practical operations of the modern commercial paper house than could conveniently be given in these earlier historical chapters. In the present chapter the organization of the commercial paper house will be described. In the remaining chapters of Part II the methods used by dealers in conducting their main operations will be considered, together with such related matters as the classes of paper bought and sold in the open market, the classes of concerns issuing such paper, the buyers of open-market obligations, the practices followed by banks in buying outside paper, and the "other operations" of commercial paper houses.

1. Legal Forms of Organization Used by Commercial Paper Houses

Most commercial paper houses in recent years have used the partnership, rather than the corporate, form of organization. Of the twenty-three houses which presumably were the largest dealers in commercial paper in 1931, in fact, fourteen were organized as partnerships and only nine as corporations.[1] Similarly, of fourteen

---

[1] The largest of these nine corporations, a Chicago house, was then using, and has since continued to use, a separate partnership for conducting its operations in New York, in which it maintains its most important branch office. On the other hand, one of the largest of the fourteen partnerships referred to above was closely affiliated with two houses which were organized as separate corporations. (Only

houses consulted in the spring of 1936, seven (including five of the leading nine dealers) were using the partnership form of organization and only five (including three leading dealers and a comparatively small house which in handling commercial paper acts as a correspondent dealer only) were organized as corporations.[2]

Several reasons may be given for the fact that the majority of commercial paper houses have preferred to use the partnership, rather than the corporate, form of organization. In the first place, some houses have been members of one or more stock exchanges whose rules do not allow concerns organized as corporations to become members thereof. Secondly, under the income tax laws of some states dealers find it to their advantage to use the partnership form of organization, rather than the corporate form.[3] Thirdly, a house organized as a partnership may inspire more confidence on the part of both its borrowing and its buying customers than a house using the corporate form of organization; for the active members of a firm assume unlimited liability, whereas the liability of a corporation is limited. The reputation of a house for integrity and financial responsibility, however, is no doubt a more important advantage than the fact that it may happen to be organized as a firm, rather than a corporation.[4] In the fourth place, the members

---

one of these two houses was included among the nine corporations referred to in the text; the other was considered as in effect a branch office of the partnership in question.)

[2] The remaining two houses were organized as single proprietorships.

[3] One of the main reasons why three New York houses, one of which had formerly been organized as a corporation, were using the partnership form of organization in 1931 was that, under the income tax laws of New York State, they found this form more advantageous than the corporate form. On the other hand, a Boston house reported about the same time that it was using the corporate form of organization because of certain advantages it offered with respect to taxation.

[4] In the event of any misappropriation of funds held by a commercial paper house for either its borrowing or its buying customers, the creditors concerned would possess greater legal advantages if the house with which they were dealing happened to be a partnership than if it had been organized as a corporation. Similarly, if commercial paper houses indorsed the paper they handle and thereby assumed responsibility for its payment at maturity, banks holding open-market paper on which payment had been defaulted would possess greater legal advantages if they had purchased such paper through a partnership than if they had bought it through a corporation. Even in such hypothetical cases as these, however, the financial responsibility of the house concerned would be more important than the particular form of organization it happened to be using.

of a firm can exercise a direct and centralized control over their business, and their operations are subject to less regulation by state and other laws than those of a house organized as a corporation. Finally, most houses adopted the partnership form of organization at the time of their establishment, and the majority of such firms have no doubt felt that there would be no particular advantages in substituting the corporate form for the type of organization they adopted when they entered the commercial paper business.

2. Types of Organizations Maintained by Dealers in Recent Years

Whether operating as partnerships or as corporations, commercial paper houses all use essentially the same methods of conducting their main operations, which consist in buying promissory notes issued by concerns with a high credit standing and then finding a market for such obligations among banks in all sections of the country. The size and complexity of the organizations they maintain for the purpose of dealing in open-market paper depend on the scope of their operations. Some small dealers who confine their activities in the main to their own immediate localities require only a single office and the services of one or two assistants. The larger houses, on the other hand, buy and sell commercial paper in a market that is nation-wide, and consequently find it necessary to maintain considerably larger and more elaborate organizations. All houses, regardless of their size, maintain a main office in a financial center of some importance. In addition to this main office, all but the smallest dealers maintain either branch offices, correspondent relations, or sales representatives in one or more other important financial centers. Some houses in recent years have depended on one only of these three agencies, in addition to their main offices, for the distribution of the open-market paper they have handled. Others have used two of these agencies concurrently, and one or two of the larger houses, in order to secure a wide distribution of their borrowing customers' paper, have made use of all three.

The extent to which different houses have relied on these three agencies in recent years varies considerably. This is shown by the following two enumerations, the first of which indicates the cities in which the main offices of twenty-three houses [5] were located in 1931, the number of dealers maintaining their main offices in each of these cities, the number of branch offices, correspondent relations, and/or sales representatives which each of the twenty-three houses was maintaining, and the cities in which such branch offices, correspondent relations, or sales representatives were being maintained; and the second of which gives corresponding data for thirteen houses (including the leading nine dealers) in the spring of 1936:

(1) Twenty-three houses, 1931

Boston: Four houses

First house: One correspondent — New York. (Was also maintaining correspondent relations with an investment banking house in Hartford, but only for the purpose of dealing in collateral loan paper.)

Second house: Two branch offices — New York and Providence. (Latter office was not handling commercial paper.) One correspondent — Chicago.

Third house: Two branch offices — New York and Chicago. Two sales representatives — Albany and Portland (Maine). (These representatives were handling securities as well as commercial paper.)

Fourth house: One branch office — New York. Three correspondents — Chicago, Minneapolis, and St. Louis. One sales representative — Portland (Oregon).

Hartford: One house: Five correspondents — Boston, Chicago, Milwaukee, St. Louis, and San Francisco. (Relations with correspondents in latter two cities were nonreciprocal.) [6]

New York: Eight houses

First house: Five branch offices — Boston, Philadelphia, Chicago, St. Louis, and San Francisco.

---

[5] These twenty-three houses are the same as those mentioned in the preceding section. As was noted above, they were presumably the largest dealers in commercial paper in the country in 1931.

[6] As is indicated below, correspondent relations between two dealers may be said to be "nonreciprocal" when one dealer sells paper originated by the other but the latter does not sell paper originated by the former; and "reciprocal" when each of the two dealers sells paper originated by the other.

Second house: Five branch offices — Chicago, St. Louis, Portland (Oregon), San Francisco, and Los Angeles. One correspondent — Boston. One sales representative — Pittsburgh.

Third house: Four branch offices — Boston, Philadelphia, Chicago, and St. Louis. Three sales representatives — Seattle, Portland (Oregon), and San Francisco.

Fourth house: Five branch offices — Boston, Hartford, Scranton, Chicago, and St. Louis. (Though considered as branches of the main office in New York, the Boston, Chicago, and St. Louis offices were virtually independent organizations. The St. Louis office was organized as a separate corporation. The New York, Boston, Chicago, and St. Louis offices, and an affiliated San Francisco house organized as a separate corporation, were operating what might be called an inter-company correspondent system; i.e., each of these organizations was handling paper originated by the others.)

Fifth house: Two branch offices — Chicago and San Francisco. Five sales representatives — Hartford, Philadelphia, Scranton, St. Louis, and Seattle.[7]

Sixth house: Two branch offices — Boston and Philadelphia. Two correspondents — Chicago and San Francisco. (Relations with both these correspondents were nonreciprocal.)

Seventh house: Two correspondents — Milwaukee and San Francisco. (Relations with San Francisco correspondent were nonreciprocal.)

Eighth house: One correspondent — Chicago. (Relations with this correspondent were nonreciprocal.)

Philadelphia: One house: One branch office — New York.

Chicago: Three houses

First house: Five branch offices — New York, Indianapolis, Milwaukee, Minneapolis, and St. Louis. Two sales representatives — Boston and Spokane.

Second house: Six correspondents — Boston, Hartford, New York (two), St. Louis, and San Francisco. (Relations with last four of these dealers were nonreciprocal.)

Third house: Three correspondents — Boston, Minneapolis, and St. Louis.

Minneapolis: One house: One branch office — St. Paul. Three correspondents — Boston, Chicago, and St. Louis.

---

[7] It would perhaps be more accurate to say that this house was maintaining small branch offices, rather than sales representatives, in Hartford, Philadelphia, Scranton, St. Louis, and Seattle in 1931.

St. Louis: One house: Five correspondents — Boston, Hartford, Chicago (two), and Minneapolis. (Relations with the Hartford correspondent and one of the two Chicago dealers were nonreciprocal.) One sales representative — Kansas City.

New Orleans: Two houses

First house: Seven branch offices — New York, Chicago, Atlanta, St. Louis, Houston, Dallas, and Los Angeles. (The St. Louis office was not handling commercial paper.)

Second house: No branch offices, correspondent relations, or sales representatives.

Wichita, Kansas: One house: One sales representative — Topeka (Kansas).

San Francisco: One house: Seven branch offices — Spokane, Seattle, Tacoma, Portland (Oregon), Oakland, San José, and Los Angeles. One sales representative — Grass Valley (California). (This house was also a member of the inter-company correspondent system mentioned in connection with the fourth New York house above.)

(2) Thirteen houses, 1936

Boston: Two houses

First house: Six branch offices — New York, Indianapolis, Chicago, St. Louis, Kansas City, and San Francisco. (The Kansas City office was not handling commercial paper.)

Second house: Two branch offices — New York and Philadelphia. Four correspondents — Chicago, Minneapolis, St. Louis, and San Francisco.

New York: Three houses

First house: Four branch offices — Boston, Philadelphia, Chicago, and St. Louis. One correspondent — San Francisco. (Relations with this correspondent were nonreciprocal.)

Second house: Eight branch offices — Hartford, Philadelphia, Scranton, Chicago, St. Louis, Kansas City, San Francisco, and Seattle.

Third house: No branch offices, correspondent relations, or sales representatives.

Philadelphia: One house: No branch offices, correspondent relations, or sales representatives.

Chicago: Three houses

First house: Five branch offices — New York, Indianapolis, Milwaukee, Minneapolis, and Sioux City.

Second house: Four correspondents — Boston, Minneapolis, St. Louis, and San Francisco. Sales representatives in two cities — Omaha and Lincoln (Nebraska).

Third house: No branch offices, correspondent relations, or sales representatives.

Minneapolis: One house: One branch office — St. Paul. Four correspondents — Boston, Chicago, St. Louis, and San Francisco.

St. Louis: One house: Four correspondents — Boston, Chicago, Minneapolis, and San Francisco.

Wichita, Kansas: One house: No branch offices, correspondent relations, or sales representatives.

San Francisco: One house: Four branch offices — Los Angeles, Portland (Oregon), Seattle, and Spokane. Four correspondents — Boston, Chicago, Minneapolis, and St. Louis. Sales representatives in six cities — Pasadena, Fresno, Sacramento, Grass Valley (California), Salem (Oregon), and Tacoma.

From an examination of the foregoing data it may be seen that ten different types of organization were being used by dealers in open-market paper in 1931, and six different types in 1936. A clearer view of the extent to which each of these forms of organization was being used in these two years may be gained from Table 18, in which the several different types are arranged approximately in the order of their complexity and the number of houses using each type is given.

As this table indicates, a number of houses have within the last few years adopted simpler forms of organization than those they were using in 1931. This development is a result of the decline in the volume of business handled by dealers in the years immediately following 1930. Because of the steady decline in the volume of their sales during these years, a large number of the twenty-three houses mentioned above gave up operations in commercial paper entirely, and even some of the largest of those which continued to deal in open-market paper found it advisable to replace the organizations they had previously been maintaining with simpler types which would be less expensive to operate. Since the maintenance of branch offices is one of the largest items of expense involved in dealing in open-market paper, some dealers closed at least one of their branches and substituted therefor either correspondent connections or the services of sales representatives. One or two other dealers either discontinued relations with cor-

TABLE 18

TYPES OF ORGANIZATION BEING USED BY DEALERS AND NUMBER OF HOUSES USING EACH TYPE, 1931 AND 1936

	Number of Houses Using Each Type	
TYPE OF ORGANIZATION	*1931*	*1936*
Main office only	1	4
Main office and one or more sales representatives	1	–
Main office and one or more correspondents	6	1
Main office and one or more sales representatives and correspondents	1	1
Main office and one or more branch offices	3	3
Main office and one or more sales representatives and branch offices	4	–
Main office and one or more correspondents and branch offices ..	3	3
Main office and one or more sales representatives, correspondents, and branch offices	2	1
Main office, one or more branch offices, and an inter-company correspondent system used by a group of closely affiliated dealers	1	–
Main office, one or more sales representatives and branch offices, and the same inter-company correspondent system	1	–

respondents in one or more cities or dispensed with the services of one or more sales representatives. Most effective as a means of reducing operating costs, however, was the merger of one house with another. Two such mergers were effected early in 1932.[8] One of these mergers made it possible to handle the same volume of business with a single main office and without the correspondent relations which the smaller of the two combining houses had been maintaining. As a result of the other merger, a single organization, with a single main office, four branch offices, and one correspondent, replaced two separate organizations which in 1931 were maintaining, respectively, a main office and five branches, and a main office, five branches, one correspondent connection, and one sales representative.

[8] See pp. 185, 188.

3. Functions of Main and Branch Offices, Correspondent Systems, and Sales Representatives

The main offices of commercial paper houses, which are generally under the direction of their most influential partner or executive officer, are the centers from which their operations are directed. The functions performed by such offices are essentially the same in the case of all dealers. They include the origination, purchase, and distribution of open-market notes, making credit investigations, carrying the greater part of their house's portfolio of purchased paper, and making any arrangements that may be necessary for financing purchases of open-market obligations — in short, all the main operations involved in dealing in commercial paper. One of the most important of these functions — the origination of open-market paper — in the case of the larger houses may be assigned to a special department, known as the new business department. For the equally important work of credit investigation, all the larger dealers maintain a special credit department. In addition to the personnel entrusted with the responsibility of securing new accounts and making credit investigations, the larger houses maintain a staff of clerical workers in their main offices. Such offices also serve as the headquarters of a staff of salesmen.

The main function of branch offices of commercial paper houses is selling open-market paper. Selling, in fact, is the only main operation of all branches of all houses. All branches aid the main offices of their organizations in the work of credit investigation to a greater or lesser extent, but the credit departments of dealers and their complete credit files are maintained in their main offices, and the latter offices generally make the most important decisions relating to the extension of credit. Similarly, one or more branches of a number of houses buy paper, but practically always with authority from the main office and subject to its approval as regards "names," amounts, rates, and commissions. Final authority and responsibility in the matter of buying rests with the partners or senior executives of a commercial paper house, and consequently with the main office, unless one or more of the officers of a branch happen to be resident partners or influential executives. A number of branch offices, particularly those which have the authority to buy the obligations they handle, also carry stocks of purchased paper. In general, both the range and the importance of the operations which a branch office carries on depend on whether or not its officers include one or more resident partners or other influential executives. Some branches are scarcely more than small sales offices of the organizations of which they are a part. The most important branches of a few of the larger houses, however, perform all the functions of their main offices, and are of virtually coördinate importance with the latter.[9]

The functions performed by correspondent systems are similar to those of branch offices. The purpose of maintaining correspondent relations, in fact, is to secure at least some of the advantages of branch offices without the expense of operating any of the latter agencies for the distribution of open-market paper.

Three different types of correspondent systems have been used by dealers in recent years. The simplest form is a nonreciprocal system of which two houses only are members. Where such a system is used, one of the two dealers concerned sells paper which the other has originated, but the latter does not handle paper originated by the first dealer. From the point of view of the first house, the functions performed by its correspondent are in such cases similar to those of a comparatively unimportant branch office which confines its operations almost entirely to selling. The second form is a reciprocal system with two members only. Where a system of this type is used, each house handles paper originated by the other. As this statement implies, each house also supplies the other with paper it has originated itself. Hence from the point of view of its

---

[9] As may be seen from an examination of Table 18, fourteen dealers were maintaining one or more branch offices in 1931. The branches of all fourteen of these houses were of course selling open-market paper, and were also to a greater or lesser extent aiding their main offices in making credit investigations. The branch offices of twelve of the houses were buying paper, though the branches of three of these twelve houses confined their operations in the main to selling. The remaining two houses were buying all their paper through their main offices. Eleven of the fourteen houses, either occasionally or as a regular practice, carried stocks of paper at one or more branch offices — generally at buying branches, but not necessarily at all such branches.

correspondent each house performs functions similar to those of a branch office which both buys and sells paper. Obviously such a system involves closer relations between the two dealers concerned than the system first mentioned.[10] Still closer relations among the dealers concerned are involved in the third form, which is a reciprocal system with three or more members. Each member of such a system handles paper originated by all the others, and supplies the latter with paper issued by its own borrowing customers. Consequently each of the group of associated houses performs for all the others services similar to those of a branch office authorized both to buy and to sell paper for the organization of which it is a part. Though only one such system is used by dealers at present, this is by far the most important correspondent system in the country, and the total amount of paper which the houses associated in this group obtain from one another and sell in the market is considerably larger than the amount sold through correspondents by all other dealers combined.[11]

The agreements into which the members of a correspondent system enter may be very informal — virtually no more than "gentlemen's agreements" to do and not to do certain things — or of a more formal type, embodied in a legal contract with very definite provisions, but also supplemented by informal agreements and understandings. The most important provisions of such agreements, whether informal or of the more formal type, are those

[10] Whether the relations between two correspondent houses are reciprocal or nonreciprocal depends on the supply of high-grade paper each is able to originate. If one of the houses is unable to originate a supply of desirable paper large enough to satisfy the demands of its own buying customers, relations between the dealers concerned must of necessity be nonreciprocal.

[11] The correspondent system in question is the same as that referred to in n. 74, p. 188. It was reported that the total "outstandings" of this group of houses amounted to $89,000,000 on May 31, 1930, or 16½ per cent of the total amount reported by all leading dealers to the Federal Reserve Bank of New York for the same date. The proportion of the total volume of commercial paper business which the group now handles is no doubt considerably larger than the proportion it was handling in 1930.

A large amount of paper was formerly sold through the inter-company correspondent system mentioned in Table 18. This system, however, was discontinued early in 1932, when the New York house which was its leading member gave up operations in open-market paper. An affiliated San Francisco house, which was the next most important member of this inter-company system, shortly thereafter joined the correspondent system mentioned in the preceding paragraph.

relating to the division of territory and gross profits from the sale of paper obtained through correspondents. Provisions relating to the division of territory define the area in which each correspondent house may originate open-market notes and sell both the obligations of its own customers and paper secured from its correspondents. Agreements relating to the manner in which gross commissions from the sale of notes originated by correspondents are to be divided generally provide that such commissions shall be shared equally by the originating and the selling house. Besides general agreements relating to the division of territory and commissions, special agreements are made with respect to such matters in the case of certain accounts.

With regard to the comparative advantages of branch offices and correspondent connections, there is some difference of opinion among dealers.

The advantages of a system of branch offices are said to be that such a system can be completely controlled by the main office; that it enables dealers to maintain closer contacts with both their borrowing and their buying customers; and that it makes it possible for dealers to secure a better distribution of their borrowing customers' paper than could be obtained through a correspondent system, since the members of such a system have to divide commissions from sales of notes obtained from their correspondents, and are therefore likely to be less aggressive in finding a market for such obligations than in selling paper issued by their own customers. The first of these stated advantages is undoubtedly of some importance. Probably most dealers maintaining correspondent relations, however, would regard the second and third statements as inaccurate.

In favor of maintaining correspondent connections, rather than a system of branch offices, there seem to be two main arguments: first, that a correspondent system accomplishes the main purpose of a system of branches — securing a larger supply of open-market notes for sale and a broader distribution for the paper which each house originates itself — without the overhead expense involved in operating branch offices; and second, that a correspondent system can perform the important function of credit investigation and analysis more efficiently than a system of branch offices, and can therefore offer its buying customers paper of a higher grade. In support of this second argument, it is said that the credit standing of concerns issuing paper handled by the members of a correspondent system is investigated by all the houses concerned, and that in "checking" paper offered by its correspondents each house can use the services of an efficient credit department in its main office. The notes which a member house purchases from its correspondents, moreover, are bought "on option"; that is, each member of the system has the right, within a certain period, to return to the originating house from which it obtained them any notes which, after a careful credit investigation, it may consider unsatisfactory. Both these arguments have force, though some of the larger houses would no doubt contest the validity of both.

Whether in fact it is more advantageous for any particular house to operate a system of branches, or, instead, to maintain correspondent relations with other dealers, would seem to depend mainly on its ability to secure capable managers for branch offices, and to a lesser extent on the volume of its business. If it can secure able managers for each of its offices, and handles a large volume of business each year, it will probably find a system of branches more satisfactory than correspondent connections. This is all the more likely to be the case if the house in question also deals in securities, and maintains offices in important financial centers for this purpose; for in that event the use of branch offices for handling commercial paper will involve comparatively little increase in its overhead expense. A correspondent system, on the other hand, is likely to be better adapted to the requirements of a house which handles a comparatively small volume of business than a system of branch offices would be.[12]

[12] As is indicated by Table 18, fourteen houses were maintaining one or more branch offices in 1931, and fourteen were maintaining one or more correspondent connections. Seven houses were maintaining one or more branches, without any correspondent connections, seven were maintaining one or more correspondent connections but no branches, and an equal number of houses were maintaining both

Nine houses were maintaining sales representatives in one or more cities in 1931, and two houses were using the services of such representatives in the spring of 1936. Such representatives are to be distinguished from regular salesmen who make the main office or some branch office of their organization their headquarters. The cities in which they are maintained are generally at some distance from the main offices of the houses which employ their services, and are comparatively unimportant markets for the paper handled by such houses. In some cases sales representatives devote only a part of their time to selling open-market paper for the houses which use their services. In a few cases they handle securities as well as commercial paper. Some representatives, however, have devoted all their time to handling open-market notes for the houses with which they have been connected. In such cases they perform functions similar to those of a comparatively unimportant branch office which sells open-market paper but does not buy the obligations it handles.

4. Division of Territory in the Commercial Paper Business

In connection with the origination and distribution of open-market paper, practically all dealers except those whose operations are confined in the main to their own immediate localities divide the area in which they operate into certain more or less definite territories. The territorial divisions they use, which depend largely

---

one or more branches and one or more correspondent connections. Some of the largest houses in the country were not using such connections in 1931. On the other hand, seven large houses were then maintaining correspondent relations with other dealers, and a year or so later a New York house which previously had maintained no such relations established a correspondent connection with a dealer in San Francisco and closed a branch office which it had been maintaining in that city. This house is probably the largest dealer in the country. Most of the larger houses were using one or more branch offices in 1931, though two large dealers had no branches at all and a third large house had a single branch only. About a year later, however, the latter house, which is now probably the second or third largest dealer in the country, established an additional branch office.

In the spring of 1936, seven of the nine houses which were at that time the leading dealers in commercial paper were maintaining one or more branch offices, six were maintaining one or more correspondent relations, and four were maintaining both one or more branches and one or more correspondent connections.

upon the types of organization they maintain, may conveniently be considered at this point.

Three different classes of territorial divisions are used by dealers in connection with the distribution of open-market notes: divisions of territory between their main offices and any branches or sales representatives they may maintain, those between or among the members of a correspondent system, and those between two houses which handle the account — known as a "split" or "divided" account — of a concern which sells its obligations through more than one dealer.

Houses which maintain branch offices and sales representatives assign more or less definite territories to their main offices and to each of their branches and representatives. Most of the larger houses maintain their main offices in New York, Boston, or Chicago, though three large dealers maintain such offices in other financial centers which are important markets for commercial paper.[13] These main offices sell most of the paper they handle in the financial center in which they are located and in the surrounding territory. Branch offices and sales representatives are generally maintained in cities at some distance from the main offices of the houses with which they are connected. Since convenience in selling and proximity to important sources of demand for open-market paper are the main considerations determining where they shall be established, they are maintained, just as dealers' main offices are, in the financial centers of districts in which commercial banks ordinarily buy a considerable volume of outside paper each year, either for their own account or for the account of correspondent banks. Like main offices, they also sell paper mainly in the center in which they are located and in the territory adjoining. Divisions

---

[13] In 1931 four houses were maintaining their main offices in Boston, eight in New York, and three in Chicago; in 1936 two houses (both being among the largest nine dealers) were maintaining such offices in Boston, three (including two of the leading nine dealers) in New York, and four (including two of the largest nine dealers) in Chicago. Both in 1931 and in 1936 the only leading houses which were not maintaining their main offices in one of these three cities were the three houses referred to just above in the text. The main offices of these three dealers are located, respectively, in Minneapolis, St. Louis, and San Francisco. Each of these cities is an important market for commercial paper.

of territory between main offices and branches or sales representatives, however, are not necessarily hard and fast, and both main offices and branches or sales representatives may sell paper in the same territory.

Since dealers assign a separate territory to each of their offices and sales representatives, the number of territorial divisions they use depends on the number of offices and representatives they maintain. Thus a Boston house whose operations are nation-wide was maintaining in 1931, in addition to its main office, two branches and two sales representatives, and consequently was using five different territorial divisions; whereas a New York house which also buys and sells open-market paper throughout the country was maintaining, besides its main office, two branches and five representatives, and accordingly was using eight territorial divisions.

Territorial divisions of the kind just mentioned are based on the number and location of the offices and sales representatives maintained by dealers. In the case of some of the larger houses all but the largest of such divisions may be included within certain broader geographical divisions of territory. The broadest of these larger divisions are known as the East and the West. The amount of territory included in these two divisions by different dealers of course varies to some extent. The Boston house mentioned just above includes the states east of Ohio, Kentucky, Tennessee, and Mississippi in the East, and all other states in the West. Other leading dealers do not include Alabama in the East, and one large dealer includes Pittsburgh and western Pennsylvania in the West; but all the larger houses include roughly the same amounts of territory in these two divisions as the Boston house does. The East may be further subdivided into New England territory, with Boston as its center, New York territory, and Philadelphia territory. Similarly, the West is subdivided by a number of dealers into several smaller areas. The subdivisions most commonly used are the West, or Chicago territory, the South, or St. Louis territory, and the Far West, or San Francisco territory. The territory included in these three areas by a leading Chicago dealer in 1931 was as follows: Pittsburgh and western Pennsylvania, and all states north of Kentucky, Missouri, Kansas, and New Mexico in the West; Kentucky, Tennessee, Alabama, Mississippi, Missouri, Arkansas, Louisiana, Kansas, Oklahoma, Texas, and New Mexico in the South; and Idaho, Utah, Arizona, and all states to the west of these in the Far West. Other leading dealers included somewhat different amounts of territory in each of these areas, but in general divided Western territory, as distinguished from Eastern, in roughly the same way as the Chicago house did.[14]

[14] A more comprehensive view of the manner in which a large commercial paper house divides the country into geographical districts and apportions territory among its various offices may perhaps be gained if the practice followed in such matters by a leading New York house in 1931 is indicated. This house, which at present is presumably the largest dealer in open-market paper in the United States, divided the area in which it operated into four main geographical divisions. These were the East — which was further subdivided into Boston territory, New York territory, and Philadelphia territory — and the West, the South, and the Far West. New York was the center of the East, Chicago of the West, St. Louis of the South, and San Francisco of the Far West. In addition to its main office in New York, this house maintained five branch offices — one in each of the other cities mentioned above. Territory was apportioned among its various offices as follows:

Boston office: Maine, New Hampshire, Vermont, Massachusetts, Rhode Island, and the part of Connecticut east of 72°15'.

New York: Canada, the part of Connecticut west of 72°15', New York, and northern New Jersey.

Philadelphia: The part of New Jersey not assigned to New York (including Trenton and Phillipsburg, and Salem, Camden, Gloucester, Burlington, Cumberland, Atlantic, and Cape May Counties), Pennsylvania, Delaware, Maryland, Washington (D.C.), Virginia, West Virginia, North Carolina, South Carolina, Georgia, Florida, and the part of Tennessee east of the Cumberland Mountains, including Knoxville and Chattanooga.

Chicago: Ohio, Kentucky (except Paducah), Indiana, Michigan, Illinois (except ten towns assigned to the St. Louis branch office), Iowa, Wisconsin, Minnesota, North Dakota, South Dakota, Nebraska, and Colorado.

St. Louis: Certain towns in Illinois (Downs, Jerseyville, Alton, East St. Louis, Bellevue, Cairo, Murphysboro, Granite City, Edwardsville, and Pinckneyville), Paducah (Kentucky), the part of Tennessee west of the Cumberland Mountains, Alabama, Mississippi, Louisiana, Arkansas, Missouri, Kansas, Oklahoma, and Texas.

San Francisco: New Mexico, Arizona, Utah, Wyoming, Montana, Idaho, Nevada, California, Oregon, Washington, Alaska, and Hawaii.

This house at present uses practically the same divisions of territory as it was using in 1931. Since 1931, however, it has closed its branch office in San Francisco and substituted therefor correspondent relations with another house in the same city. The latter house formerly acted as correspondent for a number of other dealers but now maintains correspondent connections with the New York house alone. It originates no paper of its own.

In 1931 fourteen houses were maintaining one or more correspondent connections. The greater number of such connections being maintained at that time were those between a New England or New York house of moderate size and a house of about the same size in Chicago, St. Louis, or San Francisco. Divisions of territory between or among the members of different correspondent systems differed to some extent, but in general each house which maintained reciprocal relations with its correspondent sold its own and its correspondent's paper throughout the territory surrounding the centers in which it maintained one or more offices or sales representatives. Thus a New England or a New York house would confine its operations in the main to Eastern territory, and a Chicago correspondent would sell paper mainly in the seventh Federal Reserve district and the territory adjoining, though in special cases each house might sell some paper in the other's territory. Through an arrangement of this sort, each house would specialize in handling paper in the area in which its contacts both with borrowing and with buying customers were the closest, and both houses would be able to secure the advantages of an effective and economical territorial division of labor.

More important than correspondent connections between houses of moderate size were two larger and more elaborate correspondent systems which were also being used in 1931. The first of these was an inter-company correspondent system whose members included a leading New York house, a group of branch offices, three of which were virtually independent organizations, and an affiliated San Francisco house. This group of dealers divided the country into the four broad geographical districts — East, West, South, and Far West — which, as noted above, were being used by other large dealers at the same time; and, like other large dealers, further subdivided these four main districts into smaller territorial divisions, each of which was assigned to some office or a sales representative. The second of these systems was an association of four leading houses whose main offices were located, respectively, in Boston, Chicago, Minneapolis, and St. Louis. These dealers divided the country into five main districts, which might be designated the East, the Chicago district, the Minneapolis district, the St. Louis district, and the Northwest. The East, which was assigned to the Boston house, included the states east of Ohio, Kentucky, Arkansas, and Louisiana. The Northwest was also assigned to this Boston house. It included Idaho, Washington, and Oregon. Each of the remaining three districts was assigned to the dealer whose main office was located therein. The Chicago district included Michigan, Ohio, Kentucky, Indiana, the northern half of Illinois, approximately two-thirds of Wisconsin (all but a section in the northwestern part of the state), Iowa, Nebraska, Wyoming, Utah, Nevada, and California. Northwestern Wisconsin, Minnesota, North Dakota, South Dakota, and Montana were included in the Minneapolis district. The St. Louis district included the rest of the country. The Eastern district and the Minneapolis and St. Louis districts were further subdivided into two smaller districts, each of which was assigned to a particular office or a sales representative. Each of the associated houses in general handled paper in the territory assigned to it, though in special cases each might handle some paper in a part of the territory of one or more of the other houses.[15]

In case a concern borrowing in the open market uses the services of two or more dealers, each house handling the split or divided account is assigned a definite territory in which it may sell paper issued by the concern in question. The territory assigned to each house is that in which it can presumably secure the broadest distribution for its borrowing customer's paper. The number of separate territories assigned of course depends on the number of dealers handling the divided account. Since even the largest borrowers have required comparatively little short-term credit accommodation in recent years, whether in the form of direct loans from banks or in that of indirect loans through dealers, few con-

---

[15] The first of these two correspondent systems was discontinued early in 1932, and the San Francisco house which had been one of its members joined the second of the two systems. The latter house was then assigned Idaho, Utah, Arizona (except the part of this state included in the Dallas Federal Reserve district, which was retained by the St. Louis house mentioned above), and all states to the west of these.

cerns borrowing in the market have used the services of more than
two houses. In case a concern borrows through no more than two
dealers, it generally authorizes one dealer to handle its paper in
the East and the other to sell its notes in the West. The dividing
line between these two districts may differ somewhat in different
cases, but in general these geographical divisions contain about the
same area as corresponding divisions used by the larger houses in
dividing territory between Eastern and Western offices, and by
New England and New York houses in dividing territory with
Western correspondents. In some cases each dealer may be assigned several Federal Reserve districts. Still smaller divisions of
territory have been used also. Thus in 1931 one Boston house was
selling the paper of one of its borrowing customers in Boston, and
another dealer of the same city was selling notes of the same concern in the rest of New England. In any case each house, as a
New York dealer expressed it, "takes all the territory it can get." [16]

In connection with the origination of open-market notes, divisions of territory similar to those used in connection with the
distribution of such obligations are made between dealers' main
offices and any of their branch offices which are authorized to buy
the paper they handle,[17] and also between or among the members
of correspondent systems. Divisions of territory between dealers'
main offices and such of their branches as are authorized to buy
paper, however, may not be of any particular significance in connection with originating open-market notes. Both their main
offices and their branches originate paper mainly in the territory

[16] According to a New Orleans dealer, some concerns borrowing in the market
have sometimes allowed two houses to handle their paper in the same locality.
There have been cases, moreover, in which dealers have violated agreements relating
to territory and sold paper in localities assigned to other dealers. In general, however, all three parties to the commercial paper market — borrowing concerns, intermediary dealers, and banks buying outside paper — prefer to have all open-market
notes issued by any one concern and sold in any one territory handled by a single
house only; and as a rule dealers are careful not to "poach" on each other's territory.
  For further data relating to divided accounts, see n. 14, p. 281.

[17] In case a house maintains no branches which are authorized to buy open-
market notes, its main office will of course have to assume full responsibility for
securing an adequate supply of such obligations, and consequently will solicit new
accounts throughout the entire area in which it operates.

in which they sell, but responsibility for securing new business is entrusted largely to the partners or executive officers who have the best contacts and connections, and executives connected with any one office may solicit new accounts in territory assigned to any other office. Correspondent dealers may also originate some paper in each other's territory, though they are likely to confine their endeavors to secure new business in the main to the area in which their contacts both with borrowing and with buying customers can be the closest — that is, to their own territory. Such a policy is followed by the members of the most important correspondent system in use at present. Each of the five houses associated in this system originates open-market notes mainly in the territory in which it sells paper, but by special agreement each may solicit new accounts in territory assigned to some other member of the system.[18]

[18] A New York house and a Chicago house, both of which maintained correspondent relations with one or more other dealers, reported in 1930 that they were free to solicit new business in all parts of the country, including territory assigned to their correspondents. One of the five houses associated in the correspondent system mentioned above reported in the same year that, with their consent, it could solicit new accounts in territory assigned to its correspondents. If it sold in its own territory notes which it had originated in territory assigned to a correspondent, it was allowed to keep the full commission on sales of such paper. If, on the other hand, paper thus originated was sold by a correspondent dealer in the latter's territory, the commission was divided equally between the two houses concerned.

CHAPTER V

CLASSES OF PAPER HANDLED BY DEALERS

THE short-term credit instruments which dealers have handled in recent years have consisted almost entirely of promissory notes.[1] Such obligations may be classified into certain broad groups, irrespective of the sources from which they are obtained. On the basis of the number of indorsements they bear, for instance, they may be classified into single-name and double-name instruments; and on a different basis, into the equally broad groups of secured and unsecured paper. In the present chapter, only these broad groups of open-market notes and the denominations and maturities they bear will be considered, without special reference to the classes of concerns from which they are secured. The sources from

[1] After the passage of the Federal Reserve Act, Section 13 of which authorized member banks to accept bills of exchange, a number of dealers began to handle both trade and bank acceptances. Profits from dealing in acceptances were so small, however, that practically all commercial paper houses discontinued operations in both trade and bankers' bills within a few years after the close of the World War. Of the twenty-three houses which presumably were the largest dealers in commercial paper in 1931, only one, a comparatively small New York house, was dealing in acceptances. This house reported that it handled from $3,000,000 to $5,000,000 of trade bills a year. It indorsed these acceptances without recourse before selling them. This house retired from business in the spring of 1931, and at present no commercial paper house handles either trade or bankers' bills.

The following reasons have been given for the "failure of the trade acceptance to come to the open market":

1. Concerns possessing adequate capital and a good credit standing prefer to pay cash and take discounts offered.
2. The amounts of acceptances which concerns had available for discount did not often coincide with the amounts of "borrowed capital funds" they required.
3. Trade acceptances drawn for small and uneven amounts were less satisfactory for sale in the open market than single-name promissory notes, the denominations of which could be adjusted to the requirements of banks buying commercial paper.
4. The maturities of trade acceptances, "determined by competition and trade custom," were often unsuited to the requirements of the open market.
5. Checking two names would involve double work.

(S. P. Meech, "Recent Tendencies in Credit Relations between Commercial Paper Houses and Business Concerns," *Univ. Jour. Bus.*, Dec. 1923, pp. 69–70.)

which dealers obtain their stock in trade, that is, the various classes of concerns which issue open-market obligations, will be considered in the chapter following.

1. SINGLE-NAME AND DOUBLE-NAME PAPER

Practically all promissory notes handled by dealers are "straight" or "plain" paper, that is, paper bearing only the blank indorsement of the issuing concern. Of twenty leading dealers interviewed in 1930 and 1931, two stated that all the paper they handled was single-name, three that 95 per cent or more of the notes they sold were indorsed by the makers only, one that the only double-name paper it handled was a small amount of textile mill paper with the indorsement of a commission house, and all the rest that the bulk of the obligations they sold were single-name. One house reported that it required two indorsements on paper issued by concerns which were just beginning to borrow in the market, and a number of dealers stated that they required indorsements on the open-market obligations of concerns which secured indorsements on notes issued in connection with direct loans from banks. According to several dealers, paper issued by small close corporations was also frequently indorsed, the indorsement generally given in such cases being the personal indorsement of some officer of the company in question.[2] Only two houses, both in New York, stated specifically that they dealt in double-name trade paper. The first of these houses, which was a comparatively small concern, handled also a small amount of trade acceptances. The second of the two houses, which was one of the largest dealers in the country, reported that it handled a limited amount of "jewelry receivables," but no other class of double-name paper. Comparatively small amounts of double-name obligations and guaranteed paper are still being issued, but probably more than 90 per cent of the promissory notes handled by the larger houses at present are single-name paper.[3]

[2] Some concerns, instead of securing indorsements on their open-market notes, arrange to have the payment of such obligations guaranteed by their officers or by other companies.

[3] Of four leading houses consulted in the spring of 1936, one reported that it handled single-name obligations only, and the remaining three that about 95 per

Such notes are classed as single-name obligations because they bear the indorsement of the maker only. As a rule they are made payable to the order of "ourselves," that is, the borrowing concern, and signed and indorsed in blank by the latter. They thus become freely negotiable without further indorsement.

In some cases notes have been made payable to bearer or to the commercial paper house handling the account concerned.[4] In cases of the former sort, they are of course negotiable without indorsement. If made payable to the house through which they are sold, they are indorsed without recourse by the latter.

Only in exceptional cases are notes indorsed by dealers in any other manner; for dealers ordinarily do not assume the responsibility of guaranteeing the payment of the paper they sell,[5] though

cent or more of the notes they were handling were single-name paper. A comparatively small New York house also reported that it was dealing in such paper only.

According to the National Credit Office of New York, of the 654 concerns which borrowed through dealers in 1935, 491, or 75.1 per cent, issued "straight" paper; 74, or 11.3 per cent, indorsed notes; 45, or 6.9 per cent, guaranteed obligations; and 44, or 6.7 per cent, paper secured by collateral. In the following year, 692 concerns borrowed in the open market. The records of the National Credit Office show that, of these 692 concerns, 525, or 75.9 per cent, issued "straight" paper; 72, or 10.4 per cent, indorsed notes; 46, or 6.6 per cent, guaranteed obligations; and 49, or 7.1 per cent, paper secured by collateral. Presumably not only "straight" notes but also guaranteed and secured obligations, so long as not indorsed, should be classed as single-name paper; and, if so, 88.7 per cent of the concerns which borrowed in the market in 1935, and 89.6 per cent of those which borrowed through dealers in 1936, issued such paper.

[4] In 1931 two houses were handling some paper made payable to bearer, and in 1936 one of the larger dealers in New York stated that finance companies' notes are occasionally made payable to bearer. A New Orleans house, which might more accurately be described as a commercial bank which operated a commercial paper department, reported in 1930 that most of the paper it sold in the market was made payable to itself. One of the larger New York houses stated about the same time that the notes it handled were occasionally made payable to itself.

[5] A leading New York house reported that it sometimes guarantees that certain notes coming due within a short period — ordinarily within one month — will be paid at maturity if banks holding such notes agree to purchase new obligations to be issued by the same borrower on the maturity of the paper then outstanding. In such cases this house guarantees payment only of such an amount of the notes held by any particular bank as the latter is willing to purchase of the new paper to be issued by the concern in question. Another leading New York house occasionally follows a similar practice. At present, cases such as these are probably about the only cases in which dealers guarantee payment of the paper they handle.

Several years ago, however, two dealers are said to have indorsed the paper they sold. It is reported that the first of these two dealers charged about ¼ of 1 per cent of the face of the notes which he handled for assuming the responsibility of indors-

they do guarantee, implicitly at least, that the signatures on all notes they handle are genuine and that all such obligations are what they purport to be. They of course also assume the moral responsibility of offering for sale only such notes as are reasonably certain to be paid at maturity, and of coöperating to the fullest extent possible with their buying customers in an endeavor to reduce to a minimum any losses that may have to be sustained on purchased paper.

2. SECURED AND UNSECURED PAPER

Most promissory notes handled by dealers are not only single-name but also unsecured obligations. Twenty-three houses consulted in 1930 and 1931 reported that the bulk of the paper they handled was unsecured, though a dealer of Minneapolis stated that nearly as much secured as unsecured paper was sold in that district.

The secured obligations which these dealers were then handling were of three main classes: collateral trust notes issued by finance companies, notes secured by stocks, or by stocks and bonds, and paper secured by various classes of commodities stored in warehouses. Figures indicating the relative importance of these classes of paper are not available, but a Chicago dealer estimated that all three classes combined constituted about 12 to 15 per cent of the total amount of commercial paper being sold in the market in 1930. This same dealer, as well as a dealer of St. Louis, estimated that commercial paper houses were then handling a greater volume of finance companies' obligations than of notes of the second class, and that their sales of the latter class of paper were greater than their sales of notes secured by commodities.

---

ing them. Banks realized, however, that his indorsement was of no great value, since he could not have met any more than a small proportion of the contingent liabilities he assumed by adding his signature to the notes he sold. As a consequence, he is said to have discontinued the practice of indorsing such obligations about six months after he adopted it. The other dealer carried on his operations in a town in South Carolina. He handled mainly the notes of Southern textile mills. His charge for indorsing such paper is said to have been at the rate of 1 per cent of the face thereof a year. It is reported that he incurred some fairly heavy losses as a result of the liabilities he assumed through indorsement. He is said to have discontinued operations in commercial paper by about the middle of 1930.

Eleven houses reported that they were selling finance companies' paper, and six other dealers that they had handled such paper in earlier years. Such obligations constituted about 90 per cent of the open-market paper which a New Orleans house was handling. The security offered as collateral in the case of collateral trust notes generally consisted of installment notes which were trusteed with some bank or trust company, though a San Francisco house stated that conditional sales contracts were pledged as collateral in the case of the automobile finance companies' paper which it was handling. Two dealers reported that some of the notes they were selling for the latter class of concerns were guaranteed by bonding or surety companies.[6]

Fourteen houses were handling at least some obligations of the second main class mentioned above, which are known as "collateral loan" paper.[7] Such notes were being issued both by stock brokerage houses and by individuals. The purposes for which they were being issued were to purchase or to carry securities, and to pay off brokers' loans or other collateral loans obtained from banks direct. Strictly speaking, therefore, they should not be classed as "commercial paper" in the ordinary sense of the term.[8] The security offered as collateral for these notes consisted mainly of stocks, though some borrowers offered both stocks and bonds. A Boston dealer stated that real estate mortgages were also accepted as security.

Five houses reported that they were handling notes secured by warehouse or trust receipts for commodities stored in cold storage warehouses, and two other houses that they formerly handled such paper. The commodities in question included butter, eggs, apples,

[6] By no means all the finance companies' notes which dealers were handling in 1930 and 1931 were secured. The New Orleans house mentioned just above stated that about 80 per cent of the paper of this class which it was selling was unsecured, and that finance companies were obtaining an increasing proportion of their short-term credit requirements on their unsecured notes.

[7] Such obligations are also handled by a number of houses which deal in no other classes of open-market paper and therefore are not classed as commercial paper houses.

[8] On the other hand, business corporations occasionally borrow in the open market for commercial purposes on notes secured in the same manner as collateral loan paper issued for the purposes specified above.

and other produce. The paper of this class which these dealers were selling was originated mainly in Chicago, though cold storage warehouses in New York and Boston were also borrowing in the open market at that time.

Besides those already mentioned, dealers were handling a few other classes of secured obligations in 1930 and 1931. A Chicago dealer stated that some paper secured by such warehoused commodities as canned goods and even stoves was then being sold. A comparatively small New York house was handling a limited amount of paper secured by first mortgages on real estate. Two houses were selling notes issued by cattle loan companies, and two other dealers reported that they formerly sold such obligations.[9] The cattle loan paper handled by one of the former two houses was secured by notes which stock-growers gave the loan company in question, and these notes were secured by cattle. Two houses were handling paper issued by grain elevator companies. According to a Minneapolis dealer, a considerable amount of such paper was being bought and sold in that district. Obligations of this class are customarily secured by registered terminal grain elevator receipts.[10]

Since 1930 the volume of secured notes handled by dealers, as well as the amount of unsecured obligations they have placed with

---

[9] Since each of the former two houses had only one cattle loan company account, apparently there were only two such companies which were borrowing in the open market in 1930 and 1931. According to one of these two dealers, the supply of cattle loan company paper had shrunk to a small figure by 1930, mainly because the functions of such companies had largely been taken over by the Federal Intermediate Credit banks. The same dealer stated that the demand for such paper had also decreased to a considerable extent, largely because of the failure of a number of poorly managed cattle loan companies after about 1920.

[10] In addition to the classes of secured obligations mentioned above, dealers formerly handled a certain amount of secured cotton paper. A New York house which formerly specialized in handling the paper of cotton merchants and cotton textile mills stated that as late as 1926 it was selling each year about $2,000,000 of notes issued by cotton merchants for carrying their stock in trade. These notes were secured by warehouse receipts. Three other dealers also reported that they formerly sold secured cotton paper, but apparently no such paper has been handled by dealers in more recent years. A St. Louis house which was selling some unsecured notes issued by cotton factors in the South stated in 1930 that factors who were good credit risks were borrowing on their "straight" notes and keeping their warehouse receipts themselves. The storage and marketing of cotton are of course financed through the use of acceptances also.

banks, has declined considerably. One of the largest houses handles no secured paper at all, and three other leading dealers estimated in the spring of 1936 that 95 per cent or more of the notes they were handling were unsecured. Probably no cattle loan paper at all has been sold by dealers during the last few years. On the other hand, a number of houses have continued to deal in collateral loan notes, finance companies' obligations, and/or paper secured by grain or by commodities stored in cold storage warehouses.[11]

In practically all cases in which secured notes are sold in the open market, arrangements are made for the maintenance of an adequate margin between the face value of such obligations and the market value of the collateral offered as security therefor. In 1930 and 1931 dealers reported that margins of 10 to 25 per cent were customarily maintained on finance companies' paper; margins of 20 to 25 per cent on collateral loan paper; margins of about 20 per cent on obligations secured by cold storage warehouse receipts; "substantial" margins on cattle loan companies' paper; and margins of at least 10 per cent on notes secured by terminal grain elevator company receipts.[12]

[11] At least nine houses, including six of the leading nine dealers, were handling collateral loan notes in 1936, and at least five leading houses were dealing in finance companies' paper. A comparatively small Chicago house reported that it specializes in handling these two classes of obligations.

As was indicated in n. 3, p. 224, 44, or 6.7 per cent, of the 654 concerns which borrowed in the open market in 1935, and 49, or 7.1 per cent, of the 692 companies which borrowed through dealers in 1936, issued notes secured by some sort of collateral.

[12] Despite the fact that the various classes of notes mentioned above are well secured, most of them sell at higher rates than unsecured single-name paper of the highest grade. Finance companies' obligations may sell to yield ¼ of 1 per cent to 1 per cent more than unsecured prime paper. Dealers consulted in 1930 and 1931 stated that rates on collateral loan paper are ordinarily from ¼ of 1 per cent to 2 per cent higher than rates on prime unsecured notes, depending on the character of the securities offered as collateral; and that rates on both cattle loan companies' obligations and notes secured by cold storage warehouse receipts are ordinarily ½ of 1 per cent higher than those on unsecured prime paper. (Such rate-differentials of course vary with changes in rates in the money market in general. With the general decline in short-term money rates which began toward the close of 1929, the "spreads" between rates on prime unsecured paper and rates on various classes of secured obligations have narrowed to some extent.) A Minneapolis dealer, however, reported that "demand notes" secured by registered terminal grain elevator company receipts normally sell at rates below those on unsecured paper of the highest grade. One reason why finance companies' notes and notes secured by stocks

If banks expect them to, dealers assume the responsibility of seeing that adequate margins are maintained. They are under no legal obligation to do so, however; and in cases where collateral is trusteed the trustee is ordinarily expected to assume this responsibility.

3. DENOMINATIONS OF OPEN-MARKET NOTES

The denominations in which commercial paper is issued depend partly on the size of the borrowing concern and the amounts it borrows in the open market, but are determined mainly by the requirements of the commercial banks which buy practically all the paper handled by dealers.

The denominations which have been used in recent years include $1,000, $1,500, $2,500, $5,000, $10,000, $25,000, $50,000, $100,000, $200,000, and $250,000. Notes with denominations as low as $1,000 and $1,500 have been sold in recent years by the leading dealer in the Minneapolis district, which is said to be the most important market for small notes in the country; and, according to a Chicago dealer, some finance companies' notes have been issued for amounts as small as $1,500.[13] Obligations secured by stocks or by stocks and bonds have been issued by stock brokers within recent years for amounts as high as $200,000 and $250,000. Some years ago unsecured commercial paper was occasionally issued in denominations as high as $1,000,000.[14] Comparatively few notes, however, are made out either for smaller amounts than $2,500 or for larger amounts than $50,000. Of these various denominations, twenty-one dealers reported in 1930 and 1931 that $5,000 was the most common. This is considered the most convenient denomination, and is the smallest for which a

---

and bonds ordinarily sell at rates higher than those on prime unsecured paper is that the former two classes of obligations are not eligible for rediscount at Federal Reserve banks. Demand notes, on the other hand, sell at relatively low rates, both because they are so well secured that they are a practically "riskless" investment and because they are payable on demand. (For further data relating to demand notes, see n. 13, p. 244.)

[13] One of the leading finance companies reported in 1930 that it would issue its open-market notes in about any denominations which would be suited to the requirements of banks — including amounts as small as $500, if necessary.

[14] R. A. Foulke, *The Commercial Paper Market*, p. 148. See also n. 19, p. 251.

number of borrowers will issue paper to be sold in the market. The next most common denominations were $2,500 and $10,000. It is probable that more $2,500 than $10,000 notes were being issued in 1930 and 1931, but a number of dealers reported that they ordinarily sold a greater total *amount* of paper in the form of $10,000 notes than in that of obligations made out for $2,500. In 1936, according to the leading dealers in Boston and New York, the most common denominations in which open-market paper was currently being issued were $5,000, $10,000, and $25,000.

Notes with the denomination of $2,500, because made out for less than $5,000, are known as "split" notes. These obligations are issued largely to meet the requirements of banks which have only a small amount of capital. Because of legal restrictions limiting their loans to any one borrower to 10 per cent of their capital and surplus, such banks are not in a position to purchase notes of large denominations. Split notes also have the advantage of enabling banks to secure a greater diversification of their holdings of outside paper than would be possible with notes of larger denominations. From the point of view of the borrowing concern, $2,500 notes have the advantage of enabling it to secure a broader distribution for its paper — an advantage which is likely to be particularly important in periods of high money rates — and consequently more free advertising than it would otherwise obtain.

The proportion of notes of each of these various denominations which any particular house handles of course depends both upon the financial requirements of its borrowing customers and upon the size of the majority of banks to which it sells open-market paper. If its borrowing customers seek large amounts of credit in the open market, if it handles a relatively large amount of paper secured by stocks and bonds, and if it sells open-market obligations mainly to banks in the larger financial centers, it will handle only a relatively small proportion of notes bearing denominations smaller than $5,000.[15] If, on the other hand, it handles a large number of small accounts and little or no collateral loan paper, and if its buying customers consist largely of country banks, as

[15] A Boston house reported in 1930 that it handled no split notes at all.

much as 25 per cent of its total sales of open-market paper are
likely to be in the form of split notes.

4. Maturities of Commercial Paper

The greater part of the open-market obligations handled by
dealers bear some definite maturity.[16] The maturities which have
been used in recent years include the following: thirty days, sixty
days, three months, four months, five months, six months, seven
months, nine months, one year, and eighteen months. Maturities
shorter than ninety days and longer than six months are not common. Notes running for periods as short as thirty days and as long
as eighteen months have been issued by finance companies, which
can practically make both the maturities and the denominations of
their open-market obligations "to order." Some indorsed textile
mill paper with a maturity as long as one year has been sold within
recent years, and some collateral loan paper is issued with the
same maturity.[17] Most paper sold in the market, however, runs
for periods of four months, five months, or six months. Of these
three maturities, the last is ordinarily the most common, though it
is somewhat longer than the average maturity of all notes sold in
the market over a period of several years would be. Several
dealers estimated, both about six years ago and in 1936, that the
average maturity is about five months. This estimate would seem
to be at least roughly accurate.[18]

[16] The secured demand notes issued by terminal grain elevator companies, particularly in the ninth Federal Reserve district, are payable on demand. According
to a Boston dealer, some collateral loan notes also are made payable on demand.
Presumably these are the only two classes of open-market obligations which are
issued without definite maturities.

[17] A Boston house which handles a considerable volume of such paper reported
that collateral loan notes usually run for six months, if discounted, but for longer
periods if the interest on them is payable at maturity. This same house some years
ago used to handle one-year notes issued by several other classes of borrowers, including watch-manufacturing companies and Southern cotton mills.

According to another Boston dealer, a New England electric light and power
company has within the last few years issued open-market paper running for one
year, and some notes with a maturity even as long as two years.

[18] Of twenty-three houses consulted in 1930 and 1931, ten stated that the most
common maturity borne by the paper they handled was six months. Seven of these
houses estimated the relative importance of such paper. Their estimates of the pro-

The maturities for which open-market notes are issued, like their denominations, are determined partly by the requirements of the concerns which borrow through dealers and partly by those of the banks which buy outside paper.

The credit requirements of concerns which borrow in the market depend on such factors as the nature of their business, the extent to which their purchases and sales are seasonal, the rate of turnover of their inventory, and the length of their collection period. Concerns whose requirements are more or less continuous throughout the year prefer to borrow for periods of six months or longer, especially when money is cheap, and thus avoid the necessity of paying dealers' commissions more than twice a year.[19] On the

---

portion which this class of paper constituted of the total amount of paper they were handling ranged from 60 to 90 per cent. The maturities reported as most common by the other thirteen dealers, together with the number of houses specifying each of the maturity classes in question, were as follows: ninety days, one house (a commercial bank of New Orleans, which was a comparatively small dealer in open-market paper); four months, three houses (all comparatively small dealers); four, five, and six months, two houses; four and six months, one house; five months, three houses; five and six months, three houses. In the spring of 1936, according to a number of Eastern houses, six months was still the most common maturity.

About twenty years ago shorter maturities for both open-market notes and those issued in connection with direct loans from banks were advocated by a leading New York banker and by the Federal Reserve Board. The president of the National Bank of Commerce of New York recommended in July 1917 that both classes of notes should be issued for ninety days, instead of six months, as a means of increasing the proportion of such notes eligible for rediscount at Federal Reserve banks and consequently of bringing about a "more liquid banking position" ("James S. Alexander Urges Use of Commercial Paper Not More than Three Months," *C. and F. Chron.*, July 28, 1917, p. 333). In September of the same year the Federal Reserve Board sent a letter to the Federal Reserve banks in which, for similar reasons, it advocated the use of notes running for "not longer than four instead of six months." A large Eastern bank to which this letter was sent endeavored to interest a New York dealer in charging a "preferential commission" in the case of short-term notes. This bank stated that a much larger volume of commercial paper could probably be sold in the market, particularly in times of tight money, if dealers would buy three- and four-months' notes at a net rate and make their profit by selling such notes at a lower rate, or if they would accept a commission of, say 3/32 of 1 per cent, on 3-months' paper ("Short-Time Commercial Paper," *Fed. Res. Bull.*, Oct. 1917, pp. 739–740). It is doubtful that any of these recommendations in favor of shorter maturities had any appreciable effect on the maturities of open-market paper actually used.

[19] The dealer's commission is commonly (though not always) figured as a percentage of the face amounts of the notes he handles, irrespective of their maturities. Other things equal, therefore, it is generally to the advantage of a concern which borrows in the market more or less continuously to issue its notes for relatively long

other hand, many companies whose requirements are more seasonal in character find it to their advantage to borrow for shorter periods. If they issue their notes for periods as short as ninety days, they may be able to obtain slightly more favorable rates than those prevailing on four- to six-months' paper. Many companies, moreover, follow the policy of "cleaning up" all or the greater part of their open-market notes payable before their statement dates, and in accordance with this policy may find it necessary at certain seasons to issue no paper with maturities in excess of ninety days or four months.[20]

Banks find it comparatively easy to select the maturities which are best adapted to their requirements, whether they buy open-market obligations continuously or merely invest temporarily surplus funds in outside paper at certain seasons of the year. By purchasing notes with appropriate maturities they can arrange to have paper maturing in any month in which they expect to be in need of relatively large amounts of funds for the purpose of meeting seasonal withdrawals of deposits — as, for instance, withdrawals of Christmas club savings deposits in December — or for any other purpose.[21] Some banks ordinarily prefer six-months' paper. Others as a rule purchase ninety-day notes, since they are eligible paper and therefore more liquid than obligations with longer maturities. The maturities preferred at any particular time may depend to some extent on conditions in the money market. Thus a number of dealers reported that their buying customers generally prefer short maturities in periods of tight money, and buy notes with maturities as short as possible when rates tend to

---

periods. Rates on notes with maturities of not more than ninety days, however, may be somewhat lower than those on paper with longer maturities, and in such cases the saving in interest charges made possible by borrowing for shorter periods may offset the costs of paying dealers' commissions more often. From the point of view of the dealer, of course, shorter maturities are preferable.

[20] According to a Chicago dealer, in the years before 1914, when seasonal fluctuations in money rates were wider than they have been since the establishment of the Federal Reserve system, rates on open-market paper generally fell to the lowest levels of the year in January, February, May, and June; and shrewd borrowers who were aware of this fact would issue their notes to mature in these months, with the expectation of renewing them at favorable rates.

[21] In this connection, however, see n. 31, p. 324.

rise, and as long as possible when rates tend to fall. Other dealers, on the other hand, stated that the effects of rates on the maturities preferred by banks may be the reverse of those just indicated; and two leading houses reported that rates have no appreciable effects on the maturities preferred.

CHAPTER VI

BORROWING CUSTOMERS OF DEALERS: CLASSES OF CONCERNS USING THE OPEN MARKET

IN THE present chapter the sources from which dealers obtain the various classes of paper mentioned in the preceding chapter will be considered, together with the purposes for which their borrowing customers seek credit in the market and the advantages and disadvantages of the open-market system of financing from the point of view of the borrower.

1. QUALIFICATIONS REQUIRED FOR BORROWING IN THE OPEN MARKET

As was pointed out in the preceding chapter, the greater part of the promissory notes sold in the market are single-name obligations with no security whatsoever. Such obligations are nevertheless sold throughout the entire country, many of them to banks located in towns and cities thousands of miles distant from the main center of operations of the issuing concern. Hence the use of the open market is restricted to a comparatively small number of companies which are exceptionally good credit risks. A New York dealer estimated in 1930 that only about 2 to 4 per cent of all the business concerns in the United States were able to borrow in the market. As a matter of fact, the proportion would undoubtedly be much smaller than this estimate, if only for the reason that most concerns are too small to sell their notes through dealers.

Companies which obtain credit in the open market must as a rule conform to certain definite requirements. The qualifications which they must possess were specified by a New York dealer in 1927 as follows: Such concerns must be "in good financial and trade standing, which implies adequate banking connections and correct handling" of their merchandise obligations. They must be engaged in a line of business which lends itself readily to the open-market system of financing — "something involving merchandising, whether with manufacturing or with trading, rather than service." The funds they obtain in the open market they must use directly in their current operations, and not for investment in plant or other permanent assets. Their financial statements should be audited by "recognized outside accountants." Their balance sheets must show a satisfactory current ratio and "a reasonable amount" — generally not less than $200,000 — of invested capital.[1] Their profit and loss statements must show earnings "in fair proportion to volume as compared with similar concerns." Above all, the managements of such companies must be "of unquestionable integrity, experienced, capable."[2] To these require-

---

[1] The following table shows a percentage distribution of open-market borrowers in 1923, 1925, and 1935 according to their net worth:

Net Worth	Per Cent of Total Number of Concerns Using the Open Market		
	1923	1925	1935
Below $250,000	4.5	2.9	2.5
$ 250,000 to $ 500,000	18.9	19.1	10.1
$ 500,000 to $ 1,000,000	25.4	27.1	24.6
$ 1,000,000 to $ 2,500,000	26.7	28.4	34.4
$ 2,500,000 to $ 5,000,000	11.4	11.8	14.2
$ 5,000,000 to $10,000,000	{10.5	5.2	{12.4
$10,000,000 to $25,000,000		3.7	
Above $25,000,000	2.6	1.8	1.8
Total	100.0	100.0	100.0

(Figures for 1923 and 1925 are given in R. A. Foulke, *The Commercial Paper Market*, p. 51; those for 1935 were supplied by the National Credit Office of New York.)

It will be noted that the proportion of concerns with a net worth of less than $250,000 was very small in each of the three years for which figures are included in the table and that it decreased both in 1925 and in 1935.

Some dealers still handle the accounts of a few concerns with a net worth of less than $250,000, and a Boston house has within recent years sold notes issued by one or two public utility companies with a net worth as small as $200,000; but all dealers prefer to handle the paper of concerns whose net worth is $500,000 or more. Paper issued by comparatively small companies may yield rates as much as ¼ of 1 per cent to 1 per cent higher than rates on the obligations of larger concerns, and is therefore popular with the smaller banks. The notes of large concerns, however, generally have a broader market than paper issued by small borrowers. Some of the larger city banks do not like to go to the bother of investigating the credit standing of concerns which are too small to borrow substantial amounts of funds in the open market each year.

[2] C. V. Childs, "Commercial Paper and Its Advantages to the Borrower," *N. Y. Cred. Men's Assoc. Bull.*, Nov. 12, 1927, p. 367.

ments should be added one other, which is no less important than the foregoing — namely, that such concerns must borrow on the average not much less than $200,000 in the market each year. Handling the accounts of companies which borrow less than $200,-000 a year may involve as much work and expense as dealing in the paper of considerably larger concerns, and is likely to be unprofitable to the dealer.[3]

From this statement of the qualifications required for borrowing in the market, it follows that certain classes of concerns are as a rule unable to sell their notes through dealers. As Lincoln has pointed out, concerns of the following classes, for instance, are generally excluded from the open market as a source of short-term credit: Companies of small size, whose credit requirements can be readily supplied by their own banks; concerns which produce or deal in luxuries, goods highly subject to style changes and the like; those whose inventory turnover is very slow; those dealing in products subject to very rapid price changes or for which the demand is uncertain; and comparatively new concerns which have not yet demonstrated their earning power, even though they may be dealing in staple commodities.[4]

As a matter of fact, however, not all companies of such classes are excluded from the open market; nor are all concerns which borrow through dealers able to conform to all the requirements specified above. Some concerns which cannot conform to all these requirements may nevertheless be perfectly safe credit risks, and therefore able to sell their notes in the market, provided they are of sufficient size to make the handling of their account profitable to a dealer.[5]

[3] Figures of the average annual borrowings of concerns using the open market in recent years are given in Table 19. As this table shows, the average open-market borrowings per concern during each of the years from 1920 to 1936 were much larger than $200,000.

[4] E. E. Lincoln, *Applied Business Finance*, 4th rev. ed., pp. 429–430.

[5] In this connection see S. P. Meech, "Recent Tendencies in Credit Relations between Commercial Paper Houses and Business Concerns," *Univ. Jour. Bus.*, Dec. 1923, pp. 52–56.

2. Number and Location of Concerns Borrowing through Dealers

The estimated number of concerns which sold their notes through dealers during the years from 1920 to 1936 is shown in Table 19, together with estimated total sales by dealers and average borrowings per concern in each of these years.[6] It will be noted that both the number of concerns using the open market and total sales by dealers declined to a considerable extent after 1920, and fell to the lowest figures for the entire period in 1933. In twelve of the fifteen years following 1920 changes in the number of open-market borrowers were in the same direction as those in total sales of commercial paper. The changes in these two sets of figures were

TABLE 19

Number of Concerns Borrowing in the Open Market, Total Sales by Dealers, and Average Borrowings Per Concern, 1920–1935 *

Year	Number of Concerns Borrowing in the Market	Total Sales by Dealers (Millions of Dollars)	Average Borrowings per Concern (Thousands of Dollars)
1920	4,395	2,671	608
1921	3,676	1,798	489
1922	2,259	1,843	816
1923	2,171	2,002	922
1924	2,705	2,095	774
1925	2,754	1,783	647
1926	2,743	1,510	550
1927	2,490	1,404	564
1928	2,354	1,186	504
1929	1,653	773	468
1930	1,674	1,174	701
1931	1,239	641	517
1932	651	252	387
1933	548	228	416
1934	625	374	598
1935	654	418	639

*Figures in the last three columns of this table are estimates. Those in the second column were supplied by the National Credit Office of New York. Figures in the third column were taken from Table 3.

[6] In 1919 it was estimated that a total of "about 7,000 names" were "regularly in the hands of commercial-paper brokers" (note on "Credit Barometrics," *Jour. Pol. Econ.*, April 1919, p. 316). Since this figure seems rather exaggerated, it was not included in Table 19.

never more than roughly proportionate, however, and hence the average borrowings per concern fluctuated considerably.

Borrowing through dealers is not restricted to any particular section of the country. On the contrary, it is probable that at least a few concerns in practically every state in the country have within recent years obtained credit in the open market. While dealers secure the greater part of the obligations they handle in the districts in which they maintain their main offices, even individual houses, in fact, have originated open-market notes in nearly every state in the Union. The number of open-market borrowers in different sections of the country of course varies to a considerable extent. In general, the largest numbers of such borrowers are to be found in important trading and industrial centers, such as New York, Chicago, and Boston, and the smallest in the newer and less developed sections of the country, such as certain parts of the Northwest and the Southwest.

For the years 1922–1927 and 1930–1935 estimated figures of the total number of concerns borrowing through dealers in each of the twelve Federal Reserve districts are available. For the latter six years figures of Canadian concerns borrowing in the open market are available also. These two classes of figures are shown in Table 20, and a percentage distribution of concerns borrowing in the open market according to their location is given in Table 21. These tables show that, while the total number of open-market borrowers in each of the Federal Reserve districts declined to a considerable extent after 1926 or 1927, the proportion of such borrowers in each of the twelve districts remained roughly about the same throughout the twelve years for which figures are available; that throughout these twelve years the number of borrowers was largest in the Boston, New York, and Chicago districts, and smallest in the Minneapolis district; that the borrowers in the Boston, New York, and Chicago districts combined constituted on the average about 45 per cent of the total number of concerns using the open market during the years 1930–1935; and that Canadian borrowers on the average constituted only about ½ of 1 per cent of such concerns.

TABLE 20

DISTRIBUTION OF OPEN-MARKET BORROWERS ACCORDING TO THEIR LOCATION, 1922–1927 AND 1930–1935 *

Location of Borrowing Concerns	Number of Concerns Using Open Market											
	1922	1923	1924	1925	1926	1927	1930	1931	1932	1933	1934	1935
Federal Reserve districts												
Boston	273	257	347	325	312	249	193	166	117	114	104	89
New York	373	376	382	408	412	388	233	170	93	75	82	88
Philadelphia	119	114	177	173	161	156	104	78	32	33	41	50
Cleveland	113	104	138	135	138	114	83	88	42	27	27	28
Richmond	138	140	209	223	234	204	134	77	38	47	72	79
Atlanta	179	168	228	246	213	206	122	85	42	38	49	48
Chicago	410	438	464	492	489	445	295	245	101	77	95	107
St. Louis	144	119	158	174	188	150	109	64	32	26	29	35
Minneapolis	96	58	102	89	94	86	47	32	27	24	16	18
Kansas City	150	154	197	163	188	195	140	95	63	34	45	46
Dallas	118	124	153	150	149	151	108	51	24	16	22	23
San Francisco	146	119	150	176	165	146	97	79	35	32	41	42
Canada	....	....	....	....	....	....	9	9	5	5	2	1
Total	2,259	2,171	2,705	2,754	2,743	2,490	1,674	1,239	651	548	625	654

* Figures in this table are estimates prepared by the National Credit Office of New York. They include practically all concerns which borrowed through dealers in the years indicated. Figures for 1922–1927 are given in R. A. Foulke, *The Commercial Paper Market*, p. 43; those for 1930 were derived from figures given in L. M. Read, *The Story of Commercial Paper* (pamphlet), p. 2; those for 1931–1935 were furnished by the National Credit Office.

TABLE 21

PERCENTAGE DISTRIBUTION OF OPEN-MARKET BORROWERS ACCORDING TO THEIR LOCATION, 1922–1927 AND 1930–1935 *

Location of Borrowing Concerns	Per Cent of Total Number of Concerns Using Open Market											
	1922	1923	1924	1925	1926	1927	1930	1931	1932	1933	1934	1935
Federal Reserve districts												
Boston	12.1	11.8	12.9	11.8	11.4	10.0	11.5	13.4	18.0	20.8	16.7	13.6
New York	16.5	17.3	14.1	14.8	15.0	15.6	13.9	13.7	14.3	13.7	13.1	13.5
Philadelphia	5.3	5.2	6.5	6.3	5.9	6.3	6.2	6.3	4.9	6.0	6.6	7.6
Cleveland	5.0	5.0	5.1	4.9	5.0	4.6	5.0	7.1	6.5	4.9	4.3	4.3
Richmond	6.1	6.5	7.7	8.1	8.5	8.2	8.0	6.2	5.8	8.6	11.5	12.1
Atlanta	7.9	7.7	8.4	8.9	7.8	8.2	7.3	6.9	6.5	6.9	7.8	7.3
Chicago	18.2	20.2	17.2	17.8	18.0	17.9	17.6	19.7	15.5	14.1	15.2	16.4
St. Louis	6.4	5.4	5.8	6.3	6.8	6.0	6.5	5.2	4.9	4.8	4.6	5.3
Minneapolis	4.2	2.7	3.8	3.2	3.4	3.5	2.8	2.6	4.1	4.4	2.6	2.8
Kansas City	6.6	7.1	7.3	6.0	6.8	7.8	8.4	7.7	9.6	6.2	7.2	7.0
Dallas	5.2	5.7	5.7	5.5	5.4	6.0	6.5	4.1	3.7	2.9	3.5	3.5
San Francisco	6.5	5.4	5.5	6.4	6.0	5.9	5.8	6.4	5.4	5.8	6.6	6.4
Canada	...	...	...	...	...	...	0.5	0.7	0.8	0.9	0.3	0.2
Total	100.	100.	100.	100.	100.	100.	100.	100.	100.	100.	100.	100.

* Figures for 1922–1927 are given in R. A. Foulke, *The Commercial Paper Market*, p. 48; those for 1930 were computed from figures given in L. M. Read, *The Story of Commercial Paper* (pamphlet), p. 2, and those for 1931–1935 from figures supplied by the National Credit Office of New York.

Though the number of concerns borrowing in the market was greater in the Chicago district than in the New York district, it is said that there are more open-market borrowers in New York City than in Chicago. Presumably a substantial proportion of the concerns in the first Federal Reserve district which borrow through dealers are located in Boston, for the latter city is said to rank next after Chicago in the number of open-market borrowers.[7]

Late in 1930 two New York houses reported that they were handling the open-market notes of a few Canadian customers, and four other dealers that they had originated some such paper in earlier years; and in the spring of 1936 a large Boston house was handling the accounts of three Canadian companies. The number of Canadian concerns which have sold their notes through American dealers, however, has never been very large.[8] One reason why only a comparatively small volume of such obligations has been sold in this country is that, under Sections 88 and 89 of the Canadian Bank Act, Canadian banks which make direct loans to wholesale purchasers, shippers, dealers, or manufacturers are permitted to secure a first and preferential lien on certain classes of the current assets of such borrowers.[9] Another reason, according to a Minneapolis dealer, is that both the supply of Canadian paper and the demand for it on the part of American banks are limited by risks of losses from fluctuations in exchange rates between Canada and the United States; and American banks can of course "check"

[7] R. A. Foulke, *The Commercial Paper Market*, p. 43.

[8] Canadian concerns which have sold their open-market obligations through American dealers include such classes of borrowers as the following: a copper company, a steel company, grain dealers, flour-milling companies, lumber mills, a manufacturer of rugs, a company manufacturing silverware, one manufacturing clothing, a wholesale grocery company, and department stores. Canadian stock brokers have also sold their open-market notes in the United States in recent years. A Boston house reported in 1931 that it was then handling a considerable amount of collateral loan paper issued by Canadian stock brokerage houses, and that it had been dealing in such paper since 1915.

[9] H. P. Willis and B. H. Beckhart (editors), *Foreign Banking Systems*, pp. 419–421. See also W. M. Langston, "Section 88 of the Canadian Bank Act," *Mo. Bull. Robert Morris Associates*, Jan. 1933, pp. 210–224, and "Assignments of Accounts Receivable in Canada," *ibid.*, Mar. 1933, pp. 256–258.

American paper more readily than obligations issued by Canadian borrowers.[10]

3. CLASSES OF CONCERNS USING THE OPEN MARKET

Despite the fact that both dealers' annual sales and the number of open-market borrowers have declined to a very considerable extent since 1925, a wide variety of concerns have continued to borrow through commercial paper houses in recent years. The greater number of such borrowers may be classed as either manufacturing or trading concerns. The first of these classes includes such concerns as manufacturers of agricultural implements, clothing, cotton, woolen, and other textile products,[11] dairy products, drugs, chemicals, paint, furniture, and leather, metal, and tobacco products. Included in the second class, which probably contains about as many borrowers as the first group,[12] are such concerns as department stores, grocery and other chain stores, chain lumber-yard companies, mail order houses, seed companies, and wholesale dry goods, furniture, grocery, and hardware dealers. In addition to these two main groups of concerns, a number of other classes

[10] One or two companies in Hawaii have also sold their notes in the open market within fairly recent years. With the exception of such companies and the Canadian borrowers mentioned above, all concerns which have borrowed through American dealers have been located in this country.

[11] Some years ago notes issued by New England or Southern textile mills and indorsed by New York or Boston commission houses or selling agents were one of the most important classes of paper sold by dealers in the East. Large amounts of such paper were purchased by New England banks, including both commercial and savings banks. In more recent years, however, only a small volume of "mill paper" with commission house indorsement has been issued. A number of the larger and stronger textile mills have assumed the functions of marketing their own products and arranging for their own financing, and consequently no longer require the services of commission houses or selling agents.

[12] It was estimated that 52 per cent of the borrowers in the open market in 1924 were manufacturing concerns and that the remaining 48 per cent were trading concerns, "that is, concerns that do not change the condition of the product while in their possession" (National Credit Office, *History of Commercial Paper for the Years 1920–1924* — pamphlet — p. 5). Both "manufacturing concerns" and "trading concerns" would of course have to be given a rather broad definition if all open-market borrowers — including cold storage warehouses, oil refineries, finance companies, individuals and stock brokerage houses issuing collateral loan paper, and public utility companies — were to be classified into one or the other of these two groups.

of borrowers have also used the open market in recent years. Among these other classes, the following may be mentioned: cold storage warehouses, grain elevator companies,[13] flour-milling companies, meat packers, packers of fruits and vegetables, lumber mills, oil refineries, finance companies, individuals and stock brokerage houses issuing collateral loan paper, and even a number of public utility companies.[14]

[13] Notes of grain elevator and flour-milling companies are originated mainly in the Minneapolis and Kansas City Federal Reserve districts. In the former district a special class of grain paper, known as "demand notes," is originated. The following information relating to these notes, which in some respects differ from every other class of paper issued by concerns borrowing in the open market, was furnished by a Minneapolis dealer in 1930:

Demand notes are originated only in the ninth Federal Reserve district. They are issued mainly by terminal grain elevators, but to a small extent also by line elevators and grain commission houses.

The demand notes of terminal grain elevator companies are secured by registered terminal grain elevator receipts, with a margin of 10 per cent. These receipts are trusteed with some well-known bank, which also holds sufficient fire insurance to cover the total amount of loans secured by such receipts. All grain stored in terminal elevators in Minneapolis is inspected by deputies both of the Minnesota State Railroad and Warehouse Commission and of the Minneapolis Chamber of Commerce, and all grain stored in or removed from such elevators is certified. Hence the demand notes of these elevators are a practically "riskless" investment.

These notes are sold in denominations of $2,500 and multiples thereof. As their name indicates, they are payable on demand, and therefore have no definite maturity. They are issued without any definite maturity because terminal grain elevator companies do not know in advance just when they will be in a position to pay their demand notes from proceeds of sales of grain. Such companies sell for future delivery all grain which is used as security for these notes. As the delivery date approaches, they may find that there will be a favorable charge for carrying grain until the next delivery date, and that it will therefore be profitable to carry their grain until the next "option." In such cases they will not receive payment for grain sold, and consequently will not call their demand notes, until the later delivery date.

As long as demand notes remain outstanding, both the interest on these obligations and the dealer's commission for handling them are collected at least once every quarter. The dealer's commission, which is at the rate of ½ of 1 per cent a year, is included in the gross rate of interest paid by the borrowing concern. Thus if the gross rate of interest on any particular note happened to be 3½ per cent, the dealer would collect interest at the rate of 3½ per cent a year on the face of the note at the end of each quarter, pay 3 per cent to the holder of the note, and keep the remaining ½ of 1 per cent as his commission. Because of changes in money market conditions, the rate of interest on notes which run for several quarters may be changed several times before they are called.

In the spring of 1936 the Minneapolis dealer referred to above reported that the volume of demand notes bought and sold in the ninth Federal Reserve district has declined to a very considerable extent since 1930.

[14] An instance of borrowing in the open market by a small New England water

For the years 1922–1927, 1930, and 1933–1935 figures of the number of borrowers belonging to each of certain broad industrial groups into which concerns using the open market may be classified have been collected. These figures are given in Table 22, and a percentage distribution based on the same figures is shown in Table 23. Table 24 gives a classification of open-market borrowers in 1930 both by industries and by location.[15] The first two of these tables show that throughout the ten years referred to above borrowers in three industries alone — textiles and dry goods, foodstuffs, and metals and hardware — constituted approximately two-thirds of the total number of concerns using the open market. Borrowers in the first of these three groups made up roughly about one-third, those in the second about one-fifth, and those in the third about one-sixth, of the total number of concerns.[16] Table 24 shows that in 1930 open-market borrowers in the textile industry were most numerous in the Boston, New York, and Rich-

---

company, presumably within recent years, is mentioned in A. S. Dewing, *Corporation Finance* (rev. ed., 1931), p. 120.

Two Boston houses reported in 1931 that they were handling the open-market notes of a number of public utility companies. The paper of this class which one of these dealers was handling was issued mainly by Massachusetts electric light and power or gas companies. The other house was at that time dealing also in the open-market obligations of a few public utility companies located in other states than Massachusetts, and in more recent years has continued to handle notes issued by Massachusetts and New York utility companies.

[15] Classifications of open-market borrowers both by industries and by Federal Reserve districts for the years 1925–1927 are given in Foulke, *op. cit.*, pp. 45–47. For the year 1925 Foulke has also given a classification of such borrowers by industries and by net worth (p. 53).

[16] One reason why the first group — textiles and dry goods — contained so large a proportion of the total number of open-market borrowers is that this group included a rather wide variety of trading and manufacturing concerns, some of which were neither textile nor dry goods concerns. The 743 borrowers which were classed in this group in 1927, for instance, included such concerns as the following: cotton factors and dealers, converters of cotton goods, cotton cloth mills, cotton goods commission merchants, cotton yarn mills, and manufacturers of cotton gloves, hosiery, knit goods, underwear, pajamas, shade cloth, shirts and collars, tent awnings, and work clothing; converters of silk goods, jobbers of silk hosiery, jobbers of silks, and manufacturers of broad silks, narrow silks, silk hosiery, silk neckwear, plush, and upholstery fabric; dealers in wool, jobbers of woolen piece goods, jobbers of men's clothing, manufacturers of men's cloth and women's wear, and woolen mills; and chain stores, factors, importers of linens, jobbers of hats and millinery, mail order houses, manufacturers of corsets and hats, and wholesale and retail dealers in men's furnishings (Foulke, *op. cit.*, pp. 36–37).

TABLE 22

CLASSIFICATION OF OPEN-MARKET BORROWERS BY INDUSTRIES, 1922–1927, 1930, AND 1933–1935 *

Industry	Number of Concerns Using Open Market									
	1922	1923	1924	1925	1926	1927	1930	1933	1934	1935
Automotives and machinery	..	..	..	..	..	..	..	6	6	16
Building materials ..	18	16	26	31	28	35	37	7	7	3
Drugs and chemicals	109	102	115	122	114	125	69	39	32	29
Finance companies ..	9	32	55	74	86	85	54	24	31	60
Foodstuffs	516	405	563	585	554	507	317	131	157	171
Leather and shoes ..	182	171	148	144	136	121	90	25	32	37
Lumber and furniture	148	148	243	245	252	258	153	17	18	21
Metals and hardware	411	357	456	462	450	391	289	56	63	66
Paper and woodpulp	40	38	58	57	70	55	41	10	15	12
Public utility	..	..	..	..	..	..	..	24	15	11
Rubber goods	20	9	11	15	22	17	..	..	..	..
Textiles and dry goods	734	732	882	851	855	743	495	156	197	200
Tobacco products ...	22	26	28	30	27	21	23	12	13	6
Miscellaneous	50	135	120	138	149	132	106	41	39	22
Total	2,259	2,171	2,705	2,754	2,743	2,490	1,674	548	625	654

* Figures in this table were collected by the National Credit Office of New York. Figures for 1922–1927 are given in R. A. Foulke, *The Commercial Paper Market*, p. 32; those for 1930 were derived from figures given in L. M. Read, *The Story of Commercial Paper* (pamphlet), p. 2; those for 1933–1935 were supplied by the National Credit Office.

TABLE 23

PERCENTAGE DISTRIBUTION OF OPEN-MARKET BORROWERS BY INDUSTRIES, 1922–1927, 1930, AND 1933–1935 *

Industry	Per Cent of Total Number of Concerns Using Open Market									
	1922	1923	1924	1925	1926	1927	1930	1933	1934	1935
Automotives and machinery	..	..	..	..	..	..	..	1.1	1.0	2.4
Building materials	0.8	0.8	1.0	1.1	1.0	1.4	2.2	1.3	1.1	0.5
Drugs and chemicals	4.8	4.7	4.2	4.4	4.2	5.0	4.1	7.1	5.1	4.4
Finance companies	0.4	1.5	2.0	2.6	3.2	3.4	3.2	4.4	5.0	9.2
Foodstuffs	22.8	18.6	20.8	21.3	20.3	20.4	18.9	23.9	25.1	26.1
Leather and shoes	8.1	7.9	5.5	5.2	5.0	5.0	5.4	4.6	5.1	5.7
Lumber and furniture	6.5	6.8	9.0	8.9	9.2	10.3	9.2	3.1	2.9	3.2
Metals and hardware	18.2	16.5	16.9	16.8	16.5	15.7	17.2	10.2	10.1	10.1
Paper and woodpulp	1.8	1.7	2.2	2.1	2.0	2.2	2.5	1.8	2.4	1.8
Public utility	..	..	..	..	..	..	..	4.4	2.4	1.7
Rubber goods	0.9	0.4	0.4	0.5	0.9	0.7	..	..	..	..
Textiles and dry goods	32.5	33.7	32.6	31.0	31.2	29.8	29.6	28.4	31.5	30.6
Tobacco products	1.0	1.2	1.0	1.1	1.0	0.9	1.4	2.2	2.1	0.9
Miscellaneous	2.2	6.2	4.4	5.0	5.5	5.2	6.3	7.5	6.2	3.4
Total	100.	100.	100.	100.	100.	100.	100.	100.	100.	100.

* Figures for 1922–1927 are given in R. A. Foulke, *The Commercial Paper Market*, p. 33; those for 1930 were computed from figures given in L. M. Read, *The Story of Commercial Paper* (pamphlet), p. 2, and those for 1933–1935 from figures supplied by the National Credit Office of New York.

TABLE 24

CLASSIFICATION OF OPEN-MARKET BORROWERS BY INDUSTRIES AND LOCATION, 1930*

FEDERAL RESERVE DISTRICTS

INDUSTRY	Boston	New York	Philadelphia	Cleveland	Richmond	Atlanta	Chicago	St. Louis	Minneapolis	Kansas City	Dallas	San Francisco	Canada	Total United States and Canada
Textiles	73	102	31	18	73	50	50	25	8	21	24	15	5	495
Foodstuffs	23	13	12	11	15	34	53	25	21	48	30	30	2	317
Metals	22	30	25	17	12	13	80	22	9	22	21	16	..	289
Lumber	10	5	4	3	15	8	31	16	3	30	16	11	1	153
Leather	18	20	6	3	6	5	16	5	1	7	4	5	..	90
Chemicals	6	10	5	9	6	3	12	3	..	7	5	3	..	69
Finance	4	11	2	2	5	1	19	2	..	4	..	4	..	54
Paper	5	4	5	5	..	1	12	2	1	..	1	5	..	41
Building materials ...	2	2	1	6	..	2	5	3	..	4	5	6	1	37
Tobacco	3	7	6	..	1	1	1	3	..	..	..	1	..	23
Miscellaneous .	27	29	7	9	1	4	16	3	4	3	2	1	..	106
Total	193	233	104	83	134	122	295	109	47	140	108	97	9	1,674

* Figures in this table, except totals, are given in L. M. Read, *The Story of Commercial Paper* (pamphlet), p. 2.

mond Federal Reserve districts, those in the foodstuffs industry in the Chicago and Kansas City districts, and those in the metal industry in the Chicago district.

4. PURPOSES OF OPEN-MARKET BORROWING

The purposes for which funds are borrowed through dealers are in general the same as those for which trading and manufacturing concerns borrow directly from their own banks.

Loans obtained through dealers are used to a large extent for making prompt payments for raw materials and merchandise inventories purchased, in order to take advantage of cash discounts, and for paying wages and other current operating expenses. Working capital requirements such as these may be either seasonal or more or less continuous.

Concerns whose requirements are largely of a seasonal character, such as grain elevators, flour mills, concerns handling dairy products, seed companies, packers of fruits and vegetables, and manufacturers of clothing, shoes, and various other classes of products, as a rule borrow in the market during certain months only, and generally arrange to "clean up" all or the greater part of their open-market indebtedness within a few months after the peak of their borrowing requirements has been reached.[17] Loans to such classes of concerns are generally considered "self-liquidating" in the sense that the means of repaying them is ordinarily furnished within a comparatively short time by the sale of commodities purchased or manufactured with the aid of the borrowed funds.

Various other classes of concerns, whose operations are less subject to seasonal influences, borrow in the market for the purposes mentioned above, but more or less continuously throughout the year. That a substantial volume of what may be called permanent working capital is obtained through dealers each year

[17] Companies handling dairy products begin to borrow in the market in the spring and repay their open-market loans in the fall. Grain dealers and flour-milling companies borrow through dealers during the summer and fall. They liquidate their open-market obligations in the following spring (*Method of Seasonal Financing and Hedging in the Grain Industry* — pamphlet published by Bond and Goodwin, Inc. — pp. 2, 5). Numerous other examples of seasonal borrowing through dealers are given in "The Commercial Paper Business," *Fed. Res. Bull.*, Aug. 1921, p. 924.

is indicated by the fact that a fairly large proportion of the paper sold in the market is issued to replace maturing notes. Various dealers have estimated that the proportion is as high as 40 to 65 per cent.[18] It does not follow, however, that loans extended to concerns of this second group are necessarily less "self-liquidating" than advances to borrowers whose working capital requirements are temporary only. On the contrary, many trading and manufacturing companies belonging to the second group are able to liquidate their open-market indebtedness, with the proceeds of sales of the products they deal in or manufacture, at shorter intervals than various classes of borrowers of the first group. As a matter of fact, most concerns even of the second group reduce their notes payable to a considerable extent at least once a year; and if they remain "in the market" for longer periods than borrowers of the first group, it is because they find it profitable to "trade on the equity" more or less continuously, whereas borrowers of the first group are able to employ open-market funds advantageously during certain seasons of the year only.[19]

[18] Borrowing in the market more or less continuously has for many years been a rather common practice. The practice was criticized by various writers as early as 1913 and 1917. (See, for example, J. A. Broderick, "Registration of Commercial Paper," *Bankers' Home Mag.*, Nov. 1913, p. 43, and F. K. Houston, *Commercial Paper — Its Uses and Abuses* — pamphlet — pp. 16–17.) In 1921 it was estimated that the proportion of maturing commercial paper which was replaced with new open-market notes was as high as 50 to 75 per cent ("The Commercial Paper Business," *Fed. Res. Bull.*, Sept. 1921, p. 1054). About a year later a Boston dealer stated that the larger concerns borrowing through dealers seldom liquidate their open-market indebtedness entirely, "even though their business be seasonal" (A. P. Brown, "Commercial Paper" — typewritten paper — p. 18). In 1923 a St. Louis dealer stated that the majority of concerns using the open market are "constant borrowers," and that some of the best accounts his house was handling were those of companies which had not "cleaned up" their open-market loans for fifteen years (James McCluney, "Distribution of Commercial Paper" — typewritten paper — p. 2). It may be noted that direct loans from banks are used even more extensively than loans obtained through dealers are as a means of raising "permanent" working capital.

[19] Some years ago concerns which wished to make sure in advance that they would be able to borrow a definite amount of working capital in the market over a period of a year or so sometimes made use of a device known as a "revolving credit" or "long-term credit." A concern wishing to use a revolving credit entered into a contract with its dealer by which the latter guaranteed to purchase, over some definite period, commonly a period of one year, commercial paper of the former in amounts up to some stipulated maximum. The borrowing concern issued its notes

Few open-market borrowers, whether their credit requirements for working capital purposes are seasonal only or more or less continuous, endeavor to secure exclusively through dealers all the credit accommodation they require. Most concerns, instead, either borrow through dealers and their own banks at the same time or arrange to "rotate" their open-market loans and their bank loans,

---

in accordance with its requirements for working capital, and maturing notes were replaced, if necessary, with new issues of open-market obligations. As a rule, the rates at which the borrower's paper was to be discounted were not specified in the contract, but were determined, instead, by conditions in the money market at the time of issue. If unable to sell his borrowing customer's notes, the dealer had to carry them to maturity. For assuming this risk he received an underwriting commission which, in case the period stipulated in the contract ran for one year, commonly amounted to 2 per cent of the maximum amount of the guarantee; and, in addition, a selling commission of ½ of 1 per cent of the amounts of paper actually issued. The dealer generally secured the coöperation of local banks in underwriting the guaranteed maximum amount specified in the contract, and in such cases shared the underwriting commission with these co-insurers. In selling his customer's paper, however, he received no assistance from the underwriting banks (S. P. Meech, "Recent Tendencies in Credit Relations between Commercial Paper Houses and Business Concerns," *Univ. Jour. Bus.*, Dec. 1923, pp. 66–67).

Probably the most important revolving credit ever used in this country was one for which arrangements were made by a Boston commercial paper house and two banks, one of New York and the other of Boston, in July 1919. The following information relating to this credit was furnished by the Boston dealer:

This revolving credit was arranged for a large motor company. The chief purpose of establishing the credit was to enable the majority stockholders of the company to take over the interests of certain minority stockholders.

The amount of the credit was to be $75,000,000. This amount was to be obtained by the motor company through the issue of its unsecured ninety-day notes, which were to be renewed for three periods of 90 days each. Actually, however, the company used only $60,000,000 of the credit, and the notes were renewed only twice. Hence the company's open-market borrowing was limited to $60,000,000 for nine months.

Some of the borrowing concern's notes were issued with denominations as large as $1,000,000. Though unsecured, unindorsed, and not issued for the purpose of securing working capital, these notes were considered prime paper, and were sold to banks throughout the country. Some banks even purchased them in advance of their issue.

For underwriting the motor company's notes to the amount of $75,000,000, the commercial paper house received an underwriting commission of 2 per cent and the dealer's selling commission, and each of the two banks an underwriting commission of ½ of 1 per cent.

The amount the company borrowed through the Boston dealer — $60,000,000 — is probably the largest amount which any one concern has ever borrowed in the market at any one time.

It is probable that very few concerns, if any, have made use of revolving credits in more recent years.

using the open market for a few months and then "cleaning up" their open-market obligations and shifting their borrowing to their own banks. They may borrow mainly through dealers for periods of some length, of course, if the cost of open-market financing during such periods remains appreciably below the cost of borrowing from banks direct, but in such cases they are as a rule careful to maintain satisfactory average balances and open lines of credit with their banks.[20]

While most paper handled by dealers is issued for the purpose of securing working capital, funds borrowed in the open market are used to some extent also, just as direct advances from banks are, either for fixed capital purposes or to replace working capital which has been converted into fixed capital.[21] Perhaps the best example that may be given of borrowing through dealers for such purposes in recent years is the open-market financing of certain Massachusetts public utility companies, including both electric light and power companies and gas companies. These companies

---

[20] The following example of the manner in which a borrowing concern may "rotate" its bank loans and coördinate its borrowing from its own banks with its open-market financing was given in an address by a New York dealer in 1921: A nationally-known manufacturing company which in 1921 had a capital and surplus of approximately $40,000,000, quick assets of about $32,000,000, current liabilities of about $13,000,000, and no funded debt, maintained accounts with about twenty different banks. It had lines of credit with these banks amounting in the aggregate to $25,000,000, and kept bank balances equal to 20 per cent of its credit lines. While it never borrowed from any one bank less than its full line of credit with that bank, the company planned to stay out of debt to each of its banks for six months of each year and made it a practice never to use at any one time more than 50 per cent of its total credit lines. As soon as its credit requirements exceeded that figure it began to borrow in the open market, even though the rate on its open-market paper may have been higher than the rate at which it could borrow from one of its own banks. In no event would it allow the total amount of its notes payable to exceed $25,000,000. Thus it always had available open bank lines equal to the maximum amount of its open-market borrowing. In periods of exceptionally low money rates the company might borrow the entire amount of its credit requirements in the market. In such cases, however, it always maintained the usual 20 per cent balances, in order to make sure that it would always have open and available bank lines sufficient to enable it, if necessary, to "clean up" all its open-market obligations (W. E. Sachs, *Commercial Paper and Its Place in Our Banking System* — pamphlet — pp. 5–6).

[21] An instance of open-market borrowing by a manufacturing concern in 1918 for the purpose of replenishing working capital which was invested in new plant and equipment is given in Meech, *op. cit.*, pp. 54–55.

borrow in the market partly for the purpose of securing current working capital but also for such purposes as making improvements and expansions of plant and purchasing new plants. According to a Boston dealer, their use of open-market loans for fixed capital purposes is encouraged by state laws requiring that improvements and additions to plant must be completed before they can be "capitalized" by such companies.

As was indicated in the preceding chapter, funds secured through dealers are also used, both by stock brokerage houses and by individuals, for purchasing and carrying securities and for paying collateral loans obtained from banks direct.

5. Advantages and Disadvantages of Open-Market Financing from the Point of View of the Borrower

To concerns whose credit position is strong enough to enable them to borrow through dealers, open-market financing, especially when it is properly coördinated with borrowing from banks direct, offers a number of advantages as a means of raising short-term capital.

One of the most important of these advantages in the case of most borrowing customers of dealers is that the cost of raising short-term capital in the open market is ordinarily less than that of borrowing from banks direct.

Except in periods of high money rates, like 1920, the first half of 1921, and the greater part of 1929, rates on prime commercial paper are likely to be appreciably lower than rates charged on direct loans to customers even by the larger city banks. Some of the larger banks, to be sure, are willing to offer preferential rates to such of their borrowing customers as are able to obtain credit in the open market, and in periods of very low money rates have advanced credits to some such customers on terms favorable enough to make the cost of borrowing in the customers' loan market even lower than that of raising funds in the commercial paper market. Nevertheless most borrowing concerns, as Chart IV indicates, have in recent years generally had to pay on direct loans from banks rates distinctly higher than those on prime commercial paper.[22]

To make a fair comparison of the costs of borrowing in the market and from banks direct, however, allowance must of course be made for the dealer's commission and for the cost of maintaining idle bank balances. The commission charged by the dealer is generally (though not always) figured as a percentage of the face amounts of the notes he handles, irrespective of their maturities. This percentage varies, but is commonly ¼ of 1 per cent. Hence if open-market notes are issued with a maturity of six months, commission charges amounting to ½ of 1 per cent a year must commonly be included in the cost of borrowing in the market. If shorter maturities are used, the commission charges increase accordingly, unless the dealer is willing to accept a somewhat lower rate of compensation for handling notes running for shorter periods. Similarly, the cost of keeping unused bank balances must be included in the total cost of borrowing from banks direct. The average balances which commercial banks require their borrowing customers to maintain vary to some extent, and the cost of keeping such balances of course varies directly with the average balance ratio required. Thus if a concern obtains at a discount rate of 6 per cent a loan from a bank with which it is required to maintain average balances equal to 15 per cent of its borrowings, the actual

[22] Chart IV shows that during all but about four years of the period from 1919 to 1936 rates on prime commercial paper in New York were appreciably lower than rates charged on direct loans to customers by banks in a number of principal cities in the United States.

Reliable figures of rates charged by banks on direct loans during the years preceding 1919 are not available, but it is well known that rates charged on such loans even by the larger city banks have for many years generally been higher than rates on open-market paper. Yearly average rates on prime commercial paper in New York for the fifty-three years preceding 1919 are given in Table 1. If figures of average rates charged by banks on direct loans to customers were available for these years, they would undoubtedly be higher than the figures in Table 1.

The president of a drug company of Memphis, who was also a banker, reported that his concern was able to borrow in the market during the years from about 1900 to about 1926 "at a less average rate than the average rate charged by banks to first risk borrowing customers who keep proper bank balances" (R. R. Ellis, *Why I Use a Commercial Paper Broker* — pamphlet — p. 1). The experience of this company in this respect was no doubt typical of that of most other open-market borrowers during the same period.

cost of its loan will be, not 6 per cent, but 7.06 per cent, a year; and if the required average balance ratio were 20 instead of 15 per cent, the cost of the loan would be 7½ per cent.

Since rates on open-market notes are generally lower than the rates which concerns issuing such obligations would have to pay on direct loans from banks, and since the cost of keeping unused bank balances is likely to be appreciably greater than dealers' commission charges, it would seem that the cost of open-market financing would generally be considerably lower than that of borrowing directly from banks. It has been assumed in the foregoing discussion, however, that no bank balances need to be maintained in connection with loans obtained through dealers; and such is not the case. It is true that open-market borrowers are not required to keep balances with the banks which purchase their commercial paper, but practically all such borrowers realize the importance of keeping ample lines of credit at their own banks open and available if needed, and consequently maintain ample balances with the latter institutions even when not borrowing from them. Hence the cost of keeping idle balances must be included in the total costs of borrowing through dealers, as well as from banks direct. After the necessary allowances are made for differences in discount rates, for dealers' commission charges, and for the differences between these two methods of financing so far as the costs of maintaining unused bank balances are concerned,[23] the cost of borrowing in the market is no doubt generally lower than that of borrowing direct from banks, though not so much lower as might at first be supposed.[24]

[23] In case a concern borrowing in the open market follows the same policies with regard to keeping unused bank balances as the company mentioned in n. 20, p. 252, the cost of maintaining such balances is the same whether it borrows through a dealer or from its own banks direct. The majority of open-market borrowers, however, no doubt consider it unnecessary to keep idle bank balances in connection with their open-market financing as large as those they would maintain if they were borrowing the same amounts directly from their own banks. For this reason the cost of keeping unused balances involved in borrowing through dealers is doubtless smaller as a rule than the corresponding cost of borrowing from banks direct.

[24] While the comparatively low cost of borrowing through dealers is undoubtedly regarded by many concerns as the main advantage of this method of financing, the importance of this advantage has sometimes been overemphasized. In the case of

Another advantage of open-market financing is that the ability to sell its notes through dealers in a market that is nation-wide gives a company a certain amount of bargaining power in dealing with its own banks. The accounts of most concerns which are able to borrow in the market are considered choice accounts by commercial banks, and there is keen competition among the larger banks, as well as between banks and dealers, for the accounts of such concerns. Many banks, in fact, have bought open-market paper with the primary purpose of endeavoring to secure desirable borrowing accounts later on. Because of the active competition of other banks, as well as between banks and dealers, for the opportunity of supplying the short-term credit accommodation they require, many concerns which are able to sell their notes in the market are in a position to borrow on more favorable terms from their own banks than would ordinarily be possible otherwise.

A third advantage of using the open market is that, if properly coördinated with direct borrowing from banks, it enables a borrowing concern to "clean up" its bank loans at more or less regular intervals. The extent to which open-market borrowing is used for this purpose can only be estimated, and of course in any case varies with different concerns and with conditions in the money market, but it is known that a substantial proportion of the funds obtained in the market are used for paying off direct loans from banks. Dealers have estimated that the proportion is as high as 40 to 50 per cent. The reduction or complete liquidation of bank loans in this manner, like the converse process of discharging open-market obligations with funds borrowed from banks direct, of course in-

---

many open-market borrowers, some of the other advantages mentioned in the text below are considered more important. As a matter of fact, the cost of borrowing in the market in recent years, particularly since 1932, has by no means always been lower than the cost of borrowing from banks direct; for some of the larger city banks, confronted with the problem of finding safe and liquid short-term investments for surplus loanable funds, have offered certain prime open-market "names" rates on direct loans low enough to make the cost of borrowing directly from banks lower than that of borrowing indirectly through dealers. Many of the borrowing customers of a leading Eastern house, however, despite the fact that they have been able to obtain advances from their own banks on more favorable terms, have preferred to secure in the market at least a part of the borrowed funds they require.

volves no ultimate settlement of the borrowing concern's indebtedness, but merely a shifting of its short-term borrowings from one group of banks to another. From the point of view of the individual bank, however, the fact that the liquidity of its loans to a borrowing customer at any particular time may depend largely on their "shiftability" is of no great consequence. If a concern is able to "clean up" its bank loans at least once a year, even though it obtains the funds required for this purpose in the open market, it shows that it is in a strong enough position to borrow from other sources than its own banks, and it enables the latter to increase their loans to other customers; and hence its borrowing account will be considered a highly desirable account by its own banks.

In the fourth place, use of the open market enables concerns whose own banks are unable to supply the full amount of their credit requirements to obtain the additional accommodation they need in a market that is nation-wide. Many concerns originally began to borrow in the market because their own local banks were not in a position to extend them loans commensurate with their requirements. In more recent years use of the open market for this reason has become less common, for concerns able to borrow through dealers encounter little difficulty in establishing bank lines sufficient to meet their peak requirements for borrowed funds. At the same time, loans of national banks to any one borrower are limited to 10 per cent of their capital and surplus,[25] and loans of state banks are restricted in a similar manner by the banking statutes of many states. Many banks, moreover, both state and national, find it necessary to limit their advances to individual borrowers in order to secure a proper diversification of their loans. Hence some concerns are still unable to obtain all the accommodation they require from the banks with which they have established lines of credit, and therefore find it expedient to supplement borrowing from their own banks with borrowing through dealers.

---

[25] In recent years such loans have been restricted further by Section 26 (a) of the Banking Act of 1933, which provides that, in determining the maximum amount which a national bank may advance to a corporation, all obligations of all subsidiaries "in which such corporation owns or controls a majority interest" shall be included in the obligations of the latter company.

If they wished to, such concerns as these could of course establish additional lines of credit sufficient to enable them to obtain through direct loans from banks all the short-term accommodation they require. Some concerns, however, do not establish additional bank lines because it is unquestionably more convenient to borrow indirectly through a single commercial paper house than directly through a large number of banks in different parts of the country. This greater convenience of open-market borrowing is a minor advantage in its favor.

Much more important in the case of many concerns is a sixth advantage of borrowing through commercial paper houses — namely, that open-market borrowers are able to obtain valuable financial advice from their dealers. Furnishing such information is in fact one of the most important functions which commercial paper houses perform. It is a function, moreover, which the larger dealers are particularly well qualified to perform, for the nature of their operations requires them to keep in close touch with conditions in many different lines of business, as well as with money market conditions, in all sections of the country.[26]

A seventh advantage of open-market financing is that companies which continually maintain a credit position strong enough to enable them to borrow through dealers acquire financial prestige and obtain favorable publicity in all sections of the country in which their notes are purchased. According to a New England dealer, some concerns consider this advantage so important that they even sell their notes in the market at times when they are not in need of borrowed funds, and may lend funds so obtained out again at rates lower than those which they pay for them.[27]

[26] Dealers' financial advice to their borrowing customers is discussed in Chap. VII, § 3.

[27] While the financial prestige secured by financing through dealers may be shared more or less equally by all open-market borrowers, the advantages of borrowing through dealers are of course most important, so far as publicity is concerned, in the case of manufacturing companies. Concerns handling food products and manufacturers of blankets, shoes, silverware, clocks, and various other products have considered the free advertising obtained by borrowing in the market as one of the main advantages of this method of financing.

It has been estimated that each open-market note, from the time of its issue until its payment and cancellation, passes through the hands of about seventy

Finally, a concern which, by selling its notes through dealers, has shown its ability to obtain unsecured short-term loans from banks in all sections of the country is in a favorable position for raising such long-term capital as it may require from time to time. It may even be able to arrange for the issue of long-term securities through its dealer, for a number of commercial paper houses originate and sell such securities as well as short-term paper.[28]

The foregoing advantages of open-market financing are not offset by any important disadvantages from the point of view of the comparatively small number of concerns whose credit standing is high enough to enable them to borrow through dealers. Certain alleged disadvantages of open-market borrowing have nevertheless been adduced by various writers as objections against this method of obtaining short-term credit accommodation. On careful analysis, however, these supposed disadvantages turn out to be either nonexistent or of little consequence.

One of the most commonly mentioned of such disadvantages is that a concern borrowing in the market may become independent of its bankers, be deprived of their counsel, and consequently overexpand its business.[29] It is true that cases of this sort were not uncommon years ago, but few such cases, if any at all, have

different persons, including bank directors, bank officers, credit men, discount clerks, paying tellers, and bookkeepers. The individual notes included in a single large issue of open-market paper, moreover, have been sold to more than a thousand different banks, located in all sections of the country. (Sachs, *op. cit.*, p. 7.) Hence the sale of notes ·in the market is probably more effective as a means of securing free advertising than would at first be supposed.

[28] It is sometimes said that one of the advantages of open-market financing is that it enables a borrowing concern to save its bank lines for "emergency purposes." This can hardly be considered as an exclusive advantage of open-market borrowing, however, for obviously a concern which borrows from its own banks alone can also save bank lines for emergency purposes, provided it has established adequate banking connections. As a matter of fact, a company which has been obtaining from its own banks at least a part of the accommodation it requires is more likely to find its bank lines available in an emergency than one which has been borrowing exclusively through dealers; for in the former case the banks will have a stake in their borrowing customer's business, whereas in the latter case they may not feel under any particular obligation to come to the aid of the borrowing concern. As more than one company has discovered to its embarrassment, the full amount of a line of credit established at some earlier date is not necessarily available in a time of emergency.

[29] E. E. Lincoln, *Applied Business Finance*, 4th rev. ed., p. 446.

occurred in recent years. Even in earlier years losses from over-expansion encouraged by liberal extensions of credit to banks' own customers were no doubt considerably greater than losses from overtrading facilitated by the ease of selling promissory notes in the market. At present dealers do not allow their borrowing customers to become independent of their bankers, and are in a position to give their clients better financial advice than the latter could obtain from many commercial banks. The credit departments of both banks and commercial paper houses, moreover, have become so proficient in investigating the credit standing of concerns seeking accommodation in the market that only a comparatively small number of companies, which are regarded as unusually good credit risks, are able to sell their notes through dealers. It would be practically impossible at present for any concern to borrow in the market through a reputable dealer for the purpose of undertaking any ill-advised expansion of its business.

Another alleged disadvantage of open-market financing is that a company which borrows heavily in the market "to the neglect of proper banking connections" is "almost certain to encounter financial difficulties in times of panic and uncertainty." [30] Concerns which do not maintain adequate banking connections at present, however, cannot sell their paper in the market through responsible commercial paper houses. Dealers realize fully the importance of making sure that their borrowing customers keep their issues of open-market paper within reasonable limits, and that

[30] Lincoln, *Applied Business Finance*, p. 447. The disadvantage in question is often indicated by the statement that commercial paper houses are "fair-weather friends" only. The market for commercial paper was unquestionably restricted during the periods of financial strain which occurred in 1873, 1883, 1893, and 1907. It was also restricted, though to a lesser extent, during similar periods in 1914 and 1920. The difficulty in borrowing in the market at such times resulted largely from the facts that banks felt obligated to supply the credit needs of their own customers first and did not have large amounts of surplus funds available for the purchase of outside paper. Even in such times, however, dealers have succeeded in marketing a volume of commercial paper large enough to provide for the financial requirements of at least some of their borrowing customers. In fact, a large Eastern house reported that it was unable to satisfy the demands of its buying customers for outside paper during such periods of financial stringency as occurred in 1920, 1929, 1932, and 1933; and that in February 1933 it placed open-market notes for several concerns which could not secure accommodation from some of their own banks.

such customers shall at all times keep adequate bank lines open and available for use in an emergency. Some concerns which borrow in the market of course get into financial difficulties even at present, but in such cases commercial paper houses coöperate to the fullest extent possible with banks holding notes issued by such concerns in assisting the latter to work out of their difficulties and meet their obligations. It may be added that a great many concerns which do not borrow in the market at all, and not a few banks themselves, are practically certain to encounter financial difficulties in times of panic and uncertainty.

It is stated also that it is sometimes more convenient for borrowing concerns to deal directly with their local banks than with a commercial paper house. This is unquestionably true in some cases. On the other hand, representatives of some of the larger commercial paper houses generally arrange to call on all their borrowing customers at least once a year, and it is possible to keep in close touch with the affairs of such customers by correspondence, telephone, and telegraph. Moreover, companies whose credit requirements can be supplied by their own local banks are not likely to be in need of the services of dealers. Concerns whose local banks cannot supply all the credit they need must obtain the additional accommodation they require by borrowing direct from banks in other localities, by using the open market, or by resorting to some other method of short-term financing; and, as was pointed out above, it is more convenient to borrow through a single dealer than through any considerable number of different banks.

A fourth alleged disadvantage of open-market financing is that companies which borrow through commercial paper houses are subjected to the inconvenience and expense of answering innumerable credit inquiries by prospective and actual buyers of their paper, and that their credit may be impaired by false rumors resulting from such inquiries. Companies using the open market must of course expect to answer credit inquiries, but these come mainly from their dealers and one or two credit-reporting agencies, rather than from banks contemplating the purchase of their paper. Answers to credit inquiries, moreover, are regarded as confidential information, and the possibility that false rumors might be started as a result of such inquiries has probably deterred no concern from borrowing through dealers in recent years. In the case of companies which have become "seasoned" borrowers in the open market and issue audited financial statements containing detailed information at least once a year, this fourth objection against borrowing through dealers is particularly unimportant.

In the fifth place, it is said that if a concern in any particular industry becomes financially embarrassed, country banks, which have purchased substantial amounts of open-market obligations in recent years, will often refuse to buy paper issued by other concerns in the same industry. It is said also that if a well-known company in a given city fails or is reported to be seriously embarrassed, such banks will sometimes even "boycott" the obligations of concerns engaged in entirely different lines of business in the same locality.[31] In answer to this objection it may be said that there are at present few country banks to which these statements would apply. The force of the objection is weakened still further by the facts that the number of concerns using the open market which have become financially embarrassed in recent years is extremely small,[32] that many country banks still entrust their correspondent banks or dealers themselves with the responsibility of selecting the paper they purchase, and that there is practically always an active market for the notes of concerns which are really in a position to borrow through dealers, whether or not such obligations are purchased by particular country banks.

A final alleged disadvantage of open-market financing is that commercial paper houses interfere with the management of their borrowing customers' businesses. It is true that dealers do require more detailed information concerning the affairs of their customers than the latter furnish their own banks, expect companies whose accounts they handle to maintain satisfactory average balances with their banks and to keep adequate bank lines open and available, exercise a certain amount of control over their borrowing,

---

[31] Lincoln, *Applied Business Finance*, pp. 448–449.
[32] See p. 312.

both from their own banks and in the open market, and insist that they follow sound business policies in general. It is probable, however, that dealers interfere in their clients' affairs to no greater extent than well-managed commercial banks, and to a smaller extent than investment banking houses. Concerns using the open market, moreover, realize that any criticisms of their operating methods or recommendations of changes in their policies on the part of their dealers are offered for the purpose of improving their credit standing, and hence as a rule welcome the constructive criticism and advice which their dealers are able to offer them.

CHAPTER VII

PRACTICES FOLLOWED BY DEALERS IN SELECTING AND BUYING COMMERCIAL PAPER

MODERN commercial paper houses, as distinguished from the note brokers of earlier years, purchase outright the greater part of the promissory notes they handle. If these obligations are carefully selected, they can generally be sold as soon as issued, and dealers can therefore turn their capital very quickly. If, on the other hand, any notes should be selected without sufficient care, most banks to which they were offered for sale would reject them as unsatisfactory, and the originating house would consequently have to carry a substantial proportion of such obligations to maturity. Moreover, some losses might have to be incurred on these notes. If banks should have to bear any part of such losses, the reputation of the originating house would be adversely affected. If the originating house should happen to be carrying the entire issue of notes at maturity, or should take up any unpaid notes held by its buying customers, it would have to absorb all such losses itself. Hence of all the operations involved in dealing in promissory notes, the selection of such obligations is one of the most important. The practices followed by leading dealers in selecting and buying the paper they handle will be considered in this chapter.

1. ORIGINATING OPEN-MARKET PAPER

The most difficult problem encountered by commercial paper houses is that of securing an adequate supply of high-grade open-market obligations.

In recent years, for the following three reasons, this problem has probably become more serious than in any preceding period in the history of the commercial paper business: In the first place, as both banks and dealers have become more proficient in making credit investigations, the standards to which concerns wishing to borrow in the open market must conform have constantly become higher. Secondly, many concerns of the class able to borrow through commercial paper houses have needed but little short-term credit. Thirdly, competition in supplying such reduced amounts of credit as concerns of this class have required, both among dealers themselves and between banks and dealers, has become more active than in earlier years.

At the same time, commercial paper houses have been unable to reduce their overhead and other expenses to any great extent, or to increase their commission charges — which ordinarily do not exceed ¼ of 1 per cent of the face amounts of the notes they handle — and consequently must still handle a large volume of business each year if they are to operate at a profit. Hence success in the commercial paper business at present depends to a greater extent than in any earlier period upon the ability of dealers to secure an adequate supply of high-grade notes. And for the same reason "finding" or originating open-market paper, to take the place of that issued by concerns which for one reason or another discontinue the practice of borrowing through dealers, has become an increasingly important function of the comparatively small number of houses which have continued to buy and sell promissory notes in the market.

In order to originate open-market paper — that is, to select notes issued by companies whose accounts they have not previously handled — dealers as a rule must first select concerns whose paper they wish to purchase and then actively solicit the borrowing accounts of these prospective customers. They cannot wait for new borrowing customers to come to them, for most concerns which have not yet borrowed in the market know very little about this method of financing and consequently do not realize its advantages; and, besides, competition in the commercial paper business is very active, and each individual house knows that other dealers are likely to secure accounts which it does not solicit itself.[1]

---

[1] In some cases, however, dealers do secure new accounts which they have not solicited. Occasionally concerns whose credit requirements become so large that they cannot secure all the accommodation they need from their local banks are advised by the latter to supplement their bank loans with loans obtained through dealers. Moreover, when houses which have been dealing in open-market notes discontinue

Since only commercial paper of high grade can be readily sold in the open market, dealers must select very carefully the companies whose borrowing accounts they endeavor to secure. These concerns, in whatever line of business they may be engaged, must possess certain general qualifications for borrowing in the market. They must have a net worth of not less than about $250,000, must be able to use on the average about $200,000 or more of borrowed funds each year, and must have, or be able to secure, adequate banking connections; their management must be able and of unquestionable integrity; and they must have an unusually high credit standing. Moreover, they should be companies which in all probability will be able to carry on their operations profitably, and remain unusually good credit risks, for some years to come, for commercial paper houses prefer to establish enduring connections with the concerns whose obligations they undertake to handle.[2]

---

operations in commercial paper they turn over to other dealers, either gratuitously or for some form of compensation, the accounts of their borrowing customers who wish to continue to use the open market. In some cases concerns which have not previously borrowed in the market voluntarily offer their accounts to dealers, and companies which have been using the open market discontinue their relations with the houses which have been handling their paper and offer their accounts to other dealers. The houses to which such accounts are offered, however, reject a large proportion of them. Concerns of the first class seldom possess the qualifications required for borrowing through dealers, as is indicated by the fact that a New York house consulted in 1930 reported that it ordinarily rejected about 75 per cent of the new accounts which were offered to it voluntarily. Companies of the second class are generally concerns whose paper has not been of a particularly high grade, and has therefore been moving slowly and only at comparatively high rates. Such companies sometimes erroneously conclude that not their own credit standing, but the lack of sufficient activity on the part of their dealers, has been responsible for the failure of their notes to move more rapidly, and consequently hope to secure a better distribution for their paper by turning their accounts over to other houses.

[2] All dealers prefer, so far as possible, to secure the accounts of companies with which they can establish enduring connections, because it is more profitable to handle the paper of such concerns than that of companies which borrow in the market only at infrequent intervals or discontinue their borrowing through dealers entirely after a few years. Concerns of the former class are likely to issue relatively large amounts of open-market obligations each year, their paper becomes well known in the market, their business policies are likely to require but little supervision on the part of their dealers, and it is relatively easy for the latter to keep in touch with their affairs. Hence the gross profits from selling their paper are relatively large and the expenses involved in handling their accounts relatively small. Since connections established with large companies are more likely to be enduring than those estab-

Though comparatively few companies possess the qualifications indicated, some such concerns are to be found in practically every state in the Union and in practically all the more important trades and industries. Some of the larger commercial paper houses accordingly select concerns in all sections of the country and in many different lines of business as prospective borrowing customers whose accounts they wish to solicit. Even the larger dealers, however, originate the greater part of the paper they handle in the territory adjacent to the centers in which they maintain their main offices and their most important branch offices. The area throughout which smaller houses which maintain no branch offices can conveniently originate open-market notes, and consequently the range of industries among which they can readily seek new borrowing customers, is of course more restricted. Hence such houses generally specialize to a greater extent than the larger dealers in handling the paper of certain classes of concerns.[3] Since in all sections of the country some classes of paper are more in demand than others, all houses, whether large or small, must be careful in originating open-market notes to select classes of obligations which are popular with banks in the districts in which they are to be offered for sale.

In case dealers maintain no branch offices, the accounts of all concerns which they have selected as prospective borrowing customers must of course be solicited by their main offices. If they maintain one or more branches in addition to their main offices, these branches inform the latter offices of opportunities for securing new accounts and in most cases also solicit new business themselves. The final decision with respect to buying new paper as a

---

lished with concerns of comparatively small size, some of the larger houses do not actively solicit the accounts of small companies.

In 1930 a New York house was selling open-market paper for some borrowing customers whose accounts it and several predecessor firms had been handling for about thirty years; and a Boston house was still handling paper for some customers whose accounts it secured when it entered the commercial paper business some fifty years earlier.

[3] In 1930, for example, a house which was buying and selling commercial paper mainly in a few states in the Kansas City Federal Reserve district reported that about 80 per cent of the obligations it was then handling were notes issued by flour-milling concerns.

rule rests with their main offices, but branches which are managed by resident partners or other influential executives may have the same authority as their main offices in originating and buying open-market notes. Some of the larger houses assign the function of originating such obligations to special departments, known as new business departments, which they maintain in their main offices. These dealers, however, use substantially the same methods of selecting new paper as other houses which do not maintain special departments for this purpose. In the case of a number of houses, both large and small, all partners or officers, and all salesmen as well, solicit new accounts. In the case of other houses, particularly those of smaller size, new business is solicited by partners or officers only. Thus different dealers follow somewhat different policies in soliciting new business. In the case of all houses, however, the responsibility for originating open-market notes is assumed mainly by partners or influential executives; for contacts are an important aid in securing new accounts, and the partners or officers of commercial paper houses have the most valuable contacts.

2. METHODS OF CREDIT INVESTIGATION USED BY DEALERS

Before deciding whether to solicit the account of any company which they are considering as a prospective borrowing customer, dealers first make a careful and detailed investigation of its qualifications for borrowing in the open market.[4] For this purpose they maintain in their main office a special credit department which coöperates very closely with their new business department or, if they do not maintain a special new business department, with all members of their organization who are entrusted with the responsibility of securing new business. They must of course also keep in close touch with the affairs of all their customers after they have

---

[4] A leading New England house reported in 1931 that it rarely solicits the account of a prospective borrowing customer whose affairs it has not been following for at least several years. On the other hand, the credit investigation which a commercial paper house makes before deciding whether to solicit the borrowing account of a prospective customer may be relatively brief and simple if the concern in question happens to be either a company for which it has already brought out long-term securities or a "seasoned" open-market borrower whose paper is currently being handled by some other dealer.

secured their accounts, in order to determine whether the latter are following sound business policies and whether any concern wishing to borrow in the market at any particular time has maintained a credit standing high enough to enable it to use this method of financing. Hence they assign to their credit department the further function of collecting and classifying in systematically arranged credit files detailed and up-to-date information relating to the credit standing of every company whose account they handle.[5]

The methods used by different houses in investigating the qualifications of prospective customers for borrowing in the market, as well as in determining whether customers whose accounts they have already obtained are in a position to use this system of financing at any particular time, differ to some extent. All dealers, however, secure information of the same general character with respect to the concerns which they are considering as prospective borrowing customers, as well as those whose accounts they are already handling.

As was pointed out above, commercial paper houses prefer to secure as new borrowing customers companies with which they can establish enduring connections. For this reason the investigations which some of the larger dealers make before deciding to solicit the accounts of concerns which they are considering as prospective borrowing clients are of the same character as the investigations which they would conduct before deciding whether to bring out an issue of long-term securities. Thus some of these houses may begin an inquiry undertaken for the purpose of enabling them to decide whether they wish to solicit the account of a prospective customer by making a careful survey of existing and probable

---

[5] As early as 1917 a Texas banker stated that dealers in commercial paper "have the most highly specialized credit systems which are known" (J. G. McNary, "The Business Man, the Obligations of the Business Man from the Standpoint of the Banker," *Proc. Ariz. Bankers' Assoc.*, 1917, p. 52).

Some commercial banks in the South, as well as the investment banking affiliate of a Southern bank, were dealing in commercial paper as recently as 1931. The former institutions were of course able to use the facilities of their bank credit departments in making the credit investigations necessary in connection with their operations in open-market paper. Similarly, the investment banking affiliate, instead of organizing a credit department of its own, used the facilities of the credit department of the bank with which it was connected.

future conditions in the industry or line of business in which the company in question is engaged. After making this industrial survey, they are ready to determine the position of the concern in the industry. For this purpose they make what may be called an engineering examination of the company's plant and equipment, as well as a careful investigation of its general scheme of organization and its personnel. They then make a detailed examination of its current financial condition and its credit standing with its banks and the concerns from which it purchases supplies and raw materials or the merchandise or other products which it handles.

Though practically all dealers obtain more or less detailed information of the kinds just indicated before deciding whether to solicit the account of a prospective customer, not all houses follow the same order of procedure in conducting their investigations.[6]

Most dealers, in fact, secure first of all complete information with respect to the character of the management of a company which they are considering as a prospective client. Since the credit standing of a borrowing concern depends to a considerable extent on the reliability and integrity of its management, information of the kind in question must be collected very carefully. Such information may be secured by personal interviews with officers of the company whose affairs are being investigated and by interviews or correspondence with concerns from which it makes purchases, with its banks, and with individuals who are acquainted with its management.

If satisfied with the results of this preliminary investigation, dealers must next ascertain whether the company's officers are following sound policies and managing its affairs successfully, and whether it is in a strong enough financial position to enable it to borrow in the market. The information required for such purposes is obtained through trade and bank "checkings" and, in some cases, reports of credit agencies, through a careful and detailed analysis of the company's balance sheets and operating statements as of the

---

[6] The order of procedure outlined above was being followed by a leading Middle-Western house in 1923 (A. G. Becker, *Commercial Paper* — pamphlet — pp. 13–17). At least some of the larger houses have used similar methods of credit investigation in more recent years.

latest statement date and for several preceding years, through credit questionnaires, and through interviews with the company's officers.

From the concerns from which it buys its supplies and raw materials or the merchandise or products it handles, dealers find out what terms of purchase are offered to the company, what lines of credit it is allowed, whether it pays its trade obligations promptly, whether it takes all cash discounts offered, and in general whether it is considered a good credit risk in trade circles. They are particularly careful to ascertain whether their prospective customer is taking cash discounts offered, for failure to take such discounts would indicate that the financial affairs of the company were not being prudently managed. They may also obtain useful information of a historical character from its trade creditors, and other valuable information concerning its affairs from its competitors.

From the company's banks dealers ascertain what lines of credit it has established, the amount it is currently borrowing from each of its banks, whether it has paid its bank loans promptly, whether it has maintained satisfactory average balances, whether the notes on which it has borrowed from its banks have been secured by any form of collateral or indorsed or guaranteed, and whether all the banks from which it has been borrowing regard it as a good credit risk. Since its own banks will probably not wish to divulge information of a confidential nature with respect to its affairs, dealers may also consider it advisable to "check" the company's credit standing with several banks with which it does not have a borrowing account.

If they wish to, houses considering the advisability of soliciting a new borrowing account may compare the information received from the sources already mentioned with reports prepared by credit agencies on the credit standing of the concern in question. As a rule, however, particularly if the prospective customer has not previously been borrowing in the market, such reports are likely to contain little information which cannot be secured from these other sources.

In addition to the data obtained from the sources mentioned above, dealers require information which will enable them to make their own independent investigation of the credit standing of a company which they are considering as a prospective borrowing customer. Hence they secure the concern's balance sheet and operating statement figures as of the latest date for which they are available, as well as for several years preceding, and subject these figures to a detailed and careful analysis. The information gained as a result of this examination may be supplemented by data obtained through a credit questionnaire which they ask their prospective client to fill out. Any additional data required are secured by personal interviews or correspondence with the company's officers.

Some of the larger houses have arranged to have recorded on a credit questionnaire form a large part of the information they need in order to make an independent investigation of a prospective customer's credit standing. The nature of the information required for this purpose is indicated by Exhibit 16, which is a copy of a questionnaire form used for some years before 1934 by a leading New England house.[7] As may be seen from an examination of this exhibit, this New England dealer, in order to make an independent appraisal of the credit standing of a prospective client, secures answers to such questions as the following:

What items are included in the company's current assets, and what is the total amount of such assets? What is the amount of its good accounts receivable from customers, what amount of such "receivables" is not yet due, and what amounts are past due, respectively, fewer than thirty days, thirty to sixty days, sixty to ninety days, and more than ninety days? What are the company's usual trade terms to customers? What is the amount of its good

[7] This questionnaire form probably requests more detailed information than similar forms used by other dealers. Its use was discontinued about the beginning of 1934. At that time it was only one of twenty forms contained in the credit file for each concern whose paper the New England house was handling. The other forms were used for recording balance sheet and operating statement figures, information secured through bank and trade "checkings," and the like. Since this house now obtains complete audits from all its borrowing customers at least once a year, it makes less use of credit forms at present than was customary several years ago.

EXHIBIT 16

CREDIT QUESTIONNAIRE FORM USED BY A NEW ENGLAND DEALER

CORPORATION FORM   **CONFIDENTIAL**

For the purpose of procuring credit from time to time with you, on our negotiable paper or otherwise we furnish the following as a true and correct statement of our financial condition on .... 19........ , and hereby agree to notify you immediately in writing of any materially unfavorable change in our financial condition. In the absence of such notice or a new and full written statement, this is to be considered as a continuing statement, and that our responsibility has not fallen below the condition herein set forth.

NOTE. Please Answer all Questions. Insert Ciphers or the word "None" in the absence of amount.

ASSETS	DOLLARS	CTS.	LIABILITIES	DOLLARS	CTS.
Cash on Hand and in Bank			Notes Payable for Merchandise		
Cash Surrender Value of Life Insurance on Officers			Trade Acceptances—Payable		
Accounts Receivable of Customers—Good for Merchandise Only			Notes Payable to Banks and Brokers		
Trade Acceptances of Customers—			Notes Payable to Officers, Directors and Stock-holders—Not Endorsers		
Notes Receivable of Customers—Good and Collectable			Notes Payable to Others—Individuals		
Merchandise—Finished			Trade Accounts Payable—Not Due		
Merchandise—In Process—Unfinished			Trade Accounts Payable—Past Due		
Merchandise—Raw Material			Accounts Payable to Officers, Directors and Stockholders—Not Endorsers		
Merchandise in Transit or on Hand against which Drafts are Drawn under Acceptance Agreements			Amounts Due—Endorsers of Companies' Notes		
U. S. Government Obligations			Deposits of Money with this Company		
Other Active Assets—(Itemize on page 2)			Provision for Federal Taxes		
			Accrued Interest, Other Taxes, etc.		
TOTAL QUICK ASSETS			Mortgages Payable within 12 Months		
Due from Controlled or Subsidiary Concerns (Itemize on Page 2) { For Merchandise / For Advances			Drafts Drawn under Acceptance Agreements		
Stocks, Bonds and Investments (Itemize on page 2)			Any Other Quick Liabilities—(Itemize on p. 3)		
Land (Itemize on Page 2)			**TOTAL QUICK LIABILITIES**		
			Mortgages or Liens on Real Estate Due Beyond 12 Months—When Due		
Buildings (Itemize on Page 2)			Bonded Debt—When Due		
Machinery, Equipment and Fixtures			Chattel Mortgages		
Horses, Wagons and Automobiles			Any Other Liabilities (Itemize on Page 2)		
Notes Receivable—Due from Officers, Stock-holders and Employees			Total Liabilities		
Accounts Receivable—Due from Officers, Stockholders and Employees			Reserves—Depreciation on Buildings, Machinery and Equipment		
Notes and Accounts Receivable of Customers—Doubtful			Other Reserves		
Goodwill, Patents and Trade Marks					
Stores, Supplies, Etc.			Capital Stock—Preferred Outstanding		
Deferred Assets—Itemize			Capital Stock—Common Outstanding		
Other Assets—(Itemize on Page 2)			Capital Stock—No. Shares—No Par value		
			Undivided Surplus—See Page 2		
Total			Total		

CONTINGENT LIABILITY—(Federal Reserve Bank Requirement)

Liability upon trade acceptances and/or notes receivable discounted or sold		
Liability upon trade acceptances and/or notes receivable assigned or pledged		
Liability upon customers' accounts sold, assigned or pledged		
Liability upon accommodation paper or endorsements or upon notes exchanged with others		
Liability as guarantor for others on notes, accounts or contracts		
Liability for bonds or unfinished contracts		
Liability for Federal Taxes assessed by government for past years		
Any other contingent liability		
Are trade acceptances or notes receivable ever discounted? Total contingent liabilities		

Hereby solemnly declare and certify this to be a true and correct statement of the financial condition

of the .... **Company**

      Please sign Corporation name

at the close of business... 19 ....

Date .... 19 ....   By ....

Books audited by...   Official Capacity ....

The following Confidential Information is furnished for the purpose of obtaining credit and is explanatory and supplementary to foregoing statement of condition. (The form has been prepared to meet the requirements of the Federal Reserve Bank Act.)

Name.. Business..

Main Office Address .... Date Established................................

Branches Located at.. Plant Location...............................

Incorporated under the Laws of.. Date ....

REGARDING ACCOUNTS RECEIVABLE:

Total Amount Current not due.. $ _____

Total Amount less than 30 days past due..

Total Amount 30 to 60 days past due..

Total Amount 60 to 90 days past due..

Total Amount over 90 days past due...

Largest amount of credit extended to any one account...

Amount due from this account at the statement date...

Number of active accounts at the statement date..

What are your usual trade terms to customers?..

MERCHANDISE: On what basis was merchandise inventoried?...

Goods in process of manufacture; how valued?...................................... Raw materials?..................

Amount of merchandise held on consignment (included in inventory) $ .... Held under Trust Receipts $.............

During what month is your merchandise stock usually the heaviest?.................... When the lightest?............

Is statement based on actual physical inventory, or merchandise estimated as to quantities?.....................

What amount of merchandise contracted for but not appearing in statement?.........................

OTHER ACTIVE ASSETS—Itemize..

....

DUE FROM CONTROLLED OR SUBSIDIARY CONCERNS:—

Name of Concern	Location	For Advances	When Due	For Merchandise	Terms
		$		$	
		$		$	
		$		$	

STOCKS, BONDS AND INVESTMENTS—Give description and values (if space printed not adequate append list.)

....

LAND AND BUILDINGS:

Description and Location	Title in Whose Name	Assessed Value	Appraised Value	Mortgages	When Due	Name of Mortgagees
		$	$	$		

Do you contemplate any building operations, plant extensions or the acquisition of other properties?.................... If so, please give

details, amount already expended, and estimated total amount involved..

If book value has decreased or increased during the year, please account for same...

MACHINERY, EQUIPMENT AND FIXTURES:—Are they carried on statement at assessed value, appraised value, or cost?..............

What amount has been charged to depreciation during the last year on this item?..

What amount is owing for machinery, equipment, etc.?...

NOTES AND ACCOUNTS RECEIVABLE—DUE FROM OFFICERS, STOCKHOLDERS AND EMPLOYEES:—

Name	Amount	Date	Date Due	Is it secured?	How?	Represents what?
	$					

OTHER ASSETS—Itemize ....

....

....

Are any of your assets as shown in the foregoing statement pledged as security for loans, advances or other liabilities?....................

If so, to what extent and in what manner?..

ENDORSERS HAVE OTHER ASSETS OUTSIDE OF THE CORPORATION AS FOLLOWS:

Name	Description of assets	Personal Assets	Personal Liabilities	Net Worth outside of this business
		$	$	$
		$	$	$
		$	$	$
		$	$	$

Do you give above endorsements when borrowing from your banks, or guarantees of the same persons or others?......................

Do the endorsers guarantee or endorse for any person, firm or other corporation?..............................If so, for whom and to what amount?...

DETAILS RELATIVE TO LIABILITIES

DEPOSITARY BANKS	ADDRESS	Lines Granted	What are you owing them now	What amount owing at statement date
		$	$	$
		$	$	$
		$	$	$
		$	$	$
		$	$	$
		$	$	$

Are the Notes held by your banking connections in the same form as those offered through broker?...........................

If otherwise, what is the difference?...

State maximum amount borrowed from all sources at any one time during fiscal year $...................Date.........

State minimum amount borrowed from all sources at any one time during fiscal year $...................Date.........

Do your branches or subsidiary concerns borrow locally?...........................Where?.........................

Amount of your notes payable secured by collateral $...................Describe the collateral.........................

Through what banks or brokers did you finance yourself last year?...

Do you ever give notes for merchandise?...

ACCOUNTS PAYABLE—What are your average terms of purchase?...

Do you take advantage of the best trade discounts?...

Give names and addresses of some of the concerns from which you buy:—

Name	Street Address	City and State

DEPOSITS OF MONEY WITH THIS COMPANY—By whom?...

on time or demand?...................Amount secured by collateral $.........................

OTHER CURRENT LIABILITIES—Itemize...

MORTGAGE DEBT—$...................Rate of interest...................%. When due.........................

Who holds the mortgage?...

Property covered?...

Are current assets as well as plant assets pledged as security under the indenture?.........................

BONDS—Description...

Amount authorized $...................Rate of interest...................%. Maturity.........................

Who is Trustee for the bondholders?...

Amount pledged as security for loans $...................Provision for retirement.........................

ANY OTHER LIABILITIES—Itemize...

CONDENSED INCOME OR PROFIT AND LOSS STATEMENT FOR FISCAL YEAR ENDING_____ 19___
(Federal Reserve Bank Requirement)

Costs and Expenses			Income		
Cost of Material or Merchandise consumed......			Net Sales...........		
Expense of Conducting Business..............			From Investments.............		
Salaries Paid to Officers.......................			From Discounts on Purchases........		
Interest on Borrowed Money, Bonds, etc......			From Other Sources (Itemize)........		
Bad Debts Charged Off..........................					
Depreciation Charged Off.......................					
Reserved for Federal Taxes for Current Year..					
Net Profits (after above charges).............					
Total			Total		

RECONCILEMENT OF SURPLUS
(Federal Reserve Bank Requirement)

Balance Undivided Surplus at Close of Previous Year ....

Charges not Applicable to Current Year (Include Federal Taxes for Previous Years paid during Current Year)

Any other Charges (please designate) ....

Add Net Profits as above ....

Less Dividends, Preferred_____Per cent ....$

         Common_____Per cent ....$

Surplus as per Balance Sheet ....

What dividends have been declared out of Surplus Account as it stands in balance sheet payable during current year? ....

" " are to be " " " " " " " " " " " " ....

Are dividends on Preferred Stock cumulative?....................................Are any dividends on Preferred Stock past due?....................................

Purpose of Borrowing: (Federal Reserve Bank Requirement)

Are the proceeds of your loans to be used:

(1) In the Production, Manufacture and Distribution of Commodities of Agriculture, Industry or Commerce ....

(2) For Investment in Securities, Lands, Plants, Buildings, Machinery, Improvements or Equipment? ....

Are Officers or Managers interested in other companies engaged in this or other lines of business? If so, please give names of companies and character of business. ....

Please give names and location of subsidiary or allied companies or branches stating whether financed entirely by parent corporation, borrowing individually or both:

Name and Location	How Financed

Are there any Judgments Unsatisfied, or Suits Pending against your Corporation, and for what Amount?....................................

Insurance: On Plant.................... On Merchandise $ .... Machinery $ ....

Insurance carried for the benefit of the corporation $.................... On the life of ....

Other forms $....................

    $....................

By-Laws: Please send us a copy of your By-Laws, or a copy of the article or section that specifies which of your officers are empowered to execute notes in behalf of your corporation, and sign checks.

Is there any provision in your State Laws, By-Laws or Charter limiting the amount you can borrow? ....

If so, what is the limitation? $....................In which of the foregoing is the provision contained?....................

Officers	Number of Shares Owned by Each
President	
Vice-President	
Secretary	
Treasurer	

Directors	Address

and collectible notes receivable from customers, and what amount of its accounts and notes receivable from customers is of doubtful collectibility? How much did it charge off as losses from bad debts during the last fiscal period? Was an actual physical inventory of its merchandise taken, or were the quantities of its merchandise merely estimated? How were the finished goods, the goods in process, and the raw materials included in its merchandise valued? During what month is its merchandise stock usually the heaviest? When is its merchandise inventory usually the lightest? What amounts are due the company from controlled or subsidiary concerns, and for what purposes were credits advanced to such concerns? What amounts of notes and accounts receivable are due from stockholders, officers, and employees; how, if at all, are such "receivables" secured; and for what purposes were credits advanced to such individuals? What is the assessed value of the company's land and buildings? What is the appraised value thereof? If the company is contemplating any building operations, plant extensions, or the acquisition of other properties, what is the estimated total amount to be expended for such purposes, and what amount has been expended already? How are any changes in the book value of land and buildings during the last year accounted for? How are machinery, equipment, and fixtures valued? What amount has been charged off for depreciation of buildings, plant, etc., during the last year? What insurance is carried on merchandise, plant, machinery, lives of officers for benefit of the company, etc.? Are any assets pledged for loans, advances, or any other liabilities?

What items are included in the company's current liabilities, and what is the total amount of such liabilities? What is the amount of its trade accounts payable not yet due and the amount already past due? What are its average terms of purchase? Does it take advantage of the best trade discounts offered? What are the names and addresses of some of the concerns from which it buys? What are the amounts of its accounts payable and its notes payable to officers, directors, and stockholders? Does it ever give notes for merchandise? Has it outstanding at present any notes payable for merchandise? What are the amounts of its notes payable to banks, commercial paper dealers, and others? What amount of its notes payable is secured by collateral, and what is the collateral? What are the names and addresses of its depositary banks, what line of credit has it with each of these banks, what is the amount of its notes payable to each at present, and what was the corresponding amount at the company's last statement date? Does it give indorsements or guarantees when borrowing from banks? Who are its indorsers, and what is the "outside" net worth (that is, net personal assets exclusive of any interest in the company) of each? Do these indorsers guarantee or indorse notes for any other borrowers? If so, to what amount in each case? Are the notes on which the company borrows from its banks in the same form as the notes, if any, which it offers through commercial paper dealers? If not, what is the difference in form between these two classes of notes? What was the maximum amount, and what the minimum amount, of the company's borrowings from all sources at any one time during its last fiscal year? On what date were its total borrowings at a maximum? When were they at a minimum? What contingent liabilities has the company? Are there any judgments unsatisfied or any suits pending against the company? If so, for what amounts?

What were the company's operating and other expenses, its income from all sources, and its net profits for the last fiscal year? What dividends did it pay?

What are the names and locations of its subsidiary or allied companies, or the locations of its branches, and how are such companies or branches financed? For what purposes does the company plan to use the proceeds of its loans? [8] Are any of the company's officers interested in any other companies? If so, what are the

[8] The Middle-Western house mentioned in n. 6, p. 270, has sometimes made an independent estimate or forecast of the credit requirements of a prospective borrowing customer. For this purpose it has prepared independently from its own data, "derived from internal examination of the business under study, a budget of income and expenses, receipts and disbursements." By means of such a budget it has been able to "check the reasonableness" of its client's offerings of open-market paper, and so to "avoid the risk of having paper loans go into bricks and mortar." (Becker, *op. cit.*, p. 17.)

names of these companies, and in what lines of business are they engaged?

From figures recorded on such questionnaires or taken from the prospective borrower's balance sheets and operating statements, dealers can of course compute the net working capital and the net worth of the concern whose affairs they are investigating. They can also compute certain ratios which give some indication of how efficiently the company's affairs are being managed. Among such ratios, probably the most significant are the current ratio, which should be at least as good as the current ratio which commercial banks ordinarily expect their borrowing customers to maintain — that is, not less than two to one; the "acid-test ratio" (cash and "receivables" to current liabilities), which of course indicates more accurately than the preceding ratio the company's ability to meet its current obligations; the ratio of the cost of goods sold during the last fiscal period to the average merchandise inventory during that period, which shows the rate of turnover of the company's merchandise; the ratio of net sales to the average amount of accounts receivable, which indicates the length of the company's collection period, and, if considered in connection with its terms of sale to its trade customers, its efficiency in collecting its "receivables"; the ratio of net worth to fixed assets, which shows to what extent the stockholders' investment in the company is represented by land, buildings, machinery, and other fixed assets; the ratio of net worth to debt, which indicates to what extent the owners of the company are supplying the capital it requires and to what extent such capital is being furnished by outsiders; the ratio of net profits to net worth, which shows the return the business is able to earn on the stockholders' investment; and the ratio of net profits to net sales, which shows the return the company is able to earn on a given volume of business, and therefore indicates more accurately than the preceding ratio the efficiency with which its affairs are being managed.

The trends shown by a company's balance sheet and operating statement figures are of course more significant than figures prepared for any one statement date. Similarly, the trends shown by ratios computed from balance sheet and income account figures for several years are more significant than ratio figures computed from data for a single fiscal period only. Hence in investigating the credit standing of a concern which they are considering as a prospective client dealers find it advisable to compare the company's latest available financial figures with those for several earlier years, and ratios based on the latest balance sheet and operating figures with those computed from figures for several fiscal periods preceding. They may also compare such financial figures and ratios with similar data relating to other concerns, engaged in the same line of business, whose accounts they are already handling. Some of the ratio figures they prepare, moreover, may be compared with similar figures, based on an examination of the balance sheets and operating statements of a large number of concerns in certain selected lines of business, which are published each year by the Robert Morris Associates.[9]

If the results of both their preliminary investigation of the qualifications of their prospective customer for borrowing in the market and their own independent investigation of the company's credit standing prove to be satisfactory, dealers then actively solicit the concern's account. If, on the contrary, they decide for the time being not to try to establish connections with the company, they can of course watch its future progress with a view to considering its qualifications for borrowing in the market at some later date.

After they have secured the accounts of new customers, dealers must keep in close touch with their affairs, for they must always be ready to decide without unnecessary delay whether customers wishing to borrow in the market at any particular time are in a position to use this method of financing, and to suggest any changes in policy or offer any other advice which they believe will be of benefit to any company whose account they are handling. Hence the work of credit investigation which they begin when they first consider the advisability of soliciting new accounts must be kept up continuously after they have established connections with new customers.

[9] See n. 7, pp. 341–342.

For the purpose of keeping informed as to the qualifications of their customers for borrowing in the open market, they continue to use the same general methods as they employed in determining the advisability of soliciting the accounts of these concerns in the beginning. The reports which certain credit agencies prepare on the credit standing of such concerns, particularly the special reports prepared each year by the National Credit Office of New York, are of some value to dealers as a means of checking their own appraisals of the credit standings of their borrowing customers with the results of investigations carried out by organizations which specialize in evaluating credit risks. In most cases, however, the reports of such agencies are of more value to banks contemplating the purchase of outside paper than to the houses offering promissory notes for sale. Dealers also secure balance sheets and operating statements from practically all their borrowing customers at least once a year, and from many of their customers every quarter; and at least one house obtains in addition monthly trial balances from many of the companies whose obligations it handles. Though they handle the paper of some concerns which do not issue audited statements, most dealers nevertheless obtain such statements at least once a year from the majority of their customers.[10] For pur-

[10] See n. 78, p. 191. Dealers realize the importance of securing audited financial statements from their borrowing clients, and endeavor to obtain such statements from as many of their customers as possible at least once a year. At the same time, they realize also the limitations of analyzing audited balance sheet and operating statement figures as a method of credit investigation. As early as 1915 a number of dealers consulted by an Ohio banker as to the use of audited financial statements in investigating the credit standing of concerns wishing to borrow in the market replied as follows:

"(1) Failures almost invariably have in them an element of misrepresentation, either deliberate or through ignorance. . . .

"(2) Audits probably disclose such a state of affairs sooner and are in that measure a safeguard, but an audit is not an infallible rule by any means. Some of the bad failures were made by concerns whose reports were audited.

"(3) . . . 'There is a world-wide difference between a competent and honest auditor and an incompetent and less conscientious one. It is quite as important to determine that the auditors are able, honest and fearless, as it is to determine the character of the borrowing concern.'

"(4) 'While auditing makes dishonesty in statements more difficult, it is not the financial panacea. . . . It should not be considered . . . the sole source of credit information.'"

(L. F. Kiesewetter, *Audited Statements* — pamphlet — pp. 13–14.)

It is partly because of the limitations of analyzing financial statements as a method of credit investigation that many houses, in order to determine the advis-

poses of comparison, they keep balance sheet and income account figures for the last five years or so in most of their credit files. Information gained from reports of credit agencies and the analysis of financial statements is supplemented by that obtained from trade and bank "checkings" and by correspondence and personal interviews of dealers with their borrowing customers. Of all the methods they use for keeping in close touch with their customers' affairs, personal interviews are undoubtedly the most effective. Practically all the leading dealers now arrange for at least two such interviews each year with most, if not all, the concerns whose paper they handle. A leading New England house, it is said, has even discontinued relations with some of its borrowing clients because the expense of sending representatives to call on them twice a year was too great;[11] and the necessity of maintaining close personal contacts with the companies whose obligations they handle of course limits also the extent of the territory in which other houses can carry on their operations effectively. In the personal interviews which are the most effective means of maintaining such contacts, dealers can secure confidential information not obtainable in any other manner, can discuss important problems and policies with their customers, and can offer the latter any financial or other advice which they believe will be of benefit to them.

---

ability of purchasing the paper of a prospective borrowing customer, endeavor first of all to secure complete information with respect to the character of the management of the company in question. The final decision with regard to purchasing the obligations of such a concern must of course depend to a large extent on the dealer's individual judgment of the character and ability of its officers. This was indicated as follows in an address by a New York dealer in 1924:

". . . credit methods do little more than confirm the individual judgment of the banker or broker as to the character, energy and business ability of the borrower. . . . if a credit man bears it [this statement] in mind when making an investigation, he can save himself a great deal of unnecessary labor and trouble in avoiding investigating details that really do not count in aiding him to measure his man" (H. C. Smith, *Development of the Commercial Paper Broker and His Place in Banking* — pamphlet — p. 6).

[11] The officers and credit men of this house hold a meeting one night each week to discuss the condition of any of its borrowing customers about whose credit standing any question may have come up during the week immediately preceding. Unless all those present at the meeting are convinced that a company whose condition is being discussed is a good credit risk, has a good future, and is or can be made the kind of concern with which their organization wishes to be connected over a period of years, this house discontinues relations with the customer in question.

3. Financial Advice of Dealers to their Borrowing Customers

Since only enduring connections with their borrowing clients are profitable, dealers wish if possible to make sure that concerns whose accounts they have secured will at all times keep themselves in the strong financial position which is required for borrowing in the open market. Hence they not only keep in close touch with their customers but also from time to time offer them any financial or other advice which they believe will be of value to them. In many cases they are better qualified to offer such advice than their customers' own banks are; for they are in a position to secure more detailed and confidential information with respect to the affairs of their clients than the latter furnish their own banks,[12] and they find it necessary to keep in close touch with conditions in many different lines of business, and with money market conditions as well, in all sections of the country, and consequently can consider their customers' problems and policies from a broader point of view than that of such banks. The leading houses, in fact, endeavor to give the companies whose paper they handle a service which a New England dealer has described as "a specialized banking service," the purpose of which is to enable their clients to reach a credit position so strong that they will be considered preferred risks in a market in which only concerns with an unusually high credit standing can borrow. In case notes which they have sold for any of their customers are returned by the purchasing banks under the customary option agreement, all dealers, whether large or small, examine carefully the reasons for the return of such

[12] Borrowing concerns are willing to give dealers more confidential information relating to their affairs than they furnish their own banks because they realize that commercial paper houses need such information in order to be able to answer the credit inquiries of banks which are contemplating the purchase of their notes. Another reason why dealers need such information is that many banks leave the selection of the open-market notes they purchase entirely to the houses from which they buy such obligations, and in selecting paper for these banks dealers wish to be particularly careful. In many cases in which banks wish to secure more confidential information than they already possess with regard to the affairs of their own customers, but do not consider it expedient to ask the latter for such information directly, they are able to obtain the data required from the houses handling the accounts of the companies in question.

paper. The reasons given may not be valid, but in any case dealers can discuss with the companies whose paper has been returned any criticisms expressed by the purchasing banks, and they can often suggest changes in practices or policies which will strengthen the credit of their customers not only in the open market but also with their own banks and the concerns from which they purchase supplies and raw materials or the merchandise they handle. Because of their close personal contacts with their clients and their familiarity with money market conditions and business conditions in general, dealers are also in a position to offer the companies whose paper they handle valuable advice with respect to such matters as purchasing raw materials or merchandise, expanding or contracting their operations, securing additional capital, whether short-term or long-term, and the best means of obtaining any additional capital they may require.[13]

In order to perform efficiently their function of acting as financial advisers, dealers must of course secure detailed and up-to-date information as to the financial condition of their clients; and to make sure that their customers' financial affairs will be prudently managed, they may exercise a certain amount of control over some of their policies. They are particularly careful to keep informed as to the total amount of their clients' borrowings from all sources. In most cases they can easily keep a daily record of the open-market borrowings of their own customers, and they can also ascer-

---

[13] An officer of a New York house was informed that certain financial advice which he gave a borrowing customer in the fall of 1929 saved the latter $150,000. Another New York house has been told by its clients from time to time that its financial advice has saved them more than the commissions it has charged for handling their paper have cost them. Examples of the manner in which dealers have assisted borrowing customers in shaping their financial policies are given in C. V. Childs, "Commercial Paper and Its Advantages to the Borrower," *N. Y. Cred. Men's Assoc. Bull.*, Nov. 12, 1927, pp. 368–369.

It has been reported that certain houses used to make a charge for acting as financial counselors to their borrowing customers or for establishing new lines of credit for them with commercial banks. Probably no such charges have been made in recent years, however, despite the fact that dealers' financial advice has not infrequently saved their borrowing customers thousands of dollars. At any rate, none of twenty-three leading houses consulted in 1930 and 1931 was able to give any actual instance in which a charge had been made for either of the two classes of services mentioned.

tain at frequent intervals the total amounts of the open-market loans of concerns whose paper they secure from correspondent houses. In case they handle any divided accounts, they find it more difficult to keep informed as to the total amount which the companies in question are borrowing in the market at any particular time. At present, however, there are comparatively few divided accounts.[14] Such accounts, moreover, are handled only by the larger houses, and probably most of these houses find out at least once a month, through bank "checkings" or directly from the issuing concerns themselves, the total amounts which all their customers who use the services of more than one dealer are currently borrowing in the market. Probably most houses also find out every month the total borrowings of their clients from all sources, and all dealers are careful to keep informed as to the contingent liabilities of the companies whose obligations they handle. They are also careful to make sure that the total borrowings of such concerns from all sources are kept within reasonable

[14] It will be recalled that a "divided" account is the account of a concern which sells its open-market paper through two or more houses which are not correspondents. Some years ago a large packing company is said to have used the services of as many as six dealers at the same time. In more recent years, however, few borrowers, if any, have sold their notes through more than two houses — one in the East and one in the West — at any one time. The companies which have used the services of two or more dealers concurrently have done so for either one or both of two reasons: first, because they have thought that it would be to their advantage to have their open-market notes handled in each section of the country by the house which could secure the broadest distribution for such obligations in that section; and second, because they have believed that the competition of two or more dealers for the opportunity of selling their notes would enable them to borrow at the lowest rates obtainable in the open market. The first of these two advantages of borrowing through two or more houses at the same time has been less important in recent years than formerly, for since about 1925 the credit requirements of concerns using the open market have been comparatively small, and probably no company has issued a greater volume of paper than any one of the larger houses could readily have sold to its own customers. The second of the two advantages indicated above is probably of some importance still. Competition among dealers for accounts which are not divided is still very active, however, and for this reason as well as others all houses always endeavor to secure the best possible rates for all their borrowing customers. Hence if any concern, as a result of using the services of two or more houses concurrently, succeeds in selling its paper in the market at lower rates than it would otherwise be able to obtain, it probably does so by inducing its dealers to accept for their services a compensation lower than the customary $\frac{1}{4}$ of 1 per cent. In the future the practice of borrowing through two or more houses at the same time is likely to become less common.

bounds and, if necessary to prevent overexpansion, or for any other reason, would definitely limit the amount of open-market notes they would allow a particular customer to have outstanding at any one time.[15] All houses, moreover, either expect or require their customers to carry adequate insurance on their inventories and plants, as well as any other kinds of insurance that may be necessary, to maintain satisfactory average balances with their depositary banks, to keep open and available lines of bank credit large enough to protect the buyers of their open-market paper, and to maintain satisfactory current and other financial ratios.[16]

Many concerns which borrow in the open market regard the possibility of obtaining financial and other business advice from their dealers as one of the main advantages of using this method of financing. Probably most dealers themselves consider the offering of such advice no less important than the closely related func-

[15] A New York house reported in 1930 that it often limited the amount of paper it would take from individual borrowing customers at a single time. On the other hand, a Minneapolis house reported that it set no definite limits on the amount of paper it would take from grain elevator companies, for the open-market notes it handles for such concerns are customarily secured by terminal warehouse receipts for grain.

[16] Probably most open-market borrowers at present have bank lines of credit equal to the maximum amount of their open-market notes payable outstanding each year. If necessary, dealers arrange to establish additional lines of credit for any of their customers whose banking connections appear to be inadequate. In some cases concerns which, on their advice or with their assistance, have arranged to establish additional bank lines, have subsequently obtained from their own banks a greater proportion of the short-term credit accommodation they have required, and a correspondingly smaller proportion through open-market loans. It is of course fully as important to make sure that bank lines once established are open and available if needed as it is to establish adequate banking connections in the beginning. For this reason a Boston house, if it had any doubts as to the availability of the bank lines of any of its borrowing customers, used to have the companies in question borrow from their own banks and thereby find out how much of their established lines of credit with the latter were really available.

While dealers expect their customers to maintain satisfactory current and other financial ratios, they of course do not attempt to apply any hard and fast rules in such matters. Probably most dealers expect or require most concerns whose paper they handle to maintain a current ratio of at least 2 to 1, but in some cases a lower ratio is considered satisfactory. Thus a leading Chicago house reported that it has handled the paper of wool dealers and packers whose current ratios have been as low as 1.3 to 1 and 1.5 to 1, respectively; a New Orleans house, that it did not require a current ratio of 2 to 1 in the case of finance companies; and two houses which were handling large amounts of grain paper, that they did not require such a current ratio in the case of grain elevator companies.

tion of making credit investigations.[17] That they have attained a high degree of proficiency in performing both these functions is shown by the fact that losses on open-market paper have for a number of years amounted to no more than a small fraction of 1 per cent.[18]

4. Practices Followed by Dealers in Buying Commercial Paper

Once dealers have decided to purchase the open-market notes of a borrowing customer, whether a concern whose account they have just secured or one whose paper they have been handling for some time, the actual buying of such obligations is largely a routine operation.

In case they maintain no branch offices, they must of course purchase through their main offices all the notes they handle. If they maintain one or more branches in addition to their main offices, the more important of these branches also buy paper, but practically always with authority from their main offices and subject to the approval of the latter as regards "names," amounts, rates, and commissions.

In buying open-market obligations issued by their borrowing customers, dealers use one or more of four different methods: outright buying, known also as purchase on a "fixed-rate" or "named-rate" basis; buying on an "open-rate" basis, known also as purchase on a "check-on-account" basis; buying on an open-rate basis "with limited protection"; and buying on a consignment or brokerage basis.

In case they buy paper outright, they remit payment for the face amount thereof, less the discount and their commission charges, as soon as they receive their customers' obligations. This method of payment is ordinarily the most satisfactory from the

[17] In 1930 a New York house reported that one of the members of its organization was devoting the greater part of his time to acting as the business adviser of its borrowing clients. Six years earlier a leading New York dealer expressed the opinion that the greatest service of the commercial paper house consists in gathering and distributing credit information and in acting as the financial adviser of the concerns whose obligations it handles. (Smith, *op. cit.*, pp. 9–10.)

[18] See pp. 307–314.

point of view of their customers, for it enables the latter to obtain a definite amount of funds without delay. It requires dealers themselves, however, to assume the risk of losses from a rise in money rates between the time at which they purchase and that at which they sell an issue of open-market notes, though of course they also have the opportunity of making a speculative trading profit if commercial paper rates, instead of rising, happen to fall.[19] Of the four methods of purchasing paper mentioned above, outright buying is the most commonly used. Six of twenty-two leading dealers consulted in 1930 and 1931 reported that they bought open-market notes on an outright basis only,[20] eleven that they bought outright in the main or as a rule, one that it bought outright about 25 per cent of the obligations it handled, or all such obligations except those which it bought on a consignment basis, and four that, though they purchased on an open-rate basis a large proportion of the notes they handled, they also bought some paper outright. In the spring of 1936 practically all dealers were purchasing outright either all or the greater part of the paper they were handling. In general, houses which buy both on an outright and on an open-rate basis are likely to purchase outright the obligations of their larger customers and of other concerns whose credit standing is exceptionally high, and to buy paper on an open-rate basis when money rates are uncertain and are expected to rise in the near future. The manner in which dealers purchase their customers' notes, as well as the rates at which they discount such obligations and the commissions they receive for their services, are matters for negotiation between themselves and their customers,

[19] It has been said that houses which buy open-market notes outright at a definite rate have to protect themselves against the risk of losses from rising money rates by charging somewhat higher discount rates than they would charge if they purchased the same obligations on an open-rate basis. As a matter of fact, however, the risk of losses from rising rates is not so great as might be supposed; for changes in commercial paper rates are generally gradual, and the turnover of carefully selected paper is very rapid. It is probable that such losses as dealers incur in handling open-market notes are more likely to result from errors in judgment with respect to their buying rates than from rising money rates.

[20] One of these houses, however, reported that when money rates were uncertain and changing it sometimes made the price it paid for its customers' paper depend on changes in rates. Purchases made under such conditions are really purchases on an open-rate basis.

and companies whose credit rating is exceptionally high have enough bargaining power at times not only to insist that their paper be purchased outright but also to dictate the rates at which it shall be discounted.

Such concerns may insist that their notes be purchased outright at a flat or net discount rate, without any commission charges. From their point of view, this method of purchase has the advantage of enabling them to determine more directly the total costs of borrowing in the market. They of course also hope that it will enable them to reduce these costs to some extent. Whether in fact it does or not depends on the comparative bargaining power of themselves and their dealers. In many cases they undoubtedly do succeed in reducing the total costs of open-market financing through selling their obligations at a net rate. Like the outright purchase of paper at a fixed discount rate with a commission charge in addition, the purchase of open-market notes at a flat rate with no commission charge requires dealers to assume the risk of losses from rising money rates, but also offers them the opportunity of making a speculative trading profit from the sale of commercial paper at rates lower than those at which they have purchased it.[21] Though the latter method of buying was by no means so common before 1931 as it has been since, it was nevertheless used occasionally by practically all houses;[22] and during

[21] When buying open-market notes at a flat rate, dealers endeavor to acquire such paper at rates high enough to protect themselves against losses from a rise in money rates and to indemnify themselves for the loss of their customary commission. As is implied in the text above, in many cases the trading profit they make from selling notes bought at a net rate is less than the compensation they would receive if they bought the same obligations at a stated rate, sold them at the same rate, and charged the customary commission of ¼ of 1 per cent for their services.

[22] Of twenty-two leading houses consulted in 1930 and 1931, all but one reported that they occasionally bought open-market notes at a net rate, without any commission charge. A Chicago house stated that it is sometimes practically compelled to buy paper in this manner when money rates are low, offerings of open-market obligations are scarce and easy to sell, and the cost of borrowing in the market would otherwise be considered too high by some of its customers. A Minneapolis dealer reported that the paper of grain elevator companies is more commonly purchased at a flat rate than obligations issued by other classes of borrowers. A Southern house — which was the "commercial paper department" of a commercial bank — stated that it bought all the paper it handled, except notes issued by one of its borrowing customers, at a net rate.

the last few years it has been employed as commonly by some dealers as buying outright at a stated rate plus commission. In general, its use is likely to be most common in connection with the purchase of notes issued with maturities of four months or shorter, and at times when rates on prime paper are at unusually low levels.

After outright buying at a fixed rate, buying on an open-rate basis is the next most common method used by dealers in purchasing their stock in trade. When they use the latter method of buying paper, they often do not remit payment at once for the face amount thereof, less the discount and their commission charges, as they do when buying outright at a fixed rate; but, instead, leave the rate of discount open, make their customers a substantial advance against their notes, sell these notes at the best rates obtainable, and then make an adjustment with their customers for any balance due to or from the latter. The advance is generally a round amount approximately equal to the face amount of the paper purchased, less the dealer's commission and discount at the rate at which it is expected such paper will be sold.[23] In other cases they make payment for open-market notes just as they would if they were buying at a fixed rate, but leave the final rate of discount open until they have sold such paper, and then make an adjustment for any balance due to their customers or to themselves as a result of a difference between their buying and selling rates. From the point of view of some borrowing concerns, buying on an open-rate basis is less satisfactory than buying outright at a fixed rate; for when their notes are purchased on an open-rate basis they cannot tell in advance what their total costs of using the open market will be. Moreover,

---

[23] A leading New York house reported in 1930 that it customarily advanced 90 per cent of the face amount of notes purchased on an open-rate basis and paid the remaining 10 per cent, less the discount and its commission charges, after it had sold such obligations. Three other dealers at the same time were advancing amounts equal, respectively, to 96 per cent, 97 per cent, and 98 per cent of the face amount of the paper they were buying on the same basis. If necessary, dealers can borrow from commercial banks, with commercial paper as collateral, all or the greater part of the capital required for making such advances. If required to maintain a margin of 10 per cent in connection with loans so secured, they can borrow approximately $91 for every $100 of purchased paper they can offer as security for such loans.

if their obligations are purchased under the first of the two methods of open-rate buying mentioned above, they of course do not receive the full amount of the net proceeds of their open-market loans until after their paper has been sold by their dealers. On the other hand, dealers always sell at the lowest rates possible all notes they buy on an open-rate basis, and in at least some cases would no doubt consider it necessary, as a means of protecting themselves against losses from rising rates, to charge somewhat higher discount rates if they bought the same paper at a fixed rate instead. Furthermore, if they assume the risks of loss involved in buying at a fixed rate, they can fairly expect to keep for themselves any trading profits they may be able to make from differences between their buying and selling rates. Consequently, most houses do not as a rule reduce by such differences the discount rates they charge customers whose obligations they succeed in selling at rates lower than those at which they bought them.[24] For these reasons a number of open-market borrowers prefer to sell their notes on an open-rate basis. From the point of view of dealers, buying on the latter basis has the advantage of enabling them to avoid the risk of losses from rising rates. As was indicated above, eleven of twenty-two leading houses interviewed in 1930 and 1931 were buying on an open-rate basis a comparatively small proportion of the notes they were handling — their purchases on this basis being made in the main at times when money rates were uncertain and were expected to rise in the near future — and four houses were buying on the same basis the greater part of the open-market obligations in

[24] Occasionally, however, some houses do give customers whose paper they have bought outright at a fixed rate and sold at a lower rate the advantage of the lower rate. And at least a few houses have occasionally made arrangements whereby certain customers whose notes they have bought on the same basis have protected them against losses from selling such obligations at rates higher than those at which they were purchased. In cases of this sort the borrowing concerns have agreed that the rates of discount they would be charged would be the rates at which their dealers could sell their notes, even though the latter rates should be higher than those at which these dealers actually bought such paper. In all cases of this sort, as well as in all cases in which dealers give their customers the benefit of selling rates which are lower than their buying rates, paper is in effect bought on an open-rate basis, even though it is actually discounted at a fixed rate.

which they were dealing. The proportion of such obligations which three of the latter four houses were buying on an open-rate basis ranged from about 90 to about 95 per cent.

The third method of purchasing open-market paper mentioned above, or open-rate buying with limited protection, is a method in accordance with which it is agreed that the dealer's buying rate shall be left open but shall not exceed a certain definite figure as a maximum. Thus, to give an example, if a dealer thought he could sell an issue of a certain customer's paper at $3\frac{1}{4}$ to $3\frac{1}{2}$ per cent, and wished to buy this paper on an open-rate basis with limited protection, he would agree to purchase the issue at a rate not to exceed $3\frac{1}{2}$ per cent as a maximum. He would then endeavor to sell the paper at a rate of $3\frac{1}{4}$ per cent or lower, and would give his customer the benefit of the lowest rate obtainable. If he should find it necessary to sell the issue at a rate higher than $3\frac{1}{2}$ per cent, he would have to stand the loss himself. When this method of buying is used, the dealer advances a round amount against his customer's notes and makes any necessary adjustments for sums due to or from the borrowing concern after the latter's obligations have been sold, just as he does when he purchases paper on an open-rate basis. Open-rate buying with limited protection is obviously intermediate between buying outright at a fixed rate and buying on an open-rate basis. It enables a concern wishing to sell an issue of notes in the open market to ascertain in advance what the maximum cost of using this method of financing will be, and the dealer to reduce, but not to avoid entirely, the risk of losses from differences between his buying and selling rates. It is used less commonly than buying on an open-rate basis, and much less commonly than buying outright at a fixed rate.[25]

The last of the four methods of buying mentioned above — buying on a consignment or brokerage basis — was the only method used by most dealers until after the close of the Civil War period. When they use this method of purchasing, dealers merely accept

[25] Three houses consulted in 1930 reported that they occasionally bought paper on an open-rate basis with limited protection. A branch office of a fourth house reported at the same time that it bought in this manner about 25 per cent of the open-market obligations it handled.

paper of their clients for sale, sell it at the best rates obtainable, and remit payment for the face amount of such paper, less the discount and commission charges, after they have sold it. Houses which use this method of buying do so for one or more of three different purposes. The first of these is to avoid the risk of losses from differences between their buying and selling rates. In some cases open-market borrowers wish to sell their paper at rates lower than those at which their dealers believe their notes can be marketed. In such cases dealers sometimes take paper on consignment and endeavor to sell it at rates which will be satisfactory to their customers. If unable to sell it at such rates, they either return it to the issuing concerns or try to induce the latter to accept rates somewhat higher. The second of the three purposes for which they buy on consignment is to avoid investing any considerable amount of capital in open-market notes for which there may be no active market, as, for instance, notes issued by comparatively small concerns or by companies which have not yet become well known as borrowers in the open market. The paper of finance companies has probably been purchased on the same basis even more commonly than the obligations of concerns of the latter two classes; for finance companies' notes have been issued in a wide variety of denominations and maturities, and dealers cannot always ascertain in advance just what maturities and denominations are likely to be preferred by their buying customers. The third purpose for which they buy on consignment is to accommodate customers who wish to secure funds in advance of their actual requirements for borrowed capital. The concerns in question may wish to borrow in this manner at times when the market for commercial paper is comparatively inactive or when rates are steadily rising. The funds so obtained may be used for various purposes, including the repayment of direct loans from banks as well as the financing of current operations. In recent years only a small proportion of the total volume of paper bought and sold in the open market has been purchased on a brokerage basis. Of twenty-three leading houses consulted in 1930 and 1931, thirteen reported that they were buying no notes at all on consignment, nine that they were buying on this basis only a comparatively small volume of open-market paper,[26] and only one that it was buying on a brokerage basis exclusively.[27]

Two of the twenty-three houses reported that they used a modified form of consignment buying in purchasing some of the paper they handled. In accordance with this method, they accepted notes for sale in advance of the issuing concerns' actual requirements for borrowed funds, but agreed to remit payment for such obligations by a specified date.[28]

In addition to the open-market notes they originate themselves, some five or six houses at present buy paper from correspondent dealers. In earlier years notes secured from correspondents were commonly purchased only as they were sold to the customers of the buying house, but at present practically all such paper is bought outright. The selling house always allows the buying house options similar to those granted by dealers to the banks which are the ultimate investors in open-market paper.

5. METHODS USED BY DEALERS IN PAYING FOR OPEN-MARKET PAPER

In paying for open-market notes, as well as in buying such paper, dealers use several different methods. In case the borrowing concern is located in the city in which he maintains his main office, the dealer as a rule sends a check on a local bank direct to his customer

[26] One of these nine houses reported that it bought no notes on a consignment basis except the obligations of finance companies; one that it purchased on this basis only notes of the latter class and collateral loan paper issued by stock brokerage houses; two that they bought paper on consignment only or mainly when they believed that it could not be marketed at rates as low as those at which the issuing concerns wished to borrow; and one that the only notes it purchased on a brokerage basis were those issued by finance companies or by concerns which wished to borrow at rates below those at which it believed their paper could be sold in the market.

[27] This house discontinued operations in 1931.

[28] Presumably one of the main purposes for which these two houses used this method of buying was to reduce the amount of capital required for financing their purchases of open-market notes, particularly at times when the rates charged on loans from their banks were higher than those at which they were purchasing their customers' paper. At any rate, one of the two houses stated that at such times it bought in this manner a larger proportion of the open-market notes it handled than in times when it could borrow from banks at rates lower than its buying rates.

or to some local bank in which the latter has a deposit account.[29]
In paying for notes issued by out-of-town customers, dealers in
recent years have used at least six different methods, as follows:
sending a check drawn on one of their local banks direct to the
borrowing customer;[30] depositing a check for the account of the
borrowing concern in a local bank in which it has an account, the
check being made payable to this bank;[31] depositing a check in a
local bank which is the correspondent of one of the customer's local
banks; sending their check to an out-of-town bank in which both
they and the borrowing company have an account, the check being
made payable to this bank for the account of the borrower; sending
their customer a draft drawn on a bank in New York, Boston,
Philadelphia, or some other financial center; and allowing the borrowing concern to draw a sight draft on them.[32]

[29] A Hartford house reported in 1930 that it occasionally paid for notes issued by
Boston wool commission houses with drafts on Boston banks, but paid for all other
paper it handled, irrespective of the location of the issuing concern, by means of
checks on a New York bank.

[30] A leading New York house reported that customers whose paper it pays for in
this manner sometimes have it send them a check for the face amount of an issue of
open-market notes and then send it in return a check for the discount and commission charges.

[31] If the borrowing concern wishes to use the borrowed funds at once, the bank
can either notify this concern by wire that its account has been credited with the
amount of the check or wire funds to its correspondent in the city in which the
borrowing company is located.

[32] The methods used by banks in paying for open-market notes, and the manner
in which they in turn collect the amounts due them at the maturity of such obligations, are indicated in Chap. X, § 4.

CHAPTER VIII

BUYING CUSTOMERS OF DEALERS: BANKS AND OTHER BUYERS OF OPEN–MARKET PAPER

IN THE present chapter the various classes of buyers of open-market paper, the relative importance of each of these classes, and the advantages of commercial paper as an investment for the surplus funds of banks and other buying customers of dealers will be indicated.

1. BUYING CUSTOMERS OF DEALERS

The buyers of open-market paper in recent years have included commercial banks and trust companies, savings banks, insurance companies, investment trusts, other classes of business corporations, educational institutions, trustees, private investors, banks located in territories or insular possessions of the United States, and foreign banking institutions.

The commercial banks, whether organized as national, state, or private banks, have included institutions in all sections of the country. Even individual houses, in fact, have within recent years sold commercial paper to banks in practically every state in the Union.[1] Commercial banks in some states have of course bought considerably larger amounts of outside paper than similar institutions in other states. Purchases by banks in Massachusetts, New York, Pennsylvania, Illinois, Minnesota, Missouri, Texas, and California, for instance, have been comparatively large in recent years, whereas banks in such states as Vermont, Delaware, North Carolina, Louisiana, Wyoming, Utah, Arizona, and Nevada have bought relatively little outside paper.[2]

---

[1] Several years ago — presumably about the end of 1925 — the open-market notes of even a single borrowing client of a leading New York house were being held by one or more banks in every state in the United States except Utah and Oklahoma, and in Hawaii as well (C. V. Childs, *Commercial Paper and the Broker's Function* — pamphlet — pp. 4–5).

[2] These conclusions are based on figures of the amounts of purchased commercial

Table 25 shows the commercial paper holdings on selected call dates in recent years of national banks in the ten cities whose national banks held the largest amounts of such paper. Though it includes figures for national banks only, this table indicates that purchases of outside paper have been largest in such cities as Boston, New York, Philadelphia, Chicago, St. Louis, Milwaukee, Minneapolis, St. Joseph, Omaha, and San Francisco. The first five of these cities and Minneapolis and San Francisco may be regarded as the primary commercial paper markets. These are the cities in which either the main offices or the most important branch offices of the leading dealers are maintained; and banks in these cities purchase relatively large amounts of open-market notes for their country correspondent banks, as well as for their own account.[3]

Table 26 shows the amounts of outside paper held on the call dates mentioned just above by "country" national banks in the five states in which the commercial paper holdings of such banks were largest. As this table indicates, purchases of open-market notes by these banks in recent years have been largest in such states as Massachusetts, Rhode Island, Connecticut, New York, Pennsylvania, and Illinois.

Total purchases by commercial banks within the United States, including both the larger city institutions and the much larger number of country banks, probably constitute more than 95 per

---

paper held by central reserve city, reserve city, and "country" national banks on the following call dates: Dec. 31, 1928, June 29, 1929, Dec. 31, 1929, June 30, 1930, Dec. 31, 1930, June 30, 1931, Dec. 31, 1931, June 30, 1932, June 30, 1933, June 30, 1934, and June 29, 1935. These figures are given in the *Annual Report of the Comptroller of the Currency*, 1929–1935.

[3] For some years before 1931 a St. Louis national bank was one of the largest buyers of commercial paper in the United States. During a part of August 1929, when rates on New York Stock Exchange call loans were appreciably higher than those on prime paper, this bank held no open-market obligations at all. The period in question, however, was the first one in twenty years in which it carried none of its earning assets in the form of outside paper. During the five years from 1923 to 1928 it bought some $226,000,000 of such paper. At the end of July 1930 its holdings of open-market obligations amounted approximately to $18,000,000, or about 20 per cent of its total loans and discounts. In more recent years this bank, like certain other large city banks, has bought little or no outside paper.

According to a Chicago dealer, the importance of San Francisco as a market for commercial paper has declined considerably since the development of branch banking in California.

TABLE 25

OPEN-MARKET COMMERCIAL PAPER HELD BY NATIONAL BANKS IN LEADING TEN
CITIES ON SELECTED CALL DATES, 1928–1935

(Thousands of Dollars)

Call Date	Leading Ten Cities	Commercial Paper Held by National Banks in Each City
Dec. 31, 1928	1 Boston	18,178
	2 St. Louis	16,133
	3 St. Paul	8,382
	4 New York	7,828
	5 Chicago	7,820
	6 Philadelphia	7,690
	7 St. Joseph	5,855
	8 Milwaukee	3,760
	9 San Francisco	3,290
	10 Indianapolis	3,182
June 29, 1929	1 Boston	13,674
	2 St. Louis	5,550
	3 Chicago	5,549
	4 Philadelphia	5,193
	5 St. Joseph	4,968
	6 New York	4,646
	7 Omaha	3,522
	8 Portland (Ore.)	2,898
	9 San Francisco	2,630
	10 Milwaukee	2,017
June 30, 1930	1 Boston	50,791
	2 Chicago	39,449
	3 Philadelphia	29,888
	4 St. Louis	22,360
	5 New York	14,994
	6 San Francisco	13,844
	7 Pittsburgh	6,793
	8 St. Joseph	5,328
	9 Omaha	4,782
	10 Milwaukee	4,639
June 30, 1931	1 New York	52,455
	2 Boston	26,408
	3 Philadelphia	25,841
	4 St. Louis	13,765
	5 Chicago	9,060
	6 San Francisco	6,905
	7 Minneapolis	6,808
	8 St. Joseph	5,379
	9 Omaha	3,663
	10 Cedar Rapids	3,037

TABLE 25 (*Continued*)

Call Date	Leading Ten Cities	Commercial Paper Held by National Banks in Each City
June 30, 1932	1 Boston	12,817
	2 New York	12,356
	3 Washington	3,220
	4 St. Louis	2,895
	5 Chicago	2,636
	6 Philadelphia	2,268
	7 St. Joseph	2,262
	8 San Francisco	1,613
	9 Richmond	1,450
	10 Minneapolis	1,432
June 30, 1933 *	1 Boston	10,208
	2 Philadelphia	2,124
	3 St. Joseph	2,023
	4 Detroit	1,833
	5 Peoria	1,666
	6 St. Louis	1,109
	7 Louisville	1,095
	8 Cedar Rapids	1,045
	9 Washington	1,021
	10 Omaha	925
June 30, 1934 *	1 Boston	14,460
	2 Chicago	7,812
	3 Philadelphia	5,810
	4 St. Joseph	3,830
	5 Detroit	3,630
	6 New York	3,563
	7 Cedar Rapids	3,551
	8 Kansas City (Mo.)	2,870
	9 Peoria	2,849
	10 Louisville	2,513
June 29, 1935	1 Philadelphia	13,005
	2 Boston	10,019
	3 Chicago	5,655
	4 Detroit	4,398
	5 Kansas City (Mo.)	3,768
	6 St. Joseph	3,540
	7 Lincoln	3,508
	8 Louisville	2,863
	9 Cedar Rapids	2,785
	10 San Francisco	2,659

* Figures for this date relate to licensed national banks only, i.e., those operating on an unrestricted basis.

Source: *Annual Report of the Comptroller of the Currency*, 1929–1935.

TABLE 26

OPEN-MARKET COMMERCIAL PAPER HELD BY "COUNTRY" NATIONAL BANKS * IN
LEADING FIVE STATES ON SELECTED CALL DATES, 1928–1935

(Thousands of Dollars)

Call Date	Leading Five States		Commercial Paper Held by "Country" National Banks in Each State
Dec. 31, 1928	1	Texas	18,165
	2	Massachusetts	16,338
	3	Pennsylvania	16,320
	4	Illinois	11,702
	5	New York	9,025
June 29, 1929	1	Massachusetts	12,785
	2	Pennsylvania	11,374
	3	Illinois	10,608
	4	New Jersey	7,225
	5	New York	7,032
June 30, 1930	1	New York	16,183
	2	Massachusetts	15,808
	3	Pennsylvania	10,934
	4	Illinois	9,653
	5	Wisconsin	7,853
June 30, 1931	1	Massachusetts	12,517
	2	New York	12,079
	3	Pennsylvania	5,672
	4	Rhode Island	4,334
	5	Wisconsin	4,322
June 30, 1932	1	New York	5,479
	2	Massachusetts	5,113
	3	Pennsylvania	3,578
	4	Connecticut	2,119
	5	Rhode Island	1,881
June 30, 1933 †	1	Massachusetts	4,166
	2	Pennsylvania	3,268
	3	New York	3,211
	4	Connecticut	3,167
	5	Rhode Island	2,149
June 30, 1934 †	1	Massachusetts	13,318
	2	Connecticut	4,863
	3	Rhode Island	4,529
	4	New York	4,466
	5	Pennsylvania	3,176
June 29, 1935	1	Massachusetts	13,604
	2	New York	6,741
	3	Pennsylvania	6,459
	4	Illinois	5,921
	5	Connecticut	5,564

* National banks located in towns and cities other than central reserve and reserve cities.

† Figures for this date relate to licensed national banks only, i.e., those operating on an unrestricted basis.

Source: *Annual Report of the Comptroller of the Currency*, 1929–1935.

cent of all the open-market paper sold by dealers each year.[4] The distribution of such purchases between purchases by the larger city banks and those by country banks of course varies from time to time. Some dealers as a rule sell mainly to city banks, others to country banks; and some houses ordinarily sell roughly about the

[4] Though commercial banks have purchased practically all the open-market obligations which have been sold in recent years, their holdings of outside paper have constituted but a small proportion of their earning assets. On June 30, 1922, the estimated amount of such paper held by all banks in the United States made up only 2 per cent of their total loans and investments. Five years later the proportion was only 1 per cent. (See the table shown in n. 13, p. 123.) As is shown by Table 17, the proportion of the commercial paper holdings of Federal Reserve member banks to their total loans was less than 2 per cent on all but eight of the twenty-two call dates from Oct. 3, 1928, to Dec. 31, 1935, inclusive. Holdings of outside paper have also constituted but a small proportion of the total loans and discounts of national banks on selected call dates in recent years, as the following table indicates:

OPEN-MARKET COMMERCIAL PAPER HELD BY NATIONAL BANKS
ON SELECTED CALL DATES, 1928–1935

(Amounts in thousands of dollars)

Call Date	Amount	Per Cent of Total Loans and Discounts
Dec. 31, 1928	301,231	1.97
June 29, 1929	195,666	1.32
June 30, 1930	381,470	2.56
June 30, 1931	269,215	2.04
June 30, 1932	83,251	0.81
June 30, 1933	59,840 *	0.74
June 30, 1934	136,360 *	1.77
June 29, 1935	180,548	2.45

* Amount reported by licensed national banks only, i.e., those operating on an unrestricted basis.

Source: *Annual Report of the Comptroller of the Currency*, 1929, 1932, and 1935.

The proportion which the commercial paper holdings of individual banks have constituted of their earning assets, however, has at various times been much higher than the percentage figures given in this table or referred to just above. It is said that the New York Life Insurance and Trust Company some twenty-five or thirty years ago used to carry about one-third of its assets in the form of purchased paper (E. D. Page, "Commercial Paper as an Investment," *Bankers' Mag.*, Aug. 1911, p. 169). In 1916 the Third National Bank of St. Louis bought $17,500,000 of open-market paper, "out of total loans of approximately one hundred million." During certain seasons of the year the proportion of its commercial paper holdings to its total loans "ran over 33⅓%" (F. K. Houston, *Commercial Paper — Its Uses and Abuses* — pamphlet — p. 2). Another national bank of the same city, as was stated in the preceding footnote, was carrying about 20 per cent of its total loans and discounts in the form of open-market obligations at the end of July, 1930. According to a St. Louis dealer, banks in St. Joseph (Missouri) and one bank in Wichita (Kansas) were also carrying fairly large percentages of their total loans and discounts in the form of outside paper at that time. The proportion which such paper

same amounts of open-market notes to each of these two classes of buyers. In general, city banks tend to purchase larger amounts of such obligations than country banks in periods of low money rates, and smaller amounts than the latter class of banks when rates on commercial paper are relatively high.

Some evidence of such a tendency in recent years may be derived from an examination of Chart II and Table 27, which show, respectively, rates on prime commercial paper in New York and the distribution of the commercial paper holdings of all Federal Reserve member banks on selected call dates among central reserve city banks, reserve city banks, and "country" banks. The "country" banks include not only institutions located in small towns but also all other member banks except those located in New York, Chicago, and some sixty reserve cities. Nevertheless, Table 27 indicates that holdings of open-market notes by the larger city banks were comparatively small, and by the smaller country banks were comparatively large, in the latter part of 1928, in 1929, in the earlier part of 1930, and in the latter part of 1931, when commercial paper rates were relatively high; and that during the rest of the period from the latter part of 1928 to 1934, when such rates were comparatively low, the larger city banks were holding relatively large amounts and the smaller country banks relatively small amounts of outside paper.[5]

---

has constituted of the earning assets of commercial banks in more recent years would undoubtedly have been greater if a larger supply of open-market obligations had been available. It should be added, however, that percentage figures showing member banks' holdings of open-market commercial paper on call dates in recent years are no doubt higher than they would be if based exclusively on their holdings of notes purchased through commercial paper houses; for a number of banks class as open-market paper notes which they buy directly from two or three large finance companies.

[5] The tendency in question was also observed in the years from 1918 to 1922, a period during the greater part of which commercial paper rates were relatively high. Many country banks are said to have "learned to buy" open-market obligations in 1918, 1919, and 1920 (James McCluney, "Distribution of Commercial Paper" — typewritten paper — p. 2). From about April 1920 until November 1921 such banks were the main buyers of commercial paper (Federal Reserve Bank of New York, *Report on Business Conditions*, April–July 1920, and *Mo. Rev.*, Aug. 1920–May 1921, and Dec. 1921). It should be noted that, for the following reasons, such evidence of the tendency under consideration as may be derived from comparing the amounts of open-market notes held by the three classes of member banks on call

TABLE 27

DISTRIBUTION OF HOLDINGS OF OPEN-MARKET COMMERCIAL PAPER AMONG ALL FEDERAL RESERVE MEMBER BANKS ON CALL DATES, 1928–1935

(Amounts in Millions of Dollars)

| CALL DATE | TOTAL | CENTRAL RESERVE CITY BANKS | | | RESERVE CITY BANKS | COUNTRY BANKS | PER CENT OF TOTAL HELD BY EACH CLASS | | |
		New York	Chicago	Total			Central Reserve City Banks	Reserve City Banks	Country Banks
1928 — Oct. 3	457	63	21	84	178	195	18.4	38.9	42.7
Dec. 31	390	29	14	43	136	211	11.0	34.9	54.1
1929 — Mar. 27	376	37	10	47	136	192	13.0	36.0	51.0
June 29	249	21	6	27	83	140	11.0	33.0	56.0
Oct. 4	228	8	4	12	71	144	5.0	31.0	64.0
Dec. 31	291	21	5	26	102	163	8.9	35.1	56.0
1930 — Mar. 27	499	49	33	82	209	207	16.5	42.0	41.5
June 30	507	35	56	91	245	171	18.0	48.3	33.7
Sept. 24	523	22	42	64	295	164	12.2	56.4	31.4
Dec. 31	366	34	18	52	194	120	14.2	53.0	32.8
1931 — Mar. 25	361	35	21	56	191	114	15.5	52.9	31.6
June 30	384	94	21	115	168	101	30.0	43.7	26.3
Sept. 29	296	48	24	72	143	81	24.3	48.3	27.4
Dec. 31	140	29	9	38	53	48	27.3	38.2	34.5
1932 — June 30	122	23	11	34	50	36	28.2	41.5	30.3
Sept. 30	115	14	12	26	53	36	22.6	46.1	31.3
Dec. 31	93	19	9	28	36	28	30.0	40.0	30.0
1933 — June 30 *	87	10	12	22	38	27	25.3	43.7	31.0
Oct. 25	164	27	19	46	72	46	28.0	44.0	28.0
Dec. 30	132	19	16	35	61	34	27.0	46.7	26.3
1934 — Mar. 5	157	14	17	31	72	54	19.7	45.9	34.4
June 30	200	13	18	31	97	72	15.5	48.5	36.0
Oct. 17	253	8	25	33	126	95	13.0	50.0	37.0
Dec. 31	232	6	27	33	108	92	14.1	46.4	39.5
1935 — Mar. 4	255	4	21	25	122	109	9.7	47.7	42.6
June 29	247	5	14	19	112	116	7.7	45.3	47.0
Nov. 1	260	4	13	17	111	132	6.5	42.7	50.8
Dec. 31	272	5	12	17	120	135	6.3	44.1	49.6

* Beginning with June 1933 figures relate to licensed national banks only, i.e., those operating on an unrestricted basis.

Source (of figures other than percentage figures in last three columns): *Annual Report of the Federal Reserve Board*, 1931, pp. 98–99, and 1934, pp. 150–151; and *Member Bank Call Report*, nos. 65–68.

Such evidence of the tendency mentioned above as is furnished by Chart II and Table 27 was supported until about the close of 1933 by the experience of practically all dealers in open-market notes. Twenty leading houses reported, either in 1930 or 1931, that city banks buy such obligations mainly in periods when commercial paper rates are relatively low, eighteen of the same houses that country banks buy mainly in periods when rates are comparatively high,[6] and twenty-two dealers that purchases by the latter class of banks are reduced appreciably when rates fall to 4 per cent or lower.[7]

---

dates with fluctuations in commercial paper rates cannot be regarded as conclusive: (1) The reported figures of member banks' holdings of open-market notes are merely the amounts of such obligations they happen to be holding on three or four dates each year; (2) the greater part of the commercial paper they are holding at any particular time was actually purchased from a few days to six months or more earlier; (3) the figures reported by a number of banks include their holdings of notes they have purchased directly from one or more large finance companies; (4) many institutions classed as "country" banks are in fact located in fairly large cities and are of substantial size.

[6] According to a St. Louis house whose buying customers in 1930 included some 3,000 country banks, purchases by banks of this class are largest when the yield on open-market paper rises to a figure as high as 8 per cent. On the other hand, a Minneapolis house reported that country banks in the ninth Federal Reserve district buy large amounts of demand notes, issued by terminal grain elevators, on which the yields are ordinarily lower than those on most other classes of paper; a San Francisco house that in August 1930, when rates on prime open-market obligations were as low as 3 per cent, it was selling as much commercial paper to country banks in Washington and Oregon as these banks ordinarily purchased from it at any other time; and two other houses, one in Boston and one in Chicago, that country banks buy open-market notes more steadily than city banks, irrespective of rates on such obligations.

[7] Dealers in New York, St. Louis, and Wichita (Kansas) reported in 1930 that, if rates on open-market paper fall to 3 per cent, country banks prefer to increase their balances with their city correspondents, and accept 2 per cent interest on such deposits, rather than assume the risk of buying outside paper for a return only 1 per cent higher. In more recent years, however, the payment by Federal Reserve member banks of interest on demand deposits has been prohibited by Section 11 (b) of the Banking Act of 1933. Hence country banks can no longer consider such deposits with member bank correspondents as an alternative form of investment for surplus funds. As a consequence, Section 11 (b) has doubtless had the effect of increasing the demand for open-market obligations by country banks, to some extent at least, despite the abnormally low rates on such paper since June 1933, when the Act was passed.

Country banks still endeavor to secure relatively high rates of return on their loans and investments, including open-market obligations. Many such banks, however, would not consider a rate of 4 per cent, or even 3 per cent, on prime commercial paper unattractive at present, even though they would have bought little or no

On the other hand, since the close of 1933 the tendency under consideration seems to have become less pronounced. As Table 27 indicates, the proportion of "country" banks' holdings of open-market notes to the total amounts held on call dates by member banks of all three classes increased substantially in 1934 and 1935 — both years in which rates on prime paper were at extremely low levels; whereas the proportion held by reserve city banks remained about the same and that held by central reserve city banks decreased considerably. Moreover, a leading Eastern house, which has offices or correspondents in all the principal commercial paper markets in the United States, reported in the spring of 1936 that country banks were buying outside paper as actively as the larger city banks, despite the low rates then prevailing. It is probable, however, that the larger city banks' holdings of open-market obligations have declined relatively to those of country banks since the close of 1933 mainly because of abnormal and presumably temporary conditions in the short-term money market;[8] and that, after rates on prime paper have again reached

---

outside paper at such rates in 1930. The rates obtainable on any one class of loan or investment considered by itself have no particular significance. Much more significant is the relation of such rates to those obtainable on alternative classes of loans or investments. At a time when opportunities for making desirable loans to their own customers are definitely limited, and when prime ninety-day bankers' bills yield only $\frac{1}{4}$ of 1 per cent, stock exchange call and time loans only 1 per cent, and 182-day Treasury bills less than $\frac{1}{4}$ of 1 per cent — as was the case toward the end of August, 1934 — even as low a rate on prime four- to six-months' commercial paper as 1 per cent is relatively attractive not only to many city banks but to many of the smaller country banks as well.

[8] According to Eastern dealers, a number of the larger New York banks, by agreement among themselves, have bought no open-market notes yielding less than $1\frac{1}{2}$ per cent since about the beginning of 1934, and some of the larger Chicago banks have likewise bought little or no outside paper during the same period. These facts presumably account for the decline in the proportion of central reserve city banks' holdings of open-market notes to the total amounts of such obligations held by member banks on call dates in 1934 and 1935.

There seem to be two main reasons why some of the larger banks, not only in New York and Chicago but also in other financial centers, have bought little or no commercial paper since about the close of 1933. In the first place, they have wished to avoid "breaking the rate" obtainable on open-market notes in a period when commercial paper yields have been the lowest ever recorded. So long as they keep their loanable funds invested, however, it would seem that they can avoid "breaking" the rate in question only at the cost of reducing the yield obtainable on some other class of earning assets. Secondly, they have by no means welcomed the active

levels comparable to those which prevailed from 1900 to 1931, city banks will again tend to buy larger amounts of open-market notes than country banks in periods of comparatively low money rates and smaller amounts than banks of the latter class at times when rates are relatively high.

The main reasons why city banks ordinarily buy open-market notes most actively in periods when commercial paper rates are relatively low, whereas purchases by country banks are generally largest in periods when rates are comparatively high, are probably as follows: Demands for accommodation on the part of city banks' customers are likely to fluctuate with general business conditions to a greater extent than demands for direct loans on the part of country banks' customers. City banks accordingly have larger amounts of surplus loanable funds than country banks at times when both business activity and money rates are at a low level. Moreover, they are likely at such times to be more interested than country banks are in keeping their earning assets in a liquid condition, and hence are more likely than banks of the latter class to place a larger proportion of their loanable funds in open-market paper. Country banks endeavor even at such times to secure relatively high rates of return on their loans and investments, partly because they are accustomed to charge higher rates than city banks on direct loans to customers, and partly because they have to obtain relatively high yields on their earning assets in order to pay the interest rates they have customarily offered on savings deposits. When the opposite conditions prevail — that is, when business is active and money rates have risen to relatively high levels — demands for direct loans on the part of their own customers absorb such a large proportion of the loanable funds of city banks that the latter can purchase but limited amounts of outside paper. Demands for accommodation on the part of country banks' customers also increase at such times, but are likely to increase to a smaller extent than those of city banks' customers. Moreover,

competition which dealers have offered them in supplying the requirements of concerns of high credit standing for short-term funds, and consequently have wished to avoid promoting an increase in the volume of open-market financing.

commercial paper at such times may offer yields as high, or nearly as high, as those which country banks are obtaining on customers' loans involving distinctly greater risks. Under such conditions, many country banks increase their purchases of open-market notes to a considerable extent.

As was indicated above, purchases by the remaining classes of buyers probably constitute less than 5 per cent of the total amount of open-market paper sold by dealers each year. There are three main reasons why purchases by these other classes of buyers have been so small in recent years. In the first place, dealers have been unable to secure enough paper to meet the demands of the American commercial banks which are their best customers, and consequently as a rule have preferred to apportion among these customers such supplies of open-market notes as they have been able to obtain, rather than offer paper to other classes of possible buyers. In the second place, relatively few potential buyers of other classes are aware of the existence of an open market for commercial paper or familiar with the advantages of such paper as a short-term investment. Lastly, open-market obligations are not so well suited to the investment requirements of other classes of buyers as to those of American commercial banks.

Purchases of commercial paper by savings banks have been confined to institutions located in certain states only, for such paper is not a legal investment for savings banks in a number of states.[9] Insurance companies have purchased but small amounts of open-market notes, partly because most such companies are not authorized by their charters to buy commercial paper, and partly

[9] The only states in which dealers consulted in 1930 and 1931 reported that they sell open-market notes to savings banks are Massachusetts, Rhode Island, and California. According to these dealers, commercial paper is not a legal investment for savings banks in such states as New York, Ohio, and Illinois, and may not be purchased by Massachusetts savings banks unless it bears two indorsements.

Massachusetts savings banks as a rule prefer paper with long maturities. About fourteen years ago they were "large investors in the year notes of Massachusetts corporations with a responsible endorser, and in [textile] mill notes with selling house endorsements" (A. P. Brown, "Commercial Paper" — typewritten paper — p. 4). In more recent years they have purchased substantial amounts of collateral loan paper from Boston dealers. Some savings banks in California have also bought such paper from a Boston dealer.

because long-term securities are as a rule better suited to their investment requirements.[10] Investment trusts occasionally buy open-market obligations, including collateral loan paper. So far, however, they have bought only limited amounts of such obligations, partly because open-market notes, unless payable on demand — as some collateral loan paper is — are not so well adapted to their requirements as bankers' bills, government obligations, and listed corporation securities, for which there is an active resale market. Business corporations of other classes also buy commercial paper, but purchases by such corporations are probably much smaller at present than they were about fifteen years ago.[11] Purchases by educational institutions, trustees, and private investors are also smaller at present than they were some years ago.[12]

Banks in Alaska and Hawaii occasionally buy open-market notes, and banks in Guam, the Philippine Islands, and Puerto Rico

[10] A house in Hartford, Connecticut, in which a number of well-known insurance companies maintain their main offices, reported in 1930 that it had never sold open-market paper to any such companies.

[11] Some fourteen years ago "a surprisingly large number of business houses and corporations" used to invest their surplus funds in commercial paper. One of these concerns not only bought fairly large amounts of such paper but also sold considerable amounts of its own obligations through a Boston house during the season of the year when its requirements for borrowed funds were the greatest (Brown, *op. cit.*, p. 3). This concern may have been a textile mill. At any rate, some of the more prosperous New England textile mills were buying commercial paper, including collateral loan paper, about the same time from the Boston house just mentioned. In 1930 a Chicago house reported that corporations had been buying fairly large amounts of open-market notes that year, and a St. Louis house that it was still selling a considerable amount of such obligations to one corporation. In the summer of 1933 a leading Chicago house stated that one corporation had bought as much as $1,000,000 of open-market paper a year from it during the preceding year or so.

[12] About fourteen years ago a Boston house occasionally used to sell large amounts of open-market paper, particularly notes issued by Massachusetts textile mills, to trustees in that city (*ibid.*, p. 3). A Boston dealer reported in the summer of 1931 that a leading New England university, which had been buying open-market notes for years, was still purchasing textile mill paper with commission house indorsement. In 1930 a former dealer of Philadelphia stated that some years ago private investors used to buy a substantial proportion of the open-market paper sold in that district, and that even in recent years he had sold a considerable amount of such paper to an individual investor; and a Minneapolis house that it was selling a fairly large amount of open-market notes to individuals. Private investors, as well as investment trusts and other business corporations, occasionally buy collateral loan paper from a Boston house which handles a relatively large amount of such paper.

used to buy such obligations some years ago.[13] Purchases by banks in Alaska and Hawaii are generally made through correspondent banks in San Francisco or Seattle, and the latter institutions in most cases probably hold the purchased paper for their correspondents to maturity. Some years ago Canadian banks occasionally bought substantial amounts of open-market notes from American dealers. In more recent years, however, they have purchased only a very small volume of such obligations, and such purchases as they have made have as a rule been effected through their branch offices in Chicago or New York, rather than their main offices.[14] A few other foreign banks have also bought small

[13] In 1930 three houses stated that they occasionally sold open-market notes to banks in Alaska and Hawaii; one of these three that it also sold such obligations to a bank in Guam from time to time and had formerly sold paper to banks in the Philippine Islands; one house that its New York correspondent sold open-market notes to Alaskan and Hawaiian banks; and one house that it had in the past sold such paper to banks in Alaska. In 1931 the New York agency of a Philippine bank reported that the latter institution some years ago occasionally bought commercial paper from a New York dealer but had purchased no open-market notes since about 1918. In 1936 a New York house stated that it sold commercial paper to banks in Puerto Rico some years ago.

The following table shows the amounts of purchased paper held by banks in Alaska and Hawaii on selected dates in recent years:

OPEN-MARKET COMMERCIAL PAPER HELD BY BANKS IN ALASKA
AND HAWAII ON SELECTED CALL DATES, 1928–1935

(Thousands of Dollars)

Call Date	Held by Banks in Alaska	Held by Banks in Hawaii
Dec. 31, 1928	881	...
June 29, 1929	617	...
Dec. 31, 1929	687	100
Mar. 27, 1930	546	700
June 30, 1930	572	300
Sept. 24, 1930	752	275
Dec. 31, 1930	656	250
Mar. 25, 1931	557	300
June 30, 1931	421	500
Sept. 29, 1931	392	...
Dec. 31, 1931	331	...
June 30, 1932	317	...
June 30, 1933	16	...
June 30, 1934	30	...
June 29, 1935	50	120

Source: *Annual Report of the Comptroller of the Currency*, 1929–1935.

[14] Canadian banks were purchasing open-market notes issued by American con-

amounts of open-market paper within recent years. They have generally purchased such paper through their branches or agencies in New York, or through some New York correspondent bank or banking house which has held the purchased obligations to maturity.[15]

---

cerns at least as early as 1884 (George Hague, "One-Name Paper," *Proc. Amer. Bankers' Assoc.*, 1884, p. 68). During the following twenty-five years their purchases of such obligations probably increased appreciably. A former dealer in New York reported that he sold paper to a bank in Montreal and one in Toronto also from about 1905 to 1910. His sales to the latter institution during this period amounted approximately to $1,000,000 a year. In 1930 dealers in Boston, Chicago, and Minneapolis stated that they had formerly sold open-market notes to Canadian banks or to the American branch offices or banking correspondents of the latter, but were making no sales to such banks currently. The Minneapolis house just referred to reported that it used to sell to Canadian banks directly, and that the paper it sold them had to be made payable in Canada. According to this house and a dealer in Chicago also, Canadian banks, or their American branches or banking correspondents, were still buying some open-market obligations in 1930. In the summer of 1931 none of the branch offices which five Canadian banks were maintaining in New York City were buying commercial paper. Three of the five branches, however, reported that they had formerly bought open-market notes, and one of these three that the Chicago branch of its bank was still buying such obligations. Two reasons were given for the fact that none of the five New York branches were buying commercial paper in 1931. The first reason was that, while such branches are allowed under the state banking laws of New York to purchase acceptances, they apparently are not allowed to buy open-market notes; the second, that Canadian banks consider funds used in their New York branches as secondary reserves, wish to keep such funds in very liquid investments, and therefore prefer to invest them in call loans (which they could then convert into gold quickly if they needed it). They may also have been deterred from purchasing commercial paper by the risk of losses from fluctuations in exchange rates and by the fact that Canadian banks can generally obtain higher rates on direct loans to their own customers than on open-market notes.

[15] Dealers apparently were selling some open-market obligations to European buyers, presumably banks or banking houses, as early as 1913 (Ralph Van Vechten, address as president of Clearing House Section, American Bankers' Association, *Proc. Amer. Bankers' Assoc.*, 1913, p. 522). Some years later a bank in Mexico and one in Formosa are said to have bought commercial paper in the United States, the former through a California bank and the latter through a bank in New York. About 1924 a New York dealer sold some ninety-day paper to the Berlin branch of a British banking house. In 1930 another New York house, through its London office, sold some open-market notes of the highest grade to a bank in England and to a bank in France also. In the same year one of the largest houses in the country reported that it sometimes sold short-term paper of the highest grade to certain European buyers — presumably banks or banking houses. In such cases it guaranteed payment of the purchased obligations and held them to maturity for its buying customers. In the spring of 1931 a Boston dealer sold some open-market notes to a local investment banking house which presumably purchased them for the account of some foreign banking house. In the summer of 1931 the New York branch offices

2. Advantages of Open-Market Paper as an Investment for Banks' Funds

Both as an investment for their secondary reserves and as an outlet for surplus loanable funds which, either at certain seasons or more or less continuously throughout the year, they are unable to employ advantageously in direct advances to their own customers, carefully selected open-market notes offer several important advantages to the commercial banks which are the main buyers of such obligations.

One of the most important of these advantages is that open-market paper is an exceptionally secure form of investment. In fact, if judiciously selected, such paper is practically as safe an investment as bankers' acceptances, stock exchange call and time loans, and United States government bonds; and even if selected at random it is a distinctly more secure form of investment than the direct loans which banks make to their own customers and the

---

of one Mexican bank, one Belgian bank, three British banks, and one bank of South Africa reported that they were buying no commercial paper. The branch of the Belgian bank, however, stated that it had bought such paper as recently as about 1927, and the branch of one of the British banks that it would purchase open-market notes if allowed to do so by the state banking laws of New York. The fact that apparently they were not permitted to purchase such obligations under these laws was given by practically all these branches, except that of the Belgian bank, as a reason why they were not buying commercial paper at that time. The Mexican branch gave as an additional reason the fact that the funds of its bank could be used more profitably in Mexico, where legal rates of interest were as high as 12 to 18 per cent a year. In 1936 a leading New York house reported that it sold commercial paper to French and English banks some twenty years ago, and that it sold some such paper to a New York bank for the account of a French bank in 1935.

It is said that some twenty years ago dealers were "obliged to lend their guarantee in some form" when they sold paper to European purchasers (Van Vechten, *loc. cit.*). In more recent years also some foreign buyers have arranged to have the open-market notes they have purchased guaranteed in some manner. As was noted in the preceding paragraph, one of the larger houses stated in 1930 that it customarily guaranteed payment of the short-term paper it occasionally sold to certain European buyers. The New York branch office of a Canadian bank which formerly bought open-market notes from time to time used to arrange to have such paper indorsed by a bank. For its indorsement the bank made a charge which was at the rate of ¼ of 1 per cent of the face amount of the paper a year. This charge was of course in the nature of an insurance premium which reduced the yield on six-months' notes by ⅛ of 1 per cent. At present such a premium would be considered distinctly more than commensurate with the risk involved in purchasing carefully selected paper.

long-term securities (other than United States government bonds) in which they have placed a large proportion of their earning assets in recent years.[16]

Table 28 shows estimated commercial paper "outstandings," annual sales by dealers, and losses on purchased paper during the fourteen years ending with 1935. As may be seen from an examination of this table, estimated losses on purchased paper in none of these fourteen years except 1930 amounted to as much as ⅛ of 1 per cent of the estimated average amount of open-market obligations outstanding or 1/20 of 1 per cent of estimated annual sales by dealers. For the period from 1922 to 1936 as a whole, the estimated average annual loss on purchased paper amounted only to about 0.05 per cent of estimated average "outstandings," and the proportion of estimated total losses to estimated total sales by dealers, which is a more significant figure, to less than 0.03 per cent. The percentages of losses which national banks (excluding failed banks) charged off on both their securities and their loans and discounts during the eighteen years ending with June 30, 1935, were much greater, as is shown by Table 29. In none of these years were the losses charged off on "bonds and securities" and loans and discounts less than 0.41 per cent and 0.23 per cent, respectively. On the average the losses charged off during the eighteen-year period amounted to about 1.19 per cent in the case of "bonds and securities" and to about 1.27 per cent in the case of loans and discounts. These figures are, respectively, about twenty-four and twenty-five times as large as the estimated average annual loss on open-market notes expressed as a percentage of the estimated average amount of commercial paper outstanding during the fourteen years from 1922 to 1936.[17]

---

[16] In this connection it may be noted that an authority on investments has classed prime commercial paper as a practically riskless investment. (See D. C. Rose, *A Scientific Approach to Investment Management*, p. 62, and *The Practical Application of Investment Management*, p. 25.)

[17] While Tables 28 and 29 undoubtedly indicate that open-market notes have in recent years been a much more secure form of investment than national banks' "bonds and securities" and loans and discounts, the data contained in these tables do not furnish an entirely satisfactory basis for precise statements as to the comparative safety of these alternative outlets for banks' loanable funds.

The figures of commercial paper outstanding, sales by dealers, and losses on

TABLE 28

Estimated Average Amounts of Commercial Paper Outstanding, Annual Sales by Dealers, and Losses on Purchased Paper, 1922–1935 *

Year	Estimated Average Amounts of Commercial Paper Outstanding	Estimated Annual Sales by Dealers	Estimated Losses on Purchased Paper	Proportion of Estimated Losses to Estimated Average "Outstandings"	Proportion of Estimated Losses to Estimated Annual Sales
1922	$768,000,000	$1,843,000,000	$112,500	0.0146%	0.0061%
1923	834,000,000	2,002,000,000	212,500	0.0255	0.0106
1924	873,000,000	2,095,000,000	996,250	0.1141	0.0476
1925	743,000,000	1,783,000,000	789,700	0.1063	0.0443
1926	629,000,000	1,510,000,000	304,750	0.0484	0.0202
1927	585,000,000	1,404,000,000	610,875	0.1044	0.0435
1928	494,000,000	1,186,000,000	None	.....	.....
1929	322,000,000	773,000,000	118,575	0.0368	0.0153
1930	489,000,000	1,174,000,000	915,875	0.1873	0.0780
1931	267,000,000	641,000,000	200,000	0.0749	0.0312
1932	105,000,000	252,000,000	52,500	0.0500	0.0208
1933	95,000,000	228,000,000	None	.....	.....
1934	156,000,000	374,000,000	None	.....	.....
1935	174,000,000	418,000,000	None	.....	.....

* Figures of estimated average commercial paper "outstandings" and annual sales by dealers were taken from Table 3. Figures of estimated losses on purchased paper were supplied by the National Credit Office of New York. Losses for the years 1930–1932 are estimates as of December 1, 1935. Final losses for these three years are likely to be at least somewhat smaller than the estimates given in this table.

TABLE 29

NATIONAL BANKS' INVESTMENTS IN SECURITIES, LOANS AND DISCOUNTS, AND LOSSES CHARGED OFF ON SECURITIES AND LOANS AND DISCOUNTS, YEARS ENDED JUNE 30, 1918–1935

(Amounts in Thousands of Dollars)

Year Ended June 30—	United States Government Securities Owned	Other Bonds and Securities Owned	Total Bonds and Securities Owned	Loans and Discounts (Including Rediscounts)	Losses Charged off on Bonds and Securities Owned	Losses Charged off on Loans and Discounts	Percentage of Losses Charged off — On Bonds and Securities to Total Bonds and Securities Owned	Percentage of Losses Charged off — On Account Loans and Discounts to Total Loans and Discounts
1918	2,129,283	1,840,487	3,969,770	10,135,842	44,350	33,964	1.12	0.34
1919	3,176,314	1,875,609	5,051,923	11,010,206	27,819	35,440	0.55	0.32
1920	2,269,575	1,916,890	4,186,465	13,611,416	61,790	31,284	1.48	0.23
1921	2,019,497	2,005,584	4,025,081	12,004,515	76,179	76,210	1.89	0.63
1922	2,285,459	2,277,866	4,563,325	11,248,214	33,444	135,208	0.73	1.20
1923	2,693,846	2,375,857	5,069,703	11,817,671	21,890	120,438	0.43	1.02
1924	2,481,778	2,660,550	5,142,328	11,978,728	24,642	102,814	0.48	0.86
1925	2,536,767	3,193,677	5,730,444	12,674,067	25,301	95,552	0.44	0.75
1926	2,469,268	3,372,985	5,842,253	13,417,674	23,783	93,605	0.41	0.70
1927	2,596,178	3,797,040	6,393,218	13,955,696	27,579	86,512	0.43	0.62
1928	2,891,167	4,256,281	7,147,448	15,144,995	29,191	92,106	0.41	0.61
1929	2,803,860	3,852,675	6,656,535	14,801,130	43,458	86,815	0.65	0.59
1930	2,753,941	4,134,230	6,888,171	14,887,752	61,371	103,817	0.89	0.70
1931	3,256,268	4,418,569	7,674,837	13,177,485	119,294	186,864	1.55	1.42
1932	3,352,666	3,843,986	7,196,652	10,281,676	201,848	259,478	2.80	2.52
1933	4,031,576	3,340,055	7,371,631	8,116,972	236,557	231,420	3.21	2.85
1934	6,003,652	3,344,901	9,348,553	7,694,749	241,789	379,294	2.59	4.93
1935	7,173,007	3,543,379	10,716,386	7,365,226	136,743	188,237	1.28	2.56

Source: *Annual Report of the Comptroller of the Currency*, 1935, p. 95.

It will be noted that the total estimated losses on open-market notes, including obligations of all grades handled by dealers, were merely nominal throughout the period 1922–1935, and that no final losses at all were recorded for 1928 or any of the three years

purchased paper, given in Table 28, are all estimates, and the figures of losses for the years 1930–1932 will probably have to be revised downward to some extent as a result of the payment at some later date of at least some part of the open-market obligations which remained unpaid at the time when such figures were collected. Figures of total annual losses on purchased paper are not available for the years preceding 1922; hence comparisons of such losses with those on national banks' security holdings and loans and discounts in these earlier years cannot be made. Losses on commercial paper may have been heavier in 1920 and 1921, and in 1918 and 1919 also, than in any years since 1921, though, according to an estimate given in an address by a Boston dealer, the losses on some $4,000,000,000 of paper sold during the eighteen months ending with July 1921 amounted only to 0.047 per cent (R. E. Anderson, Jr., *The Future of Commercial Paper* — pamphlet containing reprint of an address before the New Jersey Bankers' Association, Jan. 19, 1934 — pp. 1–2). Hence if figures of such losses for the entire period from 1918 to 1936 were available, percentage figures based on such data might be somewhat larger than those given in the text above.

Table 29 does not show separate figures for losses on United States government securities and for those on other securities, and the figures of losses which it shows are expressed merely as percentages of the amounts of securities and loans and discounts which national banks happened to be carrying on their books on one particular date in each year. The losses shown in this table may be reduced to some extent as a result of recoveries in later years.

It should be noted that the figures of loans and discounts given in Table 29 include national banks' holdings of open-market notes, and that the losses on loans and discounts shown in this table include losses (if any) on such obligations as well as on direct loans of these banks to their own customers. Hence losses on the latter class of advances were in most years actually somewhat lower in absolute amounts than Table 29 indicates. On the other hand, since the percentage of losses on purchased paper is much smaller than that on banks' direct advances to their own customers, and no losses at all were reported on open-market notes for four of the eighteen years from 1918 to 1936, the percentages of losses incurred by national banks on direct advances to their own customers alone were actually somewhat higher than might be inferred from an examination of this table. Similarly, if separate percentage figures of losses incurred by these banks on their investments in securities other than United States government obligations were available, such figures would no doubt be appreciably higher than the percentage figures of losses on "bonds and securities" given in Table 29.

The figures given in Table 29 relate only to national banks which were in operation on June 30 of each year, i.e., do not include losses of failed national banks. If losses of the latter class of banks had been included, the percentage figures shown in the last two columns of this table would no doubt have been higher, particularly in such years as 1931–1933, when the number of national bank failures was abnormally large. If figures for state banks were available, they would very probably show that the percentages of losses incurred by such banks on both their investments and their loans and discounts were higher than those suffered by national banks.

ending with 1935.[18] Both the number of financial embarrassments among open-market borrowers and the proportion of the number of such embarrassments to the total number of concerns using the open market have likewise been extremely small since 1922.[19] On

[18] The National Credit Office of New York has recently reported that no losses were incurred on open-market commercial paper in 1936, either.

[19] These conclusions are based on the following two tables:

CLASSIFICATION OF FINANCIAL EMBARRASSMENTS AMONG OPEN-MARKET BORROWERS BY LINES OF BUSINESS, 1922–1935 *

Line of Business	1922	1923	1924	1925	1926	1927	1928	1929	1930	1931	1932	1933	1934	1935	Total
Textile:															
(a) Mills	..	1	1	1	2	..	..	2	1	..	..	2	..	..	10
(b) Wholesalers	..	..	1	1	1	1	..	..	1	2	1	..	..	..	8
(c) Retailers ..	1	1	2	1	..	..	..	..	3	2	..	..	..	..	10
(d) Cutters ...	..	1	3	..	..	1	..	1	..	1	..	..	..	..	7
Foodstuffs	3	1	4	2	..	1	..	2	5	1	..	..	..	..	19
Leather	..	..	2	..	..	..	2	..	..	1	..	..	..	..	5
Lumber	..	..	1	1	..	..	..	..	1	..	..	1	..	..	4
Metals	1	2	1	1	..	..	..	2	1	1	2	1	..	..	12
Finance companies	1	..	1	1	..	2	..	..	..	..	..	..	..	..	5
Miscellaneous ...	1	1	2	1	1	..	..	1	1	1	..	..	..	..	9
Total	7	7	16	11	4	5	2	7	13	9	4	4	0	0	89

* Figures in this table were collected by the National Credit Office of New York. A classification of financial embarrassments among open-market borrowers by Federal Reserve districts for the period from 1922 to July 1, 1931, is given in L. M. Read, *The Story of Commercial Paper* (pamphlet), p. 4.

NUMBER OF FINANCIAL EMBARRASSMENTS AMONG OPEN-MARKET BORROWERS COMPARED WITH NUMBER OF CONCERNS USING THE OPEN MARKET, 1922–1935 *

Year	Number of Financial Embarrassments	Number of Concerns Using Open Market	Proportion of Embarrassments to Number of Concerns Using Open Market
1922	7	2,259	0.31%
1923	7	2,171	0.32
1924	16	2,705	0.59
1925	11	2,754	0.40
1926	4	2,743	0.15
1927	5	2,490	0.20
1928	2	2,354	0.08
1929	7	1,653	0.42
1930	13	1,674	0.78
1931	9	1,239	0.73
1932	4	651	0.61
1933	4	548	0.73
1934	0	625	0.00
1935	0	654	0.00

* Figures in the second and third columns of this table were collected by the National Credit Office. The records of the latter show that there were no financial embarrassments at all among open-market borrowers in 1936.

From the figures given in the table immediately above it may be computed that on the average about one out of every 275 concerns using the open market became

the other hand, at least some losses were incurred on bankers' acceptances in 1931, and on both bankers' bills and bankers' balances maintained with city correspondent banks in 1933; and percentage losses of national banks were particularly heavy on "bonds and securities" in 1932, 1933, and 1934, and on loans and discounts in each of the four years ending with 1935. Some banks, moreover, have within the last few years suffered appreciable losses even on United States government bonds, as a result of having to sell such obligations at lower prices than those at which they purchased them.[20] In some cases the percentage of losses on sales of these securities has been much greater than the estimated proportion of losses on the open-market notes sold by dealers dur-

temporarily embarrassed — i.e., failed to meet its notes at maturity — in each of the fourteen years from 1922 to 1936. It does not follow, however, that none of the concerns which defaulted payment of the principal of their obligations at maturity were able to liquidate any part of their open-market indebtedness at some later date. On the contrary, the proportion of the total amount of defaulted open-market notes which is eventually paid is as a rule higher than might be supposed. During the five years ending with 1933, for instance, according to the records of the National Credit Office, payment was defaulted on a total of $8,647,000 of commercial paper at maturity, but all but $1,286,950, or approximately 15 per cent, of this indebtedness had been liquidated by about Dec. 1, 1935. In a number of cases concerns which have failed to meet their open-market notes at maturity, but have taken them up at some later date, have also paid interest on such defaulted obligations at the rate of 6 per cent a year.

[20] It is sometimes said that one of the advantages of open-market paper as an investment is that it is always worth its face value, whereas the prices of bonds and other securities are continually fluctuating. It is true that one special class of paper — the demand notes issued by grain elevator companies and grain commission houses in the Minneapolis Federal Reserve district — is always worth its face value, since such paper is amply secured and "callable both ways," and the interest on it, instead of being deducted in advance, is collected either when such paper is called or at regular intervals after its issue. Collateral loan notes also are sometimes made payable on demand, and in such cases are always worth their face value, provided adequate margins are always maintained on the collateral. Other classes of paper handled by dealers, however, are ordinarily not worth their *face* value until maturity; and, if carried to maturity, as most commercial paper is, even bonds which have previously been selling below par will then be worth less than their face value, unless the issuing concern is unable to meet its obligations. If open-market notes, instead of being carried to maturity by the purchasers, were bought and sold a number of times before they became due and payable, their market prices would fluctuate both with changes in money rates and in accordance with the length of time between their purchase and their maturity dates, just as the market prices of bonds do. In a period of rapidly rising money rates it is possible that some banks might incur slight losses even on commercial paper of the highest grade if they should find it necessary to rediscount such paper with correspondent banks.

ing the years from 1922 to 1936, which amounted only to about 1/40 of 1 per cent. On the basis of the foregoing data it may be concluded that commercial paper, even if selected at random, is about as safe an investment as any in which banks can place their loanable funds.[21]

There are three main reasons why open-market notes, though as a rule unindorsed and entirely unsecured, are among the safest

[21] No losses at all have been incurred on the demand notes mentioned in the preceding footnote, and a number of banks have sustained no losses on any other classes of obligations which they have purchased from dealers. Ten city banks reported, either in 1930 or in 1931, that they had sustained no losses at all on outside paper for a number of years. These institutions included two leading banks in New York, two in Boston, and one each in Springfield (Massachusetts), Richmond, Atlanta, Minneapolis, Kansas City, and Los Angeles. The number of years during which they had been buying open-market obligations with no losses ranged from five to thirty, and the amounts of such paper they had purchased from about $7,000,000 to several hundred million dollars. Seventeen other city banks, including two leading institutions each in Boston, Richmond, Minneapolis, and Dallas, and one each in New York, Philadelphia, Baltimore, Washington, St. Louis, Kansas City, San Francisco, Portland (Oregon), and Seattle, reported that they had incurred practically no losses at all on outside paper purchased over periods of time ranging from one year to thirty years. The amounts of such paper which these banks had bought ranged from about $11,000,000 to about $500,000,000 (including paper purchased for correspondent banks). Two of the seventeen banks, one a national bank of St. Louis and the other a national bank of Portland (Oregon), kept careful records of their purchases and losses for a number of years preceding 1930. The St. Louis bank, which was formerly one of the largest buyers of open-market obligations in the country, reported that it purchased $226,125,000 of outside paper for its own account during the five years ending with 1927, and that its losses on such paper amounted to $33,000, or 0.0146 per cent of its purchases. The Portland bank reported that it bought $143,007,000 of open-market notes during the fifteen years from 1915 to 1930, and that its losses on such obligations amounted to $12,183, or 0.0085 per cent of its purchases. Numerous other cases could be cited in which banks have incurred either no losses whatsoever, or losses so small as to be negligible, on purchases of large amounts of outside paper over periods of some years.

Further data relating to the safety of open-market obligations as an investment were supplied by dealers themselves. An officer of a leading Chicago house stated in 1923 that no losses at all were incurred on the "hundreds of millions of dollars of paper" which his house sold from 1907 to 1920, and that even in "the trying days of 1920 and 1921" there were "but two real failures" among the borrowing customers of this house (A. G. Becker, *Commercial Paper* — pamphlet — pp. 12, 19). Of sixteen leading dealers consulted in 1930, five reported that no losses had been incurred on any of the open-market notes they had sold, one house that no losses had been sustained on the paper it had sold since about the beginning of 1921, and the remaining ten houses that the final losses on the open-market obligations which they had sold since they entered the commercial paper business amounted only to a small fraction of 1 per cent. Losses on paper sold by eight other leading dealers were also so small as to be insignificant.

of all investments for the surplus funds of banks. In the first place, they are very carefully selected by the houses which deal in such obligations. Secondly, most commercial banks themselves are in a position to investigate carefully the credit standing of all concerns whose paper they may be interested in purchasing. Buying banks are ordinarily granted an option period of seven to ten days or more in which to make their credit investigations, and, if not satisfied with the results of their inquiries, are allowed to return paper purchased under the customary option agreement to the house from which they bought it. As a rule, they can secure all or most of the credit information they really need from the dealer concerned. If they wish to, they can also "check" the credit standing of an open-market borrower with the latter's depositary banks and trade creditors, with credit-reporting agencies, and with their own correspondent banks. If they do not have efficient credit departments of their own, they can entrust the latter banks with the responsibility of selecting outside paper for them. Moreover, the purchase of open-market notes is a wholly impersonal transaction. Bankers buy such paper exclusively on the basis of its merits as an investment; whereas, in considering applications for loans made by their own customers, they are not infrequently influenced by personal friendships, deposit balances maintained, and other factors having no particular bearing on the ability of prospective borrowers to meet their obligations at maturity. There can be no question that open-market notes are selected more carefully than the notes on which banks extend direct loans to their own customers. So carefully, in fact, are obligations of the former class selected that practically the only cases of final losses on open-market paper are those resulting from fraud or willful misrepresentation.[22] In the third place, if concerns which borrow in the open market get into financial difficulties before an issue of their open-market notes falls due, they will make every possible effort to meet such obligations at maturity. It is clearly to their interest to

---

[22] F. W. Crane, "Commercial Paper Purchased from Brokers," *Proc. Ill. Bankers' Assoc.*, 1916, p. 135; H. C. Smith, *The Federal Reserve Regulations as to Commercial Paper and Their Application to Existing Methods of Credit* (pamphlet), p. 13.

do so, for their paper is likely to be held by banks in many different sections of the country, the news of their failure to meet their
notes at maturity would spread throughout the country in a very
short time, and as a consequence their credit might suffer irrepa-
rable injury.[23]

A second advantage of open-market notes as an investment for
banks' funds is that such obligations possess a high degree of
liquidity. That is, they are practically always paid promptly at
maturity, without requests for extensions or renewals, and the
banks holding them can generally convert them into cash before
maturity by rediscounting them with the Federal Reserve banks
or with correspondent banks. Most open-market paper, if it
matures within ninety days, is eligible for rediscount with the
Reserve banks. As a rule, member banks prefer to rediscount such
paper, rather than obligations of their own customers, with the
Reserve banks, for outside paper is of high grade, is generally
"acceptable" as well as eligible, and is made out in round amounts.
Member banks holding commercial paper with a maturity exceeding ninety days, and non-member banks wishing to realize
open-market obligations before maturity, can generally arrange to
rediscount outside paper with correspondent banks. In most cases,

---

[23] The importance of meeting open-market obligations promptly at maturity was
indicated in an address by a well-known New York banker some twenty years ago
as follows: ". . . about the best asset in existence is the honor and integrity of our
great merchants, individuals and firms, together with those large corporations whose
management regards highly their contracts and the strong position which they oc-
cupy in the commercial and industrial world. A single note going to protest may
mean bankruptcy and business death" (J. H. Case, "The Desirability of Commercial
Paper as a Bank Investment," *Proc. N. J. Bankers' Assoc.*, 1912, pp. 33–34).

It is sometimes said that commercial paper is a safe investment because it is
issued by concerns in all sections of the country and in many different lines of business, and the purchase of such paper enables banks to diversify their loans both
geographically and industrially. The fact that the purchase of open-market notes
makes possible such a diversification, however, is rather a reason why many individual banks find it to their advantage to carry at least some part of their earning
assets in the form of such obligations than an explanation of why commercial paper
is a safe investment. So far as any one investor is concerned, diversification is undoubtedly a means of reducing losses in cases where some losses are inevitable; but
it does not make possible any reduction in the total losses which must be borne by
investors as a whole.

moreover, such paper can be rediscounted without loss.[24] Open-market obligations unquestionably possess a higher degree of liquidity than most direct loans of banks to their own customers and many corporation bonds. Prime paper which is eligible for rediscount at a Federal Reserve bank is more liquid than stock exchange time loans, but ordinarily somewhat less liquid than prime bankers' acceptances and United States government bonds, for which there are broader resale markets. During the financial crises of 1907 and 1914, however, high-grade commercial paper proved more liquid than call loans, and it is said that during a part of the financial crisis of March 1933 a number of banks found that such paper was even more liquid than United States government bonds and some bankers' acceptances. Moreover, at least two classes of open-market obligations — collateral loan paper when it is made payable on demand, and the demand notes issued by grain elevator companies and grain commission houses in the ninth Federal Reserve district — are as liquid as stock exchange call loans, prime bankers' acceptances, and United States government bonds. In the matter of liquidity, therefore, high-grade commercial paper compares favorably with any other earning assets which banks carry as secondary reserves.

It has been pointed out, however, that the liquidity of open-market notes is in no small measure due to their "shiftability." As was stated in Chapter VI, a fairly large proportion of the paper sold in the market each year is issued to replace maturing notes. This means that the issuing concerns, whether or not they are able to meet their maturing paper with the proceeds of sales of goods

[24] If a bank should find it necessary, because of a rise in money rates or for any other reason, to rediscount open-market notes at rates higher than those at which it purchased them, it would of course suffer some loss on the rediscounting transaction. The amount of any such loss would depend partly on the differences between the rates at which the notes in question were purchased and those at which they were rediscounted, and partly on the length of time the buying bank held the notes before rediscounting them. Since changes in money rates are ordinarily gradual, and open-market paper as a rule is issued with comparatively short maturities, any losses from such rediscounting transactions are not likely to constitute more than a very small proportion of the face amount of the paper rediscounted.

purchased or manufactured with the aid of funds obtained through dealers, are in fact meeting their obligations by continuing to borrow from banks which already hold these obligations, by borrowing from other banks which purchase their paper, or by obtaining advances from both groups of banks concurrently. Open-market borrowers may also "rotate" their open-market loans and the loans they secure directly from their own banks, using advances from their own banks to pay their open-market loans, and conversely. It does not follow, of course, that concerns which meet maturing open-market obligations with new issues of notes or with direct advances from their own banks would not be able, if necessary, to pay their open-market loans without the aid of borrowed funds. Many concerns whose credit standing is unusually strong, in fact, use the open market as a means of raising what may be called permanent working capital because they find it profitable to "trade on the equity" in this manner more or less continuously throughout the year. There are cases, however, in which open-market borrowers find it difficult, or even impossible, to meet their maturing notes promptly without the aid of funds obtained by borrowing from their own banks or by selling new notes to banks which do not hold any of the maturing paper. In such cases the liquidity of the maturing open-market loans clearly depends on their "shiftability." It is equally clear that the liquidity of commercial paper depends on its "shiftability" if the term "liquidity" is used to mean ready convertibility into cash or its equivalent; for banks which realize open-market notes by rediscounting them with Federal Reserve banks or correspondent banks merely shift to these other institutions the loans which give rise to such obligations.

It should be noted, however, that the liquidity of all other earning assets of banks also depends, to some extent at least, on their "shiftability." The prompt payment at maturity of some even of the most liquid of banks' direct loans to their own customers in some cases depends on the ability of the borrowing concerns to obtain direct loans from other banks or to sell their notes in the market through dealers. Similarly, bankers' acceptances are sometimes paid with borrowed funds, and the liquidity of stock exchange call and time loans at times depends to a large extent on the ability and willingness of the larger city banks to advance the funds required for paying these loans. Moreover, if banks wish to realize any of the four main classes of their earning assets, other than outside paper, which are more or less readily convertible into cash or its equivalent before maturity, they find it necessary to shift such earning assets either to other banks or to some other class of buyers. Thus they must rediscount their own customers' notes with a Federal Reserve bank or some correspondent bank, rediscount bankers' bills or sell them to a Federal Reserve bank or in the open market, sell United States government obligations to a Federal Reserve bank or in the open market, and sell bonds other than government obligations in the security markets.

Hence so far as liquidity is concerned, commercial paper does not differ essentially from the other assets in which banks place their loanable funds. From the point of view of the individual bank, both open-market paper and these other classes of assets may possess a high degree of liquidity. From the standpoint of the banking system as a whole, however, the liquidity both of open-market paper and of these other classes of assets depends to a greater or lesser extent upon the ease with which earning assets can be shifted from individual banks to other banks in the system or to some other class of lenders.[25]

A third advantage which outside paper offers as an investment for banks' funds is that the net yields obtainable on open-market obligations compare favorably with those which may be secured on most alternative investments for such funds. The average rate on prime commercial paper in New York City was 4.39 per cent for the period 1900–1935 and 4.02 per cent for the seventeen years from 1919 to 1936. These figures may be regarded as conservative estimates of the average net yields obtainable on open-market

---

[25] Certain classes of commercial banks' earning assets, including prime commercial paper, prime bankers' bills, high-grade listed bonds, and obligations of the United States government, can of course be shifted, to some extent at least, to such other classes of lenders as individual investors, business corporations, savings banks, and foreign banking institutions.

notes during these two periods: for they are average yields which were secured on obligations of the highest grade, whereas returns ranging from ¼ of 1 per cent to 1 per cent or more higher were obtainable on the average during the same periods on notes given a lower rating than "prime"; and no deduction for losses needs to be made from the two figures given above, since losses on paper of all grades sold by dealers since 1900 have amounted only to a small fraction of 1 per cent.

The average rates on prime paper for the years 1900–1935 and 1919–1935 were undoubtedly lower than the average rates charged by banks on direct loans to their own customers during the same periods. From the available figures of rates charged in thirty-six selected cities it may be estimated that the average of the rates charged on all such loans made by commercial banks during the second of these two periods was probably not less than 5½ per cent; and for the years 1900–1935 the average would no doubt be somewhat higher. To ascertain the net yields on loans of this class it would of course be necessary to adjust to some extent the rates actually charged. Such rates would have to be increased somewhat because borrowers are customarily expected, if not required, to maintain average deposit balances equal to a certain percentage of the amounts borrowed, and actual yields on direct loans are consequently somewhat higher than the rates charged on such loans. On the other hand, the rates actually charged would have to be reduced somewhat because of losses on direct loans, which in the case of national banks (excluding failed banks) amounted to about 1¼ per cent during the years from 1918 to 1936. The adjustments necessary for the reasons indicated would of course vary considerably with different banks. If adjusted figures for all banks for the years 1900–1935 and 1919–1935 were available, and averages of these figures were taken, these averages would probably be ½ of 1 per cent or more higher than the average yield on prime commercial paper during both of these periods.

The latter yield compares more favorably, however, with yields on other earning assets of banks. The average yield on prime ninety-day bankers' acceptances in New York City during the years from 1919 to 1936 was 3.06 per cent, or nearly 1 per cent less than the average yield (4.02 per cent) on prime commercial paper for the same period. Since both these classes of investments are purchased on a discount basis, and losses on both have been negligible, no adjustment of these yield figures needs to be made. Prime commercial paper therefore proved to be a distinctly more remunerative investment than prime ninety-day bankers' bills during the seventeen years ending with 1935. The average yield on Liberty and Treasury bonds during the same period was 3.92 per cent, or slightly less than the average yield on prime paper. During the thirty-six-year period 1900–1935 the average yield on New York Stock Exchange call loans was 3.79 per cent, on New York Stock Exchange sixty- to ninety-day time loans [26] was 4.12 per cent, and on sixty high-grade corporation and municipal bonds (fifteen industrial, fifteen railroad, fifteen public utility, and fifteen municipal bonds) was 4.68 per cent, as compared with an average rate of 4.39 per cent on prime open-market notes. Yields on "Street loans" and bonds, however, must be adjusted before they can be compared with the yield on open-market paper. No adjustment for losses is necessary in the case of yields on "Street loans," but some such adjustment should be made in the yields of the bonds mentioned above, for banks incur losses on their purchases and sales even of United States government obligations and high-grade corporation bonds.[27] On the other hand, any reductions in

[26] The terms "New York Stock Exchange call loans" and "New York Stock Exchange time loans" are used above, as well as elsewhere in this study, merely to designate open-market loans on Stock Exchange collateral in the New York money market. Actually, only a part, and at present only a comparatively small part, of the total volume of call loans made in the open market in New York on Stock Exchange collateral are obtained at the money desk of the Exchange; and no time loans are made at the money desk.

[27] Losses of all commercial banks in the United States on United States government bonds and high-grade corporation bonds during the years from 1918 to 1936 may have amounted to as much as ½ of 1 per cent of their average holdings of such obligations. At any rate, as was indicated above, the losses charged off by national banks (excluding failed banks) on their "bonds and securities," including United States government obligations, during this period amounted on the average to about 1.19 per cent of their holdings of such securities on June 30 for the years in question; and losses of state banks on their securities were no doubt greater than those of national banks. If the average yield on sixty corporation bonds of medium grade

net yield figures made necessary by such losses would be offset to at least some extent in the case of government bonds by tax exemption provisions. Allowances would also have to be made for the facts (1) that commercial paper is purchased on a discount basis, whereas the interest on open-market call and time loans on Stock Exchange collateral in the New York money market, so long as such loans remain outstanding, is charged to the account of the borrower at the end of each month, and the interest on bonds also is paid on an "interest-to-follow" basis, as a rule semiannually;[28] and (2) that banks incur no brokerage charges when they purchase open-market notes, whereas a charge is made by New York Clearing House banks for placing funds of out-of-town banks in "Street loans," and when they buy or sell bonds or other securities through brokers banks must pay the usual commission charges.[29] If all the adjustments necessary for the reasons indi-

---

during the years from 1900 to 1936 had been computed, it would of course have been higher than 4.68 per cent, which was the average return during the same period on the sixty high-grade bonds referred to in the text above. On the other hand, the average return on bonds of medium grade would probably have to be reduced by 2 per cent or more, because of losses on such securities, before the average net yield on bonds of this grade could be ascertained.

[28] Thus the (gross) yield on 5 per cent bonds bought at par and on funds placed by out-of-town banks in "Street loans" in New York at 5 per cent would be just 5 per cent a year, whereas the (net) yield on commercial paper discounted at 5 per cent would be 5.26 per cent a year. (To convert the foregoing yield figures into comparative net yield figures, adjustments would of course have to be made to allow for the charges incurred in buying and selling bonds and in placing funds in "Street loans," and for losses on bonds.)

[29] Early in 1926 an amendment to the constitution of the New York Clearing House Association was adopted which provided that, for placing funds of out-of-town banks and other lenders in "Street loans," all Clearing House member banks, and all non-members clearing through such member banks, should make a charge of not less than 5 per cent of the interest or discount received on such loans. This amendment became effective on Mar. 1, 1926. Before the adoption of this amendment, New York banks had not followed any uniform policy with respect to the charges made for placing funds of out-of-town correspondents or customers in "Street loans." Some banks had made no such charges at all. Others had charged fees which depended largely on the size of customers' balances and the attractiveness of their business. The maximum charge had been about ¼ of 1 per cent (presumably ¼ of 1 per cent a year on the principal of the loan) (*C. and F. Chron.*, Feb. 27, 1926, pp. 1113–1114). An amendment adopted by the association on Apr. 10, 1929, which became effective forthwith, provided that the charge of not less than 5 per cent of the interest or discount received on "Street loans" should be changed to ½ of 1 per cent a year on the principal of such loans (*ibid.*, Apr. 13,

cated were made, the average net yield on prime open-market notes during the years 1900–1935 would actually be higher than that on the sixty high-grade corporation and municipal bonds mentioned above. The average net return on prime paper would also be higher than the average net yields on New York Stock Exchange call and time loans during the same period, as well as higher than the average net return on Liberty and Treasury bonds during the years 1919–1935, by greater percentages than the unadjusted yield figures given above would indicate.[30]

1929, p. 2394). This latter charge was higher than the former so long as rates obtainable on "Street loans" remained below 10 per cent a year, lower than the earlier charge if rates rose above 10 per cent, and exactly the same as the earlier charge if the rate obtainable on "Street loans" happened to be 10 per cent. On Sept. 19, 1933, the association adopted an amendment which provided for modifying the charge then in effect to the extent that "when the rate of interest or discount earned on the loan . . . is less than 2%, the charge shall be 25% of the amount of the interest or discount collected, with a minimum charge of 1/4 of 1% per annum upon the amount of such loan" (*ibid.*, Sept. 23, 1933, p. 2196). On Oct. 25, 1935, the charge for placing "Street loans" was restored to a minimum of 1/2 of 1 per cent a year on the principal thereof by an amendment rescinding the amendment of Sept. 19, 1933 (*ibid.*, Oct. 26, 1935, pp. 2663–2664). Out-of-town banks sometimes accept "participations" in collateral loans with New York City banks, but even in such cases the charge of 1/2 of 1 per cent just referred to is made for placing their funds in "Street loans."

The brokerage charges for buying and selling bonds at present (October 1936) are as follows: United States government obligations, $1.00 for each $1,000 bond, and 50 cents each for bonds of any smaller principal amount; corporation bonds, $2.50 for each $1,000 bond, $1.25 for each $500 bond, and $1.00 for each $100 bond. (The foregoing figures were furnished by a Boston brokerage house. The minimum brokerage charges of certain other houses are somewhat higher than the figures given above. In addition to the regular brokerage charge, a federal tax charge of 40 cents for each $1,000 is incurred on the sale of corporation bonds.) Hence if banks or other investors sell either government or corporation bonds within a short period after they have purchased them, brokerage charges are likely to absorb all or the greater part of the interest earned on such securities between the date of their purchase and the date of their sale.

[30] The average yields mentioned in the text above were computed from figures given in Tables 1, 5, 6, 7, 8, and 9. The figures from which the average of the rates charged by commercial banks on direct loans to customers was estimated are given in Table 4. Comparisons of prime commercial paper rates with rates charged customers by banks in thirty-six leading cities, with rates on prime bankers' bills and New York Stock Exchange call and time loans, and with yields on Liberty and Treasury bonds and sixty high-grade corporation and municipal bonds, are shown by Charts IV, V, and VI, respectively. The figures plotted on these charts, however, would have to be adjusted in the manner indicated in the text above before the net yields on other earning assets of commercial banks could be compared with the net return on open-market paper. Hence the three charts do not make possible any

Thus over a period of some years high-grade commercial paper has proved to be not only one of the safest and most liquid but also one of the most remunerative investments in which commercial banks have placed their loanable funds.

The fact that they are issued with convenient denominations and maturities constitutes a fourth advantage of open-market notes as an investment for such funds. By selecting outside paper in varying amounts and with varying maturities, banks which need relatively large amounts of liquid resources at certain seasons of the year can arrange to have notes maturing at such times in the required amounts. They can thus keep surplus funds profitably employed until needed for meeting increased demands for cash on the part of depositors or for credit on the part of their own borrowing customers, and they can rest assured that the funds required for such purposes are practically certain to be available when needed.[31]

Two indirect advantages which commercial banks derive from investing surplus funds in outside paper are also of some importance. The first of these indirect advantages is that the purchase of open-market obligations sometimes facilitates the acquisition of profitable new accounts. A number of banks, in fact, have in recent years bought commercial paper with the express purpose of endeavoring to induce the issuing concerns to open accounts with them at some later date.[32] Moreover, the banks which customarily

---

accurate comparison of the net yield received by banks on commercial paper with the net returns received on other classes of their earning assets. The comparison of the yield on open-market notes with that on bankers' bills which can be made with the aid of Chart V is approximately accurate; but the commercial paper and acceptance rates plotted on this chart are only those on prime notes, with maturities ranging from sixty days to six months, and prime bankers' bills with a maturity of ninety days.

[31] It should be noted, however, that no great number of banks can make use of open-market loans as a means of adjusting their cash position in the manner indicated in years when the available supply of commercial paper is so small as it has been since about the end of 1930.

[32] Other things being equal, banks prefer to extend direct loans to borrowing concerns, rather than purchase open-market obligations issued by the latter, for they can generally charge somewhat higher rates on direct loans to their own customers than those at which the same borrowers can obtain credit in the open market, and only their own customers maintain balances with them.

buy open-market notes are those which have the closest contacts with commercial paper houses, and such contacts are sometimes of value in enabling city banks to secure desirable new accounts. For concerns which borrow in the market occasionally find it advisable to establish additional banking connections, and in such cases dealers are in a position to recommend that the new connections be established with banks to which they sell open-market paper. The second of the two indirect advantages referred to above is that in investigating the credit standing of concerns which borrow in the open market bankers acquire a training and experience which is often of considerable value in enabling them to appraise the risks involved in extending credits to their own customers.[33]

[33] The main advantages of open-market paper as an investment for the funds of other classes of buyers than banking institutions are its safety, its relatively attractive yield, and its convenient denominations and maturities. It is somewhat less liquid from the point of view of these other classes of buyers than from the standpoint of commercial banks, for it can be rediscounted by the latter more readily than by any other class of buyers.

CHAPTER IX

DISTRIBUTION OF COMMERCIAL PAPER

THE advantages of outside paper both as an investment for their secondary reserves and as an outlet for their surplus loanable funds are now recognized by bankers in all sections of the country, and many banks purchase relatively large amounts of open-market notes each year of their own accord. In marketing such obligations, however, as well as in originating their stock in trade, dealers take the initiative, instead of waiting for prospective customers to come to them.[1] The practices they follow in placing open-market paper with the banks which are their main buying customers will be indicated in the present chapter.

1. SELLING METHODS OF DEALERS

Distribution of commercial paper is effected mainly through the main offices of dealers. Houses which maintain, in addition to their main offices, one or more branches, correspondent connections, and/or sales representatives, of course use these other agencies also for the same purpose. Stocks of paper are carried mainly at main offices. To facilitate prompt delivery of paper to their buying customers, however, houses which maintain branch as well as main offices generally carry inventories of open-market notes at one or more of their branches also — particularly at branches which are authorized to originate such obligations.[2]

Practically all dealers make use of four different methods of distribution: selling through personal solicitation of salesmen, by telephone, by telegraph, and by mail.

[1] A comparatively small Philadelphia house, which succeeded a firm established in 1866, reported in 1930 that it had never employed salesmen to call on prospective buying customers. Somewhat later in the same year this house retired from business. Its failure to show greater initiative in its selling methods was no doubt at least partly responsible for a considerable decline in its business during the years immediately preceding 1931.

[2] Instead of sending open-market notes which they have originated or purchased to the main offices of their organizations, branch offices of the latter class may, with the approval of the main offices concerned, sell an entire issue of such notes to customers in their own territory.

The main offices of all dealers serve as headquarters for a staff of salesmen who call on banks in the sales territory assigned to such offices. In the case of houses which maintain one or more branch offices, each of these branches is assigned a sales territory of its own, and maintains its own staff of salesmen. Whether connected with a branch office or with the main office of their organization, salesmen as a rule call on both city and country banks, though a few salesmen connected with the main offices of some of the larger houses have within recent years sold paper exclusively in the cities in which such main offices are located. At least some regular salesmen of a number of houses which deal in long-term securities as well as open-market notes, and also one or more sales representatives of some of the houses which have used the services of such representatives,[3] have in recent years sold bonds or other securities in addition to commercial paper. Besides selling open-market obligations to banks in the territory assigned to them, salesmen of a number of houses, including both large and small organizations, also solicit new borrowing accounts in the same territory. In the case of other houses, the sales staff is considerably larger than the personnel entrusted with the responsibility of securing new accounts.[4]

Selling through personal solicitation of salesmen is probably the most effective method of distribution used by dealers, but it is also a relatively expensive method of placing open-market notes with their buying customers, particularly with country banks located in towns which are at some distance from their main offices and any branch offices they may maintain. Because of the active demand for outside paper as an investment for banks' funds, moreover, it has been relatively easy to market the limited supplies of open-market notes which have been available in recent years through

[3] As was stated in Chap. IV, sales representatives are to be distinguished from the regular salesmen who make the main office or some branch office of a commercial paper house their headquarters.

[4] In the case of some of the smaller houses, both the number of individuals who assume the responsibility of originating open-market notes and the selling staff may be very small. Thus in 1930 all buying in the case of at least three houses was being done by the head of the firm or by a single officer, and in the case of at least three other houses by no more than two or three officers or partners; and in the case of at least four houses practically all selling was being done either by the head of the firm or by no more than two or three officers or partners.

the other three methods of distribution mentioned above. For these reasons dealers have made greater use of these other methods since about 1925, and have relied somewhat less than formerly on personal solicitation by salesmen as a means of securing a broad distribution for the obligations of their borrowing customers. Selling by telephone is a method used extensively by all houses. The larger houses sell substantial amounts of paper each year by telegraph also. When open-market notes are offered for sale by wire, they are likely to be obligations of the highest grade, and the banks to which such notes are offered are likely to be institutions which are relatively large buyers of outside paper. These banks and others wishing to purchase such paper are permitted to telephone or telegraph orders at the expense of the selling house. The last of the methods of distribution mentioned above — selling by mail — is used more or less extensively by all the larger houses, particularly for placing paper with banks in towns or cities which are at some distance from their main offices and any branch offices they maintain. This method of distribution includes both selling by direct correspondence and selling through the issue of note offering lists. In 1930 a large Chicago house reported that it was circularizing some 14,000 banks periodically: some, every day; other active buyers, at least once a month; and the remaining banks, which included about one-half the total number, once every three months. Some years ago practically all dealers used to send note offering lists out to a large number of banks about once a week. In more recent years, however, because of the limited supplies of open-market paper available, such offering sheets have been sent out infrequently, and have listed a few selected "names" only.

2. Options Allowed in Connection with the Sale of Open-Market Paper

Practically all open-market notes handled by dealers are sold "on option." That is, banks which have purchased outside paper are generally given from a week to seventeen days to investigate the credit standing of the issuing concerns, and are allowed the option of either keeping such paper or returning it to the selling house before the expiration of the option period, in case they are not satisfied with the results of their credit inquiries, and receiving a check for the face amount less the discount to maturity.[5] Some such arrangement as this is practically necessary in connection with the sale of most paper except that issued by well-known concerns whose credit standing is unquestioned; for, if banks had to make their credit investigations before buying open-market notes, many of them would often find that obligations which they wished to purchase had already been sold to other buyers, and that consequently they had merely wasted their time in "checking" such paper.[6]

The length of the option periods allowed by dealers varies from about seven to seventeen days, depending on the distance of the buying bank from the selling house and the necessary sources of credit information. The most common period is ten days. Options running for more than ten days are as a rule granted only to Eastern banks buying paper issued by concerns in the Far West, or to Pacific Coast banks buying notes of Eastern borrowers. A few years ago the option period allowed in such cases was seventeen, twenty, or twenty-one days. In more recent years there has been a tendency, even in such cases, to shorten option periods so far as possible. Thus in the summer of 1933 one of the largest houses in the country was as a rule allowing options running for not more than ten days even in connection with sales of Pacific Coast paper to Eastern banks, and Eastern paper to banks in the Far West, and another leading dealer was allowing an option period of not more than fourteen days in such cases. Occasionally dealers are willing to extend their usual option periods for a few days, but

[5] The discount rates at which dealers buy back returned notes in such cases are the same as those at which such obligations were purchased by the banks concerned.

[6] As was pointed out in Chap. IV, when a dealer buys paper from a correspondent, the buying house is allowed an option similar to those customarily granted to banks which purchase open-market notes. If for any reason it is unable to sell to its own customers paper which it has bought outright from a correspondent, the buying house sells such paper back to the issuing house. The buying house may also rediscount notes with the originating house if the latter wishes to repurchase paper with a view to selling it to its own customers.

as a rule extensions are granted only when they appear to be warranted by special circumstances.[7]

When buying notes issued by concerns whose paper they have recently held, or by large companies whose credit standing is unusually strong, banks may not ask for the options customarily allowed by dealers. In most cases, however, the majority of banks do ask for the usual options.[8] It is understood by the purchasers of open-market notes that options are allowed for the purpose of credit investigation only, and that purchased paper is not to be returned to the selling house by the buyer unless the results of the latter's investigation of the credit standing of the issuing concern prove unsatisfactory.[9] Most banks at present are careful to observe the terms of option agreements, but even in recent years some banks have either shown carelessness in this matter or deliberately abused the option privilege.[10]

[7] Banks sometimes ask to have options extended when concerns whose paper they have purchased are about ready to issue new financial statements. As a rule, however, dealers do not grant extensions for the purpose of allowing buying customers to examine statements which have not yet been issued. Even if such extensions were granted as a matter of course, the buying banks in the great majority of cases would no doubt decide to keep the paper in question.

[8] A St. Louis house reported in 1930 that the larger city banks always do, while country banks often do not, ask for options, and that some country banks to which it sells open-market paper ask for no options at all.

[9] The terms of option agreements are customarily printed or stamped on the dealer's bill of sale. The following is the form of agreement used by a leading New England house: "This option is given and accepted with the understanding that paper returned under its provision is to be for adverse credit reasons only. The above notes *if unmarked* may be returned by giving notice to our office during banking hours on or before the dates as specified against each note on this bill."

[10] Some years ago failure on the part of buying banks to observe the terms of option agreements was a by no means uncommon practice. According to former Boston dealers, abuse of the option privilege by banks in New York and St. Louis was particularly common. One Boston house discontinued selling open-market paper to certain banks in the latter city because of their persistent failure to observe the terms of option agreements. A New York dealer reported in 1930 that certain Southern banks used to buy open-market notes from his organization with the express purpose of investing surplus funds in such obligations for the duration of the option periods only. Since the house in question realized that these banks were buying outside paper for the purpose mentioned, it was in effect selling such paper to them with a repurchase agreement. Abuse of the option privilege by other banks has been most common in periods of rising money rates. By returning open-market notes in such periods, banks which are not overscrupulous about observing the terms of option agreements can sometimes reinvest at somewhat higher rates the

3. Allotting Open-Market Paper to Prospective Buyers

Some fifteen years ago the problem of finding a market for all the commercial paper they were able to originate was regarded by dealers as more difficult than that of securing an adequate supply of open-market obligations. In more recent years the situation has been reversed: the credit requirements of concerns using the open market have declined to a considerable extent, whereas the demand for outside paper as an investment for banks' funds has remained very active, and dealers have consequently experienced much greater difficulty in originating than in marketing commercial paper. During the greater part of the period since about the beginning of 1926, in fact, they have been unable to meet the demands of their buying customers for open-market notes.

Under these circumstances, instead of endeavoring to supply each individual bank with as much outside paper as it wishes to purchase, a number of the leading houses have followed the policy of apportioning such limited supplies of short-term notes as they have been able to secure from their borrowing customers among a large number of banks.[11] It is of course easier and less expensive to dispose of open-market paper by selling it to a comparatively small number of banks in as large blocks as they wish to purchase than by distributing it in smaller amounts among a larger number of buyers. On the other hand, dealers realize that the best interests of their borrowing clients require that the market for obligations issued by the latter shall be broad and continuous, and that

---

funds which were previously invested in outside paper. The dealer, on the other hand, agrees to repurchase returned notes at the rates at which he sold such obligations to the buying bank. Consequently, unless he is willing to carry the returned notes to maturity, which it is not his function to do, he may have to sell them at rates higher than those at which he bought them. In the latter case he will of course incur a loss varying with the differences between his buying and selling rates and the maturities of the notes returned.

As was pointed out in Chap. III, certain recommendations with respect to the policies which dealers should follow in the matter of allowing options were made early in 1926 by the Commercial Credits Committee of the Investment Bankers' Association of America. (See pp. 196–197.)

[11] The houses in question first apportion stocks of paper among their various offices and/or correspondents, and the latter in turn make allotments to their buying customers.

they can maintain such a market more effectively over a period of years if, at times when available supplies of their stock in trade are insufficient to meet the demands therefor, they allot paper in relatively small amounts to a large number of buyers. Though some banks dislike to go to the trouble and expense of maintaining credit files on companies whose obligations can be purchased in small amounts only, the policy of allotting open-market notes wins the goodwill of the majority of buyers of such obligations, for it enables dealers to supply a large number of banks with at least some paper and to treat all their buying customers alike. Hence the latter are willing to buy larger amounts of outside paper at times when the demand for open-market notes is comparatively light than they would purchase if dealers did not follow the policy of allotting such obligations at times when available supplies of commercial paper are relatively smaller.[12]

4. Price Policies of Dealers

Dealers sell all the open-market notes they handle on a discount basis. Accordingly, the prices at which they offer such obligations for sale are always equal to the face amounts thereof less the discount to maturity, and vary inversely with the rates of discount at which they are willing to sell open-market paper.

The rates, and therefore the prices, at which they offer to sell their borrowing customers' obligations, depend partly on conditions in the short-term money market and partly on their appraisal of the credit standing of the issuing concerns. In all cases they endeavor to secure the highest possible prices for the paper they

[12] A Boston house adopted the policy of allotting open-market notes to its buying customers as early as 1922. So far as practicable, this house apportions such obligations among its customers on a *pro rata* basis. Thus at a time when banks are ordering about twice as much outside paper as it is able to supply it allots each bank only about half the amount of such paper the latter wishes to purchase. According to an officer of this house, its allotment policy enabled it to increase the proportion of its sales to total sales by dealers both in 1929 and in 1931. In 1929, when many banks were not buying outside paper at all, it had a broader market for its borrowing customers' obligations than it would have had if it had not followed the policy of allotting paper in the years preceding; and consequently a number of its customers were willing to borrow larger amounts of funds in the market in 1931, when dealers found it very difficult to secure open-market paper, than they would have borrowed otherwise.

handle, or, in other words, to enable their customers to borrow in the market on the most favorable terms possible. Ordinarily they offer to sell open-market paper which they buy outright at the same rates as those at which they purchase it, and to sell notes of the same concern at the same rate in all markets at any given time.

There are exceptions, however, to both of these rules. Exceptions to the first rule occur in cases in which dealers buy paper at a flat or net rate, without commission; and exceptions to both rules as a result of changes in short-term money rates and of bargaining between dealers and banks with regard to the former's selling rates. In cases in which they buy paper at a flat or net rate, dealers try to sell such paper at a rate at least somewhat lower than their buying rate, and thus make at least a small selling profit in compensation for relinquishing their usual commission. Moreover, they sometimes find it possible to sell open-market notes at rates lower than their buying rates because of changes in conditions in short-term money markets, though for the same reason they also find it necessary at other times to sell paper at rates higher than those at which they purchased it. Exceptions to the second rule as a result of changes in money rates occur in cases in which such rates change in an important financial center like New York, but do not immediately spread to certain other centers. In such cases dealers sometimes sell notes of the same concern at slightly different rates in different markets at the same time. The more important markets for commercial paper are all so closely connected at present, however, and competition in the commercial paper business is so active, that changes in rates on open-market obligations in a leading financial center like New York are likely to spread rather rapidly to other centers.[13] Exceptions to the two rules in question as a result of bargaining between dealers and banks with regard to the former's selling rates are no doubt less

[13] A San Francisco house reported in 1930, however, that it has sometimes continued to sell paper at rates below those prevailing in New York for nearly a week after rates in the latter city have risen. Some time is required, of course, for the main offices of commercial paper houses to notify their branch offices of changes in rates. Hence the same house may for a short time sell the same paper in different cities at slightly different rates.

common now than they were some years ago, but nevertheless still occur from time to time. Thus in case a leading Chicago bank should offer to buy at 3⅞ per cent paper which a Boston house had purchased, and was currently selling, at 3¾ per cent, the Boston house might accept the offer, provided it had not previously sold the Chicago bank any open-market notes issued by the same concern and was especially interested in broadening the market for the paper in question by placing some of it with that particular bank. Transactions of this sort — known as "trades" — of course involve a "splitting" of the dealer's commission with the buying bank. Partly for this reason, such "trades" are likely to be made only in special cases and only in connection with the sale of notes for which the demand is less active than that for prime paper.[14]

[14] In some cases notes of concerns which have used the services of two or more dealers concurrently have been sold at different rates by these dealers not only in different markets but also in the same market. Even individual houses have occasionally sold the same paper at different rates in the same market on the same day. Instances of the latter sort are rare, however, for dealers prefer so far as possible to offer the same notes at the same rates to all buyers in the same market, and of course all their buying customers prefer to be treated alike. In some cases selling the same paper at different rates in the same market on the same day is practically unavoidable. Thus in 1930 a dealer sold some notes of one of his borrowing customers to a New York bank at 4 per cent, but later in the day found it necessary, in order to "move" the obligations of the issuing concern, to sell the same paper to another New York bank at 4¼ per cent. The first bank found out later that the second bank had purchased this paper at 4¼ per cent. It thereupon insisted on receiving a "refund" of ¼ of 1 per cent on its own purchase, though the dealer had bought the paper in question to sell at 4 per cent, and had sold part of it at a slightly higher rate only because under the circumstances he had found it necessary to do so.

CHAPTER X

PRACTICES FOLLOWED BY BANKS IN SELECTING AND BUYING OUTSIDE PAPER

THE practices followed by dealers in purchasing open-market notes from their borrowing customers were considered in Chapter VII, and their practices in placing such obligations with the commercial banks which are their main buying customers in Chapter IX. In order to complete the account, which was begun in the earlier and continued in the later of these two chapters, of the manner in which commercial paper is bought and sold in the open market, the practices followed by banks in selecting and buying outside paper will be described in the present chapter.

1. SELECTING OUTSIDE PAPER

In selecting open-market obligations for purchase, different banks show preferences for somewhat different classes of paper.

All buying customers of dealers, to be sure, endeavor to select obligations which will be paid promptly at maturity, but by no means all banks confine their purchases to notes given a "prime" rating. Most city banks, it is true, do show a preference for obligations of the latter class. Many country banks, on the other hand, follow the policy of buying "for rate," that is, of selecting classes of paper offering the highest yields. At least some city banks follow a policy which may be regarded as intermediate between the two just mentioned — namely, the policy of buying notes which, though not classed as "prime," are nevertheless practically as safe an investment as prime paper is, and at the same time offer yields as much as $\frac{1}{4}$ to $\frac{1}{2}$ of 1 per cent higher than those obtainable on obligations of the latter class. Carrying out such a policy successfully of course requires greater skill in credit analysis than buying merely prime paper or buying "for rate."

Most banks prefer to select notes which either are or within a relatively short time will be eligible for rediscount with the Federal

Reserve banks. The rates on such notes are ordinarily somewhat lower than those on non-eligible classes of paper, however, and consequently banks which buy "for rate" are likely to show a preference for obligations of the latter classes.

Practically all banks which buy open-market paper have to meet increased demands for cash on the part of depositors, as well as for credit on the part of borrowing customers, at certain seasons of the year. Hence they customarily select notes with the maturities and in the amounts best adapted to enabling them to meet, in part, at least, the increased demands made on their resources at such times.

Probably most banks which buy relatively large amounts of outside paper dislike to maintain credit files on companies which make but a limited use of the open market, and therefore prefer to select obligations of concerns whose paper may be purchased in substantial amounts each year. On the other hand, banks which purchase no more than one or two $5,000 notes of any one company in the course of an entire year show no particular preference for the notes of concerns which raise large amounts of short-term capital in the open market.

In order to diversify their loans, practically all the buying customers of dealers select at least some open-market paper issued by concerns engaged in lines of business different from those of their own customers, and located in different sections of the country. At the same time, bankers can more readily "check" notes issued by companies in their own locality than those of concerns located in other sections of the country, and hence often prefer to purchase obligations of the former class. Under certain conditions some banks will purchase open-market notes issued by their own customers, but as a rule most banks prefer to buy paper issued by concerns to which they do not make direct loans.[1]

[1] Probably the main reason why banks as a rule prefer to confine their purchases of outside paper for their own account to notes issued by concerns to which they do not make direct loans is that, if asked to extend a direct loan to a company whose open-market paper they already held, they might not be able to grant the accommodation requested without increasing their total loans to this concern to an amount in excess of its line of credit. In such cases, moreover, it might be impossible to grant the loan requested without violating provisions of banking laws limiting the amount of credit that may be advanced to any one borrower. Never-

The methods which banks use in selecting outside paper also differ to a certain extent. A large number of the buying customers of dealers, indeed, can scarcely be said to have used any method of selecting open-market notes in recent years at all, for some banks have left the selection of such obligations entirely to dealers,[2] many others have depended on correspondent banks to buy outside paper for them,[3] and some member banks have even had Federal

---

theless some banks occasionally do buy for their own account open-market notes issued by their own customers, particularly if they can make sure that the latter will not need to make any extensive use of their bank lines before the maturity of the open-market obligations in question; and city banks often purchase notes of their own customers for the account of country correspondents. In cases in which they do buy for their own account open-market notes issued by their own customers, the rates which banks receive on such obligations are generally somewhat lower than those at which they would be willing to make direct loans to the issuing concerns. Hence they would generally prefer to extend credit to such companies directly, rather than indirectly through purchasing their notes in the open market. At least one commercial paper house will not sell open-market notes issued by its customers to banks with which the borrowing concerns have direct lines of credit, unless it first secures its customers' consent and unless it is distinctly understood that the purchase of such paper will not reduce the issuing concern's line of direct credit with the buying bank.

[2] In such cases dealers customarily select high-grade paper for their buying customers. Banks have probably incurred no losses at all on notes which dealers have selected for them in recent years.

[3] Country banks in all sections of the country have for years depended on city correspondents to purchase open-market notes for them. The practice of depending on correspondent banks for this service apparently is less common in the Boston, New York, and Philadelphia Federal Reserve districts than in other sections of the country, and is probably becoming somewhat less common in all Federal Reserve districts.

A country bank wishing to purchase open-market notes through a city correspondent may merely state the amount of paper it wants to buy and leave the selection thereof entirely to the city bank; or it may specify the rates, denominations, and maturities it prefers, in addition to the amount it wishes to invest in outside paper. Some years ago a large bank in New York used to buy open-market notes in advance of the demands of its country correspondents for such obligations, in order to make sure it would have enough paper on hand when the latter banks wanted it. Certain other city banks have followed the same practice in more recent years.

City banks which select outside paper for country correspondents always buy such paper for the "account and risk" of the latter. They nevertheless select open-market notes for their correspondents as carefully as they buy paper for their own account. Performing this service for their correspondents of course involves extra work and expense on the part of the larger city banks. For this reason New York City banks are said to have made a charge of ⅛ of 1 per cent, from about 1920 to about 1924, for buying paper for the account of correspondent banks. In more recent years, however, city banks have performed the service in question without charge.

At least some country banks in all sections of the country have within recent

Reserve banks purchase such paper for their account.[4] A number of country banks which have purchased open-market notes on their own account have nevertheless depended on their city correspondents to "check" such obligations for them, instead of attempting to conduct any careful credit investigations of their own. Both city banks and country banks which do their own "checking" often buy certain classes of outside paper without any very careful credit investigation — for instance, prime unsecured paper issued by nationally known trading and manufacturing concerns, and secured obligations of the same grade issued by grain elevator companies and grain commission houses in the Northwest. As a rule, however, banks which themselves "check" the commercial paper they purchase base their selection of all notes issued by concerns whose obligations they have not previously held, or by other companies on which they do not have up-to-date credit files, on a careful investigation of the credit standing of the issuing concern. The methods of credit investigation used by these banks in connection with the purchase of such classes of paper will be indicated in the following section.

2. Methods of Credit Investigation Used by Banks

The main purpose of the credit investigations on which banks base the selection of the outside paper they purchase is of course to make sure that such paper is reasonably certain to be paid at maturity. The information they require for this purpose is essentially the same, though as a rule it need not be so detailed, as that on which dealers base their own selection of open-market obligations. The methods which they use in securing such information are also similar to those employed by dealers.

---

years depended on their city correspondents not only to select open-market notes for them but also to maintain a market for such paper by repurchasing it from them; and some banks of the same class have sold purchased paper back to the houses from which they bought it. Occasionally country banks, instead of rediscounting outside paper with correspondent banks or dealers, offer open-market notes as collateral for loans they obtain from the banks which bought these notes for their account and risk.

[4] H. P. Willis and W. H. Steiner, *Federal Reserve Banking Practice*, pp. 103, 107–108.

The credit information which dealers collect was considered at some length in Chapter VII. Since banks require essentially the same data as a basis for their selection of outside paper, this information need not be described in detail again. Some of the more important data which bankers generally consider it advisable to secure before deciding whether or not to invest loanable funds in the open-market notes of any particular company (or to keep notes already purchased "on option"), however, may be summarized at this point. Such information can be indicated most concisely by listing some of the more important questions raised by banks when investigating the credit standing of a concern whose notes they may wish to purchase (or have already bought "on option") in the open market. The following are questions of this class:

Are general business conditions in the trade territory served by the borrowing company favorable at present? Are they likely to remain favorable during the next few months? Has the present management of the company demonstrated its ability? Is the integrity of its managing officers beyond question? Is the company's financial condition satisfactory? What proportion of its accounts and notes receivable are really collectible and are likely to be collected within the next few months? On what basis is its inventory valued? How are its fixed assets valued? Are any of its assets pledged as security for loans or any other liabilities? Does it carry adequate insurance on its plant, machinery, etc.? What lines of credit is it allowed by trade creditors? Does it pay its trade obligations promptly, and take the best trade discounts offered? What lines of bank credit does it have, what is the total amount of its bank lines which are really open and available, and what amount is it borrowing from its own banks at present? Is it considered a good credit risk by all these banks? What is the amount of its open-market notes payable at present? What was its maximum debt during its last fiscal period? Its minimum debt? On what date was its debt at a maximum? At a minimum? What is its present net worth? Are its open-market loans self-liquidating? Are its open-market notes eligible for rediscount with Federal Reserve banks? Is there any difference between the notes it gives its own banks and its open-market obligations with regard to indorsement, guarantee, or security? Does it discount its "receivables"? Has it any other class of contingent liabilities? What were its sales, expenses, net profits, and dividends during the last few years? Are its balance sheet and operating statement figures audited by a reliable firm of accountants? Are simultaneous audits of its subsidiary and/or affiliated companies, if any, available? Is it planning any expansion in the near future? [5]

In some cases bankers are in a position to secure credit information relating to open-market borrowers by means of personal interviews with officers of such concerns. They cannot, however, maintain with companies whose notes they purchase through dealers the close personal contacts which they establish with their own customers, unless they are willing to buy open-market obligations issued by the latter. In most cases, therefore, they find it necessary to secure through other means than personal interviews the data on which they base their selection of outside paper. If they purchase notes handled by the larger commercial paper houses, they are generally able to obtain from the latter all the information they really need for purposes of credit investigation, including audited balance sheets and operating statements as of the most recent statement dates and other pertinent financial data.[6] They nevertheless customarily supplement such data with information obtained through certain other sources, such as the borrowing concern's banks of deposit, other banks in the same locality, one or more of their own correspondent banks, concerns from which the borrowing company purchases raw materials, supplies, or the merchandise it handles, and concerns which are competitors of the borrower. They may also use the services of credit-reporting

[5] Some of the larger city banks in recent years have recorded information secured by such questions as the foregoing on credit questionnaire forms similar to those used by dealers. Like the latter, however, banks make less use of such questionnaire forms at present than was customary some years ago.

[6] In case they are contemplating the purchase of notes handled by a commercial paper house with which they have had no previous dealings, bankers may consider it advisable first to make sure that the selling house shows care and good judgment in selecting the paper it handles, and has sufficient financial responsibility to repurchase any notes that may be returned to it under the customary option agreement.

agencies, particularly those of the National Credit Office of New York, which specializes in reporting on the credit standing of companies whose notes are sold in the market. Such services are of course of more value to banks in the smaller towns and cities than to the larger city banks.

Banks of the latter class subject to careful analysis the balance sheets and operating statements which they customarily secure from dealers. The methods which their credit departments use in analyzing financial data are practically the same as those used by the credit departments of commercial paper houses. Their credit analyses in most cases are likely to be somewhat less thorough and detailed than those of the larger commercial paper houses, however, partly because they are interested primarily in the ability of companies whose notes they have purchased to meet such obligations at maturity, and therefore in the financial condition of the issuing concerns in the near future; whereas dealers are interested in establishing enduring connections with their borrowing customers, and therefore in selecting for purchase, so far as possible, paper issued by companies which are likely to be able to maintain over a period of years the high credit standing required for borrowing in the market. Bankers nevertheless consider, just as dealers do, the trends shown by the balance sheet and operating statement figures of concerns whose credit standing they are investigating. They often take into account also the trends shown by certain ratios which may be computed from these figures and used as a basis for judging the efficiency with which the affairs of such companies are being managed. Like dealers, moreover, they may find it to their advantage in certain cases to compare balance sheet and operating statement figures of these concerns, as well as selected financial ratios computed from such figures, with similar figures which are published each year by the Robert Morris Associates.[7]

[7] The Robert Morris Associates is the name of a corporation "of the first class not for profit" which was organized under the laws of Pennsylvania in 1919 (*The Robert Morris Associates — A Brief History* — pamphlet — p. 9). The membership of the Associates is composed mainly of commercial banks and bankers, but includes a number of commercial paper houses also.

The Associates publish each year "common size" balance sheets for more than 100 different industries and trades; nine selected ratio figures for each of about 100

3. OTHER PRACTICES FOLLOWED BY BANKS IN BUYING COMMERCIAL PAPER

It has already been pointed out that banks may purchase outside paper for secondary reserve purposes, as a temporary investment for surplus funds which they cannot advantageously employ in direct advances to their own customers, or primarily for the purpose of securing desirable new deposit and borrowing accounts; that different banks select different classes of open-market notes and use different methods of selecting such obligations; that, while many banks ordinarily buy relatively large amounts of outside paper each year of their own accord, others allow the dealer to take the initiative in finding a market for the obligations he handles; and that banks customarily buy open-market notes "on

---

different lines of business; and "common size" profit and loss statements for a limited number of different industries and trades.

The manner in which the "common size" balance sheets are prepared is as follows: Balance sheets of a number of companies in the same industry or trade are secured; all similar items of each class shown on these financial statements are added together to make a single consolidated or composite balance sheet; and each item on the consolidated statement is then expressed as a percentage of the total assets shown on that statement. The resulting composite percentage balance sheet is called a "common size statement" (*ibid.*, p. 23).

The nine ratio figures mentioned above are as follows: The ratio of current assets to current liabilities, of net worth to fixed assets, of net worth to total debt, of sales to "receivables," of sales to merchandise inventory, of sales to fixed assets, of sales to net worth, of profits to sales, and of profits to net worth. These ratios are computed from consolidated balance sheet figures and consolidated figures for sales and profits. If a comparatively large number of companies are included in any particular industry or trade whose figures are analyzed, the nine ratios are computed for each of these companies separately, the resulting figures are tabulated, and the quartile and median figures for each of the nine ratios are given (*ibid.*, p. 24).

In a few cases in which figures for a large number of companies are available, "common size" profit and loss statements are published. These are composite percentage statements prepared in the same manner as the "common size" balance sheets.

The number of companies included in the different lines of business whose figures are analyzed varies to a considerable extent. In some cases it is so small that significant comparisons can hardly be made between the figures for any one company in a particular trade or industry and those for the entire group of companies included in the same line of business. The number of concerns included in each line of business is stated, however, and any necessary allowances can therefore be made when figures for any one company are being compared with those for a group of companies in the same industry or trade.

option." Certain other practices which they follow in purchasing commercial paper will now be indicated.

Ordinarily the amounts of outside paper which banks purchase vary with business conditions, being largest in years when business is active and commodity prices are relatively high and smallest in years when business activity is at a low level and prices are comparatively low. This relation between business conditions and banks' purchases of open-market notes is hardly to be explained in terms of changes in the total demand for such obligations on the part of dealers' buying customers, however, for there is practically always an active demand for high-grade commercial paper, irrespective of prevailing business conditions. The reason for the relation in question is, rather, that available supplies of such obligations ordinarily are considerably larger in years when business is active and prices are relatively high than in years when the opposite conditions prevail.[8]

In various sections of the country in which agriculture is one of the most important industries, banks' purchases of open-market notes show certain seasonal fluctuations. Thus purchases by certain banks in Maine are likely to reach a maximum after the potato crop has been marketed in the fall; the demand for outside paper by banks in the Minneapolis Federal Reserve district is generally most active from August through November, after grain and other agricultural staples of that district have been sold; purchases by

[8] Banks' purchases of open-market notes declined considerably in 1928 and 1929, though business activity was above normal during the greater part of both these years. Because of the fact that unusually high yields could be obtained on New York Stock Exchange call and time loans in 1928 and 1929, the demand for outside paper on the part of many banks decreased, to some extent at least, in these two years. The main reason for the decline in banks' purchases of open-market notes in 1928 and 1929, however, was the fact that in both these years the supplies of such obligations which dealers were able to secure from their borrowing customers decreased to a considerable extent.

It has already been pointed out that banks' purchases of commercial paper have decreased considerably during financial crises, partly because at such times demands for accommodation on the part of their own customers have been unusually heavy. According to a Boston dealer, however, certain banks which at other times purchase but little outside paper buy relatively large amounts of open-market notes in periods of business uncertainty, as a means of keeping a larger proportion of their earning assets in a highly liquid condition.

certain banks in the Kansas City Federal Reserve district ordinarily are largest in July and August, after the wheat crop has been marketed; and the demand for open-market paper by country banks in Texas is generally most active in the fall, after the cotton crop has been sold. Purchases by banks in other Southern states, and by certain banks in the St. Louis Federal Reserve district, also show a seasonal tendency.[9]

In such sections of the country the amounts of outside paper which many banks purchase depend to a large extent on the size of the crops and the prices of the leading agricultural staples. Thus purchases by certain banks in the Kansas City Federal Reserve district decline considerably in years in which the wheat crop in that district fails, banks in southern Louisiana are said to buy but little open-market paper except in years when the "sugar crop" is good, and purchases by certain banks in Texas and other Southern states are largest in years in which the cotton crop is good and the price of cotton is relatively high.

In regions in which industry is more diversified and agriculture is relatively less important, purchases of open-market notes are less subject to seasonal influences. When they *are* "in the market," the larger city banks, and even country banks in New England, New York, Pennsylvania, and certain parts of the Middle West tend to buy outside paper more or less continuously. According to a Boston dealer, banks in Idaho, Oregon, and Washington have also bought such paper continuously in recent years. Purchases by banks in such regions as these fluctuate mainly with changes in general business conditions and conditions in the money market.

The data which would be required in order to determine whether or not, over a period of years, the larger city banks buy open-market notes more continuously than country banks, are not available. It might at first be supposed that purchases by city banks would be the more continuous. It is true that purchases by such

[9] Other examples of seasonal purchases of outside paper by banks in districts in which agriculture is an important industry are given in "The Commercial Paper Business," *Fed. Res. Bull.*, Aug. 1921, pp. 922–923.

Purchases by certain banks in Florida and California also show seasonal variations, reaching a maximum at times when the "tourist trade" is most active.

banks are less subject to seasonal influences than those of country banks, and a number of city banks have bought outside paper more or less continuously for some years. On the other hand, purchases of country banks from at least several of the larger commercial paper houses have been more continuous over periods of some years than those of city banks. In any case, as was pointed out in Chapter VIII, city banks ordinarily buy open-market notes most actively in periods when commercial paper rates are relatively low, whereas purchases by country banks are generally largest in periods when rates are comparatively high.

4. Paying for Outside Paper and Collecting Payment of Open-Market Notes at Maturity

Banks which have purchased open-market paper arrange to have it forwarded to them either directly from the dealer or indirectly through some correspondent bank to which the dealer makes delivery.

Like dealers themselves, banks use several different methods of paying for the notes they purchase. In case the buying bank is located in the same city as the selling office of the dealer, payment is most commonly made by a cashier's check or by a credit to the account of the dealer if the latter has an account with the bank concerned.[10] In case the buyer is an out-of-town bank, payment is commonly made by exchange on the city in which the dealer's selling office is located, or on some other financial center, by a cashier's check on the buying bank or on a correspondent bank located in the same city as the dealer's selling office, or by a credit to the account of the dealer if he has an account with such a correspondent bank.[11] If the correspondent bank gives its own check to the dealer, or credits his account, it of course charges the account of the buying bank with the amount involved.

In some cases open-market notes are made payable at the office

---

[10] Payment in cases of this sort has also been made by drafts and by cash; and, in Philadelphia, by "due bills" payable at the Philadelphia Clearing House one day after issued, but treated as cash by banks in that city.

[11] Checks on Federal Reserve banks are also used sometimes by out-of-town member banks as a means of payment for purchased paper.

of the commercial paper house through which they are sold. In such cases payment of maturing notes is of course collected from the selling house itself. Most open-market paper, however, is made payable at some bank in New York or in some other leading financial center. Hence in most cases payment is collected from a designated bank. Maturing obligations can of course be presented for collection directly by the holding banks if the latter are located in the same city as the office of the selling house or the bank at which such paper is payable. If the holding banks are located in other cities, they customarily forward maturing notes to their correspondent banks in the centers in which such obligations are payable. Their correspondent banks then collect payment for the forwarding banks and credit the accounts of the latter for the amounts collected.

CHAPTER XI

FINANCIAL POLICIES OF DEALERS

IN THE present chapter the compensation received by dealers for marketing the obligations of their borrowing customers, the manner in which they finance their operations in open-market paper, and certain related financial policies which they follow will be considered.

1. COMPENSATION RECEIVED BY DEALERS FOR HANDLING OPEN-MARKET PAPER

For handling the open-market obligations of their borrowing customers, dealers have for years followed the policy of charging a commission of ¼ of 1 per cent of the face amount of such paper. This commission or "service charge," as it is sometimes called, is customarily deducted, together with the discount, at the time when the dealer remits payment for notes which he has purchased. Since it is paid by the borrowing concern, it increases the cost of borrowing in the market by an equivalent amount. In many cases, though not in all, the rate of commission charged remains the same, irrespective of the maturity of open-market paper. In such cases, therefore, the shorter the maturity of such paper, the greater the cost of borrowing in the market. For this reason, borrowing concerns, other things being equal, find it to their advantage to issue notes with maturities of six months or longer, whereas dealers of course find it most profitable to handle paper with shorter maturities.

Though ¼ of 1 per cent may be regarded as the customary service charge for handling open-market notes, the rate of commission which dealers receive for marketing such obligations in practice is by no means uniform. In fact, it may be fully twice as high, or less than one-half as high, as ¼ of 1 per cent, the rate actually charged being dependent in many cases on the comparative bargaining power of the dealer and his borrowing customers.

In 1920, because of increasing costs of distribution, certain dealers raised their commission charge to ½ of 1 per cent.[1] In at least some cases, however, these dealers no doubt found it necessary later on to reduce their charge to the rate they had previously received. During a part of the period from 1920 to 1930 several dealers used a sliding scale of commission charges. In such cases the commission varied either with the maturity or with the amounts of the paper they handled for certain of their customers.[2] In 1929 two houses in the Middle West raised the commission they were charging certain of their clients — comparatively small companies or other concerns whose obligations it was relatively difficult to market —to ⅜ or ½ of 1 per cent. After the decline in commercial paper rates which took place later in the same year, however, one of these two houses reduced the rate it charged such customers to ¼ of 1 per cent, and the other in a number of cases lowered its charge to the same figure. In the fall of 1930 the latter

---

[1] Federal Reserve Bank of New York, *Report on Business Conditions*, June 30, 1920, p. 4; and "The Commercial Paper Business," *Fed. Res. Bull.*, Sept. 1921, p. 1055. In some cases a similar result was accomplished by the dealer's "insisting upon" maturities as short as three months (*ibid.*).

It will be recalled that the Commercial Credits Committee of the Investment Bankers' Association of America became interested in the matter of raising commissions in 1925, but in the following year abandoned "any concerted effort" to increase the charges which dealers were making for their services. (See pp. 193–196.)

As was pointed out in Chap. VI, dealers some years ago occasionally provided "revolving credits" for their borrowing customers, and in such cases commonly received an underwriting commission of 2 per cent, in addition to a selling commission of ½ of 1 per cent of the amounts of paper actually issued by their clients. (See n. 19, pp. 250–251.)

[2] As late as 1925 a Southern dealer was using the following scale of commission charges for handling four-months' paper issued by a Chicago packing company:

1/16 of 1 per cent on the first $250,000.

⅛ of 1 per cent on the second $250,000.

¼ of 1 per cent on the third $250,000.

⅜ of 1 per cent on an issue of $1,000,000 or more.

According to this dealer, another house in a different section of the country used the same scale of charges for handling the paper of the same company.

A New York house as late as 1929 used the following scale of charges for marketing the obligations of one of its customers:

¼ of 1 per cent on 3-months' paper.

5/16 of 1 per cent on 4-months' paper.

⅜ of 1 per cent on 5-months' paper.

½ of 1 per cent on 6-months' paper.

house was still charging certain of its customers rates as high as ⅜ to ½ of 1 per cent, and two affiliated houses, one in New York and one in San Francisco, were charging a fairly large proportion of their customers the same rates. Various other dealers were also charging rates as high as ⅜ to ½ of 1 per cent for handling the paper of certain of their clients, particularly finance companies and concerns of comparatively small size.[3] In the spring of 1936 at least four houses were likewise charging rates as high as ½ of 1 per cent for marketing notes issued by certain of their borrowing customers.

On the other hand, the compensation which dealers receive often amounts to less than ¼ of 1 per cent of their sales. It is generally less than the latter figure when paper is sold through a correspondent house, for in such cases the commission as a rule is divided equally between the two dealers concerned.[4] The rate charged "seasoned" open-market borrowers whose obligations are classed as prime paper is often no higher than ⅛ of 1 per cent. Occasionally rates of less than ¼ of 1 per cent are also charged for handling high-grade paper which is issued with maturities of four

---

[3] A New York house as late as 1928 was receiving a commission of ¾ of 1 per cent on its sales of a certain finance company's notes through its own offices, and ¼ of 1 per cent on sales of such paper through correspondent dealers. The obligations of this company were issued with maturities of nine months.

A Southern house reported in 1930 that it was sometimes able to sell finance companies' notes at rates ½ of 1 per cent below its buying rates. A rate differential of this amount on six-months' paper would make possible a trading profit which would be equal to a commission of ¼ of 1 per cent.

[4] For instance, the commissions received by a New England house on sales of $16,017,500 of open-market paper through its correspondents during the four years from 1926 to 1930 amounted approximately to $17,486, or about 0.11 per cent of such sales. Sales of this house through its own offices during the same period amounted to $98,931,900, on which its commissions were approximately $176,750, or about 0.18 per cent of the former figure. Its total sales were $114,949,400, and its total commissions approximately $194,236, or about 0.17 per cent of such sales. A correspondent house in the Middle West received an average commission of about 0.19 per cent, or $9.33 for each $5,000 note, on its total sales during the five years from 1925 to 1930. The average rate of commission received by the latter house on its total sales for the first six months of 1930 was about 0.17 per cent, or $8.40 for each $5,000 note. Since the dealer's regular service charge is 0.25 per cent, or $12.50 for each $5,000 note, the average rate of commission received by these houses on their total sales for the years mentioned amounted only to about three-fourths of the regular rate, and the average rate received by the New England house on sales through its correspondents to less than one-half of the latter rate.

months or shorter.[5] Moreover, as was pointed out in Chapter VII, some houses during the last few years have bought open-market notes at a net rate, without any commission charge, as commonly as at a stated rate plus commission. When they buy paper at a net rate, dealers of course endeavor to sell it at rates low enough to indemnify themselves for the loss of their regular commission, but as a rule any trading profit they are able to make on the sale of high-grade notes is likely to amount to less than the equivalent of a commission of ¼ of 1 per cent. Finally, even if they charge their borrowing customers the regular rate of ¼ of 1 per cent, the rate of compensation which dealers actually receive may amount to less than the regular rate; for they sometimes find it necessary to sell paper at rates higher than their buying rates,[6] and they may occasionally incur at least some losses on open-market obligations which are not paid promptly at maturity.

Thus the compensation actually received by dealers ranges from ⅛ of 1 per cent, or less, to ½ of 1 per cent of the total amount of open-market paper they handle for their borrowing customers. On the average it is probably somewhat less than ¼ of 1 per cent of their sales. The rates of compensation mentioned above, moreover, are gross rates. Since the expenses of maintaining their offices and carrying on their operations are likely to absorb at least one-half of the gross earnings of commercial paper houses, even in years when they handle a relatively large volume of open-market obligations, it is probable that their net compensation is generally somewhat less than ⅛ of 1 per cent of their sales. In years when their sales volume is comparatively small their net earnings shrink to a con-

---

[5] Thus a large New York house reported a few years ago that it sometimes charged only ⅙ of 1 per cent for marketing high-grade notes maturing in four months, or only two-thirds of the rate for handling six-months' paper issued by the same concern.

[6] The trading losses they incur in such cases may result from their purchasing open-market notes at rates below the market, in order to secure choice accounts or to retain accounts they are already handling; from a rise in short-term money rates which makes it necessary for them to raise their selling rates in general; or from raising their selling rates in order to "move" paper for which there is no very active demand or to place notes of some particular company with a particular bank. Their practice of offering selling rates above their buying rates, especially for the latter two purposes, is known as "splitting" their commissions with their buying customers.

siderable extent. Hence operations in commercial paper, like dealings in acceptances, can be carried on to advantage only by houses which are able to secure a large volume of business each year.

2. FINANCING OPERATIONS IN COMMERCIAL PAPER

Dealers require capital both for financing the purchase of open-market notes from their borrowing customers and for meeting their current operating expenses. The amounts of capital they require for such purposes vary with their inventories of purchased paper, with the proportion of their total purchases which they buy outright, rather than on a consignment basis, and with the size of the organizations they maintain. Since they generally endeavor to sell their borrowing customers' obligations as rapidly as they purchase them, and there is almost always an active demand for high-grade open-market notes, the turnover of their portfolios of purchased paper is ordinarily very rapid, and the average amount of capital they have invested in inventories of such paper constitutes only a small proportion of their total sales each year. In recent years, in fact, dealers have been able in many cases to turn over their limited portfolios of open-market notes every day, though a number of the leading houses, in order to allot purchased paper among their different offices and/or correspondents, have purposely held their borrowing customers' obligations for one day, instead of marketing them at once. It has therefore been possible to turn over capital invested in inventories of commercial paper at a rate as rapid as 180 times or more a year. In case dealers borrow a part of the funds which they use for purchasing their stock in trade, the turnover of their own capital is of course even more rapid than that of the total amount of capital which they use for this purpose. By following the policy of turning over their inventories of purchased paper, and therefore the capital invested in such inventories, as rapidly as possible, they are of course able to reduce to a minimum the interest costs involved in handling a given volume of business. If they could buy on a brokerage or consignment basis all the obligations they handle, they would obviously require no capital at all for purchasing their stock in trade. As was pointed out in Chapter VII, however, only a small proportion of the paper which has been bought and sold in the market in recent years has been purchased on consignment. Hence the use of this method of buying has not reduced to any considerable extent the amounts of capital which dealers have required for financing their purchases of open-market paper.

Dealers themselves in most cases furnish a substantial proportion of the capital they require for carrying on their operations in such paper. Any additional funds they may need for this purpose they secure almost entirely from commercial banks.

The proportion of their own capital to the total capital they use depends partly on their own financial resources and partly on the volume of business they are handling at any particular time, and therefore varies to a considerable extent. Some dealers have borrowed from eight to ten times as much capital as they have furnished themselves. On the other hand, probably few houses, if any, have found it necessary in recent years to borrow at any one time more than four times as much as their own capital, and some of the larger houses have for several years required only a limited amount of borrowed funds. Even in 1930, when total sales by dealers were much larger than they have been in any succeeding year, a leading New York house reported that it sometimes for periods of several months at a time relied entirely on its own capital for financing its operations. Other dealers also occasionally finance their operations without the aid of borrowed funds at times when supplies of open-market notes are limited and the demand for outside paper on the part of their buying customers is very active;[7] and some houses occasionally have surplus funds of their own available for investment.[8]

[7] Dealers occasionally hold for their borrowing customers for short periods substantial amounts of funds which they have received from their buying customers in payment for outside paper. Such funds, until transferred to their borrowing customers, in effect constitute a part of their own capital.

A New England house stated in 1931 that it has held funds for its customers for periods as long as three months, and that it sometimes allows interest on such funds at the rates at which it purchased the notes of the customers concerned. A Middle-Western house reported in 1930 that it allows interest on funds it holds for customers at the rates at which it obtains demand loans from its banks.

[8] Such houses have probably placed surplus funds in call loans more often than in any other form of investment. They have sometimes used temporary surpluses for carrying commercial paper or invested them in government bonds or acceptances.

Though dealers in recent years have themselves customarily furnished a substantial proportion of the capital they have used, all houses nevertheless borrow from commercial banks, either more or less regularly or occasionally, at least some part of the funds they require for financing their purchases of open-market paper. Practically all houses which secure funds in this manner, moreover, borrow from commercial banks only, and most houses borrow only from banks with which they already maintain deposit accounts.[9] In most cases dealers can secure all the credit they require from their own depositary banks, and they prefer to borrow from the latter because they are likely to be able to secure from their own banks the most favorable terms with respect to rates, average balances to be maintained, and the margins, if any, to be maintained on collateral offered as security for loans. They can also expect to place larger amounts of commercial paper with their own banks of deposit than with institutions with which they do not regularly maintain deposit accounts.[10]

The number of banks with which they maintain such accounts varies with the amounts of borrowed funds they require, the number of their offices which are authorized to buy and/or carry stocks of open-market notes, and the extent to which they use banking connections as a means of increasing the demand for the obligations they handle. All houses maintain accounts with a number of the leading banks in the cities in which their main offices are located and with one or more banks in the cities in which they maintain branch offices. Accordingly, the cities in which the number of accounts maintained by dealers is the largest are such financial centers as New York, Boston, and Chicago. For the convenience

[9] A Boston house reported in 1931 that it sometimes obtains loans running for six months to one year from New England savings banks, particularly at times when it is expected that short-term money rates will rise in the near future. As collateral for such loans, it offers commercial paper and/or one or more classes of securities, such as stocks, bonds, and municipal notes.

Besides this Boston house, six other dealers reported about the same time that they occasionally borrowed from non-depositary banks. Within a year or so later, however, three of these six houses retired from business.

[10] Dealers expect banks with which they maintain profitable deposit and borrowing accounts to buy at least some outside paper from them each year. In some cases they have discontinued their accounts with banks which purchased but little or no open-market paper from them.

of borrowing customers whose notes are made payable in New York, two or three Middle-Western houses maintain accounts with one or more banks in that city, though they have no offices in New York and obtain from banks in other cities all or the greater part of the credit they require for financing their operations in open-market paper.

Dealers borrow mainly from banks in cities in which they maintain their main offices and any important branch offices which they authorize to buy and carry stocks of commercial paper, though some houses borrow from banks in all cities in which they maintain deposit accounts. In general, dealers endeavor to distribute their borrowings more or less equally among the various banks from which they secure credit. Some houses maintain deposit accounts with certain banks primarily for the purpose of increasing the demand for the open-market paper they handle, and consequently obtain but small amounts of short-term capital, if any at all, from such banks.

While dealers are not required to maintain balances amounting to any definite percentage of the loans they obtain from their banks, the latter generally expect them to maintain satisfactory average balances, which may be as low as 10 per cent or as high as 20 per cent of their borrowings. In any case, dealers customarily maintain satisfactory average balances of their own accord. A leading New England house generally maintains balances in excess of its bank loans, and the deposits of other dealers at times may amount to as much as 50 per cent of their borrowings. The balances of practically all houses with at least some of their banks are increased to a considerable extent from time to time by deposits of funds which they hold temporarily for their borrowing customers.

Practically all loans which dealers secure from commercial banks are demand loans, though a few houses have occasionally made use of time loans also, particularly in periods of rising money rates. These demand loans are not called by the banks from which they are obtained, but are paid at the convenience of the borrower. They are generally of short duration, about three or four days being the average length of time for which they remain outstanding, according to several Eastern dealers. In many cases they are supposed to have just one day to run, or, at any rate, are paid on the day on which they are obtained. In such cases they are known as "day loans."

Most loans which banks extend to dealers, whether demand or time loans, are secured by some form of collateral, though four houses reported in 1930 or 1931 that they occasionally borrowed on their unsecured notes also. The collateral which is offered as security for such loans is generally commercial paper which dealers have recently purchased from their borrowing customers. As notes offered as collateral are sold, they are of course replaced with new obligations. Some houses which deal in long-term securities, as well as open-market paper, also use stocks and bonds as collateral. The practices which dealers follow with respect to maintaining margins on the collateral they offer as security for their bank loans vary to a considerable extent. Seven houses stated in 1930 that they customarily borrowed "flat" — that is, up to the full face value of commercial paper (or market value of long-term securities) offered as security for their loans. Nine other houses, on the other hand, reported that, either voluntarily or at the request of their banks, they gave margins considered satisfactory by the latter. The margins which they maintained ranged from 5 per cent to about 25 per cent in the case of commercial paper, the margin most commonly given being about 10 per cent.[11] The margins they gave in case they offered securities as collateral also varied to some extent. Several dealers stated that margins of 10 per cent were commonly maintained when bonds were offered as collateral, and a large Chicago house that banks were willing to advance up to 75 per cent of the market value of stocks which dealers offered as security for their loans.

---

[11] Since open-market paper is bought and sold on a discount basis, it is not worth its face value until maturity. The actual margin of protection which a bank has when it makes a loan on the security of such paper is therefore less than the stated margin. Thus if a dealer borrowed $100,000 on $105,000 of six-months' paper which could be sold in the market at a discount of 4 per cent, the stated margin he would give would be $5,000, or 5 per cent, whereas the actual margin at that time would be only $2,900, or 2.9 per cent. If, instead, he borrowed "flat" — i.e., gave no margin at all — the actual value of the notes he would offer as security would at that time be only $98,000.

Since they always maintain satisfactory average deposit balances, commonly borrow for short periods, and generally offer highly liquid collateral as security for their loans, dealers are able to borrow from their banks at preferential rates. A Boston house reported in 1930 that the rates at which it borrowed from its local banks fluctuated with call loan renewal rates in that city. Four New York houses stated about the same time that dealers in that city customarily borrow from local banks at the New York Stock Exchange call loan renewal rate. According to one of these houses, however, if the latter rate rises above 6 per cent the rates charged by such banks are determined by agreement between themselves and the dealers concerned. A considerably larger number of houses reported that the rates at which they obtain bank loans fluctuate rather closely with the rates at which commercial paper is currently selling in the open market. For short periods the rates charged dealers may be either higher or lower than their buying and selling rates by as much as ¼ of 1 per cent or more. When the rates they pay for borrowed funds are above prevailing commercial paper rates they endeavor to reduce their borrowings, in order to minimize the losses involved in carrying their portfolios. If their borrowing rates fall ¼ of 1 per cent or more below their buying rates, they may find it profitable under certain conditions to carry notes purchased with borrowed funds. Two Eastern houses stated that some years ago they could borrow at rates as much as ½ of 1 per cent below prevailing commercial paper rates, and consequently could carry at a profit notes which they purchased with funds obtained from their banks. In more recent years, however, dealers have probably not been able very often to borrow at rates much more than about ¼ of 1 per cent below their buying rates, and have generally found it to their advantage to turn over their portfolios as rapidly as possible, rather than carry paper with the aid of borrowed capital.[12]

[12] Carrying open-market notes involves greater risks of trading losses from changes in commercial paper rates than marketing such obligations as rapidly as possible. On the other hand, it also offers greater opportunities for making trading profits. Trading losses are most likely to be incurred at times when commercial paper rates are rising, while the probabilities of making trading profits are greatest at times when rates are falling. Other things being equal, therefore, dealers are most likely to carry paper in periods of falling rates.

CHAPTER XII

"OTHER OPERATIONS" OF DEALERS

OF THE twenty-three houses which at the end of 1930 were handling practically all the commercial paper being sold in the open market, only one was confining its operations exclusively to buying and selling open-market paper. The remaining twenty-two houses, in addition to dealing in promissory notes, were engaged also in one or more other classes of operations. At that time the "other operations" of about half of these twenty-two houses were more important than their dealings in commercial paper. After 1930 a fairly large number of dealers retired from business. Of the limited number of houses which have continued to buy and sell promissory notes in the market in more recent years, only about five or six restrict their operations exclusively to dealing in such obligations. While buying and selling open-market notes is the most important class of dealings in which one or two other houses engage, even these houses carry on one or more other classes of operations. The "other operations" in which dealers have engaged in recent years include dealings in long-term securities, buying and selling securities on a brokerage basis, and a miscellaneous group of operations none of which has been of any particular importance in the case of more than one or two houses. The relative importance of these various classes of "other operations" will be indicated in the present chapter.

1. DEALINGS IN SECURITIES

The most important class of "other operations" in which commercial paper houses have engaged in recent years is dealing in long-term securities. At the end of 1930 seventeen dealers were engaged in originating, wholesaling, or retailing securities. Only a few houses were acting as retail dealers in stocks and bonds, however, and still fewer were carrying on all three classes of operations in securities. In the spring of 1936, at least nine or ten houses were engaged in the distribution of stocks and/or bonds. Eight of these

houses were originating, six were wholesaling, and seven were retailing long-term securities; and six were carrying on all three of
these classes of operations.

Five of the twenty-three houses mentioned above reported that
they occasionally engaged in underwriting (as distinguished from
distributing) security issues. At least five dealers were also carrying on operations of this class in 1936.

Combining investment banking operations with handling commercial paper is said to offer the houses which follow this policy
three advantages which cannot be obtained by houses that deal in
long-term securities or open-market obligations only. In the first
place, houses which engage in both classes of operations are in a
position to aid their borrowing clients in securing not only short-
term funds but also any long-term capital they may require. Secondly, through their contacts with the concerns whose paper they
sell in the open market they are able to avail themselves of opportunities they would not otherwise have for originating security
issues. Bringing out new securities of concerns whose open-market
obligations they are already handling involves comparatively little
preliminary investigation work or expense, and has often been
much more profitable than buying and selling commercial paper.
Some investment banking houses have considered the opportunities for originating security issues which arise in connection with
dealing in open-market obligations important enough to justify
them in continuing to buy and sell promissory notes even at times
when operations in commercial paper, as such, have been unprofitable. Finally, earnings from dealings in bonds — if not as a rule,
at least in a number of cases — have been comparatively large at
times when business activity and money rates have been at a low
level, supplies of open-market notes have been limited, and earnings from operations in such obligations have been small; whereas
earnings from the latter class of operations are greatest at times
when business is active and comparatively large supplies of commercial paper are available. Hence the earnings of houses which
have followed the policy of combining investment banking operations with dealing in open-market notes have been more stable than

they would have been had these houses confined their operations to dealings in long-term securities or commercial paper alone.

On the other hand, houses which carry on both classes of operations are likely to neglect their commercial paper business at times when dealings in securities are more profitable, as was the case from about 1925 to about 1930. Moreover, houses which confine their operations almost exclusively to buying and selling open-market notes, and are therefore interested chiefly in the latter class of dealings, are likely to handle their commercial paper business more efficiently than those which deal in long-term securities as well as open-market paper. They also avoid the losses which houses of the latter class sometimes have to take as a result of shrinkages in the value of their inventories of securities in times of depression.

2. SECURITY BROKERAGE OPERATIONS

In addition to buying and selling open-market notes and originating, distributing, or underwriting securities, eight dealers were buying and selling securities on a brokerage basis in 1930, and in 1931 another house began operations of the latter class. Such operations were comparatively unimportant, however, in the case of all but three or four of these nine houses. Four of the nine dealers later retired from business, and the house which began security brokerage operations in 1931 discontinued its brokerage business within less than a month. In the spring of 1936 five dealers reported that they were carrying on operations of this class. One of these five houses and a partner in each of two others are members of the New York Stock Exchange and one or more other leading security exchanges. While handling securities on a brokerage basis is a fairly important part of the business of one or two of these five dealers, none of the latter would be considered large brokerage houses.

3. OTHER CLASSES OF "OTHER OPERATIONS"

Dealing in or underwriting long-term securities and buying and selling such securities on a brokerage basis are the "other operations" in which commercial paper houses have most commonly engaged in recent years. Other classes of "other operations" in which one or more dealers have engaged include the following: acting as an acceptance house; dealing in foreign exchange; holding foreign deposits and acting as the correspondent of foreign banking houses; carrying on a commercial banking business; handling insurance; buying and selling mortgage notes; selling mortgages on a brokerage basis; reorganizing and refinancing business concerns; and maintaining an investment management department.

A New York house reported in 1930 that, besides originating and wholesaling securities, it was acting as an acceptance house, dealing in foreign exchange, holding foreign deposits, and acting as the correspondent of foreign banking houses. In the spring of 1936 this house, which is now probably the largest commercial paper dealer in the country, was still carrying on the operations just mentioned, except that of holding foreign deposits. It was also underwriting and retailing long-term securities and maintaining an investment management department. Two Southern dealers, through wholly-owned subsidiary mortgage companies, were selling collateral trust mortgage notes in 1930. The first of these houses was also carrying on a commercial banking business and handling insurance, and the second was dealing in long-term securities. The "other operations" of both these dealers were much more important than their dealings in commercial paper at that time; and about three years later both houses discontinued the latter class of dealings. A Middle-Western house was also selling mortgage notes in 1930, in addition to dealing in long-term securities. As compared with its dealings in commercial paper, however, these other two classes of operations were relatively unimportant. A leading New England house, besides originating, wholesaling, and retailing long-term securities and acting as a broker in buying and selling stocks and bonds, was also selling mortgages on a brokerage basis in 1931. These other classes of operations were at that time, and have since remained, more important than its dealings in commercial paper. A New York house reported in 1930 that, in addition to dealing in short-term municipal notes and underwriting security issues, it had also occasionally made arrangements for reorganizing and refinancing business concerns. The "other operations" of this house, however, were comparatively unimportant at that time, and were later discontinued. Finally, a Chicago house, besides originating, wholesaling, and retailing long-term securities, also maintains an investment management department. Though this house is one of the larger dealers in open-market notes, its "other operations" have for some years been considerably more important than its dealings in commercial paper.

PART III

ECONOMIC SIGNIFICANCE OF THE COMMERCIAL PAPER HOUSE

CHAPTER XIII

THE PLACE OF THE COMMERCIAL PAPER HOUSE IN THE FINANCIAL SYSTEM

IN THE historical chapters which constitute the first part of this study an account was given of the main developments relating to the methods of operation used by dealers from the beginning of the commercial paper business in the eighteenth century to the close of 1935, and in certain of the chapters included in Part II the practical operations of the commercial paper house were described in some detail. With the factual material presented in these earlier historical and descriptive chapters as a background, we may now consider the economic significance of an institution which, though it has no precise counterpart in any other country, has for many years rendered important services both to borrowing concerns and to commercial banks in all sections of the United States. In the first of the two chapters included in Part III a more comprehensive view of the rôle which the commercial paper house plays in the functioning of the financial system will be given than was presented in the preceding chapters. In Chapter XIV an appraisal of the work of the commercial paper house will be given.

The purpose of the present chapter, more specifically, is to indicate the nature of the functions performed by dealers in promissory notes; to describe briefly the market in which they carry on their operations in such paper, and to point out certain similarities, as well as certain differences, between this market and some of the most important of the other short-term open markets for money; to show the relations which the commercial paper house has with the money market as a whole; and to present a comparison of the operations of the commercial paper house with those of certain other financial institutions whose functions in certain respects resemble more or less closely the functions performed by dealers in open-market notes.

1. Functions of the Commercial Paper House

In all sections of the country there are a number of concerns of high credit standing which are unable to secure from their own banks as much short-term capital as they require, or find it to their advantage in any case to supplement borrowing directly from such institutions with borrowing indirectly, through the sale of their notes in the open market, from a much larger number of banks located in other sections of the country. At the same time there are commercial banks in all parts of the United States which, either at certain seasons of the year or from one year to another, have surplus loanable funds which they can employ more advantageously in other forms of investment than in direct advances to their own customers. The function of the commercial paper house is to serve as an intermediary in bringing these potential borrowers and lenders together. It fulfills this function by purchasing short-term notes issued by its borrowing customers and finding a market for these obligations among the commercial banks which are its main buying customers.

In performing this function the commercial paper house acts as a merchant in so far as it buys and sells open-market notes outright. Some houses buy and sell on a consignment basis a small proportion of the paper they handle. In handling notes on this basis they of course act as a broker only. Since all dealers furnish at least some part of the capital required for financing their purchases of such obligations, and their portfolios of purchased paper represent advances of corresponding amounts of short-term funds to their borrowing customers, they also perform a banking function. Another function they perform — that of acting as financial advisers to their borrowing customers — may likewise be regarded as a banking function.[1]

---

[1] As was pointed out in the preceding chapter, a number of houses, in addition to dealing in open-market paper, engage also in one or more classes of other operations, the most important of which are dealing in and underwriting long-term securities and buying and selling such securities on a brokerage basis. Houses which deal in long-term securities perform merchandising and banking functions similar to those which they fulfill in buying and selling commercial paper outright; houses which buy and sell stocks and bonds on a brokerage basis, a function similar to that performed by

2. THE COMMERCIAL PAPER MARKET

The market in which dealers buy and sell the promissory notes which constitute their stock in trade is commonly referred to as the commercial paper market.

As has been indicated already, this market is made up of a large group of borrowers, a still larger group of lenders, and the comparatively small number of commercial paper houses which act as intermediary dealers in bringing these borrowers and lenders together. The borrowers are business concerns of high credit standing which wish to supplement direct borrowing from their own banks with borrowing indirectly through dealers as a means of raising short-term capital. Most of these concerns are engaged in trading or manufacturing enterprises, though borrowers of other classes also obtain funds in the market. The lenders include both commercial banks and investors of a few other classes wishing to place surplus funds in a safe and highly liquid form of investment.

Most paper which dealers purchase from their borrowing customers and sell to commercial banks and other buying customers is issued with maturities of six months or shorter. Hence the commercial paper market is a short-term market. It may be described further as a nation-wide open market. It is a nation-wide market because dealers purchase the notes they handle from concerns in all sections of the country and sell these obligations to banks in all parts of the United States. It is an open market not only because it is a broad market in which there are many borrowers and lenders but also because it is one in which relations between borrowers and lenders are indirect and impersonal.[2] The borrowing concerns and

---

dealers who act merely as brokers in handling certain classes of paper; and houses which underwrite securities, an insurance function similar to that performed by dealers who some years ago used to provide "revolving credits" for certain of their borrowing customers. (See n. 19, pp. 250–251.)

[2] It has been said that an open market "is characterized primarily by the fact that in it the operations of borrowing and lending are impersonal" (W. W. Riefler, *Money Rates and Money Markets in the United States*, pp. 9–10). But in most cases relations between borrowers and lenders are not likely to be strictly impersonal unless borrowing and lending operations are effected indirectly through the intermediation of some sort of dealer. At any rate, about the only short-term open markets for money in this country in which such operations are effected without the

the banks which purchase practically all the promissory notes sold in the market do not deal with each other directly with regard to the terms of open-market loans; extension of credit to open-market borrowers is effected, instead, only indirectly through the intermediation of the dealers in commercial paper. Hence the rates at which funds are borrowed in the market are not determined, as are rates on direct loans from banks, by negotiation between borrowers and lenders. They are determined, instead, by all the forces affecting the supply of short-term funds and the demand therefor throughout the country as a whole, and the rate at which any particular concern borrows on its open-market paper is ordinarily the same throughout the entire country at any given time.

The commercial paper market is only one of a number of smaller separate markets which are included in the money market as a whole, or the funds market. The funds market may be divided into the long-term market and the short-term market, and the latter into the customers' loan market and the open market. The short-term open market may be subdivided into a number of smaller markets, among the most important of which are the market for United States Treasury obligations (including bills, notes, and, formerly, certificates of indebtedness [3]), for New York Stock Ex-

aid of intermediary dealers are the market for notes issued directly to the purchasers thereof by several of the large finance companies and the market for United States Treasury obligations; and secondary distribution even of government obligations is effected through dealers. Besides being a market in which relations between borrowers and lenders are impersonal and in most cases indirect, an open money market is characterized further by the fact that in it the number of lenders is relatively large and competition among lenders is active, with the result that the rate at which any one borrower obtains credit at any particular time is ordinarily the same throughout the entire market. In this respect as well as others, however, the difference between an open market and the customers' loan market, in which borrowers obtain "over-the-counter" advances direct from their own banks, may be regarded as only a difference of degree.

[3] At the end of December 1936 the total amount of Treasury bills outstanding was $2,203,000,000, compared with $10,804,000,000 of notes. Certificates of indebtedness amounting to $117,000,000 were also outstanding as of the same date, but the Treasury has issued no certificates for general financing purposes since January 1934, and such certificates as have been outstanding since December 15, 1934, were issued to provide an investment for special government funds. Hence there has been no open market for certificates since about the end of 1934. The Treasury has been issuing Treasury bills since about the middle of 1929. These have taken the place of certificates because they offer a more convenient and

change call and time loans on security collateral, for bankers' ac-ceptances, and for commercial paper.[4] Thus the commercial paper market is only one of five of the more important short-term open money markets in the United States.

Of these five markets, the market for commercial paper is the oldest. It may also be regarded as the broadest. For both bor-rowers and lenders in the commercial paper market are to be found in all sections of the country; the number of borrowers in this market is much larger than that of the borrowers in the market for short-term Treasury obligations (in which there is of course but a single borrower), and ordinarily is probably about as large as the number of borrowers in either of the New York collateral loan markets or the acceptance market; the variety of borrowers in the commercial paper market is probably somewhat greater than that of borrowers in the acceptance market, and is much greater than that of borrowers in the remaining three markets; the number of lenders in the commercial paper market, while it may be somewhat smaller than that of lenders in the market for short-term Treasury obligations, is generally greater than the number of lenders in the acceptance market, and in recent years has presumably been con-siderably larger than that of lenders in either of the New York collateral loan markets; and though commercial banks purchase practically all the obligations sold in the commercial paper mar-ket, the variety of lenders in this market is about as great as that

economical means of raising short-term funds for general financing purposes. For a discussion of Treasury bills, which, unlike other Treasury obligations, are sold on a discount basis to the highest bidder, see Belmont Towbin, "Treasury Bills," *Harv. Bus. Rev.*, July 1933, pp. 507–511.

[4] Other short-term open markets for money in the United States include the market for "Federal funds," for obligations of municipalities, and for notes issued by several of the larger finance companies and sold to banks and other investors in all sections of the country.

The limited market for call loans secured by acceptances has also been considered an open market. Because of the relations between the borrowers and the lenders therein, however, it would seem that this market may more accurately be regarded as essentially a subdivision of the short-term customers' loan market. Until about 1921 there was a fairly active open market for cattle loan paper. After the drastic decline in live-stock prices which took place in 1920 and 1921, however, and re-sulted in the failure of many cattle loan companies and heavy losses to holders of cattle loan paper, the annual volume of such paper sold by cattle loan companies in the open market declined to a very considerable extent.

of the lenders in any of the other four short-term open markets.

Though the oldest and the broadest of these five markets, the market for commercial paper is at present probably the least important so far as the volume of funds advanced to borrowers each year is concerned. The importance of the latter market is greater, however, than would be indicated by the annual volume of commercial paper financing alone, for there is active competition between lenders in the commercial paper market and those in the customers' loan market, and commercial paper rates influence directly the rates which commercial banks charge on over-the-counter loans to customers of the highest credit standing. Moreover, the commercial paper market is the only open market in this country in which the rates charged on short-term commercial and industrial loans are determined by the free play of the forces of supply and demand, uninfluenced by any kind of artificial control.

The market for commercial paper is similar to all the other four in being a market in which the investment of loanable funds is unusually safe and advances to borrowers are highly liquid. It has already been shown, in Chapter VIII, that open-market notes are a practically riskless investment. Loans extended to borrowers in the commercial paper market may therefore be considered virtually as secure as advances to borrowers in any of the other four markets. It was also pointed out in Chapter VIII that advances to concerns borrowing in the commercial paper market possess a high degree of liquidity. Since most commercial paper having a maturity of not more than ninety days is eligible for rediscount at the Federal Reserve banks, loans advanced to borrowers in the latter market may be regarded as more liquid than loans in the time loan market. On the other hand, loans extended to concerns borrowing in the commercial paper market are generally considered somewhat less liquid than advances to borrowers in the markets for call loans, bankers' acceptances, and short-term Treasury obligations; for call loans can be called, and acceptances and Treasury obligations can be sold to the Federal Reserve banks or to dealers. So long as brokers and dealers in securities are able to pay their call loans on demand, even though in order to do so they may find it necessary to shift their borrowing from one group of lenders to another in the same or some other market, the call loan market is virtually a "two-way" market. Similarly, the markets for acceptances and Treasury obligations are also "two-way" markets, so long as acceptances and government obligations can be sold to the Federal Reserve banks or to dealers. As contrasted with the latter markets, the commercial paper market may be regarded as a "one-way" market only. The difference between the commercial paper market and these other markets in this respect, however, is only a difference of degree; for banks which have purchased open-market notes occasionally resell such obligations to their correspondent banks or to the dealer handling the paper in question.

The open market for commercial paper is also similar to all the other four in being a market in which the majority of the lenders are commercial banks. Both in the commercial paper market and the two markets for "Street loans," however, the proportion of the total amounts borrowed which is advanced by such banks is greater than that ordinarily supplied by commercial banks either to borrowers in the acceptance market or to the Federal government in the market for Treasury obligations. None of the funds advanced to borrowers in the former three markets are supplied by the Federal Reserve banks (though the latter of course furnish a rediscount market for eligible commercial paper held by member banks). The Reserve banks, on the other hand, ordinarily supply a relatively large proportion of the funds placed in the bankers' acceptance market,[5] at times hold fairly large amounts of short-term Treasury obligations also, and by means of their buying

[5] During most of the period since about the middle of 1932, however, the Reserve banks have held only a small proportion of the total volume of bankers' (dollar) acceptances outstanding, or no such bills at all, whether for their own account or for the account of foreign correspondents. By far the greater part of the total amount of bankers' bills outstanding in recent years has been held, instead, by commercial banks. A number of banks, faced with the problem of finding employment for surplus loanable funds, have held relatively large amounts of bills which they themselves have accepted. When short-term money rates have again reached levels which may be regarded as more nearly "normal," it is probable that the Reserve banks will again feel called upon to purchase relatively large amounts of bankers' acceptances.

policies keep rates on bankers' bills at artificially low levels and yields on Treasury obligations at levels at least somewhat lower than those which would prevail if they did not make a market for obligations of this class. Hence the markets for commercial paper and call and time loans stand on their own feet, so to speak, whereas the other two markets receive a certain amount of artificial support.

So far as rates are concerned, two other similarities may be noted between the market for commercial paper and the other four markets. The first is that rates in the commercial paper market, like those in the other four, are particularly "sensitive" rates, responding quickly to changes in either the supply of or the demand for loanable funds. It is in these markets that changes in money rates generally appear first, and the changes initiated in these markets spread only subsequently to the customers' loan market and the market for long-term bonds. The second similarity referred to above is that changes in rates in the commercial paper market, as well as those in the other four markets, are governed largely by changes in the volume of member banks' indebtedness at the Federal Reserve banks and the discount policies and open-market operations of the Federal Reserve system.

The commercial paper market is similar to that for Treasury obligations, but differs from the other three, in so far as it is a market in which the loans advanced are unsecured. In being a market in which borrowing operations show distinct seasonal fluctuations, it is similar to the acceptance market but differs from the collateral loan markets and the market for Treasury bills and notes.

Finally, the commercial paper market differs from all the other four in that it is a market in which most of the borrowers may be classified either as trading or as manufacturing concerns.

3. Relations of the Commercial Paper House with the Money Market

While the buying and selling operations through which it brings borrowers and lenders together are carried on only in the commercial paper market itself, the commercial paper house nevertheless has either indirect relations or direct contacts with certain other subdivisions of the market for funds, including both customers' loan markets and all the important open markets.

With lenders in customers' loan markets and with dealers or lenders in the acceptance market, in collateral loan markets, and in the market for long-term securities, it has indirect relations as a competitor in providing a method of financing for concerns which are considered preferred credit risks. In supplying an attractive short-term investment for commercial banks and other investors, it has similar relations with dealers or borrowers in the leading open markets for money.

Through buying and selling the promissory notes of their borrowing customers, dealers enable the latter to use a highly satisfactory method of short-term financing. They thus enter into competition with commercial banks in advancing short-term funds to borrowing concerns of high credit standing. To the extent that they handle collateral loan paper, they compete both with banks which make loans on security collateral in the customers' loan market — that is, direct to their own customers — and with those which place funds in the New York Stock Exchange call and time loan markets. In so far as open-market financing is used for purposes for which acceptance financing or financing through finance companies is also being used, or could be employed, dealers in commercial paper compete against discount houses and finance companies also. As was indicated in Chapter III, however, competition between commercial paper houses and the latter two classes of institutions in supplying short-term credit accommodation has been relatively unimportant in recent years. Finally, to the extent that they advance short-term funds to concerns which would otherwise raise capital through the issue of long-term securities, commercial paper houses compete against investment banking houses. Since short-term and long-term financing are commonly employed for different purposes, however, their competition with investment banking houses is less active than their competition with commercial banks.

In addition to supplying short-term credit for their borrowing customers, commercial paper houses also make available for commercial banks and a few other classes of investors a safe and highly liquid form of short-term investment. In performing the latter service they enter into competition with dealers or borrowers who offer alternative investments for banks' funds in other open markets, such as dealers in the acceptance market, finance companies which sell their own obligations direct to banks and other investors, dealers in government obligations, dealers in other classes of securities, and borrowers in the New York Stock Exchange call and time loan markets.

With the most important class of lenders in the customers' loan market the commercial paper house has direct contacts as a borrower, for dealers in open-market notes obtain from commercial banks practically all the borrowed capital they require for carrying on their operations. Since they maintain deposit accounts with a number of banks, and coöperate with these and many other banks in the exchange of credit information, they also have other direct contacts with the customers' loan market.

Occasionally the commercial paper house has maintained direct contacts as a lender with the collateral loan market, the market for United States government obligations, or the market for acceptances, for dealers in open-market paper have at times invested surplus funds in call loans, government bonds, or bankers' bills.[6]

[6] Dealers also borrow from and make loans to their own borrowing customers. They occasionally hold for the latter for short periods funds which they have received from their buying customers in payment for open-market paper. If they use these funds in their own business they are of course for the time being actually borrowing equivalent amounts from their borrowing customers, though such funds in effect constitute a part of their own capital. In addition to borrowing from the concerns whose paper they handle, dealers are always making short-term advances to the latter, for they always furnish a part of the capital required for carrying their portfolios of unsold paper. Occasionally they carry purchased notes as an investment for surplus funds of their own. In such cases their advances to their borrowing customers run for somewhat longer periods. In case they carry purchased paper with funds borrowed from banks in order to make a carrying profit, they act as a borrower in the customers' loan market and as a lender in the commercial paper market at the same time.

Commercial paper houses which also deal in long-term securities or buy and sell such securities on a brokerage basis have certain other relations with the money market. These other relations, however, are more or less similar to those involved in dealing in commercial paper. Thus houses which deal in long-term securities have

Unlike commercial banks, dealers in United States government obligations, and acceptance dealers, commercial paper houses have no direct contacts with the Federal Reserve banks.

Both member and non-member banks sell acceptances to the Reserve banks, and member banks rediscount acceptances and commercial paper (including both open-market obligations and notes issued by their own customers) with the Reserve banks and obtain advances from the latter on their own promissory notes secured by acceptances, government obligations, or commercial paper. Dealers in government obligations sell such securities to the Reserve banks and can borrow from the latter through selling them Treasury bills or notes which they agree to repurchase within fifteen days. Discount houses also maintain close direct relations with the Reserve banks. The American discount market, in fact, has grown up under the support of the Federal Reserve system, and depends for its existence upon the continued support of the Reserve banks. Though the latter ordinarily do not take the initiative in buying bankers' bills, they always stand ready to purchase at their established buying rates eligible acceptances offered them by dealers or other holders, and they have generally held a substantial proportion of the total amount of dollar acceptances outstanding.[7] Besides purchasing relatively large amounts of bills outright, the Reserve banks have supported the discount market by enabling acceptance dealers to finance the purchase of their inventories. These dealers themselves furnish only a part of the capital required for carrying on their operations. While they also borrow from incorporated banks, private banks, and acceptance houses on call loans secured by acceptances, they ordinarily obtain the greater

---

indirect relations with commercial banks as competitors in providing a method of financing for concerns requiring substantial amounts of borrowed funds, and with dealers or borrowers in the acceptance market, in collateral loan markets, and in the market for short-term Treasury obligations as competitors in supplying investments for banks and certain other classes of investors. They also have direct relations with commercial banks as borrowers and depositors; with lenders in collateral loan markets as borrowers; and, if they have surplus funds of their own to invest, with borrowers in one or more money markets as lenders. Houses which carry on stock brokerage operations have the same direct relations with the money market as those just mentioned.

[7] In this connection, however, see n. 5, p. 371.

part of the borrowed funds they require for purchasing and carrying their portfolios by selling to the Reserve banks acceptances which they agree to repurchase within a stated period, commonly fifteen days. The discount rates at which they borrow through entering into repurchase agreements with the Reserve banks are generally enough below their buying rates to enable them to avoid losses in carrying inventories of unsold bills; and either by selling acceptances to the Reserve banks outright, at the latter's buying rates, or by making use of repurchase agreements, they can also generally avoid losses from rising money rates.

Commercial paper houses, on the other hand, neither sell open-market obligations to the Reserve banks nor receive from the latter any assistance in financing their operations or any protection against shrinkages in the value of their inventories resulting from changes in money rates. As has been pointed out already, they sell practically all the paper they handle to commercial banks, and obtain from such institutions practically all the borrowed capital they require for carrying on their operations in open-market notes. Thus the open-market system of financing is itself financed by the commercial banking system, and neither the purchase of outside paper by commercial banks nor their advances to dealers in promissory notes have any direct effect in increasing the amount of Federal Reserve credit outstanding; whereas the acceptance system of financing ordinarily is financed to a considerable extent by the Reserve banking system, and both the outright purchase of bills by the Reserve banks and their purchase of acceptances under resale agreements with bill brokers result directly in increasing the amount of funds which the Reserve system releases to the money market.

As a matter of fact, neither in finding a market for their stock in trade nor in financing their operations do commercial paper houses encounter the problems which arise in the business of dealing in acceptances. Hence they require no support from the Reserve banks of the kind which bill brokers, if they are to stand ready to buy and sell acceptances at all times, are likely to find indispensable so long as the Reserve system follows the policy of keeping rates in the bill market at artificially low levels. Even if the Reserve banks for any reason considered it advisable to do so, they could not offer commercial paper houses support of the kind on which discount houses regularly depend; for they are not authorized to purchase commercial paper in the open market, though they may discount eligible paper for member banks and grant short-term advances on promissory notes of the latter secured by such paper. Since they can neither buy nor sell commercial paper in the open market, they cannot use open-market operations in such paper as a means of accomplishing policy objectives, whereas they can make use of open-market operations for this purpose both in the bill market and in the market for United States government obligations.

Though the commercial paper house has no direct contacts with the Reserve banking system, the volume of paper handled by dealers each year is affected indirectly by the discount policies and open-market operations of the Reserve banks, in so far as such policies and operations influence commodity prices and the volume of business activity and bring about changes in rates in the money market which alter the relative advantages of open-market financing and other means of raising short-term capital and the comparative attractiveness of commercial paper and alternative investments for surplus funds of banks.

4. COMPARISON OF THE OPERATIONS OF THE COMMERCIAL PAPER HOUSE WITH THOSE OF CERTAIN OTHER FINANCIAL INSTITUTIONS

In some respects the operations of the commercial paper house resemble those of commercial banks, acceptance dealers, and such other financial institutions as cattle loan companies, some of the larger finance companies which sell their own notes in the open market, investment banking houses, and the London discount houses, or bill brokers.

The operations of commercial banks are closely similar in a number of respects to those carried on by dealers in commercial paper. Both banks and dealers extend short-term credit in the main to the same classes of borrowers — that is, commercial and industrial concerns — though banks in recent years have invested relatively large proportions of their earning assets in long-term securities and in loans secured by stocks and bonds and by real estate, which are likely to run for longer periods than advances to open-market borrowers. The methods of credit investigation used by the larger city banks are essentially the same as those used by dealers, and both these banks and dealers render their borrowing customers an important service by acting as their financial advisers. From a broader social point of view, both also perform the important function of selecting a large number of the business concerns to which short-term credit is to be advanced, thereby apportioning among the borrowers who presumably can make the most effective use of such funds a substantial part of the community's supplies of liquid capital available for short-term investment. Dealers do not accept or "create" deposits, or perform certain other functions of banks, but they occasionally do hold substantial amounts of funds for their borrowing customers for short periods. It may be said, of course, that dealers act only as intermediaries, whereas banks are the ultimate lenders in the commercial paper market — since they purchase practically all the obligations handled by dealers and furnish practically all the borrowed funds required by the latter for financing their operations — as well as in various other money markets. The difference between banks and dealers in this respect, however, may be regarded as merely a difference of degree; for banks in effect borrow from their depositors, including commercial paper houses, the greater part of the funds on which their advances to their own customers and to other borrowers, including those whose paper they purchase in the open market, are based; and dealers always have capital of their own invested in portfolios of paper which they have purchased outright from their borrowing customers and have not yet sold to their buying customers, and to that extent perform the banking function of acting as lenders in the commercial paper market themselves. Accordingly commercial paper houses have been called "quasi bankers" and "banks at large." [8] Finally, as

[8] Walter McAvoy, "The Economic Importance of the Commercial Paper House," *Jour. Pol. Econ.*, Feb. 1922, pp. 79, 84. Another writer has called the commercial

recently as about 1926 a number of banks were acting as commercial paper dealers themselves; and even in more recent years some banks have occasionally sold at a profit, to correspondent or other banks, notes which they have discounted for their own customers, and have thus in effect acted as dealers on a small scale.

From a broad functional point of view the operations of dealers may be regarded as analogous to those of a nation-wide system of branch banks, for commercial paper houses, like such a branch banking system, collect loanable funds in parts of the country in which they are comparatively abundant and distribute them in sections in which they are relatively scarce. Thus the operations of both bring about a redistribution of available supplies of short-term capital in accordance with the relative needs of borrowers in all parts of the country. They tend accordingly to make the rates charged in different sections for the use of short-term funds more nearly uniform, as well as to bring about a more effective utilization of the country's productive resources.

The operations of American discount houses or acceptance dealers in certain respects resemble those of commercial paper houses very closely. Like dealers in commercial paper, discount houses buy and sell short-term credit instruments outright in an open market, and in performing this merchandising function act as intermediaries in bringing borrowers and lenders together; and they perform a banking function in so far as they carry their portfolios of purchased paper with their own capital. On the other hand, their operations differ from those of commercial paper houses in that the short-term credit instruments in which they deal are bills of exchange,[9] instead of promissory notes, and are used mainly

---

paper house "a bank of discount" (H. W. Murray, "What Is Commercial Paper?" *Mid-Continent Banker*, Aug. 1925, p. 23). There would seem to be as good reasons for calling commercial paper houses "commercial paper bankers" as for calling dealers in long-term securities "investment bankers"; and a large Eastern house which deals exclusively in open-market notes does in fact refer to its operations as those of "commercial paper bankers." It may be noted also that at least twelve commercial paper houses were members of the American Bankers' Association in 1931, and that in 1936 a number of houses were members of the latter association, some state bankers' association, and/or one or more associations of bank credit men, such as the Robert Morris Associates and the Bank Credit Associates of New York.

[9] A few of the leading bill brokers deal in short-term Treasury obligations as well as acceptances. The New York corporation which is the largest discount house

for financing the shipment or storage of agricultural products and raw materials, particularly those which enter into foreign trade; and in that they ordinarily depend to a large extent on the Federal Reserve banks to furnish a market for their stock in trade and to finance their operations.

Like commercial paper houses and acceptance dealers also, cattle loan companies act as intermediaries in bringing borrowers and lenders together through performing the merchandising function of buying and selling short-term credit instruments in the open market, and as bankers in so far as they invest their own capital in the paper they handle. Like the system of financing through commercial paper houses, moreover, the cattle loan system is itself financed largely by the commercial banking system, for cattle loan companies sell the paper of their borrowing customers to commercial banks and obtain from the latter the greater part of the borrowed capital they require for carrying on their operations.[10] The business of the cattle loan company differs from that of the commercial paper house, however, in that the cattle loan company secures all the paper it handles from borrowers who are engaged in the business of raising or feeding live stock, deals almost entirely in notes which are secured by chattel mortgages, customarily indorses these obligations itself, and carries on its operations in a market which is by no means so broad as the market for commercial paper.

Several of the larger finance companies sell short-term notes with convenient denominations and maturities to commercial banks and a few other classes of investors in all sections of the country. In this respect their operations resemble those of commercial paper houses.[11] Unlike the latter, however, these finance companies do

---

in the country deals in long-term United States government securities and "Federal funds" also. A large Boston house deals in both short-term and long-term government obligations and other long-term securities, in addition to buying and selling acceptances.

[10] Cattle loan companies may also dispose of purchased paper by rediscounting it at the Federal Intermediate Credit banks.

[11] One of these companies reported in 1931 that sales of its obligations to banks alone in recent years had amounted to about $20,000,000 a year. It may be noted that sales of this company's open-market notes were being handled by its "com-

not act as intermediary dealers in open-market obligations; for they themselves issue all the paper they place with banks and other investors, and they sell their notes in the market as a means of raising the borrowed capital they require for financing the operations of their own borrowing customers.

Investment banking houses of course deal mainly in long-term securities, instead of short-term credit instruments, but in other respects their operations are closely similar to those of commercial paper houses. Like the latter, they buy and sell their stock in trade outright in the open market, and in performing this merchandising function act as intermediaries in bringing prospective borrowers and investors together. They thus assume the responsibility of determining to what uses a substantial part of the savings of the community shall be applied. They also perform a banking function in so far as they invest their own capital in the securities they handle. Like dealers in commercial paper, however, they act primarily as distributors of available supplies of loanable funds, rather than ultimate lenders in the money market. Since they obtain in the customers' loan market and in the open market for collateral loans (in which the lenders are mainly commercial banks) the borrowed funds they require for carrying on their

mercial paper department" in New York and by "commercial paper offices" which it maintained in other financial centers.

The extent to which another large finance company has relied on open-market financing as a means of raising short-term capital in recent years is indicated by the following table, which shows the total annual sales of this company's short-term notes direct to banks and other purchasers in the open market for the ten years ending with 1935:

Year	Total Sales of Company's Notes Direct to Purchasers in Open Market
1926	$ 96,519,000
1927	133,000,000
1928	178,000,000
1929	207,000,000
1930	417,000,000
1931	208,000,000
1932	135,000,000
1933	71,000,000
1934	182,000,000
1935	183,000,000

operations, and sell a substantial part of their stock in trade to commercial banks, the system of financing through dealers in long-term securities, like that of financing through dealers in commercial paper, is itself financed to a large extent by the commercial banking system.[12]

The commercial paper house is a distinctively American institution. Its closest counterpart in foreign countries is the London discount house, certain of whose operations are analogous to those of American dealers in commercial paper. Like the latter, the London discount houses — or "bill brokers"[13] — buy and sell short-term credit instruments outright in an open market; in performing this merchandising function, act as intermediaries in bringing borrowers and lenders together; and fulfill a banking function in so far as they invest their own capital in their inventories of purchased paper. Moreover, they sell such paper to commercial banks, and secure from the latter a substantial proportion of the borrowed capital they require for conducting their operations. Hence the system of financing through London dealers in acceptances, like that of financing through American dealers in promissory notes, is itself financed (in part, at least) by a commercial banking system. On the other hand, the operations of the London discount houses differ from those of American commercial paper houses in that dealers of the former class, instead of handling promissory notes, deal in acceptances, which are drawn mainly in connection with the financing of foreign-trade transactions; in

[12] Since the majority of the leading dealers in commercial paper deal also in long-term securities, the functions performed by "commercial paper houses" and those fulfilled by "investment banking houses" are in many cases actually identical (except in so far as certain houses carry on one or more classes of other operations in which other houses do not engage). It would be more realistic in such cases, therefore, to point out similarities and differences between dealing in commercial paper and dealing in long-term securities than to compare "commercial paper houses" with "investment banking houses" with respect to the functions they perform.

[13] The terms "discount houses" and "bill brokers" seem to be used interchangeably in England as well as in this country. Strictly speaking, however, a distinction should be made between the London discount houses, which buy and sell acceptances outright for their own account, and the "running brokers" of the same city, who act as brokers only (*Report of the Committee on Finance and Industry* [the "Macmillan Report"], Cmd. 3897, 1931, p. 43; and W. F. Spalding, *The London Money Market*, 3d ed., p. 124).

that such dealers guarantee payment of the paper they handle; in that they are more likely than commercial paper houses are to depend on carrying such paper at a profit with borrowed funds, rather than turning their portfolios over as rapidly as possible, as the main source of their earnings; in that they accept deposits, and thus perform a second banking function; and in that they borrow from the central banking institution — though only as a last resort, since they can obtain accommodation from the Bank of England only at rates higher than their own buying rates for bills.

CHAPTER XIV

AN APPRAISAL OF THE WORK OF THE COMMERCIAL PAPER HOUSE

In the present chapter an evaluation of the services performed by dealers in commercial paper will be given. This appraisal of the work of the commercial paper house will be based on a consideration of the advantages of the open-market system of financing as a whole and of certain criticisms of this system which have been expressed from time to time.

1. ADVANTAGES OF THE OPEN-MARKET SYSTEM OF FINANCING

This system of financing has certain definite advantages from the point of view of the borrowers, as well as that of the lenders, in the commercial paper market, and also from a broader social point of view. Some of these advantages have been considered in earlier chapters, and will therefore merely be restated in this section.

From the point of view of the comparatively small number of concerns which possess the qualifications required for borrowing in the open market, some of the main advantages of this method of financing are as follows: Except in periods of unusually high money rates it is generally a less expensive method of raising short-term capital than borrowing from commercial banks direct; it enables borrowing concerns to secure accommodation in a market that is nation-wide, and therefore to borrow on somewhat more favorable terms from their own banks than they would ordinarily be able to obtain otherwise; it permits a periodic "clean-up" of bank loans, especially if it is properly coördinated with direct borrowing from banks; it enables concerns whose own banks are unable to supply the full amount of the borrowed funds they require to obtain the additional accommodation they need in a market that is considerably broader than the customers' loan market; it is a more convenient method of financing than borrowing directly from a large number of banks in different sections of the country; it enables many borrowers to obtain valuable financial advice from the dealers who handle their paper; it is a means of securing favorable publicity; and concerns which are able to use this method of financing are in a favorable position for raising such long-term capital as they may require from time to time.

Thus borrowing indirectly through dealers, though it cannot be relied on exclusively as a means of obtaining short-term capital, but should rather be considered as a method of financing supplementary to borrowing from banks direct, offers certain advantages as compared with the latter method of obtaining short-term funds. It also possesses advantages as compared with certain other methods of financing, whether short-term or long-term.

It is generally a much less expensive method of securing short-term funds than financing through discount or finance companies. In all cases where substantial discounts are offered for prompt cash payments it is also a less costly method of financing than accepting time bills of exchange or arranging for some bank to accept such bills. Moreover, the fact that a concern borrows through discount companies or allows its trade creditors to draw time bills of exchange on it often indicates either that its financial affairs are not being managed efficiently or that its credit standing is such that it is unable to make use of less expensive methods of financing; and resort to the former more expensive methods of financing is likely to impair its credit standing still further. Bankers' acceptances are of course practically indispensable for financing certain foreign-trade transactions, but when drawn for this purpose do not enter into active competition with open-market notes, since the latter are used mainly for financing transactions within the United States. Bankers' acceptances are also used, however, for financing the storage or shipment within this country of certain agricultural staples. When used for this purpose, acceptance financing competes to some extent with borrowing through dealers in open-market notes, and is generally somewhat less expensive than the latter method of financing, largely because the Federal Reserve banks still follow the policy of supporting the acceptance market by keeping rates on bankers' bills at artificially low levels.[1]

Long-term financing, like acceptance financing, is customarily used for different purposes from those for which funds are borrowed through dealers in commercial paper. As has been indicated already, however, a number of concerns raise what is in effect long-term capital by borrowing in the commercial paper market more or less continuously throughout the year. This method of financing is of course less conservative than issuing common or preferred stock, and the borrower's open-market indebtedness must be discharged on the average about twice a year (though the funds required for this purpose are often secured by replacing maturing notes with new obligations), whereas only the interest (or interest and sinking fund charges) on an issue of bonds must be met in any year preceding that in which such obligations mature. On the other hand, raising long-term capital through the sale of stock to outside interests may result in reducing the control which the original owners of a business are able to exercise over its affairs, and

---

[1] In the fall of 1933, however, the cost of borrowing in the commercial paper market fell below that of acceptance financing — for the first time, it is said, since 1914, when national banks began to accept bills of exchange (but see n. 51, p. 178). Prevailing rates on prime ninety-day bankers' bills in New York in October 1933 were ⅜ per cent bid, ¼ per cent asked. The prevailing rate on prime commercial paper with maturities of four to six months was then 1¼ per cent. Since the commission charged by banks for accepting prime ninety-day bankers' bills was then 1½ per cent a year, the cost of acceptance financing to concerns regarded as prime credit risks was 1⅞ per cent a year ("Acceptance Credit Costs," *Accept. Bull.*, Oct. 1933, pp. 1–2). On the assumption that the commission charged by commercial paper houses for handling prime six-months' notes was ¼ of 1 per cent of the face amounts of such obligations, and therefore equivalent to ½ of 1 per cent a year, the cost of borrowing in the commercial paper market to concerns which were rated as prime credit risks was then 1¾ per cent a year, or ⅛ of 1 per cent less than the cost of acceptance financing to concerns of comparable credit standing. Moreover, as was pointed out in Chap. III, in all cases where the commercial paper house's commission charge has been ¼ of 1 per cent or less, and the accepting bank has charged not less than the prevailing minimum commission of 1½ per cent a year for its services, the cost of borrowing through commercial paper houses on six-months' notes has remained less than that of acceptance financing during the greater part of the period since the fall of 1933. (The figure of 1⅞ per cent, given above as the cost of acceptance financing in October 1933, was based on the assumption that the borrowing concerns — that is, those which sold or discounted the bills in the first instance — were the concerns for which these bills were accepted by the banks on which they were drawn. Otherwise the direct cost of this method of financing to the concerns for which the bills were accepted would have been only 1½ per cent a year, the commission charge of the accepting banks.)

necessitates sharing the net earnings of the business with these outside interests; and, other things being equal, a concern with a long-term debt represented by mortgage bonds is considered less satisfactory as a bank credit risk than a company with no fixed-charge obligations having a prior lien on its assets. Moreover, raising what may be called permanent working capital by borrowing in the open market is a more flexible method of financing than issuing stocks or bonds; for open-market notes can be issued with the maturities and in the amounts which are best adapted to the varying requirements of the borrowing concern throughout the year.

From the point of view of the commercial banks which buy practically all the commercial paper handled by dealers, the main advantage of the open-market system of financing is that it provides them with an attractive investment for their secondary reserves, as well as for surplus funds which they cannot employ to advantage in direct loans to their own customers. As was shown in Chapter VIII, commercial paper is practically as safe an investment as bankers' acceptances, New York Stock Exchange call and time loans, and United States government obligations, and is a distinctly safer investment than direct loans of banks to their own customers and long-term securities, other than government bonds, of the classes which they have purchased in recent years; compares favorably as to liquidity and yield with alternative investments for their secondary reserves; and is issued in convenient denominations and with maturities adapted to banks' requirements.

Banks also derive two indirect advantages from buying open-market obligations, for the purchase of outside paper sometimes facilitates the acquisition of profitable new accounts, and the training and experience which bankers acquire in investigating the credit standing of concerns whose obligations are offered for sale in the market are of value in enabling them to judge the risks involved in extending direct loans to their own customers.

Two remaining advantages which banks derive from the open-market system of financing are that they are sometimes able to obtain valuable information relating to their own customers from dealers who handle the open-market paper of the latter, and that, at times when demands for customers' loans are unusually heavy, certain banks may find it expedient to relieve the pressure of such demands on their own resources by inducing some of their customers to obtain a part of the accommodation they require by borrowing in the open market.

From a broader social point of view, the main advantage of the open-market system of financing is that the operations of dealers bring about a more effective utilization of the country's productive resources than would result from the functioning of our independent unit system of banking alone. In a country as large as the United States, with its great diversity of industrial activity, both the available supply of short-term loanable funds and the demand therefor differ to a considerable extent as among different sections at any particular time. They also vary to a greater or lesser extent within the same sections at different seasons of the year. If a nation-wide branch banking system existed in the United States, a single large banking organization, by a process of transferring funds from regions in which they were relatively abundant to regions in which they were comparatively scarce, could readily effect a smooth and continuous adjustment of available supplies of short-term capital to the varying demands therefor in all parts of the country. Such a pooling of credit resources, and their redistribution in accordance with the relative needs of different regions, can be effected on a smaller scale by a state-wide system of branch banking, and also by a large group or chain banking organization. Even under our present independent unit system of banking credit resources can in effect be pooled and redistributed over a fairly wide area through correspondent banking relationships, as well as by a single large bank which receives deposits from different parts of the country and makes direct loans to customers throughout a wider territory than that included in its own immediate locality. There are, nevertheless, at least some concerns of high credit standing in all sections of the United States which, either at certain seasons or more or less continuously, require more short-term credit accommodation than they can secure from the banks with which they have lines of credit — or, at any rate, are unable to obtain accommodation from these banks on terms which they consider sufficiently favorable. There are also in all parts of the United States banks which, either for a few months of each year or more or less continuously throughout the year, have surplus funds which they can employ more advantageously in outside loans than in direct advances to their own customers. In a country as large as the United States, however, these potential borrowers and lenders may be thousands of miles apart, and obviously would encounter considerable difficulty if they tried to negotiate with each other directly. They can clearly be brought together much more effectively through the intermediation of a class of dealers who make it their business to keep in touch with concerns which are in a position to supplement borrowing from their own banks with borrowing in a broader market, and with banks possessing surplus funds which they are willing to place in outside loans. Commercial paper houses act as such intermediary dealers, collecting short-term loanable funds in regions in which they are comparatively abundant and redistributing them in sections in which they are relatively scarce, and thus making the supply of such funds available at any particular time more flexible and mobile. In performing this function they enable concerns of high credit standing in all sections of the country to borrow in the cheapest market, and therefore to reduce their costs of operation, and at the same time provide a safe and relatively remunerative investment for the surplus funds of banks in all parts of the United States. Hence the open-market system of financing as a whole operates to bring about a more continuous and effective utilization of the country's productive resources than would otherwise be possible under our independent unit system of banking. This fact constitutes both the fundamental reason for the existence of a system of financing found in no other country than the United States and the ultimate justification of the operations of the houses which make this system of financing possible.

Indirectly, at least, the open-market system of financing also contributes to bringing about a more effective utilization of the funds available for short-term advances to borrowers in the customers' loan market. As was indicated in Chapter II, dealers in open-market notes probably began to organize credit departments and secure financial statements from their borrowing customers during the decade of the 1890's, a few years before some even of the larger city banks in the East took similar steps. The increase in their efficiency in selecting open-market paper which resulted from the improved methods of credit investigation they were able to employ thereafter no doubt stimulated at least some of their buying customers to follow their example. At any rate, a fairly large number of banks established credit departments between 1892 and 1911, and at least some of the banks which took the lead in adopting improved methods of credit investigation organized such departments largely for the purpose of increasing their proficiency in selecting outside paper. Their adoption of improved methods of credit investigation, whether or not primarily for the latter purpose, the training in credit analysis they have acquired from the selection of open-market notes for purchase, and the close coöperation they have received from dealers in the exchange of credit information have all enabled bankers to select to better advantage the paper on which they make direct loans to their own customers. Thus the open-market system of financing not only makes possible a nation-wide open market in which loanable funds are apportioned among the concerns which presumably can use such funds to the greatest advantage, but also operates to bring about a more effective distribution of short-term capital among potential borrowers in the customers' loan market.

2. Some Criticisms of the Open-Market System

Despite the fact that dealers have for many years rendered important services both to their borrowing and to their buying customers, the system of financing which their operations make possible has in the past been subjected to a considerable amount of criticism. Since a number of the weaknesses of the system against which censure was formerly directed have in more recent years been practically eliminated, criticism of the operations of dealers is much less common at present than it was some years ago. Even in recent years, however, it has been argued that the open-market system of financing has certain disadvantages, not only from the standpoint of the borrowers and the lenders in the commercial paper market but also from a broader social point of view. The grounds on which this system has been criticized from time to time will now be considered.

The borrowing customers of dealers have expressed but little criticism of the open-market system of financing. Indeed, when properly used, this system has no disadvantages of any consequence from their point of view. Even within recent years, however, it has been maintained that the ease with which unsecured notes may be floated in the open market facilitates and encourages overtrading. It has also been stated that concerns which borrow in the market are likely to discover to their embarrassment that dealers are "fair-weather friends" only — that is, are unable to market the obligations of their borrowing clients at times when the latter are most in need of borrowed funds.

There can be no question that in earlier years, before either dealers or banks had adopted effective methods of credit investigation, the practice of borrowing in the market was often abused by concerns which were only too eager to take advantage of opportunities to expand their operations by means of borrowed funds, and as a consequence sooner or later found themselves unable to meet their obligations.[2] Even as late as 1914 and 1920 at least some cases of overtrading with the aid of open-market loans

---

[2] Criticism of the open-market system of financing on the ground that it facilitated overtrading was rather common in earlier years. Examples of such criticism may be found in the following: George Hague, "One-Name Paper," *Proc. Amer. Bankers' Assoc.*, 1884, pp. 67–70; A. S. Bolles, *Practical Banking* (11th ed., 1903), p. 114; J. T. Talbert, "Commercial Paper," *Proc. Minn. Bankers' Assoc.*, 1908, p. 43; and J. B. McCargar, "Buying Commercial Paper," *Bankers' Home Mag.*, Dec. 1915, p. 38.

On the other hand, a New York banker who was considered an authority on bank credits expressed the opinion in 1908 that a merchant who "sells his paper" (in the open market) is "much more apt to use prudence regarding his own credits," and is likely to be a better credit risk, than he would be if he borrowed from his own banks alone (J. G. Cannon, *Buying Commercial Paper* — pamphlet — pp. 15–16).

occurred. It should be noted, however, that the banks which purchased the notes issued by the borrowers concerned were as much to blame for the unfortunate consequences of such over-trading as the dealers who sold these notes in the market; for these banks were by no means so careful in selecting outside paper for purchase as well-managed banks are at present. Moreover, it is said that even about as late as 1912 "some of the largest and what afterwards proved to be the least desirable lines of [open-market] paper" were "forced out into the hands of confiding bankers in the smaller cities by the large banks whose direct extensions of credit to the makers of the paper had already passed safe limits." [3] In more recent years both dealers and bankers have become more proficient in selecting open-market obligations, and at present it would be difficult indeed for any concern to borrow excessive amounts of short-term funds through any reputable dealer for the purpose of undertaking any unwise expansion of its operations. It is obviously to the dealer's interest to watch carefully the total amounts of his clients' borrowings from all sources, with a view to making sure that such borrowings will be kept within reasonable limits. Banks also scrutinize the total amounts being borrowed by concerns whose open-market notes they are considering for purchase, and in general "check" such notes more carefully than they select the paper on which they extend direct loans to their own customers. Consequently, concerns whose credit position is strong enough to enable them to borrow in the open market are much less likely to issue excessive amounts of short-term obligations than those whose borrowings are confined to the customers' loan market.

It is true also that dealers are at times unable to find a market for paper issued by certain of their borrowing customers.

If a concern which has been borrowing through dealers gets into financial difficulties, it obviously cannot expect to borrow in the market again unless it can recover its former status as a preferred credit risk. At present, however, commercial paper is so carefully

[3] R. L. Crampton, "A Central Bureau of Credit Information," *Proc. Amer. Bankers' Assoc.*, 1912, p. 581.

selected, both by dealers and by their buying customers, that only a very small proportion of the concerns which borrow in the market become financially embarrassed.[4] Even if they do become embarrassed, most such concerns, with the aid of their dealers and their banks, are able to deal successfully with the problems which arise at such times. In such situations their dealers have sometimes advanced them credits, and always coöperate very closely with their banks in aiding them to work out of their difficulties. Hence in most cases inability to sell their notes in the open market at such times does not result in serious consequences for these concerns if they have maintained adequate banking connections — and concerns which do not maintain such connections at present cannot borrow in the market through responsible dealers. From the standpoint of dealers' borrowing customers, therefore, the fact that concerns which have become financially embarrassed cannot sell their notes in the market constitutes no serious objection against the open-market system of financing.

Before 1920, however, even concerns in a comparatively strong financial condition found it difficult to sell their notes through dealers during financial crises or periods of pronounced stringency in the money market. Purchases of open-market obligations were reduced considerably in 1913 and during the financial crisis which followed the outbreak of the World War in 1914; and during previous crises, such as those which occurred in 1893 and 1907, the market for commercial paper is said to have been "completely suspended." [5]

The decline in the market for commercial paper at such times was due in large part to the imperfect functioning of our banking system during periods of financial strain. In such periods practically all maturing commercial paper was paid in full promptly at maturity, and the payment of such paper provided at least some banks with surplus funds which were available for reinvestment in open-market obligations. The real difficulty at such times was not that of collecting and redistributing such funds as were avail-

[4] See p. 312.
[5] See pp. 61–62.

able for this purpose among concerns wishing to borrow through dealers, but rather the fact that available supplies of short-term credit were not sufficient to meet the combined demands of concerns applying for loans in the customers' loan market and those wishing to borrow in the open market for commercial paper. Demands for direct loans on the part of most banks' own customers have been unusually heavy in periods of financial strain, and consequently many banks have had no surplus funds available for investment in outside paper at such times. Had there been a reserve of lending power somewhere in the banking system, the situation would obviously have been different. No such reserve of lending power was provided, however, until the Federal Reserve system was established and made the country's available supplies of short-term credit both more mobile and more flexible.

A number of concerns found it difficult to borrow through dealers even in 1920, nearly six years after the new banking system began to function. The market for commercial paper apparently was much less restricted in that year, however, than it had been in 1907, 1913, and 1914, for in 1920 the estimated annual volume of sales by dealers reached the highest figure which has yet been recorded. Moreover, according to a leading Eastern commercial paper house, dealers were unable to supply the demands of their buying customers for open-market notes in 1933, including the period of the banking holiday, and the market for commercial paper during the latter period was distinctly more active even than that for United States government bonds.

So long as member banks, by drawing on the central banking system's reserve of lending power, can expand their loans in an emergency, it is likely that the market for commercial paper will also prove to be broader and more active during any future period of financial strain than it was in such years as 1907, 1913, and 1914. Hence the fact that it has been difficult in the past to borrow in the open market during financial crises or periods of marked stringency in the money market can hardly be considered an important objection against the open-market system of financing from the point of view of any concern which maintains a strong financial position, has adequate banking connections, keeps satisfactory average balances with its banks, and properly coördinates its open-market borrowing with borrowing in the customers' loan market.

Certain other supposed disadvantages of open-market financing from the standpoint of dealers' borrowing customers were considered in Chapter VI. Since these supposed disadvantages are of little or no importance, they need not be restated here; and, since the two objections against the open-market system of financing which have just been considered are likewise of but little consequence at present, it may be concluded that there are no important disadvantages of this system from the point of view of the borrowers in the commercial paper market.

Though but few of these borrowers have had occasion, in recent years at least, to find fault with the system of financing through dealers, this system has been exposed to a considerable amount of criticism by commercial bankers. The censure of the latter has in the past been directed against a number of different weaknesses, actual or supposed, of the open-market system. Most of the objections they have raised against the system of financing through dealers, however, can be comprehended under, or are closely connected with, two main criticisms of this system. The first of these criticisms is that dealers handle at least some paper issued by concerns which do not possess the proper qualifications for borrowing in the open market; the second, that, in buying and selling promissory notes in the market, dealers enter into direct competition with commercial banks themselves.

In earlier years criticism of the open-market system on the first of the two grounds just mentioned was no doubt amply justified.[6] The percentages of losses incurred by banks on purchased paper

---

[6] Examples of criticism of the open-market system on this ground may be found in the following: T. H. Hinchman, "English and American Banking," *Proc. Amer. Bankers' Assoc.*, 1887, p. 49; W. H. Peck, *The Value of Commercial Paper as Quick Assets* (pamphlet), p. 8; E. M. Stevens, "Commercial Paper," *Proc. N. D. Bankers' Assoc.*, 1903, p. 30; G. A. Rogers, "Loaning Money," *Proc. Kan. Bankers' Assoc.*, 1905, p. 139; and H. A. Wheeler, "A Central Bureau of Credit Information," *Proc. Indiana Bankers' Assoc.*, 1912, p. 149, and "Bank Credits under the Federal Reserve Act," *Proc. Tenn. Bankers' Assoc.*, 1914, p. 102.

were doubtless appreciably greater years ago than they have been in more recent years, though they were very probably much smaller than the corresponding figures for losses sustained by these same banks on direct loans to their own customers. Figures of total losses on open-market obligations are not available for any year preceding 1922. It is known, however, that individual banks suffered fairly heavy losses on outside paper about as late as 1914; and losses to banks as a whole during the period from 1880 to 1922 were at least serious enough to give rise to numerous proposals for making commercial paper a safer investment, such as insurance against losses on open-market notes,[7] requiring commercial paper dealers to indorse the notes they handle,[8] the organization of central credit bureaus for collecting and making available to banks information relating to the credit standing of open-market borrowers,[9] the establishment by clearing houses, particularly those

[7] Such insurance was advocated by a Wisconsin banker in 1907 and for several years thereafter (John Schuette, address — without title — *Proc. Okla. Bankers' Assoc.*, 1911, p. 104). Apparently, however, no insurance company has ever undertaken to guarantee the payment of any commercial paper at maturity. The proposal in question is open to the objections that (1) concerns whose notes cannot safely be purchased without insurance protection should not borrow in the open market at all; (2) if such concerns were allowed to borrow in the market, it would be difficult to determine premium charges properly adjusted to the risks involved in purchasing their paper; (3) as a rule, neither borrowing concerns nor dealers' buying customers would want to absorb the premium charges; and (4) insurance of the kind proposed would tend to make borrowing concerns less careful to maintain their status as preferred credit risks and banks less careful in the selection of outside paper.

[8] C. F. Bentley, "Commercial Paper as an Investment for Country Bankers," *Proc. Neb. Bankers' Assoc.*, 1903, p. 185, and Ralph Van Vechten, address as president of Clearing House Section, American Bankers' Association, *Proc. Amer. Bankers' Assoc.*, 1913, p. 521. See also H. P. Willis, "The Status of Commercial Paper under the Federal Reserve Act," *Proc. N. J. Bankers' Assoc.*, 1914, p. 53. If dealers were required to indorse the notes they handle, it would seem that they could fairly expect to receive some form of compensation for assuming the responsibility they would thereby incur. As was pointed out in Chap. VIII, foreign purchasers of open-market commercial paper issued by American concerns have occasionally paid American banks a premium of ¼ of 1 per cent a year for indorsing such paper. Most American banks, however, would probably be unwilling to pay commercial paper houses a premium of this amount for indorsement, particularly in periods of low money rates.

[9] "Commercial Credits," *Rhodes' Jour. of Banking*, Nov. 1894, p. 1082; Robert McCurdy, "Committee on Credits," *Proc. Amer. Bankers' Assoc.*, 1899, pp. 95–97; Report of Committee on Credits, *ibid.*, p. 98; Report of Committee on Credit Information, *Proc. Amer. Bankers' Assoc.*, 1908, p. 195; "Exchange of Credit Informa-

in the central reserve cities, of departments for performing the same function,[10] and the registration with banks, clearing houses, or other agencies, of all notes issued for sale in the open market.[11]

In explanation of the fact that losses on purchased paper were proportionately greater in earlier years than they have been since about 1914, several reasons may be given. In the first place, a number of the dealers in open-market obligations in earlier years were irresponsible brokers who apparently were more interested in the quantity than in the quality of the paper they handled.[12]

tion between Banks," *Proc. N. J. Bankers' Assoc.*, 1909, pp. 49–53; and R. L. Crampton, "A Central Bureau of Credit Information," *Proc. Amer. Bankers' Assoc.*, 1912, pp. 577–589. In 1912 the New York State Banking Department established a central credit bureau in its New York City branch office. One of the functions which this bureau performed was aiding New York banks in the selection of open-market paper (New York State Superintendent of Banks, *Report on Banks of Deposit and Discount*, 1912, pp. 8–10, and J. A. Broderick, "A Central Credit Bureau in Operation," *Bankers' Home Mag.*, Oct. 1912, pp. 14–17).

[10] H. M. Priest, "Clearing-House Inspection of Credits," *Bankers' Mag.*, June 1913, pp. 697–698.

[11] Agitation in favor of the registration of commercial paper became active about as early as 1907. Probably few open-market borrowers, if any, however, actually began to register their notes before 1911. In February of the latter year the International Paper Company announced that all notes it issued for sale through dealers in the future would be registered, and by March 1911 more than forty other large corporations are said to have announced their intention of having future issues of their open-market paper registered ("More Paper Registration," *N. Y. Times*, Oct. 16, 1914, p. 14; Owen Shepherd, "Commercial Paper Registration," *Trust Companies*, Mar. 1911, p. 178). In the same year a New York banker stated that it "would seem to be safe to predict that this system of protection will soon be generally recognized as being necessary to those who desire to issue commercial paper" (F. I. Kent, "Registration of Commercial Paper," *Proc. Amer. Bankers' Assoc.*, 1911, p. 534). Even as late as 1924 and 1926 it was recommended that all notes issued for sale in the open market be registered with the Federal Reserve banks ("Have Commercial Paper Registered," *Forbes*, Nov. 1, 1924, p. 155; "Would Register Commercial Paper," *N. Y. Times*, Jan. 26, 1926, p. 35). While a few additional concerns began to register their open-market notes after 1911, and at least three companies were registering such obligations with commercial banks a few years ago, registration has for a number of years been a dead issue. It involves some bother, delay, and expense (1/10 of 1 per cent of the face amount of notes registered being the fee charged by an Eastern bank a few years ago), and in most cases does not make available any credit information which cannot be obtained directly from the dealer handling the borrowing account concerned. For these and other reasons most concerns borrowing in the open market, as well as commercial paper houses themselves, have been distinctly less interested in registration than certain Eastern banks wishing to earn registration fees.

[12] S. R. Flynn, "A Twentieth Century Credit System," *Proc. Mich. Bankers' Assoc.*, 1901, p. 32; Report of Committee on Credit Information, *Proc. Amer. Bankers' Assoc.*, 1908, p. 197; Broderick, *op. cit.*, p. 16, and "Registration of Com-

Secondly, even reputable commercial paper houses which purchased their stock in trade outright were less proficient, and also less careful, in selecting the paper they handled than responsible dealers are at present. In the third place, banks themselves were often careless in selecting outside paper for purchase, as was admitted by a number of bankers.[13] Lastly, bank "checkings" in earlier years could not always be relied on.[14] Since notes which bankers consider unsatisfactory for purchase cannot be sold in the market, and banks often purchased open-market obligations without any careful investigation of the credit standing of the makers, it seems fair to say that the buying customers of dealers were themselves chiefly to blame for the fact that fairly large amounts of low-grade paper were sold in the market in earlier years.

In more recent years there has been but little criticism of the open-market system on the ground under consideration. Some dealers, it is said, in an endeavor to secure a volume of business large enough to be profitable, have induced comparatively small concerns whose borrowings should have been confined to their own banks to seek accommodation in the open market.[15] Since a number of banks have been willing to purchase such obligations, a few small dealers have doubtless handled some open-market notes issued by concerns of this class. Only negligible amounts of such paper have been offered for sale in the market in recent years, however, for neither reputable commercial paper houses nor well-managed banks select the obligations of such concerns for purchase.[16]

---

mercial Paper," *Bankers' Home Mag.*, Nov. 1913, pp. 43–44; Report of New York State Superintendent of Banks, 1913, p. 9; and F. K. Houston, *Commercial Paper — Its Uses and Abuses* (pamphlet), pp. 14–15.

[13] McCurdy, *op. cit.*, p. 97; Flynn, *op. cit.*, p. 44; Report of Committee on Credit Information, *Proc. Amer. Bankers' Assoc.*, 1908, p. 199; Talbert, "Commercial Credits," *Proc. N. Y. Bankers' Assoc.*, 1908, p. 86; and Wheeler, "A Central Bureau of Credit Information," *Proc. Indiana Bankers' Assoc.*, 1912, p. 149.

[14] Flynn, *op. cit.*, p. 32, and J. H. Puelicher, "Bank Reserves," *Proc. Wis. Bankers' Assoc.*, 1910, p. 113.

[15] C. Q. Chandler, "Bank Investment Policies," *Proc. Mid-Western Bank Management Conference*, Kansas City, Mo., Mar. 19–20, 1931, p. 69; D. W. Hogan, "Commercial Paper, Bankers' Acceptances, and Call Loans," *ibid.*, p. 75; and Mitchell Ives, "The Low Rates on Prime Commercial Credit," *A.B.A. Jour.*, April 1934, p. 35.

[16] As a Boston banker has pointed out, dealers have also been criticized in recent

Much more important from the point of view of bankers than the objection which has just been considered is the second of their main two criticisms of the open-market system — namely, that commercial paper houses enter into direct competition with commercial banks. Bankers have for many years criticized the open-market system of financing on the ground that dealers, by offering prospective borrowers rates of discount below those prevailing in the customers' loan market, particularly in periods of low money rates, induce many of the best customers of banks to borrow in the open market substantial amounts of funds which they would otherwise borrow directly from their own banks. Many bankers have complained also that, in thus entering into direct competition with them, dealers not only deprive them of opportunities for making loans to their best customers but also force discount rates throughout the customers' loan market down to lower levels than would otherwise prevail. In the past, at least, bankers have maintained, further, that the open-market system encourages borrowing concerns to become independent of their own banks, particularly during periods of low money rates, but is unable to furnish the accommodation required by such concerns when they get into financial difficulties, or during periods of financial strain; and that consequently demands for direct accommodation on the part of these concerns are heaviest at the very times when the latter are least desirable as credit risks from the point of view of their own banks.[17]

---

years for offering for sale notes of companies "which have only *recently recovered from an unsatisfactory financial condition* through which they had to be carried by the banks" (J. N. Eaton, "Rate Competition," *Mo. Bull. Robert Morris Associates,* July 1936, p. 46). The criticism in question, however, is directed not so much against the quality of the paper offered for sale by dealers as against their competition with banks. The present writer is inclined to agree with the banker just referred to that if a company "has worked out of a frozen position to the point where it is in good shape, and there is reasonable prospect for its continuing in that condition, and banks are willing to buy the paper, there is little reason for criticizing the broker for taking on such an account" (Eaton, *loc. cit.*).

[17] The following extract from an address by a St. Paul banker in 1901 no doubt reflects the attitude which many bankers in the past have taken toward advancing credits to such concerns in periods of financial strain: "There is the merchant with his fixed line [of bank credit] at home, who keeps it open until the exigencies of a tight money-market or a panic bring him to his deposit bank seeking escape from

There can be no doubt that competition among dealers themselves, as well as between dealers and banks, has for years been very active. During the last few years, when bankers have encountered unusual difficulties in finding profitable employment for short-term funds, even at abnormally low rates of return, competition between dealers and banks has probably been more active than in any preceding period since the beginning of the commercial paper business.[18] It is not surprising, therefore, that many bankers feel that the commercial paper house deprives them of opportunities for employing their loanable funds in direct advances to their own customers. It is easy to understand also why bankers should dislike to have to aid the commercial paper house in selling their own customers' obligations in the open market, as they often must do if they are to send truthful replies to the credit inquiries of other bankers who are contemplating the purchase of such paper.[19]

---

ruin. . . . During the time his paper is in active demand, this merchant gives the profit to the outside brokers or banks. As soon as the pinch comes, or his condition gives rise to apprehension, then he remembers his line. When he becomes an extrahazardous risk, this merchant will generously give to his home bank the opportunity to make a very little or to lose a great deal. If the merchant survives the period of stringency, the home bank will make five or six per cent on the venture; and if he fails, the bank will lose from 25 per cent up. . . . I wonder that they [such merchants] are not told more often when they seek to fall back on their lines at such times: 'Line! Oh, yes, you had a line; it was a "good-times" line. Sorry you couldn't use it. Can't help you now. We are not making loans'" (Flynn, *op. cit.*, p. 29).

[18] It was no doubt because of this situation that the Committee on Credit Practices of the Association of Reserve City Bankers, in its report for 1935, made the "recommendation" that "firms and corporations selling paper in the open market should have current borrowings from their line of credit banks in excess of the amount sold in the open market at all times" (Report of the Committee on Credit Practices, *Proc. Assoc. Reserve City Bankers*, 1935, p. 26). This recommendation has presumably had no important practical effects. Most concerns which are able to borrow in the open market would no doubt be strongly opposed to any such "regimentation" of their financial affairs as a practical application of the recommendation in question would involve, and the financial policies of such concerns cannot be dictated by their line-of-credit banks, particularly in periods of low money rates.

[19] The fact that bankers are thus called on, willingly or unwillingly, to aid the commercial paper house in selling notes of their own customers in the market has been called "one of the anomalies of the financial world" (Talbert, *op. cit.*, p. 86). The attitude of many bankers toward this anomaly is suggested in the following excerpt from an address by a Michigan banker about thirty-five years ago: ". . . it is a queer sensation that creeps over the bank cashier as he opens the mail in the morning and reads one letter after another inquiring about the standing,

Many bankers, however, including at least some who buy substantial amounts of outside paper for the account of their own institutions, apparently have overlooked certain facts in connection with the open-market system of financing.

They seem to have failed to realize, for instance, that the commercial paper house performs the function of an intermediary dealer, and can sell no paper which bankers are not willing of their own accord to purchase; and that the ultimate competition is not between dealers and banks but between lenders in the customers' loan market and those in the commercial paper market, or, more specifically, between banks which make direct loans to certain borrowing concerns and a larger number of banks, located in all sections of the country, which are willing to buy the short-term notes of these same concerns in the open market.

Moreover, individual bankers who have criticized the open-market system of financing on the ground that it restricts the volume of their loans to their own customers have been inclined to judge this system of financing primarily on the basis of its effects on their own operations in the customers' loan market, rather than on the basis of its advantages and disadvantages as a whole. They have therefore apparently overlooked the fact that it has important advantages both to borrowing concerns and to banks themselves.

Borrowing concerns can hardly be blamed for securing indirectly through dealers at least a part of the credit accommodation they require, for this method of raising short-term capital (in addition to offering them a number of other advantages) is ordinarily less expensive than borrowing directly from their own banks. Since they are under a strong compulsion to meet open-market obliga-

---

reputation, character, and responsibility, — of whom? The best customers he has got; the very men that he depends upon to maintain his business, and by whom, perhaps, he has stood in . . . times of testing . . . in the years gone by, and by whom he expects to stand in the years to come. . . . What . . . answer is he to . . . write back to the banker in Chicago or New York about that customer? Give him a good bill of credit, put him in good credit in his local town? Why yes, he is entitled to it. But what does it mean? What is that inquiry for? . . .

"The paper has been offered to or placed in some bank in Chicago or New York, and your report will be the basis of their taking that paper, which is being sent there in good times and at reduced rates of interest" (J. R. Wylie, address before the Michigan Bankers' Association, *Proc. Mich. Bankers' Assoc.*, 1901, p. 36).

tions promptly at maturity, whereas they are often able to secure renewals or extensions of loans obtained in the customers' loan market, it is no more than reasonable that they should be able to borrow in the open market at rates below those at which their own banks are willing to advance credits to them.

While the open-market borrowing of such concerns reduces correspondingly the amounts of "over-the-counter" accommodation they require, the very fact that they are able to supplement their borrowings in the customers' loan market with funds obtained through dealers may be of considerable advantage to their own banks when demands for loans on the part of other customers of these banks are unusually heavy. Moreover, companies which secure in the open market a part of the borrowed funds they require practically always maintain satisfactory average balances with their own banks, and the free use of these balances compensates these banks, to some extent at least, for any reduction in the volume of their customers' loans resulting from the competition of the commercial paper market. Banks also derive other advantages from the open-market system. Commercial paper houses make available a choice investment for the surplus funds of banks in all sections of the country, yet make no charge whatsoever to their buying customers for this service. Had no special class of intermediary dealers arisen to render this service, commercial banks in the larger cities, as was noted by a Boston banker in 1916, "would have to send highly paid men of good judgment over the country in search of parties to whom they could lend money whenever a surplus of funds occurred." [20] Dealers also coöperate closely with bankers in the exchange of credit information, and aid them in securing desirable new accounts; keep substantial average balances in the banks with which they maintain deposit accounts; and, at least in years in which the commercial paper business is active, borrow large amounts from the latter banks each year. Not all banks, of course, are in a position to avail themselves of the advantages offered by the open-market system to the same extent,

[20] T. P. Beal, Jr., "Effect of Increased Operations of Note Brokers upon the Earnings of Commercial Banks," *Proc. Amer. Bankers' Assoc.*, 1916, p. 503.

and individual bankers may have reasons for believing that these advantages are insufficient to compensate them for the fact that the volume of their loans to their own customers is restricted to some extent by the competition of the dealer. Any disadvantages experienced by individual banks as a result of such competition, however, are greatly outweighed by the advantages of the open-market system to the banking system as a whole.

It may be noted also that, however active the competition of dealers with banks has been, the competition of banks against dealers, as well as that among banks themselves, has at times been no less active.

Competition of banks with dealers has taken several different forms. As late as about 1926 a number of banks were themselves acting as dealers, though in most cases they were carrying on their operations in open-market paper in a comparatively restricted territory. A much larger number of banks have sold notes of their own customers to correspondent banks, sometimes at rates lower than those at which these notes were discounted in the first instance.[21] In some cases banks have "exchanged" loans; that is,

---

[21] A Boston bank reported in 1931 that it used to sell large amounts of high-grade notes of its own customers to correspondent banks in New England. As late as about 1927 this bank had about as much as $5,000,000 of these obligations "outstanding," and sold such paper to as many as twenty-five different banks at a time. It also sold its customers' notes to individuals and to a Boston business concern. It generally sold these notes at the rates at which it discounted them for its customers, though occasionally it rediscounted them at rates somewhat lower than its buying rates, thereby realizing a small selling profit. Contrary to the usual practice in such cases, it customarily indorsed such obligations before selling them.

About twenty years ago individual officers of a number of Kansas banks were in effect acting as dealers, as the following extract from an address by a banker of that state indicates: "Many a managing officer of a Kansas bank is in the brokerage business today on the reputation of and at the expense of his bank. He makes loans in his own name at 8% and discounts them with the city correspondent of his bank at the lowest rate obtainable, endorsing same as an individual, and the profit therefrom he puts into his own pocket. There is no secret about the transaction; quite likely the board of directors know all about it. . . . The city bank would not discount the paper for the cashier except for his official position . . . if the paper is not cared for at maturity the city bank will discover that they are relying not on the cashier as an individual but on the bank, and they will promptly charge the dishonored paper to the [selling] bank's account. . . . The profits arising from such transactions are the bank's. The bank has paid for the officer's time used in the transaction; the outlet for such paper has been furnished by the bank; in fact the very loan itself has probably been furnished by one of the bank's customers and the

each of two banks which have been unable, because of legal limitations on the amount of accommodation that may be extended to any one borrower, to supply the full amounts of credit required by certain of their customers, has discounted notes of such customers with the other.[22] Whatever the reasons for inter-

---

transaction has taken place in the bank's place of business . . ." (W. A. Matson, "Slack and Slip-shod Banking," *Proc. Kan. Bankers' Assoc.*, 1916, p. 112).

Inter-bank rediscounting became "a recognized practice" in the United States "at least as early as the establishment of the national banking system" (O. C. Lockhart, "The Development of Interbank Borrowing in the National System, 1869–1914," *Jour. Pol. Econ.*, Feb. 1921, p. 139). Conservative bankers, particularly in the larger cities of the East and the North, have nevertheless generally disapproved of banks' rediscounting notes of their own customers with other banks, especially when such rediscounting is resorted to by the selling banks as a means of borrowing. Objections which bankers themselves have raised against banks' selling customers' notes to correspondent institutions are that such notes are likely to be sold when the selling banks are in an extended condition; that such rediscounting is likely to result in the extension of excessive amounts of credit to the makers of the rediscounted obligations; and that the selling banks must stand ready to buy such obligations back from their correspondents, even though they have not agreed to do so. The selling banks, moreover, have found that country correspondents are likely to return rediscounted notes which are not met at maturity by the makers. Cf. the following: ". . . it [customers' paper which has been sold to country correspondent banks] always comes back when least welcome, and it makes no difference if you sell it 'without recourse.' If the holder crowds your customer, you have to take it up to protect him just the same" (T. M. Wingo, address — without title — before the Arizona Bankers' Association, *Proc. Ariz. Bankers' Assoc.*, 1922, p. 36).

[22] This practice, which is doubtless less common now than it was in earlier years, is known also as "swapping notes." It is open to both of the first two objections against inter-bank rediscounting which were mentioned in the preceding footnote. Some years ago the directors of certain banks which engaged in the practice of "swapping" notes used to guarantee personally the paper which their institutions rediscounted with the banks from which they in turn purchased customers' notes. In case any losses had to be incurred on paper so guaranteed, however, such losses were not assumed by the directors concerned. They were sustained, instead, by the selling banks, despite the fact that the latter had assumed no legal or moral responsibility with respect to the paper guaranteed by their directors (J. E. Cosgriff, "Troublesome Problems in Banking," *Proc. Idaho Bankers' Assoc.*, 1913, p. 95).

From about 1901 to about 1909 a committee of the Kansas Bankers' Association, called the "Committee on Loan Exchange," acted as an intermediary agency for the interchange of customers' notes among banks belonging to the association. In its report for 1902 the committee intimated that it would be willing to arrange for the interchange of paper discounted by Kansas banks and notes discounted by banks in Missouri, Oklahoma, and the Indian Territory. In addition to customers' notes obtained from banks, the committee offered for sale limited amounts of paper issued by milling concerns and jobbing and wholesale houses. The total amounts of paper handled by the committee from 1902 to 1909 were reported as follows: 1902, $90,000; 1903, $104,000; 1904, $124,000; 1905, $219,000; 1906, $388,000, including $97,000 of paper (presumably issued by milling companies) "secured by warehouse

bank rediscounting may be, the purchase of customers' notes from correspondent or other banks tends to reduce the demand of the buying bank for open-market obligations, though of course it may also release funds which the selling bank will be in a position to invest in outside paper. The commercial loan "participations" in which banks engage, like inter-bank rediscounting operations, also provide outlets for loanable funds which might otherwise be placed in open-market loans.[23] Moreover, banks have often tried to eliminate the services of the commercial paper house by dealing with borrowing concerns directly. While such direct dealings have not proved entirely satisfactory from the point of view of either the borrowers or the lenders concerned, banks in the past have purchased at least limited amounts of paper directly from the issuing companies. A leading packing company which had been dealing directly with banks for some years is said to have raised considerable amounts of short-term capital in this manner as recently as about 1928. The ultimate objective of banks which endeavor to deal directly with borrowing concerns is commonly to secure profitable new accounts. Many bankers, including some who have been most active in expressing their disapproval of the competition of

---

receipts"; 1907, $620,000; 1908, $1,006,000, including $682,000 of "rediscounts from the various banks" and $324,000 of "commercial paper" (Report of Committee on Loan Exchange, *Proc. Kan. Bankers' Assoc.*, 1902, pp. 96–97; 1903, pp. 106–107; 1904, pp. 34–35; 1905, pp. 33–34; 1906, pp. 39–40; 1907, p. 53; and 1908, p. 106). Though it operated on a small scale only, the committee was obviously performing some of the functions of a commercial paper house.

In 1914 it was proposed that a somewhat similar agency be established by the Maryland Bankers' Association. The proposed "credit bureau" was to undertake to make available to banks "on the Eastern Shore" of Maryland the "surplus accumulations" of banks in the "northern counties" (Claude Gilbert, "Country Credit Methods," *Proc. Md. Bankers' Assoc.*, 1914, pp. 52–53).

[23] An Indianapolis bank undertook, presumably in 1923, to supply its correspondents with "participations in commercial paper," i.e., to sell them participations in notes which it discounted in connection with direct loans to its own customers. It was stated that its purpose in assuming this function was to increase its list of correspondents, rather than to make a profit from selling them participations in customers' loans; and that, in performing the service mentioned, the bank intended to supplement the services of commercial paper houses, rather than to compete against the latter (W. B. Schiltges, "Small Bank Participation in Commercial Paper," *Bankers' Monthly*, Nov. 1923, p. 92). In selling such participations, however, it was clearly providing an investment for funds which might otherwise have been placed in paper handled by regular dealers in open-market obligations.

the commercial paper house, have purchased open-market obligations primarily for the same purpose. Finally, some of the larger city banks in recent years have offered direct loans to concerns of high credit standing at rates low enough to make the cost of borrowing in the customers' loan market even lower than that of raising funds in the open market for commercial paper.

Competition between banks and dealers is particularly active during periods of low money rates. In such periods competition among banks themselves is also unusually active. A well-informed New York banker observed as early as 1908 that such competition was at times no less active than that between dealers and bankers.[24] Since that time competition among banks for profitable deposit and borrowing accounts has undoubtedly become much more active.[25] All the larger city banks now maintain new business departments for the express purpose of securing profitable new accounts. In the majority of cases no one bank can secure such accounts without depriving some other bank or banks, for the time

[24] This banker made the following statement in this connection: "Much has been said about the note brokers' competition with each other, the cutting of rates, the solicitations of paper and drawing it away from banks, but I wish to testify from an experience of over twenty-five years, in which time I have been dealing with note brokerage houses all over the United States, that there is no more cutting of rates, or unbusinesslike methods practiced in this line of business than there is at times among the banks themselves" (J. G. Cannon, *Buying Commercial Paper* — pamphlet — p. 11). (See also Beal, *op. cit.*, p. 501.)

[25] The following extract from an address by a North Carolina banker in 1935 indicates the lengths to which competition among banks themselves has gone in recent years:

"Bankers are to-day seriously cutting each other's income by a senseless bidding for loans at low rates. Many bankers are going outside of their regular trade areas, offering money to non-customers at lower rates than they are willing to offer their regular customers, simply to employ their idle money. . . . As a result, many borrowers are shopping around to get the best possible rates, and in order to make any loans at all, banks have had to reduce rates almost to the vanishing point" (R. M. Hanes, "The Problem of Bank Earnings," *Proc. Amer. Bankers' Assoc.*, 1935, published in *C. and F. Chron.*, American Bankers' Convention Section, Nov. 30, 1935, p. 75).

In the following year a Boston banker who was formerly connected with a leading Eastern commercial paper house pointed out that, while competition between banks and "brokers" (commercial paper dealers) had for several years been more active than rate-competition among dealers themselves, "competition in rates . . . *between the banks* themselves" was then "more serious" than competition between banks and dealers, and had been "particularly severe during the last two years" (Eaton, *op. cit.*, pp. 45, 47).

being at least, of opportunities for employing loanable funds to advantage. Probably for this reason it is said that relations between dealers and bankers are often "more friendly and more cordial" than those "between banks carrying the same account." [26]

As was noted above, bankers who have disapproved of the competition of dealers have expressed two remaining objections against the open-market system; namely, that such competition forces rates on direct loans to customers down to lower levels than would otherwise prevail, and that dealers have proved to be "fair-weather friends" only, with the result that the demands of open-market borrowers for direct loans from their own banks have been heaviest at the very times when these banks have been the least anxious to extend credit to such borrowers.

The competition of dealers undoubtedly does tend to depress the level of rates prevailing in the customers' loan market. It is doubtful, however, whether such competition has any greater tendency to reduce rates charged on direct loans to customers than that which results from competition among banks themselves.[27] It should be noted also that, if banks were unable to purchase outside paper, they would have to seek alternative investments for surplus loanable funds. At the same time, concerns which now secure in the open market a part of their requirements for borrowed funds would under such circumstances presumably increase their direct borrowings from their own banks by an amount no greater than that of the funds which they now obtain through dealers. Under these conditions the increase in the supply of funds available for investment in the customers' loan market would be at least equal to the increase in the demand for such funds. Rates charged on customers' loans would therefore probably be no higher than they are under existing conditions. Consequently it hardly seems accurate to say that the competition of dealers forces rates in the

[26] C. R. Burnett, "Commercial Paper" (lecture to the credit class of the Richmond Chapter, American Institute of Banking, Dec. 8, 1921).

[27] Cf. the following: "During a period of declining rates we frequently hear the brokers blamed for cheap money and criticised for what is commonly referred to as *breaking rates*. Records show that during the last two years, at least, when such comments have been particularly marked, the decline in paper rates has followed, rather than led, rates made by the banks" (Eaton, *op. cit.*, p. 45).

customers' loan market down to levels below those which would otherwise prevail.

The second objection mentioned just above is of but little consequence at present, however important it may have been in earlier years. Reputable dealers do not allow their borrowing customers to become independent of their own banks. On the contrary, they expect concerns whose paper they handle to maintain adequate banking connections, to keep satisfactory average balances with their banks, and to use open-market financing, not as an exclusive means of raising short-term capital, but rather as a means of supplementing their borrowing in the customers' loan market. Hence if such concerns get into financial difficulties they can fairly expect their depositary banks to come to their aid. As a matter of fact, however, banks are seldom called on to come to the aid of companies which have become financially embarrassed and therefore are unable to sell their paper in the market; for only a very small proportion of the concerns which borrow through dealers get into financial difficulties. Moreover, demands for direct loans from banks on the part of open-market borrowers during periods of financial strain have been relatively lighter since 1914 than they were in earlier years; for, as was indicated above, the market for commercial paper during such periods has been more active since the establishment of the Federal Reserve banking system than it was in preceding years. Even if open-market borrowers do find it necessary to make relatively large use of their bank lines in periods of financial strain, they are in any case likely to be more desirable as bank credit risks at such times than the majority of concerns which do not borrow in the open market.

There are still individual bankers who disapprove of the competition of the commercial paper house. However, most bankers who are really familiar with the operations of the open-market system as a whole, and have considered carefully the true nature of the competition between dealers and commercial banks, would probably agree that any disadvantages of the open-market system from the point of view of individual banks are greatly outweighed by its advantages to the banking system.

If the open-market system has no important disadvantages from the point of view of either the borrowers or the lenders in the commercial paper market, it presumably has no such disadvantages from a broader social point of view. It has nevertheless been maintained that there are certain disadvantages of the system from such a point of view. Four such disadvantages, actual or supposed, may be considered here. These are that open-market borrowing is resorted to as a means of securing what may be called permanent working capital;[28] that when banks find it necessary, in order to utilize surplus funds, to buy open-market paper issued by their own customers, there is "no economic justification for the use of the open market," but, rather, "a distinct economic loss, resulting from the wasted effort in placing the paper";[29] that the ease of borrowing in the open market encourages overtrading, and is therefore likely to aggravate the "increasing intensity of commercial crises";[30] and that under "our system of note brokerage and independent banking those banks holding a minimum of local loans and a maximum of broker's paper are relieved of strain in a stringency, while others with less paper and heavier local loans meet the demands of their borrowers with less ease" — whereas under a branch banking system the demand for loanable funds and the supply thereof are so equated that "every part or unit of the system bears its proper share of strain when strain comes." [31]

It was pointed out in Chapter VI that a substantial volume of "permanent" working capital in fact is obtained through dealers by concerns which borrow in the market more or less continuously throughout the year, and that funds borrowed in the market are used to some extent also for fixed capital purposes or to replace working capital which has been converted into fixed capital. Direct loans from banks are also used for the same purposes, and more extensively than open-market loans are. Those who believe that commercial banks should advance only such credits as will prove

[28] C. A. Phillips, *Bank Credit*, pp. 8, 283–285.

[29] E. E. Lincoln, *Applied Business Finance*, 4th rev. ed., p. 452.

[30] Note on the "note-broker and his function," *Jour. Pol. Econ.*, Dec. 1892, pp. 105–106.

[31] Phillips, *op. cit.*, pp. 140–141.

to be "self-liquidating" in short periods of a few months will of course disapprove of borrowing either in the commercial paper market or in the customers' loan market for these other purposes. It would seem, however, that the main criteria by which the desirability of the various possible classes of bank loans should be determined are their comparative safety and liquidity. Since carefully selected open-market paper, even when issued for the purposes under consideration, is practically as safe and liquid an investment as bankers' acceptances and United States government securities, it would seem, further, that borrowing through dealers for these other purposes may be regarded as a proper use of the open market, provided the borrowers are responsible concerns which are able to make profitable use of the funds so obtained.

The second of the four stated disadvantages of the open-market system from a social point of view is of no consequence. As a rule most banks do not select for purchase open-market obligations issued by concerns to which they make direct loans. Even if banks do purchase open-market notes issued by their own customers, it can hardly be said that any "distinct economic loss" or "wasted effort" is involved in the purchase and sale of such obligations. Placing commercial paper with banks which make direct advances to the issuing concerns, provided these banks wish to purchase such paper, requires no more effort than finding a market among other banks for obligations of the same borrowers. Moreover, the issuing concerns can in most cases borrow through dealers no less conveniently than they can borrow from their own depositary banks. Even though they may find it more convenient in some cases to borrow direct from their own banks, the latter ordinarily are not willing to offer them rates as low as they can obtain in the open market. If such were not the case, their own banks would not need to purchase their open-market notes in order to find employment for surplus loanable funds. Finally, if the banks concerned do not purchase such obligations they must find other outlets for their loanable funds, and selecting high-grade investments of most other classes requires practically as much effort as "checking" open-market paper issued by their own customers.

The validity of the third objection against the open-market system from a social point of view of course depends on the validity of the assumption that the ease of borrowing through dealers encourages overtrading. Criticism of the open-market system on the ground that it encourages overtrading has already been considered. As was pointed out above, this criticism has but little force at present, however valid it may have been in earlier years. It may be argued, indeed, that even in earlier years the net effect of the open-market system in encouraging overtrading, and consequently in aggravating the "increasing intensity of commercial crises," was less than has sometimes been supposed. It is true that some dealers and a considerably larger number of banks, through carelessness in selecting notes for purchase, in effect did encourage excessive borrowing in the open market, and that as a result a number of banks incurred substantial losses on outside paper. If these same banks, however, instead of buying open-market obligations, had placed equivalent amounts of loanable funds in direct advances to their own customers or in long-term securities, they would probably have been equally careless in selecting such alternative investments. Moreover, open-market notes offered a safe investment for large amounts of funds which banks would have placed in earning assets of lower grade if the open-market system of financing had not developed in this country. Hence even in earlier years the existence of this system tended to reduce the number of bank failures; and its influence in this direction operated to offset any tendency it had to encourage overtrading.

The last of the four stated disadvantages of the open-market system from a social point of view is not a disadvantage which is necessarily inherent in the open-market system of financing and the independent unit system of banking under which the open-market system developed. The fundamental difficulty in times of financial strain has been the lack of a sufficient reserve of lending power, rather than the inability of the open-market system and our independent unit system of banking to shift available supplies of short-term capital from sections in which loanable funds have been relatively abundant to those in which they have been comparatively scarce. A nation-wide system of branch banking no doubt could adjust available supplies of loanable funds to the varying demands therefor in different sections of the country more expeditiously and more smoothly than the open-market system and our independent unit system of banking; but in times of severe financial strain even a large branch banking system is likely to fail to function efficiently unless it can draw upon a reserve of lending power provided by a central banking system or some other organization.[32] Since such a reserve of lending power was provided in this country by the establishment of the Federal Reserve banking system, the disadvantage under consideration has been of less importance since 1914 than it was in earlier years, at least so far as member banks are concerned. In any case it is clearly not a disadvantage of the open-market system as such.

Since neither those which have just been considered nor any other supposed disadvantages of the open-market system from a social point of view are of any consequence at present, it may be concluded that the advantages of this system from such a point of view are not offset by any important disadvantages.

3. Conclusions

The system of financing which the operations of dealers make possible has developed in the United States largely because of the existence in this country of a commercial banking system made up of a large number of widely scattered and comparatively small independent unit banks. If, as a result of the removal of restrictive legislation, a nation-wide system of branch banking should develop in this country, the functions now performed by the commercial paper house would no longer be necessary.

At present, however, dealers in open-market paper undoubtedly render important services to hundreds of borrowing concerns of high credit standing and to a much larger number of commercial banks. They enable their borrowing customers to supplement borrowing in the customers' loan market with a method of financ-

[32] In this connection see J. F. Ebersole, "One Year of the Reconstruction Finance Corporation," *Quar. Jour. Econ.*, May 1933, pp. 478–479.

ing that is equally convenient and flexible and generally somewhat less expensive. They are also in a position to offer the concerns whose paper they handle valuable financial advice. For the commercial banks which are their main buying customers they provide a short-term investment which is highly liquid and unusually secure and compares favorably as to yield with other earning assets in which surplus funds of such banks are customarily invested.

In fulfilling these functions they make the country's available supplies of short-term loanable funds more mobile, assume the responsibility of apportioning substantial amounts of such funds among the borrowing concerns which presumably can make the most advantageous uses of short-term credit accommodation, and thus bring about a more effective utilization of the productive resources of the country than would result from the functioning of our independent unit system of banking alone. Hence they not only render valuable services to the individual borrowers and lenders in the commercial paper market but also perform functions which are important from a broader social point of view.

The advantages of the open-market system of financing are offset by no disadvantages of any consequence from the point of view of dealers' borrowing customers or from a social point of view.

From the point of view of individual commercial banks the only important disadvantage of this system at present is that dealers enter into direct competition with them in advancing short-term loans to concerns with a high credit standing. Strictly speaking, the competition in question is really not between dealers and banks, but, rather, between banks wishing to make direct loans to borrowing concerns and those willing to make somewhat safer indirect advances to the same concerns at correspondingly lower rates. The ultimate lenders in the commercial paper market, in other words, are commercial banks themselves, and no commercial paper can be sold to these banks which they are not willing of their own accord to purchase. Moreover, if there were no dealers in open-market notes at least some banks would have to incur considerable expense in order to find equally safe and attractive alternative investments for surplus loanable funds, and some banks would suffer appreciable losses as a result of placing such funds in less secure forms of investment than commercial paper. It is doubtful, furthermore, whether "competition" between dealers and banks forces rates in the customers' loan market down to levels appreciably below those which would prevail if no such competition existed. For in periods of low money rates, when complaints of bankers against the competition of the "broker" are loudest, competition among banks themselves is likely to be fully as active as that between banks and dealers; and, if there were no commercial paper houses, competition among banks in making over-the-counter loans would become even more active than it is at present. In view of these facts, the conclusion seems warranted that the only important disadvantage of the open-market system of financing from the point of view of individual banks is greatly outweighed by its advantages to the banking system as a whole.

BIBLIOGRAPHY

BIBLIOGRAPHY

Books

Adams, J. T., *Provincial Society — 1690–1763* (New York: The Macmillan Company, 1927).

American Acceptance Council, *Bankers' Acceptances — Volume and Rates in the Discount and Money Markets* (New York, 1928).

——, *Facts and Figures Relating to the American Money Market* (New York, 1931).

American Institute of Banking, *Bank Management* (New York, 1931), Chap. VI.

——, *Credit Management* (New York, 1931), Chaps. IV, V, VIII.

——, *Credits* (New York, 1924), Chap. VIII.

Atkins, P. M., *Bank Secondary Reserve and Investment Policies* (New York: The Bankers' Publishing Company, 1930).

Babson, R. W., and May, Ralph, *Commercial Paper*, 3rd ed. (Wellesley Hills, Massachusetts: Babson Institute, 1920).

Bagehot, Walter, *Lombard Street*, 14th ed. (London: John Murray, 1915).

Balabanis, H. P., *The American Discount Market* (Chicago: The University of Chicago Press, 1935).

The Bankers' Directory of the United States and Canada, 1876–77, (Chicago: Rand McNally and Company, 1876).

Banking Law Journal, *Commercial Paper and Bills of Exchange of the World* (New York, 1915).

Barrett, Walter, *see* Scoville, J. A.

Beckhart, B. H., *The Discount Policy of the Federal Reserve System* (New York: Henry Holt and Company, 1924).

——, *The New York Money Market* (New York: Columbia University Press, 1932), vol. III.

Beckhart, B. H., and Smith, J. G., *The New York Money Market* (New York: Columbia University Press, 1932), vol. II.

Beckhart, B. H., Smith, J. G., and Brown, W. A., Jr., *The New York Money Market* (New York: Columbia University Press, 1932), vol. IV.

Bishop, A. L., *The Financing of Business Enterprises* (New York: Harper and Brothers, 1929), Chap. XXIX.

Blodget, Samuel, *Economica: A Statistical Manual for the United States of America* (Washington, D. C., 1806).

Bogart, E. L., *Economic History of the American People* (New York: Longmans, Green and Company, 1931).

Bolles, A. S., *Practical Banking* (New York: Homans Publishing Company, 1884).

——, *Practical Banking*, 11th ed. (Indianapolis: Levey Brothers and Company, 1903).

The Boston Almanac for the Year 1857 (Boston: John P. Jewett and Company, 1857).

Bradford, F. A., *Money and Banking*, 2nd ed. (New York: Longmans, Green and Company, 1935), Chap. XVIII.

Bryan, A. C., *History of State Banking in Maryland* (Baltimore: The Johns Hopkins Press, 1899).

Burgess, W. R., *The Reserve Banks and the Money Market* (New York: Harper and Brothers, 1927).

——, *The Reserve Banks and the Money Market*, rev. ed. (New York: Harper and Brothers, 1936).

Burtchett, F. F., *Corporation Finance* (New York: Harper and Brothers, 1934), pp. 272–273.

Clark, L. E., *Central Banking under the Federal Reserve System* (New York: The Macmillan Company, 1935), Chap. XVIII.

Cleveland, F. A., *Funds and Their Uses, rev. ed.* (New York: D. Appleton and Company, 1922), pp. 386–389.

Clews, Henry, *Fifty Years in Wall Street* (New York: Irving Publishing Company, 1908).

——, *Twenty-eight Years in Wall Street* (New York: Irving Publishing Company, 1888).

Conway, Thomas, Jr., and Patterson, E. M., *The Operation of the New Bank Act* (Philadelphia: J. B. Lippincott Company, 1914).

Dewey, D. R., *Financial History of the United States*, 9th ed. (New York: Longmans, Green and Company, 1924).

——, *State Banking Before the Civil War* (Washington: Government Printing Office, 1910).

Dewing, A. S., *Corporation Finance*, rev. ed. (New York: The Ronald Press Company, 1931), Chap. XI.

——, *The Financial Policy of Corporations*, 3rd rev. ed. (New York: The Ronald Press Company, 1934).

Digest of Decisions Relating to National Banks, 1864–1926 (Washington: Government Printing Office, 1927), vol. I, pp. 503–504; vol. II, p. 316.

Edwards, G. W., *Principles of Banking and Finance* (New York: The Ronald Press Company, 1932), pp. 79–81.

Foster, B. F., *A Practical Summary of the Law and Usage of Bills of Exchange and Promissory Notes* (Boston: Perkins and Marvin, 1837).

Foster, M. B., and Rodgers, Raymond, eds., *Money and Banking* (New York: Prentice-Hall, Inc., 1936), Chap. XVIII.

Foulke, R. A., *The Commercial Paper Market* (New York: The Bankers' Publishing Company, 1931).

Fraser, C. E., *Finance*, vol. X of *The Manuals of Business Management* (Chicago: A. W. Shaw Company, 1927), Chap. XI.

Freedley, E. T., *A Practical Treatise on Business* (Philadelphia: Lippincott, Grambo and Company, 1854).

Garis, R. L., *Principles of Money, Credit, and Banking* (New York: The Macmillan Company, 1934), pp. 972–976.

Gerstenberg, C. W., *Financial Organization and Management of Business*, rev. ed. (New York: Prentice-Hall, Inc., 1933), Chap. XXIV.

Gibbons, J. S., *The Banks of New York, Their Dealers, the Clearing House, and the Panic of 1857* (New York: D. Appleton and Company, 1858).

Greendlinger, Leo, and Johnston, P. H., *Financing* (New York: Alexander Hamilton Institute, 1927), Chap. XVI.

Haney, L. H., Logan, L. S., and Gavens, H. S., *Brokers' Loans* (New York: Harper and Brothers, 1932).

Hardy, C. O., *Credit Policies of the Federal Reserve System* (Washington: The Brookings Institution, 1932), Chaps. XII–XV, XVII.

Harr, Luther, and Harris, W. C., *Banking Theory and Practice* (New York: McGraw-Hill Book Company, Inc., 1930), Chap. XXXIV.

Harris, S. E., *Twenty Years of Federal Reserve Policy*, two vols. (Cambridge: Harvard University Press, 1933).

Holdsworth, J. T., *Money and Banking*, 5th ed. (New York: D. Appleton and Company, 1928), Chap. XVI.

Howard, E. D., and Johnson, J. F., *Money and Banking* (New York: Alexander Hamilton Institute, 1911), Chap. XXIII.

James, F. C., *The Economics of Money, Credit and Banking*, 2nd ed. (New York: The Ronald Press Company, 1935), Chap. XII.

Jolliffe, M. F., *The United States as a Financial Centre, 1919–1933* (Cardiff: University of Wales Press Board, 1935), Chaps. II, IV–VII, X.

Kavanaugh, T. J., *Bank Credit Methods and Practice* (New York: The Bankers' Publishing Company, 1921), Chap. IV.

Kilborne, R. D., *Principles of Money and Banking*, 3rd ed. (New York: McGraw-Hill Book Company, Inc., 1932), Chap. XXVI.

Kirkbride, F. B., Sterrett, J. E., and Willis, H. P., *The Modern Trust Company*, 6th ed. (New York: The Macmillan Company, 1925), Chap. XVII.

Kniffin, W. H., *Commercial Banking*, two vols. (New York: McGraw-Hill Book Company, Inc., 1923), Chap. XXI.

——, *Commercial Paper, Acceptances, and the Analysis of Credit Statements* (New York: The Bankers' Publishing Company, 1918).

——, *The Practical Work of a Bank* (New York: The Bankers' Publishing Company, 1928), Chap. XIV.

Lincoln, E. E., *Applied Business Finance*, 4th ed. (New York: McGraw-Hill Book Company, Inc., 1929), Chap. XVI.

Lyon, L. S., *Hand-to-Mouth Buying* (Washington: The Brookings Institution, 1929).

Madden, J. T., and Nadler, Marcus, *The International Money Markets* (New York: Prentice-Hall, Inc., 1935), Chap. VII.

McKinsey, J. O., and Meech, S. P., *Controlling the Finances of a Business* (New York: The Ronald Press Company, 1923), Chap. XXI.

Miller, H. E., *Banking Theories in the United States Before 1860* (Cambridge: Harvard University Press, 1927).

Miller, M. D., *Bank Loans on Statement and Character* (New York: The Ronald Press Company, 1927), Chap. XVIII.

Mitchell, W. C., *A History of the Greenbacks* (Chicago: The University of Chicago Press, 1903).

Mitchell, W. F., *The Uses of Bank Funds* (Chicago: The University of Chicago Press, 1925).

Moulton, H. G., *Principles of Money and Banking* (Chicago: The University of Chicago Press, 1916).

——, *The Financial Organization of Society*, 3rd ed. (Chicago: The University of Chicago Press, 1930), Chap. XXI.

Munn, G. G., *Bank Credit* (New York: McGraw-Hill Book Company, Inc., 1925), Chap. VI, XIV.

Myers, M. G., *The New York Money Market* (New York: Columbia University Press, 1931), vol. I.

Patten, C. B., *The Methods and Machinery of Practical Banking*, 7th ed. (New York: Bradford Rhodes and Company, 1896), Chap. VII.

Phillips, C. A., *Bank Credit* (New York: The Macmillan Company, 1926), Chaps. VII, XVI.

Prudden, R. F., *The Bank Credit Investigator* (New York: The Bankers' Publishing Company, 1922), Chap. IX.

Raguet, Condy, *A Treatise on Currency and Banking* (Philadelphia: Grigg and Elliot, 1840).

Recent Economic Changes in the United States. Report of the Committee on Recent Economic Changes of the President's Conference on Unemployment. Two vols. (New York: McGraw-Hill Book Company, Inc., 1929), vol. I, Chap. V; vol. II, Chap. X.

Reed, H. L., *Principles of Corporation Finance* (Boston: Houghton Mifflin Company, 1925), Chap. XI.

Richardson, A. P., ed., *The Influence of Accountants' Certificates on Commercial Credit* (New York: American Association of Public Accountants, 1913).

Riefler, W. W., *Money Rates and Money Markets in the United States* (New York: Harper and Brothers, 1930). Chaps. I–V.

Rodkey, R. G., *The Banking Process* (New York: The Macmillan Company, 1928), Chap. XII.

Rose, D. C., *A Scientific Approach to Investment Management* (New York: Harper and Brothers, 1928), page 62.

——, *The Practical Application of Investment Management* (New York: Harper and Brothers, 1933), page 25.

Rufener, L. A., *Money and Banking in the United States* (Boston: Houghton Mifflin Company, 1934), pp. 359–361.

Scoville, J. A., *The Old Merchants of New York City*, 1st and 2nd ser. (New York: George W. Carleton, 1863).

Smith, J. G., *The Development of Trust Companies in the United States* (New York: Henry Holt and Company, 1928), Chap. XIV.

Spalding, W. F., *The London Money Market*, 3rd ed. (London: Sir Isaac Pitman and Sons, Ltd., 1924), Chap. VII.

Sprague, O. M. W., *History of Crises under the National Banking System.* Senate Document no. 538, 61st Congress, 2d Session: vol. 5, no. 3, National Monetary Commission (Washington: Government Printing Office, 1910).

Steiner, W. H., *Money and Banking* (New York: Henry Holt and Company, 1933), Chap. XIII.

Sumner, W. G., *A History of Banking in the United States*, vol. I of *A History of Banking in All the Leading Nations* (New York: *Journal of Commerce and Commercial Bulletin*, 1896).

Vanderblue, H. B., *Problems in Business Economics* (Chicago: A. W. Shaw Company, 1924), pp. 75–80.

Wall, Alexander, *Analytical Credits* (Indianapolis: The Bobbs-Merrill Company, 1921), Chap. XV.

——, *The Banker's Credit Manual* (Indianapolis: The Bobbs-Merrill Company, 1919), Chap. IX.

Warburg, P. M., *The Federal Reserve System — Its Origin and Growth*, two vols. (New York: The Macmillan Company, 1930).

Watkins, L. L., *Bankers' Balances* (Chicago: A. W. Shaw Company, 1929), Chaps. VIII–X.

Westerfield, R. B., *Banking Principles and Practice*, five vols. (New York: The Ronald Press Company, 1921).

White, Horace, *Money and Banking*, 5th ed. (Boston: Ginn and Company, 1914).

——, *Money and Banking*, new ed., revised by C. S. Tippetts and L. A. Froman (Boston: Ginn and Company, 1935), pp. 312, 658–662.

Whitney, Caroline, *Experiments in Credit Control — The Federal Reserve System* (New York: Columbia University Press, 1934), pp. 73, 76–80, 169–171, 175.

Willis, H. P., *The Federal Reserve System* (New York: The Ronald Press Company, 1923), Chap. XLII.

——, *The Theory and Practice of Central Banking* (New York: Harper and Brothers, 1936), Chaps. VII, XI.

Willis, H. P., and Beckhart, B. H., eds., *Foreign Banking Systems* (New York: Henry Holt and Company, 1929), Chap. V.

Willis, H. P., and Bogen, J. I., *Investment Banking* (New York: Harper and Brothers, 1929), Chap. X.

——, *Investment Banking*, rev. ed. (New York: Harper and Brothers, 1936), Chap. XI.

Willis, H. P., Chapman, J. M., and Robey, R. W., *Contemporary Banking* (New York: Harper and Brothers, 1933), pp. 438–439, 551, 560–561.

Willis, H. P., and Steiner, W. H., *Federal Reserve Banking Practice* (New York: D. Appleton and Company, 1926), Chap. IX.

Woodward, P. H., *One Hundred Years of the Hartford Bank* (Hartford, Conn.: Case, Lockwood and Brainard Company, 1892).

Wright, Ivan, *Readings in Money, Credit, and Banking Principles* (New York: Harper and Brothers, 1926), Chap. XV.

ARTICLES IN PERIODICALS

Acceptance Bulletin:

"Acceptance Credit Costs," October 1933, pp. 1–2.

"The Monthly Review," October 1933, pp. 9–10.

Agger, E. E., "Commercial Paper and the Federal Reserve Board," *Annals of the American Academy of Political and Social Science,* vol. LXIII (January 1916), pp. 105–121.

——, "Educational Campaign Concerning Commercial Paper," *American Economic Review,* March 1917, pp. 200–202.

——, "The Commercial Paper Debate," *Journal of Political Economy,* July 1914, pp. 661–683.

——, "The Credit Basis of Commercial Paper," *American Bankers' Association Journal,* November 1917, pp. 344–345.

——, "The Development of an Open Market for Commercial Paper," *Annals of the American Academy of Political and Social Science,* January 1922, pp. 209–217.

——, "The Field for Bankers' Acceptances in Domestic Trade," *American Bankers' Association Journal,* March 1926, pp. 621, 656–659.

Alexander, J. S., "Commercial Paper and Its Part in Present-Day Financing," *Bankers' Monthly,* September 1926, pp. 11, 59.

Alexander, W. O., "Should Country Banks Purchase Commercial Paper?" *American Bankers' Association Journal,* April 1926, pp. 700, 723–724.

Allen, H. H., "Investing the Other 25 Billions," *American Bankers' Association Journal,* June 1928, pp. 953, 1001–1004.

American Bankers' Association Journal:

"Commercial Paper," February 1927, p. 558.

"Credit Clearing Houses or the Registering of Commercial Paper," February 1911, p. 459.

"Credit Information," July 1908, p. 9.

"Credit Information," August 1911, p. 78.

"Mercantile Failures and Commercial Paper," June 1916, p. 1072.

"Note Kiting," April 1909, p. 353.

"Purchase of Paper through Note Brokers," November 1908, p. 161.

"Registration of Commercial Paper," May 1911, p. 667.

"Resolutions of the 54th Convention," October 1928, pp. 361, 414.

"The New Importance of Commercial Paper," January 1934, pp. 36, 56–57.

Anderson, B. M., Jr., "Paper in National Banks Available for Rediscount with Federal Reserve Banks Decreasing," *Annalist*, Jan. 21, 1927, p. 133.

——, "Paper in National Banks Available for Rediscount with Federal Reserve Banks," *Chase Economic Bulletin*, Apr. 8, 1927, pp. 17–20.

Annalist (New York Times):
"Commercial Paper," Mar. 9, 1914, pp. 293–294.
"Commercial Paper under Federal Reserve Act," Feb. 23, 1914, pp. 252–253.
"H. B. Claflin Company Failure," June 29, 1914, p. 834.

Axe, E. W., and Houghton, Ruth, "Commercial Paper as a Stock Market Barometer: A Statistical Survey of the Entire Period 1884–1926," *Annalist*, Sept. 24, 1926, pp. 398–399, 418.

Badger, R. E., "Call Money's Effect on Business," *American Bankers' Association Journal*, August 1929, pp. 145–146, 149–150.

Badger, R. E., and Behrens, C. F., "Financing by Stock Rights," *Investment Banking*, April 1931, pp. 37–40.

Bankers' Magazine (New York):
"Commercial Paper under the Federal Reserve Act," April 1914, pp. 454–460.
"Registration of Commercial Paper," May 1911, pp. 572–573.
"Registration of Commercial Paper," December 1911, pp. 718–719.

Bankers' Magazine (and State Financial Register):
"Exchanges, Stock, &c.," June 1847, pp. 735–736.
"Notes on the Money Market," February 1848, pp. 511–512; February 1849, p. 528; May 1849, pp. 707–708.
"Review of the Month," April 1849, pp. 644–648.

Bankers' Magazine (and Statistical Register):
"A Discount Registry," December 1875, p. 480.
"Banking in Cincinnati," May 1851, pp. 881–882.
"Banking in the United States. II. Of Bills of Exchange and Promissory Notes," September 1860, pp. 169–176.
"Banks of the City of New York," January 1860, pp. 556–557.
"Brokers' Board," March 1856, pp. 694–695.
"Correspondence of the Bankers' Magazine. I. List of Note Brokers," July 1859, p. 58.
"Increase of Banking Capital," May 1857, p. 902.
"Information Concerning Bank Credits," November 1885, pp. 359–361.
"Inquiries of Correspondents. III. The Purchase of Notes by National Banks," June 1878, pp. 984–985.

"Legal Miscellany. I. Liabilities of Note Brokers — Forgeries," December 1856, pp. 459–462.

"Liabilities of Brokers in the Negotiation of Forged Mercantile Paper," December 1856, pp. 488–489.

"National Banks and Purchased Notes," September 1881, pp. 166–168.

"Note Brokers," January 1884, p. 552.

"Notes on the Money Market," January, February, April, June, August, September, 1850; February, May, July, October, 1851; January, March, April, May, December, 1852; September, November, 1853; June, 1854; March, April, October, 1855; May, October-December, 1856; December, 1857; October, 1858; February, March, May-September, December, 1859; March, June-August, December, 1860; January-April, June, August, October-December, 1861; February, March, 1862; February, 1866; July, 1867; December, 1869; August, 1870; September, 1872; December, 1873; August, September, 1884.

"Out-Door Capital," December 1850, p. 505.

"Permanent Investment," January 1858, p. 577.

"Philadelphia Money Market," February 1850, p. 676.

"Shaving Notes without any Capital," January 1858, p. 577.

"The New York Banks and Their Customers," August 1884, pp. 81–84.

Bankers' Weekly Circular and Statistical Record:

Article on New Orleans money market, Feb. 10, 1846, p. 260.

"Money Market," Dec. 30, 1845, p. 162.

"Money Market — January 20, 1846," Jan. 20, 1846, p. 209.

"Money Market. — N. O. December 2," Dec. 23, 1845, p. 155.

"Money Market. — Nov. 11, 1845," Nov. 11, 1845, p. 58.

"Money Market. — 18th November, 1845," Nov. 18, 1845, p. 74.

"The Money Market," Apr. 14, 1846, p. 415.

Banking, "Selecting Commercial Paper," April 1935, p. 61.

Banking Law Journal:

"A Commercial Paper Credit Company," September 1909, pp. 645–646.

"Mercantile Credits," July 1894, pp. 3–4.

"Remedies on Commercial Paper of Insolvent Concerns," January 1895, pp. 45–47.

"The Liability of Investment Brokers in the Sale of Commercial Paper," May 1894, pp. 387–390.

Bashore, M. A., "How to Buy Commercial Paper," *Bankers' Magazine*, July 1918, pp. 37–38.

Bayne, Paul, "Commercial Paper the Most Liquid Asset," *Bankers' Home Magazine*, December 1912, pp. 32–34.

Bean, R. H., "Acceptance Market Facts," *Acceptance Bulletin*, January 1929, pp. 1–4.

——, "Acceptances for Short Term Investments," *American Bankers' Association Journal*, September 1929, pp. 230, 277–278.

Blinn, C. P., Jr., "Purchase of Securities as Related to Commercial Paper," *Monthly Bulletin of the Robert Morris Associates*, February 1927, pp. 301–306.

——, "The Practical Problem of Unemployed Funds," *Acceptance Bulletin*, May 1936, pp. 1–9.

Bolles, A. S., "Notes on Banking in New York City," *Bankers' Magazine*, April 1889, pp. 721–727.

Bradford, F. A., "Cash Burdened Corporations," *American Bankers' Association Journal*, January 1932, pp. 465–466, 481.

Bradstreet's, "Banks and Commercial Paper," Dec. 31, 1892, p. 838.

Breckenridge, R. M., "Branch Banking and Discount Rates," *Bankers' Magazine*, January 1899, pp. 38–52.

——, "Discount Rates in the United States," *Political Science Quarterly*, March 1898, pp. 119–142.

Broderick, J. A., "A Central Credit Bureau in Operation," *Bankers' Home Magazine*, October 1912, pp. 14–17.

——, "Registration of Commercial Paper," *Bankers' Home Magazine*, November 1913, pp. 42–45.

Burgess, W. R., "Steadier Interest Rates under the Federal Reserve System," *American Bankers' Association Journal*, July 1925, pp. 12–15, 20.

——, "The Banker's Bill and the Federal Reserve Banks," *American Bankers' Association Journal*, November 1925, pp. 329–330, 386–387.

Burke, H. C., Jr., "Credit Risk in Commercial Paper," *Texas Bankers' Record*, June 1926, pp. 61–62, 64.

Burritt, Francis, "Banking on Short Dated Paper," *Bankers' Magazine*, January 1859, pp. 532–533.

Burroughs, J. H., "Investing in Commercial Paper," *Bankers' Home Magazine*, February 1907, pp. 38–40.

Business Week, "Commercial Paper Comes Back with Banks as Biggest Buyers," May 21, 1930, p. 10.

Cabell, H. C., "Banking at the South, with Reference to New York City," *Hunt's Merchants' Magazine*, March 1860, pp. 311–323.

Caldwell, G. B., "Credit and the Federal Reserve," *Bankers' Monthly*, July 1914, pp. 11–20.

Case, J. H., "Commercial Paper as a Bank Investment," *Northwestern Banker*, March 1927, pp. 60–62.

Chester, F. D., "On Early Moslem Promissory Notes," *Journal of the American Oriental Society*, vol. XVI (1896), pp. xliii–xlvii.

Childs, C. V., "Commercial Paper and Its Advantages to the Borrower," *New York Credit Men's Association Bulletin*, Nov. 12, 1927, pp. 366–370.

Cole, A. H., "Evolution of the Foreign-Exchange Market of the United States," *Journal of Economic and Business History*, May 1929, pp. 384–421.

Commercial and Financial Chronicle:
"Argues in Favor of the Registration of Commercial Paper," Feb. 1, 1919, p. 415.
"Brokers' Loans in Relation to Commercial Paper," Nov. 17, 1928, pp. 2743–2744.
"Clearing-House Definition of Commercial Paper Acceptable under Federal Reserve Act," Mar. 7, 1914, pp. 729–731.
"Commercial Paper Market Enjoying Distinct Revival — Amount Outstanding Rises Above $300,000,000, Dealers Say," Jan. 11, 1930, p. 224.
"Corporation Balance Sheets, End of 1928, Show Improvement," June 1, 1929, p. 3591.
"James S. Alexander Urges Use of Commercial Paper Not More than Three Months," July 28, 1917, p. 333.
News item relating to the establishment of a "central credit bureau" in Washington, D. C., Oct. 1, 1910, p. 842.
"Reserve Board Favors Short Time Commercial Paper," Sept. 22, 1917, p. 1154.
"Suggestion by Harriman National Bank that Commercial Paper be Registered by Federal Reserve Bank," Feb. 6, 1926, p. 693.
"The Financial Situation," July 29, 1893, pp. 162–164.
"The Present State of Trade and Credit," Sept. 9, 1865, pp. 325–326.

Conant, C. A., "The Development of Credit," *Journal of Political Economy*, March 1899, pp. 161–181.

Conder, G. H., "Bills of Exchange: The Part They Have Played in English Banking, Past and Present," *Journal of the Institute of Bankers*, October 1889, pp. 415–441.

Conover, S. S., "The Credit Man in a Bank," *Banking Law Journal*, April 1906, pp. 309–313.

Conway, Thomas, Jr., "The Influence of the Federal Reserve Act upon Commercial Borrowing," *Annals of the American Academy of Political and Social Science*, May 1915, pp. 226–235.

Crum, W. L., "Cycles of Rates on Commercial Paper," *Review of Economic Statistics*, January 1923, pp. 17–27.

Current Opinion, "Recent Abuses of Commercial Paper," September 1914, pp. 215–216.

Currie, L. B., "The Decline of the Commercial Loan," *Quarterly Journal of Economics*, August 1931, pp. 698–709.

Dailey, D. M., "Bank Credit during the Last Decade," *Bankers' Magazine*, October 1930, pp. 497–502.

Dakan, C. S., "The Changing Uses of Credit," *American Bankers' Association Journal*, August 1929, pp. 134, 181–182.

Davenport, Bruce, "The Shrinkage in Borrowing on the Open Market," *American Bankers' Association Journal*, December 1925, pp. 415, 459–460.

Demmery, Joseph, "Correspondent Banks and the Federal Reserve System," *University Journal of Business*, June 1924, pp. 288–309.

Eaton, J. N., "Effect of the Federal Reserve Act on the Commercial Paper Market," *American Bankers' Association Journal*, August 1916, pp. 179–183.

——, "Rate Competition," *Monthly Bulletin of the Robert Morris Associates*, July 1936, pp. 45–48.

Ebersole, J. F., "One Year of the Reconstruction Finance Corporation," *Quarterly Journal of Economics*, May 1933, pp. 464–492.

Edwards, G. W., "The Changing Investment Policy of American Banks," *Bankers' Magazine*, February 1927, pp. 155–159.

Ellsworth, D. W., "Commercial Paper Rates Resume Upward Movement; Bond Prices at New Low," *Annalist*, Mar. 1, 1929, pp. 427–428.

Escher, Franklin, "The New Era in Discounts," *Annalist*, June 22, 1914, pp. 776–777.

Facinelli, V. J., "The Principles and Uses of Commercial Paper," *Mountain States Banker*, February 1927, pp. 5–6.

Federal Reserve Bulletin:
"Dealing in Acceptances," October 1921, pp. 1166–1170.
"Paper Eligible for Rediscount at Federal Reserve Banks," July 1930, pp. 400–410.

"Purchase of Brokers' Paper," August 1916, pp. 375–376.
"Short-Time Commercial Paper," October 1917, pp. 739–740.
"The Commercial Paper Business," August 1921, pp. 920–926; September 1921, pp. 1052–1057.

Forbes:
  "Governors to Consider Registering All Paper," Nov. 15, 1924, p. 216.
  "Have Commercial Paper Registered," Nov. 1, 1924, p. 155.

Forgan, J. B., "A Good Note," *Bulletin of the American Institute of Banking*, January 1925, pp. 31–39.

——, "Evolution in Banking Thought during the Past Generation," *Bulletin of the National Association of Credit Men*, October 1917, pp. 935–938.

Foster, Hugh, "What Constitutes Eligible Paper," *Southern Banker*, April 1929, pp. 21–22.

Foulds, M. H., "The Massachusetts Bank, 1784–1865," *Journal of Economic and Business History*, February 1930, pp. 256–270.

Foulke, R. A., "Better Days for Commercial Paper," *Banking*, March 1937, p. 26.

——, "Commercial Paper Analysis Shows Small Losses," *Bankers' Monthly*, October 1926, pp. 46–47.

——, "Commercial Paper and Its Market," *Mid-Western Banker*, September 1926, pp. 12–13, 35–36.

——, "Commercial Paper in the Banking System," *Banking*, February 1935, pp. 26–29.

——, "Commercial Paper — The Healthy Bank Investment for Trying Times," *Dun and Bradstreet Monthly Review*, July 1933, pp. 6–7.

——, "Losses on Commercial Paper, and on Bonds and Securities," *Bank Director*, February 1927, pp. 9–10.

——, "No Losses on Open Market Commercial Paper in 1933," *Dun and Bradstreet Monthly Review*, April 1934, pp. 8–11.

——, "The Commercial Paper Market," *Bank Director*, April 1927, pp. 40–42.

——, "The Paper Market — Coordinator of Credit Thought and Research," *American Bankers' Association Journal*, May 1926, pp. 755–756, 793–794.

Fry, M. H., "The Future of the Acceptance Market," *Acceptance Bulletin*, February 1923, pp. 9–10.

Geddes, J. J., "Rules for Buying Commercial Paper," *Bank Director*, August 1925, pp. 57–61.

430   *BIBLIOGRAPHY*

Gossett, C. R., "Postal Savings vs. Commercial Paper," *Northwestern Banker*, July 1934, p. 15.

Grover, Lawrence, "The New Situation Confronting Commercial Banking," *Annalist*, June 24, 1927, pp. 891–892.

Gumbel, Irving, "The Place of Commercial Paper in the Bank's Portfolio," *Southern Banker*, April 1928, pp. 25–26, 38.

Harvard Business Review:
    "Bank Investments," October 1922, pp. 100–105.
    "Judging the Value of Commercial Paper," July 1927, pp. 468–481.

Hazlewood, C. B., "Commercial Paper as Secondary Reserve," *American Bankers' Association Journal*, August 1913, pp. 114–116.

——, "Modern Tendencies in Commercial Banking," *Journal of Business of the University of Chicago*, January 1930, pp. 1–15.

——, "Rules for the Selection of Commercial Paper," *Bankers' Magazine*, September 1913, pp. 254–256.

Henson, G. N., "Selection of Loans," *Bankers' Magazine*, February 1894, pp. 613–616.

Hilgard [Hilyard ?], H. L., "Making the Bank Secondary Reserve Liquid," *Bankers' Monthly*, September 1924, pp. 32–35.

Holdsworth, W. A., "The Origins and Early History of Negotiable Instruments," *Law Quarterly Review*, January 1915, pp. 12–29; April 1915, pp. 173–186; October 1915, pp. 376–388; January 1916, pp. 20–37.

Hubbard, J. B., "A Weekly Index of Money Rates: 1922–25," *Review of Economic Statistics*, January 1926, pp. 23–28.

——, "Commercial-Paper Rates and Bond Yields," *Review of Economic Statistics*, February 1931, pp. 34–35.

——, "Open-Market Money Rates," *Harvard Business Review*, April 1926, pp. 319–325.

Huckins, A. K., "Commercial Paper from the Standpoint of the Note Broker," *Monthly Bulletin of the Robert Morris Associates*, June 1922, pp. 9–12.

Hunt's Merchants' Magazine:
    "Cincinnati Money and Exchange Market in 1853–4," November 1854, pp. 615–616.
    "Commercial Chronicle and Review," January 1859, pp. 76–82; January 1861, pp. 75–84.
    "Liabilities of Brokers in the Negotiation of Forged Notes," December 1856, pp. 737–738.
    "Long Credits," June 1860, pp. 768–769.

"Monthly Commercial Chronicle," April 1843, pp. 365–371; June 1844, pp. 559–564.

"National Banks Not Authorized to Establish Branches, or to Buy Commercial Paper at More Than Seven Per Cent," February 1867, pp. 167–168.

"Notes and Drafts Given as Collateral Security for a Loan," October 1853, p. 455.

"Of Paying Extra Interest for Money," August 1857, pp. 262–263.

"The Wall Street Note Brokers," November 1851, p. 622.

Ives, Mitchell, "The Low Rates on Prime Commercial Credit," *American Bankers' Association Journal*, April 1934, pp. 34–35, 51.

Jenks, Edward, "On the Early History of Negotiable Instruments," *Law Quarterly Review*, vol. IX (January, 1893), pp. 70–85.

Journal of Political Economy:
Note on the "note-broker and his function," December 1892, pp. 105–106.
Note on "Credit Barometrics," April 1919, pp. 315–316.

Kavanaugh, T. J., "A Central Bank Credit Bureau," *Bankers' Home Magazine*, October 1915, pp. 31–36.

Kilborne, R. D., "Crowding out Commercial Loans," *American Bankers' Association Journal*, February 1929, pp. 779–780, 798.

Klein, J. J., "Commercial Importance of Single Name Paper," *Annalist*, Mar. 23, 1914, p. 361.

——, "The Development of Mercantile Instruments of Credit in the United States," *Journal of Accountancy*, vol. XII (September–December, 1911), pp. 321–345, 422–449, 526–537, 594–607; vol. XIII (January–March, 1912), pp. 44–50, 122–132, 207–217.

Knight, T. S., "Commercial Paper in Modern Finance," *Coast Banker*, March 1923, pp. 270–273.

Kuhns, W. R., "What Spurs Commercial Paper?" *American Bankers' Association Journal*, May 1930, pp. 1045–1046, 1090–1091.

Lang, G. L., "Commercial Paper as a Secondary Reserve," *Ninth District Banker*, February 15, 1925, pp. 28–30.

Langston, W. M., "Assignments of Accounts Receivable in Canada," *Monthly Bulletin of the Robert Morris Associates*, March 1933, pp. 256–258.

——, "Section 88 of the Canadian Bank Act," *Monthly Bulletin of the Robert Morris Associates*, January 1933, pp. 210–224.

Larson, Henrietta M., "S. & M. Allen — Lottery, Exchange, and Stock Brokerage," *Journal of Economic and Business History*, May 1931, pp. 424–445.

Laughlin, J. L., "The Aldrich-Vreeland Act," *Journal of Political Economy*, October 1908, pp. 489–513.

——, "The Banking and Currency Act of 1913. II," *Journal of Political Economy*, May 1914, pp. 405–435.

Lee, V. P., "Country Bank Investment Trends," *Bankers' Magazine*, February 1930, pp. 183–187.

Lockhart, O. C., "The Development of Interbank Borrowing in the National System, 1869–1914," *Journal of Political Economy*, February 1921, pp. 138–160; March 1921, pp. 222–240.

Magazine of Wall Street, "A Tendency to Guard against in the Commercial Paper Market," May 24, 1924, p. 132.

Mandeville, C. H. W., "Commercial Paper from the Standpoint of the Bank," *Monthly Bulletin of the Robert Morris Associates*, June 1922, pp. 13–22.

Martin, B. F., "Recent Movements in the Commercial-paper Market," *Harvard Business Review*, April 1931, pp. 360–370.

McAvoy, Walter, "The Economic Importance of the Commercial Paper House," *Journal of Political Economy*, February 1922, pp. 78–87.

McCargar, J. B., "Buying Commercial Paper," *Bankers' Home Magazine*, December 1915, pp. 36–39.

Meech, S. P., "Recent Tendencies in Credit Relations Between Commercial Paper Houses and Business Concerns," *University Journal of Business*, December 1923, pp. 52–71.

Miller, M. D., "Making Commercial Paper Pass the Acid Test," *Bankers' Monthly*, July 1925, pp. 36–37, 77.

Mortimer, F. C., "Some Phases of Loans and Discounts," *Bankers' Magazine*, April 1912, pp. 511–517.

Moulton, H. G., "Commercial Banking and Capital Formation," *Journal of Political Economy*, vol. XXVI (May, June, July, and November 1918), pp. 484–508, 638–663, 705–731, 849–881.

Muhlbach, Walter, "Security Investments of National Banks," *American Bankers' Association Journal*, November 1924, pp. 307–308.

Munn, G. G., "New Problems of Investing Bank Funds," *Bankers' Magazine*, January 1929, pp. 15–17.

——, "The Commercial Paper System," *Bankers' Magazine*, May 1925, pp. 883–889.

——, "The Trend toward Long Term Investments," *Bankers' Magazine*, February 1929, pp. 181–185.

Murray, H. W., "What is Commercial Paper?" *Mid-Continent Banker*, August 1925, pp. 23–25.

Nahm, M. B., "Safe Secondary Reserves," *American Bankers' Association Journal*, April 1929, pp. 974, 1045–1046.

Naumburg, E., "A Danger in Two-Name Paper," *Annalist*, March 23, 1914, p. 361.

Newfang, Oscar, "The Selection of Commercial Paper," *Bankers' Magazine*, December 1912, pp. 665–666.

——, "Undesirable Commercial Paper," *Bankers' Monthly*, August 1913, pp. 28–30.

Nicholson, H. C., "33 Points on Selecting Purchased Investments," *Bankers' Monthly*, February 1929, pp. 19–21, 40–41.

Niles' Weekly Register:
"Brokers," vol. XVI (May 8, 1819), p. 179.
"Description!," vol. XVII (Nov. 20, 1819), p. 185.
"Paper System. The Farmer and the Broker," vol. XIV (Aug. 22, 1818), pp. 426–428.
"Shaving," vol. XVII (Oct. 9, 1819), p. 85.
"The Paper System — No. I" (and Nos. II–VII), vol. XIV: No. I, Apr. 25, 1818, pp. 141–142; No. II, May 2, 1818, pp. 153–156; No. III, May 9, 1818, pp. 180–184; No. IV, May 16, 1818, pp. 194–199; No. V, June 6, 1818, pp. 242–246; No. VI, June 13, 1818, pp. 273–277; No. VII, June 20, 1818, pp. 284–287.

Norris, G. W., "Changed Methods of Financing Business," *Commercial and Financial Chronicle*, Feb. 2, 1929, p. 668.

North Pacific Banker, "Secondary Reserve Policies," Sept. 23, 1927, pp. 1, 12.

Northwestern National Bank, Minneapolis, *Northwestern National Bank Review*, March 1917, pp. 3–4.

O'Hara, R. M., "Creating and Marketing of Bankers' Acceptances," *Bulletin of the American Institute of Banking*, October 1925, pp. 397–403.

Orr, W. W., "A Return to Commercial Paper Borrowing," *Credit Executive*, November 1932, p. 29.

Page, E. D., "Commercial Paper as an Investment," *Bankers' Magazine*, August 1911, pp. 163–169.

——, "Single-Name Commercial Paper under New Banking System — The Merchant's Viewpoint," *Trust Companies*, March 1914, pp. 206–208.

——, "The Proposal to Dehumanize Trade," *Annalist*, Mar. 16, 1914, pp. 324–325.

Patton, F. F., "Commercial Paper for the Bank's Secondary Reserve," *Mid-Western Banker*, February 1929, pp. 30, 61.

Peddie, J. W., "Bankers' Acceptances and Commercial Paper," *Acceptance Bulletin*, November 1921, pp. 2–3.

Persons, W. M., and Frickey, Edwin, "Money Rates and Security Prices," *Review of Economic Statistics*, January 1926, pp. 29–46.

Peterson, J. M., "The Customers' Loan Market and the Open-Market Supply of Loanable Funds," *Journal of Political Economy*, February 1933, pp. 80–94.

Post, William, "The Loan and Credit Department. I," *Bulletin of the American Institute of Bank Clerks*, July 15, 1903, pp. 100–102.

Price, T. H., "Commercial Paper," *Outlook*, Apr. 25, 1914, pp. 948–950.

Priest, H. M., "Clearing-House Inspection of Credits," *Bankers' Magazine*, June 1913, pp. 697–698.

Pruessner, A. H., "The Earliest Traces of Negotiable Instruments," *American Journal of Semitic Languages and Literature*, January 1928, pp. 88–107.

Read, Frederick, "The Origin, Early History, and Later Development of Bills of Exchange and Certain Other Negotiable Instruments," *Canadian Bar Review*, September 1926, pp. 440–459; December 1926, pp. 665–682.

Review of Economic Statistics, "Rates on Prime Commercial Paper in New York, 1866–1922," January 1923, pp. 28–29.

Rhodes' Journal of Banking:
> Article on discounting paper at banks, April 1883, p. 292.
> "Banking Practice," August 1889, pp. 723–724.
> "Can National Banks Buy Paper?" October 1886, p. 796.
> "Commercial Credits," November 1894, pp. 1081–1083.
> "Commercial Paper," May 1887, p. 501.
> "Credit Associations," January 1887, pp. 79–80.
> "Heavy Failure of a Note Broker," October 1882, p. 741.
> "How to Determine the Value of Paper Offered for Discount" (Article I), April 1893, pp. 371–374.
> "Out-of-Town Paper," June 1889, p. 521.
> "Paper in Market," May 1887, pp. 515–516.
> "Practical Banking" (Part XVIII), January 1886, pp. 14–28.
> "Scrutiny of Commercial Paper," December 1883, p. 1048.

Riefler, W. W., "Differentials in Rates Charged Customers," *Federal Reserve Bulletin*, December 1927, pp. 803–817.

Robert Morris Associates, *Monthly Bulletin:*
"Domiciliation of Open-Market Paper," May 1925, pp. 415–416;
February 1926, pp. 336–337; March 1926, pp. 352–355.
Editorial recommending that commercial paper dealers furnish more
detailed information concerning proposed uses of open-market
funds, May 1925, pp. 417–418.

Rovensky, J. E., "Commercial Paper and Bankers' Acceptances," *Fourth District Finance and Industry*, Mar. 22, 1930, pp. 11–12.

——, "Commercial Paper and Bankers' Acceptances as Secondary Reserves," *Bankers' Monthly*, May 1930, pp. 16, 39.

——, "The Market for Money," *Bankers' Magazine*, July 1930, pp. 65–68.

——, "The Relation and Interdependence of Interest Rates," *Monthly Bulletin of the Robert Morris Associates*, June 1930, pp. 18–22.

Sachs, W. E., "From the Commercial Paper House to the Country Bank," *Bankers' Home Magazine*, October 1921, pp. 7–11.

Schaffner, R. C., "The Relation of the New Currency Act to the Work of Commercial Paper Houses," *Journal of Political Economy*, April 1914, pp. 358–364.

Schiltges, W. B., "Small Bank Participation in Commercial Paper," *Bankers' Monthly*, November 1923, p. 92.

Schmidt, J. H., "Commercial Paper," *Bulletin of the American Institute of Banking*, December 1907, pp. 530–533.

Sensenich, E. H., "Commercial Paper as a Reserve," *Bankers' Monthly*, August 1914, pp. 17–22.

Shepherd, Owen, "Commercial Paper Registration," *Trust Companies*, March 1911, pp. 178–182.

——, "Registration of Commercial Paper by Trust Companies," *Trust Companies*, April 1912, pp. 283–288.

Snyder, Carl, "The Influence of the Interest Rate on the Business Cycle," *American Economic Review*, December 1925, pp. 684–699.

Sprague, O. M. W., "Commercial Paper and the Federal Reserve Banks," *Journal of Political Economy*, May 1914, pp. 436–443.

——, "The Crisis of 1914 in the United States," *American Economic Review*, September 1915, pp. 499–533.

——, "The Federal Reserve Act of 1913," *Quarterly Journal of Economics*, February 1914, pp. 213–254.

Steiner, W. H., "Development of American Bank Credit Methods," *University Journal of Business*, August 1923, pp. 441–450.

Steiner, W. H., "Paper Eligible for Rediscount at Federal Reserve Banks: Theories Underlying Federal Reserve Board Rulings," *Journal of Political Economy*, June 1926, pp. 327–348.

——, "The Classification of Financial Institutions," *Journal of Political Economy*, February 1922, pp. 119–123.

Stevens, E. M., "Why Banks Have Been Increasing Their Bond Accounts," *Bankers' Magazine*, September 1927, pp. 259–262.

Stuart, E. C., "How to Protect Your Bank in Commercial Paper Buying," *Bankers' Monthly*, September 1926, pp. 27, 74–75, 80.

Swartwout, R. H., "Bank Purchases of Commercial Paper," *Moody's Magazine*, January 1907, pp. 174–177.

System, "Financing through the Note Broker," March 1926, pp. 379–381, 420.

Thralls, Jerome, "The American Discount Market," *Bulletin of the American Institute of Banking*, April 1925, pp. 140–145.

Time, "Cash & Comeback," Nov. 9, 1936, pp. 62, 64, 66.

Tosdal, H. R., "Hand-to-Mouth Buying," *Harvard Business Review*, April 1933, pp. 299–306.

Towbin, Belmont, "Treasury Bills," *Harvard Business Review*, July 1933, pp. 507–511.

Trudeau, P. W., "Commercial Paper," *Monthly Bulletin of the Robert Morris Associates*, September 1925, pp. 118–126.

Trust Companies, "Registration of Commercial Paper," April 1911, p. 271.

United States Democratic Review, "Monthly Financial and Commercial Article," October 1842, pp. 433–438.

Usher, A. P., "The Origin of the Bill of Exchange," *Journal of Political Economy*, June 1914, pp. 566–576.

——, "The Parisian Bill Market in the Seventeenth Century," *Journal of Political Economy*, December 1916, pp. 985–1002.

Welsh, Prentice, "Commercial Paper from the Borrower's Standpoint," *Bankers' Magazine*, July 1930, pp. 31–37.

——, "Getting Back to Commercial Paper," *Bankers' Magazine*, June 1930, pp. 811–819.

——, "Problems of the Bank Credit Correspondent," *Monthly Bulletin of the Robert Morris Associates*, April 1933, pp. 289–292.

Westerfield, R. B., "The Trend to Secured Loans," *Journal of Business* (University of Chicago), January 1932, pp. 1–18.

Whitney, A. D., "Investing Bank Reserves," *Bankers' Monthly*, November 1928, pp. 60–63.

Wohlers, H. R., "The Registration of Commercial Paper," *Bankers' Magazine*, April 1911, pp. 480–481.

Wright, Ivan, "Loans to Brokers and Dealers for Account of Others," *Journal of Business* (University of Chicago), April 1929, pp. 117–136.

——, "Where the Real Danger Lies in the Growth of Loans 'For Account of Others,' " *Annalist*, Sept. 21, 1928, p. 431.

REPORTS

Annual Report of the Bank Commissioners of Massachusetts, 1860.

Annual Report of the Board of Governors of the Federal Reserve System. Gives figures of member banks' holdings of acceptances, commercial paper, and other classes of earning assets on call dates; of the volume of bankers' (dollar) acceptances and commercial paper outstanding at the end of each month; of rates charged on direct loans to customers by member banks in principal cities of the United States; of short-term and long-term open-market money rates, etc.

Annual Report of the Comptroller of the Currency. Gives figures of member banks' holdings of acceptances, commercial paper, and other classes of earning assets on call dates; figures of national banks' losses on loans and discounts and on bonds and other securities, etc.

Annual Report of the Federal Reserve Bank of New York, 1924, p. 20.

Annual Report of the Federal Reserve Board, 1926, pp. 7–10.

Annual Report of the Secretary of the Treasury, 1865, p. 11.

Commercial Credits Committee, Investment Bankers' Association of America:
First annual report. Reprinted in part in *Bankers' Magazine*, January 1926, p. 89.
"Interim Report, Commercial Credits Committee," *Investment Bankers' Association of America Bulletin*, Mar. 31, 1925, p. 179.
"Interim Report of the Commercial Credits Committee," *Investment Bankers' Association of America Bulletin*, May 29, 1929, p. 73.
"Report of Commercial Credits Committee," *Investment Bankers' Association of America Bulletin*, Feb. 28, 1925, p. 151; Feb. 20, 1926, p. 94; Apr. 30, 1926, p. 145; May 29, 1926, pp. 212–213; and *Proceedings of the Investment Bankers' Association of America*, 1926, pp. 109–112; 1927, p. 166; 1929, pp. 141–142; 1930, pp. 144–145; 1931, pp. 105–106; 1934, pp. 53–55.

Hardy, C. O. and Viner, Jacob, *Report on the Availability of Bank Credit in the Seventh Federal Reserve District* (Washington: Government Printing Office, 1935).

New York State Superintendent of Banks, *Report on Banks of Deposit and Discount*, 1912, 1913.

Report of Clearing House Section, American Bankers' Association, 1920, *American Bankers' Association Journal*, November 1920, pp. 240–241.

Report of Committee on Credit Information, *Proceedings of the American Bankers' Association*, 1908, pp. 195–207.

Report of Committee on Credits, *Proceedings of the American Bankers' Association*, 1899, p. 98.

Report of Committee on Loan Exchange, *Proceedings of the Kansas Bankers' Association:* 1902, pp. 96–97; 1903, pp. 106–107; 1904, pp. 34–35; 1905, pp. 33–34; 1906, pp. 39–40; 1907, p. 53; 1908, p. 106.

Report of Committee on Registration of Commercial Paper, *Proceedings of the Minnesota Bankers' Association*, 1912, pp. 130–132.

Report of Economic Policy Commission, American Bankers' Association, May 7, 1930.

Report of Economic Policy Commission, American Bankers' Association, 1932 and 1936, published in *Commercial and Financial Chronicle*, American Bankers' Convention Section, Oct. 22, 1932, pp. 32–34, and Oct. 10, 1936, pp. 36–37.

Report of Executive Council, *Proceedings of the American Bankers' Association*, 1908, pp. 60–63.

"Report of Mr. J. S. Norris, of Maryland" (on the title of national banks to notes bought in the open market), *Proceedings of the American Bankers' Association*, 1881, pp. 90–91.

Report of the Committee Appointed by the Legislature to Visit and Examine the Banks in Connecticut, 1837.

Report of the Committee on Credit Practices, *Proceedings of the Association of Reserve City Bankers*, 1934, p. 27, and 1935, p. 26.

Report of the Committee on Finance and Industry [The "Macmillan Report"], Cmd. 3897 (London: H. M. Stationery Office, 1931), pp. 43–45.

Report of the Secretary, *Proceedings of the Illinois Bankers' Association*, 1911, pp. 99–101.

ADDRESSES, ETC., PUBLISHED IN PROCEEDINGS OF BANKERS'
ASSOCIATIONS OR CONFERENCES

Adams, A. E., "As to the Efficiency of Our Present System," *Proceedings of the Ohio Bankers' Association*, 1914, pp. 43–55.

Anderson, A. C., Presidential address, *Proceedings of the Minnesota Bankers' Association*, 1904, pp. 8–18.

Andrew, T. W., "Banking Methods — Ancient and Modern," *Proceedings of the South Carolina Bankers' Association*, 1905, pp. 69–86.

Baker, W. H., "Commercial Paper," *Proceedings of the American Bankers' Association*, 1887, pp. 45–47.

Beal, T. P., Jr., "Effect of Increased Operations of Note Brokers upon the Earnings of Commercial Banks," *Proceedings of the American Bankers' Association*, 1916, pp. 499–506. (Beal's address is followed by a discussion, pp. 506–514.)

Bentley, C. F., "Commercial Paper as an Investment for Country Bankers," *Proceedings of the Nebraska Bankers' Association*, 1903, pp. 174–185.

Black, J. P. A., Presidential address, *Proceedings of the Nebraska Bankers' Association*, 1908, pp. 30–34.

Bohne, E. C., "Banking in Europe," *Proceedings of the Kentucky Bankers' Association*, 1906, pp. 103–119.

Brokaw, C. L., "A Study in Bank Investments," *Proceedings of the Kansas Bankers' Association*, 1908, pp. 37–48.

Burnham, S. H., address on commercial paper, *Proceedings of the Nebraska Bankers' Association*, 1903, pp. 188–189.

Cannon, J. G., "Uniform Statement Blanks and Credit Department Methods," *Proceedings of the American Bankers' Association*, 1899, pp. 170–177.

Case, J. H., "The Desirability of Commercial Paper as a Bank Investment," *Proceedings of the New Jersey Bankers' Association*, 1912, pp. 30–40.

Chandler, C. Q., "Bank Investment Policies," *Proceedings Mid-Western Bank Management Conference*, Kansas City, Mo., Mar. 19–20, 1931, pp. 66–71.

Chase, K. S., "Registration of Commercial Paper," *Proceedings of the Minnesota Bankers' Association*, 1911, pp. 30–44.

Conant, C. A., "Exchange of Credit Information between Banks," *Proceedings of the New Jersey Bankers' Association*, 1909, pp. 47–54.

Cosgriff, J. E., "Troublesome Problems in Banking," *Proceedings of the Idaho Bankers' Association*, 1913, pp. 90–98.

Crampton, R. L., "A Central Bureau of Credit Information," *Proceedings of the American Bankers' Association*, 1912, pp. 577–589.

Crandall, Noble, address on commercial paper, *Proceedings of the Nebraska Bankers' Association*, 1903, pp. 185–188.

Crane, F. W., "Commercial Paper Purchased from Brokers," *Proceedings of the Illinois Bankers' Association*, 1916, pp. 130–139.

Deming, J. K., "Modern Methods of Soliciting Business," *Proceedings of the Iowa Bankers' Association*, 1892, pp. 19–22.

Flynn, S. R., "A Twentieth Century Credit System," *Proceedings of the Michigan Bankers' Association*, 1901, pp. 28–35. (Flynn's address is followed by a discussion, pp. 36–45.)

Franklin, N. E., "Commercial Paper," *Proceedings of the South Dakota Bankers' Association*, 1912, pp. 126–131.

Gilbert, Claude, "Country Credit Methods," *Proceedings of the Maryland Bankers' Association*, 1914, pp. 43–53.

Gordon, C. A., "Collateral Loans and Commercial Paper," *Proceedings Second Southern Bank Management Conference*, Nashville, Tenn., Nov. 5–6, 1931, pp. 30–33, 59.

Greenwood, G. H., "Secondary Reserves," *Proceedings of the Oregon Bankers' Association*, 1929, pp. 90–97.

Hague, George, "One-Name Paper," *Proceedings of the American Bankers' Association*, 1884, pp. 64–70.

Hanes, R. M., "The Problem of Bank Earnings," *Proceedings of the American Bankers' Association*, 1935, published in the *Commercial and Financial Chronicle*, American Bankers' Convention Section, Nov. 30, 1935, p. 75.

Hazlewood, C. B., "Commercial Paper as a Secondary Reserve for West Virginia Banks," *Proceedings of the West Virginia Bankers' Association*, 1913, pp. 83–92.

Heller, E. H., "Commercial Paper, Bankers' Acceptances, and Call Loans," *Proceedings Southern Bank Management Conference*, Atlanta, Ga., Mar. 25–26, 1930, pp. 71–73.

Hilliard, H. P., address (without title), *Proceedings of the Michigan Bankers' Association*, 1904, pp. 66–75.

Hilyard, H. L., "Commercial Paper as Secondary Reserve," *Proceedings*, Departmental Conferences, American Institute of Banking, Baltimore, July 1924, pp. 476–482.

Hinchman, T. H., "English and American Banking," *Proceedings of the American Bankers' Association*, 1887, pp. 49–51.

Hogan, D. W., "Commercial Paper, Bankers' Acceptances, and Call Loans," *Proceedings Mid-Western Bank Management Conference*, Kansas City, Mo., Mar. 19–20, 1931, pp. 73–76.

Hurst, J. M., "Interest on Balances and Its Regulation by Open Market Rates," *Proceedings of the Idaho Bankers' Association*, 1916, pp. 59–67.

Jones, W. O., "The Ideal Country Banker," *Proceedings of the Oregon Bankers' Association*, 1908, pp. 47–70.

——, "The Ideal Country Banker," *Proceedings of the North Carolina Bankers' Association*, 1909, pp. 123–142.

Kent, F. I., "Registration of Commercial Paper," *Proceedings of the American Bankers' Association*, 1911, pp. 526–534.

King, E. C., "How Banks Should Buy Commercial Paper," *Proceedings of the New Jersey Bankers' Association*, 1924, pp. 68–72.

Law, W. A., "Coöperation in Commercial Credits," *Proceedings of the Pennsylvania Bankers' Association*, 1908, pp. 40–49.

Leathers, J. H., "Is a Credit Bureau, or Bureau of Information to Prevent Losses from Bad Debts, Feasible Among Banks?" *Proceedings of the American Bankers' Association*, 1897, pp. 86–88.

Lee, W. H., "Clearing House Bank Examinations," *Proceedings of the Missouri Bankers' Association*, 1910, pp. 94–105.

Lynch, J. K., "Modern Tendencies and Ancient Principles," *Proceedings of the Arizona Bankers' Association*, 1909, pp. 42–53.

——, "Seven Years' Financial Schooling," *Proceedings of the Arizona Bankers' Association*, 1914, pp. 32–43.

Martindale, J. B., "The Business of a Commercial Bank and How to Safeguard the Investment of Its Funds," *Proceedings of the American Bankers' Association*, 1911, pp. 696–705.

Matson, W. A., "Slack and Slip-shod Banking," *Proceedings of the Kansas Bankers' Association*, 1916, pp. 111–114.

Matthews, James, "Condensed Statements," *Proceedings of the American Bankers' Association*, 1918, pp. 633–637.

McCurdy, Robert, "Committee on Credits," *Proceedings of the American Bankers' Association*, 1899, pp. 94–97.

McLane, W. F., "Whom to Trust," *Proceedings of the South Dakota Bankers' Association*, 1910, pp. 58–69.

McNary, J. G., "The Business Man, the Obligations of the Business Man from the Standpoint of the Banker," *Proceedings of the Arizona Bankers' Association*, 1917, pp. 45–58.

Meek, C. E., address on credit, *Proceedings of the Kentucky Bankers' Association*, 1914, pp. 47–59.

Nahm, M. B., "Balancing an Investment Program with Particular Reference to Commercial Paper and Call Loans," *Proceedings Mississippi Valley Conference on Commercial Bank Management*, Chicago, Mar. 28–29, 1929, pp. 108–110.

Padgett, A. E., "The Multiplication of Banks," *Proceedings of the South Carolina Bankers' Association*, 1908, pp. 125–134.

Puelicher, J. H., "Bank Reserves," *Proceedings of the Wisconsin Bankers' Association*, 1910, pp. 108–123.

Randall, J. W., "The Centenary of Maryland's First Banking Corporations," *Proceedings of the Maryland Bankers' Association*, 1904, pp. 42–62.

Rogers, G. A., "Loaning Money," *Proceedings of the Kansas Bankers' Association*, 1905, pp. 133–140.

Rovensky, J. E., "Commercial Paper and Bankers' Acceptances," *Proceedings Central Atlantic States Bank Management Conference*, Philadelphia, Mar. 14–15, 1930, pp. 65–69.

Royce, J. Q., "An Analysis of Banking Conditions in Kansas," *Proceedings of the Kansas Bankers' Association*, 1906, pp. 57–67.

Royse, E., "The Critical Season in Banking in Nebraska," *Proceedings of the Nebraska Bankers' Association*, 1903, pp. 364–367.

Schroeder, W. G., address (without title), *Proceedings of the Oklahoma-Indian Territory Bankers' Association*, 1907, pp. 63–64.

Schuette, John, address (without title), *Proceedings of the Oklahoma Bankers' Association*, 1911, pp. 100–105.

Sensenich, E. H., "Commercial Paper as a Secondary Reserve," *Proceedings of the Idaho Bankers' Association*, 1914, pp. 112–117.

——, "Convertible Assets, the Secret of the Strong Bank," *Proceedings of the Montana Bankers' Association*, 1914, pp. 29–34.

Stevens, E. M., "Commercial Paper," *Proceedings of the North Dakota Bankers' Association*, 1903, pp. 29–31.

——, "The Function of the Commercial Bank," *Proceedings of the American Bankers' Association*, 1931, published in the *Commercial and Financial Chronicle*, American Bankers' Convention Section, Oct. 24, 1931, pp. 42–45.

Stevens, H. C., "Paper Eligible for Rediscount," *Proceedings of the Association of Reserve City Bankers*, 1932, pp. 85–87.

Talbert, J. T., "Commercial Credits," *Proceedings of the New York Bankers' Association*, 1908, pp. 76–91.

——, "Commercial Paper," *Proceedings of the Minnesota Bankers' Association*, 1908, pp. 36–53.

——, "The Clearing System," *Proceedings of the Kentucky Bankers' Association*, 1908, pp. 89–119.

——, "The New Currency Law," *Proceedings of the Ohio Bankers' Association*, 1908, pp. 70–81.

Van Vechten, Ralph, address as president of Clearing House Section, American Bankers' Association, *Proceedings of the American Bankers' Association*, 1913, pp. 516–524.

Wade, F. J., "What Causes Fluctuation in Money Rates?" *Proceedings of the New York State Bankers' Association*, 1906, pp. 35–41.

Wattles, G. W., "Quick Assets," *Proceedings of the Nebraska Bankers' Association*, 1904, pp. 115–118.

Welch, H. L., "Important Factors in Purchasing Commercial Paper," *Proceedings*, Departmental Conferences, American Institute of Banking, Tulsa, Oklahoma, June, 1929, pp. 401–414.

Wexler, Sol, "Lessons of the Recent Panic," *Proceedings of the Alabama Bankers' Association*, 1908, pp. 95–101.

Wheeler, H. A., "A Central Bureau of Credit Information," *Proceedings of the Indiana Bankers' Association*, 1912, pp. 142–150.

——, "Bank Credits under the Federal Reserve Act," *Proceedings of the Tennessee Bankers' Association*, 1914, pp. 95–109.

Willis, H. P., "The Status of Commercial Paper under the Federal Reserve Act," *Proceedings of the New Jersey Bankers' Association*, 1914, pp. 45–57.

Wingo, T. M., address (without title), *Proceedings of the Arizona Bankers' Association*, 1922, pp. 34–40.

ARTICLES IN NEWSPAPERS

American Banker:

"Commercial Paper Inquiries Reflect Easy Money Market," Nov. 19, 1929, pp. 1–2.

"Commercial Paper Rate Seems Easing Slightly as Year Ends," Nov. 23, 1928, pp. 1, 7.

"Record High Commercial Paper Rates Fail to Improve Market," May 28, 1929, p. 1.

"Use of Bankers' Acceptances Lessens Sale of Commercial Paper," June 22, 1928, p. 1.

Beckhart, B. H., "Gold Base Shifts Laid to Erratic Capital Exports by U. S.," *New York Evening Post, Annual Survey — Finance and Business*, Jan. 4, 1932, pp. 8, 10, 20, 37.

Gray, W. L., "For Wider Use of Trade Acceptances," *Barron's*, Mar. 13, 1933, p. 16.

Journal of Commerce (New York):
"Commercial Paper Comes Back," July 23, 1934, p. 2.
"Commercial Paper Market Enjoying Distinct Revival," Jan. 7, 1930, p. 1.
" 'Eligible' Paper," Mar. 18, 1927, p. 6.

May, Ralph, "Commercial Paper, an Investment for Individuals," *Barron's* Aug. 20, 1923, pp. 3, 12.

Naumburg, W. W., "Commercial Paper," *Annual Financial Review*, *New York Times*, Jan. 7, 1912, p. 25.

——, "Commercial Paper Output Limited," *Journal of Commerce*, Financial and Commercial Section, Jan. 3, 1922, p. 5.

New York Evening Post, "Double-Name Paper," Mar. 14, 1914, p. 3.

New York Sun, "Commercial Paper Now Popular," June 2, 1934, p. 42.

New York Times:
"Explains Change in Credit Methods," June 8, 1930, § 1, p. 25.
"For Check on Notes," Sept. 21, 1913, Pt. 7, p. 15.
"Heavy Borrowing," Feb. 8, 1914, § 8, p. 9.
"Merger Arranged by Goldman Sachs," Feb. 9, 1932, p. 37.
"More Discounting Paper," Mar. 16, 1930, p. 20 N.
"More Paper Registration," Oct. 16, 1914, p. 14.
"Registering Commercial Paper," Jan. 1, 1915, p. 21.
"Registration of Commercial Paper," Sept. 28, 1913, Pt. 8, p. 16.
"Securities Firms to Co-operate," Oct. 11, 1923, p. 32.
"Would Register Commercial Paper," Jan. 26, 1926, p. 35.
"99 Per Cent. One-Name Paper," Feb. 11, 1914, p. 13.

Wall Street Journal, "Commercial Paper Increase Probable," Aug. 28, 1933, p. 7.

PAMPHLETS

Anderson, R. E., Jr., *The Future of Commercial Paper*, reprint of an address before the New Jersey Bankers' Association, Jan. 19, 1934.

Basis of Sound Banking, reprint of a letter written by Charles A. Conant on Oct. 24, 1907, to the *New York Evening Post*.

Becker, A. G., *Commercial Paper*, reprint of a paper read before the Chicago and Cook County Bankers' Association, Feb. 15, 1923.

Becker, A. G., and Company, *Commercial Paper* (*c.* 1927).

Bond and Goodwin, Inc., *Method of Seasonal Financing and Hedging in the Grain Industry* (*c.* 1927).

Cannon, J. G., *An Ideal Bank*, reprint of an address before the Institute of Accounts, New York, January 1891.

——, *Bank Credits*, reprint of an address delivered at Drexel Institute, Philadelphia, Nov. 17, 1892.

——, *Bank Credits. No. 2*, reprint of an address before the New Jersey State Bankers' Association, Atlantic City, Mar. 17, 1905.

——, *Buying Commercial Paper*, reprint of an address before the Illinois State Bankers' Association, 1908.

——, *Clearing House Loan Certificates and Substitutes for Money Used during the Panic of 1907*, reprint of an address before the Finance Forum, New York City, Mar. 30, 1910.

——, *Losses From Bad Debts*, reprint of an address before the New York State Bankers' Association, Saratoga, New York, July 11, 1895.

Chamber of Commerce of the United States, *Trade Acceptances — Supporting and Opposing Arguments* (Washington, D. C., 1918).

Childs, C. V., *Commercial Paper and the Broker's Function*, reprint of an address before the Reserve City Bankers' Association, Atlanta, Apr. 28, 1926.

Eaton, J. N., *Commercial Paper — Its History and Development and the Probable Effect of the Federal Reserve Act*, reprint of an address before the Providence Chapter, American Institute of Banking, Jan. 27, 1916 (New York: Bankers' Publishing Company, 1916).

Ellis, R. R., *Why I Use a Commercial Paper Broker* (c. 1926).

Hemmen, George, *The Big Idea* (issued by G. H. Burr and Company, Seattle, Washington, May 1931).

Houston, F. K., *Commercial Paper — Its Uses and Abuses*, reprint of an address before the Convention of Reserve City Bankers, Baltimore, Apr. 26, 1917.

Jacobs, L. M., *Bank Acceptances*, Senate Document no. 569, 61st Congress, 2d Session (Washington: Government Printing Office, 1910). (Published in vol. XX of *Publications of National Monetary Commission*, Washington, 1911.)

Kiesewetter, L. F., *Audited Statements*, reprint of a paper read at a meeting of the Association of Reserve City Bankers, Louisville, Kentucky, Apr. 20, 1915.

Lindsay, A. H., *Commercial Paper*, reprint of an address before the members of Group 7, Wisconsin Bankers' Association, La Crosse, Wis., May 28, 1913.

McCluney and Company, pamphlet containing statements of bankers as to their experience with commercial paper during the fall of 1907.

McVickar, John, *Considerations upon the Expediency of Abolishing Damages on Protested Bills of Exchange* (New York: Elliott and Palmer, 1829).

National Credit Office, New York:
> *A Study of Specialized Finance Companies*, prepared by R. A. Foulke, Manager, Bank Service Department, December 1927.
> *History of Commercial Paper for the Years 1920–1924* (1925 ?).
> *Relative Advantages of Investing in Commercial Paper Compared with High Grade Bonds*, November 1925.
> *The Story of Commercial Paper — Its Attributes from the Viewpoint of the Banker.* A series of four pamphlets prepared by R. A. Foulke, Manager, Bank Service Department, 1926 and 1927.

Naumburg, E., *Basis of Sound Banking.*

Oliver, W. B., *Commercial Paper*, reprint of an address before the Anthracite Association of Bankers. No date.

Peck, W. H., *Commercial Credits and Federal Reserve Bank Requirements as to Rediscounts by Member Banks*, reprint of an address before Group 2, Pennsylvania Bankers' Association, Philadelphia, Feb. 12, 1915.

——, *Panics and Reserves*, reprint of an address before the Scranton (Pennsylvania) Chapter, American Institute of Banking, May 12, 1910.

——, *The Value of Commercial Paper as Quick Assets*, reprint of an address before Group 3, Pennsylvania Bankers' Association, Wilkes-Barre, Pennsylvania, July 21, 1897.

Pimm, A. B., *Commercial Paper — Past, Present, and Future.* No date.

Read, L. M., *The Story of Commercial Paper*, reprint of an article in *Dun's Review*, Aug. 1, 1931, pp. 1–4 and Aug. 8, 1931, pp. 1–4 (New York: R. G. Dun and Company, 1931).

Sachs, W. E., *Commercial Paper and Its Place in Our Banking System*, reprint of an address before the Kentucky Bankers' Association, Louisville, Kentucky, Aug. 24, 1921.

Sands, O. J., *Commercial Paper as a National Asset*, reprint of an address before the National Association of Credit Men, Cincinnati, Ohio, June 19, 1913.

Smith, H. C., *Development of the Commercial Paper Broker and His Place in Banking*, reprint of an address before the American Institute of Banking Credits Conference, Baltimore, July 1924.

——, *The Federal Reserve Regulations as to Commercial Paper and Their Application to Existing Methods of Credit*, reprint of an address before the Philadelphia Association of Credit Men, Philadelphia, Jan. 26, 1915.

The Robert Morris Associates, *The Robert Morris Associates — A Brief History* (1933).

Weil, McKey, Pearson and Company, *Commercial Paper from the Standpoint of the Borrower*, April 1934.

CASES OR PROBLEMS IN FINANCE INVOLVING COMMERCIAL PAPER OR COMMERCIAL PAPER HOUSES

Biddle, C. P., and Bates, G. E., *Investment Banking — A Case Book* (New York: McGraw-Hill Book Company, Inc., 1931), pp. 130–131.

Ebersole, J. F., *Bank Management — A Case Book* (New York: McGraw-Hill Book Company, Inc., 1931), Part I: § 2, pp. 76–103; § 5, pp. 162–179.

——, *Bank Management — A Case Book*, 2nd ed. (New York: McGraw-Hill Book Company, Inc., 1935), Part I: § 2, pp. 47–51; § 5, pp. 91–102.

Fraser, C. E., *Problems in Finance* (Chicago: A. W. Shaw Company, 1927), § 8, pp. 433–472.

——, *Problems in Finance*, 2nd rev. ed. (New York: McGraw-Hill Book Company, Inc., 1930), § 6, pp. 388–408.

Harvard Business Reports (Chicago: A. W. Shaw Company, 1926), vol. II, pp. 362–366.

Lincoln, E. E., *Problems in Business Finance* (Chicago: A. W. Shaw Company, 1921), pp. 46–49.

Meech, S. P., "Financing a Change of Business through Commercial Paper Issues," *Journal of Political Economy*, April 1923, pp. 294–298.

——, "Financing Expansion at the Peak of the Cycle by Short Term Loans," *University Journal of Business*, February 1923, pp. 221–229.

Mints, L. W., "Expansion of Fixed and Working Capital by Open Market Borrowing," *Journal of Political Economy*, April 1923, pp. 299–302.

——, "Open Market Borrowing to Finance the Production of Goods Sold for Future Delivery," *Journal of Political Economy*, February 1923, pp. 128–138.

Vanderblue, H. B., *Economic Principles — A Case Book* (Chicago: A. W. Shaw Company, 1927), pp. 206–209.

——, *Problems in Business Economics* (Chicago: A. W. Shaw Company, 1924), pp. 177–183.

——, *Problems in Business Economics*, 2nd rev. ed. (New York: Mc-Graw-Hill Book Company, Inc., 1929), pp. 316–328, 334–337, 413–416, 422–424.

Unpublished cases in files of Harvard Graduate School of Business Administration:
Atlas Motor Oil Company (Finance 344).
Danville Packing Company (Finance 334).
Hampton, McLaren and Company (Finance 425).
Simpson, Thomas and Company (Finance 262).

LEGAL CASES

Atlantic State Bank v. Savery *et al.*, 82 N. Y. 291 (1880).

Atlas National Bank v. Savery, 127 Mass. 75 (1879).

Bank of Columbia v. Fitzhugh, 1 Harris and Gill (Md.) 239 (1827).

Attleborough National Bank v. Rogers, 125 Mass. 339 (1878).

Baxter v. Duren, 29 Me. 434 (1849).

Boardman v. Gore *et al.*, 15 Mass. 331 (1819).

Brown v. Montgomery, 20 N. Y. 287 (1859).

Churchill v. Suter, 4 Mass. 156 (1808).

Conrey v. Hoover, 10 La. Ann. 437 (1855).

Dana v. Underwood, 19 Pickering (Mass.) 99 (1837).

Danforth *et al.* v. National State Bank of Elizabeth, 48 Fed. 271 (1891).

Farmers' and Mechanics' Bank v. Baldwin, 23 Minn. 198 (1876).

First National Bank of Greenville v. Sherburne, 14 Bradwell (Ill.) 566 (1884).

First National Bank of Pierre v. Smith *et al.*, 8 S. Dak. 7 (1895).

First National Bank of Rochester v. Pierson, 24 Minn. 140 (1877).

Fisher v. Rieman *et al.*, 12 Md. 497 (1859).

Fleckner v. The Bank of the United States, 8 Wheaton 338 (1823).

Foltz v. Mey, 1 Bay (S. Car.) 486 (1795).

Fonda v. Garland, 7 La. Ann. 201 (1852).

Gaither v. Lee, 2 Cranch C. C. 205; 9 Fed. Cases 1066 (1820).

Greenwood v. Lowe, 7 La. Ann. 197 (1852).

Hamlin v. Abell, 120 Mo. 188 (1893).

Jones v. Hake, 2 Johnson (N. Y.) 60 (1800).

Lazear v. National Union Bank of Md., 52 Md. 78 (1879).

Lobdell v. Baker, 1 Metcalf (Mass.) 193 (1840); 3 Metcalf 469 (1842).

Merchants' National Bank of St. Paul v. Hanson, 33 Minn. 40 (1884).

Morris v. Third National Bank of Springfield, Mass., 142 Fed. 25 (1905).

Munn v. Commission Co., 15 Johnson (N. Y.) 44 (1818).

Mussi v. Lorain the younger, 2 Browne (Penn.) 55 (1811).

National Pemberton Bank v. Porter, 125 Mass. 333 (1878).

Nevins *et al.* v. De Grand, 15 Mass. 436 (1819).

Niagara County Bank v. Baker *et al.*, 15 Ohio St. 68 (1864).

Nott v. Papet, 15 La. 306 (1840).

Pape v. Capitol Bank of Topeka, 20 Kans. 440 (1878).

Payne v. Trezevant, 2 Bay (S. Car.) 23 (1796).

Prescott National Bank of Lowell v. Butler, 157 Mass. 548 (1893).

Roubieu v. Palmer, 10 La. Ann. 320 (1855).

Sauerwein v. Brunner, 1 Harris and Gill (Md.) 477 (1827).

Séré v. Faurès, 15 La. Ann. 189 (1860).

Smith v. The Exchange Bank of Pittsburg, 26 Ohio St. 141 (1875).

Steward v. Atlantic National Bank of Boston, 27 Fed. 224 (1928).

Thompson v. McCullough, 31 Mo. 224 (1860).

Thompson v. St. Nicholas National Bank, 146 U. S. 240 (1892).

Tracy v. Talmage, 18 Barbour (N. Y.) 456 (1854).

Wachusett National Bank v. Sioux City Stove Works, 56 Fed. 321 (1893).

Widgery v. Munroe *et al.*, 6 Mass. 449 (1810).

Wilkie v. Roosevelt, 3 Johnson (N. Y.) 66; 206 (1802).

Winston v. Tufts, 10 La. Ann. 23 (1855).

Woodhull v. Holmes, 10 Johnson (N. Y.) 231 (1813).

MISCELLANEOUS

Babson, R. W., "The Selection of Commercial Paper," special letter, *Babson's Reports*, Aug. 29, 1910.

Blake Brothers and Company, "A Word About Blake Brothers & Co.," typewritten paper. No date.

Boehmler, E. W., *Commercial Paper*, reprint of five articles from the *Chicago Journal of Commerce* (Chicago: *Chicago Journal of Commerce*, March 1932).

Brown, A. P., "Commercial Paper," typewritten paper — copy of an address at the Harvard Graduate School of Business Administration, *c.* 1922.

Brown, P. M., "Bankers' Acceptances and the Discount Market," unpublished doctoral thesis, Harvard University, 1931.

Burnett, C. R., "Commercial Paper," lecture to the credit class of the Richmond Chapter, American Institute of Banking, Dec. 8, 1921.

"Commercial Paper — Its History, Its Functions, and Its Possibilities," typewritten paper, anonymous, *c.* 1914.

Costello, G. R., "Commercial Paper — Hints and Suggestions," typewritten paper, 1925.

Currie, L. B., "Bank Assets and Banking Theory," unpublished doctoral thesis, Harvard University, 1931.

Federal Reserve Bank of New York, *Monthly Review of Credit and Business Conditions*, 1919 to date. (Called *Report on Business Conditions* until August, 1920.) Each issue gives a review of the bill market and the commercial paper market.

Federal Reserve Bulletin. Gives figures of member banks' holdings of acceptances, commercial paper, and other classes of earning assets on call dates; of the volume of bankers' (dollar) acceptances and commercial paper outstanding at the end of each month; of rates charged on direct loans to customers by member banks in principal cities of the United States; of short-term and long-term open-market money rates, etc.

Forgan, J. B., "Branch Banking." Address before the Bankers' Club of Milwaukee, May 1902. Reprinted in W. H. Hull (ed.), *Practical Problems in Banking and Currency* (New York: The Macmillan Company, 1907), pp. 238–254.

Goldman, William, *Why I Use a Commercial Paper Broker*, reprint of an article published in *Credit Craft*, July 1926.

Investment Banking in Chicago, Bulletin No. 39, Bureau of Business Research, University of Illinois (Urbana: University of Illinois, Oct. 13, 1931).

Library of Congress (Division of Bibliography). *Select List of References on Negotiable Instruments*, Dec. 12, 1910. Has supplementary list of later references.

McCluney, James, "Distribution of Commercial Paper," typewritten paper, 1923 (?).

Merchants' Association of New York, "Brief of the Merchants' Association of New York on Commercial Paper for Discount by the Federal Reserve Banks," typewritten paper, *c.* 1914.

Minnesota Bankers' Association, resolutions relating to audited financial statements and/or the registration of commercial paper, *Proceedings of the Minnesota Bankers' Association*, 1910, pp. 166, 173, 183.

Naumburg, W. W., *Commercial Paper*, reprint of an article published in *Credit Craft*, June (?) 1926.

Operation of the National and Federal Reserve Banking Systems, Hearings before a Subcommittee of the Committee on Banking and Currency, United States Senate, Seventy-first Congress, Third Session, pursuant to Sen. Res. 71. Parts 3 and 6 (Washington: Government Printing Office, 1931).

Raguet, Condy (editor), *The Financial Register of the United States*. (Philadelphia: Wirtz and Tatem, etc., 1838), vol. I, July 1837–June 1838; vol. II, July 1838–December 1838.

Stuart, E. D., "Is It Desirable for a Concern Borrowing a Substantial Amount on the Open Market to Keep Its Lines Entirely Open?", typewritten paper. No date.

Weil, McKey, Pearson and Company, *Command of Credit*, advertising letter issued in February 1937.

——, *Commercial Paper*, advertising letter issued in February, 1933.

——, *"Commercial Paper" — By Companies Using It*, advertising letter issued in April 1935.

INDEX

INDEX